THE GADAMER READER

Topics in Historical Philosophy

General Editors David Kolb
John McCumber

Associate Editor Anthony J. Steinbock

THE GADAMER READER

A Bouquet of the Later Writings

Hans-Georg Gadamer

Edited by Richard E. Palmer
Translated from the German

Northwestern University Press
Evanston, Illinois

Northwestern University Press
www.nupress.northwestern.edu

Printed in the United States of America

10   9   8   7   6   5   4   3

Library of Congress Cataloging-in-Publication Data

Gadamer, Hans Georg, 1900–2002.
    [Selections. English. 2007]
    The Gadamer reader : a bouquet of the later writings / Hans-Georg
Gadamer ; edited by Richard E. Palmer.
        p. cm. — (Topics in historical philosophy)
    A translation of the 1997 Gadamer Lesebuch, augmented by three essays
not included in the Lesebuch.
    Includes bibliographical references and index.
    ISBN-13: 978-0-8101-1987-1 (cloth : alk. paper)
    ISBN-10: 0-8101-1987-0 (cloth : alk. paper)
    ISBN-13: 978-0-8101-1988-8 (pbk. : alk. paper)
    ISBN-10: 0-8101-1988-9 (pbk. : alk. paper)
    1. Hermeneutics. 2. Aesthetics, Modern—20th century. 3. Philosophy,
Modern—20th century. I. Palmer, Richard E., 1933– II. Title. III. Series:
Northwestern University topics in historical philosophy.
B3248.G32E5 2007
193—dc22

                                                            2007006139

Contents

Preface

On a sunny 1997 summer day in Heidelberg I stepped into Ziehank's bookstore and as usual went straight to the shelf of books by and about Gadamer. A small red paperback with the title *Gadamer Lesebuch* immediately caught my eye. My friend Jean Grondin was the editor, and it was a University Paperback, UTB 1972. A round, yellow smiley face sticker on the cover announced: "For Gadamer's 97th birthday, February 1997. Special price 12 DM for three months only." On the back was a blurb saying that this book offered a representative selection of important writings by Gadamer on hermeneutics, ethics, aesthetics, and the history of philosophy, rounded off by a self-presentation at the beginning and a dialogue with Grondin at the end.

Looking through the contents, I immediately decided to translate it. Half the sixteen essays were not yet translated into English, and bringing them together in a single volume would offer an up-to-date anthology of Gadamer's writings. I told Jim Risser of my plans, and he said he also was preparing to publish a collection of Gadamer's essays in English! He gave me his projected table of contents. His collection had more essays related to *Truth and Method* and four selections were on practical philosophy, but it also contained many of the same selections. He generously said he would step aside if I wanted to translate the *Gadamer Lesebuch,* but he suggested adding a couple of essays in practical philosophy, since that was a topic of great interest in America. This would widen the coverage and make it more valuable as a textbook, so I accepted his suggestion. He generously stepped aside. On my own I added one other text, Gadamer's last essay on Derrida and deconstruction, and voilà, you have *The Gadamer Reader* in English!

Teaching duties, speaking engagements at home and abroad, and a debilitating health condition delayed my completion of the volume, but it is here at last. A note about my providing introductions to each of the essays: When I ventured to show my draft translation of Gadamer's "On the Possibility of a Philosophical Ethics" to the Central Illinois Philosophers Group, which meets every three weeks or so, they found the essay slow going until I explained several things about it and in it, at which time it became much more clear, they said. They urged me for the reader's sake to write an introduction to each essay, smoothing the path to understanding Gadamer. So for each essay I have offered a few introductory remarks, telling the occasion on which Gadamer presented it, explaining why it is an important essay, and defining key terms. An explanatory hermeneutical function, you might say. Those who prefer to read only the "thing itself" can skip the introductions. And even so, you are stuck with a translation and not the original German text.

Which brings up the topic of my translation style: Herbert Spiegelberg once told me that my 1970 translation of the full uncut, unchanged version of Husserl's 1927 *Britannica* article on "Phenomenology" that had finally been published in 1962 was clearer than the original German! (Later, Karl Schuhmann in the Netherlands found several mistakes in it when he taught a course using it, for which I thanked him and which I hastened to correct for later reprintings.) For the present translations, I have followed Gadamer's advice to first understand what is being said and then put it into ordinary English usage. When adding a connective word at the beginning of a sentence would make its meaning clear, or when using a more familiar phrase to say the same thing in English, I have not hesitated to do so. My apologies to the purists, but I had Gadamer's permission! I have profited from my general knowledge of Gadamer's philosophy, and I would recheck a rendering when it seemed to contradict his general view on the matter. My aim has been to make Gadamer's thought as available as possible in English.

Acknowledgments

I wish to thank MacMurray College for letting me keep an office here on campus and eat in the cafeteria after my retirement in 1999 so I could work on this translation. An endless sabbatical! I wish to thank my activist wife for allowing me the solitude to work full time on this project while she concentrates on really helping people in Guatemala and Chiapas. And to my beautiful friends and fellow colleagues in the Central Illinois Philosophers Group—Larry Shiner, Peter Wenz, Meredith Cargill, Peter Boltuc, Robert Kunath, Berndt Estabrook, Jose Arce, Rosina Neginsky, Marcia Salner, Robert Gallagher, and Harry Berman—you have my gratitude and thanks for many helpful suggestions. At Mohr Siebeck in Tübingen, Germany, I thank Jill Sopper for her patience and help, and at Northwestern University Press, I am grateful to Susan Betz, Anne Gendler, Rachel Delaney, Stephanie Frerich, and especially my amazing, super copy editor, Paul Mendelson, who saved me from many embarrassing mistakes and inconsistencies. Also, the financial commitment of Northwestern University Press to cover the necessary permission fees made possible this translation of the widely read *Gadamer Lesebuch*.

I am grateful for the fine translation work done by those who came before, especially the translations of David E. Linge, Frederick G. Lawrence, Joel Weinsheimer, and Jamey Findling and Snezhina Gabova, who have greatly enhanced this volume. All the remaining translations and all introductions are by me. Thanks go first to MIT Press for permission to reprint three essays: "The Heritage of Hegel," "Hermeneutics as Practical Philosophy," and "Hermeneutics as a Theoretical and Practical Task," translated by Frederick G. Lawrence in *Reason in the Age of Science* (1981). The German text of "Hermeneutik als praktische und theoretische Aufgabe," added to our volume to enhance its coverage of practical philosophy, was originally published in the *Rechtstheoretische Zeitschrift für Logik, Methodenlehre, Kybernetik und Soziologie des Rechts,* 6, Heft 3(1978): 257–74. Thanks for permission to reprint the MIT translation of this essay—granted by Claudia Blomberg, Foreign Rights Department, Duncker and Humblot, GmbH. I thank University of California

Press at Berkeley for permission to reprint three essays translated by David E. Linge: "The Universality of the Hermeneutical Problem," "Aesthetics and Hermeneutics," and "Heidegger and the Language of Metaphysics" in his *Philosophical Hermeneutics*. I thank the *Continental Philosophy Review*, published by Kluwer Academic Publishers, for "Plato as Portraitist," translated by Jamey Findling and Snezhina Gabova in volume 33, number 3 (July 2000), pp. 245–74, and I thank the Yale University Press for the translation of "On the Possibility of a Philosophical Ethics" by Joel Weinsheimer in his *Hermeneutics, Religion, and Ethics* (1999), pp. 18–36.

In addition to these, I myself have already published several of the translations and reprint them here with permission: 1) "Autobiographical Reflections" was parts 1 and 3 of the longer essay "Reflections on My Philosophical Journey" in *The Philosophy of Hans-Georg Gadamer*, edited by Lewis E. Hahn (Open Court Press), pp. 3–18, 26–40. Thanks go to Open Court Press for permission to reprint these parts. 2) "From Word to Concept: The Task of Hermeneutics as Philosophy" has been reprinted from *Gadamer's Repercussions: Reconsidering Philosophical Hermeneutics*, edited by Bruce Krajewski (Berkeley: University of California Press, 2004), pp. 1–12, where it served as the introduction to the volume. 3) My translation of "On the Truth of the Word" previously appeared in a special issue of *Symposium: Journal of the Canadian Society for Hermeneutics and Postmodern Thought*, volume 6, number 2 (Fall 2002), pp. 115–34, dedicated to "Gadamer's Philosophical Legacy." I regret that I was not aware at the time that Lawrence K. Schmidt had already translated this essay in *The Specter of Relativism* (Evanston: Northwestern University Press, 1995), pp. 135–55. 4) "Text and Interpretation," which I translated with Dennis Schmidt, is reprinted here with permission from *Dialogue and Deconstruction: The Gadamer-Derrida Encounter*, edited by Diane P. Michelfelder and Richard E. Palmer, published by the State University of New York Press, copyright 1989 State University of New York, pp. 21–51. All rights reserved. 5) Four of my new translations of essays that were to appear here for the first time in English appeared as a preview and advance notice of this book in a special issue dedicated to Gadamer of the English journal *Theory, Culture, and Society* 23, 1 (January 2006), pp. 1–100. They are: "Language and Understanding," "Classical and Philosophical Hermeneutics," "Artworks in Word and Image: 'So True, So Full of Being!' (1992) Goethe Quotation," and the concluding dialogue with Jean Grondin, "Looking Back with Gadamer Over His Writings and Their Effective History." They are reprinted here by special arrangement with Sage Publications.

I want to thank my wonderful Peace Brigades International and SiPaz activist wife, Louise, for her idealism, inspiration, and support, and Iranian graduate student in literature and Beckett expert Vahid Norouzalibeik, for many suggestions and for encouragement. Finally, I would like to thank my son Kent for indispensable computer help in preparing the index for this volume.

Richard E. Palmer
September 2006

THE GADAMER READER

1

Autobiographical Reflections

This essay was written during Gadamer's midseventies to comply with a request that he write an autobiographical sketch as one of three for a book, *Philosophie in Selbstdarstellungen* (*Philosophy in Self-Presentations*).[1] It is one of a very few autobiographical essays he wrote. He preferred to discuss ideas and appreciations of other persons, but not to go into the details of his own life. He loved debate. He did publish in the same year (1977), however, a book-length account of his younger years, *Philosophical Apprenticeships*, which recollects his life in Marburg in the 1920s but also focuses on a series of memorable portraits of well-known figures, some his teachers, others his colleagues.[2]

Today, those who wish to learn more of the details of Gadamer's life and writings may consult a recent definitive biography by Jean Grondin, now translated into English: *Hans-Georg Gadamer: A Biography*.[3] This volume furnishes an impeccably documented scholarly account of Gadamer's life, including three chapters on his experiences during the Nazi period. "Autobiographical Reflections" first appeared in English as parts 1 and 3 of the much longer essay "Reflections on My Philosophical Journey," written as the required intellectual autobiography for the 1997 "Library of Living Philosophers" volume on Gadamer, *The Philosophy of Hans-Georg Gadamer*.[4] That translation has been extensively corrected and reworded for the present volume and further explanatory footnotes have been added to make it more accessible to English-speaking readers.

As the opening text in this volume, this essay is an ideal general introduction to Gadamer's thought. It offers us an account by Gadamer himself of his life beginning in 1918 and his writings beginning in 1922 and running up to the mid-1970s. This was well after the publication of his masterwork, and in this essay he ventures to reply to some of his critics. It could have been titled "In His Own Words" or "Apologia pro vita sua." He recalls entering university life, his teachers in Marburg, many of them famous in classical philosophy, the philosophical currents of the time, and even some general books that expressed the mood of the time. He explains his decision to obtain a teaching certificate in classical philology in 1927, studying under Paul Friedländer in order to give himself the solid foundation he needed to stand his ground against the powerful interpretations of Greek texts being put forward by Heidegger, under whom he served as an assistant in Marburg from 1923 to 1928 (when Heidegger was called back to Freiburg to take Husserl's chair). While Gadamer admired the way that Heidegger brought Greek texts back to life, he wanted to develop an independent standpoint of his own as a scholar of ancient Greek. Both his 1922 dissertation and his 1929 habilitation were on Plato, and Platonic dialogue remained a distinctive and integral factor in his later hermeneutical philosophy. His study under the famous Marburg Platonists Paul Natorp and Paul Friedländer strengthened his credentials in classical philology.

In this essay Gadamer offers a chronological review of his major works up to and including his masterwork, *Truth and Method* (1960). He discusses his experiences living in Germany during the despairing 1920s and its search for a new start, his study under Heidegger and his relationship to him, his struggles through the desperate and dominated 1930s when he sought for cover in the irrelevance of teaching Greek philosophy, and on into the 1940s, when he refers to being elected rector of Leipzig University after the war because he was not a Nazi. His lucky move from the Russian zone of Germany to Frankfurt in the Western zone plunged him for two years into a struggle to deal with student needs after the war, and only after he was called to Heidelberg in 1949 could he teach courses that would lay the foundation for his masterwork in hermeneutics.

Gadamer enhances the philosophical interest of this essay by explaining and defending some of the key terms and ideas in his philosophy: the truth of art and poetry, the personal concept of experience in contrast to the scientific concept of it, dialogue, *phronesis* and *energeia*, the historical character of consciousness, the key role of language in understanding, the importance of the different kinds of speaking, and his criticism of the prevailing concepts of self-consciousness stemming from Hegel. He also goes into his famous dialogue with Jürgen Habermas regarding his hermeneutics, and he ends the essay with a reference to his 1973 book on Celan, written in response to the poet's tragic death, and illustrating the importance of poetry to his philosophical hermeneutics. Truly this essay offers a good general introduction to the life and thought of Gadamer, and in his own words.

But it does not tell the whole story. For this you will need to read the lively essays in the rest of this *Gadamer Reader,* most of which date from after 1977. These essays present more detailed elaborations of his major concepts, such as *phronesis* (practical philosophy); they explore some Greek concepts and help us understand the hermeneutic experience and the experience of art; they showcase Gadamer's view of Hegel;

and they include the first English translation of his lengthy final essay on Derrida and deconstruction, "Hermeneutics Tracking the Trace" (1995).

I am indebted to Professor Gadamer himself for reading and occasionally correcting my translation of this essay when it was put together to be two parts of his fuller four-part "Reflections on My Philosophical Journey" in the 1997 volume *The Philosophy of Hans-Georg Gadamer* (La-Salle and Chicago: Open Press, 1997). At that time Jean Grondin was living in Heidelberg and also made suggestions. I have also consulted his eloquent translation of 1977 "Selbstdarstellung" into French as "Auto-présentation," which appeared with other significant Gadamer essays in his collection *La philosophie herméneutique* (Paris: PUF, 1996), 11–62. I also thank Carsten Dutt of Heidelberg University for valuable corrections of my translation of Gadamer's "Reflections on My Philosophical Journey" and Meredith Cargill for his help in proofreading my reworked translation of this essay for the present volume.

* * *

Autobiographical Reflections

In 1918, with the First World War in its last year, I graduated from the Holy Spirit Gymnasium in Breslau and enrolled in Breslau University. At that time, as I looked around, I had no idea that my path would eventually lead me into philosophy.[1]

My father was a university researcher in the natural sciences, and was basically averse to all book knowledge, although his own knowledge of Horace was excellent. During my childhood he sought to interest me in the natural sciences in a variety of ways, and I must say he was very disappointed at his lack of success. The fact that I liked what those "chattering professors" [*Schwatzprofessoren*] (as Dad called them) were saying was clear from the beginning. But he let me have my way, although for the rest of his life [he died in 1928] he remained unhappy about my choice.

My studies in those days were like the first episodes in a long odyssey. A whole range of things enticed me and I ventured to taste many of them. If, in the end, it was the philosophical interest that gained the upper hand, rather than my genuine interest in the study of literature, history, or art history, this was really less a turning away from one of them and toward the others so much as it was a gradual pressing further and further into the discipline of scholarly work as such. In the confusion which the First World War and its end had brought to the whole German scene, to try to mold oneself unquestioningly into the surviving tradition was simply no longer possible. And the perplexity we were experiencing was in itself already an impetus to philosophical questioning.

In philosophy, it was obvious that merely accepting and continuing what the older generation had accomplished was no longer feasible for us in the younger generation. In the First World War's grisly trench warfare and heavy artillery battles for position, the neo-Kantianism which had up to then been accorded a truly worldwide acceptance, though not undisputed, was just as thoroughly defeated as was the proud cultural consciousness of that whole liberal age, with its faith in scientifically based progress. In a disoriented world, we who were young at that time were searching for a new orientation. In our search we were limited, in practice, to the intra-German scene, where bitterness, mania for innovation, poverty, hopelessness, and yet also the unbroken will to live, all competed with each other in the youth of the time. Expressionism was at that time the reigning force in life as well as art, and while the natural sciences continued their upswing—with the Einsteinian theory of relativity in particular causing a great deal of discussion—still, in those areas of study and research that were conditioned by the reigning worldview, namely writing and scholarship, truly a mood of catastrophe was spreading more and more, and this was bringing about a break with the old traditions. *The Collapse of German Idealism,* an oft-cited book of that time by Paul Ernst,[2] was one side of the new "mood of the times" [*Zeitgefühl*]—the academic side. The other and far more encompassing side of this *Zeitgefühl* found its expression in the sensational success of Oswald Spengler's *The Decline of the West.*[3] This "romance," as I think it must be called, made up partly of scholarship and mostly of world-historical fantasy, was "much admired, much reviled," but in the end it would seem to be just as much the inscription of a world-historical mood of pessimism as it was a genuine putting in question of the modern faith in progress and its proud ideal of proficiency and "accomplishing things." In this situation it is hardly surprising that a completely second-rate book of the times had a truly profound effect on me: Theodor Lessing's *Europe and Asia.* This [1926] book, based on the wisdom of the East, put the totality of European accomplishment-oriented thinking in question. Regrettably, a little later in a still more chaotic time, Lessing was assassinated by German nationalists. In any case, for the first time in my experience the all-encompassing horizon which I had grown into through birth, education, schooling, and, indeed, the whole world around me, became relativized. And in this way for me something like *thinking* began.

Of course, a number of significant authors had already given me a certain first introduction to thinking. I remember the powerful impression that Thomas Mann's *Reflections of an Unpolitical Man* made on me during my final year of high school. His fanciful but enthusiastic opposition between art and life as it was expressed in "Tonio Kröger" also touched me deeply, and I remember being enchanted by the melancholy tone of Hermann Hesse's early novels. My first introduction to the art of conceptual thinking, on the other hand, came from Richard Honigswald, whose chiseled dialectic elegantly, although a little monotonously, defended the transcendental idealistic position of neo-Kantianism against all psychologism. I very faithfully took down his lecture course, "Basic Questions in the Theory of Knowledge," word for word in shorthand and then translated it into longhand. My two notebooks containing this lecture course have since been donated to the Honigswald Archive in Würzburg, which was brought into being by Hans Wagner. In any case, these lectures offered me a good introduction to transcendental philosophy. So in 1919 when I came to Marburg, I at least already had a fair preparation in transcendental philosophy.

In Marburg I was soon confronted with new academic experiences. Unlike the universities in the large cities, the "small" universities of that time still had a real academic life—a "life of ideas" as Humboldt intended that phrase—and in the philosophical faculty there was in every area and with every professor a "circle," so one was soon drawn in several directions toward a variety of interests. At that time the critique of historical theology following in the footsteps of Karl Barth's *Commentary on the Letter to the Romans* [1919] was just beginning in Marburg, a critique which was later to become the so-called dialectical theology. Among more and more young people in those days, there was sharp criticism of the "methodologism" in the neo-Kantian school, and over against this, there was acclaim for Husserl's art of phenomenological description. But what took hold of our whole feeling for life, above all, was "life-philosophy"—behind which stood the European event of Friedrich Nietzsche. And the problem of historical relativism connected with this preoccupied the minds of many young people, whose discussion of it related especially to the works of Wilhelm Dilthey[4] and Ernst Troeltsch.[5]

In addition to these developments in theology and philosophy, about that time the influence of the circle around the poet Stefan George, in particular, began to penetrate into the general academic world, and it should also be remarked that the extremely effective and fascinating books of Friedrich Gundolf brought a new artistic sensitivity into the scholarly interaction with poetry. In general, everything that came out of the George circle—Gundolf's books as well as the Nietzsche book of Ernst Bertram, Wolters's skillful pamphlet rhetoric, Salin's crystalline delicacy, and finally, Erich Kahler's exceptionally explicit declamatory attack on Max Weber's famous speech on "Science as a Profession"—amounted to a single great provocation. These were the voices of a strongly held critique of the culture. And I had the feeling that, in this case, in contrast to similar tones of protest from other sides—which, in light of my being a typically dissatisfied beginning student, also gained a certain hearing from me—there was definitely something to it. A certain power seemed to stand behind these often monotonous declamations. The fact that a poet like George could, with the magical sound of his verse and the force of his personality, exercise such a powerful effect on people posed a nagging question for many thoughtful persons, and represented a never completely forgotten corrective to the play with concepts that I was encountering in my philosophical study.

Even then, I myself simply could not ignore the fact that the experience of art had something to do with philosophy. The philosophers in the German Romantic period, right up to the end of the era of idealism, held that art was a true instrument of philosophy, if not its superior adversary, and they found in this truth their all-encompassing task. Indeed, the price that the university philosophy of the post-Hegelian era had to pay for its failure to recognize this truth—was barrenness. The same thing also applied and applies for neo-Kantianism, and indeed it also applies to positivism right up to the present-day [1977], the so-called "new positivism." In my view then and still today, the reclaiming of this truth about the relevance of art to philosophy is the task that our historical heritage has assigned to us.

But certainly the task of appealing to the truth of art against the doubt which historical relativism had already attached to the conceptual truth-claims of philosophy was not an easy one. The experience of art possesses a kind of evidence which is both too strong and at the same time not strong enough. It is too strong in the sense that probably no one would venture to extend his faith in scientific progress to the heights of art by trying, for instance, to see in Shakespeare an advance over Sophocles, or to see in Michelangelo an advance beyond Phidias. On the other hand, the evidence of art is also too weak in the sense that the artwork withholds the very truth that it embodies and this prevents it from becoming conceptually precise. In any case, by the time I was in Marburg, the form of cultural education—of the aesthetic consciousness as well as of historical consciousness—had degenerated into the study of "worldviews." For me, of course, this did not mean that either art or the encounter with the historical tradition of thought had lost their fascination. On the contrary, the assertions of art, like those of the great philosophers, raised for me a claim to truth then more than ever, confused but unavoidable, which would not allow itself to be neutralized by any Kantian "history of problems," nor to be subordinated to the rules of rigorous scientific exactitude and methodical progress.

Rather, the claim to truth at that time, under the influence of a new reception of Kierkegaard in Germany, called itself "existential." Existentialism dealt with a truth which was supposed to be demonstrated not so much in terms of universally held propositions or knowledge but rather in the immediacy of one's own experience and in the absolute unsubstitutability of one's own existence. Dostoevsky, above all others, seemed to us to have known about this. The red Piper volumes of the Dostoyevskian novels flamed on every writing desk. The letters of van Gogh and Kierkegaard's *Either/Or,* which he wrote against Hegel, beckoned to us, and of course, behind all the boldness and riskiness of our existential engagement—as a then scarcely visible threat to the Romantic traditionalism of our culture—stood the gigantic form of Friedrich Nietzsche with his ecstatic critique of everything, including all the illusions of self-consciousness. Where, we wondered, was a thinker whose philosophical power was adequate to the powerful initiatives that had been put forward by Nietzsche?

In the Marburg school of philosophy, the new feeling which had arisen during that time was causing new ground to be broken.[6] Paul Natorp, the brilliant methodologist of the Marburg school, who in his older days sought with muselike enthusiasm to penetrate into the mystical unsayability of the primordially concrete, left lasting impressions behind him. Natorp conjured up not only Plato and Dostoyevsky but Beethoven and Rabindranath Tagore, and also the mystical tradition from Plotinus and Meister Eckhart up to the Quakers. No less impressive at that time was the daemonism of Max Scheler, who, as guest lecturer in Marburg, demonstrated his penetrating phenomenological gifts, which had directed him into unexpected and very new fields of exploration. And there was also the cool acuteness with which Nicolai Hartmann, a thinker and teacher of imposing perseverance, sought to strip away his own idealistic past through critical argumentation with it. When I wrote my Plato dissertation and in 1922 received my first doctorate while far too young, I still stood under the influence of Nicolai Hartmann above all, who had come out in opposition to Natorp's system-oriented, idealistic style.

At that time we also lived in the expectation of a new philosophical orientation, which was particularly tied to the dark, magical word "phenomenology." But when Husserl himself, who with all his analytical genius and inexhaustible descriptive patience that continuously pressed on for final evidence, had envisioned no better philosophical support for his thinking than a neo-Kantian transcendental idealism, where was help for real thinking to come from? Heidegger brought it. Some followers built their interpretation of Marx on Heidegger, others their interpretation of Freud on Heidegger, and all of us, in the end, our interpretation of what Nietzsche was. I myself suddenly realized from Heidegger that we could only "fetch back" [*wiederholen*, repeat] the philosophizing of the Greeks after we had forfeited that *fundamentum inconcussum* of philosophy on the basis of which Hegel had written his story of philosophy and the neo-Kantians their history of problems—namely, *self-consciousness*.

From that point on I had a glimpse of what I wanted, and obviously it had nothing to do with the idea of some new, all-encompassing system. After all, I had not forgotten Kierkegaard's critique of Hegel. In my early essay "On the Idea of System in Philosophy," written for the Festschrift celebrating Natorp's seventieth birthday,[7] I attempted to refute the new idea that philosophy can be reduced to basic experiences that carry human existence and that philosophy can be explained somewhere beyond all historicism. Although it was a document of my immaturity, this essay also gave evidence of my new involvement with Heidegger and the inspiration he had already become for me. Because this essay appeared in 1924, it has sometimes been interpreted as an anticipation of Heidegger's turn against transcendental idealism—a view which I think is completely wrong. As a matter of fact, the three months in the summer of 1923 that I spent in Freiburg studying with Heidegger would in themselves scarcely have led me to this "inspiration" if there were not already all sorts of things in place in my mind and ready to receive it. Certainly Heidegger was the one who permitted me to have the necessary distance from the work of my two other Marburg teachers: Natorp's construction of encompassing systems, and the naive objectivism of Hartmann's categorial research. My essay, at that point, was of course quite impertinent stuff. As I came to know more, I began to remain silent. In fact, at the time of my habilitation in 1928, I could only present as philosophical publications, in addition to my habilitation, one other equally impertinent publication from 1923 on Hartmann's *Metaphysics of Knowledge (Metaphysik der Erkenntnis),* published in *Logos.*[8] I had in the meantime, however, been studying classical philology, and I was later able to develop an essay from my entry paper in the philological seminar of Paul Friedländer, namely, "The Aristotelian *Protreptikos* and Aristotelian Ethics from the Standpoint of Their Developmental History," which Richard Heinze accepted for publication in *Hermes.*[9] It was a critique of Werner Jaeger. The success of this essay gained me recognition in philological circles, even though I only professed to be a student of Heidegger.

What was it that so attracted me and others to Heidegger? At the time, of course, I could not tell you. Today I would put it as follows. In Heidegger the development of thought in the philosophical tradition came to life because it was understood as answers to real questions. The disclosure of the history of the motivation of these philosophical questions lent to them a certain inevitability. And questions that are understood cannot simply pass into one's stock of knowledge. They become one's own questions. Indeed, it had also been the claim of the neo-Kantian "history of problems" approach to recognize in those problems one's own questions. But their claim to fetch back these supertemporal, "eternal" problems in ever-new systematic contexts was not shown to be correct, and these "identical" problems actually were purloined with full naïveté from the building materials of neo-Kantian and German idealist philosophy. The objection lodged by historical relativist skepticism against the claims of supertemporality is persuasive, I think, and cannot simply be gainsaid. Only after I learned from Heidegger how to bring historical thinking into recovering our own questions did this make the old questions of the tradition understandable and so alive that they became our own questions. Today, I would call what I am describing here simply the fundamental experience in hermeneutics.

Above all, it was the intensity with which Heidegger evoked Greek philosophy that worked on us like a magical spell. The fact that such a spell was more a counterexample than an example of what his own questioning was intending to do was something we were scarcely aware of at the time. Heidegger's *Destruktion* of Greek metaphysics was concerned not just with the consciousness-based idealism of the modern age, but likewise with its origins in Greek metaphysics. Heidegger's "destruction" and radical critique also called into question the Christian character of theology as well as the scientific character of philosophy. What a contrast to the bloodless academic philosophizing of the time, which moved within an alienated Kantian or Hegelian language and attempted once again either to bring transcendental idealism to perfection or else to overcome it! Suddenly Plato and Aristotle appeared as co-conspirators and comrades in arms to everyone who had found that playing around with systems in academic philosophy had become obsolete—even in the form of the open system of problems, categories, and values, on the basis of which both the phenomenological research into essences [*Wesenforschung*] and the analysis of categories in the history of problems understood themselves. From the Greeks one could learn that thinking in philosophy does not, in order to be responsible, have to adopt the thought as system-guiding, that there must be a final grounding for philosophy in a highest principle; on the contrary, it stands always under the guiding thought that philosophy must base itself on primordial world experience achieved through the conceptual and intuitive power of the language in which we live. The secret of the Platonic dialogues, it seems to me, is that they teach us this.

Among German Plato scholars at that time, it was Julius Stenzel whose work pointed in a direction similar to my own. Taking note of the dead end of self-consciousness, in which both idealism and its critics found themselves trapped, Stenzel observed in the Greeks the "restraining of subjectivity."[10] This idea occurred to me also, even before Heidegger began to teach it to me, as being a superiority of the Greeks; yet it is a puzzling superiority in which out of self-forgetful surrender they abandoned themselves in boundless innocence to the passion of thinking.

Already very early, and on the same basis, I had taken an interest in Hegel, so far as I understood him, and precisely because I only understood him that far. Above all, his *Logic* really possessed, for me, something of Greek innocence; also his genial *Lectures on the History of Philosophy* (unfortunately poorly edited) provided a bridge to a nonhistorical but truly speculative understanding of Platonic and Aristotelian thinking.

The thing that was most important for me, however, I learned from Heidegger. And this came in the first seminar in which I participated in 1923, when Heidegger was still in Freiburg. It was a seminar on the sixth book of the *Nicomachean Ethics*. At that time, *phronesis*—the virtue of "practical reason," that *allo eidos gnoseos,* that is, that "other form of cognition"—was for me truly a magical word. Certainly, it was an immediate provocation to me when Heidegger one day analyzed the demarcation between *techne* and *phronesis* and then, in reference to the sentence, *phroneseos de ouk esti lethe*[11] (in practical reason there is no forgetting), explained, "That is conscience!" But this bit of spontaneous pedagogical exaggeration focused on a decisive point, by means of which Heidegger himself was preparing for his new posing of the being-question later in *Being and Time*. One thinks especially of terms like *Gewissen-Habenwollen* [the will-to-have-conscience] in *Being and Time,* sections 54ff.

What was by no means clear to me at the time was that Heidegger's remark could also be understood in a completely different way, namely, as a covert critique of the Greeks! This saying then means that Greek thought was only able to think the primordial human phenomenon of conscience as a form of knowledge whose certainty was unthreatened by any forgetting. In any case, Heidegger's provocative remark stimulated me to make alien questions my own, and at the same time it made me aware of anticipation within concepts [*Vorgreiflichkeit*].

The second essential point I gained from Heidegger's instruction was one which Heidegger demonstrated to me from Aristotle's text in some private encounters, namely how untenable it was to allege the "realism" of Aristotle, and that Aristotle ultimately stood on the same ground of the logos for which Plato had prepared him in his discipleship to Socrates. Many years later—following a paper given in one of my seminars—Heidegger discussed with us the fact that this new common ground in the logos, and therewith in dialectical philosophizing between Plato and Aristotle not only supports Aristotle's doctrine of the categories but also enables one to sort out the differences between *dynamis* and *energeia*.[12]

What I have described above was, in reality, my first introduction to the universality of hermeneutics. This was, of course, not clear to me at the time. Only slowly did it dawn on me that the Aristotle who had been strongly pressed on us by Heidegger, an Aristotle whose conceptual precision was filled to the limit with intuition and experience, did not just express Aristotle's new thinking. Heidegger followed the principle put forward in Plato's *Sophist,* that one should make the dialogical partner stronger. Heidegger did this so well that he almost appeared like an *Aristoteles redivivus* [Aristotle brought back to life], an Aristotle who, through the power of intuition and the boldness of his highly original conceptuality, cast a spell over everyone. Nevertheless, the sense of identification to which Heidegger's interpretations forced us posed a powerful challenge to me personally. I was acutely aware that my diverse studies up to that time, studies which had ranged through many areas, literature and art history, and even my studies in the field of ancient philosophy, in which I had written my dissertation, were of no use to me in coming to grips with the challenge of Heidegger's interpretations. So I began a new, systematically laid-out study of classical philology under the direction of Paul Friedländer, a plan of study in which, along with the Greek philosophers, the radiant figure of Pindar, who had been put in a new light by the then-new edition of Hölderlin, attracted me above all—not to mention ancient rhetoric, whose complementary function to philosophy dawned on me then and has accompanied me as I developed my philosophical hermeneutics. All things considered, I feel strongly indebted to these early studies because they made the strong identification with Aristotle, to which Heidegger had invited us, ever more difficult for me. For the more or less conscious guiding theme of all my studies was: in becoming aware of the otherness of the Greeks, to be at the same time loyal to them, to discover truths in their "being-other" that have perhaps been covered over but perhaps were still operative and unmastered today. In Heidegger's interpretation of the Greeks lay a problem that especially in his works after *Being and Time* [1927] kept bothering me. Certainly it was possible in terms of Heidegger's purposes at that time to contrast the existential concept of "Dasein" with "what is merely on hand" [*Vorhandenheit,* just being (objectively) "on hand"] as its counter-concept and extremist derivation without differentiating between this Greek understanding of being and the "concept of object in the natural sciences." But for me there lay in this practice a strong provocation to test the validity of this point in Heidegger, and from this stimulus I went so far as to immerse myself for a time in studying the Aristotelian concept of nature and the rise of modern science, above all in Galileo.

Of course, the hermeneutical situation which I took as a starting point was given first through the shattering of the idealistic and second, the Romantic search for a restoration of unity. But the claim of being able to integrate even the empirical sciences of modern times into the unity of philosophical sciences, a claim which found expression in the concept of a "speculative physics" (a journal even carried this name!), was simply unfulfillable. Any new effort at an integrative claim obviously could not be a repeat of that earlier, failed attempt. But in order to know more clearly the reasons for this impossibility, the concept of science in modern times must present itself in a sharper profile, and the Greek concept of "science" based on the concept of purpose must do so as well, for this was a concept that German idealism had undertaken to renew. It is self-evident that Kant's *Critique of Judgment,* in particular its critique of "teleological judgment," becomes significant in connection with this problem, and a number of my students have undertaken to work this question out further.

The history of Greek science is apparently quite different from the history of modern science in this respect. Plato succeeded in joining together the path of enlightenment, that is, the path of free research and rational explanations of the world, with the traditional world of Greek religion and the Greek view of life. Plato and Aristotle, not Democritus, held sway over the history of science in late antiquity, and this was by no means a history of decline in the sciences. Specialized science [*Fachwissenschaft*], as we now call it, did not have to defend itself against philosophy and its prejudices in Hellenistic times, but rather received its emancipation *by means of* Greek philosophy, through the *Timaeus* and the Aristotelian philosophy of nature, as I tried to show in a paper titled "Is There Matter?" (1973).[13] Actually, even the counter-project of Galilean and Newtonian physics still remained conditioned by Greek philosophy. My study on "Ancient Atomic Theory" (1935) is the only piece from this area of studies that I published at that time.[14] It should help to correct the childish preference which modern science has had for the great unknown figure of Democritus. I should also add that this does not in the least detract from the greatness of Democritus himself.

But of course Plato was at the center of my studies in those days. My first Plato book, *Plato's Dialectical Ethics*,[15] based on my habilitation thesis, was an Aristotle book that got stuck, because my starting point was actually Aristotle's two treatises on "pleasure" in the *Nicomachean Ethics* (book VII: 10–13 and book X: 1–5). However, the problem is scarcely solvable if one takes a genetic approach, so I argued that the problem should be posed in a phenomenological way. Even though I could not "explain" this juxtaposition historically-genetically, I wanted, if possible, to demonstrate that it could be justified anyway. But this could not be done without relating both treatises to the Platonic *Philebus*, and so it was with this intention that I undertook a phenomenological interpretation of this dialogue. In those days I was not yet able to appreciate the universal significance of the *Philebus* for the Platonic doctrine of numbers and in general for the relationship of idea and "reality."[16] Rather, the two things I had in mind both had to do with method: first, to understand the function of Platonic dialectic from a phenomenology of the dialogue; and second, to explain the teaching about pleasure and its forms of appearance from a phenomenological analysis of real phenomena found in life. The phenomenological art of description which I had tried to learn from Husserl (in Freiburg in 1923) and also from Heidegger was supposed to yield an interpretation of ancient texts that was oriented "to the things themselves." My treatise had relative success and received some recognition, though of course not from the specialized historians, who indeed always live in the delusion that it is trivial to understand what is simply there. What should be investigated, they think, is what lies behind it. So Hans Leisegang in his review of current Plato research in the 1932 *Archiv für Geschichte der Philosophie* cast my work aside with a disdainful reference to a sentence from my introduction: "Its relationship to historical criticism is then already a positive one, if such criticism—taking the view that no progress is going to be made from our interpretation—finds that what I say in my interpretation [of what the text says] is self-evident."[17] In reality, however, I was well-grounded in classical philology. I had in the mid-1920s pursued a rigorous course of studies to become certified as a classical philologist and had passed a state exam in it in 1927. I was habilitated in philosophy very soon thereafter (1928–29). What is at issue here is a contrast in methodological standpoints which I undertook to clarify later through my hermeneutical analyses—obviously without success, according to all those who are not ready for the work of reflection but can only regard one's research as "positive" if something new is produced (even if it remains as "un-understood" as the old approach that it replaced).

Nevertheless, it was a successful start. As a teacher of philosophy I learned new things every semester. In those days, even under the poverty-stricken conditions of a foundation-supported scholar or a commissioned and authorized teacher [*Lehrbeauftragter*], my teaching could also be completely in line with my own research plans. So I entered into Plato's thought ever more deeply. In this connection, I was greatly helped by working with Jakob Klein in the area of ancient mathematics and number theory. It was in those times that Klein's classic treatise, "Greek Logistics and the Rise of Algebra" (1936), was first published. I certainly will not claim that the mathematics-oriented studies of mine, which extended over a decade, reflected in any meaningful way the horrible drama of the events of that time. At most they did so indirectly, because in light of the situation after 1933, I purposely abandoned a larger study of the Sophistic and Platonic doctrines of the state, although I did publish two partial aspects of it: "Plato and the Poets" (1934) and "Plato's Educational State" (1942).[18]

Each of these two essays has its story. The first little piece developed an interpretation of the *Republic* by which I still stand today as the only correct one: that the Platonic ideal state presents a conscious utopia which has more to do with Jonathan Swift than with "political science."[19] My publication of this essay in 1934 also subtly documents my position vis-à-vis National Socialism by means of the motto I placed at the beginning: "Whoever philosophizes will not be in agreement with the conceptions of the times." As a quotation from Goethe it was indeed well masked, since it was in continuity with Goethe's characterization of the Platonic writings. But even if one does not want to make a martyr of oneself or voluntarily choose emigration, such a motto can nevertheless convey a certain emphasis to the understanding reader in a time of enforced conformity, an affirmation of one's own viewpoint—similar to Karl Reinhardt's inscription at the end of the preface to his book on the Greek tragedian Sophocles: "In January and September 1933." Indeed, from that time on, the fact that one strenuously avoided politically relevant themes (and publication in journals outside one's special field) was in accord with the same law of self-preservation. It remains true even to this day that a state which, in philosophical questions, designates a single "doctrine" about the state as "correct" must know that its best people will move into other fields where they will not be censured by politicians—which in effect means by laymen. In this case, it makes no difference whether the politician is National Socialist (black) or red, no protest can change anything. So during those years I continued my work unnoticed

turned from exile and taught along with me, creating a healthy tension. There were several years of highly fruitful interaction with Jürgen Habermas, whom we called to Heidelberg as a young *Extraordinarius* after I had learned that Max Horkheimer and Theodor Adorno had gotten into an argument on his account! Well, whoever was able to separate those intellectual brothers-in-arms, Max and Teddy, even just a little bit, must really be something, and in fact the manuscript we requested confirmed the talent of the young scholar, which had been evident to me for some time. But of course there were also other students who had passionately given themselves up to philosophy. I brought a large group of students with me when I came from Frankfurt, among them Dieter Henrich, who also carried the stamp of his first experiences, which were of the Marburg arch-Kantians, J. Ebbinghaus and Klaus Reich. In Heidelberg, too, there were many others who were active in teaching or research, such as Wolfgang Bartuschat, Rüdiger Bubner, Theo Ebert, Heinz Kimmerle, Wolfgang Künne, Ruprecht Pflaumer, J. H. Trede, and Wolfgang Wieland. Others came later from Frankfurt, where Wolfgang Cramer had a strong influence: Konrad Cramer [his son], Friedrich Fulda, and Reiner Wiehl. Also, more and more students from other countries came and blended themselves into the circle of my students. From Italy, I especially remember Valerio Verra and Gianni Vattimo; from Spain, Emilio Lledo; and of course a great number of Americans, many of whom I met again during my many trips to America after 1968, who were now holding positions of responsibility. A special source of satisfaction has been the fact that from my closest circle of students many emerged who found that what they learned could be carried over into other fields, a good test of the idea of hermeneutics itself.

Over the years, what I tried to teach, above all, was hermeneutic praxis. Hermeneutics is primarily a practice, the art of understanding and of making something understood to someone else. It is the heart of all education that wants to teach how to philosophize. In it, what one has to exercise above all is the ear, the sensitivity for perceiving prior determinations, anticipations, and imprints that reside in concepts. This goes for a good part of my work in the history of concepts. With the help of the German Research Foundation I organized a series of colloquia on the history of concepts, and reported on them, and these have triggered a variety of similar endeavors.[28] Conscientiousness and reliability in the employment of concepts requires a "concept-history" kind of awareness, such that one does not fall into the arbitrariness of constructing definitions, or the illusion that one can standardize philosophical speaking into certain obligatory forms. A consciousness of the history of concepts becomes a duty of critical thinking. I have sought in other ways to accomplish this task, for instance by bringing to life, in conjunction with Helmut Kuhn, the *Philosophische Rundschau,* a journal dedicated completely to critique. Helmut Kuhn's critical talent was something I already had learned to admire very early, before 1933, in the last issues of the old *Kantstudien.* Some twenty-three years of issues of the *Philosophische Rundschau* appeared under the strict leadership of my wife, Käte Lekebusch Gadamer, until it was entrusted to other, younger hands.

But the central point of all my activity in the Heidelberg years, as before, remained my teaching duties. Only after my formal retirement in 1968 did I have time to present my ideas on hermeneutics in a wider circumference and in other countries, where they met with widespread interest—above all in America.

Hermeneutics and Greek philosophy have remained the two main foci of my work, and *Truth and Method* has remained since 1960 a center of discussion and critique. In the rest of this essay, I should like first to explore the context of factors which has motivated my thinking in hermeneutics, in particular "practical philosophy," and, second, to make an effort at self-critique in relation to *Truth and Method.*

First, then, the hermeneutics I developed in *Truth and Method.*

What was this *philosophical* hermeneutics? How did it differ from the hermeneutics that arose in the Romantic tradition with Schleiermacher, who deepened a very old *theological* discipline, and which reached a high point in Dilthey's *geisteswissenschaftliche* hermeneutics, a hermeneutics intended to serve as a methodological basis for the humanities and social sciences? With what justification could my own endeavor be called a "philosophical" hermeneutics?

Regrettably, it is not a superfluous task to go into these questions, because many people have seen and do see in this hermeneutical philosophy a rejection of methodical rationality. Many others, especially after hermeneutics became a stylish slogan, and any and every kind of "interpretation" called itself "hermeneutical," have misused the word and misunderstood the issue because of which I took hold of this term. They reversed its meaning in that they saw in it a new methodology, through which they could justify methodological unclarity or furnish a legitimate cover for their ideology. Others again, belonging to the camp of the critique of ideology, recognize truth in it, but only half the truth. It is fine and good, they say, that the preconceptual operativeness of tradition has been recognized, but hermeneutics lacks the decisive thing, a critical and emancipatory reflection that would free one's consciousness from tradition.

Perhaps it would shed some light on the situation if I presented the motivation for my approach as it actually developed. In this way it may become clear that in reality, the method-fanatics and the ideology-critics are the ones who are not doing enough reflection. For the method-fanatics treat the rationality of trial and error—which is undisputed—as the ultimate measure of human reason; on the other hand, the ideology-critics recognize the ideological prejudice that such rationality contains, but they do not sufficiently ponder the ideological implications of their own critique of ideology.

When I sought to develop a philosophical hermeneutics, it was obvious to me from the prior history of hermeneutics that the disciplines based on "understanding" formed my starting point. But to them I added a not previously noticed supplement. I mean the experience of art. For both art and the historical sciences are ways of experiencing in which our own understanding of existence is immediately brought into play. Heidegger's unfolding of the existential structure of understanding in *Being and Time* offered me conceptual help in placing the problematic of "understanding" in its proper breadth. He called this displaying of the existential structure of understanding a "hermeneutic of facticity," which is to say that the human Dasein actually finds itself already embedded in "factual" existence. Using Heidegger's analysis, I offered a critique of German idealism and its Romantic traditions. On this basis it was clear to me that the inherited forms of consciousness that we have acquired historically in our education—forms I have labeled "aesthetic consciousness" and "historical consciousness"—represent only alienated forms of our true historical being. The unique, originary experiences that are mediated to us through art and history cannot be grasped within these alienated forms. The tranquil distance from its object, on the basis of which a consciousness conditioned by the usual middle-class education enjoyed its cultural privileges, does not take into account how much of *ourselves* must come into play and is at stake when we encounter works of art and studies of history.

So I sought in my hermeneutics to overcome the primacy of self-consciousness, and especially the prejudices of an idealism rooted in consciousness, by describing it in the mode of "game or play" [*Spiel*].[29] For when one plays a *game*, the game itself is never a mere object; rather, it exists in and for those who play it, even if one is only participating as a "spectator." In this context, I think, the inappropriateness of the concept of "subject" and "object" is evident, a point which Heidegger's exposition in *Being and Time* has also made clear. The factors which led Heidegger to his famous "turn" I for my part sought to describe in terms of our self-understanding coming up against its limits, that is, as "a consciousness in which history is always at work" [*wirkungsgeschichtliches Bewusstsein*], which is really "more *being* than consciousness"—*mehr Sein als Bewusstsein.*[30] What I formulated with this phrase was not so much a task to be accomplished in the practice of art history or historical scholarship—indeed, it did not have to do at all with the methodical consciousness in these disciplines—rather, it was concerned exclusively, or at least principally, with the philosophical issue of accountability. In this context I asked: in how far is method a guarantor of truth? It is the role of philosophy to make us aware that science and method have a limited place within the whole of human *Existenz* and its rationality.

My own undertaking was itself conditioned by an "effective history" [*Wirkungsgeschichte*]. Obviously it was rooted in a very definite German philosophical and cultural heritage. The so-called *Geisteswissenschaften* ["human sciences," or humanities] in Germany had really never before so completely brought together their scientific functions and their world-intuitive functions. Or, to put it more bluntly, they had never before so fully and consistently concealed their ideologically conditioned interests behind the epistemological and methodological pretensions of scientific procedures. The indissoluble unity of all human self-knowledge was expressed much more clearly elsewhere than in Germany: in France it was through the broader concept of "lettres," and in English in the newly introduced concept of the "humanities." What I wanted to bring about by insisting on the "historically effected consciousness" was a correction of the self-concept found in the historical human sciences, and here I include the study of art, namely, that they are not "sciences" in the manner of the natural sciences.

But bringing about the recognition of a "historically effected consciousness" in the human sciences was not my only goal, for the full dimensions of what I have called "the hermeneutical problem" are much broader. There is something like a hermeneutical problematic in the natural sciences, too. Their path is also not simply that of methodical, step-by-step progress. This has been persuasively shown by Thomas Kuhn and was earlier implied by Heidegger's essay "The Age of the World Picture,"[31] as well as in his interpretation of the Aristotelian view of nature in *Physics* B 1. Both make clear that the reigning "paradigm" is decisive both for the questions that research raises and for the data that it examines, and these are apparently not just the result of methodical research. Galileo had already said, "Mente concipio."[32]

Behind all this, however, a much broader dimension opens up, a dimension that is based on the fundamental linguisticality of human beings. In all human knowing of the world and in all orientation within the world, the nature of the moment of understanding has to be worked out, and in this way the universality of hermeneutics becomes quite evident. Naturally, the fundamental linguisticality of understanding cannot mean that all experiencing of the world can only take place as and in language, for we are all too well aware of those prelinguistic and metalinguistic inner awarenesses, those moments of dumbfoundedness and speaking silences in which our immediate contact with the world takes place. Of course, who would deny that there are real factors conditioning human life, such as hunger, love, labor, and domination, which are not themselves language or speaking, but which for their part furnish the space within which our speaking to each other and listening to each other can take place. This fact cannot be disputed; indeed, it is precisely these preconditions of human thinking and speaking which themselves make hermeneutic reflection necessary.

Furthermore, with a hermeneutics oriented to Socratic dialogue, as mine is, one does not have to be reminded that *doxa* is not real knowing, and that the apparent agreement-in-understanding on the basis of which one lives and speaks is not always a real agreement. But even the discovery that something is only apparently the case, which Socratic conversation brings about, takes place within the element of linguisticality. Even the total breakdown of communication, even misunderstanding and the famous admission that one does not know, presuppose that understanding is possible. The commonality that we call human rests on the linguistic constitution of our life world. Indeed, every attempt by means of critical reflection and argumentation to contend against distortions in interhuman communication only confirms this commonality.[33]

What I have called the hermeneutic aspect of human life and communication thus cannot remain limited to the hermeneutic sciences of history and to interactions with texts; nor is it enough to broaden hermeneutics to include the experience of works of art. Rather, as Schleiermacher already knew, the universality of the hermeneutical problem has to do with the whole universe of the rational; that is, with everything about which one can seek to reach an understanding. Where this seems impossible because one "speaks a different language," hermeneutics is still not at an end. Precisely here the hermeneutical task is posed in its full seriousness, namely finding a common language. Even the common language is never a fixed given. It resides in the play of language between speakers, who must enter into the game of language so that communication can begin, even where various viewpoints stand irreconcilably over against each other. The possibility of reaching an understanding between rational beings can never be denied. Even the relativism which seems to reside in the multiplicity of human languages is no barrier for reason, whose "word" [or logos] all have in common, as Heraclitus was already aware long ago. The learning of a foreign language, and likewise even the first learning of language by children, does not just involve acquiring the means of reaching an understanding. Learning to do this represents a kind of prior schematization of possible experience and its first acquisition. Growing into a language, then, is a path to knowledge of the world. Not only this kind of "learning" but every experience takes place in the constantly developing formation [*Bildung*] of our knowledge of the world. In a much deeper and more universal sense than the great philologist August Boeckh meant it when he formulated it in reference to the work of philologists, experience is always an *Erkenntnis von Erkanntem*—"a knowledge of the known." For we live in what has been handed down to us, and this is not just a specific region of our experience of the world that we call the "cultural tradition," which only consists of texts and monuments and which are able to pass on to us a linguistically constituted and historically documented sense. No, it is *the world itself* which is communicatively experienced and continuously entrusted to us as an infinitely open task to pass on. It is never the world as it was on its first day but the world as it has come down to us. The hermeneutic process is always present when we experience something, when unfamiliarity is overcome; where enlightenment, insight, and appropriation succeed, these all take place in bringing something into words and into the common consciousness. Even the monological language of modern science attains social reality *only in this way*. It is because of this that the universality of hermeneutics, which Habermas so resolutely disputed, seems to me to be well-grounded. Habermas, in my opinion, never gets past an understanding of the hermeneutical problem that one finds in German idealism, and he unjustly restricts my conception of tradition to the "cultural tradition" in the sense that Theodor Litt used this term. The extended discussion between Habermas and myself of this question is documented in the 1971 volume published by Suhrkamp entitled *Hermeneutik und Ideologiekritik*.[34]

In relation to our philosophical tradition, as well, I believe we have a similar hermeneutical task. Philosophizing, too, does not just start from point zero but rather has to think further and speak further the language we speak. What this means today, just as it did in the days of the ancient Sophists, is that the presently alienated language of philosophy must recover its original saying power and be led back to the uttering of what is meant [*das Sagen des Gemeinten*] and back to the things we have in common, the solidarities that are the bearers of our speaking [*die unser Sprechen tragenden Gemeinsamkeiten*].

Modern science has more or less blinded us to this important task, and generalizing the scientific perspective into philosophy should be resisted. In Plato's *Phaedo* Socrates puts forward the following demand: he would like to understand the structure of the world and the occurrences in nature in the same way he understands why he sits here in prison and has not accepted the offer of flight—namely because he considers it *good* to accept even an unjust sentence against him. Now, to understand nature as Socrates here understands himself, namely in terms of the Good, is a demand that in a certain way is fulfilled through Aristotle's teleological philosophy of nature. But this Socratic demand is no longer accepted today and indeed has not been since the science that developed in the seventeenth century, which was the first real "science" of nature, a science that has in some measure made the control of nature possible. But in my view, precisely because of the nonunifiability of philosophy with the modern natural sciences, hermeneutics as philosophy does not have as much to learn from the theory found in modern science as it does from older traditions, which it needs to call back to memory.

One of these is the tradition of rhetoric, a tradition Giambattista Vico, as the last representative of that older tradition, defended with strong methodological awareness against modern science, which he called *critica*.[35] Already in my classical Greek studies during the 1920s I was strongly interested in rhetoric, both as the art of speaking and its theory. For a long time rhetoric has not been sufficiently recognized. In the older tradition rhetoric was the bearer of aesthetic concepts, as still becomes quite clear in Baumgarten's articulation of aesthetics in the eighteenth century. In any case, the point that needs great emphasis today is this: the rationality of the rhetorical way of arguing, which admittedly seeks to bring emotions into play but also works with arguments and with probabilities, is and remains a far more determining factor in society than the excellence of science. For this reason, in *Truth and Method* I have expressly related myself to rhetoric, and from many sides I have found corroboration. For instance, in the work of Chaim Perelman, who takes legal practice as his starting point.[36] This does not mean that I underestimate the importance of modern science and its application in the technical civilization of today. On the contrary, there are completely new problems of mediation that are posed by living in modern civilization. But the situation has not in principle been changed by this. The hermeneutical task of integrating the monologicality of science into the communicative consciousness, a task which entails the exercise of practical, social, and political rationality, has only become more urgent with the flowering of technological civilization.

In reality this is an old problem, one that we have been aware of since Plato. You will recall that Socrates accused the statesmen and the poets, and also the real masters of the individual manual arts, of not knowing the "Good." Aristotle has determined for us the structural difference involved here through his differentiation of *techne* from *phronesis.* This is a difference that cannot just be talked away. Even if this distinction can be misused, and even if the call for "conscience" may itself often conceal unrecognized ideological commitments, it is still a misunderstanding of reason and rationality if one finds them only within the anonymity of science as science. So I was persuaded that the Socratic legacy of "human wisdom" had to be taken up again in my own hermeneutical theory-formation, a legacy which, when measured against the godlike infallibility of science, is, in the sense of *sophia,* a consciousness of not knowing. What Aristotle developed as "practical philosophy" can serve as a model for this fallible and merely human wisdom. This is the second line of the ancient tradition that, in my view, needs to be renewed.

The Aristotelian project of developing a practical science [*praktische Wissenschaft*] represents, it seems to me, the only scientific-theoretical model according to which the scholarly disciplines that are based on "understanding" [*die "verstehenden" Wissenschaften*] can be developed and thought through. Hermeneutic reflection on the conditions of understanding makes it quite clear that this type of understanding can best be articulated in a reflection that neither starts at a zero point nor ends in infinity. Aristotle has made it clear that practical reason and practical insight are not teachable as science is, but must be exercised in praxis, and this is only possible because of an inner link with the ethos—a point well worth remembering. The model provided to us by practical philosophy, then, must be put in place of these "theories" whose ontological legitimation can only be found in an infinite intellect, an intellect about which our experience of human existence, unsupported by revelation, knows nothing. This model must be invoked against all who would bend human reason into the methodical thinking that characterizes what we call "anonymous" science. To present and defend the model of rationality belonging to practical reason against the perfection of a logical self-understanding specific to the sciences seems to me the true and authentic task of philosophy today. This is especially true in light of the practical meaning of science for our life and survival today.

"Practical philosophy" is much more than merely a methodological model for the "hermeneutical" disciplines. It also offers to them something like a *sachliche Grundlage*—a content-relative foundation. The special kind of "method" that belongs to practical philosophy follows from what Aristotle worked out as "practical reason"; this is a rationality possessing a specific conceptual character. Indeed, its structure cannot be grasped by means of the modern concept of science at all. Hegel, whose dialectic was successful in rehabilitating many traditional ideas, was also able to renew many of the truths of "practical" philosophy; yet even the dialectical flexibility of Hegel threatens today to become a new, unconscious dogmatism of reflection. For example, the concept of reflection that serves as the basis for Habermas's "critique of ideology" implies a highly abstract concept of coercion-free discourse which totally loses sight of the actual conditions of human praxis. As has been well documented in my article in *Hermeneutik und Ideologiekritik,* cited previously, I had to reject Habermas's recourse to psychoanalysis as illegitimately taking the therapeutic situation of psychoanalysis for the program of critique of ideology. But in the realm of practical reason there is simply no analogy to the "knowing" analyst who guides the productive thinking processes of the analysand. With regard to the question of reflection, it seems to me that Brentano's differentiation of reflexive self-awareness from objectivizing reflection, a distinction that goes back to Aristotle, is still superior to what we find in the heritage of German idealism. The same thing also applies, in my opinion, with regard to the demand for a transcendental reflection that Karl-Otto Apel and others have directed at hermeneutics. This demand and my reply to it have also been documented in the volume on hermeneutics and critique of ideology.

So I have to say that the dialogues of Plato, even more than the works of the great thinkers of German idealism, have left their stamp on my thinking. These dialogues are my constant companions, and what a unique company they are! However much we moderns may have been taught by Nietzsche and Heidegger about how Greek concepts have anticipated everything from Aristotle to Hegel to modern logic, so that they constitute a boundary beyond which our own questions remain without answers and our intentions remain unsatisfied, it is still Plato's dialogical art which serves as an antidote to the illusion of superiority which we think we possess as inheritors of the Judeo-Christian tradition. Admittedly it was also Plato who, with the doctrine of ideas, the mathematization of nature, and the intellectualizing of what we would call "ethics," laid the foundation for the metaphysical conceptuality of our tradition. But at the same time he mimetically limited all his assertions: just as Socrates knew how to do this with his dialogue partners by using irony, so also Plato, through his art of dialogical poetry, robbed his reader of his assumed superiority. To philosophize *with* Plato, not just to criticize Plato, that is the task. To criticize Plato is perhaps just as simple-minded as to reproach Sophocles for not being Shakespeare. This may seem paradoxical, but only to someone who is blind to the philosophical relevance of Plato's poetic imagination.

One must first learn to read Plato mimetically. In our century some things have happened that make this a little easier, especially Paul

Friedländer's great three-volume study of Plato,[37] but also through many other inspired but sometimes not so well-grounded books from the circle of the poet Stefan George (by Heinrich Friedmann, Kurt Singer, and Kurt Hildebrandt, for instance), as well as the works of Leo Strauss and his friends and students. The task, however, is far from accomplished. It consists of relating the conceptual assertions that one encounters in the dialogues as exactly as possible with the dialogical reality out of which they grow. For one finds there a "Doric harmony" of deed and speaking, of *ergon* and logos, which has to do not just with the words. Rather, it is the authentic spirit of the Socratic dialogues. They are in the literal sense *hinführende Reden*—speeches that lead you somewhere. Only in these conversations does Socrates open his heart to us and let us know what he really intends, not in his art of refutation that often works sophistically and drives his partners into terrible entanglements.

Yes, if only human wisdom were such that it could be passed from one person to another like water over a thread of wool (*Symposium* 175d). But human wisdom is not like this. Wisdom is the awareness of not-knowing [*das Wissen des Nichtwissens*], *the docta ignorantia*. Through it the other person with whom Socrates is having the conversation is convicted of his own not-knowing—and this means that something dawns on him about himself and about his living with only pretended knowledge. Or, to put it in the clearer formulation from Plato's *Seventh Letter:* not just his thesis but his soul is refuted. This applies not only to the young men who believe themselves to be friends and yet do not know what friendship is (in the *Lysis*), and to the famous generals (in the *Laches*) who believe they embody in themselves bravery, the virtue of soldiers; or the ambitious statesmen (in the *Charmides*) who think they possess a knowledge of statesmanship superior to that of all others. It applies, likewise, to all those who follow the professional teachers of wisdom, and in the end it even applies to the simplest citizen who must make himself and others believe that he is a just person as salesman, dealer, banker, or craftsman. Apparently, then, a specialized knowledge is not what is involved here but another kind of knowing, a knowing that is beyond all specialized competencies and beyond all claims to superiority in knowledge, a knowing beyond all otherwise recognized *technai* and *epistemai*. This other knowledge means a *Wendung zur Idee*—a "turning to the idea"— that is, a turning to that which lies behind all mere positings by supposedly knowledgeable persons.

But this means that in the end Plato does not have a doctrine that one can simply learn from him, namely the "doctrine of ideas." And if he himself criticizes this doctrine in his *Parmenides*, this also does not mean that at that time he was beginning to have doubts about it.

Rather, it means that the acceptance of the "ideas" does not designate the acceptance of a doctrine so much as a way of questioning that the doctrine has the task of developing and discussing. This is the Platonic dialectic. Dialectic is the art of having a conversation and includes the art of having a conversation with oneself and fervently seeking an understanding of oneself. It is the art of thinking. But this means the art of seriously questioning what one really means when one thinks or says this or that. In doing so, one sets out on a journey, or better, is already on the journey. For there is something like a "natural disposition of man toward philosophy." Our thinking is never satisfied with what one means in saying this or that. Thinking constantly points beyond itself. The work that goes on in a Platonic dialogue has its way of expressing this: it points toward the One, toward Being, toward the "Good" which is present in the order of the soul, in the constitution of the city, and in the structure of the world.

Although Heidegger interprets the acceptance of Plato's doctrine of ideas as the beginning of the forgetfulness of Being, a forgetfulness which reaches its peak in a thinking merely in terms of representation and objectivation, and in a will to power which dominates the era of technology, and although his understanding that even the earliest Greek thinking of Being is a preparation for the forgetfulness of Being that occurs in metaphysics is consistent enough with this, I would argue that the authentic meaning of the Platonic dialectic of ideas is ultimately something quite different from all this. The fundamental step of going beyond all existing things in Plato is a step beyond a "simplistic" [einfaltige] acceptance of the ideas; thus, it ultimately represents a countermovement *against* the "metaphysical" interpretation of Being as merely the being of beings.

Actually, the history of metaphysics could be written as a history of Platonism. Its stages would be, say, Plotinus and Augustine, Meister Eckhart and Nicholas of Cusa, Leibniz, Kant, and Hegel; which means, of course, all those great efforts of Western thought to *go questioningly back behind* the substantial being of the Form and thus behind the whole metaphysical tradition. And in this respect, the first Platonist in the series would be none other than Aristotle himself. To defend this view, and thus to oppose the common interpretation of Aristotle's criticisms of the doctrine of ideas, and to attack also the substance metaphysics of the Western tradition, has been the goal of my writing in this area.[38] By the way, I do not stand all alone in this; Hegel also held such a view.

To make good my point would not be some kind of merely "historical" undertaking. For certainly my intention would not be to supplement the Heideggerian history of the increasing forgetfulness of being with a history of the remembering of being. That would not be meaningful. Indeed, it is certainly appropriate to speak of an increasing forgetfulness. In my view, Heidegger's great achievement was to have shaken us out of too full a forgetfulness by asking in earnest: what is being? I myself recall how in 1924 Heidegger ended a semester seminar on Cajetan's *De nominum analogia* with the question "Was ist das, das Sein?" and how we looked at each other and shook our heads over the absurdity of the question. In the meantime, we have all been reminded, in a certain sense, of the question of being. Even the defenders of the traditional metaphysical tradition, those who wish to be critics of Heidegger, find they are no longer captive to a self-evident understanding of being, an understanding grounded in the metaphysical tradition and accepted without question. Rather, they now defend the classical answer *as* an answer, which means that they have again recovered the question as a question.

Everywhere that philosophizing is attempted, one finds in this process that a recollection of being takes place. In spite of this, it seems to me there is no history of the recollection of Being. Recollection has no history. There is not an increasing recollection in the way that there is an increasing forgetfulness [of Being]. For recollection always comes to one, and comes over one, so that something is again made present. It offers, for the space of a moment, a halt to all passing away and forgetting. But the recollection of Being is not a recollection of something previously known and now present once again; rather, it is a recollection of a question previously asked, the reclaiming of a lost question. And a question which is asked again is no longer just something recollected; it becomes a question again and is now asked anew. It is no longer a recollection of something that was asked once upon a time in history, because now it is posed anew. In this way, questioning reconceptualizes [*aufhebt*, sublimates] the historicity of our thinking and knowing. In this sense philosophy has no history. The first person who wrote a history of philosophy that was really such was also the last to do so—Hegel. And in Hegel, history was canceled (and fulfilled) [*aufgehoben*] in the present-ness of absolute spirit [*des absoluten Geistes*].

But is this presentness *our* presentness? Is Hegel also still present for us? Certainly one ought not to dogmatize and dogmatically narrow Hegel down. When Hegel spoke of the end of history which is to be reached through the freedom of every one, he meant that history is at an end only in the sense that no higher principle can be put forward than the freedom of everyone. The increasing unfreedom of everyone which has begun to characterize Western civilization—perhaps as its inescapable destiny—would constitute for Hegel no valid objection to the principle of freedom. Indeed, he would say, "So much the worse for the facts." At the same time, I would ask Hegel this: is the first and last principle in which the philosophical thinking of being culminates really *Geist* [spirit, mind]? [39] Certainly, the critique by the young Hegelians was polemically directed against this. It is my conviction that Heidegger has been the first thinker since Hegel to present us with a positive alternative possibility, a possibility that gets beyond mere dialectical reversal. Heidegger's point is this: truth is not the total unconcealment whose ideal fulfillment would in the end be the presence of absolute spirit to itself. Rather, Heidegger taught us to think truth as an unconcealing and a concealing at the same time. The great efforts at thinking in the tradition, efforts in which over and over again we feel ourselves to be addressed and expressed, all stand in this tension. What is asserted is not everything. Indeed, it is the unsaid that first makes it, and lets it be, a word that can reach us. This seems to me to be compellingly true. The concepts in which thinking is formulated stand silhouetted like dark shadows on a wall. They work in a one-sided way, predetermining and prejudging. One thinks, for instance, of Greek intellectualism, or of the metaphysics of will in German idealism, or the methodologism of the neo-Kantians and neopositivists. In a process of which it is not aware, each of these formulated its highest principle without realizing the anticipatory entrapment contained in its own concepts.

For this reason, in every dialogue we have with the thinking of a thinker that we are seeking to understand, the dialogue remains an endless conversation. If it is a true conversation, a conversation in which we seek to find "our" language—to grasp what we have in common. Consciously taking up a historical distance from one's partner and placing one's partner in a historically surveyable course of events must remain subordinate movements of our effort to achieve understanding. As a matter of fact, they represent a certain self-assurance by which one actually closes oneself off from one's partner. In a genuine conversation, on the other hand, one seeks to open oneself to him or her, which means holding fast to the common subject matter as the ground on which one stands together with one's partner.

But if this is the case, then the goal of preserving one's own "position" is not a good one. On the other hand, if one takes such dialogical endlessness [*Unendlichkeit,* infinity] to its most radical extreme, does this not entail a complete relativism? But if this were so, would not this position itself be trapped in the well-known self-contradiction of all relativism? In the end, I think, the way such a dialogue goes on is very much like the way we acquire our experiences in life: a fullness of experiences, encounters, instructions, and disappointments does not just conjoin everything and in the end mean that one knows everything;

rather, it means that one is initiated and at the same time has learned a bit of modesty. In a central chapter of my book *Truth and Method* I have defended this "personal" concept of experience against the deformation that the concept of experience has suffered in being institutionalized in the empirical sciences. In this I feel myself akin to Michael Polanyi.[40] Hermeneutic philosophy, as I envision it, does not understand itself as an "absolute" position but as a path of experiencing. Its modesty consists in the fact that for it there is no higher principle than this: holding oneself open to the conversation. This means, however, constantly recognizing in advance the possibility that your partner may be right, even recognizing the possible superiority of your partner. Is this too little to expect? It seems to me that this is the kind of integrity one can demand of a professor of philosophy—and it is one which one also ought to demand.

It seems evident to me that we cannot get around a return to the original dialogicality of human being in the world and of having a world. This holds even if one is demanding some kind of final accountability or "ultimate foundation" [*Letztbegrundung*] for positing the self-realization of the spirit. The path of Hegel's thought, above all, should be newly examined. Heidegger has uncovered the Greek roots of the tradition of metaphysics, and he has at the same time recognized a radical allegiance to the Greeks in Hegel's dialectical dissolution of traditional concepts as carried out in the *Science of Logic*. But Heidegger's *Destruktion* of metaphysics has not, in my view, robbed metaphysics of its importance today. In particular, Hegel's powerful speculative leap beyond the subjectivity of subjective Spirit established this possibility and offered a way of shattering the predominance of subjectivism. Was Hegel's intention not the same as that in Heidegger's turn away from the transcendental principle of the self? Was it not also Hegel's intention to surpass the orientation to self-consciousness and the subject-object schema of a philosophy of consciousness? Or are there still differences that remain? Do my orientation to the universality of language and to an existence based on the linguisticality of our access to the world, both of which I share with Heidegger—do they really constitute a step beyond Hegel, or are they a step back behind Hegel?[41]

As a first determination of the site of my own effort at thinking, I would say that I have taken it on myself to restore to a place of honor what Hegel termed "bad infinity" [*schlechte Unendlichkeit*]—but with a decisive modification, of course. For in my view the unending [*unendliche*, infinite] dialogue of the soul with itself which thinking is, is not properly characterized by saying it is an endlessly refined determination of a world of objects that we are seeking to know, either in the neo-Kantian

sense of an infinite task or in the Hegelian dialectical sense that thinking is always moving beyond every particular limit. Rather, here I think
Heidegger showed me a new path when, as a preparation for posing the
question of Being in a new way, he turned to a critique of the metaphysical tradition, and in so doing found himself "on the way to language."
This way of language is not absorbed in making judgments and examining their claims to objective validity; rather, it is a way of language that
constantly holds itself open to the whole of Being. Totality, in my view, is
not some kind of objectivity that awaits human determination. In this respect, I find Kant's critique of the antinomies of pure reason to be correct
and are not superseded by Hegel. Totality is never an object but rather
a world-horizon which encloses us and within which we live our lives.

I did not need to follow Heidegger, who based himself on Hölderlin instead of Hegel and who interpreted the work of art as a primordial
occurrence of truth, in order to find in the poetic work a corrective
for the ideal of making an objective determination of truth, or in order to recognize the hubris that resides in concepts. On the contrary,
this was already clear to me in my own first efforts at thinking. From
early on the poetic work offered my own hermeneutic orientation constant food for thought. Likewise, the hermeneutical effort to conceive
of the nature of language on the basis of dialogue—inevitable for me
as a lifelong student of Plato—ultimately meant that every formulation
one might make was in principle surpassable in the process of conversation. The rigid fixing of things in terminology, which is fully appropriate in the realm of modern science and its effort to put knowledge
into the hands of its anonymous society of investigators, is peculiarly
suspect in relation to the realm of motion called philosophical thought.
The great early Greek thinkers were able to preserve the flexibility of
their own language even when their thinking was occasionally carried
out in conceptually fixed terms, say, in thematic analysis. On the other
hand, there is Scholasticism: ancient, medieval, modern—and the most
recent. Scholasticism follows philosophy like its shadow. That is why the
true rank of a thinker or of thinking is almost determinable according to how far the thinker or the thinking is able to break through the
fossilization represented by the usages in the inherited philosophical
language. Fundamentally, Hegel's programmatic effort at doing this,
which in his hands became the dialectical method, had many forerun-
ners. Even a thinker as ceremonially minded as Kant, who constantly
had in his mind the Latin language of late Scholasticism, established his
"own" language, a language which certainly avoided neologisms but in
which the traditional concepts gained new applications and new meanings. Likewise, Husserl's higher rank in philosophy as compared with

contemporary and older neo-Kantians consists precisely in the fact that his intellectual powers of intuition welded together the inherited technical expressions and combined them with the descriptive elasticity of his vocabulary into the unity of a personal style. And Heidegger did not hesitate to justify the novelty of his use of language by appealing to the example of Plato and Aristotle, and Heidegger is, by the way, far more followed now than the initially provocative effect and public amazement would have allowed one to expect. Philosophy, in contrast to the sciences and also to practical life, finds itself in a peculiar kind of difficulty. The language we speak in everyday use is not created for the purpose of philosophizing. Philosophy continually finds itself in a state of linguistic need [*Sprachnot*]. This is constitutive of philosophy, and this calamity, this distress, becomes all the more felt, the more boldly the philosophizer breaks new paths. One generally marks oneself as a dilettante in thinking if one arbitrarily introduces terms and zealously "defines one's concepts." No, the true philosopher awakens the intuitive power already resident in language, so every linguistic zeal, or even linguistic violence, can be in place only if this can be accepted into the language of those who want to think along with the philosopher, think further with him, and that means if his words are able to push forward, extend, or light up the horizon of communication.

It is unavoidable that the language of philosophy, which never finds its object at hand but must itself construct it, does not move within systems of propositions whose logical formalization and critical testing for conclusiveness and univocity would supposedly deepen its insights. Such a use of language will not create from the world a "revolution," not even the one proclaimed by the analysts of ordinary language. To illustrate this point with an example: if one analyzes the arguments in a Platonic dialogue with logical methods, shows logical inconsistencies, fills in gaps, unmasks false deductions, and so on, one will achieve a certain increase in clarity. But does one learn to read Plato in this way? Does doing this make his questions one's own? Does one succeed in actually learning from Plato instead of just confirming one's own superiority? What applies in this case to reading Plato applies by extension to all philosophy. Plato has in his *Seventh Letter* rightly described this once and for all: the means that one uses for philosophizing are not the same as philosophizing itself. Simple logical rigor is not everything. Not that logic does not have its own evident validity. But thematization in logic restrains the horizon of questioning in order to allow for verification, and in doing so blocks the kind of opening up of the world which takes place in our own experience of that world. This is a hermeneutical finding which I believe in the end converges with what we find in the later

Wittgenstein. In his later writings he revised the nominalistic prejudices of his *Tractatus* in favor of leading all speaking back to the context of life-praxis. Of course, the result of this proposed reduction of philosophy to a praxis-context remained for him a negative move. It consisted in a flat rejection of all the undemonstrable questions of metaphysics rather than in *winning back* these undemonstrable questions of metaphysics, however undemonstrable they might be, by detecting in them the linguistic constitution of our being-in-the-world [*In-der-Welt-Sein*]. For this, of course, far more can be learned from the words uttered by poets than from Wittgenstein.

In the case of poetry, one thing is undisputed: conceptual explication is never able to exhaust the content of a poetic image. No one disputes this. Indeed, this point has been recognized at least since Kant, if not earlier with Baumgarten's discovery of poetic truth as *cognitio sensitiva*. From a hermeneutic perspective this has to be of special interest. But in dealing with poetry, the mere separation of the aesthetic from the theoretical, and the freeing of poetry from the pressure of rules or concepts will not suffice. For poetry is still a form of speech in which concepts stand in a relationship with each other. The hermeneutical task is to learn how to determine the special place of poetry in the constraining context of language, where a conceptual element is always involved. The question is: in what manner does language become art? I do not pose this question here because the practice of interpretation always has to do with forms of speaking and because in poetry one also has to do with a linguistically created work or composition, that is, with a text. Rather, it is because poetic "structures" are text in a new sense: they are text in an "eminent" sense of that word—namely, "eminent text." In this kind of text language emerges in its full autonomy. Here language just stands on its own; it brings itself to stand before us autonomously, whereas normally its words are taken over by the intention in the speech and then after being used are just left behind.[42]

Here we have a hermeneutical problem with a difficulty of its own, for through poetry a special kind of communication takes place. In a poem, with *whom* does the communication take place? Is it with the reader? With *which* reader? Here the dialectic of question and answer which is always the basis of the hermeneutical process and which corresponds to the basic structure of dialogue undergoes a special modification. The reception and interpretation of poetry appears to imply a dialogical relationship of its own special kind.

This becomes especially evident if one studies the specific character of the various kinds of speaking. First, it is not only the poetic word that displays a wide scale of differentiation in the dialogical relationship;

for instance, epic, dramatic, and lyric poetry. But there are also other kinds of speaking in which the basic hermeneutical relationship of question and answer undergoes fundamental modifications. I am thinking, for instance, of the various forms of religious speaking, such as proclaiming, praying, preaching, blessing. One could also mention the mythic saga, the legal text, and even the more or less stammering language of philosophy. All of these forms involve the hermeneutical structure of application with which I have increasingly occupied myself since the publication of *Truth and Method*. I believe I have been able to get closer to what is involved here by approaching the problem from two sides: first, from my studies of Hegel, in whom I have pursued the role of the linguistic in relation to the logical; and second, from the side of modern hermetic poetry, to which I have dedicated a book, choosing Paul Celan's "Atemkristall" [cycle of poems] as the object of the commentary.[43] Reflection on them has served to remind me, and can constantly serve to remind us all, that Plato was no Platonist and philosophy is not Scholasticism.

Translated by Richard E. Palmer

Part 1

Defining the Idea of a Philosophical Hermeneutics

Classical and Philosophical Hermeneutics

Encyclopedia articles have served since the Enlightenment as a significant scholarly reference source. They not only give an account of a topic
and offer a wide range of important bibliographical references for further study, but also become historic intellectual landmarks. For instance,
famous predecessor encyclopedia articles that undertake to give an account of the discipline of hermeneutics are articles from 1735,[1] 1829,[2]
1899,[3] and 1959.[4] If one were to collect these four famous articles and
add Gadamer's article of 1977, one would have a picture of the evolving
definition of hermeneutics.[5] Gadamer's encyclopedia article on hermeneutics, then, culminates an evolving set of such articles on the topic.

Gadamer's article not only presents us with a fairly detailed history
of traditional hermeneutics from ancient times to the present; it also
offers an account of the development of his new philosophical hermeneutics and its reception history, both positive and negative, from 1960
to 1975. It is therefore a very important resource. He succinctly defines
his philosophical hermeneutics and replies to its principal critics. One
could compare it to Husserl's famous *Encyclopaedia Britannica* article on
"Phenomenology" (1927).[6] It does not just discuss a topic, it defines a
discipline.

"Classical and Philosophical Hermeneutics," here translated into
English for the first time, is not Gadamer's first attempt at an encyclopedia article on hermeneutics. His first attempt was a shorter article written in 1968 for the survey *Contemporary Philosophy,* edited by Raymond
Klibansky.[7] This earlier article bears little resemblance to his later encyclopedia text.[8] His second, much more extensive effort, titled simply
"Hermeneutik," appeared in the *Historisches Wörterbuch der Philosophie*
(1974). It represents a major statement both with regard to the history
of traditional hermeneutics and to what hermeneutics had become as a
result of his masterwork of 1960. When Gadamer was invited to contribute an article on hermeneutics to an Italian encyclopedia, the *Enciclopedia del Novecento* (1977),[9] he sent them the typed German manuscript
text of the 1974 article but expanded the manuscript by about two pages
at the end to devote a little more detail to Habermas and the Frankfurt

school's critique of ideology.[10] The original German manuscript of this 1977 text is what he used in volume 2 of his collected works (*Gesammelte Werke* 2: 92–117) and that is translated here. He retitled the article "Klassische und philosophische Hermeneutik" to indicate that hermeneutics is treated both as it is classically defined and understood (dedicated to the task of text interpretation) and as his philosophical hermeneutics (dedicated to the nature of the task and process of understanding) defines it.

In this rich article Gadamer first traces the etymology of the word "hermeneutics" in ancient Greek and the different dimensions of meaning it had even at that time. He discusses the key affinity in antiquity between hermeneutics and rhetoric, as well as the modern significance of this point for his own hermeneutics. He includes in his account of the discipline's historical development the juridical, rhetorical, and theological hermeneutics from ancient to modern times, although with little detail. A more extensive account of the development of theological hermeneutics can be found in the previous encyclopedia articles of 1899 and 1959 mentioned above. The main point Gadamer notes in his account of ancient hermeneutics is the importance of allegorical interpretation in Greek times and then in the Christian tradition up to the Reformation.[11] He notes that after that time, history as a factor and the methods of classical philology had an important place in the development of Protestant hermeneutics. He also calls attention in his account of traditional hermeneutics to the factor of application, especially in juridical and theological hermeneutics. This comes out in a more pronounced way than in previous historical accounts of hermeneutics. Application is something that Gadamerian philosophical hermeneutics seeks to reinstate in order to redress its absence from the tradition of philological and theological hermeneutics in the nineteenth century.

Also notable here is his clear rejection of the general hermeneutics of Schleiermacher and Dilthey, which remain methodological and in which the interpreter goes back from the text or work of art to the psychic reality of the personal experience of the creator. At this point Gadamer's article becomes less like an objective encyclopedia article and more like a defense of his own position. For instance, he makes very clear why he takes issue with Schleiermacher and Dilthey. In doing so he brings in another key element in his hermeneutics: his insistence on interpreting texts not as expressions of the soul or of emotions but rather as conveying the *Sache* (subject matter) communicated by the text. The *Sache* on which Gadamer insists in his hermeneutics is the matter, the issue, and ultimately the truth emerging from the experience of the text or work of art. Truth, a decisive element in Gadamer's philosophical hermeneutics, can only be defended as emerging if the emphasis is placed on *Sache* rather than on soul. A text, according to Gadamer, does not just express feelings or the mind of the author. In its highest forms—in sacred texts, in poetry, in law, even in works of art—the work causes truth to emerge, or in Heidegger's terms, it "brings truth to stand."[12]

To summarize this article briefly, then, in it Gadamer moves beyond previous encyclopedia articles on hermeneutics to propose and defend a new philosophical discipline. He first examines the etymology of the word "hermeneutics" at its beginnings in ancient Greece, which hold significant dimensions for a philosophical hermeneutics. He then discusses hermeneutics in various forms since ancient times. But starting with eighteenth-century aesthetics and Schleiermacher's hermeneutics, he offers a critical history of hermeneutics up to his *Truth and Method*. Thus, this article can serve as a short introduction to his masterwork. But Gadamer then goes beyond *Truth and Method* in time to take up the reactions to it since its publication in 1960 and to offer his reply to them. He considers critics like Emilio Betti, E. D. Hirsch, and Hans Albert, who bitterly attacked that work and wrote in favor of the philological tradition. He also expresses his reservations about the current of German literary criticism that offered an "aesthetics of reception" as a response to his work. For Gadamer, this response represented a rather truncated reading of his philosophical hermeneutics. And also, he notes Derrida's deconstructionist critique of philosophical hermeneutics. Gadamer's encounters with Derrida in 1980 and 1989 were dialogues that failed; they simply talked past each other.[13] And he takes up the criticisms by Habermas and the critique of ideology. At the end, he reaffirms the universality of his hermeneutics as a theory of the praxis of understanding that needs to be defended against the narrowness of many forms of scientific understanding.

Since the time of this article, Gadamer's hermeneutics has continued to unfold and to extend its influence worldwide.[14] While his encyclopedia article documents the phases of its unfolding up to that time, the influence of philosophical hermeneutics has continued to spread. Different disciplines, such as the social sciences (mentioned by Gadamer in his article), but also literature, history, and the theory of methodology continue to find in his critique of scientific reasoning and methodologies a philosophical basis for fruitful innovations. One could lament that in the classical portion of his encyclopedia article Gadamer omits a consideration of non-Western forms of classical text interpretation, such as the rich Jewish tradition, and also the Buddhist, Hindu, Chinese, and Muslim traditions. Gadamer contents himself with returning to ancient

Greece. In any case, his philosophical hermeneutics continues to attract worldwide interest, and this encyclopedia article remains a good introduction to his philosophical hermeneutics as well as a landmark in the evolving history of hermeneutics.[15]

* * *

Classical and Philosophical Hermeneutics

"Hermeneutics" is a term that covers many different levels of reflection, as is frequently the case with Greek words that have become part of the terminology in our scholarly disciplines. "Hermeneutics" refers, first of all, to a practice, an art, that requires a special skill. This points to a further Greek word, namely *techne*. Hermeneutics is the practical art, that is, a *techne,* involved in such things as preaching, interpreting other languages, explaining and explicating texts, and, as the basis of all of these, the art of understanding, an art particularly required any time the meaning of something is not clear and unambiguous.

We find even in the earliest Greek usage of the words *hermeneia* and *hermeneuein* a certain ambiguity.[1] Hermes was the messenger of the gods who brought the messages of the gods to human beings. As he is depicted in Homer, Hermes literally repeats the same words that the gods had told him to tell a human person. But often, especially in ordinary usage, the business of the *hermeneus* [interpreter] was more precisely that of translating something foreign or unintelligible into the language everybody speaks and understands. The business of translating therefore always has a certain "freedom." It assumes a full understanding of the foreign language, but still more an understanding of the true sense of what is meant in the specific expression in the target language. Any interpreter who wants to be intelligible must bring what is meant into clear linguistic expression once again. What hermeneutics accomplishes, then, is this bringing of something out of one world and into another, out of the world of the gods and into that of humans, or out of the world of a foreign language into the world of one's own language. (Human interpreters can only translate well into their own language.) However, because one's task of translation consists precisely in causing someone to be rightly oriented to something, the meaning of ερμηνευειν [*hermeneuein*] shifts back and forth between merely translating meaning and the practical giving of instructions, between mere reporting and actually demanding obedience.

Indeed, in a completely neutral sense, ερμηνεια [*hermeneia*] only means "expression of thought," but it is significant that Plato used the word to refer not just to any expression of a thought but only to the king's knowledge, the herald's knowledge, and so on, thus words having the character of commanding or giving instruction about a matter.[2] The closeness of hermeneutics to the mantic art[3] [the art of uttering truth] is to be understood in this sense: it is the art of transmitting the will of the gods, alongside the art of reading the future from signs. Nevertheless, Aristotle in his *Peri hermeneias* uses the term *hermeneias* only in the logical sense of an assertion being true or false, suggesting a purely cognitive direction of meaning, dealing as he does in this text only with the *logos apophantikos*. Corresponding to this purely cognitive sense, the terms *hermeneia* and *hermeneus* came in later Greek culture to mean one who makes a "learned explanation" and an "explainer" or "translator" [respectively]. Of course, there always still clung to hermeneutics as an art something of its older heritage in the sacred sphere:[4] hermeneutics is an art to whose saying one had to submit as something to be respected, or which one recognized with admiration because this art was able to understand and explain the hidden—speech in a foreign language or even the unexpressed conviction of another person. Hermeneutics is thus an *ars* [art], or in German a *Kunstlehre* [a teaching or doctrine of a certain art], like the art of speaking or the art of writing or the art of calculating with numbers, and as an "art" it is more a practical ability to do something [a *techne*] than a "science."

This is the case even in the modern echoes of the word in theological and juridical hermeneutics; in these this aspect of the old sense of the word seems to hold: they are both an "art" or at least an "art" in the lower sense, as a serviceable means, but more to the point, they always include a normative competence: the interpreter not only understands how to practice the art of translating, he or she also brings something normative to expression—the divine or the human law.

In contrast to this, when we use the term "hermeneutics" today we stand in the scientific tradition of the modern era. In this tradition, the usage of the term "hermeneutics" begins with the rise of modern concepts of method and science. Implicit in the meaning of the term today is always some kind of methodical consciousness at work. The interpreter not only possesses the art of exegesis [*Auslegung*]; he or she also knows how to justify his or her exegesis theoretically. For instance, in the modern era the first use of the term "hermeneutics" as a book title came in the year 1654 with J. Dannhauer's *Hermeneutica Sacra sive Methodus Exponendarum Sacrarum Litteraturum* [*Sacred Hermeneutics, or a Method of Explicating Sacred Scripture*]. Since that time the theological and philological hermeneutics have been sharply distinguished from juridical hermeneutics.

Theologically, hermeneutics signifies the art of rightly interpreting the holy scriptures, which in itself is an ancient art. Already in the early church fathers' time, interpretation was led toward a methodical consciousness, above all by Augustine in his *De doctrina Christiana.* The task of Christian dogmatics in early times was shaped by the tension between the particular history of the Jewish people and the universal proclamation Jesus put forward in the New Testament. Here methodical reflection is called on to help create solutions to this problem. With the help of notions from Plotinus, Augustine in *De doctrina Christiana* described the ascent of the spirit from the literal sense of a text to the moral meaning, and then further upward to the spiritual meaning. In this way he solved a doctrinal problem by integrating the ancient hermeneutical heritage into a single, unified standpoint.

The problem of allegorical interpretation is the core of ancient hermeneutics. Allegory as a mode of interpretation is quite old. The term originally used for the allegorical meaning in Greece was *hyponoia,* the meaning behind the literal meaning. This form of interpretation was already practiced at the time of Plato's *Sophist,* as A. Tate has rightly maintained in this century, and this point has been corroborated by ancient papyrus texts that have been recently discovered. The historical context at the base of this mode of interpretation is now clear: a new interpretive art was required the moment the Homeric epic, a work intended for a noble society, lost its compelling validity. This happened with the democratization of the cities. For them the ethics of nobility served as their patrimony. An expression of this was the educational idea of the Sophists, that Odysseus outranked Achilles. Furthermore, on the stage Odysseus often took on Sophistic tendencies. The allegorical interpretation of Homer developed into a universal method, especially in the Stoics. Christian patristic hermeneutics, epitomized by Origen and Augustine, continued to use the allegorical method. And it was systematized in the Middle Ages by John Cassian with his method of the fourfold sense [the literal, allegorical, moral, and anagogical meanings] of scripture.

A new impetus entered into hermeneutics in the Reformation when the Reformers urged a return to a focus on the literal level of the holy scriptures. Their sharp polemic was directed against the traditional method of finding multiple levels of meaning in scripture.[5] In particular the allegorical method was criticized. It should really only be applied and an allegorical understanding sought, said the Reformers, in cases where the meaning of the text, say, of a parable—in Jesus' speeches, for instance—justified it. In tandem with this Reformation polemic against allegorical interpretation, a new methodological consciousness was awakened that wanted to be objective, object-centered, and free from all subjective arbitrariness. However, the central motive was still a normative one: in both theological hermeneutics and in the humanistic hermeneutics of modern times, the aim was to get back to the correct interpretation of those texts which contained material that was authentic. In this respect, the motivation of their hermeneutical efforts was not so much what it later was in Schleiermacher, that is, to make a tradition understandable that was difficult to understand and gave rise to misunderstandings. Rather, they wanted to bring a whole new understanding to an existing tradition by uncovering its lost beginnings, the access to which had been broken off or changed. For them, the original meaning had been concealed or distorted, and this original meaning needed to be sought out and again be made like new. So in going back to original sources, hermeneutics sought everywhere to gain a new understanding of something that had been spoiled by distortion, disfigurement, or misuse—in the case of the Bible this was through the doctrinal tradition of the church; in the case of the Greek and Latin classics, this was through the barbaric Latin used in Scholasticism. And in Roman law this distortion came about through regional practices of justice. The new hermeneutical efforts at this time were not just dedicated to understanding the text more correctly; they also sought to bring interpretation to acceptance in a way that was exemplary and compelling, as for example in the proclamation of a message from God, or the interpretation of an oracle utterance, or in showing clearly a prescription of the law that compels adherence.

Along with this motivation in hermeneutics that was directed to matters of content, there was also at the beginning of modernity a more formal motivation at work. This was the method-oriented consciousness that belonged to the new science. Especially by using the language of mathematics, this new motivation was pressing for a universal doctrine of the interpretation of signs. For the sake of this universality, hermeneutics was dealt with as a part of logic.[6] In the eighteenth century, Christian Wolff's *Logic* played the decisive role in this by the inclusion of a chapter on hermeneutics in a book on logic.[7] A logical-philosophical interest was in play here, which strove to place hermeneutics firmly within the parameters of a general semantics [*einer allgemeinen Semantik*]. A basic sketch of this project was given by Georg Friedrich Meier [1718–77], whose intellectual forerunner was Chladenius [1710–59].[8] In contrast to this, during the seventeenth [previous] century the emerging discipline of hermeneutics in theology and philology remained in general fragmentary and served more didactic rather than philosophical goals. For pragmatic purposes, certainly, it developed a few basic methodical rules, which for the most part had been drawn from ancient grammar and rhetoric (Quintilian).[9] But for the most part during this time, hermeneutics remained only a collection of explanations of difficulties, which were to help open up and clarify one's understanding of scripture (or, in the humanistic realm, the classics). The customary title of such manuals was a "Clavis," or "Key," as for example, Flacius's *Clavis scripturae sacrae* of 1567.[10]

It is important to note that the conceptual vocabulary of the early Protestant hermeneutics was derived from ancient rhetoric. Melanchthon's contribution, in this regard, was epoch-making. He turned rhetoric around by directing its basic concepts to the right reading of books (*bonis auctoribus legendis*), which was the prevailing pattern and theme in rhetoric during late antiquity (e.g., in Dionysius of Halicarnassus [b. 54 BC]). Indeed, the basic demand to understand the individual part from the whole goes back to the relationship of *caput* (head) and *membra* (members of the body), which ancient rhetoric took as the pattern to follow. In Flacius this basic hermeneutical principle obviously had a highly exciting application, since the dogmatic unity of the canon, which he used in the explication of individual New Testament writings, sharply restricted Luther's basic principle regarding scripture, as we shall see.

Certainly the two general hermeneutical rules borrowed from ancient rhetoric [namely, the right reading of books and the relation of whole to part] that we have mentioned in these early modern forms of "hermeneutics" would not in themselves justify a philosophical interest in these writings. Nevertheless, we find already in the very early history of Protestant hermeneutics that a deep philosophical problematic [that of pre-understanding] arose which was only to break forth fully in the twentieth century. Now the basic Lutheran thesis of *sacra scriptura sui ipsius interpres* [sacred scripture is self-interpreting] certainly does contain a clear negation of the dogmatic tradition of the Roman Church, but at the same time this thesis did not in any way propose to put forward a naive inspiration theory. Luther needed a special principle that justified his own translation and exegetical work, the principle of *sui ipsius interpres*. This was particularly so because the Wittenberg theology as well as the great translation of the Bible that he, as a highly learned scholar, put forward brought into play a rich collection of traditional philological and exegetical tools. Of course, the paradox in this basic premise of Luther was all too apparent, and the defenders of the Catholic doctrinal tradition in the Council of Trent [1545–63] and also in Counter-Reformation writings did not fail to call attention to its theoretical weaknesses. Certainly one could not deny that Protestant exegesis of the Bible also worked with dogmatic guidelines that were in part systematically summed up in the articles of faith, and were in part suggested in the selection of their *loci praecipui* [particular locations]. The critique of Flacius by Richard Simon in his *Histoire critique du texte du Nouveau Testament* (1689) and in his *De l'inspiration des livres sacrés* (1687) importantly documents what we today call the hermeneutical problematic of "pre-understanding."[11] Also, it can be shown that this general principle conceals certain ontological implications that only became visible in the twentieth century [Heidegger].

In connection with its rejection of any doctrine of verbal inspiration in interpreting the scriptures, the theological hermeneutics of the early Enlightenment finally sought to formulate some general rules of understanding. In particular, historical criticism directed at the Bible found its first legitimation at that time. Spinoza's *Tractatus Theologico-Politicus* [Amsterdam, 1670] was a major event in this respect. Its criticism of miracles, for example, was made through the claim of reason, the claim only to recognize what is rational, that is, what is really possible. This was not just a critique of miracles. It contained at the same time a further positive application, to the extent of a general principle that what offends the reason calls for a natural explanation. This led to a turn toward the historical, that is, a turn away from a focus on the alleged (and rationally unintelligible) miracle stories to a (rationally intelligible) faith in miracles.[12]

Stepping forward during the Enlightenment to oppose the negative impact of this turn was what we call pietist hermeneutics, a mode of interpretation which, since A. H. Francke, has closely linked the meaning of texts with their edifying application. Here the tradition of ancient rhetoric and its teaching with regard to the role of emotional impact enters in, especially with regard to their doctrine of the sermon, which in Protestantism had received a new, major role. The influential hermeneutics of J. J. Rambach in the eighteenth century expressly placed *subtilitas applicandi* [sensitivity to the application] alongside *subtilitas intelligendi* [understanding] and *subtilitas explicandi* [explanation]. This certainly corresponded to the way preaching conveys the meaning of a text in a sermon.[13] The expression *subtilitas* (fineness, sensitivity) comes from the competitive-mindedness of the humanistic tradition and points in an elegant way to the fact that what is called the "methodology" of interpretation—like the application of rules as such—requires powers of judgment which cannot be secured through rules alone.[14] For the application of theory to hermeneutical practice, this was to signify a lasting curtailment. As we mentioned above, hermeneutics, having the status in the eighteenth century of a mere help-discipline in theology, had a constant struggle to be accorded equal weight with the dogmatic interest [see, for example, Ernesti and Semler].[15]

Schleiermacher's hermeneutics, prompted by Friedrich Schlegel, freed hermeneutics from all dogmatic and occasional moments by conceiving of it as a universal [*allgemeine*] doctrine of understanding and interpretation. In Schleiermacher the occasional, disciplinary elements arise only in a supplementary way; in turning to the biblical text, of course, they are given their due. With his hermeneutical theory, Schleiermacher could defend the scientific character of theology, especially against inspiration-based theologies. These theologies had fundamentally put in question the validity of understanding the holy scriptures by means of textual exegesis, historical theology, philology, and so on. But on the other hand, the interest that formed the basis of Schleiermacher's conception of a general hermeneutics was not just a political interest in forming a scientific theology, but in the background stood a philosophical impulse. One of the deepest drives of the Romantic age was a faith in dialogue as a source of truth in its own right, a source that was undogmatic and not in any way replaceable by dogmatic belief. While Kant and Fichte had designated the spontaneity of the "I think" as the highest principle of all philosophy, the Romantic generation of Schlegel and Schleiermacher, outstanding in its glowing cultivation of friendship, extended and even transformed the principle of dialogue to the point that it became a metaphysics of individuality. The inexpressibility of the individual became the basis for a turn to the historical world, a world that clearly emerged into consciousness via the break with tradition that occurred in the revolutionary era. The capacity for friendship, and with it the capacity for dialogue, for letter-writing, for communication as such—all these currents in the Romantic sense of life were combined in the interest in understanding and misunderstanding. This was the primal human experience that formed the starting point of Schleiermacher's hermeneutics. After Schleiermacher, the understanding of texts was the [Romantic] understanding of what was alien, distant, and surrounded by darkness, and an understanding of the traces of spirit congealed into writing. Thus, the living explication of literature and particularly of the holy scriptures represented important applications of Schleiermacher's universal hermeneutics.

Admittedly, Schleiermacher's hermeneutics is not completely free of the somewhat dusty classroom air found in earlier writings in hermeneutics—and likewise his genuine philosophical work is overshadowed by the other great thinkers in German idealism. His work has neither the compelling power of Fichtean deductions, nor Schelling's speculative elegance, nor the grainy headstrongness of Hegel's conceptual art—no, Schleiermacher was basically an orator, even when he philoso-phized. His books read like a set of speaker's notes. In particular, his contributions to hermeneutics are like jottings, and the work that is hermeneutically the most interesting, namely his remarks on thinking and speaking, is not found at all in his "hermeneutics" but in his lecture course on dialectics! And regrettably, according to a major book in Ital-ian on Schleiermacher in 1968, we are still waiting for a usable critical edition of these lectures.[16] In Schleiermacher, the basic meaning of the text itself, which traditionally was normative for interpretation and gave hermeneutical efforts their direction, steps into the background. For him, understanding is a reproductive repetition of the original intel-lectual act of the author's production of the meaning on the basis of the congeniality of spirit. Schleiermacher teaches this against the backdrop of his metaphysical conception of the individualizing of the life of the cosmos [*Individualizierung des All-Lebens*]. In this context, the role of lan-guage emerges in a form that fundamentally overcomes the traditional restriction of hermeneutics to what is written. Schleiermacher's ground-ing of understanding on dialogue and on interhuman understanding establishes a foundation for hermeneutics at a deeper level than before, and in a way that allows one to erect on a hermeneutical basis a sys-tem that is scientific and scholarly. Hermeneutics becomes the scholarly foundation not just for theology but for all historically based humanistic disciplines. The dogmatic presupposition of certain definitive texts on the basis of which hermeneutics performed its mediating function is gone, both in theology as well as in humanistic philology (not to men-tion legal interpretation). The way is cleared for historicism.

In the successors of Schleiermacher, his "psychological interpreta-tion" in particular was further supported by the Romantic doctrine that creativity came from the creative unconscious of a genius; this became more and more a defining theoretical basis in the human sciences. Hey-mann Steinthal's *Introduction to Psychology and Linguistics*[17] offers a highly instructive example of this, and in Dilthey it led to a systematic new grounding for the human sciences in a "descriptive and analytical psy-chology." Of course, a proper philosophical grounding for the histori-cal sciences was not something that mattered deeply to Schleiermacher. Rather, he himself belongs in the context of the transcendental ideal-ism established by Kant and Fichte. Fichte's *Foundations for the Theory of Science as a Whole*, especially, had an epochal significance comparable at the time to Kant's *Critique of Pure Reason*. As Fichte's title already indi-cates, what is being dealt with here is a derivation of all knowledge from a unitary "highest principle," that of the spontaneity of reason. (Fichte called this a *Tathandlung* [action] instead of a *Tatsache* [fact].) And this turn from Kantian "critical idealism" to "absolute idealism" was the basis of all that came later—in Schiller, Schleiermacher, Schelling, Friedrich Schlegel, and Wilhelm von Humboldt—right down to Boeckh, Ranke, Droysen, and Dilthey.

The fact that in the middle and later nineteenth century the "historical school," in spite of its rejection of any a priori construction of world history in the style of Fichte and Hegel, nevertheless shared the basic theoretical assumptions of idealist philosophy has been particularly well shown by Erich Rothacker in his *Introduction to the Human Sciences* (1930).[18] The published lectures of the famous philologist August Boeckh, titled *Encyclopedia of the Philological Sciences,* were also very influential. In this work, Boeckh determined the task of philology to be simply the "knowing of the known" [*Erkennen des Erkannten*]. He found here a very good formula for the secondary character of philology. The character of classical literature as moral example, which had been rediscovered by humanism in the Renaissance and was primarily to motivate behavior as an *imitation,* paled to historical indifference in Boeckh. The basic task of understanding as he defined it was differentiated into several different ways of interpretation: the grammatical, the literary-genre, the historical-real, and the psychological-individual.[19] And Dilthey took this approach as the starting point of his *verstehende Psychologie* [understanding-based psychology].

Of course, under the influence of the "inductive logic" of John Stuart Mill what was called the "epistemological orientation" had changed by that time, and although Dilthey was defending the idea of an "understanding-based psychology" against the ever-expanding experimental psychology based on Herbart and Fechner, he still shared with them the general inductive standpoint of taking "experience" [*Erfahrung*] as the starting point. But in Dilthey this was rather different. It was established on the "principle of consciousness" [*Satz des Bewusstseins*] and the concept of *Erlebnis* [heightened, lived experience]. Also, the philosophical-historical and even theological-historical background, on which the intellectual history written by the historian Johann Gustav Droysen was based, was a constant warning to him, as was the rigorous criticism that his friend, the speculative Lutheran thinker Yorck von Wartenburg, had made of the naive historicism of their time. Both of these contributed to the fact that in his later development Dilthey broke new ground. For example, the concept of *Erlebnis,* which had for him formed the psychological basis for hermeneutics, was supplemented by the distinction he made between *Ausdruck* [expression] and its *Bedeutung* [meaning]. This was partly influenced by the critique of psychologism he found in the prolegomena to Husserl's *Logical Investigations* [1900] and by his own rather Platonic theory of meaning. Also, it partly represents a return to Hegel's theory of objective spirit, which Dilthey had discovered from his studies of the history of Hegel's youth.[20]

Dilthey's work yielded fruit in the twentieth century. It was continued by such important figures as Georg Misch, B. Groethuysen, E. Spranger, Theodore Litt, Joachim Wach, Hans Freyer, Erich Rothacker, and Otto Bollnow, among others. Finally, the idealistic tradition of hermeneutics from Schleiermacher to Dilthey and beyond was drawn on later by the legal historian Emilio Betti in his writings on hermeneutics in the 1950s and after.[21]

Dilthey himself did not fully achieve the task he struggled so hard to accomplish, namely to mediate on the theoretical level between "historical consciousness" and the scientific claim to truth. The theologian Ernst Troeltsch's formula, "From relativity to totality," was presented as the theoretical solution to the problem of relativism in Dilthey's sense, but this formula remained entangled in the historicism it tried to overcome, as did Troeltsch's own work as a whole. It was characteristic of Troeltsch even in his three-volume work on historicism that he went off on a tangent (although brilliantly) over and over again. Dilthey did just the opposite, seeking a constant that would go back behind all relativity. To accomplish this he undertook a highly influential doctrine of "types of worldview," which was supposed to do justice to the many-sidedness of life. But such a doctrine of different types of worldview only overcame historicism in a very qualified sense. For the determinative basis of this theory of types, like every such doctrine of types, was the concept of the "worldview," that is to say, an attitude of consciousness which one cannot go behind and which one could only describe and compare with other worldviews. But ultimately a worldview could only be accepted as "the appearance of an expression of life." But this meant that "the will to know through concepts," which is the heart of philosophy's claim to truth, had to be given up in favor of "historical consciousness," a conception Dilthey presupposed dogmatically without reflecting on it. Such an approach was a world away from the great Fichte's much-misused saying, "The philosophy that one chooses depends on what kind of human being one is,"[22] a thesis that registered an unequivocal profession of faith in idealism.

This point can be shown to be the case in Dilthey's disciples. The pedagogical-anthropological, psychological, sociological, art-theoretical, and historical theories about types, which were spreading at that time, clearly demonstrated that their fruitfulness rested in each case on a concealed dogmatic base. We can see in all these typologies, put forward by Max Weber, Spranger, Litt, Pinder, Kretschmer, Jaensch, Lersch, and others, that they had only a limited truth value. At the same time they lost even this when they attempted to encompass the totality of all appearances, that is, to be complete. Such an extension of a typology into an all-encompassing basis of its essence in each case could only mean its self-dissolution, that is, the destruction of its dogmatic center. Even Jaspers's famous *Psychology of Worldviews* [1919] was not free of this problem, which is found in all typologies after Max Weber and Dilthey, as something his "philosophy" later required (and achieved). Typology as a tool of thought can in truth only be made legitimate from an extremely nominalistic standpoint. Even Max Weber's nominalistic radicality of self-asceticism was aware of its limits and supplemented itself through the fully irrational decisionistic concession that each person must choose "his god," the god he wishes to follow.[23]

In a similar way, the theological hermeneutics that began in the epoch in which Schleiermacher laid its foundation on a universal basis also remained entangled in its own dogmatic aporiae. Already Friedrich Lücke, the editor of Schleiermacher's hermeneutics lectures [published posthumously in 1838], chose to emphasize the theological element in him. Theological dogmatics in the nineteenth century as whole turned back to the early Protestant problem-horizon, where hermeneutics was something given along with the rule of faith. It was dead set against the demand for a critique of all dogmatics in the light of history. The result was an increasing indifference to the special task of theology. For this reason, in the age of liberal theology one finds basically no hermeneutical problematic that is specifically theological.

In this context, the hermeneutical reflection of Rudolf Bultmann [1884–1976] was an epochal event when, after himself passing through radical historicism and also being directly influenced by the dialectical theology of Karl Barth and Eduard Thurneysen, he introduced the theme of "demythologizing," which established the necessity of a genuine mediation between historical and dogmatic exegesis. Of course, the dilemma between carrying out an analysis that was historically individualizing and the mission of carrying forward the Christian message, the kerygma, remained theoretically insoluble, and Bultmann's concept of "mythos" quickly proved itself to be a construction absolutely full of presuppositions based in the modern Enlightenment. He negated the truth-claim that is embodied in the language of mythos—so this was a hermeneutic position that was extremely one-sided. The debate over demythologizing, which Günther Bornkamm has described with great expertise and skill,[24] nevertheless still remains of general hermeneutical interest, in that we find in it the ancient tension between dogmatism and hermeneutics now put before us in a contemporary, modified form. Bultmann's theological self-reflection moved away from idealism and in the direction of Heideggerian thinking. On the other hand, the claim that was consequently raised by Karl Barth and dialectical theology brought to general awareness the human as well as theological problem involved in "talk about God." The solution that Bultmann had sought was a positive one, that is to say, a methodologically justified solution that gave up nothing of the great accomplishment represented by historical theology. In this situation, Heidegger's existential philosophy in *Being and Time* [1927] seemed to Bultmann to offer a neutral, anthropological position, in which the self-understanding of religious faith found an ontological grounding.[25] Heidegger's analysis of the futurity of the existing being [the Dasein] either in the mode of authenticity [*Eigentlichkeit*] or, on the other side, the human decline into being entrapped in the world [*Verfallen*], could be interpreted theologically by means of the concepts of faith and sin. This was certainly not what Heidegger had in mind with his exposition of the question of Being; rather, this represented an anthropologizing of it. But the universal relevance for human existence of the question of God which Bultmann was able to ground in what Heidegger called the human ability to exist authentically [fulfilling the best possible way for the existing individual to be in the world] brought a genuine hermeneutical gain. This gain lay above all in the hermeneutical concept of pre-understanding—not to mention the rich exegetical advance represented by such a hermeneutical consciousness.

Heidegger's new philosophical approach produced results not only in terms of its positive effects on theology, but above all in being able to break with the relativism and typological rigidity that reigned in the Dilthey school. It was thanks to Georg Misch that Husserl and also Heidegger were confronted with Dilthey, and through this confrontation the deeper philosophical impulse of Dilthey was released and given a new life.[26] In spite of the fact that his life-philosophy ultimately constituted a counterposition to that of Heidegger, Dilthey's move back behind what was called the "transcendental consciousness" to what he called the "standpoint of life" was an important inspiration for Heidegger as he worked out his own philosophy. The editing by Georg Misch of the scattered writings of Dilthey into volumes 5–8 of the collected works, as well as Misch's expert introductions, made Dilthey's philosophical achievement, which had been largely overshadowed by his historical and literary accomplishments, visible for the first time in the 1920s. As the philosophical ideas of Dilthey (and Kierkegaard) entered into the foundations of twentieth-century *Existenzphilosophie,* this led to a philosophical radicalization of the hermeneutical problem. In his early thinking, Heidegger fashioned the concept of a "hermeneutics of facticity" [*Hermeneutik der Faktizität*], and in so doing against Husserl's phenomenological ontology of essences he formulated the paradoxical task of explicating the *Unvordenkliche* [Schelling: "unthinkable"] dimension of *Existenz* [the futurality of human existing]. Indeed, Heidegger interpreted *Existenz* itself as "understanding" and *Auslegung* [laying out, interpretation], and eventually defined *Existenz* as the self-projecting by the self of its possibilities. Here he reached a point at which the instrumentalistic sense of the hermeneutical phenomenon as basically methodological had to turn into a new sense of the hermeneutical as an ontological phenomenon[!] "Understanding" is no longer meant as one process of human thinking among others, a behavior that could be developed through discipline into a scientific procedure; rather, it means something that constitutes the basic being-in-motion [*Bewegtheit*, movedness] of the existing human being [Dasein]. This characterization of understanding and the special emphasis Heidegger gave to it by making understanding the basic movement of *Existenz* flowed into his concept of interpretation—a concept which Nietzsche above all had developed in its theoretical significance. This [new Nietzchean] path of thinking rests on a doubt about the assertions made in one's consciousness, about which Nietzsche expressly stated that one should doubt these assertions better than Descartes did.[27] In Nietzsche this doubt resulted in a change in his sense of truth as such, so that interpretation as a process becomes an expression of one's will to power and with this step interpretation acquires an ontological significance.

Now it seems to me that in the twentieth century a similar ontological sense is assigned to the concept of *Geschichtlichkeit* [historicality], both by the young Heidegger and by Jaspers. Historicality is no longer seen as merely a boundary phenomenon recognized by reason in its claim to grasp truth; rather, it comes to represent a positive conditioning factor in the knowledge of truth. With this move the argumentation of historical relativism loses any real basis. The idea of requiring a criterion for absolute truth is shown to be an abstract and metaphysical idol and loses any methodological significance at all. As a term, then, *Geschichtlichkeit* ceases to evoke the specter of historical relativism, against which Husserl's programmatic essay "Philosophy as Rigorous Science" [1913] had so passionately issued a warning.

Above all, this new orientation renewed the influence of Kierkegaard's thinking. It fit in well with and was operative in the highest degree in inspiring a new critique of idealism by Unamuno and others, as well as the development of the standpoint of the "thou," the other "I." One sees this in orientation in Theodor Haecker, Friedrich Gogarten,

Eduard Griesebach, Ferdinand Ebner, Martin Buber, Karl Jaspers, Viktor von Weizsäcker, and also in Karl Löwith's *The Individual in the Role of a Person with Other Persons.*[28]

The rich intellectual dialectic with which Emilio Betti sought to justify the heritage of Romantic hermeneutics in terms of "an interplay of subjective and objective" had nevertheless to appear inadequate in view of the fact that Heidegger's *Being and Time* [1927] had clearly shown that the concept of "the subject" was just a precursor of the ontological, and then it was basically exploded when Heidegger in his thinking of the "turn" completely discredited reflection within the framework of transcendental philosophy. The emergence [*Ereignis*] of truth, which according to Heidegger takes shape in the space of the interplay of disclosure and concealment, gave to all processes of disclosure—even that of the sciences based on understanding—a new ontological valence. And with this philosophical development, it became possible to address a whole new series of questions to traditional hermeneutics.

For instance, the basically psychological underpinnings of hermeneutics during the period of German idealism proved to be dubious. Is the meaning of a text really exhausted by arriving at the meaning that was psychologically "intended" by the author, the *mens auctoris* [the mind of the author]? Is understanding to be conceived of as nothing more than the reproduction of the author's original production? It is quite clear that this view cannot hold true in the case of juridical hermeneutics, which manifestly exercises a creative legal function. Also, this view [*mens auctoris*] serves to push legal hermeneutics and its normative function to one side and to treat the practical application of meaning as something that has nothing at all to do with what they call "science"! The concept of objectivity in science, after all, demands that one hold fast to a canon that was shaped by the *mens auctoris*. But can this view really be enough? For example, what about the interpretation of *works of performative art* (which often take the form of a practical production by the stage manager, the director, or the translator)? Can one really deny that the reproducing artist creatively "interprets" the original creation and does not simply reproduce it? One distinguishes very precisely between reproductive interpretations of musical or dramatic works that are appropriate and those that are "impermissible" and not in the right style. One can sense this. What justification does one have to make the claim of this sense of producing meaning any different from that of science? Does such reproduction really take place in the artist like sleepwalking, without the use of conscious knowledge? Obviously not. But the content of meaning in an artistic reproduction certainly cannot be limited to what the author may have consciously meant. The self-interpretation by the artist is of questionable validity, as is well known. And interpreting the meaning of the created work still poses for the performer the task of an unambiguous approximation. So the performance of an artwork is clearly not just completely abandoned to randomness, any more than the interpretations undertaken by science.

And what about the sense and interpretation of historical events? The consciousness of the contemporaries in a historical situation is characterized by the fact that they who undergo history do not know how it was that these events happened to them. Even when faced with this fact, Dilthey to the end held fast to the systematic consistency of his concept of *Erlebnis* [heightened personal experience]. We see this from the fact that biography and autobiography functioned as models for him in his theory with regard to the historical set of connections or context of effects [*Wirkungszusammenhang*].[29] Even in R. G. Collingwood's profound critique of positivist method-consciousness, which by the way made use of the dialectical instrument of Crocean Hegelianism,[30] we see that in using the concept of *reenactment* Collingwood too remained entrapped along with his teacher in a subjectivistic narrowing of the problem when they took as foundational a model case of historical understanding, namely the subjective reenactment of plans that had been historically carried out. Here Hegel was more consistent. His well-known claim to recognize reason in history was established on a concept of *Geist* whose essence included the fact that it "occurs within time" [not in someone's mind], and only on this basis could the *history* of *Geist* attain the specific determination of its content. Granted, there were also for Hegel "world-historical individuals" who were distinguished by being "executors for the world-spirit" and whose personal decisions and passions corresponded with what was *an der Zeit* [timely]. But for Hegel these exceptional cases did not themselves define for him the meaning of historical understanding; rather, they were themselves understood on the basis of historical necessity, a necessity whose understanding the philosopher accomplished, and this is what enabled him to define the person as exceptional. The escape hatch of expecting the historian to be congenial with his object of study, a path which Schleiermacher had already taken, manifestly also did not really take one further. In such a view, world history would be transformed into an aesthetic drama. This would mean on the one hand asking too much of the historian, and then also underestimating his task of confronting his own horizon with the complex horizon of the past.

And how does this view fit with the kerygmatic [message-bearing] sense of the holy scriptures? Schleiermacher's concept of congeniality in interpretation here leads one into what is fully absurd, for it raises the specter of inspiration theory. Moreover, even the historical exegesis of the Bible runs up against limits with this theory, especially in taking as a guiding concept the "self-understanding" of the author of different texts in holy scripture. Is not the healing meaning of scripture really and necessarily something other than what is generated through merely summing up the theological intuition of the New Testament writer? Here the pietistic hermeneutics of A. H. Francke and J. J. Rambach, among others, deserves ever more attention today because its doctrine of interpretation adds application to the moments of understanding and explication, and thereby emphasizes the relationship of the "scriptural text" itself to the present. We find within this point a central motif of a hermeneutics which takes seriously the historicality [*Geschichtlichkeit*] of human beings. Certainly idealist hermeneutics takes account of it, especially Emilio Betti with his canon of "corresponding to the sense." Yet it seems to me that only the resolute recognition of the concept of pre-understanding and the principle of history of effects offers a methodological basis for the unfolding of what we have called the consciousness of history being always at work in consciousness [*wirkungsgeschichtliches Bewusstsein*]. As a special case, for instance, the concept of a canon in New Testament theology also finds in the *wirkungsgeschichtliches Bewusstsein* a legitimation. The theological significance of the Old Testament, too, is very hard to justify if in hermeneutics one clings to the *mens auctoris* as a basis for interpretation. The great positive accomplishment of Gerhard von Rad [author of *The Theology of the Old Testament*] demonstrates this point and leaves the narrowness of this earlier perspective behind. It is in keeping with the situation today [1974] that the most recent discussions taking place in hermeneutics have also had an effect on Catholic theology (for example in Stachel, Biser, and Coreth).[31]

In literary theory something similar is represented, in part, under the title of "aesthetics of reception" (see Jauss, Iser, Gerigk). Yet precisely in this area, opposition to philosophical hermeneutics by persons in traditional philology, who are fixated on methodology and who fear that the objectivity of research will be lost, has become very vocal (E. D. Hirsch, Jr., and Thomas Seebohm).[32]

In light of this issue, the venerable tradition of juristic hermeneutics attains a new life and relevance. Within the dogmatics of modern law this tradition could only play a troubling role, seeming like a never completely avoidable stain on a self-fulfilling dogmatics. Nevertheless, one should make no mistake: jurisprudence is a normative discipline and performs the necessary dogmatic function of supplementing the law. As such, it performs an indispensable task, because it bridges the unavoidable gap between the universality of settled law and the concreteness of the individual case. In this regard, we should remember that Aristotle in his *Nicomachean Ethics* already staked out the hermeneutical space within legal doctrine for this process with his discussion of the problem of natural law and the concept of *epieikeia* [decency; *epieikes*, decent people]. Also, if we think back on the history of this concept,[33] we find that the problem of an understanding exegesis [*verstehenden Auslegung*] of the law is indissolubly linked with application. Jurisprudence was faced with such a double task, especially since the [modern] reception of Roman law and justice. At that time it was not just a matter of understanding the Roman judges, but of applying the dogmatic rules of Roman law to the cultural world of modern times.[34] Out of this situation jurisprudence developed an even closer link between the hermeneutical and the dogmatic task than that which imposed itself in theology. A doctrine regarding the exegesis of Roman law could not allow of historical alienation if Roman law was to retain its acceptance as valid. The exegesis of Roman law by Thibaut in 1806[35] therefore regards it as self-evident that the doctrine of legal exegesis [*Auslegung*] could not find support solely on the basis of the intention of the lawgiver, but must also raise the *Grund des Gesetzes* [the rational foundation of the law, the legal ground] to the status of comprising a genuine hermeneutical canon.

With the creation of modern codifications of law, the explication of Roman law, which had classically been the main task of jurisprudence, was forced to give up its dogmatic interest in the practical meaning of the law and became just one constituent part in the standpoint of a history of law. In this way, it could be seamlessly subordinated to the methodological thinking in the historical sciences. Conversely, juridical hermeneutics became only a subsidiary discipline in the dogmatics of law in the new style and was placed on the very margins of jurisprudence. Nevertheless, the fundamental problem of what was called "concretion in jurisprudence"[36] still continued to exist, and the relationship between the history of law and the normative science of law is now more complicated than just enabling the history of law to substitute for hermeneutics. Shedding light on the historical circumstances and actual concrete deliberations of the lawmakers before or at the time of the promulgation of a law may be ever so informative hermeneutically—nevertheless the significance of the *ratio legis* is not exhausted by this, and it remains an indispensable hermeneutical element in all pronouncing of legal judgments [*Jurisdiktion*, jurisdiction]. Thus the hermeneutical problem remains just as much natural and at home in all legal studies as it does in theology, and "application" always remains an important task in both.

One must therefore raise the question of whether theology and jurisprudence do not stand ready to make an essential contribution to a general hermeneutics. To unfold this question, the methodological standpoints we find immanent in theology, jurisprudence, and the historical-philological sciences will not suffice. For we have to do here 1) with pointing out the limits of the present conception in these disciplines of historical knowing and 2) with giving back to dogmatic interpretation its limited legitimacy.[37] Of course, this stands in opposition to the concept found in science of proceeding without any presuppositions [*Voraussetzungslosigkeit*] whatever.[38] These are the reasons why, when I undertook *Truth and Method,* I started out with a realm of experience which in a certain sense has to be posited in a dogmatic way, in that its claim to acceptance demands an absolute recognition and does not allow of being held in suspension—namely, *the experience of art.* Here, as a rule, to understand means to recognize or accept [*Geltenlassen*]. It means, as Emil Staiger puts it, "Begreifen, was uns ergreift"—"To grasp something that takes hold of *us.*" Certainly the objectivity of the scholarly study of art or literature continues to retain its full seriousness as a scholarly effort, but in every case it still finds that it is itself subordinate to the experiencing of specific works of art or poetry. In the authentic experiencing of art, the *applicatio* cannot be separated from the *intellectio* and *explicatio.* This cannot be without consequences for the scholarly study of art [*Kunstwissenschaft,* aesthetics and art history]. The problem involved here is first discussed by Hans Sedlmayr in his distinction between first and second *Kunstwissenschaft.*[39] The diverse methods of research which have been developed in the scholarly study of art and literature in the end have to maintain their fruitfulness by how far they bring about a heightened clarity and sense of appropriateness in the actual experience of art. In and of themselves they require hermeneutic integration. In other words, the application structure, which has its traditional home in juristic hermeneutics, necessarily becomes a valuable interpretive model here. Certainly in the reconciliation of the historical understanding of law and understanding of the law in terms of its dogmatic character which thrusts itself upon us here, the differences between them cannot be erased, which has been emphasized already by Betti and by Wieacker. However, the meaning of "application," which is a constitutive element in all understanding, does not at all consist of "applying" something from the outside and after the fact that originally exists in itself. The application of means to the accomplishment of predetermined ends, and the application of rules in our behavior as well, do not generally mean that we are subordinating something that is self-sufficient, such as a matter known in a "purely theoretical way," to some practical purpose. Rather, the means are in general determined by ends, and rules are determined by, or even abstracted from, behavior. Already Hegel in his *Phenomenology of Spirit* analyzed the dialectic of law and individual cases, in which the concrete determination is generated both from the law and vice versa [*auseinanderwirft*].

Thus we must add that the application structure of understanding which philosophical analysis discloses does not in any way mean that we place limits on our readiness to understand without presuppositions what a text itself says, nor does it in any way say, on the other hand, that one must distance the text from one's "own" senses of its meaning in order to make it serve preconceived intentions. No, hermeneutic reflection merely uncovers the conditions under which understanding *always already* and in each case operates—as our "pre-understanding"—conditions which are also operative when we concern ourselves to understand the assertion made by a text. In no way does this mean, either, that the human sciences and humanities now have to be left behind as "inexact" sciences to vegetate further in their regrettable defectiveness, insofar as they do not rise to the level of [presuppositionless] "science" and do not become a participating part of the wonderful *unity of science*. Rather, philosophical hermeneutics concludes that understanding is in fact only possible when one brings one's own presuppositions into play! The productive contribution of the interpreter belongs in an indispensable [*unaufhebbare*] way to the meaning of understanding itself. Certainly philosophical hermeneutics does not legitimize private and arbitrary subjective biases and prejudices. Why? Because for it the sole measure which it allows is the "matter" [*Sache*] being considered at the time, or the text one is seeking to understand. Certainly the ineradicable [*unaufhebbare*] and necessary distance between time periods, cultures, classes, races, or even between persons, constitutes a more than subjective [*übersubjektives*] moment that imparts life and tension to each understanding. One can describe this as follows: the interpreter and the text each possess his or her and its own horizon, and each moment of understanding represents a fusion of these horizons. Thus, in New Testament scholarship (above all in Ernst Fuchs and Gerhard Ebeling) as well as in literary criticism, and also in the further development of the Heideggerian approach, the definition of the hermeneutical problem has been fundamentally pushed away from a subjective and psychological basis and moved in the direction of an objective meaning [a meaning coming from the object] mediated by effective history [*in die Richtung des objektiven, wirkungsgeschichtlich vermittelten Sinns*].

The seminal "given" that resides in the mediating of such distances is the language in which the interpreter (or translator!) brings what he or she has understood newly to language. Theologians [*Theologen*] as well as students of poetry [*Poetologen*, poetologists] speak of something like a "language-event" [*Sprachereignis*, an emergence-event in which something emerges into language]. In doing this, perhaps hermeneutics parallels in its own way the neopositivist critique of metaphysics that arose from analytic philosophy. Since this critique no longer clings to the idea that one can free oneself of the "bewitchment of language" with the help of an artificial symbolic language that analyzes manners of speaking and reduces everything to univocal assertions, it also finds that in the end even the functioning of language in language games, as Wittgenstein's *Philosophical Investigations* has shown, does not get us back to univocal meaning. Karl-Otto Apel has rightly emphasized that the continuity of the tradition is describable with the concept of a "language game" only in a very discontinuous, interrupted way.[40] Insofar as hermeneutics overcomes the positivistic naïveté resident in the concept of "the given" by reflecting on the necessary conditions for understanding (pre-understanding, temporal priority of the question, the history of the motivation contained in every assertion), it represents a critique of the positivistic method-based mentality. The degree to which the schemas of Karl-Otto Apel's transcendental theory or the earlier Habermas's historical dialectic may follow from this is debatable.[41]

Philosophical hermeneutics, in any case, has a subject matter in its own right. This means that in spite of its formal generality, it is not legitimately classified within logic. In a certain sense like logic, it is universal, yet in a certain sense it surpasses logic even in universality. Certainly every context of connections in an assertion can be looked at in terms of its logical structure—the rules of grammar, syntax, and finally the laws of consequential logic; all of these can be applied at every moment to connections in speaking and thought. The strict demands of a logic of assertions, however, are seldom adequate to the real context of lived speaking. Speech and conversation are not statements in the sense that they consist of logical judgments whose univocity and meaning is confirmable and repeatable; rather, they have their occasional side. Assertions occur in a communication process, and in this process the monologue of scientific speaking or demonstrating something scientifically constitutes only a special case. In normal use language fulfills its mission in dialogue; this conversation may also be the dialogue of the soul with itself, as Plato characterized thinking. In this respect, philosophical hermeneutics as the theory of understanding and of reaching an understanding is of the greatest possible generality and universality [*Allgemeinheit*]. It understands every statement not merely in its logical valence but as the answer to a question, and this means that whoever understands must understand what the question is, and since understanding must gain the meaning of an utterance from the history of its motivations, it must necessarily move beyond the logically graspable content of any statement. This point is found in Hegel's dialectic of spirit and was taken up anew by Benedetto Croce, R. G. Collingwood, and others. "The Logic of Question and Answer" is a chapter extremely worth reading in Collingwood's *Autobiography*. Even a purely phenomenological analysis cannot escape the fact that there are neither isolated perceptions nor isolated judgments. This was established phenomenologically by Hans Lipps's *Hermeneutical Logic* (1938) on the basis of Husserl's doctrine of anonymous intentionalities. This was also carried out by Lipps under the influence of Heidegger's existential concept of world. In England, J. L. Austin moved in a similar direction as he carried further the turn of thought in the later Wittgenstein.

As a consequence of this movement away from the language of science and back to the language of daily life, and the move back from the "sciences of experience" to experience in the "lifeworld" (Husserl), hermeneutics, too, instead of subordinating itself to logic, had to go back and reorient itself to the older tradition of rhetoric to which, as we have shown earlier,[42] it had once been closely connected. In doing so it took up a thread of its history that had been broken off in the eighteenth century. It turned back, above all, to Giambattista Vico, who was defending the ancient rhetorical tradition, which he represented as a professor of rhetoric in Naples, against the monopolistic claim of "modern" science, which he called *critica*. Vico especially emphasized the importance of rhetoric for education and for the development of the *sensus communis*, and as a matter of fact hermeneutics shared with rhetoric an emphasis on the role that the *eikos*, the persuasive argument, had played. The great classical tradition of *eikos* in rhetoric was very fundamentally broken off in Germany during the eighteenth century despite the efforts of Herder; nevertheless, it remained alive unrecognized in the realm of aesthetics and also had an effect on hermeneutics, as Klaus Dockhorn, above all, has shown.[43] Even in our own time rhetoric and forensic rationality have, especially through the efforts of Chaim Perelman and his school,[44] offered strong resistance to the monopolistic claims of modern mathematical logic and the further expansion of its influence.

Yet a far more encompassing dimension of the hermeneutical problem is connected to this; it is the central place of language in the hermeneutic realm. Language is not just one medium among others within the world of "symbolic forms" (as Cassirer calls them); rather, it is related in a very important way to the commonality of reason. For it is reason that is communicatively actualized in language, as Richard Hönigswald has emphasized: language is not just a "fact," it is a "principle." On it rests the universality of the hermeneutical dimension. One encounters such universality already in the doctrine of meaning put forward by Saint Augustine and Saint Thomas Aquinas when they saw that the meaning of signs (of words) is surpassed in importance by the meaning of the matter being discussed, and because of this they were justified in going beyond the *sensus litteralis*. Philosophical hermeneutics today certainly cannot simply follow these two great thinkers, that is to say, it cannot simply enthrone a new form of allegorical interpretation. This would presuppose a language of creation through which God speaks to us. Whether this is the case or not, it is certainly a fact that not only in speaking and writing but in all human creation a "sense" has entered, and this poses for us the hermeneutical task of reading that sense off of them. Hegel expressed this idea with his concept of the "objective spirit" [*objektiver Geist*], and this part of his philosophy of spirit has lived on independent of the totality of his dialectical system. As examples of this, I think of Nicolai Hartmann's doctrine of the objectified spirit and the idealist philosophies of Croce and Gentile. And not only the language of art makes a legitimate claim to be understood. Every form of human cultural creation does. Indeed, the question expands. Does not everything have its place in our linguistically grasped orientation to the world?

All human knowledge of the world is linguistically mediated. Our first orientation to the world fulfills itself in the learning of language. But not only this. The linguisticality [*Sprachlichkeit*] of our being-in-the-world articulates in the end the whole realm of our experience. Although the logic of induction which Aristotle described[45] and Francis Bacon developed into the foundation of the new sciences of experience may be unsatisfactory today and in need of correction, as Popper argues,[46] its nearness in terms of content to the linguistic articulation of the world emerges brilliantly in this form. Already Themistius [317–388 AD] in his suggestive commentary on Aristotle illustrated the relevant chapter in the *Posterior Analytics* B 19 by the example of learning to speak a language, and in this area of thinking modern linguistics (Chomsky) and modern psychology (Piaget) have also taken steps forward. And yet what they are saying applies in an even wider sense! All experience takes place in our constant communicative cultural education into our knowledge of the world. It is itself continuously the "knowledge of what is known," but in a much deeper and more universal sense than August Boeckh had in mind when he made up this formula, which he intended for philologists to express what they were doing. But the heritage in and through which we live our lives is not just the so-called cultural heritage, it is not a heritage that only exists as texts and monuments and in the mediation of their linguistically grasped and historically documented sense, while the real determinants of our lives, the conditions of production in society, and so on, remain "external." No, the communicatively experienced world itself is constantly being handed over to us—*traditur*—as an open totality. It is given to us as experience and nothing but experience. It is always co-present when the world is experienced, when unfamiliarity is canceled, when something becomes clear, when insight happens, when one successfully appropriates a piece of knowledge. In the end, one could say that the primary task of hermeneutics as a philosophical theory may lie in showing what it means to integrate the knowledge we have in the sciences into the "personal knowing" of the individual's "experience," as Michael Polanyi has shown in his book *Personal Knowledge*.[47]

For this reason the hermeneutical dimension is particularly concerned with the work of the concept in philosophy, a work which has gone on through the millennia. As experience that thinks through the heritage, this hermeneutical dimension must be understood as a single great conversation that is taking place and with which every present time participates, a conversation which cannot master the present in some arrogant and superior way and bring it under critical control. That was the weakness of the discipline we call the "history of problems," which was only able to read the history of philosophy as a corroboration of its own history-of-problems approach and not as a critical partner that discloses limits in our own insights. Of course we need to ponder this problem in hermeneutical reflection as well. It teaches us that the language of philosophy always has something inappropriate about it and in its intention always pursues more than can be found in its assertions or by simply taking it at its word. The words that carry its concepts [*die Begriffsworte*], words that have been coined in it and passed down, are not firm markers and signals through which something can be univocally designated, as in the systems of symbols in mathematics and logic and their applications. Rather, they originate in the communicative movement of human interpretation of the world, a movement that takes place in language, and is further developed and transformed and enriched as time goes on; then they move into new contexts and connections that cover over the older connections; and then these sink halfway into being unthought before being brought to life again through a thinking that questions.

So all philosophical labor with concepts is based on a hermeneutical dimension; it is a labor that nowadays is rather inexactly designated by the phrase "history of concepts." For this labor with concepts is not some effort of secondary importance, and this phrase should not mean that instead of speaking about the subject matter, one will now be speaking of the means one uses in understanding it; on the contrary, philosophical labor with concepts forms the critical element in the very use of our concepts. The lay people who furiously demand univocal definitions, and likewise the experts who have a craze for univocality in their one-sided, semantic epistemology, misunderstand what language is. They do not realize that the language of concepts cannot be invented, or randomly changed, or used and then put aside; rather, concepts arise out of the element in which we live and move in our thinking. In the highly artificial form of terminology we encounter only the ossified crust of the living stream of thinking and speaking. Terminology, too, is introduced and carried along by the communication event that we bring about in speaking and on the basis of which mutual understanding and agreements are reached.[48] By the way, there seems to me to be a point of convergence between the development of analytic philosophy in English and my philosophical hermeneutics. But the parallel I see between the two still remains limited. Just as Dilthey in the nineteenth century indicted English empiricism for its lack of historical culture and education, so today the critical claim put forward by a historically reflective hermeneutics consists not so much in bringing ways of speaking under control by grasping their logical structure, which would seem to be the goal of analytic philosophy, as rather to reclaim the linguistically mediated content of utterances along with the whole treasury of historical experience that they contain.

In the logic of the social sciences as a field of study, the hermeneutical problem acquires a new importance. One must recognize the fact that the hermeneutical dimension plays a basic role in all experience of the world and therefore also plays a role even in the work of the natural sciences, as Thomas Kuhn has shown.[49] But this holds even more strongly for the social sciences. For insofar as society always has a linguistically understood existence,[50] the field of objects in the social sciences themselves (and not only its theory-formation) is governed by the hermeneutical dimension. The hermeneutical critique of naive objectivism in the human sciences and humanities has in a certain sense a parallel in the social sciences, as one finds in Habermas's critique of ideology inspired by Marx (and see also the vehement polemic directed against hermeneutics by Hans Albert).[51] One should also note that healing through dialogue is an eminently hermeneutical phenomenon. About this Jacques Lacan and Paul Ricoeur, above all, have discussed its theoretical foundations.[52] The analogy between mental illnesses and the illnesses of society, however, seems questionable to me. The position of the social scientist over against society does not seem to me to be comparable to that of the psychoanalyst in relation to his patient.[53] Furthermore, a critique of ideology that imagines it is above all ideological presuppositions is no less dogmatic than a positivistic social science that understands itself as a form of social engineering [*Sozialtechnik*]. Efforts at mediation between hermeneutics and various opposing factions do help us understand the objections of the theory of deconstruction, represented by Derrida, against hermeneutics.[54] In spite of this opposition, the hermeneutical experience still defends its own case against such a theory of the deconstruction of "sense." To seek "sense" in writing [*écriture*], in spite of Nietzsche's view, has nothing to do with metaphysics.

When one follows the approach oriented to [my] hermeneutics, every effort at grasping a meaning is in principle directed toward a possible consensus, a possible agreement in understanding; indeed, it must already rest on a general agreement in understanding that is binding, if it is to come about that one understands and is understood. This is not some dogmatic assumption but a simple phenomenological description of coming to an understanding. When there is no common ground linking two parties together, no conversation can succeed. So even the critique of ideology, in the final analysis, has to introduce rational discourse as a link which is supposed to make it possible to reach understandings in a compulsion-free way. The same holds for the therapeutic process in psychoanalysis. The success of dialogical therapy in psychoanalysis is not based simply on the patient's voluntary work in reflection. Ultimately, just to succeed through language therapy with the doctor in dissolving one's hang-ups is not the whole story. Rather, the ultimate goal is to regain one's natural capacity to communicate with others, and this means getting back to a basic understanding with others that makes it meaningful for one to talk with another person.

Here a difference between hermeneutics and the critique of ideology opens up that one cannot ignore. The critique of ideology approach claims to be an emancipatory reflection. Correspondingly, the therapeutic dialogue in psychoanalysis claims that by making one conscious of the masks worn by the unconscious it can bring release from them. Both the critique of ideology and psychoanalysis posit their own special knowledge in advance and hold this to be scientifically based. In contrast to this, hermeneutical reflection does not posit any scientific claim with specific content of this kind. Reflection in philosophical hermeneutics does not claim to know in advance that concrete social conditions allow only a distorted form of communication to take place. And included in their view is that one already knows what will be the result of their undistorted, right kind of communication. Also, the critique of ideology approach does not intend to operate like a therapist who through the reflection process will lead the patient to a higher insight into his or her life history and thereby enable one to find his or her true nature. In both the critique of ideology and psychoanalysis, the interpretation intends to be guided by a prior knowledge on the basis of which one will be freed of prior fixations and prejudices. In this sense, both are to be understood as experiences of "enlightenment." Hermeneutical experience, in contrast to this, regards with skepticism every conscious intention that employs a system of knowledge. [It is in no way like the concept of pre-understanding in philosophical hermeneutics.] The concept of pre-understanding which Bultmann introduced into theology does not have in mind this kind of advance [expert scientific, technical] knowing; rather, our prior judgments (or what I have called "prejudices" [*Vorurteile*]) are brought into play and actually put at risk in every process of understanding. In the rich concreteness of this kind of hermeneutical experience, concepts like "enlightenment," "emancipation," and "compulsion-free dialogue" are revealed to be pale abstractions. Hermeneutical experience, in contrast, realizes how deeply rooted prejudgments can be and how little even our becoming conscious of them is able to free us from their power. Descartes, one of the fathers of the Enlightenment, knew this very well when he sought less through argumentation than through meditation, that is, through always repeated reconsideration of a problem, to establish the legitimacy of his concept of method. One should not reproach this as the mere making of rhetorical constructions. Without these there is no communication; this is the case even in scientific and philosophical contributions, which all have to use rhetorical means to make good their claims to acceptance. The whole history of thought confirms the ancient view that rhetoric and hermeneutics are very close to each other.

Certainly it is also true that hermeneutics always has an element that goes beyond rhetoric: it always includes an encounter with the opinions of an other person, whose opinions come to expression in words. This encounter also takes place with texts to be understood, as well as encounters with all other cultural creations of this type. They must possess and unfold their own powers of persuasion in order to come to be understood. Hermeneutics is philosophy because it does not allow itself to be just the teaching of an art [*Kunstlehre*] that devotes itself to empathizing with the opinions of *the other person*. No, as philosophy, hermeneutical reflection includes the point that in all understanding of a matter, or of another person, the critique of oneself should also be happening. In terms of hermeneutics, one who understands does not claim to hold a superior position in advance, but instead admits that his or her own assumed truth must be put to the test in the act of understanding. This moment is included in all understanding, and for this reason every understanding of something contributes to the further development of what I call effective historical consciousness [and thus to further self-knowledge].

The basic model of reaching an understanding together is dialogue or conversation. As we know only too well, a conversation is not possible if one of the partners believes himself or herself to be in a clearly superior position in comparison with the other person, and assumes that he or she possesses a prior knowledge of the erroneous prejudgments in which the other is entangled. If one does this, one actually locks oneself into the circle of one's own prejudices. Reaching an understanding dialogically is impossible if in principle one of the partners in a dialogue does not allow himself or herself to enter into a real conversation. An example of this would be, for instance, if in a set of social interactions one played the psychologist or psychoanalyst and did not take the meaning of the statements of the other person seriously but instead claimed to see through them psychoanalytically. In such a case, the partnership in dialogue on which social life is based is destroyed. A systematic discussion of this problematic is undertaken by Paul Ricoeur, who speaks of a "conflict of interpretations." In this conflict, he places Marx, Nietzsche, and Freud on one side [as persons superior to what they analyze] and the phenomenological intentionality of understanding "symbols" on the other, and then he seeks a dialectical mediation between these two standpoints. On the one side, one seeks a genealogical derivation of the other as *archaeology;* on the other side, the orientation is toward grasping an intended sense, which he calls *teleology.* In his view, this constitutes only a preparatory distinction that a universal hermeneutics must work out. With the help of symbols these two sides would then shed light on the constitutive functions of understanding symbols and on self-understanding. But such a general hermeneutical theory seems inconsistent to me. Each of the two ways of understanding symbols which he here places side by side has in view a very different sense of the meaning of the symbol and not the same meaning, and thus each does not constitute a different meaning of the same thing; no, the one *way of understanding* excludes the other because it means something different. One approach seeks to understand what the symbol wants to say, the other seeks to understand *what the symbol is trying to conceal and mask.* The latter is a totally different sense of "understanding" from that found in hermeneutics.

Ultimately, the universality of [philosophical] hermeneutics will depend on the extent to which the theoretical and transcendental character of hermeneutics remains limited to being accepted by science, or whether it will also demonstrate the validity of the principles of common sense, the *sensus communis,* thereby showing that the way science is used is within a practical consciousness. Hermeneutics understood in this wider, universal sense moves into the region of "practical philosophy," a region which Joachim Ritter and his school, finding themselves situated in the midst of the German tradition of transcendental philosophy, tried to revive. Philosophical hermeneutics is aware of what it could mean to move in this direction.[55] A theory of the praxis of understanding is obviously theory and not practice, but a theory of praxis is still not some kind of "technique," nor is it an effort to make societal practice more scientific. Rather, hermeneutics offers a philosophical reflection on the limits of all scientific and technical control of nature and of society. These limits are truths that need to be defended against the modern concept of science, and defending these truths is one of the most important tasks of a philosophical hermeneutics.[56]

Translated by Richard E. Palmer

3

The Universality of the Hermeneutical Problem

Gadamer first gave "Die Universalität des hermeneutischen Problems" as a lecture at the academy in Walberberg on October 12, 1965, and immediately published it in a prominent journal, the *Philosophisches Jahrbuch* (1966). The next year he added it to his collection of essays, *Kleine Schriften I* (1967), and he included it in volume 2 of his collected works (1986), where he added a number of notes referring to sources or addressing objections to his argument.[1] These notes, included in the *Gadamer Lesebuch,* appear in this translation. Gadamer's decision to include the essay in this collection indicates its importance in his writings.

In arguing for the universality of the hermeneutical problem, Gadamer was expanding further the significance of what he had put forward in *Truth and Method.* There he had defined hermeneutics philosophically and not as a method of explicating texts. Hermeneutics as presented there is not only the process of historically conditioned understanding, and not only quintessentially represented in the encounter with art, but also a way of being in the world. What started out in part 1 of *Truth and Method* as an ontology of the experience of artworks, continued in part 2 as an insistence on the historical character of understanding, and ended in part 3 by asserting the centrality of language in all understanding, now goes a step further. Gadamer in this essay is sensing the broader implications of hermeneutics. He asserts provocatively that the hermeneutical problem is universal.

The new reflection in this essay is about the place and function of the understanding process not only in daily life or in the experience of literature and art, but also in the sciences. Because understanding uses the same language and follows the same linguistic rules in all of these, and because it is always situational and directed toward a goal, it is the universal basis even of science. Of course, in the sciences language may become abstract and lifeless, while in the humanities it may bring deeply realized human realities to stand, but living language is still the basis for all understanding. Hermeneutics is universal, Gadamer insists. By this he means that his philosophical analysis of understanding applies everywhere that understanding takes place as an event in human life.

Gadamer's essay on the universality of the hermeneutical problem did not go unnoticed, but in its reception history the decisive event was the dispute it provoked with Jürgen Habermas, his former student, colleague at Heidelberg, and thereafter lifelong friend.[2] Habermas's most comprehensive and best-known response to Gadamer's article and to his hermeneutics in general is "The Claim of Hermeneutics to Universality" ["Der Universalitätsanspruch der Hermeneutik"], which appeared not only in the Festschrift on Gadamer's seventieth birthday, namely *Hermeneutics and Dialectics,* but also in a mass-market paperback rather sensationally titled *Hermeneutics and the Critique of Ideology.* This paperback volume excellently documented the "Gadamer-Habermas debate" by placing it in the context of the larger debate between the Marxist critique of ideology and hermeneutics. In addition to essays by other prominent philosophers, the paperback contained a more recent essay by Gadamer titled "Rhetorik, Hermeneutik, und Ideologiekritik," and also at the end of the volume a reply by Gadamer to all the other essays. Gadamer's universality essay itself was not reprinted in the volume but nevertheless remained its provocation and thematic focus. Other contributors to the volume were Karl-Otto Apel, Claus von Bormann, Rüdiger Bubner, and Hans Joachim Giegel. It was an exciting volume and the essay by Habermas on the claim of hermeneutics to universality was its centerpiece. We will discuss Habermas's critique briefly after a short summary of Gadamer's assertions in this essay.

Gadamer's title does not fully indicate the content of his essay. In his first paragraph he says that he will try to answer "the question posed for us by the existence of modern science" (3, i.e., first page).[3] His essay, then, is a direct attack on the insufficiencies of modern science. A little later he says that his task "will be to reconnect the objective world of technology . . . with those fundamental orders of our being that are neither arbitrary nor manipulable by us" (3–4)—that is to say, hermeneutics deals with what is neither arbitrary nor manipulable by us, a contrast with science. In order to deal with this central question, Gadamer first addresses the question of clarifying what hermeneutics means and does. In doing this he promises to "elucidate several phenomena in which the universality of hermeneutics becomes evident" (4). The clarification, along with the explanation of universality, make this a valuable part of the essay, in that it offers Gadamer's own summary of his hermeneutical project in *Truth and Method* before he goes on to assert its universality. We will turn to his summary first.

To explain his hermeneutics, Gadamer does not start with a universal definition but with "two experiences of alienation that we encounter in our concrete existence" (4). The first is aesthetic alienation, and the other is alienation from history. In the modern "aesthetic conscious-ness" we focus on a dimension secondary to the truth-claim of art: the alienation of judgment in modern aesthetic consciousness. Gadamer's hermeneutics claims to lead us to the "the authentic experience that confronts us in the form of art itself" (5). The second form of alien-ation is from our always operative historical consciousness. The goal of historical objectivity since the nineteenth-century historian Leopold von Ranke has been to put us at a scientific distance from the historical object in which we try to forget totally our own historical present and lose ourselves in the past time being studied. But Gadamer notes that Nietzsche in "The Use and Abuse of History for Life" contrasts such an objective attitude with the observer's "immediate will to shape things." That is, there is a contradiction here. Gadamer points out that even historians claiming to be objective, like Mommsen in his *History of Rome,* are immediately identifiable because of their perspective. So "historical science . . . expresses only one part of our actual experience—our actual encounter—with historical tradition" (6–7).

Gadamer then contrasts his "hermeneutical consciousness" with the other two forms of consciousness. Here he regrets that Schleier-macher's "science of hermeneutics" is absorbed into the "idea of mod-ern science," and instead of simply avoiding mistakes in understand-ing, hermeneutics goes on to presuppose "a deep common accord" (7). Understanding is really closer to "reaching an understanding" on the basis of this deeper "common understanding that always precedes these situations" (7). It is not our aesthetic or historical judgments that are important but our prior judgments. Citing Heidegger's *Being and Time,* Gadamer asserts, "It is not so much our judgments as it is our prejudices that constitute our being." (Gadamer here footnotes *WM* 277, *TM* 261.) He asserts that these prejudgments "constitute the initial directedness of our whole ability to experience" (9). These prejudices "are simply con-ditions whereby we experience something—whereby what we encounter says something to us" (9). Furthermore, the attitude of objectivity is in-appropriate for describing this encounter because in this encounter we don't possess something, "we are possessed *by* something and precisely by means of it we are opened up for the new, the different, the true" (9, emphasis added). This is the hermeneutical consciousness that Ga-damer advocates. It is a consciousness that allows itself to be captured and guided by the text instead of directing scientific methods *toward* it. This is a distinctive, basically Heideggerian moment in Gadamer's hermeneutics.

Gadamer now turns to the issue of universality. What is universal-ity as he describes it? Gadamer begins by pointing to the undisclosed presuppositions of scientific knowing and technological making. He says that we have not thought through the link between the presuppositions of our knowing and those of our technological making. He asks: "If these remain in semi-darkness, won't the result be that the hands that apply this knowledge will become destructive?" (10). This is Gadamer's ominous warning. Hermeneutics, then, is not merely an exercise in philosophy; it is needed to uncover these presuppositions. Furthermore, it deals with "the basic factor in our contemporary culture, namely, science and its industrial/technological utilization" (11). In doing this, hermeneutics "encompasses the entire procedure of science," according to Gadamer (11). In particular, hermeneutics deals with inquiry in terms of question and answer: the question pre-shapes and determines the direction of the answer, so all assertions are answers to questions, and we need to be careful what questions we ask and fail to ask. Statistics and certain other disciplines illustrate "the fact that there is such a thing as methodological sterility, and that the application of a method can be to something not worth knowing" (11). The question first has to be genuine. Ultimately, it is not method, says Gadamer, but imagination that leads to knowledge worth knowing. He then asserts that "the real power of *hermeneutical* consciousness is our ability to see what is questionable" (13). Scientists *need* a hermeneutical consciousness to achieve their goal and to prevent their knowledge from becoming destructive. Hermeneutics is universal; it is prior to scientific questioning and integral to it.

In the final section, Gadamer turns to a seminal work of Johannes Lohmann on philosophy and the science of language.[4] Here he invokes a linguist to buttress his philosophical claims that language is the heart of the hermeneutical consciousness and that the hermeneutical element is universal. Language contains not merely a worldview but also "a teleology" and a theater in which things come to stand, so that "what is manifest here is the real mode of operation of our whole human experience of the world" (15). "Understanding is language-bound," says Gadamer, meaning that in and through language we have our being in the world. Language opens up a world, even in a foreign language, in what Gadamer calls the "inner infinity" (17) of a dialogue in the direction of the "truth that we are" (16). Genuine speaking in actual dialogue is what truly opens up a world. Language is integral to the universality of the hermeneutical experience.

Now to Habermas's criticisms of the "universality" of hermeneutics and the hermeneutical situation, and also of two key terms in Gadamer's hermeneutics: prejudice and authority. First, Habermas follows Gadamer in presenting a philosophy of communication, basically a hermeneutic of the logic of the social sciences, so he is indebted to Gadamer in some respects. But for Habermas true communication is not found in humans as they speak to each other or read great texts, but in communication as it occurs in an "ideal speech situation" undistorted by social forces, such as the political power of prejudice and authority. For Habermas, prejudice interferes with the emancipation of the individual person from social misunderstandings. It is the set of misunderstandings handed down by tradition that needs to be overcome. Authority, too, is another pressure on the acting individual and should be resisted in favor of a free, undistorted, socially emancipatory reflection. Thinking that is distorted should not be universalized but eventually escaped. Psychoanalysis and critical theory are emancipatory forms of reflection that are not included within the universality of Gadamer's hermeneutics. He finds Gadamer too accepting of prejudice and authority.

So Habermas finds Gadamer's hermeneutics not to be so universal as he claims, since Gadamer does not discuss these emancipatory forms of reasoning and reflection. Gadamer's basic reply is that he is describing the basic process of linguistic understanding by which meaning is constructed, a process prior to any more specialized form of thinking, such as psychoanalysis. This does not disqualify psychoanalysis, but it rebuts the objection that hermeneutics lacks universality. As regards the charge of defending prejudice, Gadamer redefines prejudice as prior understandings [*Vorverständnisse*], the understandings on the basis of which we understand the phenomena that confront us. These are necessary for understanding to take place, and they can even be labeled as "fruitful." In reply to the criticisms of cravenly accepting authority, Gadamer distinguishes between authority with no basis and authority that we have a reason to respect, such as that of a doctor, lawyer, teacher, or minister. We do not just cravenly accept their views, but we recognize that the voice of experience and tradition has some weight and should be given serious consideration. In other words, there is such a thing as "legitimate authority" and we should respect this authority. Gadamer's objection is that in the Enlightenment period, tradition was rejected out of hand when it should have been weighed against alternative views. Henry Ford embodied this Enlightenment view when he said, "History is bunk!"

We cannot do justice to either side of the debate with these capsule presentations. It would seem to be true that Gadamer's hermeneutics is not universal if that means all-inclusive. It does not include critical theory or psychoanalysis. But Gadamer means something more like "fundamental," even a condition for the possibility of understanding. He describes what is always at work in understanding. If this is the definition, we should consider his arguments fairly. On the other hand, it is true that psychoanalysis is a therapeutic technique that has liberated many persons from the chains of irrational neuroses, so one has to grant the utility of its claims. But Gadamer points out that the conversation between a therapist and patient is not a real dialogue between equals because the therapist claims a superior liberating reality not grasped by the patient. For Gadamer, the Socratic dialogue that mutually and respectfully seeks the truth and that is willing to admit errors is a model for communication, not therapy. Also, Gadamer is basing his hermeneutics on actual human experiences, not on theorizing from counterfactual, ideal speech situations that are free of distortions.

The solution that suggests itself is to accept what is useful from both thinkers and not try to prove one wrong at the expense of the other. In many ways, they are dealing with different phenomena: neuroses, social distortions, obstacles to communication, on the one hand, and on the other the attempt to offer a philosophical description of meaningful events of encounter. Paul Ricoeur contrasted a "hermeneutics of suspicion" (in Marx, Freud, and Nietzsche) that goes behind the text being interpreted to find the concealed motives at work there with, on the other hand, a "hermeneutics of disclosure" that uses the language of the text to bring truth to stand in the life of mortal human beings (interpretation of sacred texts, literature, art). It would seem that there are noble examples of each, and Habermas presents us with a "hermeneutics of suspicion" while Gadamer offers a hermeneutics closer to the function of disclosure in art, literature, deep speaking, and sacred texts.

* * *

The Universality of the Hermeneutical Problem

Why has the problem of language come to occupy the same central position in current philosophical discussions that the concept of thought, or "thought thinking itself," held in philosophy a century and a half ago? In dealing with this question, I shall try to give an answer indirectly to the central question of the modern age—a question posed for us by the existence of modern science. It is the question of how our natural view of the world—the experience of the world that we have as we simply live out our lives—is related to the unassailable and anonymous authority that confronts us in the pronouncements of science. Since the seventeenth century, the real task of philosophy has been to mediate this new employment of man's cognitive and constructive capacities with the totality of our experience of life. This task has found expression in a variety of ways, including our own generation's attempt to bring the topic of language to the center of philosophical concern. Language is the fundamental mode of operation of our being-in-the-world and the all-embracing form of the constitution of the world. Hence we always have in view the pronouncements of the sciences, which are fixed in nonverbal signs. And our task is to reconnect the objective world of technology, which the sciences place at our disposal and discretion, with those fundamental orders of our being that are neither arbitrary nor manipulable by us, but rather simply demand our respect.

I want to elucidate several phenomena in which the universality of this question becomes evident. I have called the point of view involved in this theme "hermeneutical," a term developed by Heidegger. Heidegger was continuing a perspective stemming originally from Protestant theology and transmitted into our own century by Wilhelm Dilthey.

What is hermeneutics? I would like to start from two experiences of alienation that we encounter in our concrete existence: the experience of alienation of the aesthetic consciousness and the experience of alienation of the historical consciousness. In both cases what I mean can be stated in a few words. The aesthetic consciousness realizes a possibility that as such we can neither deny nor diminish in its value, namely, that we relate ourselves, either negatively or affirmatively, to the quality of an artistic form. This statement means we are related in such a way that the judgment we make decides in the end regarding the expressive power and validity of what we judge. What we reject has nothing to say to us—or we reject it because it has nothing to say to us. This characterizes our relation to art in the broadest sense of the word, a sense that, as Hegel has shown, includes the entire religious world of the ancient Greeks, whose religion of beauty experienced the divine in concrete works of art that man creates in response to the gods. When it loses its original and unquestioned authority, this whole world of experience becomes alienated into an object of aesthetic judgment. At the same time, however, we must admit that the world of artistic tradition—the splendid contemporaneousness that we gain through art with so many human worlds—is more than a mere object of our free acceptance or rejection. Is it not true that when a work of art has seized us it no longer leaves us the freedom to push it away from us once again and to accept or reject it on our own terms? And is it not also true that these artistic creations, which come down to us through the millennia, were not created for such aesthetic acceptance or rejection? No artist of the religiously vital cultures of the past ever produced his work of art with any other intention than that his creation should be received in terms of what it says and presents and that it should have its place in the world where humans live together. The consciousness of art—the aesthetic consciousness—is always secondary to the immediate truth-claim that proceeds from the work of art itself. To this extent, when we judge a work of art on the basis of its aesthetic quality, something that is really much more intimately familiar to us is alienated. This alienation in aesthetic judgment always takes place when we have withdrawn ourselves, and are no longer open to the immediate claim of that which grasps us. Thus one point of departure for my reflections in *Truth and Method* was that the aesthetic sovereignty that claims its rights in the experience of art [in aesthetic consciousness] represents an alienation when compared to the authentic experience that confronts us in the actual encounter with the artwork.[1]

About thirty years ago, this problem cropped up in a particularly distorted form when the National Socialist politics of art, as a means to its own ends, tried to criticize formalism by arguing that art is bound to a people. Despite its misuse by the National Socialists, we cannot deny that the idea of art being bound to a people involves a real insight. A genuine artistic creation stands within a particular community, and such a community is always distinguishable from the cultured society that is informed and terrorized by art criticism.

The second mode of the experience of alienation is the historical consciousness—the noble and slowly perfected art of holding ourselves at a critical distance in dealing with witnesses to past life. Ranke's celebrated description of this idea as the extinguishing of the individual provided a popular formula for the ideal of historical thinking: the historical consciousness has the task of understanding all the witnesses of a past time from out of the spirit of that time, of extricating them from the preoccupations of our own present life, and of knowing, without moral smugness, the past as a human phenomenon.[2] In his well-known essay "The Use and Abuse of History for Life," Nietzsche formulated the contradiction between this historical distancing and the immediate will to shape things that always cleaves to the present. And at the same time he exposed many of the consequences of what he called the "Alexandrian," weakened form of the will, which is found in modern historical science. We might recall his indictment of the weakness of evaluation that has befallen the modern mind because it has become so accustomed to considering things in ever different and changing lights that it is blinded and incapable of arriving at an opinion of its own regarding the objects it studies. It is unable to determine its own position vis-à-vis what confronts it. Nietzsche traces the value-blindness of historical objectivism back to the conflict between the alienated historical world and the life-powers of the present.

To be sure, Nietzsche is an ecstatic witness. But our actual experience of the historical consciousness in the last hundred years has taught us most emphatically that there are serious difficulties involved in its claim to historical objectivity. Even in those masterworks of historical scholarship that seem to be the very consummation of the extinguishing of the individual demanded by Ranke, it is still an unquestioned principle of our scientific experience that we can classify these works with unfailing accuracy in terms of the political tendencies of the time in which they were written. When we read Mommsen's *History of Rome,* we know who alone could have written it, that is, we can identify the political situation in which this historian organized the voices of the past in a meaningful way. We know it too in the case of Treitschke or of Sybel, to choose only a few prominent names from Prussian historiography. This clearly means, first of all, that the whole reality of historical experience does not find expression in the mastery of historical method. No one disputes the fact that controlling the prejudices of our own present to such an extent that we do not misunderstand the witnesses of the past is a valid aim, but obviously such control does not completely fulfill the task of understanding the past and its transmissions. Indeed, it could very well be that only insignificant things in historical scholarship permit us to approximate this ideal of totally extinguishing individuality, while the great productive achievements of scholarship always preserve something of the splendid magic of immediately mirroring the present in the past and the past in the present. Historical science, the second experience from which I begin, expresses only one part of our actual experience—our actual encounter with historical tradition—and it knows only an alienated form of this historical tradition.

We can contrast the hermeneutical consciousness with these examples of alienation as a more comprehensive possibility that we must develop. But in the case of this hermeneutical consciousness, too, our initial task must be to overcome the epistemological truncation by which the traditional "science of hermeneutics" has been absorbed into the idea of modern science. If we consider Schleiermacher's hermeneutics, for instance, we find his view of this discipline peculiarly restricted by the modern idea of science. Schleiermacher's hermeneutics shows him to be a leading voice of historical Romanticism. But at the same time, he kept the concern of the Christian theologian clearly in mind, intending his hermeneutics, as a general doctrine of the art of understanding, to be of value in the special work of interpreting scripture. Schleiermacher defined hermeneutics as the art of avoiding misunderstanding. To exclude by controlled, methodical consideration whatever is alien and leads to misunderstanding—misunderstanding suggested to us by distance in time, change in linguistic usages, or in the meanings of words and modes of thinking—this is certainly a far from absurd description of the hermeneutical endeavor. But the question also arises as to whether the phenomenon of understanding is defined appropriately when we say that to understand is to avoid misunderstanding. Is it not, in fact, the case that every misunderstanding presupposes a "deep common accord"?

I am trying to call attention here to a common experience. We say, for instance, that understanding and misunderstanding take place between I and thou. But the formulation "I and thou" already betrays an enormous alienation. There is nothing like an "I and thou" at all—there is neither the I nor the thou as isolated, substantial realities. I may say "thou" and I may refer to myself over against a thou, but a common understanding [*Verständigung*] always precedes these situations. We all know that to say "thou" to someone presupposes a deep common accord [*tiefes Einverständnis*]. Something enduring is already present when this word is spoken. When we try to reach agreement on a matter on which we have different opinions, this deeper factor always comes into play, even if we are seldom aware of it. The science of hermeneutics would have us believe that the opinion we have to understand is something alien that seeks to lure us into misunderstanding, and our task is to exclude every element through which a misunderstanding can creep in. We accomplish this task by a controlled procedure of historical training, by historical criticism, and by a controllable method in connection with powers of psychological empathy. It seems to me that this description is valid in one respect, and yet it is only a partial description of a comprehensive life-phenomenon that constitutes the "we" that we all are. Our task, it seems to me, is to transcend the prejudices that underlie the aesthetic consciousness, the historical consciousness, and the kind of hermeneutical consciousness that has been restricted to a technique for avoiding misunderstandings and to overcome the alienations present in them all.

What is it, then, in these three experiences that seemed to us to have been left out, and what makes us so sensitive to the distinctiveness of these experiences? What is the *aesthetic* consciousness when compared to the fullness of what has already addressed us—what we call "classical" in art?[3] Is it not always already determined in this way what will be expressive for us and what we will find significant? Whenever we say with an instinctive, even if perhaps erroneous, certainty (but a certainty that is initially valid for our consciousness), "this is classical; it will endure," what we are speaking of has already preformed our possibility for aesthetic judgment. There are no purely formal criteria that can claim to judge and sanction the formative level simply on the basis of its artistic virtuosity. Rather, our sensitive-spiritual existence is an aesthetic resonance chamber that resonates with the voices that are constantly reaching us, preceding all explicit aesthetic judgment.

The situation is similar with the historical consciousness. Here, too, we must certainly admit that there are innumerable tasks of historical scholarship that have no relation to our own present and to the depths of its historical consciousness. But it seems to me there can be no doubt that the great horizon of the past, out of which our culture and our present live, influences us in everything we want, hope for, or fear in the future. History is only present to us in light of our futurity. Here we have all learned from Heidegger, for he exhibited precisely the primacy of futurity for our possible recollection and retention, and for the whole of our history.

Heidegger worked out this primacy in his doctrine of the productivity of the hermeneutical circle. I have given the following formulation to this insight: it is not so much our judgments as it is our prejudices that constitute our being.[4] This is a provocative formulation, for I am using it to restore to its rightful place a positive concept of prejudice that was driven out of our linguistic usage by the French and the English Enlightenment. It can be shown that the concept of prejudice did not originally have the meaning we have attached to it. Prejudices are not necessarily unjustified and erroneous, so that they inevitably distort the truth. In fact, the historicity of our existence entails that prejudices, in the literal sense of the word, constitute the initial directedness of our whole ability to experience. Prejudices are biases of our openness to the world. They are simply conditions whereby we experience something— whereby what we encounter says something to us. This formulation certainly does not mean that we are enclosed within a wall of prejudices and only let through the narrow portals those things that can produce a pass saying, "Nothing new will be said here." Instead we welcome just that guest who promises something new to our curiosity. But how do we know the guest we admit is one who has something *new* to say to us?[5] Is not our expectation and our readiness to hear the new also necessarily determined by the old that has already taken possession of us? The concept of prejudice is closely connected to the concept of authority, and the above image makes it clear that it is in need of hermeneutical rehabilitation. Like every image, however, this one too is misleading. The nature of the hermeneutical experience is not that something is outside and desires admission. Rather, we are possessed by something and precisely by means of it we are opened up for the new, the different, the true. Plato made this clear in his beautiful comparison of bodily foods with spiritual nourishment: while we can refuse the former (for example, on the advice of a physician), we have always taken the latter into ourselves already.[6]

But now the question arises as to how we can legitimate this hermeneutical conditionedness of our being in the face of modern science, which stands or falls with the principle of being unbiased and free of prejudice. We will certainly not accomplish this legitimation by making prescriptions for science and recommending that it toe the line—quite aside from the fact that such pronouncements always have something comical about them. Science will not do us this favor. It will continue along its own path with an inner necessity beyond its control, and it will produce more and more breathtaking knowledge and controlling power. It can be no other way. It is senseless, for instance, to hinder a genetic researcher because such research threatens to breed a superman. Hence the problem cannot appear as one in which our human consciousness ranges itself over against the world of science and presumes to develop a kind of antiscience. Nevertheless, we cannot avoid the question of whether what we are aware of in such apparently harmless examples as the aesthetic consciousness and the historical consciousness does not represent a problem that is also present in modern natural science and our technological attitude toward the world. If modern science enables us to erect a new world of technological purposes that transforms everything around us, we are not thereby suggesting that the researcher who gained the knowledge decisive for this state of affairs even considered its technical applications. The genuine researcher is motivated by a desire for knowledge and by nothing else. And yet, over against the whole of our civilization that is founded on modern science, we must ask repeatedly if something has not been omitted. If the presuppositions of these possibilities for knowing and making remain half in the dark, cannot the result be that the hand applying this knowledge will be destructive?[7]

The problem is really universal. The hermeneutical question, as I have characterized it, is not restricted to the areas from which I began in my own investigations. My only concern there was to secure a theoretical basis that would enable us to deal with the basic factor of contemporary culture, namely, science and its industrial, technological utilization. Statistics provide us with a useful example of how the hermeneutical dimension encompasses the entire procedure of science. It is an extreme example, but it shows us that science always stands under definite conditions of methodological abstraction and that the successes of modern science rest on the fact that other possibilities for questioning are concealed by abstraction. This fact comes out clearly in the case of statistics, for the anticipatory character of the questions that statistics answers make it particularly suitable for propaganda purposes. Indeed, effective propaganda must always try to initially influence the judgment of the person addressed and to restrict his possibilities of judgment. Thus what is established by statistics seems to be a language of facts, but which questions these facts answer and which facts would begin to speak if other questions were asked are hermeneutical questions. Only a hermeneutical inquiry would legitimate the meaning of these facts and thus the consequences that follow from them.

But I am anticipating, and have inadvertently used the phrase, "which answers to which questions fit the facts." This phrase is in fact the hermeneutical *Urphänomen:* no assertion is possible that cannot be understood as an answer to a question, and assertions can only be understood in this way. This does not impair the impressive methodology of modern science in the least. Whoever wants to learn a science has to learn to master its methodology. But we also know that methodology as such does not guarantee in any way the productivity of its application. Any experience of life can confirm the fact that there is such a thing as methodological sterility, that is, the application of a method to something not really worth knowing, to something that has not been made an object of investigation on the basis of a genuine question.

The methodological self-consciousness of modern science certainly stands in opposition to this argument. A historian, for example, will say in reply: it is all very nice to talk about the historical tradition in which alone the voices of the past gain their meaning and through which the prejudices that determine the present are inspired. But the situation is completely different in questions of serious historical research. How could one seriously mean, for example, that the clarification of the taxation practices of fifteenth-century cities or of the marital customs of Eskimos somehow first receive their meaning from the consciousness of the present and its anticipations? These are questions of historical knowledge that we take up as tasks quite independently of any relation to the present.

In answering this objection, one can say that the extremity of this point of view would be similar to what we find in certain large industrial research facilities, above all in America and Russia. I mean the so-called random experiment in which one simply covers the material without concern for waste or cost, taking the chance that some day one measurement among the thousands of measurements will finally yield an interesting finding; that is, it will turn out to be the answer to a question from which someone can progress. No doubt modern research in the humanities also works this way to some extent. One thinks, for instance, of the great editions and especially of the ever more perfect indexes. It must remain an open question, of course, whether by such procedures modern historical research increases the chances of actually noticing the interesting fact and thus gaining from it the corresponding enrichment of our knowledge. But even if they do, one might ask: is this an ideal, that countless research projects (that is, determinations of the connection of facts) are extracted from a thousand historians, so that the 1,001st historian can find something interesting? Of course, I am drawing a caricature of genuine scholarship. But in every caricature there is an element of truth, and this one contains an indirect answer to the question of what it is that really makes the productive scholar. That he has learned the methods? The person who never produces anything new has also done that. It is imagination [*Phantasie*] that is the decisive function of the scholar. Imagination naturally has a hermeneutical function and serves the sense for what is questionable. It serves the ability to expose real, productive questions, something in which, generally speaking, only he who masters all the methods of his science succeeds.

As a student of Plato, I particularly love those scenes in which Socrates gets into a dispute with the Sophist virtuosi and drives them to despair by his questions. Eventually they can endure his questions no longer and claim for themselves the apparently preferable role of the questioner. And what happens? They can think of nothing at all to ask. Nothing at all occurs to them that is worth going into and trying to answer.

I draw the following inference from this observation. The real power of hermeneutical consciousness is our ability to see what is questionable. Now if what we have before our eyes is not only the artistic tradition of a people, or historical tradition, or the principle of modern science in its hermeneutical preconditions, but rather the whole of our experience, then we have succeeded, I think, in joining the experience of science to our own universal and human experience of life. For we have now reached the fundamental level that we can call (with Johannes Lohmann) the "linguistic constitution of the world."[8] It presents itself as the consciousness that is effected by history [*wirkungsgeschichtliches Bewusstsein*] and that provides an initial schematization for all our possibilities of knowing. I leave out of account the fact that the scholar—even the natural scientist—is perhaps not completely free of custom and society and from all possible factors in his environment. What I mean is that precisely *within* his scientific experience it is not so much the "laws of ironclad inference" (Helmholtz) that present fruitful ideas to him, but rather unforeseen constellations that kindle the spark of scientific inspiration (for example, Newton's falling apple or some other incidental observation).

The consciousness that is effected by history has its fulfillment in what is linguistic. We can learn from the sensitive student of language that language, in its life and occurrence, must not be thought of as merely changing, but rather as something that has a teleology operating within it. This means that the words that are formed, the means of expression that appear in a language in order to say certain things, are not accidentally fixed, since they do not once again fall altogether into disuse. Instead, a definite articulation of the world is built up—a process that works as if guided and one that we can always observe in children who are learning to speak.

We can illustrate this by considering a passage in Aristotle's *Posterior Analytics* that ingeniously describes one definite aspect of language formation.[9] The passage treats what Aristotle calls the *epagoge,* that is, the formation of the universal. How does one arrive at a universal? In philosophy we say: "how do we arrive at a general concept," but even words in this sense are obviously general. How does it happen that they are "words," that is, that they have a general meaning? In his first apperception, a sensuously equipped being finds himself in a surging sea of stimuli, and finally one day he begins, as we say, to know something. Clearly we do not mean that he was previously blind. Rather, when we say "to know" [*erkennen*] we mean "to recognize" [*wiedererkennen*], that is, to pick something out [*herauserkennen*] of the stream of images flowing past as being identical. What is picked out in this fashion is clearly retained. But how? When does a child know its mother for the first time? When it sees her for the first time? No. Then when? How does it take place? Can we really say at all that there is a single event in which a first knowing extricates the child from the darkness of not knowing? It seems obvious to me that we cannot. Aristotle has described this wonderfully. He says it is the same as when an army is in flight, driven by panic, until at last someone stops and looks around to see whether the foe is still dangerously close behind. We cannot say that the army stops when one soldier has stopped. But then another stops. The army does not stop by virtue of the fact that two soldiers stop. When does it actually stop, then? Suddenly it stands its ground again. Suddenly it obeys the command once again. A subtle pun in involved in Aristotle's description, for in Greek "command" means *arche,* that is, *principium.* When is the principle present as a principle? Through what capacity? This question is in fact the question of the occurrence of the universal.

If I have not misunderstood Johannes Lohmann's exposition, precisely this same teleology operates constantly in the life of language. When Lohmann speaks of linguistic tendencies as the real agents of history in which specific forms expand, he knows of course that it occurs in these forms of realization, of "coming to a stand" [*Zum-Stehen-Kommen*], as the beautiful German phrase says. What is manifest here, I contend, is the real mode of operation of our whole human experience of the world. Learning to speak is surely a phase of special productivity, and in the course of time we have all transformed the genius of the three-year-old into a poor and meager talent. But in the utilization of the linguistic interpretation of the world that finally comes about, something of the productivity of our beginnings remains alive. We are all acquainted with this, for instance, in the attempt to translate, in practical life or in literature or wherever; that is, we are familiar with the strange, uncomfortable, and tortuous feeling we have as long as we do not have the right word. When we have found the right expression (it need not always be one word), when we are certain that we have it, then it "stands," then something has come to a "stand." Once again we have a halt in the midst of the rush of the foreign language, whose endless variation makes us lose our orientation. What I am describing is the mode of the whole human experience of the world. I call this experience hermeneutical, for the process we are describing is repeated continually throughout our familiar experience. There is always a world already interpreted, already organized in its basic relations, into which experience steps as something new, upsetting what has led our expectations and undergoing reorganization itself in the upheaval. Misunderstanding and strangeness are not the first factors; thus, avoiding misunderstanding cannot be regarded as the specific task of hermeneutics. Just the reverse is the case. Only the support of familiar and common understanding makes possible the venture into the alien, the lifting up of something out of the alien, and thus the broadening and enrichment of our own experience of the world.

This discussion shows how the claim to universality that is appropriate to the hermeneutical dimension is to be understood. Understanding is language-bound. But this assertion does not lead us into any kind of linguistic relativism. It is indeed true that we live within a language, but language is not a system of signals that we send off with the aid of a telegraphic key when we enter the office or transmission station. That is not speaking, for it does not have the infinity of the act that is linguistically creative and world-experiencing. While we live wholly within a language, the fact that we do so does not constitute linguistic relativism, because there is absolutely no captivity within a language—not even within our native language. We all experience this when we learn a foreign language, especially on journeys insofar as we master the foreign language to some extent. To master the foreign language means precisely that when we engage in speaking it in the foreign land, we do not constantly consult inwardly our own world and its vocabulary. The better we know the language, the less such a side glance at our native language is perceptible, and only because we never know foreign languages well enough do we always have something of this feeling. But it is nevertheless already speaking, even if perhaps a stammering speaking; for stammering is the obstruction of a desire to speak and is thus opened into the infinite realm of possible expression. Any language in which we live is infinite in this sense, and it is completely mistaken to infer that reason is fragmented because there are various languages. Just the opposite is the case. Precisely through our finitude, the particularity of our being, which is evident even in the variety of languages, the infinite dialogue is opened in the direction of the truth that we are.

If this is correct, then the relation of our modern industrial world, founded by science, which we described at the outset, is mirrored above all on the level of language. We live in an epoch in which increasingly a leveling of all life-forms is taking place—that is the rationally necessary requirement for maintaining life on our planet. The food problem of mankind, for example, can only be overcome by giving up the lavish wastefulness that has covered the earth. Unavoidably, the mechanical, industrial world is expanding within the life of the individual as a sort of sphere of technical perfection. When we hear modern lovers talking to each other, we often wonder if they are communicating with words or with advertising labels and technical terms from the sign language of the modern industrial world. It is inevitable that the leveled life-forms of the industrial age also affect language, and in fact the impoverishment of the vocabulary of language is making enormous progress, thus bringing about an approximation of language to a technical sign-system. Leveling tendencies of this kind are irresistible. Yet in spite of them, the simultaneous building up of our own world in language still persists whenever we want to say something to each other. The result is the actual relationship of human beings to each other. Each is at first surrounded by a kind of linguistic circle, and these linguistic circles come into contact with each other, merging more and more. In this way, language occurs once again, in vocabulary and grammar as always, and never without the inner infinity of the dialogue that is in progress between every speaker and his partner. That is the fundamental dimension of hermeneutics. Genuine speaking, which has something to say and hence does not give prearranged signals, but rather seeks words through which one reaches the other person, is the universal human task—but it is a special task for the theologian, to whom is entrusted the saying-further [*Weitersagen*] of a message that stands written.

Translated by David E. Linge

4

Language and Understanding

"Language and Understanding" was originally recorded as a lecture for radio on March 18, and broadcast on Southwest Radio (Sudwestfunk) in two parts on March 22 and March 30, 1970. This explains the absence of footnotes in this text. The first in-print publication of the lecture came during the same year in the Lutheran monthly, *Zeitwende*,[1] and it also appeared the following year in a book that Gadamer coauthored.[2] Half a dozen years later he chose to include it in *Kleine Schriften* (1967–77), a four-volume collection of his writings,[3] and in 1986 he added it without change to volume 2 of his *Gesammelte Werke*, a volume which collects his writings in the area of hermeneutics.[4] Finally, in 1997 it was included in an inexpensive one-volume paperback collection of his writings, the *Gadamer Lesebuch*. While the inclusion of this essay in both sets of collected writings affirms its place in his writings about hermeneutics, his decision to include it in the *Gadamer Lesebuch* suggests that it held a special place for Gadamer. So we must ask: why did Gadamer find this essay important enough to be included in the *Lesebuch*?

First, in this essay Gadamer redefines the nature of understanding in contrast to the usual definition, and he does so without footnotes and to a general audience. This is helpful. Second, he redefines language, also. These two redefinitions place his philosophical hermeneutics in a new and more accessible light. Together, these more accessible redefinitions give us a sense of what is new and exciting in his philosophical hermeneutics. And third, toward the end of his talk and without naming names, he goes on to clarify and defend certain matters that were initially misunderstood in his project of a philosophical hermeneutics. These three factors may be among the reasons why Gadamer chose to include this essay in the *Gadamer Lesebuch*.

In taking up the topic of understanding, Gadamer was dealing with a central issue of hermeneutics since Friedrich Schleiermacher, who redefined hermeneutics as a "general theory of understanding," when it had previously been focused on the task of overcoming difficulties in understanding texts in various disciplines, such as theology, literature, and law. Schleiermacher's interdisciplinary approach was taken up by Dilthey, who proposed to transform hermeneutics as a general method of understanding texts into the fundamental methodology of all of the humanities. Heidegger broadened the conception of hermeneutics itself even further by making understanding not just a process of understanding texts, but a process of self-understanding in the course of living one's life temporally and historically. He formulated what may be called an ontological hermeneutics, for it was an interpretation of the being of a temporally existing human being. In *Truth and Method* Gadamer took up Heidegger's concept of an existential self-understanding, and also Heidegger's subsequent ontology of the human experience of artworks. In emphasizing the inseparability of understanding and language, he is restating a key element of his own hermeneutical philosophy in *Truth and Method* and also adds Heidegger's emphasis on language and being in later essays. But Gadamer goes beyond what he says in *Truth and Method* or even what Heidegger says about language and being in his later writings, to assert the social significance of language and understanding. It is this last step in defining language and understanding that constitutes an exciting new step in his thinking, a step that makes his hermeneutics of special interest to the social sciences. And because he is addressing a radio audience, he puts the issues in terms that a layman can understand. At the same time, he is articulating a truly important theme in his later philosophy: *solidarity,* the social solidarity contained in language.

The fact that language and thinking or understanding are inseparable has been said before, but Gadamer goes further here to articulate the fact that language is a repository of a culture. In other places in his writings he says that language reveals the thoughts and thought forms of a culture, and great texts embody these ideas in a permanent and transmittable way, a way that has to be interpreted and reinterpreted in each generation, and this gives the humanities a special place in education. But in this broadcast to a radio audience, Gadamer does not mention great texts, the role of the humanities, or even "philosophical hermeneutics"; rather, he talks about understanding as a fabric, a network of understandings out of which we understand what we understand. Silent understanding, he notes, rests on a network of previous understandings, and these understandings reside in language. This is his definition of understanding.

The second major theme is language. Gadamer here seeks to show how his view of language is radically unlike scientific views of language that approach it abstractly, in terms of the contextless assertions of logic. He asserts that language is constantly building up and bearing within itself the commonality of a world orientation. It is this shared orientation, this fabric of shared understandings, this common social world that makes social solidarity possible. Gadamer contrasts his inclusion of this background of shared solidarity in understandings with the lack of such a background in the abstractness of scientific treatments of language. More importantly, he makes a political point for this audience: there is an ominous absence of controls within technological knowledge when it is separated from the context of social solidarity that makes human societies human. This is a point that is important to us even today. So in this essay, Gadamer markedly goes beyond the idea that language and understanding are inseparable to state that these shared understandings in language form the background for social solidarity. Thus they have a social, moral, normative character that is lost in the use of language by science, technology, and even in the isolating and abstract way that analytic philosophy generally deals with language.

In the final section of this essay, Gadamer replies to some misunderstandings of his philosophy that have arisen in the decade since the publication of his masterwork. For this audience, however, he does not mention his critic, Habermas, by name. His dialogue with Habermas about language and the nature of the background social fabric of understandings has continued over decades, but his defense of his philosophy always goes back to the fact that for him *language is living language and takes place in events of understanding*. Thus, language as it is used in a psychoanalytic situation is not a good general model for language and understanding,[5] nor is language as imagined in the distortion-free context of an ideal speech situation (as Habermas calls it) living language.[6] In both of these cases, Habermas sees language in the context of an emancipatory reflection needed to change social norms rather than as it functions in the ordinary processes of understanding and reaching an understanding.

Gadamer's last paragraph presents his point in a richly condensed and luminous way. He says there that we must get back to the living reality of language that both reveals and conceals, to language such as we find in religious forms of expression, but above all in poetry. His concluding sentence notes that all this is "especially clear in the poetic use of language." What Gadamer means by "living language" in this essay is not ordinary language, or language about language, or even language in interpretation. Rather, it is ultimately in poetry that language truly shines forth in all its power and beauty. As ever, he turns to poetry as "living language."

So in this essay, Gadamer elucidates in a clear and accessible way his distinctive new way of redefining language and understanding and supplements it with replies to some criticisms of his view. This essay is irreplaceable in the annals of Gadamer's writings for its accessibility and for clarifying what is new about his way of defining both language and understanding.

* * *

Language and Understanding

The problem of understanding is of increasing interest in recent years. Certainly this is not unrelated to our very uneasy social and world-political situation and the sharp increase in tensions at the present time. Everywhere one looks one finds that efforts to reach an understanding between zones within a nation, between nations, blocks of nations, and between generations, are failing. It would seem that a common language is lacking, and the concepts that generally serve as guidelines for discussion—I have in mind, for example, concepts like "democracy" and "freedom"—only function as emotional appeals that make oppositions more rigid and the tensions more extreme—the very tensions one is seeking to reduce.

So I think my general thesis here—that reaching an understanding is a problem that must succeed or fail in the medium of language—actually does not require elaborate demonstration. All the phenomena involved in reaching an understanding, the phenomena of understanding and misunderstanding which constitute the central focus of what we call "hermeneutics," clearly involve language. But in the following discussion I will propose something more radical. I wish to suggest that the general process of reaching an understanding between persons and the process of understanding per se are both language-events that resemble the inner conversation of the soul with itself, a conversation which Plato asserted was the very essence of thinking.

The claim that all understanding is linguistic in character is admittedly provocative. We need only look around ourselves and at our own experiences to find a swarm of counterexamples, or at least what seem to be. For instance, silent, wordless consent is often taken to be the highest and innermost type of understanding. Anyone who observes language carefully will immediately come across such phenomena as silent consent or guessing that something is the case without putting it into words. But I believe that even these cases are in modes of language [of *Sprachlichkeit*] in a sense. In what follows I hope to make clear why it makes sense to say this.

But what about still other phenomena—like "speechless astonishment" or being "struck dumb with admiration"—to which language may lead us? What we encounter in such moments are certainly phenomena about which we can say they "leave us speechless." Language deserts us, and it deserts us precisely because what enlightens is standing so strongly before our ever more encompassing gaze that words would not be adequate to grasp it. Is it not a really daring claim to maintain, as I do, that even when language deserts us, this too is a form of language [*Sprachlichkeit*]? Is my claim not like the absurd dogmatism of those philosophers who over and over again try to stand things on their heads when they can just as well stand on their feet? Yet I would say that when speech deserts us, what this really means is that one would like to say so much that one does not know where to begin. The breakdown of language actually testifies to one's capacity to search out an expression for everything, so I think it is really only a manner of speaking to say that language has deserted us. In actuality, speaking has not come to an end but to a beginning.

I would like to demonstrate this above all by considering the first linguistic example I mentioned, namely when one speaks of a "silent consent." What is the hermeneutical significance of this phrase? The problem of understanding, which we find discussed in so many of its dimensions, especially in all of the disciplines where exact methods of verification are available, consists basically in the fact that there we have a merely inner evidence of understanding; for example, understanding that comes to light when I suddenly understand the context of a statement used in a certain situation. That is to say, when it suddenly becomes completely clear and graspable, how justified it is that the other person says what he says, or how unjustified. Actually, such experiences of understanding clearly presuppose difficulties in understanding, the disturbance of an agreement in understanding. So all efforts at trying to understand something begin when one comes up against something that is strange, challenging, disorienting.

The Greeks had a very fine word for that which brings our understanding to a standstill. They called it the *atopon*. This word actually means "the placeless," that which cannot be fitted into the categories of expectation in our understanding and which therefore causes us to be suspicious of it. The famous Platonic doctrine that philosophizing begins with wonder has this suspicion in mind, this experience of not being able to go any further with the pre-schematized expectations of our orientation to the world, which therefore beckons to thinking. Aristotle described this very aptly when he said that what we expect depends on how much insight we have into the context, and he gave the following example. When one is amazed at the fact that the root of two is irrational, and that therefore the relationship of the diagonals and the length of the sides of a quadrangle is not rationally expressible, one sees from this that he is no mathematician, for a mathematician would be amazed that anyone could expect this relationship to be rational. The support for this conclusion is relative, is related to knowledge and deep acquaintance with the subject. All this surprise and wonder, all this not being able to get any further, is obviously always connected with getting further, with penetrating to important knowledge!

What I therefore want to maintain is that if we really want to bring into view clearly the place that the process of understanding has in the whole of our being as human beings, and also in our social being as human beings, we must consciously separate the general phenomenon of understanding from an overemphasis on disturbances in understanding. Actually, a prior agreement in understanding is presupposed wherever disturbances in this agreement arise. The relatively infrequent hindrances to agreement in understanding and to reaching agreements in understanding are supposedly what pose the task and desire to agree in understanding and thus are supposed to lead to the lifting of obstacles to understanding. In other words, when we consider the matter carefully, the example of "silent agreement" is not so much an objection to the linguistic character of understanding; instead, it is the linguistic character of understanding that assures its breadth and universality. This is a basic truth that we need to honor and restore, after having endured several centuries in which the concept of method has been posited in modern science as the absolute starting point for our self-understanding.

Modern science, which arose in the seventeenth century, is based on thought about method and the progressive accumulation of knowledge assured by method. This form of science has uniquely changed our planet by privileging a certain form of access to our world, an access that is neither the only nor the most encompassing access that we possess. It is this access to the world by means of methodical isolation and conscious interrogation—in the experiment—which has enabled particular realms in which this isolation can be accomplished to spread out and attain a special hold on our ways of doing things. This was the great accomplishment of the mathematical sciences of nature, and particularly of the Galilean mechanics of the seventeenth century. But it is well known that the intellectual achievement of discovering the laws of free-falling bodies and of inclined planes was not brought about merely by observation. There was no vacuum. Free fall is an abstraction. Everyone remembers his or her own astonishment at the experiment that he or she experienced in school, where a piece of lead and a feather, when dropped in a relative vacuum, fell at the same rate! Galileo isolated things from the conditioning factors that were found in nature, abstracting from the resistance of the medium of air. But it was such abstraction that made possible the mathematical description of factors which bring about natural events, and thereby enable man's controlling intervention in nature.

The discipline of mechanics which Galileo constructed in this way is, in fact, the mother of our technical civilization. Here a very specific methodical way of gaining knowledge arose, whose success brought about the tension between our unmethodical knowledge of the world, which encompasses our whole experience of life, and the scientific knowledge that brought it about. Kant's great achievement philosophically was that he found a persuasive conceptual solution for this tension. For philosophy in the seventeenth and eighteenth centuries had exhausted itself on the insoluble task of uniting the omniscience of the metaphysical tradition with the new science—an effort that could not bring about a viable balance between a science of reason based on concepts and a science based on experience. Kant, in contrast, found a solution. His critical restriction of reason and its conceptual knowledge to what was given in experience, a restriction he found in the English critique of metaphysics, carried with it the destruction of metaphysics as a dogmatic science. But Kant, the "crusher of everything" [*Alleszermalmer*]—as his contemporaries felt the gentle professor of Königsberg to be—was at the same time also the great founder of moral philosophy rigorously based on the principle of the autonomy of practical reason. Kant recognized freedom as a unique fact of reason, that is to say, he showed that without assuming the freedom of the practical reason of man, the moral and social existence of man could not be thought. In doing this, Kant gave to philosophical thinking a new legitimacy for the concept of freedom in the face of all the determinism that was rising from modern science. In fact, the impetus of his moral philosophy, mediated above all through Fichte, stands behind the great trailblazers of the "historical worldview" [*historische Weltanschauung*]: namely, Wilhelm von Humboldt, Ranke, and Droysen, above all. But certainly also Hegel and everyone who is positively or negatively influenced by him were also filled with Kant's idea of freedom down to the last detail, and therefore, against the method-centeredness of the historical sciences, they maintained a stream of philosophical thinking that by and large has remained a major trend in philosophy.

Nevertheless, precisely the connection between the rising new sciences and the ideal of method was also the thing that put them at a distance, so to speak, from the phenomenon of understanding. Just as for the researcher into nature nature is at first something inscrutably strange, such that through calculation and purposeful compulsion, through torture with the help of experiments, nature is compelled to make assertions; so also the sciences that employ understanding are themselves more and more seen in terms of this kind of concept of method. The result is that understanding is largely viewed as the removal of misunderstandings, as bridging the alienation between the I and the thou. But is the thou ever as alien as the object of experimental natural science by definition is? We need to recognize that agreement in understanding is more primordial than misunderstanding, so that over and over again understanding leads us back into a reconstruction of agreement in understanding. This fact, it seems to me, clearly and fully legitimates the universal character of understanding.

But why is understanding, when it comes into the open, linguistic in character? Why does the "silent agreement" among people that again and again is built up as the commonality of an orientation to the world point to what we may call "linguisticality"? The question, so posed, carries the answer implicitly in itself. Language is what is constantly building up and bearing within itself this commonality of world-orientation. To speak with one another is not primarily hashing things out with each other. It seems to me characteristic of the tensions within modernity that it loves this manner of speaking. To speak with another person is also not speaking past him or her. Rather, in speaking with another person one builds up an aspect held in common, the thing that is being talked about. The true reality of human communication is such that a conversation does not simply carry one person's opinion through against another's in argument, or even simply add one opinion to another. Genuine conversation transforms the viewpoint of both. A conversation that is truly successful is such that one cannot fall back into the disagreement that touched it off. The commonality between the partners is so very strong that the point is no longer the fact that I think this and you think that, but rather it involves *the shared interpretation of the world which makes moral and social solidarity possible* [emphasis added]. What is right and is recognized as right by both sides requires by its very nature the commonality that is built up when human beings understand each other. Agreement in opinions is in fact constantly being built up as we speak with each other, and then it sinks back into the stillness of agreement in understanding and things that both regard as self-evident. For this reason the thesis is justified which asserts that all extra-verbal forms of understanding go back to an understanding that unfolds in speaking and in speaking with another person.

When I take this insight as my starting point, as I do, this does not mean that in all understanding there resides a potential relationship to language, such that it is always possible—this is the pride of our reason—whenever a disagreement arises, that one can blaze a path to agreement in understanding through talking to each other. We will not always succeed, but our social life together is based on the presupposition that through talking things out with each other to the fullest possible extent, we will overcome being blocked off from mutual insight by remaining stuck within the compass of our own opinions. It is therefore also a serious mistake to think that the universality of understanding, which I take as my starting assumption and which I try to persuade others to assume also, includes within it something like a harmonizing attitude or a basic conservatism with regard to our social world. To "understand" the structures and ordering of our world, to understand ourselves with each other in this world, just as much presupposes critique and struggle with what has grown rigid or outdated as it does the recognition or defense of the existing orders of things.

One can see this again in the way we speak with each other and build up mutual understandings. One can observe this from generation to generation. In particular, if world history accelerates greatly, as it has done in the last decade, one nevertheless witnesses how new language arises for the occasion. New language here certainly does not mean a totally new language, nor at the same time changing the expressions we have for the same thing. With new aspects, with new goals, a new speaking is worked out and born. A new language brings disturbances in our understanding of things, but at the same time in the communicative event one can overcome the disturbance. At least that is the ideal goal of all communication. Under certain conditions this may prove to be unachievable, of course. One of such conditions is the pathological breakdown of interhuman understandings which characterizes the fact of neurosis. And the question arises as to whether social life as a whole does not in the communicative process itself serve to maintain and spread a "false consciousness." At least this is the thesis put forward by advocates of the critique of ideology, namely that the contradiction in social interests makes the communicative event practically impossible, just as is the case in mental illness. But just as the therapy in this case consists precisely in reconnecting the patient with the common set of understandings in the society, so also it is the claim of the critique of ideology that it seeks to correct the false social consciousness and by doing so establish a right agreement in understanding. Special cases of a deeply disturbed agreement in understanding with society may make necessary a reconstruction of the social understandings, based on an explicit knowledge of the nature of the disturbance of them. But this point again confirms the constitutive function of agreement in understanding as such.

Moreover, it is self-evident that language leads its tension-filled life in a certain antagonism between conventionality and revolutionary awakening. We all experienced our first linguistic training when we came to school. There everything that had seemed right to our healthy linguistic fantasy was no longer permitted. The same thing happened with our instruction in drawing, which very often led to a child losing all enjoyment of drawing. In reality one can say that the school is largely an institution for bringing about social conformity. It is only an institution among others, of course. I don't want to be misunderstood as making a complaint against the schools that they should be otherwise. Rather, I think this *is* society, this is the way society works, always teaching us standards and bringing about conformity. This does not at all mean that education in our society is merely a process of repression and education in language an instrument of such repression. But language continues to live on in spite of all such conformism. New linguistic structures and ways of expression arise from the changes in our lives and our experience. The antagonism we spoke of before lives on, an antagonism that maintains language as something we have in common and that nevertheless is always generating new impulses toward the transformation of what we have in common.

The question arises, then, as to whether this relationship between the natural tendency of society to conformity and the explosive powers connected with critical insight has not in our highly industrialized technical civilization undergone a qualitative change. There have always been subtle unnoticed changes in the life and usage of language; certain slogans and catchwords come into vogue and then die out. The decline that was taking place in especially critical times could be observed by tracing the changes in language, as Thucydides did in his famous description of the terrible consequences of the plague in beleaguered Athens. But perhaps in our present circumstances we are confronted with something qualitatively new and different that was never here before. What I have in mind is the purposeful regulation and control of language today. This is a fact that seems to have been brought about by our technical civilization. For what we call the regulation and control of language today is no longer the unintentional control by the schoolteacher or the general control exercised by public opinion, but is a consciously wielded instrument of politics. Language is now able, by means of a centrally steered communication system, to put matters in a certain suggestive light, such that the regulation of language is prescribed in advance, so to speak, to follow technological paths. A contemporary example of this, in which we just now again find ourselves in the grip of a transformation in language, is the designation of the other half of Germany as the DDR [Deutsche Demokratische Republik]. As we well know, this term was for decades scorned by official regulation of our language, and nobody could overlook the fact that the term they recommended to replace it, namely "middle Germany," had a sharply political accent. Here the focus of attention was only on a process [*Vorgang*], quite apart from any content being referenced. The technical form of shaping public opinion today gives the centrally controlled regulation of language an influence that is disabling the natural conforming powers operative in language within society. This is one of the problems we face today: how to harmonize the central control of opinion formation in the political realm with the demands that reason also makes to help determine the life of the society on the basis of free insight and critical judgment.

One may think that science will offer the solution to this problem. After all, does not science have as its distinguishing characteristic that it is able to be independent of politics and public opinion? Is not the scientist taught to form his judgments on the basis of free insight? This may in fact be a distinguishing characteristic of science in its purest realms. But does this mean that all by itself and from its own power it has an effect on the public? Science may want ever so much to escape all manipulation of its own intentions—yet the tremendously high estimation in which science is held goes completely against this. It constantly places limits on the critical freedom that it so much admires in the scientific researcher, by invoking the authority of science where in reality the issue is one of a struggle for political power.

Does science really "have its own language," a language to which one ought to listen? The question is obviously ambiguous. On the one hand, science certainly does develop its own linguistic means for describing things, fixing meanings, and communicating its understanding within the process of doing its research. In this sense science seems to have its own language. On the other hand, does it have a language that tries to reach the public consciousness and overcome the legendary unintelligibility of science? Does the communicative system that is developed within scientific research really have the character of being a language all its own? If one means this by the "language of science," then obviously one does not mean the kind of communicative system that grows out of everyday language. The best example of this is mathematics and its role in the natural sciences. What mathematics is for itself is its own private secret. The physicist does not know this at all. What mathematics knows, what its object is, what its questions are, is something unique to it. It is apparently one of the miraculous powers of human reason that unfolds within human reason itself while reason looks on and lingers to have an investigation of itself. But as a language in which the world is spoken of, mathematics is only one system of symbols among the several symbolic systems in the totality of our linguistic comportment and is not in itself a language. The physicist, who always finds himself in a highly embarrassing situation when he wants to go beyond his equations and make understandable to others or himself what he has worked out, always finds himself torn by the tensions in a task of integration. The great physicists even become poetical in this case and often in a very elegant way. How these tiny atoms do everything they do, how they capture and hold electrons and carry out other wonderful and clever processes—that is a whole fairy-tale language in which a physicist seeks to present what he depicts more exactly in equations, so that he can, within limits, make it all clearer to himself and to all of us.

Certainly mathematics is involved, but the mathematics that the physicist uses to gain his knowledge and formulate it, is not in itself a language; rather, it is only part of a very complex and diverse linguistic instrument which the physicist uses in order to bring to language what he wants to say. This means, in other words, that scientific speaking is always the mediation of a language within a certain discipline or set of disciplinary expressions—we call it a scholarly terminology—that stand within an encompassing language that is living, growing, and changing. This task of integration and mediation with the ordinary spoken language is particularly challenging for the physicist because more than all other natural scientists he speaks in and through mathematics. Precisely because the physicist represents the extreme case of employing a basically mathematical symbolism, his case is especially instructive. In his resort to poetic metaphors, we see that for physics mathematics is only a part of language, and by no means an autonomous part. Language is autonomous when, as we find to be the case in mature languages, it comes forward in its reality to light up aspects of the world in various cultures.

So the question now is how scientific and nonscientific speaking and thinking relate to each other. Is not scientific language just in the situation of only approaching but never reaching the flexible freedom of everyday speaking? If someone denies this situation, one can point out that today seemingly the older, more mature languages are indispensable. But perhaps we all need to learn a bit more about this, and then finally we will all be able to understand without words the equations of physics. Then would we need nothing but scientific language? Modern logical calculus in fact has as its goal an absolutely univocal artificial language. But this possibility is disputed. For instance, Giambattista Vico and Gottfried von Herder maintained to the contrary that poetry is the original language of the human race, and the intellectualizing that was taking place in modern languages was a poor fate for language and was not really the fulfillment of the ideal of language. The question this brings up is: can the opinion be right at all that every language is striving to move toward a more scientific language as the fulfillment of its potential?

In order to discuss this question, I would like to juxtapose two phenomena. The first is the *statement* or *assertion* [*Aussage*] and the other is the *word* [*Wort*]. First, I will explain both concepts. When I say "the word," I do not simply mean the singular form of the plural, "words," as we might find in the dictionary. I also do not mean the singular form of the plural, "words," understood as a word that with other words forms the context of a sentence. No, I mean rather the word that is always singular and never plural! This is the word that applies to you, a word that you let be said to you when someone "gives you the word." This word clearly falls within a certain life relationship, it is a word that receives its unity of meaning from a certain life context. It is good to remember that ultimately behind this singular-only "word" that cannot be plural stands the usage of this term in the New Testament. For what "in the beginning was the Word" means, was a matter over which Faust brooded [in Goethe's *Faust*, part 1] when he was trying to translate the first verse of John's gospel. This active word, this word radiant with power, is not for Goethe an individual magic formula but points (without alluding to the incarnation event) beyond itself to what binds human reason to its deep "thirst for *Existenz*."[1]

If I place "the word," understood in this sense, next to "statement," I think the meaning of the term "statement" or "assertion" becomes clearer. We speak of a statement in the logic of statements, of statement calculus in the modern mathematical formalization of logic. This self-evident way of speaking about the term ultimately goes back to the most consequential, most significant, inventions of our Western culture, and that is the construction of a logic based on statements. Aristotle, the creator of this part of logic, the masterful analyst of the process of drawing conclusions in logical thinking, accomplished this through a formalization of assertion sentences and the demonstrable conclusiveness of their connections. We remember the famous school example of a syllogism, "All human beings are mortal. Darius is a human being. Therefore Darius is mortal." What kind of achievement in abstraction is accomplished here? Apparently this: that only what is uttered as a statement really counts. All other forms of language and speaking are not made the object of analysis, only the statement. The Greek word for this use of statement is *apophansis*, or *logos apophantikos*, which means the speaking, the assertion whose only meaning is the *apophainesthai*, to bring about the self-showing of what is said. This refers to an assertion that is theoretical in the sense that it abstracts itself from everything that is not expressly said. Only that which the statement itself reveals through its being said constitutes the object of analysis and the foundation of logical consequentiality.

Now I ask you: Are there such pure statements? When and where? In any case, the statement is not the only form of speaking there is. Aristotle himself speaks about this in relation to his teaching about the statement, and it is clear in this context what one still has to consider: something like a prayer and a request, a curse and a command. One must even take into consideration one of the puzzling in-between-phenomena: the question, whose peculiar nature is that it stands closer to a statement than any of the other linguistic phenomena, and yet it allows no logic in the sense of a logic of statements. Perhaps there is a logic question. In such a logic, we could note that the answer to a question necessarily arouses new questions. Perhaps there is a logic of the request; for example, we note that the first request is never the last. But the question is whether this ought to be called "logic" or whether logic only applies to the connections between pure statements. But how do we delimit what a statement is? Can one take a statement out of its motivational context? ·

Of course, in modern scientific methodology these matters are not much discussed. For it is the very nature of scientific methodology that its assertions are like a kind of treasure house of methodically assured truths. Like every treasure house, the treasure house of science has a stockpile of things that are randomly usable. In fact, it is the nature of modern science that it is constantly adding to its stockpile of knowledge available for random use. The many problems that arise with regard to the social and human responsibility of science, problems that since Hiroshima weigh so heavily on our consciences, are rendered so severe because methodologically modern science is not in a position to control the ends to which its knowledge is applied in the same way it can control the contexts in which it acquires that knowledge. The methodical abstraction of modern science is the thing that brings about its great success, in the fact that it makes possible the practical application that we call technology. Again, technology as the application of science is, like science, not itself controllable. I am by no means a fatalist and prophet of doom when I doubt whether science could possibly place limits on itself. Rather, I believe that ultimately it is not science as such that can guide and guarantee the rational application of our technological power. No, ultimately the only thing that can do this is the human and the political capacity that belongs to us all as human beings. At any rate, this is the capacity that can lead us in such a way that we avoid the most terrible catastrophes. At the same time, I fully recognize that the isolation involved in the truth of statements and in the logic built on statements in modern science is fully legitimate. But we pay a high price for this, a price which natural science cannot by its nature save us from paying: such is the universality of science that theoretical reason and the instrumentality of science are not able in themselves to place any limits on the technological capacity that man has built up. No doubt there are in science "pure" statements, but what this means is that this knowledge is still capable of serving any and all possible purposes.

Of course, I wonder if even this example does not in reality demonstrate that the abstract, isolated statements that constitute the basis for the world-forming power of technology are never really encountered in complete isolation. For instance, does it not appear to be true here that every assertion is always motivated by something? Were not the abstraction and concentration on being able to do things that finally led in the seventeenth century to the methodical thinking found in modern science based on a separation from the religious conceptions of the medieval world and on a decision in favor of modest knowledge and self-help? That is the motivational basis here for a will to know which is at the same time the ability to do things. And in order to have this knowledge, this ability to do things, it scorns every effort to govern it or place limits on itself. In contrast to this, in the high cultures of East Asia the technological application of knowledge is governed by the binding powers of social reason, so the possibilities of realizing one's own capabilities remained unfulfilled. What powers that we lack and what enabled them to do this is a question for the researcher in religion, the cultural historian, and also the philosopher who is really at home in Chinese language and culture (it seems such a person can never be found!).

In any case, the extreme example provided by our modern scientific and technological culture seems to show us that the isolation they accord to the assertion, the total detachment from any kind of context of motivation, becomes very questionable when one looks at the whole of science. So I think I am correct in saying that a statement, as I understand it, is a motivated assertion. There are some especially suggestive phenomena one can cite to show this, such as interrogations or statements by witnesses. In the administration of justice, on the basis of wisdom and discretion or necessity in legal findings, it is the case that the witness, at least in certain cases, is asked questions of which the witness does not know the purpose. In some cases, the evidential value of an assertion that a witness makes rests solely on the fact that it cannot be desired by the witness to be either defending or incriminating the person charged, because the witness does not comprehend the context that has to be clarified. Now everyone who has been either a witness or a victim of an interrogation knows how dreadful it is when one has to answer questions without knowing why one is asked them. The fiction of a "pure" assertion apparently corresponds in this kind of witness testimony to the no less fictitious pure determination of factual statements, and it is precisely this fictitious restriction to the factual that then gives the attorneys their opportunity. So this extreme example of the assertion that is made in court teaches us that one speaks with motivation, and does not just make a statement but answers a question. Answering a question, however, entails grasping the sense of the question and therewith its background motivation. As we know only too well, nothing is so difficult as when we are supposed to answer so-called dumb questions, that is, questions that have no clear, univocal direction of meaning.

It follows from this that an assertion never contains the full content of its meaning solely within itself. In logic we have long been acquainted with this as the problem of occasionality. "Occasional" expressions, which occur in every language, are characterized by the fact that unlike other expressions, they do not contain their meaning fully in themselves. For example, when I say "here." That which is "here" is not understandable to everyone through the fact that it was uttered aloud or written down; rather, one must know where this "here" was or is. For its meaning, the "here" requires to be filled in by the occasion, the *occasio*, in which it is said. Expressions of this type have, for this reason, been of especial interest to logical-phenomenological analysis, because one can show that in the case of these meanings, they contain the situation and the occasion in the content of their meaning. The special problem posed by these "occasional" expressions appears to be that in many respects they require further elucidation [*Erweiterung*, expansion]. Hans Lipps in his *Untersuchungen zu einer hermeneutischen Logik* [*Investigations Toward a Hermeneutical Logic*][2] has elaborated on this, and the English logical analysis of J. L. Austin and his followers likewise has put forward an important standpoint represented in the expression, "How to do things with words" (How one can do something simply by using words).[3] These give us examples of forms of speaking that transcend speaking and become transactions. They offer an especially sharp contrast to the concept of assertions as existing purely in themselves.

Now let's place this concept of the isolated assertion [Aussage] with its very blurry boundaries over against the concept of the "word," but not word defined as the smallest unit of speech. The word that a real person utters or has said to him (or her) is not that grammatical element in the linguistic analysis of a sentence, for one can demonstrate in the concrete phenomena involved in learning a language how second-ary the word is compared to the linguistic melody of a sentence. The word that can truly be accepted as the smallest unit of sense is not the word one finds in breaking down a speech to its last constituent piece. This word I refer to is also not a name, and speaking it is not a naming process, because the report we get in Genesis, for example, about nam-ing conveys a false implication that we just go from one thing to another giving things names. No, the freedom of assigning names at random is not at all our basic linguistic relationship to words: there is no first word. To speak of a first word is a contradiction in itself. There is always already a system of words that is the basis for the meaning of each word. Also, I cannot say something like: "I would like to introduce a word." Certainly one finds here and there people who say this, but they greatly overestimate themselves if they do this. They are not the ones who intro-duce a word. At most they put forward an expression or coin a technical term, which they then define. But when a word comes into being, this is certainly not how it happens. A word introduces *itself*. A word only becomes a word when it breaks and enters into communicative usage. This does not happen through the introducing act of someone who has suggested the word, but apparently happens when and because it "in-troduces itself." However, the very term "language use" [*Sprachgebrauch*] always implies things that look past the real nature of our linguistic experience of the world. It suggests that words are like something one has in one's pocket and when one uses them one just pulls them out of one's pocket, as if linguistic usage were at the whim of the user of language. But language is not dependent on this or that user. In reality, language usage shows us that ultimately the language refuses to be mis-used. For it is language itself that prescribes what will be linguistically acceptable. This should not be taken to mean some kind of mythologiz-ing of language; it means, rather, that the claim of language can never be reduced to what an individual subjectively intends. It belongs to the way of being of language [*Seinsweise der Sprache*] that *we* and not just one of us but indeed all of us are the ones who are speaking.

A word is also not completely separable from what people call the "ideal unity" of the word meaning of signs or other phenomena of ex-pression. Indeed, one of the most important logical and phenomeno-logical achievements at the beginning of the twentieth century was that phenomenology, especially Husserl in his *Logical Investigations*, worked out the difference between all signs other than words and the meaning of words. He correctly showed that the meaning of a word has nothing to do with the fantasy images that practical psychology [*realpsychologischen Worstellungsbildern*] had found to be provoked by the use of a word. The idealization that a word possesses through the fact that it has one—and always this one—particular meaning distinguishes it from all other senses of "meaning," for example, the meaning a sign has. While the insight of phenomenology that the meaning of a word was not simply a psychic event was fundamental and important, it made a mistake when it spoke of the "ideal unity of a word meaning." Language is such that, whatever particular meaning a word may possess, words do not have a single unchanging meaning; rather, they possess a fluctuating range of meanings, and precisely this fluctuation constitutes the peculiar risk of speaking. Only in the process of speaking, as we speak further, as we build up the fabric of a linguistic context, do we come to fix the meanings in the moments of meaning of our speaking. Only in this way do we mutually agree on what we mean.

Especially in understanding texts in a foreign language do we find this to be the case. There everyone knows very well how the fluctuation of word meanings is gradually stabilized in the process of using them, and only slowly does one reproduce the unity of sense of a sentence. Even this is not an adequate description of the process. One needs only to contemplate the process of translation in order to see how incomplete such a description is. For the despair of translation lies in the fact that the unity of viewpoint that a sentence possesses in its own language does not permit its being arranged in the corresponding order of sentence parts in the target language. To do so produces the dreadful sentences we often find in translated books: letters without spirit [*Buchstaben ohne Geist*]. What is missing that necessarily constitutes the very nature of language is that there is a word being offered by the other person, a word that calls forth other words, so to speak, that themselves hold open the continuation of the speaking. A translated sentence that has not been worked on and fundamentally transformed by a master of translation to the extent that one no longer longs for the more vibrant original sentence, is just a pale map of a territory instead of the territory itself. The meaning of a word resides not just in the language system and in the context; rather, this "standing-in-a-context" means at the same time that the word is never completely separated from the multiple meanings it has in itself, even when the context has made clear the meaning it possesses in this particular context. Evidently, then, the meaning that a word acquires in the speaking where one encounters it is not the only thing that is present there. Other things are co-present, and it is the presence of all that is co-present there that comes together to make up the evocative power of living speech. For this reason, I think one can say that every speaking points into the Open of further speaking. More and more is going to be said in the direction that the speaking has taken.

This shows the truth of my thesis that speaking takes place in the process of a "conversation" [*Gespräch*].

If one grasps the phenomenon of language not by starting from the isolated sentence but by beginning with the totality of our behavior in the world, which at the same time is a living in conversation [*Gesprächsleben*], we can understand why the phenomenon of language is so puzzling, drawing us toward it but at the same time turning us away. Speaking is the most deeply self-forgetful action that we as rational human beings perform. Everyone has had the experience of how one stops in the midst of one's own speaking, becomes conscious of the words one has just uttered, and becoming conscious of them just at that moment continues speaking. A little story about an experience my daughter and I had illustrates this point nicely. She was supposed to write "strawberries" and asked me how to spell it. As I was telling her this, she said to me, "Isn't it comical that when I hear all this, I don't understand the word at all any more. Only when I have forgotten it does the word come back and live again in me." This being with the word in such a way that one does not treat it like an object that one uses is clearly the basic mode of all linguistic behavior. Language contains a self-protecting and self-concealing power, such that what happens in it is protected from the grasp of one's own reflection and remains hidden in the unconscious. When one comes to recognize both the revealing and the self-concealing nature of language, then one is obliged to go beyond the dimensions of sentence logic and press forward to wider horizons. Within the living unity of language, the language of science is always only a moment that is integrated into a whole, and there are all kinds of other ways that words are used, such as those we find in philosophical, religious, and poetical speaking. In all of them the word is doing something quite different from just self-forgetfully passing through the world. In words we are at home. In words there is a kind of guarantee for what they say. These things are especially clear in the poetic use of language.

Translated by Richard E. Palmer

5

From Word to Concept: The Task of Hermeneutics as Philosophy

When Gadamer was asked to give a major address for Hegel Week at Bamberg University in April 1994 and also receive an honorary doctorate from the university, he waxed eloquent and prophetic about his time and the task of hermeneutics. It was like a swan song. The local newspaper opined that "Gadamer has presented us here with a summa of his thought,"[1] and the address was quickly published by the university in a handsome volume. At a point in his life when his years numbered ninety-four, Gadamer ventured as a major philosopher to take the measure of his age and found it wanting. This age, he found, was dominated by the shallowness of scientific thinking and needed to find a balance between humane wisdom and its technological power. For this purpose, he directed his listeners back to the wisdom of the Greeks, who recognized that the statesman, the philosopher, and even the medical doctor needed not just science but a sense of "right measure" and of what was appropriate to the occasion. For this, mere calculation is not enough today. Noting the environmental problems that are closing in on us, he asserted: "Nature, too, is a reality that one cannot protect solely by means of measuring and calculating."

Looking into the future at the end of his lecture, he anticipated intercultural conversations between members of different religions. "I do not know what answers humanity will finally arrive at one day concerning how people will live together," he said, but it is clear that hermeneutics must play a role in this coming dialogue. Hermeneutics calls attention to "the powers of commonality in the family, in comradeship, in human solidarity." It always looks for a common ground for conversation, for dialogue, for negotiation.

Standing in the shadow of Hegel in the room where he was speaking, Gadamer invoked the legacy of this great dialectical thinker who recognized not just the claims of science but also the legitimate knowledge claims of law, religion, and literature, and who attempted to formulate an encompassing concept that would take in both sides. It is this kind of thinking that is needed today, said Gadamer. Instead, what we have today is a one-dimensional thinking actuated by pragmatism, greed, and the will to power, but what is called for is a path that goes beyond this way of thinking to assert the claims of another way of being in the world, a way of human solidarity and interhuman understanding. Hermeneutics shows us this path. Indeed, it is the fateful task of hermeneutics as philosophy to recall us to this more excellent way.

Gadamer's address, "Vom Wort zum Begriff: Die Aufgabe der Hermeneutik als Philosophie," first appeared in *Menschliche Endlichkeit und Kompensation: Bamberger Hegelwoche 1994,* edited by Odo Marquard (Bamberg: Verlag Frankischer Tag, 1995), 111–24, and is reprinted here with permission of the Universitätsverlag Bamberg. One year later it appeared as one of several essays in a handsome limited-edition volume: *Die Moderne und die Grenze der Vergegenständlichung,* edited by Bernd Klüser, together with contributions by Hans Belting, Gottfried Boehm, and Walther Zimmerli (Munich: Bernd Klüser, 1996), 19–40. And finally in 1997, it was included in the *Gadamer Lesebuch.* The translator wants to thank Lawrence K. Schmidt for his careful review of this translation and Meredith Cargill for many helpful suggestions.

* * *

From Word to Concept: The Task of Hermeneutics as Philosophy

I would first like briefly to justify the theme I have chosen, namely: "from word to concept." This is a subject that belongs to both philosophy and hermeneutics. Indeed, concepts are really one of the distinguishing marks of philosophy, for philosophy first entered Western culture in this form. For this reason the *concept* is the first thing I would like to discuss today. Of one thing I am sure: the concept, which very often presents itself as something strange and demanding, must begin to speak if it is really to be grasped. Therefore, I would first like to revise my topic a little to read: "Not only from word to concept, but likewise from concept to word!"

Let's go back to the beginning for a moment. The point we must start from is the fact that conceptual thinking is a basic characteristic of the Occident. But even the word "Occident" [*Abendland,* land of evening] is no longer as current as it was in my youth, when Oswald Spengler announced its decline.[1] Today we would prefer instead to speak of "Europe," but again nobody really knows what Europe will be; at most we know what we would like it to be one day. For this reason, I believe my topic is not so far from the most pressing questions of today. And I have not simply chosen to speak once again about one of my favorite topics, that is, to express my thanks for this festive occasion. Rather, I speak again because these are questions I am continuously at work on, and I want to confront them here to the best of my ability.

How did it really come about in human history, that in the very dire historical situation in which the Greek city-state culture found itself [i.e., under pressure from the Persian, the Asiatic, and later the Punic African spirit], at exactly this time conceptual thinking, the enduring intellectual creation whose bright rays have streamed out over the globe down to the present day, arose in Greek culture? You all know, of course, what I am referring to. I am speaking about *science*—about that science we all learn in school, Euclidean geometry first and foremost. What wonderful precision it displayed in logically proving things that nobody doubted, yet which nevertheless required the very highest intellectual effort for their proof! This success in proving things represents an intellectually heroic deed, a deed that moved Western thought for the first time beyond all knowledge based on experience [*Erfahrungewissen*] and founded what is now called "science" [*Wissenschaft*].

I can only speak with greatest admiration about this powerful capacity of reason. The numbers and geometry that ground the enormous edifice of mathematics are truly a miracle. I begin with the basic assumption that science had its birth in Greece and it was also from the Greeks that we inherited our thinking and reflection about the possibility of knowledge as such. If these two points are true, I would go on to pose the further question: what does knowing [*Wissen*] truly signify for us?

I think you know the answer. It lies in the form in which Socrates received his reply from the Delphic oracle: *that no human being then living was wiser than he.* His great admirer and student, Plato, has shown us what this wisdom consists of, namely knowing about our not knowing. It is the uncompromising and incorruptible way by which we humans seek, during the short span of life that ends in death, to understand the other person, the unknown, the *ignoramus* and *ignorabimus*—in other words, our not knowing our true place in the world.

If I begin to ponder the matter in this way, then the following question presses itself on me. How has this mathematizing capacity of the Greeks, this logical power, this formation of the most speakable of all languages—as Nietzsche called Greek (but in truth all languages are speakable for those who understand how to think)—how did it manage to gain preeminence throughout the known world? If we pose the question in this way, I think we come a few steps closer to our topic, "word and concept," and thus closer to what comes to mind when I focus my attention on the situation of the world today and on our conception of the world, a conception that must no longer be purely Eurocentric.

There cannot be uncertainty anymore that our science-based civilization, with its unbelievable capacity to alter nature for our own use, life, and survival, has also caused a huge worldwide problem. Indeed, this has become a very important question, a question that is addressed to us, and not just because science itself has taught us what a very short episode in time the history of humanity represents within the evolution of the universe.

Along with the privilege of our present power to transform the world, do we not also face one last great challenge? Along with this tremendous power, have we not also been presented with a task that completely exceeds the powers of our understanding? When one looks beyond what we regard as the "civilized motherland" of our European and Anglo-Saxon cultural traditions and around at the world today—Japan, China, India, South Africa, or South America—one finds that in all these cultures the same mathematized and formalized thinking is gaining the upper hand. How will this happen? How will this go together with what existed before? Will one culture dominate the other? Somehow a global transformation is emerging. I certainly don't want to argue here that the international adoption of the British bathroom betokens a revolution, or that the wearing of the European business suit as standard attire in offices from Japan to China to India is deeply significant; rather, I am saying that at least in certain realms of life a certain cultural standardization is emerging, which, like a revolution, is turning everything upside down.

In all this there is a fact worth considering: whole blocks of humanity that are quite different from each other in terms of cult, religion, and honoring their ancestors—in short, that have different collective ways of living together in conformity with their social rules—these diverse cultures are now being confronted by the resplendent methodological mastery represented by science. Indeed, we can measure our fate by how, either harmonizing or clashing, the fusing of cultures will take place, perhaps even shaping our own future. Or better—our fate will be measured *by how that future is going to be determined by us!* Our fate will be decided by how well the world that bears the stamp of science, and a world that was philosophically expressed through concepts, will be able to bring itself into harmony with the equally deep insights into the destiny of humanity that have come to expression, for example, in the dialogue of a Chinese master with his disciple, or in other kinds of testimony from religiously founded cultures that are completely strange to us.

How have we gotten into this situation? The ancient Greek world was not completely without poetry. For the oldest written evidence of

Greek conceptual thinking comes in the form of Homeric poetry—in testimonies sung in Homeric verse; so it is not philosophy but the epic that stands at the beginning of our written heritage. And we experience the power of poetry when we see in it *how the concept suddenly began to speak*—spreading suddenly from Greek city-state cultures to the whole Mediterranean world—when, embedded in the lines of a verse text, it uttered the question, *ti to on*—"What is being?" And what is it we call nothingness?

I could go on and show how this question actually became Plato's question and led to the establishing of a metaphysics, which, through Aristotle, finally came to be accepted throughout the world and left its imprint on two thousand years of Western thought, until from out of this Greek thought modern science emerged in the seventeenth century, as well as the empirical sciences on the basis of mathematics. But at this moment, perhaps it is appropriate for us to remember that we find ourselves in a room dedicated to Hegel. We have good reason to recall that it was Hegel who saw himself faced with the philosophical task of gathering together the "sciences" and everything else that did not merge with science—such as metaphysics and religion—and to raise these up into the uniting whole of an encompassing concept.

Now the modern empirical sciences, on the one hand, with their mathematical instrumentalization, and, on the other hand, the Socratic thinking that constantly questions things, seeking the Good with an attitude of not knowing—these are two ways of encountering reality that do not seem to go together. Perhaps for a moment we should venture the leap of laying out before ourselves how this great epoch of European culture had reached a certain fulfillment when Hegel sought to make persuasive a reconciliation between the truth of the sciences and that which does not arise in them: the truth of metaphysics as well as of the Christian religion.

Hegel did not bring this about through the mad delusion that science is the unconditional master of certainty cultivated through method. No, one should not forget that as Hegel strove for a great synthesis between "absolute knowledge" in metaphysics and the exact knowledge in the methodical sciences, he always envisioned as present within this synthesis the message of art and of religion. For Hegel, this synthesis was not just a matter of mastering certain areas of knowledge with the help of abstraction and measurement; it involved those forms of knowing or forms of questioning that *do not let go of us*, such as when we stand before works of art or when we are touched by poetic creations. Also, the great works that invite theological reflection, or that fulfill the pious requirement that human beings have of needing to consider their finitude, can reach a very moving intensity.

There was a time when one was well aware that this kind of knowing was quite different from that of mathematics and logic. At that time, for example, one called the study of law "jurisprudence"—that is, a kind of intelligence or wisdom in judging. Law students then were seeking to develop in themselves a capacity to make distinctions so that they could judge what was right in a balanced, differentiated, and "objective" way.

In the meantime, however, the "scientific" ideal has been able to so fully absolutize itself that in the German language one now terms the study of law the *science* of law [*Rechtswissenschaft*] and the academic study of art the *science* of art [*Kunstwissenschaft*]. Earlier, the study of art was called the history of art [*Kunstgeschichte*]. And in Germany, even today, the discipline of studying literature is called the *science* of literature [*Literaturwissenschaft*], although earlier it was called the history of literature. What the earlier term signified was that one assumed from the beginning that one cannot "know" literature in the same sense that one obtains "knowledge" through measurement and mathematics following the model of the natural sciences. A quite different capacity was required for this kind of knowledge.

When I have the honor, as now, of speaking at an institution oriented to the "sciences" of the human spirit [*Geisteswissenschaften,* meaning the humanities and also the social sciences, sometimes translated as the "human sciences"], I am well aware that these "sciences" [*Wissenschaften*] are not sciences in the rigorous mathematical and natural scientific sense. Although the social sciences have certainly applied mathematical methods in their historically developed forms of methodical-critical research, I believe they are nevertheless also guided by and determined by other things: historical models [*Vorbilder*], experience, strokes of fate, and in any case by a different kind of exactness from that in mathematical physics.

In the natural sciences one speaks of the "precision" of mathematizing. But is the precision attained by the application of mathematics to living situations ever as great as the precision attained by the ear of the musician who in tuning his or her instrument finally reaches a point of satisfaction? Are there not quite different forms of precision, forms that do not consist in the application of rules or in the use of an apparatus, but rather in a grasp of what is right that goes far beyond this? I could go into endless examples to make plausible what I mean when I say that hermeneutics is not a doctrine of methods for the humanities and social sciences [*Geisteswissenschaften*] but rather a basic insight into what thinking and knowing mean for human beings in their practical life, even if one makes use of scientific methods.

A distinctive capacity is required in human beings in order for them to make the right use of human knowledge. Plato once posed the question—and not in some context distant from my point: what really constitutes the true statesman? I venture to say that for Plato such a statesman was not just thinking of how to win the next election. Rather, Plato had something essentially different in mind, a quite specific talent: a certain instinctive feeling for balance, an instinct for creating situations of balance and for sensing the many possibilities of how to create and manage situations so as to maintain balance. In his dialogue about the true statesman [the *Statesman*], Plato at one point speaks at some length about this ability. He starts out by presupposing that two different ways of measuring are possible, and both appear to be indispensable. In the first form of measuring one goes after things with a ruler in order to make them available and controllable, like the meter ruler in Paris that all other metric measurements must follow. In this case one is clearly concerned with what the Greeks called *poson,* "quantity."

The second kind of measuring consists of striking the "right measure," of finding what is appropriate. We experience this, for example, in the wonder of harmonious tones sounding together, or in the harmonious feeling of well-being that we call "health." This concerns what the Greeks called *poion,* "quality."

I was able to elucidate this distinction not so long ago in my book *The Enigma of Health,* dealing specifically with illness as the object of medical science. Illness in itself is certainly a threat that one has to be on guard against. When one becomes ill, a doctor with knowledge and skill is needed, and one hopes that the doctor can "bring the illness under control" [*beherrschen*]. Health, on the other hand, is clearly something quite different, something we do not observe or control in the same way. Rather, it is something we follow—like a path, for example. When we are on this path we have the feeling that "now we are headed in the right direction." The path under our feet becomes a way. There are, of course, many other instances in addition to becoming physically healthy that provide a clear contrast to the ideal of scientific governance and control.

We understand the term "scientific rigor" [*Wissenschaftlichkeit*] to mean objectivity, and it is surely a good thing for us to bring under critical control the subjective presuppositions that are in play when one observes anything. Scientific results must in principle be clearly understandable and repeatable by anyone. This is what makes the idea of objective knowledge possible. All of this is fully in order. But one should also not forget what the word "object" in German means. It means "standing-against" [*Gegenstand*], that is, in a certain way *resisting* [*Widerstand*]. In the sphere of illness and health, however, we are dealing with a knowing [*Wissen*] that does not simply rule over and control objects.

For with regard to health, we cannot simply reconstruct the ways of nature. Rather, we must be content to break the resistance of the illness and to help nature prevail using her own secret ways. To do this requires the *art* of the doctor to find the "right measure." This is not just science [*Wissenschaft*] but rather a different kind of knowing that after its own fulfillment withdraws, one might say. Certainly this concept of art as something that basically only helps nature prevail is something different from what "art" is in the creative and formative arts and also the literary arts. But even here one finds something akin to how these arts are carried out, and this marks a kind of boundary between this art and what one associates with the objectivity of science. In medicine as in other arts, one is concerned with much more than the mere application of rules.

In my book *Truth and Method* I began my considerations first of all with art, and not with science or even with the "human sciences." Even within the human sciences it is *art* that brings the basic questions of human being to our awareness in such a unique way—indeed, in such a way that no resistance or objection against it arises. An artwork is like a model [*Vorbild*] for us in this regard.

By this I mean that an artwork is, so to speak, irrefutable [*unwiderleglich*]. For example, one calls poetry irrefutable. Consider what the German word *Gedicht* [poem] means. Here, once again, it helps to know a bit of Latin. *Gedicht* comes from the Latin *dicere* [to say] and also *dictare* [to dictate]. This means a poem is a *Diktat* [something dictated, as in taking dictation, or more strongly, a command]. The poem compels through the way it says what it says. Indeed, this holds for all rhetorical uses of language. But the poem compels over and over, and the better one knows it, the more compelling it is. Nobody would ever object to listening to a recitation by saying that he or she already knew the poem.

In disciplines like art history, literature, and music [*Musikwissenschaft*, the "science" of music], and likewise in the classical studies of philology and archaeology, one who never really opens himself or herself up to a work of art but still claims to be an expert in the field, who always knows it better, is not really an expert but a "philistine." In all the sciences that I understand a bit about, there comes a moment in which something is *there*, something one should not forget and cannot forget. This is not a matter of mastering an area of study. Take, for example, the discipline of art history. In art history the requirements of science, as such, appear to be satisfied in all areas where we can successfully apply historical methods. This is the reason, I think, that iconography has become so popular in the modern science of art [*Kunstwissenschaft*]. But is scientific knowing what art requires? In iconography, whether the object of questioning is a work of art or not does not matter. Hence, for iconography, kitsch is really far more interesting than art.

I am not saying that this is the case with regard to the genuine historian of art, but for understandable reasons the scientized historical method of understanding works of pictorial art continues to gain acceptance in academic circles. This should not, however, be the only permissible approach. I fully believe and hope that here, and everywhere, a balance between both forms of knowledge is attainable, a balance that accepts both the scientific and the artistic sides. In the passage from Plato's *Statesman* that we mentioned earlier, you will recall that Plato, too, expressly states that both kinds of measuring are required—the measuring that measures, and the "right measure," the appropriate [*das Angemessene*], that one tries to find. There are other cases of this kind that I would claim have an equal right to stand alongside the scientific ideal. In science, as I have said, one is generally concerned with a knowing that breaks down resistance, and only in the end does it require art [rather than science], an aptitude for art [*Kunstfertigkeit*] that I illustrated with the example of the physician. This second sort of knowing supports itself, carries within itself a capacity of its own that involves itself [*sich einsetzt*]. This is the reason I have focused on these forms of knowledge, and not just because I have a special preference for the arts. I think it is not permissible that one form should try to be the whole answer: one form of measuring is not more important than the other. Rather, both forms are important.

There is something we can also learn from the German word for measure: we say in German, for instance, "He has a measured or moderate nature [*ein gemessenes Wesen*], a nature that is always appropriate." What is expressed in these words is something like the security of a balance between open-mindedness [*Aufgeschlossenheit*] and peace within oneself. Now, in these observations I do not presume to situate myself within the social sciences. Indeed, I have no competence to talk about the social sciences in the way that, for example, a political scientist can. Nevertheless, I can consider what "politics" is in relation to the miracle of balance. What is this, really? Let me give you an example of this miracle that I myself experienced as a youth, when I learned to ride a bicycle. I had a somewhat lonely youth and received a bicycle to keep me occupied. I had to learn to ride it all by myself. There was a little hill in our backyard, and there I tried to teach myself how to ride it. I climbed up the hill and after a few failed attempts made a great discovery: as long as I held onto the handlebars as tight as I could, I always tipped over! But suddenly I stopped this and it happened as if by itself. Today, I see in this example what the politicians have learned and what their task is: they must above all create a balance if they want to steer toward and reach their goal.

If a politician wants to realize future possibilities at all, he or she must be persuasive, and this is not easy. Here the decisive point is the same as in our example. It is virtually unbelievable that a little less pressure in holding onto the handlebars, even just a wee bit less, enables one to hold the bicycle in balance and to steer it. But if you exert just a little too much pressure, then suddenly nothing goes right. I apply this experience not just to politics, however, but to all our behavior, conditioned as it is by modern forms of life where we are governed by rules, prescriptions, and orders. Yet a proper conformity to such an order is not a matter of blindly and angrily applying rules. What I am talking about here is first of all simply the consequence that follows from a well-regulated conformity to the proper rules of behavior. The reshaping of reality by modern technology now poses new tasks for us all. We must make justice our starting point and central concern, and in particular we must make right use of our knowledge and ability to do things.

Environmental problems force themselves on us here. Nature, too, is a reality that one cannot protect solely by means of measuring and calculating. Rather, it is something with which and in which one must learn to live, so that one may breathe more freely. It is essential, then, that we behave more appropriately. We all feel this in ourselves, I think, when we observe animals in their ways of life. We should hold them in respect in the same way that one holds in respect other human beings with their varied beliefs and ways of life.

These are relevant questions that we are all struggling with today, for now we see what depends on them: movements to settle inequities, to create balance, and for exchange. It is essential, therefore, to recognize all the varied forms of human life and the expressions of their particular worldviews. In doing so, we find ourselves in the realm of hermeneutics. This I call the art of understanding. But what is understanding, really? Understanding, whatever else it may mean, does not entail that one agrees with whatever or whomever one "understands." Such a meeting of the minds in understanding would be utopian. Understanding means that I am able to weigh and consider fairly *what the other person thinks!* It means that one recognizes that the other person could be right in what he or she says or actually wants to say. Understanding, therefore, is not simply mastering something that stands opposite you [*das Gegenüber*], whether it is the other person or the whole objective [*gegenständliche*] world in general. Certainly understanding can be this, so that one understands in order to master or control. Indeed, man's will to rule over nature is natural and it makes our survival possible. Even the story of creation in the Old Testament speaks of this order of the world and of humans reigning over all of nature. And yet it still remains true that ruling and the will to power are not everything.

Indeed, it is important that the extent of this ruling over nature be kept within limits by other powers, especially those of commonality— in the family, in comradeship, in human solidarity—so that one understands and also is understood. Understanding always means first of all: oh, now I understand what you want! In saying this, I have not said that you are right or that you will be judged to be correct. But only when we get to the point that we *understand* another human being, either in a political situation or a text, will we be able to communicate with one another at all. Only when we consider seriously the enormous tasks that await humanity in the future—only then, I think, will we also come to appreciate the world-political significance of *understanding.* You will recall how I pictured the world at the beginning of this lecture. A cadre of highly educated East Asians is attending German and European universities. Very often they astonish us with the tremendous discipline with which they work, and the rapidity with which they are able to produce perfectly written texts, even though oral expression is sometimes almost impossible. It is just unbelievable that many of these people speak almost unintelligibly but are able to write error-free texts! These are differences in communicative behavior that we must become aware of in their broad significance if we are to encounter other cultures. All this goes both ways, of course. The Japanese student coming here probably also finds at first that we do not speak intelligibly but only squawk and sputter.

This will be a task of the future world, of that I am sure. Just as we must realize that people speaking other languages do not just babble but are really speaking, so too they, for their part, will need at least to become familiar with our world if they want to speak and understand German and not just hear it as some kind of squawking and sputtering.

This venturesome elite of East Asian scholars is already doing a lot in this regard, and it should be self-evident to us that their efforts do not entail giving up their own inherited ways of life and their own basic religious ideas.

Of course, we do not know anything about what the great conversations of the future between members of different religions may hold in store. And while our young people today in their own stressful years of development find a guru from India fascinating, it is still essential that they should learn to understand the other ways of life as wholes, that they understand all that comprises the basis of these cultures: the view of the family, of ancestors, death, and the living on of ancestors within us, and also in these cultures such a decisive concept as their evaluation of human life. In part, all of these are controlled by forms of lawfulness quite different from those that have become natural to us through our long history of Christian education and culture. And when we define philosophy as hermeneutics, we cannot be satisfied just to re-peat the same thing as existed before, as if what hermeneutics basically wanted were simply to put forward a conservative view of the world that merely extended Christian values. Perhaps, but only perhaps, this might suffice as a European standard for arriving at an agreement on what understanding is. But such a standard is far too narrow.

I do not know what answers humanity will one day finally arrive at concerning how people will live together, either in relation to the rights of the individual versus the rights of the collective, or in relation to the violence that comes from the family or from the state. Just consider the almost unbelievable miracle that the Communist revolution in China, which surely has not dealt gently with the elders, was, even with almost unlimited power, still unable to destroy the family order. So, everywhere in the world, clearly there are individualities and customs of irreconcil-able otherness. I do venture to say, however, that if we do not acquire hermeneutic virtue—that is, if we do not realize that it is essential first of all to *understand* the other person if we are ever to see whether in the end perhaps something like the solidarity of humanity as a whole may be possible, especially in relation to our living together and surviving together—if we do not do this, then we will never be able to accomplish the essential tasks of humanity, whether on a small scale or large.

It is obvious that humankind today is in a desperate situation. For we have finally reached the point where human beings threaten to de-stroy themselves, and everyone should become aware of this. Doesn't this pose a genuine task of thinking for everyone today? To be very clear: human solidarity must be the basic presupposition under which we can work together to develop, even if only slowly, a set of common convictions [*gemeinsame Überzeugungen*]. It seems to me that while Euro-pean civilization has admirably brought to a high level of development the culture of science with its technical and organizational applications; at the same time, it has for the past three centuries neglected the law of balance.

It has come into possession of deadly weapons of mass destruction, but has it developed a level of maturity high enough to realize what responsibility our culture now bears for humanity as a whole? Is it not the case that in all such questions we are faced with tasks that require a consciousness possessed of farsightedness and carefulness [*Weitsicht und Vorsicht*], and also an openness to each other, if we are to carry out the tasks that will shape our future, tasks whose accomplishment is necessary for peace and reconciliation?

I am of the opinion that with all our technical and scientific progress, we [Europeans] still have not learned well enough how to live with each other and with our own progress. I would like to close with the following remark. What I have tried to make clear to you today is this: that hermeneutics as philosophy is not some kind of methodological dispute with other sciences, epistemologies, or such things. No, hermeneutics asserts something nobody today can deny: that we occupy a moment in history in which we must strenuously use the full powers of our *reason*, and not just keep doing science only.

Without bringing concepts to speak and without a common language, I believe we will not be able to find the words that can reach other persons. It is true that we usually move "from word to concept," but we must also be able to move "from concept to word" if we wish to reach the other person. Only if we accomplish both will we gain a rational understanding of each other. Only in this way, too, will we be able to hold ourselves back, so that we can allow the other person's views to be recognized. We have the ability to become so absorbed in something that we totally forget ourselves in it; this is one of the great blessings of the experience of art, as well as one of the great promises of religion. Indeed, this is ultimately one of the basic conditions that will allow us human beings to live together in a human way.

Translated by Richard E. Palmer

Part 2

Hermeneutics, Art, and Poetry

6

Aesthetics and Hermeneutics

Gadamer originally presented "Aesthetics and Hermeneutics" in 1964 as a lecture at the Fifth International Conference on Aesthetics, in Amsterdam, and in December of that year it appeared in a Dutch journal. It has now been translated into seven languages, including Japanese, Polish, Russian, and Chinese. In his collected works in German, it appears as the first essay in volume 8, a volume dedicated to aesthetics and poetics. Its first appearance in English was in 1976, in *Philosophical Hermeneutics,* the first general collection of Gadamer's essays in English.

Gadamer's first step in the essay is to emphasize that the "hermeneutical perspective is so comprehensive" that it includes art and nature, and especially the experience of the artwork (96).[1] In fact, he states that the area of aesthetics he is interested in is "the question of the experience of art" (97). He recognizes that hermeneutics is usually taken to involve the interpretation of historical and literary documents, but he finds that the encounter experience with art is part of the interpretive world and self-understanding of the person having the experience. He makes distinctions between historical documents and artworks which involve no words. The latter are experienced and interpreted, and both possess a kind of meaning; indeed, one can speak of the "language of art." Gadamer notes that in contrast to historical documents, artworks possess a contemporaneity that allows them to speak to us across the centuries with a special immediacy. Elements in Gadamer's hermeneutical philosophy like the anticipation of meaning apply to the encounter with artworks, as well as to texts in words. "A kind of anticipation of meaning guides the effort to understand from the very beginning," and indeed this holds "in an eminent way" for the experience of art (101). Just as an encounter with a biblical or literary text involves self-understanding, as theologians have noted, so also does an encounter with art, such that a meaningful encounter with an artwork brings increased self-understanding. Hermeneutics, then, offers itself as a way of comprehending more adequately the experience of encountering an artwork, an experience which shocks our expectations and even our self-understanding.

In closing, Gadamer invites his listeners to accept "the universality of the hermeneutical perspective" (103). Hermeneutics is the process of understanding, and all understanding, whether of nature, art, or words, takes place in the interpretive horizon of the historical person who has anticipations of meaning. In the case of artworks and documents in words, the meaningful encounter clearly takes place in language, a language that the work speaks as well as the many forms of documents do. But in certain kinds of documents and artworks, the encounter is a "joyous and frightening shock," as when a poem addresses the reader and says, "You must change your life!" Gadamer here is referring to the closing line of the famous Rilke poem, "On the Archaic Torso of Apollo" (in this case, about a work of art). Gadamer is pulling aesthetics out of the traditional realm of disinterested objectivity and into the realm of hermeneutical encounter.

* * *

Aesthetics and Hermeneutics

If we define the task of hermeneutics as the bridging of personal or historical distance between minds, then the experience of art would seem to fall entirely outside its province. For of all the things that confront us in nature and history, it is the work of art that speaks to us most directly. It possesses a mysterious intimacy that grips our entire being, as if there were no distance at all between us and the work and every encounter with it were an encounter with ourselves. We can refer to Hegel in this connection. He considered art to be one of the forms of Absolute Spirit; that is, he saw in art a form of Spirit's self-knowledge in which nothing alien and unredeemable appeared, a form in which there was no contingency of the actual, no unintelligibility of what is merely given. In fact, an absolute contemporaneousness exists between the work and its present beholder that persists unhampered despite every intensification of the historical consciousness. The reality of the work of art and its expressive power cannot be restricted to its original historical horizon, in which its beholder actually seems to become the contemporary of the creator. It seems instead to belong to the experience of art that the work of art always has its own present. Only in a limited way does it retain its historical origin within itself. The work of art is the expression of a truth that cannot be reduced to what its creator actually thought in it. Whether we call it the unconscious creation of the genius or we consider the conceptual inexhaustibility of every artistic expression from the point of view of the beholder, the aesthetic consciousness can appeal to the fact that the work of art communicates itself.

The hermeneutical perspective is so comprehensive, however, that it must even include the experience of beauty in nature and art. If it is the fundamental constitution of the historicity of human Dasein to mediate itself to itself understandingly—which necessarily means to the whole of its own experience of the world—then all tradition belongs to it. Tradition encompasses institutions and life-forms as well as texts. Above all, however, the encounter with art belongs within the process of integration that is involved in all human life that stands within traditions. Indeed, it is even a question as to whether the peculiar contemporaneousness of the work of art does not consist precisely in its being open in a limitless way to ever new integrations. The creator of a work of art may have in mind the public of his own time, but the real being of his work is what it is able to say, and this being reaches fundamentally beyond any historical confinement. In this sense, the work of art occupies a timeless present. But this statement does not mean that it involves no task of understanding, or that we do not find its historical heritage within it. The claim of historical hermeneutics is legitimated precisely by the fact that while the work of art does not intend to be understood historically and offers itself instead in an absolute presence, it nevertheless does not permit just any forms of comprehension. In all the openness and all the richness of its possibilities for comprehension, it permits—indeed even requires—the application of a standard of appropriateness. It may remain undecided whether the claim to appropriateness of comprehension raised at any particular time is correct. Kant was right in asserting that universal validity is required of the judgment of taste, though its recognition cannot be compelled by reasons. This holds true for every interpretation of works of art as well. It holds true for the active interpretation of the reproductive performer or the reader, as well as for that of the scientific interpreter.

One can ask skeptically if a concept of the work of art that regards it as being open to ever newer comprehension does not already belong to a secondary world of aesthetic cultivation. In its origins, is not a work of art the bearer of a meaningful life-function within a cultic or social context? And is it not within this context alone that it receives its full determination of meaning? It seems to me that this question can also be reversed: Is it really the case that a work of art, which comes out of a past or alien lifeworld and is transferred into our historically educated world, becomes a mere object of aesthetic-historical enjoyment and says nothing more of what it originally had to say? "To say something," "to have something to say"—are these simply metaphors grounded in an undetermined aesthetic formative value that is the real truth? Or is the reverse the case? Is the aesthetic quality of formation only the condition for the fact that the work bears its meaning within itself and has something to say to us? This question gives us access to the real problematic dimension of the theme "aesthetics and hermeneutics."

The inquiry developed here deliberately transforms the systematic problem of *aesthetics* into the question of the experience of *art*. In its actual genesis and also in the foundation Kant provided for it in his *Critique of Aesthetic Judgment*, it is certainly true that philosophical aesthetics covered a much broader area, since it included the beautiful in nature and art, indeed, even the sublime. It is also incontestable that in Kant's philosophy, natural beauty had a methodical priority for the basic determinations of the judgment of aesthetic taste, and especially for his concept of "disinterested pleasure." However, one must admit that natural beauty does not "say" anything in the sense that works of art, created by and for human beings, say something to us. One can rightly assert that a work of art does not satisfy in a "purely aesthetic" way, in the same sense as a flower or perhaps an ornament does. With respect to art, Kant speaks of an "intellectualized" pleasure. But this formulation does not help. The "impure," intellectualized pleasure that the work of art evokes is still what really interests us as aestheticians. Indeed, the sharper reflection that Hegel brought to the question of the relation of natural and artistic beauty led him to the valid conclusion that natural beauty is a reflection of the beauty of art. When something natural is regarded and enjoyed as beautiful, it is not a timeless and wordless givenness of the "purely aesthetic" object that has its exhibitive ground in the harmony of forms and colors and symmetry of design, as it might seem to a Pythagorizing, mathematical mind. How nature pleases us belongs instead to the context that is stamped and determined by the artistic creativity of a particular time. The aesthetic history of a landscape—for instance, the Alpine landscape—or the transitional phenomenon of garden art are irrefutable evidence of this. We are justified, therefore, in proceeding from the work of art rather than from natural beauty if we want to define the relation between aesthetics and hermeneutics. In any case, when we say that the work of art says something to us and that it thus belongs to the matrix of things we have to understand, our assertion is not a metaphor, but has a valid and demonstrable meaning. Thus the work of art is an object of hermeneutics.

According to its original definition, hermeneutics is the art of clarifying and mediating by our own effort of interpretation what is said by persons we encounter in tradition. Hermeneutics operates especially wherever what is said is not immediately intelligible. Yet this philological art and pedantic technique has long since assumed an altered and broadened form. Since the time of this original definition, the growing historical consciousness has made us aware of the misunderstanding and even the possible unintelligibility of all tradition. Also, the decay of Christian society in the West—in continuation of a process of individualization that began with the Reformation—has allowed the individual to become an ultimately indissoluble mystery to others. Since the time of the German Romantics, therefore, the task of hermeneutics has been defined as avoiding misunderstanding. With this definition, hermeneutics acquires a domain that in principle reaches as far as the expression of meaning as such. Expressions of meaning first of all take the form of linguistic manifestations. As the art of conveying what is said in a foreign language to the understanding of another person, hermeneutics is not without reason named after Hermes, the interpreter of the divine message to mankind. If we recall the origin of the term "hermeneutics," it becomes clear that we are dealing here with a language event, with a translation from one language to another, and therefore with the relation of two languages. But insofar as we can only translate from one language to another if we have understood the meaning of what is said and construct it anew in the medium of the other language, such a language event presupposes understanding.

These obvious conclusions become decisive for the question that concerns us here—the question of the language of art and the legitimacy of the hermeneutical point of view with respect to the experience of art. Every interpretation of the intelligible that helps others to understanding has the character of language. To that extent, the entire experience of the world is linguistically mediated, and the broadest concept of tradition is thus defined—one that includes what is not itself linguistic but is capable of linguistic interpretation. It extends from the "use" of tools, techniques, and so on through traditions of craftsmanship in the making of such things as various types of implements and ornamental forms, and through the cultivation of practices and customs to the establishing of patterns and so on. Does the work of art belong in this category, or does it occupy a special position? Insofar as it is not directly a question of *linguistic* works of art, the work of art does in fact seem to belong to such a nonlinguistic tradition. And yet the experience and understanding of a work of art is different from the understanding of the tool or the practices handed on to us from the past.

If we follow an old definition from Droysen's hermeneutics, we can distinguish between sources [*Quellen*] and vestiges [*Überrresten*]. Vestiges are fragments of a past world that have survived and assist us in the intellectual reconstruction of the world of which they are a remnant. Sources, on the other hand, constitute a linguistic tradition, and they thus serve our understanding of a linguistically interpreted world. Now where does an archaic image of a god belong, for instance? Is it a vestige, like any tool? Or is it a piece of world-interpretation, like everything that is handed on linguistically?

Sources, says Droysen, are records handed down for the purpose of recollection. Monuments are a hybrid form of sources and vestiges, and to this category he assigns "works of art of every kind," along with documents, coins, and so on. It may seem this way to the historian, but the work of art as such is a historical document neither in its intention nor in the meaning it acquires in one's experience of it as a work of art. To be sure, we talk of artistic monuments, as if the production of a work of art had a documentary intention. There is a certain truth in the assertion that permanence is essential to every work of art—in the transitory arts, of course, only in the form of their repeatability. The successful work "stands." (Even the music hall artist can say this of his act.) But the explicit aim at recollection through the presentation of something, as it is found in the genuine document, is not present in the work of art. We do not want to refer to anything that once was by means of a presentation. Just as little could this be a guarantee of the work of art's permanence, since it ultimately depends for its preservation on the approval of the taste or sense of quality of later generations. Precisely this dependence on a preserving will means that the work of art is handed down to us in the same sense as our literary sources are. At any rate, the work "speaks" not only as remnants of the past speak to the historical investigator or as do historical documents that render something permanent. What we are calling the language of the work of art, for the sake of which the work is preserved and handed on, is the language the work of art itself speaks, whether it is linguistic or not. The work of art says something to the historian; it says something to each person as if it were said especially to him, as something present and contemporaneous. Thus our task is to understand the meaning of what the work says and to make it clear to ourselves and others. Even the non-linguistic work of art, therefore, falls within the province of the proper task of hermeneutics. It must be integrated into the self-understanding of each person.[1]

In this comprehensive sense, hermeneutics includes aesthetics. Hermeneutics bridges the distance between minds and reveals the foreignness of the other mind. But revealing what is unfamiliar does not mean merely reconstructing historically the "world" in which the work had its original meaning and function. It also means apprehending what is said to us, which is always more than the declared and comprehended meaning. Whatever says something to us is like a person who says something. It is alien in the sense that it transcends us. To this extent, there is a double foreignness in the task of understanding, which in reality is one and the same foreignness. It is this way with all speech. Not only does it say something, but *someone* says something to someone else. Understanding speech is not just understanding the wording of what is said in the step-by-step execution of word meanings. Rather, it occurs in the unitary meaning of what is said—and this always transcends what is expressed by what is said. It may be difficult to understand what is said in a foreign or ancient language, but it is still more difficult to let something be said to us even if we understand what is said right away. Both of these things are the task of hermeneutics. We cannot understand without wanting to understand, that is, without wanting to let something be said. It would be an inadmissible abstraction to contend that we must first achieve a contemporaneousness with the author or the original reader by means of a reconstruction of his historical horizon before we could begin to grasp the meaning of what is said. No, a kind of anticipation of meaning guides the effort to understand from the very beginning.

But what holds in this fashion for all speaking is valid in a special way for the experience of art. It is more than an anticipation of meaning. It is what I would like to call being struck by the meaning of what is said. The experience of art does not only understand a recognizable meaning, as historical hermeneutics does in its handling of texts. The work of art that says something confronts us with ourselves. That is, it expresses something in such a way that what is said is like a discovery, a disclosure of something previously concealed. The element of being struck is based on this. "So true, so filled with being" [So wahr, so seiend] is not something one knows in any other way. Everything familiar is eclipsed. To understand what the work of art says to us is therefore a self-encounter. But as an encounter with the authentic, as a familiarity that includes surprise, the experience of art is *experience* in a real sense and must master ever anew the task that experience involves: the task of integrating it into the whole of one's own orientation to the world and one's own self-understanding. The language of art is constituted precisely by the fact that it speaks to the self-understanding of *every* person, and it does this as something ever present and by means of its own contemporaneousness. Indeed, precisely the contemporaneousness of the work allows it to come to expression in language. Everything depends on how something is said. But this does not mean we should reflect on the means of saying it. Quite the contrary: the more convincingly something is said, the more self-evident and natural the uniqueness and singularity of its declaration seems to be; that is, it concentrates the attention of the person being addressed entirely upon what is said and prevents him or her from moving to a distanced attitude of aesthetic differentiation. Over against the real intention, which aims at what is meant, reflection upon the means of the declaration is indeed always secondary and in general is excluded where people speak to each other face to face. For what is said is not something that presents itself as a kind of content of judgment, in the logical form of a judgment. Rather, it is what we want to say and what we will allow to be said to us. Understanding does not occur when we try to intercept what someone wants to say to us by claiming we already know it.

All these observations hold especially for the language of art. Naturally it is not the artist who is speaking here. The artist's own comments about what is said in one or another of his works may certainly be of possible interest, but the language of art means an excess of meaning that is present in the work itself. The inexhaustibility that distinguishes the language art speaks from all translation into concepts rests on this excess of meaning. It follows that in understanding a work of art, we cannot be satisfied with the cherished hermeneutical rule that the *mens auctoris* [author's intention] limits the task of understanding posed by a text. Rather, just the expansion of the hermeneutical perspective to include the language of art makes it obvious how little the subjectivity of the act of meaning suffices to be the object of understanding. But this fact has a general significance, and to that extent aesthetics is an important element of general hermeneutics. That should be conclusively indicated. Everything that in the broadest sense speaks to us as tradition poses the task of understanding, without understanding being taken to mean the new actualization in oneself of another person's thoughts. We learn this fact with convincing clarity not only from the experience of art (as explained above), but also from the understanding of history. For the real task of historical study is not to understand the subjective intentions, plans, and experiences of the men who are involved in history. Rather, what must be understood is the great matrix of the meaning of history, and this requires the interpretive effort of the historian. The subjective intentions of men standing within the historical process are seldom or never such that a later historical evaluation of events confirms their assessment by contemporaries. The significance of the events, their connections and their involvements as they are represented in historical retrospect, leave the *mens auctoris* behind them, just as the experience of the work of art leaves the *mens auctoris* behind it.

The universality of the hermeneutical standpoint is all-encompassing. I once formulated this idea by saying: "*Being that can be understood is language.*"[2] This is certainly not a metaphysical assertion. Instead it describes, from the medium of understanding, the unrestricted scope possessed by the hermeneutical standpoint. It would be easy to show that all historical experience satisfies this proposition, as does the experience of nature. In the last analysis, Goethe's statement "Everything is a symbol" is the most comprehensive formulation of the hermeneutical idea. It means that everything points to some other thing. This "every-thing" is not an assertion about each being, indicating what it is, but an assertion as to how it is to encounter man's understanding. There is nothing that cannot mean something to it. But the statement implies something else as well: nothing comes forth just in the one meaning that is offered to us. The impossibility of surveying all relations is just as much present in Goethe's concept of the symbolic as is the vicarious function of the particular for the representation of the whole. For only because the universal relatedness of being is concealed from human eyes does it need to be discovered. As universal as the hermeneutical idea is that corresponds to Goethe's words, in an eminent sense it is fulfilled only by the experience of art. For the distinctive mark of the language of art is that the individual artwork gathers into itself and ex-presses the symbolic character that, hermeneutically regarded, belongs to all things. In comparison with all other linguistic and nonlinguistic traditions, the work of art is the absolute present for each particular present, and at the same time it holds its word in readiness for every fu-ture. The intimacy with which the work of art touches us is at the same time, in enigmatic fashion, a shattering and demolishing of the familiar. It is not only the impact of a "This means you!" ["Das bist du!"] that is disclosed in a joyous and frightening shock; it also says to us: "You must change your life!"

Translated by David E. Linge

7

On the Truth of the Word

The truth of the word in poetry is a central theme in Gadamer's philosophical hermeneutics. For instance, when he gathered his essays together for his collected works, he found that he had given two essays this title! One essay, translated here for the first time, was given in a series of lectures in 1971 but remained unpublished until it was included in the collected works in 1993.[1] The other was given at the annual meeting of the Heidegger Society in 1988 and published under that title in the society's yearbook.[2] In order to include both essays in his collected works without confusion, Gadamer retitled the Heidegger Society essay "Thinking and Poetizing in Heidegger and in Hölderlin's 'Andenken'" in his collected writings.[3] The fact that Gadamer chose the earlier and longer essay under its original title for inclusion in the *Gadamer Lesebuch* also indicates the importance he attached to it.

Admirers of Heidegger's "Origin of the Work of Art" will also like Gadamer's essay on the truth of the word, for it offers an interpretation and commentary on Heidegger's view of truth by another expert in Greek philosophy and a leading student of Heidegger's thought. Gadamer extends, broadens, and supplements the insights of Heidegger to include the question of the truth of the word in poetry, sacred and legal texts, and even philosophy. Gadamer's definition of truth as *aletheia* is, of course, taken from Heidegger, and it is in this Heideggerian sense that the word "truth" is used. As a scholar of Greek literature and philosophy, Gadamer cites Homer and other works that corroborate Heidegger's interpretation. But instead of art, as in Heidegger, it is the word that can be true, and the essay goes into detail on the rich meaning of the word. Gadamer even brings in the ontological dimension of truth as revealing being in an event of disclosure, via the word. At the close of his essay, he sounds a theme that he will elaborate later in other works, namely, the "eminent text": poetry is text in the eminent sense because it uses words in their highest possible valence as words.

As we know, the origin of this text, according to Gadamer, is a series of lectures he presented in Toronto in 1971 but did not publish. Why not? The reason is simple: he lost the manuscript and only discovered it as he was preparing the edition of his collected works. He revised and expanded the essay for inclusion in volume 8, *Ästhetik und Poetik I:*

Kunst als Aussage (1993), which is our basis text, and this enhances its value as a late articulation of his views. I wish to thank most sincerely Jeff Mitscherling for his extensive editorial corrections and suggestions for this translation.

* * *

On the Truth of the Word

I

One hears today such expressions as "deception by language" and the "suspicion of ideology" and even "suspicion of metaphysics," so when I now propose to speak about "the truth of the word" it amounts to a provocation![1] This is especially the case if one speaks of "the" Word. For when something appears certain beyond all discussion, then to speak about truth can have to do only with what Aristotle [in *On Interpretation*] called "the combined" (*en synthesei aei*), that is, with the *sentence*.[2] And if one takes perception—as the Greeks did—to be made up of specific sense qualities, and then takes the "true"—*alethes*—as merely the "what-content" of what is intended, then it becomes pointless to speak of the truth of the word, since it is only the intended content of speaking. Of course, there would no longer be a word at all, if a word simply as a word could be false. A discourse, which is made up of words, can only be false or true when the opinion expressed by the words can be questionable with regard to what it says.

Nevertheless, "the" word is not just the individual word. Nor is it just the singular of "the words," or of the group of words that constitute the discourse. Rather, this expression is linked to a usage according to which "the word" has a collective meaning and implies a social relationship. The word that is said to you or that someone gives you, or when someone makes a promise and you say, "I have your word?" does not mean just one word; even if it is only the one word "yes," it says more and infinitely more than just giving an opinion. When Luther uses "the Word" in the prologue to the Gospel of John to translate "logos," behind this stands a whole theology of the word which stretches back at least to Augustine's explication of the Trinity. For the ordinary reader, too, it is a redeemable word, that Jesus Christ is for the believer the living promise that became flesh. So when we inquire into the truth of the word in what follows, it is not that of a particular word—not even that of the promise of salvation—whose content is meant, but one must nevertheless keep in mind that the Word "dwells among men" and that in all its forms of manifestation, in forms where it completely is what it is, it has a constant and reliable being. In the end, it is always the word that "stands," whether one keeps his word or stands by it, as the one who said it, or as the one who has taken another at his word. The word itself *stands.* In spite of its being spoken only once, the word is perduringly there: as the saving message, as blessing or curse, as prayer—or also as commandment [*Gebot,* as in the Ten Commandments] and law and proclaimed judgment, as saga written by a poet and as basic principle held by the philosopher. It seems more than a superficial fact that one can say of such a word, "it stands written" and it documents itself. It is with regard to these ways of being of a word [*des Wortseins*], of words which in accordance with their inherent validity "do things" rather than merely communicating something true, that the following question poses itself: what can it mean that these ways of being a word are true so they are true as words? In this connection I refer to J. L. Austin's well-known formulation of the question in order to clarify the ontological status of the poetic word.

In order to see the significance of this question, we must come to an understanding of what "truth" [*Wahrheit*] can mean. It is clear that the traditional concept of truth as *adequatio rei et intellectus* [agreement of thing and intellect] has no function where the word is not meant as a statement about something at all but rather, as something existing in itself, lifts and grants itself a claim to being [*Seinsanspruch*]. On the other hand, the extraordinary uniqueness, the singularity, which belongs to "the word" also contains an essential logical inadequacy within itself, in that the word points beyond itself to an inner infinity of answering words [of *Ant-worten*] which are all—and therefore none—"suitable" [*angemessen,* appropriate, adequate].[3] Here one thinks of the Greek word *aletheia,* whose seminal meaning Heidegger has taught us to see. What I am referring to is not the privative meaning of *a-letheia* as "un-concealment" [*Unverborgenheit*] or as "dis-closure" [*Entbergung*]. To point this out, as such, would not be such a new assertion, for it has long been known that in connection with verbs of saying [*mit Verben des Sagens*], *aletheia* has the sense of "unconcealment" (for example, in Humboldt): and Zeus says to Hera, "μή με λάθῃς"—"Don't go behind my back!"—and here the rich fantasy and enormous eloquence of the Greeks already in Homer had caused the characterization of *aletheia* as non-concealment to be singled out and noticed. What makes Heidegger's renewal of insight into the privative sense of the word significant is the fact that this Greek term is not limited to the sphere of discourse, but was also used where it meant "genuine" [*echt*] in the sense of "unadulterated" [*unverfälscht*]. Thus, one also says in Greek: a true friend, that is, true like genuine gold that does not give the false appearance of being gold. In such contexts *Entbergung* takes on an *ontological* meaning; that is, it characterizes not the behavior or the self-expression [*Sich-Äussern*] of someone or something but rather its *being* (for *aletheia* can also mean having sincerity or uprightness [*Aufrichtigkeit*] as a feature of one's personality). Is it not astonishing that one cannot only characterize a being [*Wesen*] that is capable of speaking, play-acting, and even lying by the word *aletheia*, but also some existent thing as such [*auch Seiendes als solches*]—like gold? What can it be that is hiding there or is obscured there, such that the non-concealing—and not through our doing—can be attributed to existing things [*Seienden*]? How must being "be" [*Wie muss Sein "sein"*] when the existent thing [*das Seiende*] "is" such that it can be false?

The answer will have to take its start from the well-grounded experience that what comes forth is something that is in it. [*Es kommt heraus, was an ihm ist.*] It is not accidental, therefore, that Heidegger paid special attention to the Aristotelian idea of *physis*, which described the ontological status of what arises from out of itself [*emporwächst*]. But what does it mean that being itself [*das Sein selbst*] is such that the existing being [*das Seiende*] must come forth as that which it is? And that it can even be "false," like false gold? What kind of *hiding* is it that belongs just as much to the existing being as to the *disclosure* through which it steps into presence? The unconcealment that comes to the existing being and in which the existing being emerges seems indeed in itself to be an absolute "there" like the light in Aristotle's description of the *nous poietikos* [mind of the creator as pure light] and like the *Lichtung* [a lighted space, a clearing like a meadow in a forest] that is formed in being and comes forth as being [*die sich im Sein und als Sein auftut*].

So long as Heidegger was still trying to pose the question of being on the basis of an existential analytic of Dasein, it was hard to avoid the conclusion that the authentic Dasein is its "there" and is "there" for the other. Heidegger was determined to contrast his analysis of the historical situation of Dasein and its structure as a "thrown project," with the idealism of transcendental subjectivity and its illusory representations. The care-structure of Dasein as well as its structure as a "thrown project" was to be fundamentally distinguished from idealism's guiding concepts of a "consciousness in general" or an "absolute knowledge." Nor should we fail to note that *both* authenticity and inauthenticity belong, and belong "equiprimordially," to the structural whole of Dasein, and therefore mere small talk [*Gerede*, prattle] belongs to Dasein just as much as does the word and remaining silent [*das Wort und das Schweigen*]. A sense of what the early Heidegger means by authenticity [*Eigentlichkeit*] or genuineness [*Echtheit*] merges with what he had called *angstbereite Entschlossenheit*—"resoluteness prepared to face anxiety." It is not only silence but the breaking of silence, the word. And indeed already in *Being and Time* he had taken up the challenge that the Greek concept of the logos had represented for the "Christian theologian." (By the way, this is a term Heidegger used in reference to himself when he was a *Privatdozent* [unsalaried lecturer] in philosophy pursuing his lifework.) Language, too, even as early as this, was thought of as an *Existential;* that is, as a determining factor [*Bestimmung*] of a Dasein singled out by its understanding of Being. But just as the essence of truth in the preservation of Dasein and its insistence on the "secret" and its absolute hiddenness were always related to Dasein's other, so also the word and language possess an existential relationship [*existentiellen Bezug*] to hearing and keeping silent. But what was "true" there and what "came forth" there was precisely one's *Existenz,* namely a Dasein with its being [*Sein*] standing before nothingness [*Nichts*]. Certainly here the word [*das Wort*] was also not merely the making of a statement as found in the Aristotelian *apophansis* [something said about something], which as something said just vanishes into what it says and points to (ἐν τω δηλύν); rather, the word in Heidegger had the temporal character of uniqueness and of an event [*Ereignis*]. But what was *Ereignis* here? And what "took place" [*ereignete sich*] there? Already at that early date Heidegger had seen clearly how the "word" [*das "Wort"*], owing to an inner necessity, had suffered a decline into "idle talk" [*Gerede*], and that it was the fate of thought to be capable of authenticity [*Eigentlichkeit*] and decline [*Verfallen*], of being and appearing. Nevertheless, the word as word is not only disclosure but must, just as much and precisely for that reason, be hiding and sheltering. This was something that could not be grasped by means of his transcendental analytic of Dasein. Even in the famous confrontation at Davos with the author of *The Philosophy of Symbolic Forms,*[4] Heidegger still defended the self-understanding of Dasein over against the between-world of forms [rather than the self-disclosing of being].

However, if disclosure and concealment are really conceived as [two] structural moments of "being" [*Sein*], and if temporality belongs to being and not just to the existing being that holds open the space for being, then "to be there" [*da zu sein*] certainly remains the distinguishing mark of man; and likewise, man is not just himself at home in language, but rather "being" [*Sein*] is there in the language that we speak with each other. All this is not just due to an existential decision that a person could also leave behind, but rather because the being-there of Dasein is resoluteness, a standing open [*Offenständigkeit*] to the "there." This does not entail that one should think only starting from this resoluteness, in the sense that the authentic word would be defined as the word belonging to *authenticity* [*das Wort der Eigentlichkeit*] and not the word of idle talk. Rather, what is authentically *word*—the word as true word [*wahres Wort*, like *wahres Geld*]—is determined from the direction of Being as *the word in which truth happens.* So one can link this point up to a later insight of Heidegger and pose the question of the truth of the word. Perhaps posing this question will allow us to move closer to Heidegger's insight in a concrete way and to understand such puzzling figures of speech as the "clearing of Being."

II

What is the "authentic" word?[5] This does not mean, for example, the word in which something true, or even the highest truth, is said, but rather what the "word" is in its most authentic sense. To be a word [in this sense] means to be a word that speaks, a *telling* [*sagend,* saying] word. [*Wort sein heisst sagend sein.*] To be able to sort out from among the innumerable kinds of words those that are most telling, let us think a bit about the distinguishing characteristics that make a word truly "a word": that *it stands* and that one *stands by it.* Obviously this already contains the idea that the word, along with what it says or does in saying, makes a lasting claim to be valid. Here I can refer already to the mystery of writtenness, which substantiates this claim. On the basis of this, it is not quite as arbitrary or absurd as it might sound if I specify that a word which truly speaks will be a "text." Of course, this term has only a methodical sense here, but I mean to dispute the genuineness, primordiality, meaning power, or decision-announcing power [*Entscheidungsgewalt*] that resides in living speech, or in prayer, in preaching, in blessing and curse, or in political speaking. By doing this, we will be allowed to isolate what it is that causes a word to truly be a word. The fact that texts regain their character as a word [*ihren Wortcharakter*] only in the living process of their being understood, delivered as lecture, or proclaimed, in no way changes the fact that it is the content of the text and nothing else that springs to life, that it is the potential word that *says something.* So, asking *how* the word is there when it is "text" will render visible its saying; that is, what its being is comprised of as saying [*sein Sagendsein ausmacht*].

I call the word's being-as-saying, which we have now isolated, a declaration, a statement [*Aussage*]. For in fact the declaration or statement, with all the problems of its use and misuse—for instance in trial procedure—is by its nature something definable. Even though such a legal declaration is not unretractable, it is accepted as valid until further notice unless it is retracted. Its validity includes that what is said holds true in itself and only for what is said, so any dispute about the unambiguous content of a statement and whether a reference to it is justified, indirectly corroborates its claim to a single meaning. It is undisputably clear, of course, that a witness's declaration before the court actually only has truth value in the context of the investigation. Precisely for this reason, the word *Aussage* [assertion] has come to be widely accepted in the hermeneutical context, for example, in theological exegesis or in literary aesthetics. Why? Because treating the text as *Aussage* makes it possible to deal purely with what is said there as such without recourse to the occasionality of the author, and to have nothing but the explication of the text itself as a whole to make its meaning clear. What is seriously missing, however, is the fact that through such a concentration on the text, which as a whole constitutes the assertion, the event-character of the word has been weakened. Yet it is only through the event that the text comes forth in its full meaning.

Now certainly there are written transcriptions of what is spoken that are not texts in the sense of being "the word that stands." For example, private written notes [*Aufzeichnungen*], reminders, and summaries of what has been spoken, all of which merely serve to assist our memory. Here it is clear that the written note gains life only with the decrease in recollection. This kind of text does not put forward its own statement and therefore would not, if it were published in itself, be anything that says something. Such a text is only the written trace of a fuller memory that already subsists in itself. In contrast to this, it becomes clear in what sense there are texts that really have the nature of *Aussage* [statements or declarations] and are a "word" in the above designated sense, a word that is *said* (and not just something that is passed on to us or conveyed). Thus we may determine more closely what the "word" as *saying* is by noting the fact that it is uttered or written as saying something. Again we ask: which word, uttered in this way, is the most telling [*sagend*] and can to this degree be called "true"?

III

I distinguish among three kinds of texts that are *Aussage* [declarations, statements]: the religious, the juridical, and the literary text. The last should perhaps be further subdivided in order to distinguish such different forms of literary assertion as the poetic word, the speculative sentence of the philosophers, and the basic logical unit of the predicative judgment. Even the predicative judgment belongs within this category because the general character of the word is to say something, and for this reason we are not allowed to exclude judgment [*Urteil*], which is the pointing that merely causes something to be present, if it stands in the context of an argument.

Now when we differentiate among these ways [*Weisen*] of the word, this should come from what resides in the character of the word itself and not from the circumstances under which it is uttered. This applies to "literature" in all its forms. For what characterizes literature is precisely the fact that its being in written form does not represent a diminution of its original living oral being, but rather its written form is the original form of its being, which, for its part, allows and in fact demands the secondary fulfillment of being read or spoken. One can categorize the three basic ways of being a text under three basic forms of saying: acceptance or promise [*Zusage*], announcement [*Ansage*], and *Aussage* taken in the narrower sense of a statement; and when *Aussage* is taken in an eminent sense it will be a saying-forth [*Aus-sage*], that is to say, saying carried to its true end, and thus the most telling word [*das am meisten sagende Wort*].

Thus *Aussage* in its full compass is not to be so limited that it excludes, for example, a religious text, or a legal text. These are also *Aussage*. They contain within the manner of their givenness as written language the specific nature of their saying. It is not the case, then, that a statement which is not yet a promise [*Zusage*] first becomes such when someone promises it *to* somebody, as, for example, in consolation and promising [*Verheissung*]. Rather, the *Zusage* is a kind of statement that has in itself the character of promise and has to be understood as a promise. But this means that in the *Zusage* language goes beyond itself. In the Old Testament or the New Testament, the promise does not fulfill itself just in being made, the way a poem fulfills itself in being read. Therefore, the announcement of a promise in a way finds its fulfillment in its acceptance in faith—as indeed every promise becomes a promise only if it is accepted. Likewise, a juridical text, formulating a law or a judgment, is binding as soon as it is enacted, but it is fulfilled as enacted not in itself but in being carried out or enforced. Also, a merely "historical" report [*historischer Bericht*] differs from a poetical statement in that the latter fulfills itself in being stated. Take the Gospel as an example. There the evangelist tells a story. A chronicler or historian could also tell such a story, or a poet. But the claim resident in the saying, which is ascertained with the "reading" of this story—and every reading [*Lesen*] of the same story is basically a lesson [*Lesung*]—possesses from the outset its own saying power, which I have called *Zusage*. For it is the Joyful

Message [*die Frohe Botschaft*]. One can certainly read the same text in a different way, say, with the interest of a historian who wants to test critically its value as a source. But if the historian were not to understand the statement of the text in its *Zusagecharakter* [its character as promise], then he would also not even be able to make a source-critically adequate use of it! As we say in hermeneutics, the text has its *scopus* [scope, range of importance, reach] on the basis of which one must understand it. Likewise, one can read the *Zusage* text in a purely literary way, looking at the artistic means which give life and color to its presentation, looking at its composition, the syntactical and semantic means used in its style, and unquestionably there is high poetry, especially in the Old Testament, whose style is striking. And yet even a text like the Song of Songs, say, stands in the context of the holy scripture, that is, it demands that one understand it as promise and acceptance—*Zusage*. Certainly it is here the context, but as that it is again a purely linguistic textual givenness, which lends a love song the character of a promise and acceptance. To the same *scopus* we must also relate texts which from a literary standpoint are very modest and artless, like the synoptic Gospels. One will have to deduce the nature of the text as affirmation or promise from the *scopus* indicated by the context.

One may ask oneself here whether it is the religious character of such texts, texts that speak from themselves, that already constitutes their character as *Zusage* [promise], or whether it is the special character of religions of revelation and redemption like Judaism, Christianity, and Islam, which are book-religions in the authentic sense of the word, which lends their scriptures their character as *Zusage*. In fact, it is possible that the world of myth, that is to say, of all religious traditions that do not have something like canonical texts, will open up a completely different hermeneutical problematic. For example, there are the *Aussagen* [assertions] that one may discover behind the poetic texts of the Greeks in their myths and legends. Admittedly, these do not yet have the structure of a *text,* that is, of the word that stands. Nevertheless, they are *Sage* [legends], that is, they speak through nothing more than their being spoken. Would we recognize or come to recognize such worlds of religious tradition at all if they were not standing, so to speak, within literary forms of tradition? With all due respect to the methods of the structuralist study of myth, I would say that the hermeneutical interest in them begins not so much with the question of what the myths betray in terms of hidden structures as rather what they say to you when you encounter them in poetry. What they say to you resides in the declaration [*Aussage*] which they are, and which necessarily presses forward toward determinate form, perhaps even crystallizing into myth-interpreting poetry.

In this way the hermeneutical problem of myth-exegesis finds its legitimate place among the forms of explicating the literary word.[6]

With regard to the character of the *Ansage*—the announcement—a similar examination can be carried out. *Ansage* seems specifically appropriate to declarations of law [*Rechtsaussagen*]. In its broad compass the category of *Aussage* includes rules and regulations that are publicly announced, the enactment of laws, and finally even books of law, written constitutions, judicial verdicts, and so forth. The many levels of text that run through this category and the way that handing down the law historically take on the character of literature, so very clearly manifest and maintain a particular way of saying [*des Sagens*]. These texts utter something that is valid in the legal sense of the word and can only be understood within the *scopus* in which they can claim to be valid. It is evident here that the claim of such a word to be valid is not just increased through its writtenness; the *codifiability* of these validities is also not accidental or extraneous. The meaning of what is said in such announcements is only to a certain extent brought to fulfillment there. The fact that a directive by the court or a general law in the fullest sense of its meaning as word can be fully fixed in writing apparently rests on something else: the fact that it is not to be altered and it is applicable to all. It stands. That it is *there* and that it *stands* there so long as it is not repealed apparently constitutes the essence of being accepted as valid which belongs to such utterances. In keeping with this one speaks of the "proclamation" of a law or its being made public as the beginning of its being accepted as valid law. That the interpretation of such a "word" or text is still a creative legal task does not change the fact that the assertion in itself intends to have a single clear meaning and that its force is legally binding. The hermeneutical task that is posed in this regard is a *juristic* task and may in a secondary way have a legal-historical and even a literary-historical side. In any case, even in this form of *Ansage* [announcing, proclaiming] the word embodied in *Aussage* [declaration] lives on, because as *word* it wants to be true.

If we turn now to *Aussage* in the eminent sense of the word, that is, to declarations or statements that belong above all to literature in the narrower sense of that term, we find in this category that the number of ways of making an *Aussage* [assertion, statement, declaration] is positively bewildering. In light of this fact, it seems to me justifiable methodologically to limit our inquiry here to what is called *schöne Literatur* [literature that is beautiful, "belles lettres"], that is to say, to texts that we do not see as belonging to any other context of meaning than literature. For example, cultic, legal, scientific, and even—although one might make a few exceptions here—philosophical texts. Ever since ancient times the sense of what is called the beautiful, the *kalon* [the fine], is that it is always desirable in itself, that is to say, it is persuasive not for the sake of something else but solely on the basis of its own occurrence, which naturally demands applause. However, this does not at all mean that the hermeneutical problem in reference to such works needs to be taken up into the realm of aesthetics. On the contrary, when we address the question of the truth of the word in reference to the literary word, we do so in full consciousness that in the realm of traditional aesthetics the question of truth has not been given any right to feel itself to be at home.

The art of the word, poetry, has been a special object of reflection since ancient times, and in any event long before other kinds of art were thematized. If one wants to count Vitruvius [a Roman authority on architecture] at all as a great ancient art theorist, or someone in the field of music, these are both doctrines with regard to practical arts, and thus basically the writings of both in these areas are *ars poetica* [arts of making]. Poetry has above all become the object of consideration for the philosophers, and this is not accidental, for poetry rivaled the claims made by philosophy. This is indicated not only by Plato's critique of the poets but also by Aristotle's special interest in poetics. In addition, poetics was generally placed in the neighborhood of rhetoric, an event which happened quite early in reflection directed to the understanding of art.[7] This was a productive association in many respects and was fundamental to the formulation of numerous concepts in the field of the investigation of art. The concept of style alone, of the *stilus scribendi*, provides persuasive evidence for this.

Nevertheless, one needs to ask whether the function of poetry has ever been given the attention it was due within the realm of aesthetics. The reigning idea for two thousand years has been that of mimesis, *imitatio*, of imitating or copying something.[8] Originally mimesis was closely linked to the transitory arts of dance, music, and poetry, and it was applied above all to the art of the theater. But already in Plato visual arts like sculpture and painting are brought in, and likewise in Aristotle. Above all, using the ocular concept of *eidos*, Plato [in the *Republic* X] interpreted the existing world as a copy, and poetry as a copy of that world, and thus as a copy of a copy. In this way, however, the concept of mimesis was completely wrested from its origins. Even Hegel's definition of the beautiful as the sensible appearance of the idea echoes Plato, and all the proclamations of a universal poetry in the Romantic period did not resolve the predicament that squeezed the art of words into a place between rhetoric and aesthetics.

So our inquiry into the truth of the word has not received any rich advance preparation. In Romanticism, and above all in Hegel's systematic placement of the arts, one finds only undeveloped beginnings. It was Heidegger's breakthrough that went beyond the traditional conceptualities of metaphysics and aesthetics and opened up a new access to fine art, in that he interpreted the artwork as the placing of truth in a work and he defended the sensory and moral unity of the artwork against all ontological dualisms.[9] In this way he brought new respect for the Romantic insight that poetry occupies a key position in relation to the other arts. On the basis of Heidegger's essay, it becomes far easier to say how in a picture the true being of the colors emerges, or in architecture the being of the stones, and to see the similar way that in poetry the true word [*wahre Wort*] comes forth.

This is the locus of our question: what does it mean to speak of the "coming forth of the word" [*das Hervorkommen des Wortes*] in poetry? Just as color in a painting is more shining than elsewhere and stone in architecture is more weight-bearing, so in the work of poetry the word as word speaks more tellingly than anywhere else. That is my thesis. If I am able to make it persuasive, then the question of the truth of the word can be answered on the basis of this, its highest form, its perfection. But what does it mean when we say that the word is "more telling" [*sagender*]? Our methodical linking together of word and text is a good preparation for this question. Obviously it is not the dead letter of the writing but the resurrected word (spoken or read) that can be assigned to the being of the work of art in poetry. Still, passing through its fall into writing gives the word the transfiguration that can mean its truth. In this context the question of the historical and genetic meaning of writtenness can be left to one side. What the passage into writing does here is simply bring to light the characteristically linguistic way-of-being of the *word,* and in particular of poetic statement. We will have now to check on whether the passing into and through writing in the case of *schöne Literatur* [belles lettres, beautiful literature] does not bring *something else* yet to light than what can be validly claimed for other forms that can truly be called a text.

First of all, what poems hold in common becomes visible: for example, the disappearance of the author or his transformation into the ideal figure of a speaker. In religious documents this ideal figure is often heightened into a fiction, as if God were the speaker, and in legal verdicts they expressly say, "In the name of the Law. . . ." To understand such texts certainly cannot mean what many people have been saying since Schleiermacher, namely, that to understand is a reproducing of the productive act of its creation. We should draw the same conclusion from this with regard to the literary text—namely, that psychological interpretation does not have the hermeneutical appropriateness that has earlier been ascribed to it. In both of these cases, the assertion made by the text is not to be understood as an "expressive phenomenon," as an expression of the author's inner soul. (In fact, the text cannot be traced back to an individual originator at all in many cases, anyway.) Likewise one may note that there is a wide variety of ideal speakers: there is the one who makes a *religious* promise to you, or the one who speaks to you in the name of the *law,* or . . . Yet at this last "or" one hesitates, one is brought up short. Should we really say: "those who as poets speak to someone"? Would it not be more appropriate if one only said that *the poetry speaks?* And I would add that the poem speaks better and more authentically through the listener, the hearer—or even just the reader—than it does through someone who is actually there speaking as the resuscitator, the actor, or someone who is reading a lecture. Such speakers doubtless find themselves performing a secondary function (even if it is the author himself, who takes on the role of a speaker or an actor), as they likewise do when compelled to give a lecture after just having read it through a single time. Also, one hopelessly mistakes what literature is when one tries to go from aspects of the literary construction back to the psychological act of intending it, to which the author gave "expression." Here we find a striking and persuasive difference between a literary text and the notes the author may have made to himself, or the communications he had with another person about it. The literary text is not secondary in comparison with a prior, original speaking that intends something, the way that notes and other communications are. Quite the reverse is the case, because every subsequent interpretation of the text—even the author's own—is oriented *to the text,* and not in such a way that the author possesses some dark recollection of something that he had wanted to say, such that he can refresh his memory by going back to his preparatory work. Certainly, having recourse to variants is often indispensable to construing the meaning of a text. Every construing of a text is preceded by an understanding of it, and whoever fears for the objectivity of interpretation because of this had better ask whether [the objectivist alternative of] tracking the meaning of a literary text back to an opinion of its original creator that is articulated in a text does not actually destroy the artistic meaning [*Kunstsinn*] of literature as such.

Admittedly, this is initially only a negative differentiation by which the autonomy of the word as text becomes persuasive. Now what do we base this autonomy on? How can the word be so very telling and say so much that even the author himself or herself does not know how to in-

terpret it but must once again listen to the word? When one determines
the autonomy of the word negatively, as we have done, we certainly do
find a first sense of the eminent being of saying [*Sinn des eminenten Sa-
gendseins*] that belongs to a literary text. What is truly unique to it is the
fact that a literary text raises its voice from itself, so to speak, and speaks
in nobody's name, not in the name of a god or a law but from itself! Now
I maintain the following: the "ideal speaker" of such a word is the ideal
reader! The next step would be to go more deeply into the matter and to
show that my thesis also entails no historical restriction. We can at least
note that it remains true that even in preliterary cultures, for example,
in the oral tradition of the epics, one finds such an "ideal reader," that
is, a listener who through all the recitations (or a single recitation) listens to what only the inner ear perceives. By this standard, he or she is
able to judge the rhapsodes, as we see in the ancient practice of competition among singers. Such an ideal listener is like the ideal reader.[10] If
we went more deeply into this matter, we could show this and also why
reading, in contrast to giving a lecture or presenting a recitation, is *not a
reproduction of an original* but rather shares in the ideality of the original;
for reading is not contingent at all on making a reproduction, and does
not require it. In this respect the investigations of the Polish phenomenologist Roman Ingarden into the schematic character of the literary
word have pointed the way for further work.

It would also be enlightening to compare the interpretation of absolute music and its notation, which has a fixed form on paper, with the
reading of an eminent text. This would show, I think, as the musicologist
Thrasybulos Georgiades has done,[11] what a difference exists between
note-script in the one case and manuscript in the other, between tone
in music and word in poetry, and therewith also between the musical
score [*Notensatz*] and the literary work. Without question music has the
characteristic that one must make the music, and that even the listener
to music must participate in the music, almost like someone who sings
a song along with the singer. Also, reading a musical score is not like
reading a linguistic text. This would be similar only if one were inwardly
performing the score while reading it, and if one, like the reader, were
not constrained but rather retained one's freedom of imagination. In
the case of music, however, the interpretation of the score is in nearly
all cases already pre-given to the listener by the performer, no matter
how great the freedom may be that the listener can exercise. The musician, as performer and in some cases as conductor, occupies a middle
position: he has to be an interpreter in the truest sense between the
composer and the listener. This is the same as what we're familiar with
in the theater: the performance is an interpretation that stands between

the text of the play and the spectator. For the spectator this isn't the same kind of task as reading something out loud. You are yourself the person who "reproduces," who sets something into being from out of yourself. When one is simply reading aloud to oneself, sotto voce, which was the way that reading was always done in antiquity and up into the Middle Ages, then in reality one is just carrying out the reading for oneself, not for another person who is listening to one read the text and understands it in his or her own way. Even reading aloud to another individual is not a real "reproducing" but a service to someone who wants to understand it as if he himself had been reading it. For this reason the text sounds quite different if one is only reading it aloud or only reciting it than if one reads it like an actor who tries to bring the text forth radiantly anew. There are admittedly borderline cases that cross over from one side to the other here. A genius at interpretive reading like Ludwig Tieck, above all when he read Shakespeare aloud, seems to have had such complete control over the possible variations in speaking that he was like a one-man theater.

But how is it with real theater, the literary theater that performs the text of a play? There, mimes have their role to play more or less in harmony with the director's concept. Only in ideal cases can the director so fully convey to his actors the whole of his own interpretation of the text that his interpretation shapes along with the actor the embodiment of an individual role. With or without the director, and with or without the conductor in the case of music, the performance becomes an interpretation that is presented to the spectator as the actor's or musician's own accomplishment.

All this must give way to the even more pressing question to be addressed to the "telling" [*sagende*] *word:* what is it that makes the word so telling when it is telling in the eminent sense? Here the range of literary and stylistic differences in literature overwhelms us: epic, lyric, and dramatic poetry; artistic prose, naively told stories, and the simple ballad; forms of expression that are mythic, fairy tale-like, didactic, meditative, reflexive, hermetic, or reportage-like, all the way to *poésie pure*. If every one of these can be called "literature," that is to say, that in all of them the word speaks as word with the autonomy described above, then the ideal speaker or reader that we were seeking to construct now completely dissolves and is no help at all with regard to the question of how the word is "telling" [*sagend*] in those occurrences we have been trying to address. Certainly not only the diversity of what the word in literature says and the different ways that it speaks its word give us pause here. It seems evident from the outset that the word that is able to address us cannot be characterized just in terms of the content to which it refers.

The same is true of the visual arts and for the same reasons. Someone who only looks at the objective content of a painting often looks right past what makes it a work of art. The nonobjective art of today makes this clear to everybody. The information value of a copy of a flower in a plant catalog, for example, is certainly far greater than the orgy of colors in a picture of flowers by Emil Nolde.[12] On the other hand, one can understand from this example why colorful compositions that leave behind all objective depiction, such as a still life of flaming flowers, can nevertheless be so appealing. Indeed, it seems as if hints of meaning, echoes, possible links to our customary objective seeing are all in play; still, they do not steer us toward themselves but turn our gaze toward new ordering structures that make such a composition of colors a picture without making it a copy of something. The practical lifeworld, which is governed by purposes of its own, does not offer us anything like this. The same thing seems to hold for the poetic word. It can never stop consisting of meanings that arise out of the words, or parts of words, that have meaning and that form a unity of a spoken whole or a totality of meanings. This is true even for the famous French *poésie pure*. The ordering structure that informs them, however, can no longer be opened up by the customary directions of meaning found in grammatical and syntactic speech, the rules that govern our forms of communication.

The extreme situation in modern visual art seems to me likewise to be methodologically helpful in dealing with the question of the truth of the work of art—and in our case, of the poetic word. It teaches us to reject a wrongheaded orientation directed basically to the communicative content. But it also protects us from the opposite mistake: assuming that what we may recognize in what is presented or said has no relevance at all. The word that speaks to most people is certainly not a word that just pops up and strikes one as a mere structure of sound. Saying is not just there in itself; rather it says *something,* and when what is said in the saying is completely *there,* then the word is telling even when what it says would be unlikely, and indeed when the sound of the word has faded away and perhaps was not even noticed.

When our attention is focused primarily on the manner of the speaking, on how beautifully it is said, then, as with all fine-sounding rhetoric, the ontological valence that resides in the word and the force of the matter being spoken of are lost. On the other hand, that a text speaks from itself necessarily depends on the how of its being said as such, though not in such a way that the structural form all by itself comprises the artistic statement, leaving totally aside any consideration of the intended meaning of the speaking or of the thing represented in the picture. Precisely the objective content of the work is raised to an absolute presence through art in language or visual art, to such a degree that all relation to real being or even past being fades away. Indeed, even the focus onto the how of the presentation fades away along with it. It seems as if the how of the artwork's being said, which doubtless distinguishes art from nonart, shows itself only to rise above itself—and this is also the case even when something is apparently "not saying anything" but is rather an ordered structure composed of images or elements of meaning and sound, as in the modern hermetic lyric. The word of a poem or the image in a picture is not made more telling through a foregrounding of form and content: *ars latet arte sua*—art loves to hide its art.[13] Scholarly methods can deal thematically with much about the work of art, but not with the one and all of its *Aussage*.

Let's linger with the word of the poem. What is it that is there in everything that is said and comes to stand before us, when the *Aussage* [assertion, declaration, statement] takes place or happens? I think it is self-presence, the being of the "there" [*Sein des "Da"*], and not what is expressed as its objective content. There are no poetic objects, only poetic presentations of objects (allowing ourselves here to alter a well-known saying of Nietzsche).

But that would be only a first step in the unfolding of our problem. For now the question arises as to how the poetically presented object is to become poetic through language. When Aristotle made the convincing statement that poetry is more philosophical than history, and he means to say that it contains more actual knowledge, more truth, because it presents things not as they really happened but as they could happen, this poses the question: How is poetry made? Does it present the idealized instead of what is concretely real? But in this case the riddle is precisely why the idealized thing emerges in the poetic word as concretely real, indeed as more real than that which is real and not, as the idealized, afflicted with the paleness of thought directed toward the universal. And in addition, how does everything that shines forth in the poetic word share in this transfiguration into the essential (which one can only hesitantly call "idealized")? To answer this question, it is necessary for us not to be confused by the diverse differentiation in poetic speaking. Differentiation makes the task more specific. We are here only asking about what it is that makes all these various ways of saying into texts, that is to say, what it is that gives them the "ideal" linguistic identity that is absolutely capable of making each of them a *text*. In this connection, then, we can pass over the wide range of modes of presentation that have developed into different genres of text, each with its own requirements. They have in common that they are all "literature." What is written is scarcely ever completely without linguistic coherence. There is, however, a type of linguistic expression fixed in written form that is a text, but that scarcely meets the basic requirement of linguistic identity which generally pertains to a "text." This kind of "text" is one whose wording is randomly changeable, as occasionally holds in the case of artless scientific prose. One can put the matter this way: it is possible for it to be translated without sacrifice, even by a computer, because it has to do only with the informative function, the informational content, of the text. This form of text may serve as an ideal boundary case. Actually, it stands on the threshold of non-language, using artificial symbols, whose employment as signs is just as random, because this use has the advantage (and disadvantage) of being unambiguous, in that the sign stands in a firmly established classification system for indicating what is designated. For this reason, in the natural sciences the publication of results in English immediately follows. But this too is very instructive as a borderline case, namely as the zero-point over against the high level of coherence and meaning that belongs to individual words in literary texts. In them the word has the very highest coherence with the whole of the text. We do not wish here to go into the different levels of coherence within literature. The breadth of difference becomes clear in the untranslatability of literature that culminates in lyric poetry and especially *poésie pure*. Our next remarks will try to make visible the bonding factor which links texts together in their linguistic identity, and we will also draw a conclusion about the "being" of such texts, that is to say, about the "truth of the word."

We have been concerned throughout our discussion with the linguistic medium, the medium by means of which language is bound back to its own or inner resounding, no matter how much in being-given-away it resolves into the spoken, and the medium which brings it about that this being-given-away possesses the unique evocative impact which characterizes literature. Rhythm belongs to these linguistic means as a pure becoming of form by time. Rhythm is also at home in music, but in the realm of language it is subject to its own tensive relationship to the meaning that is being referred to, and thus generally cannot be restricted to precise forms of repetition. It is hard to say what it is that this poetic rhythm articulates when reading something aloud such that we notice very clearly when it falls short of its goal. One can say that basically it has to do with a balance one can feel between two motions: the movement of the meaning and the movement of the sound. Both motions, which always blend into a single motion—and sometimes not without compulsion—have their specific syntactical means that they employ. In the realm of sound these means extend from the extremely blatant forms of measuring time (meter) and rhyme all the way to figurations of sound that remain below the threshold of conscious notice and are drawn over it via this more or less thick network, these more or less inexpressible logical links of meaning. What thereby comes into being in the coherence contributed by poetic language is clearly what I would like to call with Hölderlin the *tone*. The tone holds throughout the whole of the linguistic construction, exhibiting its tenacious power of determination above all in instances where discordant tones arise. A discordant tone [*Misstone*] is not only a false tone but a tone that detracts from the whole mood. In literature it is no different from in life in human society. It is, conversely, the enduring tone that holds together the unity of the construction—with all the differences and degrees of difference in sensitivity to disturbance and density of coherence that are possible. This tone, which endures, binds to one another the elements of the discourse. It joins together the construction in such a way that this kind of construction stands out against other discourses (so that we can, for example, recognize a quotation by the tone). It stands out above all against every kind of discourse that is not "literature" and that does not have its harmony in itself but must search for or find this harmony outside itself.

In critical questions, such borderline cases are always the most instructive. For instance, the way that Pindar introduces into the context of his songs the praise of the current victor contains an occasional element. But the power and coherence of the linguistic form is evident precisely in that the poetic construction knows full well how to carry this dedication, as is also the case with Hölderlin, who follows Pindar in his hymns. Still more instructive than cases of such occasional parts in a text, the same question arises where the text itself as a whole relates itself to a reality that stands outside language, for example in the historical novel or the historical drama. One cannot hold that a genuine literary work of art causes this relationship to extralinguistic reality to disappear completely. The claim to historical reality undoubtedly resonates as a kind of overtone in the formed text. The material is not simply invented, and the appeal to poetic license, which entitles the poet to alter the real relationships indicated in the historical sources, only confirms this. For the fact that the author is allowed to alter them, indeed to fabricate far beyond every limit of the actual historical relationships, shows how much in the shaping of his poetry the material of historical reality is transformed [*aufgehoben*], even where the poet is using history. This clearly differentiates the artistic element from the case demonstrated by the historian's art of representation.

Along the same lines, there is the important issue of how far the conceptuality of rhetoric is actually appropriate to the bonding-means that we have been describing in works of art. First, the devices of rhetoric are the devices of discourse, which as such is not originally "literature." An example that shows the difficulty of the problematic is the concept of metaphor. The poetic legitimation of the concept of metaphor has rightly been contested—but not because metaphor (or every other figure of speech in rhetoric) could not be used in poetry. Rather, the point is that the essence of poetry does not lie in metaphor and the use of metaphor. Poetic discourse is not attained by taking unpoetical speech and adding metaphor. When Gottfried Benn contested the use of "like" in poetry, he was certainly not mistakenly referring to the highly expressive and magnificently developed epic metaphors in Homer. Actually, in Homer metaphor and comparison are so well carried by the tone of the bard that they are completely part of the world he evokes. Poetic irony, which inheres in the contrasting tensions contained in Homeric comparisons, evidences exactly the perfection of their construction. So one can rightly say not only in the case of Kafka, that where the fictive realism of the narration especially motivates it, but also about the poetic word as a whole, that it has the character of an "absolute" metaphor (Allemann),[14] that is, it stands in contrast to everyday speech as such.

Thus poetic speaking has the indefiniteness and solemnity [*Schwebe und Getragenheit*] that result from neutralizing all assumption of existence, and thereby it brings about what I have called a "transformation into a construction." Husserl used the expression "modification of neutrality" in reference to this and said that in the case of poetry what he called the eidetic reduction was "spontaneously fulfilled," but he is still describing the situation while proceeding from the intentionality of consciousness. Such an intentionality is primarily positional. Husserl views the language of poetry as a modification of the straightforward everyday positing of being [*Seinssetzung*]. In place of the relation outward to an object, the self-referentiality of the word enters the scene, which one indeed can call self-reference. But precisely here we need to change our way of thinking, and here Heidegger's critique of transcendental phenomenology and its concept of consciousness proves to be fruitful. What language is as language, and what we here seek as the "truth of the word," cannot be grasped by taking the "natural" forms of linguistic communication as the starting point; rather, the possibilities of poetical forms of communication are better grasped by starting from poetical speaking! The forming of poetic language presupposes the dissolution of all conventionally accepted rules (see Hölderlin). This means that in fact language is in the process of becoming and is not a rule-governed application of words, not a co-constructing of something in accordance with convention. No, the poetic word *establishes* [*stiftet*] meaning. The way the word in a poem *herauskommt* [comes forth, emerges; a Heideg-gerian term] manifests a new saying-power that often remains hidden in the usage of what is commonly accepted.

To give an example, in German the word *Geräusch* is just as colorless and insignificant as "noise" is in English, which we don't even recognize as related to nausea and seasickness. We see how it comes alive in Stefan George's famous line: "Und das Geräusch der ungeheuren See"—"And the noise, the rush of tremendous seas." This is anything but a poetizing application of an everyday word. It remains the everyday word, but here it stands so suspended among relationships of rhythm, meter, and vocal-ization that it suddenly becomes more telling, it regains its original say-ing power! Through association with the word "tremendous" the word *Geräusch* [roar, noise, rushing sound] again *räuscht* [roars], and through the consonance of the "r" in *Rausch* and *-heuren* the two words intensify each other. These intensifications at the same time set the word up, display it, and thereby set it free to be itself. This setting-up allows it to interact with the other words in a new way—and certainly not without also bringing back into play with it other relationships of meaning, for example, it evokes the view of the coast of the North Sea and the world opposing it to the south.[15] Through this the word speaks more strongly, and what it says is essentially "there" more than ever. Just as in another context I have spoken of the *Seinsvalenz des Bildes* [the power or valence of being resident in an image or picture],[16] when what is represented by the picture gains being through the picture, so also here I would like to speak of a valence of being [*Seinsvalenz*] resident in the word. Of course, there is a difference: it is not so much the thing said in the sense of ex-pressing an objective content that now gains in being as rather it is *being as a whole.* There is a fundamental difference here between the way that the variegated world is transformed into an image in a work of art and the way that the word sways and plays itself out [in ordinary language]. The word is not an element of the world like colors or forms that can be fitted into a new order of things. Rather, every word is itself already an element of a new order of things and therefore is itself potentially this order in its entirety. When a word resonates, a whole language and everything it is able to say is called forth—and it knows how to say every-thing. So what comes out in the word that "speaks" more is not so much a single element of meaning in the world, but rather the presence of the whole built through language. Aristotle designated seeing as the most excellent of the faculties because this is the sense that perceives the most differences, but in fact one can perceive even more with hearing, and thus hearing can more justly qualify for this distinction because when we hear speech we are capable of perceiving simply everything that is distinguishable in it. The universal "there" of being that resides in the word is the miracle of language, and the highest possibility of saying consists in catching its passing away and escaping and in making firm its nearness to being. It is nearness or presentness not of this or that but of the possibility of everything. This is what distinguishes the poetic word. It fulfills itself within itself because it is a "holding of the near," and it becomes an empty word when it is reduced to its merely signifying function, for then it stands in need of communicatively mediated fulfillment. The self-fulfillment of the poetic word makes it clear why language can be merely a means of conveying information, but a mere means of conveying information is not language in its fullness.

We can take up here only in passing a question already touched on: whether the mythic word, the legend, and perhaps also the philosophical word in the form of the speculative proposition, do not all in truth share the distinguishing trait of the poetic word, namely, of being saying pure and simple [*das Sagende schlechthin zu sein*]. Considering this question will lead us to the final step in our presentation. The problem is clear. Legends are not written down and are not texts, although they do also enter into language and in it take on the form of a text. A legend as legend [or saga] appears not yet to have entered into the firm stability of poetical-linguistic coherence, but rather drifts back and forth on a stream of wisdom primeval in origin, which feeds on cultic thinking. At the same time, it does seem reasonable to call legend [*Sage*] *Aussage* [assertion, declaration, statement] in the excellent sense. Of course, the legend does not merit the name *Aussage* because of the linguistic organization of its means of telling a story but in its core, in the names that are used, in whose secret naming-power the telling of the tale is bathed. For it appears to me that in the names is hidden that which the legend calls forth in its telling. To see this, it suffices to mention the fact that the *name* in each story is likewise at the null point of translatability, that is, of the separability of its saying from what is said. But what else is the name than the final condensation [*Verdichtung*] in which human existing listens to itself? For it is the name that one hears and answers to, and one's own name is what one is and which one lives up to [*ausfüllt*, fills out, fills up].[17] In a similar way the word of poetry is self-fulfilling—and it stands as if before its own self-unfolding in the speech of the thinking word. It is the "syntax" of poetry to be "in the word." The degree of coherence of the words also determines their degree of translatability (see I. A. Richards).

We shall not go into a general discussion of the extent to which the philosophical statement is such a "legend" [*Sage*], but only briefly offer a clarification in reference to the "speculative sentence." The structure of the speculative sentence is an analogue to the self-referentiality which belongs to the poetic word. Hegel in fact described the nature of the speculative proposition as completely analogous to it, and in this regard he did not have in mind just his own dialectical method but the language of philosophy as such, insofar as it exists in its authentic possibility. He shows that in the speculative proposition the natural reaching out of speech toward the predicate, which is ascribed as an other to the subject, is broken and suffers a counter-impulse [*Gegenstoss*].[18] Thinking finds in the predicate not something other but rather the genuine [*eigentliche*] subject itself. Likewise the "assertion" [*Aussage*] goes back into itself, and that is what philosophical speech is for Hegel: the rigor of the concept holds fast to its *Aussage* in that this rigor "works it out" dialectically in its appropriate moments. This means, however, that it goes ever deeper into the "assertion" [the thesis]. It holds true not only for Hegel and his dialectical method, that philosophy does not march straight ahead, but instead returns in its restless striving to all of its paths and detours. The boundaries of translatability, which indicate when the saying does not conform with the thing to be said, are quickly reached here.

We call the being of the speaking [*Sagendsein*] of a word the "holding on to the near" [*Halten der Nähe*], and we have seen that it is not this or that possible content of the discourse that is near, but nearness itself [*die Nähe selbst*]. This is, of course, not limited to the work of art in the word, but applies to all art. The silence of the Chinese vase,[19] the stillness and puzzling peace [*Ruhe*] which comes toward you from every really persuasive artistic construction, testifies that (speaking with Heidegger) truth has here been "set to work." And Heidegger has shown us that the truth of the artwork is not the speaking forth [*Herausgesagtheit*] of the logos, but is rather a "that it is" and a "there" at the same time, which stand in the strife between disclosure and sheltering concealment. The question that has guided us here was how this looks especially in the artwork of words, where the sheltering and protecting in the "construction" [*Gebilde*] of the art already presupposes its being-in-language and the in-dwelling [*Insein*] of being in language. The limit of translatability [of poetry] shows us exactly how far the protection in the word stretches. In its ultimate concealedness the word is what protects, rescues, shelters.[20] Only someone who is at home in a language can experience the *Aussage* of the poetic word in its preserving itself and standing in itself, which in the unfamiliar shelters within itself another being-at-home. But who is "at home" in a language? It appears that what modern research calls "language competency" [a Habermas term] has to do with speaking when it is not at home in itself, with unlimitedness in the use of discourse—and that always prepares the way for its going unheard and unheeded [*das ist ihr allbereites Verhallen*].

For this reason, the poetic word in comparison with every other work of art seems to me to have yet another determinant. It can claim not only the breathtaking nearness of all art, but it also must be and is capable of capturing and holding within itself this nearness, that is, it is able to call a halt to what is fleeting. For speech is self-expression and escapes itself. The poetic word, too, can never stop being speech (or stammering) in order ever anew to give play to its possibilities of meaning. How else does the tone [we have spoken of] stand within the system of tones? How does a work of painting or architecture find its place? It seems to me that the poetic word has its enduring value in holding onto itself and in holding itself back, and that means in this it has its highest possibility. The word finds its fulfillment in the poetic word—and from there enters into the thought of a thinking person.

Translated by Richard E. Palmer

8

Text and Interpretation

This essay was Gadamer's position paper in the April 1981 "debate" with Derrida at a conference on "Text and Interpretation" held at the Sorbonne in Paris. In it he discusses his approach to texts and several elements of Derrida's philosophy, showing that he had read several of Derrida's major writings, and he even answers some criticisms that Heidegger "and presumably Derrida" would have of his philosophy. On the other hand, Derrida's position paper at that meeting [on Heidegger's interpretation of Nietzsche as not really going beyond metaphysics] does not even mention Gadamer.[1] So the unlikely debate, such as it was, actually only took place when Derrida chose to address three questions to Gadamer regarding his paper and Gadamer replied. Later Gadamer wrote several essays in response to Derrida, the last of which is included in this volume ("Hermeneutics Tracking the Trace"). Derrida himself did not regard the exchange as a debate and later remarked to a colleague [Oxenhandler] that "nothing happened." His final and very appreciative remarks about Gadamer came in Heidelberg in 2003, after Gadamer's death. This brought the "debate" to a close.

"Text and Interpretation" remains one of the most important mature statements by Gadamer of his hermeneutical philosophy specifically with regard to texts and their interpretation. In the essay, on a personal note he goes back to the influences that caused him to take the path he did in philosophy. He takes note of the way the definition of interpretation expanded with Heidegger's existential philosophy, and how this impacted his view of text interpretation, and his philosophical hermeneutics. But as we have said, the essay is important as Gadamer's first public statement addressing itself to Derrida's writings.

In a final fourteen-page section of the essay not presented by Gadamer in Paris but written for the German publication of the essay in 1984, he elaborates on his famous concept of the "eminent text." Such a form of text, Gadamer argues, is especially found in poetry, where language reaches its greatest compression, resonance, and power. To illustrate what he means, Gadamer takes up three forms of text that he does not really consider to be texts in this highest, eminent sense. These three forms of text are antithetical to genuine texts as such. He labels them "antitexts," "pseudotexts," and "pretexts." The last is represented by psychoanalysis, which goes behind the manifest text of a dream to its hidden meaning. All of these, Gadamer asserts, do not present us with a valid model for the process of interpretation at its best. Here he mentions Ricoeur's "hermeneutics of suspicion" and his discussion with Habermas of communication that is distorted by social forces. Finally, he goes into some depth about his own rich conception of "text." Here he discusses the poem "Salut" by Mallarmé and later goes into the dispute between Heidegger and Emil Staiger over the final line in Mörike's poem, "On a Lamp." He agrees with Heidegger. We will leave the pleasure of this discussion to the reader.

The first publication of Gadamer's paper and the oral exchange with Derrida (but not Derrida's paper itself)[2] was in French in a major French journal in 1984.[3] (Gadamer's paper was in French.) Later that same year it was published in German in a volume of papers from the conference that included Derrida's paper, but now translated into German—in a paperback volume titled *Text und Interpretation.*[4] The first English translation, by Dennis Schmidt, appeared in 1986,[5] but it translated a manuscript of the Paris talk and, like the published French text, did not contain the final fourteen pages that Gadamer added in 1983 on the topic of the "eminent text" for publication in *Text and Interpretation.*[6] The present translation smoothes, clarifies, and occasionally corrects the previous translation of the full text by Dennis Schmidt and Richard Palmer in *Dialogue and Deconstruction: The Gadamer-Derrida Encounter* (1989). It does this so extensively that it is presented here as a new translation by Richard E. Palmer, since it has not been presented to Dennis Schmidt for his review and approval, although it is of course deeply indebted to his pioneering translation.

* * *

Text and Interpretation

The problems that hermeneutics deals with were at first defined within individual areas of study, especially theology and jurisprudence, and ultimately also in the area of the historical disciplines.[1] But German Romanticism had the deep insight that understanding and interpretation not only come into play in what Dilthey later called "expressions of life fixed in writing," but have to do with the basic relationship of human beings to each other and to the world. In the German language, this insight has also left an imprint upon words that are derived from the word for understanding (*Verstehen*). For instance, the derivative *Verständnis* means comprehension, insight, appreciation. Thus, *Verstehen* also comes to mean "to have appreciation for something," to comprehend it [*für etwas Verständnis haben*].[2] The ability to understand, then, is a fundamental endowment of man, one that sustains his communal life with others and that, above all, takes place by way of language and partnership of conversation. In this respect, the universal claim of hermeneutics is beyond doubt. On the other hand, however, the linguistic character of the event of understanding [*Verständigungsgeschehen*], which is in play between people, represents an insurmountable barrier between human beings, the metaphysical significance of which was also evaluated positively for the first time by German Romanticism. It is expressed in the saying: *Individuum est ineffabile.* This sentence points to a limit in ancient ontology (at any rate, no example of this idea can be documented in the medieval period). But for the Romantic consciousness this saying meant that language can never touch upon the last, insurmountable secret of the individual person. This saying, then, expresses in a particularly telling way the feeling for life that characterized the Romantic age. It points to an inherent law of linguistic expression, a law which not only sets limits for linguistic expression but also determines its importance in forming the common element that unites people.

I believe it is helpful to recall these historical antecedents to the standpoint from which we presently formulate the question. Going back to Romanticism, there arose the consciousness of method that has flourished in the historical sciences, and there was pressure exerted by the successful model of the natural sciences. These led philosophical reflection to restrict the hermeneutical experience to its scientific form and deny its universality. The full scope of the fundamental hermeneutical experience is also not found in Wilhelm Dilthey—who attempted to ground the social sciences in their historical character by way of a conscious continuation of the ideas of Friedrich Schleiermacher and his Romantic compatriots—or in the neo-Kantians of the early twentieth century, who worked toward an epistemological justification of the human studies within the framework of a transcendental critique of culture and values. This lack of any standpoint that encompasses the full extent of hermeneutic experience could have been even more pronounced in this, the homeland of Kant and transcendental idealism, than in countries where literature plays a more determinative role in public life, but in the end philosophical reflection everywhere in the West went in a similar direction.

Thus, I took as my own point of departure a critique of the idealism and methodologism of an era that was dominated by epistemology. In my critique I followed Heidegger's raising of the concept of understanding to the status of an existential—that is, to a fundamental categorical determinant of human existence. This was of particular importance for me, because it was the impetus that enabled me to go beyond the discussion of method and to expand the formulation of the hermeneutic question in such a way that it not only took into account the sciences but the experience of art and history as well. Heidegger's analysis of understanding had a critical and polemical intent, and he invoked the example of the hermeneutic circle in earlier discussions, maintaining it in a positive way and conceptualizing it in his analysis of Dasein. One should not forget that at the time circularity was not dealt with as a metaphysical metaphor, but rather as the structure of a logical concept drawn from the theory of scientific proof, where it was rejected in the doctrine of the "vicious circle." The hermeneutic circle as Heidegger describes it says that in the domain of understanding there can be absolutely no derivation of one domain from the other, so that here the fallacy of circularity in logic does not represent a mistake in procedure, but rather the most appropriate description of the structure of understanding. The late nineteenth-century discussion of the hermeneutical circle by Dilthey was introduced as a means of separating himself from the post-Schleiermacherian scientific epoch. If one bears in mind along with this the true scope that the concept of understanding gains from association with the use of language, then one sees that talk about the hermeneutic circle [in Heidegger] is in fact directed toward the structure of Being-in-the-world itself; and that is, toward overcoming of the subject-object bifurcation, which was the primary thrust of Heidegger's transcendental analysis of Dasein. Just as one who uses a tool does not treat that tool as an object, but works with it, so too the understanding in and through which Dasein understands itself in its Being and in its world is not a way of comporting itself toward definite objects of knowledge, but is rather the carrying out of Being-in-the-world itself. With this move, Heidegger transformed the hermeneutical doctrine of method which he inherited from Dilthey into a "hermeneutics of facticity," a hermeneutics that was guided by his inquiry into Being and that included within it going behind both historicism and Dilthey in his questioning.

As is well known, the later Heidegger completely abandoned the concept of hermeneutics because he realized that it would not enable him to break out of the sphere of transcendental reflection. His philosophizing, which in the *Kehre* [turn] attempted to accomplish this withdrawal from the concept of the transcendental, increasingly encountered so many difficulties in expressing itself in language that many readers of Heidegger came to believe that there was more poetry than philosophical thought to be found in his work. Of course, I believe that this view was a mistake.[3] In fact, one of my own interests was to look for ways to legitimate Heidegger's discussion of that Being which is not just the being of beings. This effort led me once again to engage in intense work on the history of classical hermeneutics, and it compelled me to display the new insights I was able to bring to light by means of a critique of this history. My own contribution, it seems to me, is the discovery that no conceptual language, not even what Heidegger called the "language of metaphysics," represents an unbreakable constraint upon thought if the thinker will allow himself or herself to trust language; that is to say, if he or she engages in dialogue with other thinkers and other ways of thinking. Thus, in full agreement with Heidegger's critique of the concept of the subject, whose hidden ground he rightly revealed as substance, I have tried to conceive the primordial phenomenon and nature of language as dialogue. This effort entailed a hermeneutical reorientation of the view of the dialectic which had been developed by German idealism as the speculative method, going instead in the direction of the art of living dialogue in which the Socratic-Platonic movement of thought took place. This reorientation of the dialectic was not intended to lead to a merely negative dialectic, even though it was always conscious of the fundamental impossibility of completing the Greek dialectic. Rather, my approach represented a correction of the ideal of method that had characterized modern dialectic as reaching its fulfillment in the idealism of the Absolute. This same interest also led me to search for the hermeneutical structure of the experience of art and of history itself, which the so-called *Geisteswissenschaften* [sciences dealing with what the human mind has produced rather than natural objects] have as their "objects," rather than starting with experience as it is treated by science. For no matter how much a work of art may appear to be a historical datum, and thus a possible object of scholarly/scientific research, it is always the case that the work says something to us, and it does so in such a way that its statement can never be exhaustively expressed in a concept. Likewise, in the experience of history we find that the ideal of the objectivity that historical research offers us is only one side of the issue—in fact a secondary side, because the special feature of historical experience is that we stand in the midst of an event without knowing what is happening to us until in looking backwards we grasp what has happened. Accordingly, in every new present, history must be written anew.

Ultimately, the same point holds true for philosophy and its history. Plato, who wrote only dialogues and never dogmatic texts, is not alone in teaching us this lesson. For, in what Hegel calls the speculative element in philosophy (which was at the basis of his own observations of the history of philosophy), we are constantly faced with a challenge of bringing this same element into view in the dialectical method. Thus,

I tried to reaffirm the inexhaustibility of our experience of meaning by developing the implications for hermeneutics of the Heideggerian insight into the central significance of finitude.

In this context, dealing with the French philosophical scene represents a genuine challenge for me. In particular, Derrida has argued against the later Heidegger that Heidegger himself has not really gone beyond the logocentrism of metaphysics. Derrida's contention is that insofar as Heidegger asks about the essence of truth or the meaning of Being, he is still speaking the language of metaphysics, a language that looks upon meaning as something out there that is to be discovered. This being so, Derrida finds Nietzsche to be more radical. After all, Nietzsche's concept of interpretation does not entail the discovery of a preexisting meaning, but the constructing of meanings in the service of the "Will to Power." According to Derrida, only in this way does one go beyond the logocentrism of metaphysics. But this development and continuation of Heidegger's insights which understands itself as their radicalization must then, in order to be consistent, discard Heidegger's own presentation and critique of Nietzsche. In Derrida's view, Nietzsche is not the extreme case of the forgetfulness of Being that culminates in the concepts of value and will, as Heidegger thinks, but represents the true overcoming of metaphysics, the very metaphysics within with Heidegger remains trapped, according to Derrida, when he asks about Being, or the meaning of Being, as if it were a logos to be discovered. It was not enough that the later Heidegger developed his special quasi-poetical language in order to escape the language of metaphysics, a language that with each new essay by Heidegger seemed to be a new language and always required that the reader be constantly his or her own translator of this language. To be sure, the extent to which I succeeded in finding the language that fulfills this task is an open question, but I did confront the task, which is that of "understanding." Since my confrontation with the French continuation of Heideggerian thought [Derrida], I have become aware that my efforts to "translate" Heidegger testify to my own limits and especially indicate how deeply rooted I am in the Romantic tradition of the humanities and its humanistic heritage. But this very tradition of historicism which sustained and carried me along is that against which I have sought to take a critical stand. In a letter that has since been published,[4] Leo Strauss got to the heart of the matter by saying that for Heidegger it is Nietzsche, while for me it is Dilthey, who forms the starting point for critique. It could be that what distinguishes Heidegger's radicality is the fact that his own critique of the Husserlian brand of neo-Kantianism put him in a position to recognize in Nietzsche the extreme culmination of what he called the history of the forgetfulness of Being. But this is a significant observation, and rather than being inferior to Nietzsche's thought it goes beyond him. I find that the French followers of Nietzsche have not grasped the significance of the seductive in Nietzsche's thought. Only in this way, it seems to me, could they come to believe that the experience of Being that Heidegger tried to uncover behind metaphysics is exceeded in radicality by Nietzsche's extremism. In truth, a deep ambiguity does characterize Heidegger's image of Nietzsche, in that he follows Nietzsche into the most extreme positions and precisely at that point he finds the excesses [*Un-wesen*] of metaphysics at work, insofar as in the valuing and revaluing of all values Being itself really becomes a value-concept in the service of the "Will to Power." Heidegger's attempt to think Being goes far beyond the dissolving of metaphysics into values-thinking; or better yet, he goes back behind metaphysics itself without being satisfied with the extreme of its self-dissolution, as Nietzsche was. Such retrospective questioning does not do away with the concept of the logos and its metaphysical implications; rather, it recognizes the one-sidedness and ultimately the superficiality of such questioning. In this regard it is of decisive importance that "Being" does not display itself totally in its self-manifestation, but rather it withholds itself and withdraws itself with the same primordiality with which it manifests itself. This is the deep insight that was first put forward by Schelling in opposition to Hegel's logical idealism. Heidegger takes up this question once again in applying to it his great conceptual power, a power that Schelling lacked.

My own efforts were therefore directed toward not forgetting the limitation that resides implicitly in every hermeneutical experience of meaning. When I wrote the sentence, "Being that can be understood is language,"[5] what was implied by this was that what is can never be completely understood. This is implied insofar as everything that goes under the name of language always goes beyond whatever achieves the status of a proposition. That which is to be understood is that which comes into language, but of course it is always that which is taken as something, taken as something true [*wahr-genommen*]. This is the hermeneutical dimension—a dimension in which Being "shows itself." This is the [ontological] sense in which I retained the expression, "hermeneutics of facticity"—an expression that represents a transformation of the meaning of hermeneutics. Of course, in my attempt to describe the problems I dealt with, I took as my guiding thread the experience of meaning that takes shape in language in order to bring to light the limits within it. True, the being-toward-the-text from which I took my orientation can certainly not match in radicality the limit experience found in being-toward-death. And just as little do the never fully answerable

questions of the meaning of art, or the meaning of history as understanding that which happens to us, point to a phenomenon that is as
primordial as the question put to human Dasein about its own finitude. Therefore, I can understand why the later Heidegger (and Derrida would presumably agree with him on this point) was of the opinion
that I had never really abandoned the sphere of phenomenological immanence to which Husserl consistently held fast and which formed the
basis of my early neo-Kantian training. I can also understand why they
could believe that it is possible to find a methodological "immanence"
in the fact that I held fast to the hermeneutical circle. In fact, I continue
to think that the desire to break out of the circle cannot be fulfilled,
that indeed such a demand is truly absurd. For after all, this immanence
they refer to is nothing more than what Schleiermacher and his successor Dilthey described as what understanding is. Since Herder we recognize "understanding" to be more than merely an interpretive procedure
that uncovers a given meaning. In light of the breadth of what understanding is, the circularity that moves between the one who understands
and that which one understands can lay claim to genuine universality.
Indeed, it is precisely on this point that I believe that I have actually
followed Heidegger in his critique of the phenomenological concept of
immanence, a critique that is directed against Husserl's notion of an
ultimate transcendental justification.[6] The dialogical character of language, which I have tried to work out, leaves behind any starting point
in the subjectivity of the subject, and especially in the meaning-directed
intentions of the speaker. What we find happening in speaking is not a
mere fixing of intended meaning in words; it is an endeavor that continually modifies itself, or better: it is a continually recurring temptation
to engage oneself in something or to become involved with someone.
But that means to expose oneself and to risk oneself. True speaking
has little to do with a mere explication and assertion of our prejudices;
on the contrary, it risks our prejudices—it exposes oneself to one's own
doubts as well as to the rejoinder of the other. Who has not had the
experience—especially before the other whom we want to persuade—of
how the reasons that one has for one's own view, and even the reasons
that speak against one's own view, rush into words? The mere presence
of the other before whom we stand helps us to break up our own bias and
narrowness, even before he opens his mouth to make a reply. That which
becomes a dialogical experience for us here is not limited to the sphere
of arguments and counterarguments, the exchange and unification of
which may seem to be the goal of every confrontation. Rather, as the experiences that have been described indicate, there is something else in
this experience, namely, a potentiality for being the other [Andersseins]

that goes beyond every coming to agreement about what we have in common. This potentiality is the limit that Hegel did not transgress. To be sure, he did recognize the speculative principle that holds sway in the "logos." He even introduced proofs of this principle in dramatically concrete ways: he unfolded the structure of self-consciousness and of "self-knowledge in being an other" as the dialectic of recognition, and he sharpened this into a life-and-death struggle. In a similar fashion, Nietzsche's penetrating psychological insight brought into view the "Will to Power" that is the substratum even in all devotion and self-sacrifice. "There is a will to power even in the slave," he said. But the fact that the tension between giving up the self and affirming it continues on into the sphere of giving reasons and recognizing contrary reasons, and therewith into factual debates, and is at the same time embedded in it, represents for me a point that Heidegger made which remains decisive, and it does so precisely because he found in it what he called the "logocentrism" of Greek ontology.

A limitation in Greek models of thought can be detected here, which has been persuasively pointed out by the Old Testament, Saint Paul, Luther, and above all in the modern renewers of their thought. Even with the celebrated discovery of Socratic dialogue as the basic form of thought, this remains a dimension of dialogue that does not come into conceptual consciousness. This point fits in quite well with the fact that a writer with the poetic imagination and linguistic powers that Plato had knew how to portray the charismatic figure of a Socrates in such a way that the erotic tension that vibrates about his person is really brought into view. But although Plato's presentation of Socrates shows that when leading the conversation Socrates always demanded responsibility from others and even led them back to themselves by freeing them of their pretended wisdom, he presupposes at the same time that the logos is common to all and does not belong to himself alone. Yet, as we already indicated above, the true depth of the dialogical principle first enters philosophical consciousness in the twilight of metaphysics, in the epoch of German Romanticism, and is rehabilitated in our century in opposition to the subjective bias that characterizes idealism. This is the point from which I have proceeded to ask two further questions. First, how do the commonality of shared meaning [die Gemeinsamkeit des Sinnes], which is built up in conversation, and the impenetrable otherness of the other mediate each other? Second, what, in the final analysis, is the nature of language? Is it bridge or barrier? Is it a bridge built of things that are the same for each self over which one communicates with the other over the flowing stream of otherness? Or is it a barrier that limits our giving up of our selves [Selbstaufgabe] and that cuts us off from the possibility of ever completely expressing ourselves and communicating with others?

In the framework of our question of "Text and Interpretation," the concept of the text represents a challenge of a special kind. It is something that unites us here but perhaps also may separate me from my French colleagues. In any case, this issue motivated me to confront the theme "Text and Interpretation" once again. For instance, I would raise some questions: What is the relationship between text and language? What is it that can cross from language into text? What is basic agreement in understanding between speakers? What does it mean that something like texts can be held by us in common? What does it mean that in this process of communication with one another something emerges that, like texts, is the same for each of us? How has the concept of the text been able to undergo such a universal extension? Certainly it is obvious to anyone who has been observing the philosophical trends of our century that more is at stake in our theme than the methodology of the philological sciences. Text is more than just the subject matter and object of literary research. Interpretation is more than a technique for scientifically explicating texts. In the twentieth century, both of these concepts have acquired a new place in the equations we make about the world and our knowledge of it.

Of course, this change is connected with the role that language as a phenomenon has come to play in our thought. But such a statement is tautological. The fact that language has acquired a central position in philosophical thought is, for its part, related to the turn that philosophy took in the course of the last decades [writing in 1981]. That the ideal of scientific knowledge which modern science follows came out of the model of nature as mathematically ordered (a model that was first developed by Galileo in his mechanics) meant that the interpretation of the world centered in language, that is, an experience of the world that is linguistically sedimented in the lived-world, no longer constituted the starting point and the point of reference for asking questions or in our quest for knowledge. Now the essence of science is what can be explained by constructing rational laws. In this way, our natural language lost its unquestioned primacy, even if it did retain its own manner of seeing and speaking. A logical consequence of the implications of this mathematized modern natural science was that in modern logic and the theory of science, the model of univocal notation replaced the model of language. Thus, it was in the context of certain limited experiences that hinder the claim to universality of scientific access to the world, that in the meantime our natural language as a universal has recaptured the center of philosophy.

Of course, this does not signify that we simply return to the experiences of the lived world and their sedimentation in language, which as we know was the dominant theme of Greek metaphysics, the logical analysis of which eventually led to Aristotelian logic and to *grammatica speculativa*. On the contrary, what is being considered is not the achievements of logic, but language as language, language as it schematizes our access to the world and in doing this displaces primordial perspectives. Within the German world, this basic move is represented by a return in the twentieth century to Romantic ideas—the ideas of Friedrich Schlegel, Alexander [probably Wilhelm] von Humboldt, and others. Neither in the neo-Kantians nor in the first phenomenologists do we find the problem of language considered at all. Only in a later generation did the between-world [*Zwischenwelt*] of language become a theme; we find this in Ernst Cassirer and especially in Martin Heidegger, as well as in the interesting contributions of Hans Lipps. In the British tradition, something similar is to be found in the developments that Ludwig Wittgenstein made from his starting point in Bertrand Russell. Here the issue is not really one of a philosophy of language that is constructed upon the basis of comparative linguistics, or of the ideal of constructing a language that takes its place in a universal theory of signs; rather, the issue is the enigmatic nexus between thinking and speaking.

Thus, on the one hand, we have sign theory and linguistics, which have led to new knowledge about the way in which linguistic systems function and are constructed; and on the other hand, there is the theory of knowledge, which comes to realize that language mediates any access we have to the world. Both of these together have caused us to see a starting point for putting the philosophical justification of scientific access to the world in a new light. We see that the presupposition in this starting point is that the subject takes hold of empirical reality with methodological self-certainty by means of its rational mathematical constructions, and that it then gives expression to this reality in propositional statements. In this way the subject fulfills its epistemological task, and this fulfillment climaxes in the mathematical language with which natural science defines itself as universally valid. The between-world [*Zwischenwelt*] of language is left out of consideration here in principle. Insofar as it once again comes into view as such, it demonstrates against mathematical language the basically mediated character of all access to the world, and more than this, it demonstrates the impossibility of going beyond the linguistic schema of the world. The almost mythical status of the concept of self-consciousness—which was adopted in its apodictic self-certainty and elevated to the status of the origin and justification of all validity, and the ideal of an ultimate grounding [*Letztbegründung*] in general, a grounding which apriorism and empiricism dispute—loses its credibility, however, in the face of the priority of the domain of language, a domain that we cannot undermine and within which all consciousness and all knowledge articulate themselves. From Nietzsche we learned to doubt the grounding of truth in the self-certainty of self-consciousness. Through Freud we became acquainted with the astonishing scientific discoveries that resulted from taking these doubts seriously. And Heidegger's fundamental critique of the concept of consciousness has enabled us to see the conceptual prejudgment that stems from Greek logos-philosophy, which, in the modern turn, has put the concept of the "subject" in the center. All of this [critique] lends a certain primacy to the linguistic character of our experience of the world. In contrast with the illusion of self-consciousness as well as the naïveté of a positivist concept of facts, the between-world of language has proven itself to be the true dimension in which that which is given is given.

In light of all this, one can understand the increasing importance of the concept of interpretation. "Interpretation" is a word that originally arose in reference to the mediating relationship, the function of the intermediary between speakers of different languages; that is, it originally concerned the translator and was then used to refer to the deciphering of texts that are difficult to understand. And in the moment when the between-world of language presented itself to philosophical consciousness in its predetermined meaning, interpretation had to take a key position in philosophy. The career of the word "interpretation" began with Nietzsche and at the same time became a challenge to all positivism. Does the given exist as something from whose secure starting point one can search for the universal, the law, the rule, and so find its fulfillment? Or is the given not in fact itself the result of an interpretation? Interpretation performs the never fully complete mediation between man and world, and to this extent the fact that we understand something *as* something is the only real immediacy and givenness. The faith in certain agreed-upon theses, or *Protokollsätze* [protocol theses], as the foundation of all knowledge did not last long even in the Vienna Circle.[7] When establishing the basis of scientific knowledge even in the domain of the natural sciences, one cannot avoid the hermeneutical consequences of the fact that what is called the "given" cannot be separated from interpretation.[8]

For only in the light of interpretation does something become a fact, and only within the processes of interpretation is an observation expressible. Heidegger's critique of the phenomenological concept of consciousness was even more radical, and—similarly in Scheler—he showed that even the concept of pure perception was dogmatic. The hermeneutical understanding of something *as* something was discovered to exist even in the so-called perception itself. In the final analysis, this means that for Heidegger, interpretation is not an additional or appended procedure of knowing but comprises the basic structure of "Being-in-the-world."

Does this mean that interpretation is an insertion [*Einlegen*] of meaning and not a discovery [*Finden*] of it? This is a question, apparently posed by Nietzsche, that obviously decides the rank and extent of hermeneutics—as well as the objections of its opponents. In any case, the point that must be firmly adhered to is this: only in the context of the concept of interpretation and on the basis of it does the concept of the text come to constitute a central concept in the structure of *Sprachlichkeit* [linguisticality]; indeed, the concept of text presents itself only in the context of interpretation, and only from the point of view of interpretation is there an authentic given to be understood. This is true even in the process of coming to an understanding in dialogue: in it one takes disputed statements and repeats them and thereby pursues their intentions to a binding formulation, in a process that generally results in a transcript or protocol. In a similar manner, the interpreter of a text asks what is really there in the text. This too can lead to a biased and prejudiced response to the extent that everyone who asks a question tries to find in the answer a direct confirmation of his or her own assumptions. But in such an appeal to that which is in the text, the text itself still remains the fixed point of relation over and against the questionability, arbitrariness, or at least multiplicity of the possibilities of interpretation directed toward it.

This is once again confirmed by the history of the word. The concept of "text" entered into modern discourse essentially from two contexts. On the one hand, there is the text of scripture, whose interpretation was carried out in sermons and church doctrine; in this case, the text represents the basis of all exegesis, which in turn presupposes the truths of faith. The other natural use of the word "text" is found in connection with music. Here a text is the text for song, the basis for the musical interpretation, and here too such a text is not so much something pregiven as it is rather something that comes out of the performance of the song. Both of these natural ways of using the word "text" today point back to the use of the word by Roman jurists of late antiquity who, after the Justinian codification of the laws, used this "text" to overcome disputes in interpretation and application. From this early point the word "text" found a wider extension and was used wherever something resists integration into one's experience and where a return to the supposedly given would provide a better orientation for understanding.

The metaphorical reference to the "book of nature" rests upon the idea of a text.[9] Nature is a book whose text was written by the hand of God and the researcher is called upon to decipher it; namely, to render it readable and understandable by way of his interpretation. Thus, we find the hermeneutical relationship involved in our concept of text whenever we encounter resistance to our assumption of the primordial meaningfulness of the given. The closeness with which text and interpretation are interwoven is especially clear whenever the tradition of a text is not always pre-given as a basis for an interpretation. Indeed, it is often interpretation that leads to a critical restoration of the text. If one were able to clarify this inner relationship of interpretation and text, one would be able to realize a considerable gain methodologically.

The methodological gain that accrues from our view of language is that "text" must be understood as a hermeneutical concept. This means that the text will not be approached from the perspective of grammar and linguistics, divorced from any content that it might have. That is to say, it is not going to be viewed as an end product whose production is the object of an analysis whose intent is to explain the mechanism that allows language as such to function. In contrast, from the hermeneutical standpoint—which is the standpoint of every reader—the text is a mere intermediate product [*Zwischenprodukt*], a phase in the event of understanding that, as such, certainly includes a certain amount of abstraction, namely, the isolation and reification that is involved in this very phase. But this abstraction moves in precisely the opposite direction from the one familiar to us in linguistics. The linguistics scientist does not want to enter into the discussion of problems of understanding the topic that is spoken of in the text; rather, he wants to shed light upon the way the language as such functions, whatever the text may say. So he does not make that which is communicated in the text his focus, but instead asks how it is possible to communicate something by means of the punctuation and symbolization that are given there.

From the hermeneutical point of view, on the other hand, understanding what is said is the main and only concern. For this, the proper functioning of language is merely a precondition. Another precondition is that an expression should be acoustically intelligible, or that a printed text be decipherable, so that understanding what is spoken or written is at least possible. The text must be readable.

Once again language usage offers us an important hint. We speak of the "readability" of a text in a rather mundane sense when we merely wish to express a minimum qualification for evaluating a style or judging a translation. Naturally, this is a figurative way of speaking. But as is often the case with such speech, the negative usage makes things thoroughly clear: the corresponding negative here is unreadability, and this always means that as a written expression the text did not fulfill its task of being understood without difficulty. We find here further confirmation that we always already look ahead to an understanding of that which is said in the text. It is only from this vantage point that we grant that a text qualifies as readable.

It is well known that the task of philology is establishing a readable text. Fulfilling this task, however, always presupposes that the philologist takes as his starting point a certain understanding of the text. Only where the text has already been deciphered and the deciphered text still does not allow itself to be unhesitatingly transformed into understandability, does one raise questions about what is really in the text and whether or not the traditional reading, that is, the commonly accepted reading, is correct. The treatment of the text by the philologist who produces a readable text corresponds completely to what happens in direct, and not only acoustical, auditory transmission. We therefore say that one has "heard" when one can understand. And correspondingly, uncertainty about understanding a specific reading of a text resembles the uncertainty connected with one's grasp of an oral message. In both cases feedback [*Rückkoppelung*] comes into play. A prior understanding, an anticipation of meaning, and a great many circumstances that do not appear in the text as such play a role in one's grasp of the text [*Auffassung des Textes*]. This becomes completely clear when it is a matter of translating from a foreign language. Here the mastery of the foreign language is a precondition. If one can speak of a "text" at all in such cases, it is because one not only has to understand it but also to transform it into another language. In this case it becomes a "text," for the thing that is said is not simply understood, but rather it becomes an object. The task is reproducing that which was meant from among the multiplicity of possible meanings, and this represents still another hermeneutical relation. Every translation, even the so-called literal translation, is some kind of interpretation.

Summing up what we have said: what linguistics focuses upon, insofar as it leaves out the reaching of an agreement in understanding about a certain matter, represents in terms of the process of understanding itself only a boundary instance of dealing with language. In contrast to the view prevailing in linguistics, I believe that what advances and makes understanding possible is precisely a forgetfulness of language, that is, a forgetting of the formal elements in which the discourse or text is enclosed. Only in cases where the process of understanding is disrupted, where understanding is not succeeding, are questions asked about the wording of the text, and only then can the reconstruction of

the text become a task in its own right. In everyday speech, we differentiate between the wording and the text itself, but it is not accidental that
either of these designations can also act as a substitute for the other. In
Greek, too, both the spoken language and writing are contained in the
concept of grammar. Indeed, extending the concept of the text to include what is spoken in oral discourse is hermeneutically well grounded.
For in every case, whether the text is spoken or written, the understanding of it remains dependent upon communicative conditions that, as
such, reach beyond the merely codified meaning-content of what is said.
One can say that if one needs to focus on the wording of the text, that
is, on the text as such, this is always motivated by something unusual
having arisen in the understanding-situation.

This can be observed in the use of the word "text" today just as
clearly as it can be demonstrated in the history of that word. Doubtless
there is a vanishing point, a level of texts where we could hardly ever call
a set of words a text [*Schwundstufe*], such as one's notes that prompt one's
memory. Here the question of the text is posed only when memory fails
and the notes appear alien and incomprehensible. Then it is necessary
to refer back to the signs and writing; that is, it is necessary to refer back
to the notes as text. Generally, however, notes are not considered a text,
because they serve as the mere memory prompt, a trace that is swal-
lowed up in the return of what was intended by the entry.

But there is another extreme case of understanding where one
does not generally speak of a text. I am referring to something like a
scientific paper or communication, which presupposes certain conditions of understanding from the outset. One sees this in the direction
of address found in it. It is directed toward a person with special knowledge. As was true in the case of notes which are only for myself, so too
scientific communication, even when it is published, is not for everyone.
It only tries to be understandable by someone who is well acquainted
with the situation and language of research. When this condition is fulfilled, the partner in communication will not generally return to the
text as text. He or she only does that when the information expressed
seems to be implausible and he or she must ask whether there is a misunderstanding somewhere. This situation is, of course, different from
that of the historian of science for whom the same scientific documents
really are texts precisely because they require interpretation, in that the
interpreter is not the intended reader, so one must bridge the distance
that exists between him or her and the original reader. The concept of
the "original reader," however, is extremely vague, as I have emphasized
elsewhere.[10] Perhaps in the course of further research it will gain more
exact definition. For the same reasons, one does not generally speak

of a personal letter as a text when one is its recipient. In this case, one enters smoothly into the written situation of a conversation, as it were, so long as no special disruption of understanding makes it necessary to refer back to the exact wording of the text. For a written conversation, then, basically the same fundamental condition obtains as for an oral exchange. Both partners must have the good will to try to understand one another. Thus, the question becomes one of how far this situation can be extended and its implications applied. What if no particular addressee or group is intended, but rather a nameless reader—or perhaps an outsider who wants to understand the text? The writing of a letter is an alternative form of attempting a conversation, and as in the case of immediate linguistic contact or in all smoothly functioning exchanges, only a disruption in communication provides a motive for reaching back to the text as the "given."

In any case, like one who is in an oral conversation, the writer tries to impart what he or she means, and that includes the other with whom one shares presuppositions and upon whose understanding one relies. The other takes what is said as it is intended, that is, he understands it because he fills out and concretizes what is said and because he does not take what is said in its abstract, literal meaning. That is also the reason one cannot say certain things in letters that one can say in the immediacy of conversation, even when one sends them to a partner with whom one is very close. There is too much that is omitted in a letter that, in the immediacy of conversation, carries the proper understanding; and furthermore, in conversation one always has the opportunity to clarify or defend what was meant on the basis of some response. This is recognized especially in Socratic dialogue and the Platonic critique of writing. The logoi [sayings] which present themselves totally cut loose from any specific situation of communication [*Verständigungssituation*]—and this is true of what is written as a whole—risk misuse and misunderstanding because they have dispensed with the obvious corrections resident within living conversation.

Here an essential consequence presses itself upon us that is central for hermeneutical theory. If every printed text is restricted in this way, this implies something in regard to the intention involved in writing itself. As a writer one knows all of the problems of putting words into writing, and one is always steered by the advance picture [*Vorblick*] one has of the recipient with whom one wants to reach a similar understanding. In living conversation one tries to reach understanding through the give-and-take of discussion, which means that one searches for those words—and accompanies them with intonation and gesture—that one thinks will get through to the other. In writing, the openness that is implied in seeking the words [in oral conversation] cannot be communicated because the text is written. Therefore a "virtual" horizon of interpretation and understanding must be opened in writing the text itself, a horizon that the eventual reader has to fill out. Writing is more than fixing something spoken in writing. To be sure, everything that is fixed in writing refers back to what was originally said, but it must also and equally as much look forward. Everything that is said is always already directed toward reaching an understanding, and this necessarily includes the other.

So we speak of the "text" of a transcript because, from the start, it was intended as a document, and that means that what is fixed in it can be referred to. Precisely for this reason, a transcript requires a special mark and signature. The same is true of contracts in business and politics.

These considerations enable us to articulate a summarizing concept that serves as a basis for the constitution of all "texts," a concept which at the same time makes quite clear the embeddedness of what we call a "text" in a hermeneutical context. Every return to the "text"—whether one is dealing with a real document fixed in writing or one that is merely the repetition of what has been expressed orally in conversation— takes us back to the "original document," back to what is to be accepted as identical in meaning to what was originally announced or pronounced, and this meaning should be maintained as a meaningful entity. The task prescribed to every effort to fix something in writing is that the thing being announced should be understood. The text should set down the original announcement [*Kundgabe*] in such a way that its sense is unequivocally understandable. Here the task of the scribe corresponds to the task of the reader, addressee, interpreter—that is, to achieve such an understanding, and then to have the printed text speak once again. To this extent, reading and understanding mean that the document is led back to its original authenticity. The task of interpretation is posed when the meaning-content of what is fixed in writing is disputable and one needs to attain the correct understanding of the tidings in the document. However, these tidings, this "thing that is being conveyed" [*Kunde*], are not exactly what the speaker or writer originally said, but rather what he would have wanted to say to me if I had been his original partner in conversation. It is well known as a hermeneutical problem in the interpretation of "commands" or "orders" [*Befehlen*] that such orders are to be followed "according to their general sense" [*Sinngemäss*] and not literally. Accordingly, we must say that a text is not an object but a phase in the fulfillment of an event of understanding, of a *Verständigungsgeschehen*.

This general state of affairs is particularly well illustrated by judicial codifications of law and correspondingly can be illustrated in judicial hermeneutics. For very good reasons, judicial hermeneutics can be seen as a model for us: here the transference into written form and the continual reference to the text are especially obvious. From the outset that which is established as law serves to settle or avoid physical struggle. This is always what motivates both the seekers of justice (the parties to a dispute) as well as the finders and speakers of justice (the judges) in their return to the text. The formulation of laws, of legal contracts or legal decisions, is thus an especially exacting task, and the fact that they are fixed in writing makes it all the more so. Here a verdict or an agreement should be formulated in such a way that its legal sense emerges from the texts univocally and in such a way that misuse or distortion is avoided. "Documentation" demands precisely this: that an authentic interpretation must be possible, even if the authors themselves, the legislators or the parties to a contract, are not there. This means that from the outset the written formulation must consider the interpretive free space that arises for the "reader" of the text who has to apply it. Here it is always a matter—whether by proclamation or codification—of avoiding strife, of excluding misunderstandings and misuse, and trying to make univocal understanding possible. In contrast to the public proclamation of a law or the actual closing of a contract, fixing the law or contract in writing is only a supplementary effort at security. This implies, however, that there remains here too a free space of concretization of meaning, of interpretation that accomplishes the practical application of the law.

The claim to validity in the laying down of law, whether codified or not, rests on the fact that it is a text. Therefore law, like the statute, constantly requires interpretation for its practical application, and conversely this means that interpretation has already entered into every practical application. Legal decisions, precedents, or the prevailing administration of the law, then, always have a creative legal function. To this extent, the example of law shows with exemplary clarity just how much every construction of a text is related in advance to its interpretation, that is, to its correct application in terms of the general sense of the text. I would maintain that the hermeneutical problem is basically the same for oral and written discourse. One thinks, for example, of taking testimony from witnesses. In order to guarantee their neutrality, witnesses are not supposed to be initiated into the larger context of the investigation and the rigors of the process of making a judgment. So the question that is put to them has something like the abstractedness of a "text," and the answer that they have to give is equally abstract. This means that it is like any written utterance. The discontent of a witness with the written transcript of her testimony bears this out. She certainly cannot dispute her language, but she does not want to let it stand in such isolation and would prefer immediately to interpret it herself. It seems to the witness that the duty of the court stenographer in making the transcript is to render an account such that, when the transcript is read back, every possible justice is done to the intended meaning of the speaker. Conversely, this example of the testimony of a witness shows how the procedure of writing, namely, the written component in proceedings, feeds back into the way in which the conversation is handled. The witness, whose assertions are already placed in an isolated context, is, so to speak, already isolated because the results of the investigation will be put into written form. A similar state of affairs obviously holds true in cases where one has given a promise, an order, or a question in writing: these situations, too, contain a separation and isolation from the original communicative situation, and they need the style of the writing to bring to expression the original meaning. What remains obvious in all these cases is the need to return to the original communication situation.

Adding punctuation is one way to make easier the right understanding of the document fixed in writing. The question mark, for example, is such an indication of how the written sentence must be correctly articulated. The very appropriate Spanish custom of putting a question between two question marks makes this basic intent clear in a persuasive manner. In this way, one already knows at the beginning of the sentence how one has to articulate the relevant phrases. On the other hand, such punctuation aids were not indispensable. They were not to be found at all in most ancient cultures. This confirms how understanding is still possible solely through the fixed givenness of the text. The mere sequence of written symbols without any punctuation certainly represents an extreme form of communicative abstraction.[11]

Now I should note that doubtless there are many forms of communicative behavior in language that cannot possibly be subjected to this kind of finality. There are texts that are texts to such a degree that they are regarded as self-evidently texts even when they are encountered totally apart from a person being addressed—for example, in literary representation. On the other hand, even within the communicative event itself, we find texts that offer resistance and opposition to being texts in the normal sense. To throw into relief what it means for a text to be a text in its fullest sense and to do so in terms of specific textual forms, I should like first to distinguish three forms of opposition to textuality. These will form a backdrop that will make more accessible what it is to be text in the eminent sense. I shall call these three oppositional forms "antitexts" [*Antitexte*], "pseudotexts" [*Pseudotexte*], and "pretexts" [*Prätexte*].

By "antitexts" I have in mind forms of discourse that oppose or resist being a text in the usual sense because in them the situation of interactive speaking in which they take place is the dominant factor. In this category falls every kind of *joke*. For the fact that we do not mean something seriously but rather expect that it will be taken as a joke surely has its place in the process and event of communication. It is in this event and not in the text itself that we find the signal that this is a joke—in the tone of voice, the accompanying gesture, the social situation itself, or whatever. Furthermore, a joking remark clearly belongs to a particular moment, and when the moment passes it really cannot be repeated. Basically, the same applies to a parallel classical form based on mutual agreement in understanding, namely, *irony*. For the use of irony presupposes a common set of prior cultural understandings [*gemeinsame Vorverständigung*]. When one is able to say the opposite of what one means and still be sure that what one really means is understood, this clearly shows one is operating in a functioning communicative situation [*Verständigungsituation*]. The extent to which such "play acting" [*Verstellung*] (which really is none) is possible in the modality of writing depends on the degree of communicative pre-understanding and of reigning agreement that readers have. We know that the use of irony existed, for example, in very early aristocratic society and made a smooth transition there into writing. In this context we may mention the use of classical citations [popular in antiquity], often in a bowdlerized form. Here, too, the use of this form had the aim of societal solidarity. In this case, there was the proud rule of certain presuppositions with regard to culture, and thus they served and validated the interests of the aristocratic class. However, in cases where the relations among these preconditions for mutual understanding are not so clear, the transition into the fixity of written form becomes problematical. Just for this reason, interpreting the use of irony often poses an extraordinarily difficult hermeneutical task, and even the hypothesis that one is dealing with irony may be hard to defend. It has been said, and probably not unjustly, that to interpret something as irony often is merely a gesture of despair on the part of the interpreter. On the other hand, in our everyday life, if we use irony and are not understood, this registers a clear breakdown in mutual agreement in understanding [*Einverständnis*]. All this makes it quite clear that for a joke or irony to be possible at all, one must presuppose the existence of a *mutual understanding* that supports it [*ein tragendes Einverständnis*]. Of course, one might argue that we could build up mutual understanding among people by having everyone recast ironic expressions into straightforward expressions that could not be misunderstood. Even if that were actually possible, such straightforward and unambiguous meaning in a statement will fall far short of the communicative meaning and power that ironic discourse possesses.

The second type of text-opposed texts or "countertexts" I have labeled "pseudotexts." I refer here to the use of elements in speaking and also in writing that do not actually transmit the sense but rather are fillers [*Füllmaterial*]. These provide something like rhetorical bridges over the flow of speaking. One could define the role of rhetoric in our speech by saying it is something over and above the merely factual content of our expressions—that is to say, the meaning-content that is conveyed in the text. It is that which pertains to the purely pragmatic and ritual functions of exchange through speaking, whether oral or written. This constituent part of language which is empty of real content I label the "pseudotext." Every translator knows this phenomenon when, in transposing a text from one language into another, he or she has to recognize what is self-evidently filler material in the text and deal with it in an appropriate way. Sometimes the translator assumes there must be some authentic meaning in this filler material, but carrying over this dead wood into the target language actually destroys the flow of what is supposed to be transmitted in the text. This is a difficulty that confronts every translator. We do not deny that the translator can often find equivalent expressions for such filler material, but the true task of translating means translating only the meaning-content in the text. Meaningful translation must recognize and eradicate such filler materials. However, looking ahead, I should emphasize the following point: what we are saying about pseudotexts does not apply at all to any text with true literary quality, those that I call "texts in the eminent sense" [*eminente Texte*]. Indeed, precisely on this difference rests the limit in translatability with regard to literary texts, for there is ultimately an untranslatability in eminent texts that shows itself in the most varied nuances of meaning.

The third form of text-opposing or countertexts I call "*pre*texts." I call communicative expressions *pre*texts when one's understanding is not complete when one grasps their overt meaning. Rather, something masked comes to expression in them. *Pre*texts are texts that we interpret on the basis of something that is precisely what they do not mean overtly. What they apparently mean is merely a pretense, an excuse, behind which is concealed the hidden "meaning" [*Sinn*]. The interpretive task, then, is to see through the wall of pretense and mediate what is truly coming to expression within the text.

To this type of text also belong ideologically slanted texts that are designed to shape public opinion. The very concept of ideology tells us that there is something in the media that shape public opinion that is not really reliable information, but has a hidden guiding interest for which the information distributed serves only as a pretext. Therefore the critique of ideology strives to go back behind the thing said and to find the interests that are masked in it—for instance, the special interest of the bourgeois class in the context of capitalistic conflicts of interests. Even so, it is interesting to note that the attitude of the "critique of ideology" [*Ideologiekritik*] can itself be criticized as ideological, in that it represents anti-bourgeois interests, or whatever interests they may be, while at the same time masking its own tendentiousness as critique. One may see the general motivation of this effort to get back to the hidden, underlying interests as a concern about the breakdown of consensus, something Habermas has called "distortion of communication" [*Kommunikationsverzerrung*]. Distorted communication manifests itself as a disruption of possible agreement in understanding, and this motivates us to search for the true meaning behind the distortions. This search turns out to be something like a decoding process.

The role that dreams have played in modern depth psychology represents yet another example of interpretation as a process of going back behind a wall of pretext. It is certainly a fact that the experiences in our dream life are inconsistent. In them the logic of ordinary experience is for the most part put out of play. Of course, that does not exclude the possibility that out of the surprise-logic of dream life there can also arise an immediately attractive meaning that is comparable to the unlogic of fairy tales. In fact, narrative literature has taken as one of its possessions the genre of dreams and fairy tales, as we find, for example, in the German Romantics. But in this case it is an aesthetic quality that is enjoyed in narrative literature in the play of dream fantasy. This naturally can be interpreted in a literary-aesthetic way. In contrast, the same story in an actual dream can become the object of a totally different kind of interpretation where one seeks to go behind the fragments of dream recollection in order to reveal a true meaning, a meaning which has only disguised itself in the dream fantasies and is capable of being decoded. It is this decoding that constitutes the tremendous significance of dream recollection in psychoanalytic treatment. With the help of dream interpretation, the analysis is able to set in motion an associative conversation that removes mental blocks and ultimately frees patients of their neuroses. As is well known, this process of so-called analysis goes through many complicated stages in reconstructing the original dream text and its meaning. Certainly this meaning is something quite other than what the dreamer "intended" or even what two dream interpreters may have read out at the beginning, a deeper meaning which now, through its clarification, has resolved the unsettling element in the dream experience. What motivates the interpreter to go back behind what is consciously "meant" [*das "Gemeinte"*], behind the wall of *pre*text [*Vorwand,* which also means "excuse"], is the fact that the event [*Geschehen*] of consensual understanding on which mutual agreement rests has been totally disturbed, put out of action by what we call "neurosis."

The same general interpretive structure is also found in the well-known psychopathology of daily life, which is an area quite separate from the concern with specific neurotic disturbances. In psychopathology, actions that go wrong [*Fehlhandlungen*] are rendered suddenly quite intelligible by recourse to unconscious feelings and impulses. Here again the motivation for going back to the unconscious is the incoherence, the basic incomprehensibility of the action in question [the *Fehlhandlung*]. Through the light that is shed on it, the puzzling action is rendered comprehensible and loses its irritating quality.

The relation between text and interpretation, which I have taken as the theme of this essay, takes a special form in these instances, a form which Ricoeur has named the "hermeneutics of suspicion." However, I believe it is a mistake to privilege these rare forms of distorted intelligibility, of neurotic derangement, as constituting the normal case in textual interpretation.[12]

The ultimate goal in everything I have discussed so far has been to show that the relation between text and interpretation is fundamentally changed when one deals with what is called the "literary text." In all the cases we have discussed so far, we have seen the motivation for interpretation come to light; something in the communicative process was constituted as a text, yes, but the interpretation, like the "text itself," was subordinated and ordered to a certain process of reaching agreement in understanding [*das Geschehen der Verständigung*]. This corresponds perfectly, of course, to the literal meaning of the term *interpres,* which refers to someone who stands between and therefore has first of all the primordial function of the interpreter of languages, someone who stands between speakers of various languages and through intermediary speaking brings the separated persons together. In the same way as an interpreter overcomes the barrier of a foreign language, so also within one's own language, when disturbances of agreement in understanding arise, something like this translation procedure is required, whereby the identity of what is being asserted is found by going back to the communicative event, and this means by dealing with it as a text.

In this form of interpretation, whatever is alienating in a text, whatever makes the text unintelligible, is overcome and thereby canceled out by the interpreter. The interpreter steps in and speaks, however, only when the text (the discourse) is not able to do what it is supposed to do, namely, be heard and understood on its own. The interpreter, then, has no other function than to disappear completely when full harmony in understanding [*Verständigung*] is achieved. The discourse of the interpreter, therefore, is itself not a text; rather, it *serves* a text. This does not mean, however, that the contribution of the interpreter to the manner in which the text is heard would completely disappear. The contribution is just not thematic, not something as objective as the text; rather, it has entered into the text. In general, this is the way the relation of text and interpretation is usually characterized. Interestingly enough, this is the point at which a hermeneutically structural moment pushes itself forward and comes into bold relief. This stepping between and speaking [*Dazwischenreden*] has the structure of dialogue. The interpreter of a foreign language, who is mediating between two parties, cannot avoid experiencing his or her own distance between the two positions as a kind of superiority over the partial perspective of each side. His or her help in reaching agreement in understanding is therefore not limited to the purely linguistic level; rather, it always gets into mediating the matter itself, and also seeking to bring about a settlement of the claims and boundaries between both parties. The one who was merely an "interlocutor" [*Der Dazwischenredende*] actually becomes a "negotiator" [*Unterhändler*]. Now it seems to me that a similar relationship exists between text and reader. When the text interpreter overcomes what is alienating in the text and thereby helps the reader to an understanding of the text, his or her own stepping back is not a disappearance in any negative sense; rather, it is an entering into the communication in such a way that the tension between the horizon of the text and the horizon of the reader is resolved. I have called this a "fusion of horizons" [*Horizontverschmelzung*]. The separated horizons, like the different standpoints, merge with each other. Indeed, the process of understanding a text tends to captivate and take the reader up into that which the text says, and in this fusion the text disappears!

But not in the case of *literature!* That is to say, there are texts that do not disappear in our act of understanding them, but instead stand there confronting our understanding with normative claims, and stand continually before every new way the text can speak. Now what is it that distinguishes these texts from all others? What does it betoken for the mediating discourse of the interpreter that a text can be "there" in this way?[13]

My thesis is this: these texts are only authentically there when they come back into themselves. And when they do, they are *texts* in the original and authentic sense. The words of such texts are authentically there only in coming back to themselves. They fulfill the true meaning of the text, so to speak, from out of themselves: they speak. Literary texts are such texts that in reading them aloud one must also listen to them, if only with the inner ear; and if one recites the text, one not only listens but inwardly speaks with them. These texts attain their true existence only when one has learned them "by heart." Then they live in memory, in remembrance by the great bards, the chanting choruses [*Choreuten*], the lyric singers. As if written in the soul, they are on their way to *Schriftlichkeit* [scripturality]! Thus, it is not surprising at all that in cultures that read, such distinguished texts are called "literature" [what is written].

A literary text is not just the rendering of a spoken language into a fixed form. Indeed, a literary text does not refer back to an already spoken word at all. This fact has hermeneutic consequences. In this case, interpretation is no longer merely a means of getting back to an original expression of something [*ursprungliche Äusserung*] and mediating it to the present. Instead, the literary text is text in a most special sense, text in the highest degree, precisely because it does *not* point back to the repetition of some primordial act of oral utterance. Rather, a poetic text in its own right prescribes all repetitions and speech-acts out of itself. No speaking can ever completely fulfill what is prescribed in a poetic text. The text of a poem exercises a normative function that does not refer back either to an original utterance or to the intention of the speaker but is something that seems to originate in itself, so that in the felicity of its success, the poem surprises and overwhelms even its author.

Thus, it is by no means accidental that the word "literature" has acquired a very positive value, so that something which belongs to the category of literature possess a special distinction. A text of this kind represents not just a translation of discourse into a fixed form; no, a literary text possesses its own authenticity in itself. When we look at the basic nature of ordinary discourse, we find that what constitutes it is that the listener needs both to follow it from beginning to end and at the same time to be focused on what the discourse is conveying to him or her. But in literature we find that *language itself* comes to appearance in a very special way.

This self-presentation of words is not easy to grasp correctly. Words in literary texts obviously still maintain their discursive meaning and carry the sense of a discourse that means something. The quality of a literary text is necessarily such that it leaves untouched this primacy of the content belonging to all discourse; in fact, the primacy of the discursive meaning increases so much that the relation of its assertions to actuality is suspended. This does not mean, however, that one should overemphasize how a text is said [*das Wie des Gasagtseins,* the how of its being said]. For then we end up speaking not of the art of the words but of the artistry, not of a certain tone that prescribes how a song is to be sung but rather about matters of poetizing imitation. That is to say, we would then be speaking not of a style whose incomparability we may rightly admire but rather of its manner, whose presence now is disturbingly noticeable. Nevertheless, it is true that a literary text demands to become present in its linguistic appearance and not just to carry out its function of conveying a message. It must not only be read, it must also be listened to—even if mostly with our inner ear.

Thus, it is in the literary text that the word first attains its full self-presence [*Selbstpräsenz*]. In a literary text not only does the word make what is said present; it also makes it present in its radiant actuality as sound. Just as style constitutes a very effective factor in a good text and yet such a text does not put itself forward as a piece of stylistic decoration [*als ein Stilkunststück*], so too the actuality of words and of discourse as sound is always indissolubly bound up with the transmission of meaning. Nevertheless, there is a profound difference between the functioning of words in ordinary discourse and in literature. On the one hand, in discourse as such we are continually running ahead in thought searching for the meaning, so that we let the appearance of the words disappear as we read and listen for the meaning being conveyed; on the other hand, with a literary text the self-manifestation of each and every word has a meaning in its sonority, and the melody of the sound is also used by the discourse to augment what is said through the words. In a literary work, a peculiar tension is generated between the directedness to meaning inherent in discourse and the self-presentation inherent in its appearing. Every part of speech, every member, every individual word that submits to the unity of meaning in the sentence, represents in itself a kind of unity of meaning insofar as through its meaning something meant is evoked. So far as the word issues forth from the play within its own unity and does not function merely as a means of conveying the meaning of the discourse as a whole [*Redesinn*], to that extent the multiplicity of meaning within the word's own naming power is allowed to unfold. Thus, in a literary text we refer to connotations that also speak along with a word when the word shines forth in its full meaning.

But the individual word as carrier of its own meaning and as co-carrier of the meaning of the discourse [*Redesinn*] is still only a very abstract moment in the discourse. Everything must be seen in the larger whole of syntax. Of course, in a literary text this is a syntax that is not unconditionally and not only the customary grammar. Just as the speaker enjoys certain syntactic freedoms that the hearer is able to accommodate because he or she is also taking in all the modulations and gesticulations of the speaker, so also the poetic text—with all the nuances which it shows—has its own freedoms. These nuances are so subordinated to the actuality of sound that they help the whole of the text to a greatly strengthened power of meaning. Indeed, even in the realm of ordinary prose we know that a discourse is not the same thing as a written document [*eine Rede keine "Schreibe" ist*], and a mere talk or lecture [*Vortrag*] given is not the same thing as a whole series of lectures [*Vorlesung*]—that is to say, it is not a [scholarly] "paper." This applies even more strongly in the case of literature in the eminent sense of the term. It overcomes the abstractness of being written not only in such a way that the text becomes readable, that is to say, intelligible in its meaning. Rather, a literary text possesses its own status. Its linguistic presence as text is such as to demand repetition of its words in the original power of their sound—not in such a way as to reach back to the original speaking of the words, but looking forward toward a new, ideal speaking. The web of connections between meanings is never exhausted in the relations that exist between the main meanings of the words. In fact, it is precisely the accompanying play of relations of meaning, a play that is not bound up with discursive meaning-teleology, that gives the literary sentence its volume. Certainly, these relations of meaning would never come to appearance at all if the whole of the discourse did not, so to speak, "hold onto itself" [*an sich hielte*], inviting the reader or hearer to tarry, and impelling the reader or hearer to become a listener more and more. This process of becoming a listener nevertheless remains, like every listening, a listening to something, to something that is grasped as the pattern or totality of meaning of a discourse [*die Sinngestalt einer Rede*].

It is very difficult to assign cause and effect here. That is to say: Is it the enhancement in volume that suspends a text's referential and message-conveying function and makes it a literary text? Or is it the reverse: that the suspension of any positing of reality is that which characterizes a text as poetry, and this means as the self-manifestation of language, and lets the fullness of meaning first emerge in its total volume? Manifestly the two factors are inseparable, and in the continuum between artistic prose and pure poetry, the place the text occupies will depend in each individual case on how strong a role is played by the manifestation of language in the totality of the meaning.

How complex the role of orderly sequence in discourse is in achieving unity, and how important the placement is of its building blocks, that is, the words, becomes clear in extreme cases—for example, when a word in its polyvalence suddenly pops up and asserts itself as an autonomous bearer of meaning. Something like this happens in what we call a "play on words" [*Wortspiel*]. For instance, it is not to be denied that often a play on words is used only as a kind of decoration in the discourse [*Redeschmuck*]—an ornament that allows the spirit of the speaker to radiate forth, while it remains fully subordinated to the intended meaning of the discourse. However, the play on words can also elevate itself to a kind of autonomy [*Selbständigkeit*] and declare its independence. In that case, the result is that what the discourse as a whole is supposed to mean suddenly is disturbed, and the clarity of its intention is lost. Behind the unity of the manifestation of the word in sound there suddenly shines forth the hidden unity of variegated and even opposing meanings. In this context, we recall that Hegel spoke of the dialectical instinct of language, and Heraclitus found in the play of words one of the best tools for illustrating his basic insight that opposed things are in truth one and the same. But that is a philosophical manner of speaking. Here too, it is a matter of breakdowns in the natural tendencies of meaning in discourse, which are productive for philosophical thinking precisely because language is in this way compelled to give up its immediate signifying of objects and to help bring to appearance mental mirrorings, mirrorings of thought [*gedanklichen Spiegelungen*]. The multiplicity of meanings found in wordplay represents the densest form in which speculative thinking comes to appearance, a thinking that explains judgments which oppose each other. Dialectic is the representation of the speculative, as Hegel says.

For the literary text it is a different matter, however, for precisely the following reason: the function of mere wordplay is just not compatible with the many riches and dimensions [*vielsagenden Vielstelligkeit*] of the poetic word. In a literary text, the accompanying meanings that go along with a main meaning are certainly what give the language its literary volume, but they are able to do this by virtue of the fact that they are subordinated to the unity of meaning of the discourse and the other meanings are only suggested. Plays on words, however, are not simply plays on the polyvalence of words out of which poetic discourse is shaped; rather, in them independent meanings are played off against each other. For this reason, a play on words actually shatters the unity of discourse and demands to be understood in a higher relation of reflective meanings. That is why, if someone persists in the use of wordplay and witticisms, we become irritated because it disrupts the unity of the discourse. Certainly in a song or a lyric poem, indeed everywhere that the melodic figuration of the language predominates, the insertion of a play on words does not enhance the effect. Of course it is somewhat different in the case of dramatic speaking, where the interaction is there to govern the scene. One thinks, for instance, of stichomythia in Greek drama, or in a drama where the self-destruction of the hero is already announced as a play on words in the hero's own name.[14] And again it is quite different where the poetic discourse takes the shape neither of the flow of narrative, nor the stream of song, nor dramatic presentation, but rather consciously engages in the mental play of reflection, to which obviously belongs the shattering of one's discursive expectations. Thus, in a very reflective lyric, the play on words can take on a productive function. One thinks, for instance, of the hermetic lyrics of Paul Celan. Yet one must also ask oneself here if the path of placing such a reflexive burden on the words does not in the end become no longer passable. It is quite clear that Mallarmé, for instance, tried out wordplays in some of his prose pieces, like "Igitur," but when he came to the full body of sound in poetic forms, he hardly plays with words at all. The verses of his "Salut" are certainly many-layered and fulfill expectations of meaning on various levels such as a drinker's toast and a balance sheet of life, wavering between the foam of champagne in the glass and the trail left in the waves by the ship of life. But both dimensions of meaning can be carried out as the same melodious gesture of language and in the same unit of discourse. The sonnet of Mallarmé, of which I offer an artless German paraphrase [represented here in English translation],[15] runs as follows:

Rien, cette écume, vierge vers	Nothing, this foam, innocent verse
A ne désigner que la coupe;	Points only to the edge of the cup;
Telle loin se noie une troupe	In the farther distance splash a troop
De sirènes mainte à l'envers.	Of sirens, mostly turned away.
Nous naviguons, ô mes divers	We travel thence, my many
Amis, moi déjà sur la poupe	Friends—I, already at the stern,
Vous l'avant fasteaux qui coupe	You at the proud bow which cuts
Le flot de foudres et d'hivers;	The flux of lightning and storms;
Une ivresse belle m'engage	A fine intoxication lets me
Sans craindre même son tangage	Without even fearing its oscillation
De porter debout ce salut	Offer, standing, this salute
Solitude, récif, étoile	Solitude, cliff, star
A n'importe ce qui valut	May be whatever it may be
Le blanc souci de noire toile.	Wherever the care of the white sail leads us.

This point also holds true for the *metaphor*. In a poem, a metaphor is so bound up with the play of sounds, word meanings, and the overall meaning that it does not really stand out as a metaphor. For in a poem the prose of ordinary discourse is not found at all. Even in poetic prose [*dichterische Prosa*] metaphor scarcely has a place. Metaphor disappears when the intellectual insight which it serves is awakened. Actually, rhetoric is the realm where metaphor holds sway. In rhetoric one enjoys metaphor as metaphor. In poetry, a theory of metaphor as little deserves a place of honor as a theory of wordplay.

This brief digression teaches us how multileveled and differentiated the interplay of sound and meaning is in speaking and in writing when it becomes literature. In fact, one begins to wonder how the mediating discourse of the interpreter could be taken over into the act of interpreting the poetic text at all. The answer to this question can only be approached in a very radical way. For in contrast to all other texts, the literary text is not interrupted by the dialogical and intermediary speaking of the interpreter; rather, it is simply accompanied by the interpreter's constant co-speaking. This allows the structure of its temporal character [*Zeitlichkeit*] which belongs to all discourse to be annulled. Indeed, the categories of time that we use in connection with discourse and works of art in language constitute a peculiar difficulty when it comes to literary texts. One speaks of "presence" in relation to literary texts and even of the self-presentation of the poetic word, as I myself did above. But I must emphasize: one draws a false conclusion if one thinks one can understand such presence with the language of metaphysics as presence-at-hand [*des Vorhandenen*], or with the concept of objectifiability. Objectifiability is not at all the presentness which belongs to the literary work; indeed, it does not belong to any text at all. Language and writing always exist in their referential function [*Verweisung*]. They *are* not, but rather they *mean,* and that also applies even when the thing meant is nowhere else than in the appearing word. Poetic speaking comes to fulfillment only in speaking [*Vollzug des Sprechens*] or reading itself, and of course this entails that it is not there without being understood.

The temporal structure of speaking and of reading is a phenomenon that has not been researched. The fact that one cannot apply the simple schema of succession here becomes immediately clear when one observes that such a schema really describes the process of spelling but not that of reading. And someone who wants to read by spelling things out is not reading. In general, the same principles apply to silent reading as to reading aloud. To read aloud well to another means to so mediate the interplay of meaning and sound that it seems to occur for itself and to come forth anew. When one reads aloud one reads to someone, that means one turns and addresses him or her. And the hearer belongs to the text. Reading out loud, like lecturing, remains "dialogical"

[*Vorsprechen wie Vorlesen bleibt "dialogisch"*]. Even the simple act of reading in which one reads something to oneself remains dialogical in that in it one must bring the sound and the meaning into harmony as much as possible.

The art of reciting poetry is not fundamentally different from this. It only demands a special technique because the audience is an anonymous mixture of people and yet it is necessary that the poetic text be taken up and realized in each individual listener. We are all familiar with a reciting practice we call *Aufsagen* [simply saying] that actually corresponds to spelling out what we read. Again, this is not really speaking but merely arranging a series of fragments of meaning one after another. In Germany, this happens when children learn lines of poetry by heart and recite them to the joy of the parents. In contrast, a person truly skilled in recitation, or a great artist, will render a linguistic gestalt fully present, like the actor who must play his role as if the words had been newly found at that very moment. This cannot be a mere series of pieces of discourse; rather it must be a whole, made up of meaning and sound, which "stands" in itself. For this reason, the ideal speaker will make not himself or herself but only the text present, which must in its full power reach even a blind person who cannot see his gestures. Goethe once said, "There is no higher and purer pleasure than with closed eyes to have someone recite to you—not declaim—a piece of Shakespeare in a naturally right voice." [16] One must ask, however, whether this kind of recitation is possible for every type of poetic text. Are there perhaps some where it is not possible at all? What about meditative poetry? Even in the history of lyric poetry this question arises. Choral lyrics, and in general every musical piece that invites one to sing with the singer, are completely different from the kind of tone one finds in the elegy. Reading meditative poetry seems possible only alone, only as a solitary process.

In any case, one sees that the time-schema of serial succession is totally out of place here. It is instructive to recall what in Latin class was called "construing," an art one learned in connection with parsing Latin prose. The student must look for the verb and then the subject, and from there work with the whole collection of words until elements that at the outset seemed disparate suddenly come together into a meaning. Aristotle once described the freezing of a liquid when it is shaken as a *schlagartigen Umschlag*, a sudden transformation. It is like this also with the suddenness of understanding, as the disordered fragments of the sentence, the words, suddenly crystallize into the unity of meaning of the whole sentence. Listening and reading apparently both have the time structure of understanding, whose circular character counts among the earliest insights of rhetoric and hermeneutics.

This general structure applies to all listening and all reading. In the case of *literary texts* the situation [*Sachlage*] is far more complex. There we do not just have to do with gleaning the information transmitted by a text. In reading a literary text one does not hurry impatiently and unswervingly to the end-meaning, the grasping of which signals that one has gotten the message. It is true that there is often something like a sudden instant of understanding here in which the whole formulation is illuminated. We find this phenomenon both in relation to the poetic text as well as the artistic image [in painting or sculpture]. Relations of meaning are recognized—even if they are vague and fragmentary. In both of these cases the process of copying the real is suspended. The text with its charge of meaning [*Sinnbezug*] constitutes the only present. When we utter or read literary texts, we are thrown back on the meaning and sound relations that articulate the framework of the whole, not just once but each time. We leaf back through the text, begin again, read anew, discover new dimensions of meaning. At the end what stands is not the secure consciousness of having understood the matter so that now one can leave the text behind, but rather just the opposite. The deeper one goes into the text, the more the charges of meaning and sound in it enter into our consciousness. We do not leave the text behind us but allow ourselves to enter into it. We are then in the text, just as everyone who speaks is in the words he or she says and does not hold them at a distance as if they were tools that one uses and then puts away. For this reason, to speak in terms of "applying" words is incorrect in a rather curious way. This usage does not come to grips with actual speaking, but instead deals with speaking as if speaking were like using the lexicon of a foreign language. When one is dealing with actual speaking, one must set fundamental limits on all discourse about rules and prescriptions. This applies with a vengeance to the literary text. The literary text is not "right" because it says what anyone and everyone would have said; no, it has a new, unique kind of rightness that distinguishes it as a work of art. Every word "sits" there in such a way that it appears almost without possibility of substitution, and in a certain way there really can be no substitute.

It was Wilhelm Dilthey who, in a later development of Romantic idealism, really pointed the way for us in this matter. In trying to defend himself against the prevailing monopoly of causal thinking, he spoke of a *Wirkungszusammenhang*—a context of effects instead of a simple cause and effect, that is, of a set of relationships existing among the effects themselves, leaving fully aside the fact that they each had their causes. For this purpose he introduced the concept of "structure," which later came to be highly regarded, and he showed how the understanding of structures necessarily has a circular form. Taking his cue from musical listening—for which absolute music with its extreme lack of conceptual content [*Begriffslosigkeit*] provides a prime example because it positively excludes all theory of representation—he spoke of a concentration into a middle point, and he made the temporal structure of understanding a major theme of his thinking. This has a parallel in aesthetics where, whether in reference to a literary text, painting, or sculpture, one speaks of its "structure" [*Gebilde*].[17] The general meaning of *Gebilde* suggests something not understood from the vantage point of a preplanned, finished state that one already knows in advance, but rather something that has developed into its own pattern from within and thus is perhaps to be grasped in a further formation [*Bildung*]. To understand this idea is, in itself, clearly an important task. The task is to build up and establish what a *Gebilde* is; to construe something that is not "constructed"—and that means that all efforts at construction are withdrawn. While it is true that for reading in general, the unity of understanding and reading can only be accomplished in a reading that understands and at that moment leaves behind the linguistic appearance of the text; for in the case of literary texts something else is there that constantly makes present the changing relationships of sound and meaning. The temporal structure of this movement [*die Zeitstruktur der Bewegtheit*] is something I call "whiling" [*Verweilen*, tarrying, lingering], a lingering that occupies this presentness and into which all mediatory discourse of interpretation must enter. Without the readiness of the person who is receiving and assimilating [*des Aufnehmenden*] the text to be "all ears" [*ganz Ohr zu sein*], no poetical text will speak.

In closing, perhaps a famous example may serve as an illustration. It is the final line of a poem by Mörike, "Auf eine Lampe" ["On a Lamp"].

[Mörike's poem reads as follows:

Noch unverrückt, o schöne Lampe, *schmückest du,*	Still undisturbed, oh beautiful lamp, thou adornst
An leichten Ketten zierlich *aufgehangen hier.*	On a light chain gracefully hung here.
Die Decke des nun fast vergessnen *Lustgemachs.*	The ceiling of a now almost forgotten pleasure room.
Auf deiner weissen Marmorschale, *deren Rand*	On your white marble skin, whose border
Der Efeukranz von goldengrünem *Erz umflicht*	The ivy wreath of golden green metal woven round

Schlingt fröhlich eine Kinderschar	A troop of children joyfully
den Ringelreihn.	twist in the ring dance.
Wie reizend alles! lachend, und	How attractive everything is!
ein sanfter Geist	Laughing, and a gentle spirit
Des Ernstes doch ergossen um	Of seriousness indeed suffuses
die ganze Form—	the whole form—
Ein Kunstgebild der echten Art.	An artistic shape of the authentic kind.
Wer achtet sein?	Being noticed by whom?
Was aber schön ist, selig scheint	But what is beautiful shines
es in ihm selbst.	blissfully in itself.]

The final line reads: "Was aber schön ist, selig scheint es in ihm selbst." ("But what is beautiful shines blissfully in itself.") This particular line was the focus of a discussion between Emil Staiger and Martin Heidegger.[18] I am interested in it here, however, only as an exemplary case. In this verse, one encounters two apparently trivial and commonplace words: *scheint es*. This can be understood in the sense of *anscheinend* [apparently], *dokei* [Greek: it appears], *videtur* [Latin], *il semble* [French], "it seems," *pare* [Italian], and so on. This prosaic understanding of the phrase certainly makes sense, and for this reason it has found its defenders. But one also notices that it does not obey the law of verse [*Gesetz des Verses*]. This will allow us to show why "scheint es" here means "it shines," or *splender* [Latin: radiates]. In this case, a hermeneutical principle can be applied: in cases of conflict [*bei Anstössen*], the larger context should decide the issue. Every double possibility of understanding, however, is an offense [*Anstoss*]. Here it is decisively evident that the word "beautiful" in the line is applied to a lamp. That is what the poem as a whole is asserting and is a message that should be understood throughout the poem. A lamp that does not light up any more because it has become an old-fashioned and bygone thing hanging in a *Lustgemach* [pleasure room] ("Who notices it now?"), here gains its own brightness *because it is a work of art*. There is little doubt that *das Scheinen* here was said of the lamp, a lamp which shines even when no one is using it.

In a very scholarly contribution to this whole discussion, Leo Spitzer described in great detail the *literary genre* of such thing-poems, and he presented in a very persuasive way their place in literary history. Heidegger, for his part, correctly explored the conceptual connection between *schön* and *scheinen*, which is reminiscent of Hegel's famous phrase about the "sensory appearing/shining forth of the Idea" [*sinnlichen Scheinen der Idee*]. But there are also other grounds for this interpretation that are immanent in the text. It is precisely the way the sound and meaning of the words work together that provides us with a clear further point that is decisive. The "s"-sounds in this final line form a firm web [*Was aber schön ist, selig scheint es in ihm selbst*], and together with the metric modulation of the line (a metric accent falls on *schön, selig, scheint, in,* and *selbst*), this constitutes a melodic unity of phrase that leaves absolutely no place for a reflexive irruption such as what *scheint es* in its prosaic sense would be. For in general we speak prose all the time, as Molière's Monsieur Jourdain learns to his surprise. In fact, precisely this has led contemporary poetry to extremely hermetic styles in order not to let prose break in. Here in Mörike's poem, such a wavering in the direction of prose is never far away. Several times the language of this poem actually gets close to prose (*wer achtet sein?*). Given the place of this line in the whole, namely that it is the conclusion of the poem, it has a specially gnomic weight. In fact, the poem illustrates through its own assertion why the gold of this line is not of the order of some kind of official monetary note, like a banknote, or a piece of information, but itself has its own value. This shining is not only understood but radiates out over the whole of the appearing [*Erscheinung*] of this lamp that hangs unnoticed in a forgotten pleasure room. And it never shines more brightly than in these verses. The inner ear hears the correspondences between *schön* and *selig* and *scheinen* and *selbst;* moreover, the *selbst* with which the rhythm ends and falls silent, lets the silent motion resound within our inner ear. It allows our inner eye to see the quiet self-streaming-away of the light [*Sich-Verströmen des Lichtes*], which we name "shining" [*scheinen*]. Thus, our understanding understands not only what is said about the beautiful and what is expressed there about the autonomy of the work of art, which does not depend on any context of use; our ear hears, and our understanding takes in, the shining of the beautiful [*den Schein des Schönen*] as its true nature. The interpreter gives his reasons, disappears, and the text speaks.

Translated by Richard E. Palmer

9

The Artwork in Word and Image: "So True, So Full of Being!"

"Wort und Bild" [translated here as "The Artwork in Word and Image"] can be considered Gadamer's definitive last statement on the philosophy of art. Written in 1992, it appeared for the first time in 1993 in volume 8 of his collected works, as one of two long essays at the end of a volume which contains 35 other essays on aesthetics and poetics. This essay brings together several themes that are headings for whole groups of essays in volume 8: aesthetics and truth, the actuality and transcendence of the beautiful, hermeneutics and art, and the limits of language. In other words, it is a summation of Gadamer's thinking on art. It is not quite as long as another major essay, "The Relevance of the Beautiful"—which was revised and enlarged from its 1974 publication and offered as a small Reclam paperback in 1977—but it is three times as long as the average of all the remaining essays in volume 8. This indicates its importance for Gadamer.

On Gadamer's philosophy of art, the three most important sources are his masterwork, *Truth and Method* (1960, trans. 1975, rev. 1989), his major essay, "The Relevance of the Beautiful," and this late essay.[1] This essay has an advantage over *Truth and Method* in not being distributed over five hundred pages of hermeneutical theory and other matters, and an advantage over "The Relevance of the Beautiful" in being more comprehensive in scope, and written two decades later. It is Gadamer's final argument for why artworks, whether in word or image, whether verbal or nonverbal, can claim to be deeply true.[2] Also, the two other works are readily available in English as books, but this essay appears here for the first time in English.[3] It is therefore an excellent choice for the present volume and was also chosen by Gadamer and Grondin for inclusion in our source volume, the German *Gadamer Lesebuch*.

Although the German text itself has no subsections, in a text of this length, the translator thought they might be helpful. He has invented and inserted eight section headings in brackets for the convenience of the reader. These are only approximate and never fully adequate indications of the content of the sections. Additional headings could and perhaps should have been devised, but the translator thought these would at least give a general indication of the content of the essay. The headings inserted are:

Introduction
The Absoluteness and *Gleichzeitigkeit* of Art
Some Greek Words and Concepts That Help Describe Our Encounter
    with an Artwork
A Closer Look at the Concept of the Beautiful
What Is Common to All Art
The Experience of Art
The Truth of Art, *Vollzug,* and Reading an Artwork
On Architecture and Decorative Art: Concluding Remarks

Two German terms, *Gleichzeitigkeit* and *Vollzug,* in the headings above could be defined here in at least an introductory way. *Gleich* in German means "like" or "the same." *Zeit* means "time," and *Zeitigkeit* means something like "temporality" or even "temporally vivid." So *Gleichzeitigkeit* refers to the fact that a work of art overcomes the passage of time, in effect, and remains as temporally vivid, speaks as powerfully now as in the time of its creation. *Gleichzeitigkeit* is sometimes translated as "contemporaneity," but Gadamer told me he preferred the word "simultaneity." But neither of these terms is quite equal to the range of the meaning of this key term. Gadamer explains it in some detail in the essay. *Vollzug* has an importance far beyond what might be assumed by the fact that it shares one of the headings above with two other terms. *Vollzug* is a word that pervades the last third of the essay. The word in German points to the "execution" or carrying out of an action, especially a mandated action, the actual consummation of a marriage beyond the mere ceremony, and the performance of a musical work at a time and place. It refers to the fact that the finite "beingness" in time of an artwork is not just a combination of its parts, but is the process and experience of their being encountered by a viewer or listener or reader. In the moment of their uptake the work is realized, it speaks, its *Sache* (matter) emerges, one understands, one even says "Aha!" Here we see the hermeneutical character of Gadamer's thinking about art. It is in the *interpretation* that the work has its being.

Two Greek words are also of particular importance in the essay: *to kalon* and *energeia.* The Greek word *kalon* is usually translated as "beautiful," and *to kalon* as "the beautiful." But the richness of this word in the Greek language and especially in Plato creates connections with the good, and with the fine as in a "fine statue," and with the true and right, as in right proportions. Gadamer asserts that one can say of a work of art that it is fitting, right, and even true. This is the sense of *kalon*. Here the word "true" has a broader meaning than a correspondence of an assertion with a state of affairs. It has overtones of rightness, proportionality, and even the good. Gadamer spells out these connections in Greek and uses them to enrich our conception of the experience of art. In fact, in Gadamer's essay, *to kalon* has a further significance because it is what both verbal and nonverbal forms of art *share*. They are impressive, fine, right, beautiful. *To kalon* is the factor that brings together both forms of art under one heading, a term with wondrous richness in Greek that deepens our understanding of art.

Energeia is a term in Aristotle associated with motion, energy, and ultimately aliveness. It is the energy of a person or an animal in being alive: aliveness. Gadamer associates this term, too, with the experience of the work of art. Its "being" as it emerges in an encounter experience has the aliveness that Aristotle captures in the word *energeia*, to which as Gadamer notes, he gives a special meaning in Greek. It is a part of Heidegger's philosophy and also Gadamer's to lament the loss of Greek overtones when such terms are translated into Latin, and by extension in modern times we have lost these connections, which Gadamer seeks to restore.

In translating this essay into English, the translator has followed Gadamer's preference for a free translation of his thought and not just of his words. Sometimes, to show the direction of his thought, connectives have been added that are unspoken but self-evident in the German but not in English, and tenses are changed to increase the clarity of the text. Occasionally an endnote has been added to provide data on sources familiar to German readers that is not included in the original text, and occasionally first names and birth and death dates not in the German have been added in the notes. Any errors in capturing the author's thought are sincerely regretted. The text has been submitted to a German student of Gadamer for review, as well as to a local group of philosophers in the Springfield and Jacksonville (Illinois) area, to see where more clarity was needed. Since the focus of the essay is on artworks, the translator has changed the title from "Word and Image" to "*The Artwork in* Word and Image," in part because the German words *Wort* and *Bild* have a resonance and meanings that they do not have in English; for instance, *Bild* often simply means "picture," but in German and in this essay it also refers to other works of art such as sculpture, painting, and other visual arts, so he has translated *Bild* as image.

* * *

The Artwork in Word and Image: "So True, So Full of Being!"

It may have come as a surprise to many readers that part 1 of my 1960 work, *Truth and Method*, does not take as its object of study the human sciences and humanities [*Geisteswissenschaften*] in the totality of their various disciplines, although the appearance of the term "hermeneutics" in the book's subtitle might lead one to expect this—but rather *art*—art itself.[1] In making art my starting point, I was, in truth, responding to the experience I had in my own teaching, namely, that my real interest in the so-called *Geisteswissenschaften* was not in their character as sciences [*Wissenschaften*], but rather in how they dealt with *art*—art in all its realms: literature, the visual arts, architecture, and music. For I believe that the arts, taken as a whole, quietly govern the metaphysical heritage of our Western tradition. And the *Geisteswissenschaften* stand in a particularly close and interactive relationship with receptivity and sensitivity to art. For this reason I believe they are able to claim a philosophical authenticity of their own. This is why the general topic of "artworks in word and image"[2] has occupied my thinking from early on and why, again and again, I have sought to deal with it.

As everyone knows, the relationship of nonverbal art to verbal art is an old, classical topic with which we moderns have been very familiar at least since Gotthold Lessing's *Laocoon* (1766). Lessing's famous analysis—of how the poetic word and the pictorial shape, in this case a statue, were able to bring something to statement in contrasting ways—was directed towards differentiating between them. If Lessing wanted to trace the pictorial arts back to next-to-each-otherness in space and poetry back to succession in time, then Herder already contradicted him. What keenly interested me, however, in contrast to Lessing, was trying to work out what the art of making a picture or sculptural image and the art of making a poem have in common, and to take this common element and place it within a more general classification that says art is a "statement of truth."

In taking up the topic of artworks in word and image, I do not propose to deal with the important hermeneutic question of how an interpreter can capture pictorial or sculptural works in words or how it is possible to find a pointing word that does not just express thoughts prompted by a picture, but rather leads to a better seeing of the work itself. Certainly this is a topic that has an important place in the theory of interpretation. But what will occupy me here is the question of how word and image, the art of the word and all the visual arts, share in a common endeavor, and how, within this commonality, the role is determined that the one or the other will play in forming our culture.

Now in what does the true commonality between art in images and poetry consist? Certainly we call both creations "works of art," and by this we understand that they are marked by an immediate presentness in time and at the same time by a rising above time. To the extent that we are familiar with its language, a literary work that we recognize as worthy of being called "literature" speaks to us across all temporal distance. Similarly, a picture or sculpture that is worthy of being called a "work of art" has the power to affect us now. Both forms of art require that one tarry with its form as one views or hears it, and in both cases— to speak with Kant—there is much that is completely unnameable to which the work directs our thinking.

In my own effort at developing a hermeneutical philosophy, I have sought to validate the claim of art to truth and to show the significance of this for the human sciences. In connection with this I have, among other things, also tried to refute the idea that the art image is a mere copy of something. In poetic language there is also something that corresponds to this. I took this matter up and made it thematic in part 3 of *Truth and Method* under the vantage point of arguing for the linguistic character of art. What truth can mean in this context was only prepared for there and was further developed in my 1984 essay, "Text and Interpretation." [3]

So the classical posing of the question by Lessing in his famous *Laocoon* essay on the relationship of plastic and literary art takes a different form for me, and I have over the years dedicated many essays to concretizing this question. What we call "art" today is obviously not limited to this classical pair of arts. The question of truth also arises in other forms of art: in music, dance, theater, and especially in architecture. Along with the arts we have just named, there are arts in which one cannot speak of the self-presentation of the work of art in the same way, because their works are classified according to the purposes they serve in the praxis of life. These forms of art can at best claim a kind of co-presence for their artistic dimension, which remains in the background. In this category of arts, above all, are oratory, architecture, and all decorative art. To make the conclusions of our argument here more persuasive, we will touch upon these cases, too. But art in the form of the poetic word and in the form of the shaped image will remain central.

[The Absoluteness and *Gleichzeitigkeit* of Art]

The nature of hermeneutical reflection requires a constant return to the praxis of hermeneutic experience. Schleiermacher confessed quite candidly, "I hate all theory that does not grow out of practice." To me, this statement was an important confirmation of my own way of proceeding. In my own early studies in art history, literary history, and in my training as a classical philologist, whatever the limits of all these may have been, I found myself led more and more, if I wanted to prove the claim of art to truth, into the study of the pictorial and plastic arts and the art of poetry. Certainly the pictorial magic of the early cave paintings or other prehistoric plastic images is deeply significant, and, on the side of language, the earliest saying in art is in the prior mythic world that stands behind our literary heritage and fades back into the distance; both have remained a part of the picture for me. For all of these, I find that the same affirmation still applies that we often utter as we recognize a work of art is "right," namely, "So ist es!" ["That's it!" or "Yes, that's the way things are!"].

This leads me to one of the fundamental concepts of modern philosophy, a term which originated in the Neoplatonism of late antiquity and attained the status of a key word in German idealism. It had survived since antiquity and enjoyed an afterlife in which it was, for the most part, accorded no thought, but in our context here it reclaims its original sense. It is the concept of the "Absolute." The word in its general Latin root simply means that which is independent. In classical Latin it serves as the counter-concept to the relative. The term "absolute" means independence from all restrictive conditioning. Thus, Hegel speaks of "absolute Spirit" [absolute Geist] as that which is a constant, full presence to itself and which is fulfilled in absolute knowledge. And for Hegel art attains its timeless presentness because, like religion and philosophy, it is detached from and independent of all historical-social conditions. Art also claims absoluteness because it transcends all historical differences between eras. So we understand at once why Hegel maintained the inner closeness to each other of art, religion, and philosophy. In all three cases it had to do with a certainty of being that was absolute.

Christian theology understands the eschatological validity of the Christian message in terms of its contemporaneity [Gleichzeitigkeit], of its being the very same now, in the here and now—that is to say, in terms of the promised return of the Redeemer that truly occurs now, today in the acceptance of the faith. This is something of which Kierkegaard has reminded both his century and the twentieth century, which were dedicated to historical thinking. This contemporaneity also holds for philosophy because it is in constant dialogue with all the great thinkers in our Western tradition as if they were contemporary with us. And it is the same in the history of art. When one views the whole of art, it is certainly not possible to think in terms of some kind of historical "progress" toward an ultimate completion. Even though one can see the development of one-point perspective in art as progress, as the solution by painting of the problem of space, this certainly is not the final consummation of pictorial art as such. Even Hegel's construction of world history, according to which everything that happens is directed toward freedom, is basically a description of what the struggle of world history is at its core. And this concept also applies to philosophy, which poses the old questions about ultimate things in ever new ways and therefore these questions remain contemporaneous with us. This is the reason that Hegel himself arranged the history of philosophy as the dialectical unfolding of philosophical knowledge.

But what is the "time" of this contemporaneousness or "simultaneity"?[4] First, what is our own "present time"? Are we not somehow always aware of it? The word for present, *Gegenwart* [*warten* = waiting], already points to the fact that in it the future is in play. The future, as what is coming, is the present that "waits" for us, and that we await. All expectation of the future as such, however, rests on experience. Therefore, in every present moment not only is a horizon of the future opened up, but also the horizon of the past is in play. Even so, the present is less memory and backward-looking thought than it is present experience! In much the same way, both philosophy and art attune themselves to their own present time. In art and philosophy one does not have to know from what distance in the past, or from what foreignness, what one encounters comes. Each has its presence and is not gazed at as strange; rather, it draws you into its path—even if there may also be much that is foreign in it to be overcome.

Every present moment has its own life-space and its own tradition, which are manifested in its forms of life, in its morals and customs, and in all the institutions of social life; everywhere elements of one's religious heritage accompany one and one's own heritage and they are a part of one's distinctive character. It is characteristic that every religion is convinced of the absoluteness of its own truth. Religions find themselves constantly setting up boundaries between themselves and other religions, whose adherents are the "unbelievers." In our enlightened times this is still with us in the debate with a growing atheism. This poses new difficulties. Today we need to unite the claim to absoluteness which belongs to the nature of all holy knowledge with the recognition of other traditions and even to develop a solidarity with social structures that are completely hostile to religion.

This is a task facing humanity today, and it is a task for which the experience of art can strengthen our resolve. Certainly in the realm of art there are certain respected traditions and firmly established tastes.

And the artistic creations of other ages or distant cultures many times cannot reach us very easily. But in the long run, art in all its innumerable forms gains our acceptance, even the most strange. This demonstrates, I think, the absolute presentness of art to all times and places. An artwork is able to build bridges that reach beyond the enclosure and space in which it originated. This is shown most impressively today in music. In just a few decades East Asians have appropriated Mozart and Schubert and works of European music, so fully indeed that interpreters of music who come from there now number among the leading figures of our musical life. On the other hand, as we well know, Europe has taken to itself many of the musical languages of Africa.

Obviously in our world of many languages, the barrier of language remains difficult to overcome when one is dealing with a work of art that is being presented in another language. Yet even in literature our literary age has attained a kind of contemporaneousness with other cultures in what we call "world literature." Partly because of translations and partly because an ever greater circle of readers is familiar with foreign languages, one can speak of a vivid presentness and also contemporaneousness [*Gegenwärtigkeit und Gleichzeitigkeit*] even in the literary arts. Of course, for the pictorial and plastic arts the barriers of language do not enter in as much, or at least they can easily be overcome.

In pictorial art, of course, what is foreign will affect one in a strange way. But precisely an effect of strangeness is able to trigger its own power to attract, which leads to the viewer's appropriation. From time immemorial, there has existed a continuous interaction between cultures and ages. Every tradition appropriates what it encounters in order to move forward in the continuous process of enriching its tradition. But we should not forget that this appropriating does not mean just *knowing* but also *being.*

In the European tradition to which we belong, a "historical consciousness" has gotten more and more highly developed, although the path has been long. And this has brought an increasing refinement of our historical sense. With the development of trade and travel throughout the world, especially since the nineteenth century, and with new techniques of transmitting the news which have also refined our sense of the world, it seems that we have entered into something like an "age of reproductions." Nietzsche, in his famous essay titled "On the Advantages and Disadvantages of History for Life," was the first to see a problem in this. According to Nietzsche, the combination of historical research and a basically scientific consciousness has led to a weakening of the general mythos in our culture, which is the only thing able to give it style and shape. In the shifting light that is falling over them, things lose their own weight. We can see this in the fact that even the experience of art has come to be seen as merely one of the pleasures belonging to a historically refined education. We encounter this phenomenon, for example, when visitors in a museum congratulate themselves on recognizing a master or a familiar motif as coming from a given period. But this recognition does not at all represent the real immediacy of a genuine experience of art. For experience in its deeper sense as experience is never merely a confirmation of expectations but a surprise of them. Even at the high point of the "historically cultured" education of the nineteenth century, one was never able to see the artistic creations of a past age through the eyes of that past age. And actually to do so cannot and should not be one's goal. No, it is the vivid presentness and contemporaneousness of art that constitute and maintain its power. Indeed, I find something repellent in the very idea that art, which possesses such a captivating presentness, could become a mere object of historical research. Just for this reason, I wish to pose here the question of what it is that establishes art's superiority over time, a superiority that defies all restrictions.

Certainly I do not wish to exclude the possibility that scientific research, which undertakes many very important historical tasks, can also accomplish something with regard to the experience of art. But the kind of knowing in science remains, as such, something quite different from experiencing the presentness of art. Schleiermacher once said that a religious picture from a bygone century which we admire in the museum always has burn marks on it, as if it had been rescued from a fire. Such a picture, we know very well, has lost its place-in-life in a church or palace or wherever it was once at home. And certainly we don't just recognize this today; we also learn to see in the picture itself, for example, how it has been painted for a certain place in the world and for a certain cultic function. And with this we learn to see the relationships of light and shadow and to have in mind the circumstances which had influenced the shaping of the picture. All this can teach us to see better. This is even more true, of course, with regard to the very detailed knowledge we now have in the religious and profane realms of study for which we are indebted to the methods of science. But I believe the remark of Hegel still holds today: we no longer bow down before crucifix or Madonna.

Still, much else will be speaking to us along with the statement made by the work of art, and this will enrich it, in some cases more and in others less. For instance, the prior influences of one's religious heritage or of one's own historical experiences are always operative in one's experience of an artwork. Nevertheless, what grips us in a picture or stage play or poem suffers no substantial restriction if one has only "a little" background knowledge. So we ask: what is it that makes a picture or a poem into a work of art that has such an absolute presentness for us? Certainly it is not the noisy waves of the constant flow of information in this age of reproducibility. Rather, this reproducibility actually threatens to disintegrate the "aura" of the work of art, as Walter Benjamin has noted.

[Some Greek Words and Concepts That Help Describe Our Encounter with an Artwork]

In order to deal with the question that concerns us here, I would like to begin with a linguistic observation that will throw some light on this question. In Greek, the word *poiesis*, in which we recognize our German word *Poesie* [poetry], has a double meaning. The word means, first of all, "to make," that is, the construction or production of something that did not exist before. This word encompasses the entire realm of producing things that we call works of *handi*craft [hand*werk*], but it also includes the further development of ways of producing things right up to industrial production in modern times.

Along with this, however, the same word *poiesis* has the special meaning of the art of composing poetry. To compose poetry is in a certain sense also a making, a producing. But this word does not refer either to a lecture given only once, or to the writing down which takes place in the case of poetry. Rather, the making of which we are speaking in the case of poetry is the making of a "text." In this making whole worlds are able to rise up out of nothingness, and nonbeing comes to be being. This is almost more than making. With making in general go concrete materials, at least, that have to be given to the craftsman in advance and from which he constructs something. Mnemosyne [goddess of memory, mother of the nine Muses], however, does not need these. In the pictorial arts, the making is a real making insofar as it does require concrete material out of which the picture is constructed. In contrast, poetry appears to exist only in the airy breath of language and in the miracle of memory. For the Greeks, it shares this with music, which, however, only accompanies the poetic song. Nevertheless, both poetry and music are as if not made from matter. It remains a secondary moment when poetry is finally fixed in writing and become "literature" [something that can be read] and music becomes a score. This writtenness is secondary in both cases and is not a necessary condition either to poetry or to music. What is necessary to them is that the written texts as such attain to speaking and come to be heard. The German use of the word *schöpferisch*—"creative"—signifies this. It retains an echo of the religious concept of the Creation, which was not making in the sense of making an object by hand. In the beginning was the word, the *verbum creans*—the creating word.

Another semantic fact pointing in the same direction is linked with the word "work." This word is encountered first of all in the vicinity of what the word *techne* means in Greek. What *techne* means, however, is not the act of making or producing but rather the mental capacity for devising, planning, undertaking something—in short, the knowledge that actually *guides* the making. In such a context one can always say that the action, the *ergon*, brings something about; still, we scarcely call it a "work" in such a case! The fact is that when one is not dealing with art, one does not speak of a "work." Why is this? One does still speak of "handiwork" in the case of craftsmanship. Apparently the reason is that the handiwork—a work of craftsmanship, like industrial production, but not of art—is not truly there for itself but stands in a serving function. It has been constructed for some purpose. In contrast to this, an artist, even if he or she uses mechanical means of production, constructs something that is for itself and is there only to be contemplated. One allows an artwork to be exhibited or would like to see it exhibited, and that is all. And precisely *then* is it a *work*. And it remains a work *by* the artist, which, as a work by the artist, can be signed.

This is the case even when something like an organ improvisation, the work of a creative instant, becomes so persuasive that it makes a "lasting" impression. Likewise, plastic arts like painting or sculpture go through the same thing that is expressed in linguistic terms of passing from *poiesis* [producing] to *poesie* [a thing made]. For the poet, too, his or her creation creates and shows us a world that is there for itself and as such. In the modern world we say that the work "is published." Of course, the term "published" is used not only for what is poetic but also in reference to the publication of science and other forms of information. But it has a special sonority when the work being published belongs to what we call "literature." In this case, the term "literature" has a sound telling of existence and validity, a tone different from when the literature is only pop literature or merely the specialized "literature" of a scholarly discipline.

Beginning with some observations about how words are used, we are able to confirm that when we speak of the absoluteness of art, this has an exact and literal meaning. What we observed to be the semantically distinguishing marks of the poet and of poetry for the Greeks has, as has been shown, its parallels with the resonance that the word for "art" has attained in modern times. The same thing holds for the modern derivatives of the Latin word for "art" in other languages. What we find running through these word usages accurately describes the path that leads from a producing that is directed toward and determined by a certain use and benefit, to a producing that brings about nothing useful, something that is not used for anything. And the "freedom" this work has is truly a distinguishing mark of the beautiful. This is the reason why the expression "fine art"—*schöne Kunst* [beautiful art]—has also been used in reference to art. The beautiful is something about which it is never appropriate to ask what it is "for."

These remarks on the concept of the "fine arts" supplement the analysis put forward in *Truth and Method* where my summing-up in the last pages deals with the contrasting Greek concepts of *kalon* (fine) and *chresimon* (useful). In the concept of arts that are free of useful purpose one already senses the closeness between the theoretical and the aesthetic, and therewith the closeness between the experience of contemplating the beautiful and knowing the true. The concept of the beautiful [*kalon*, fine] in Greek thought is very closely connected with the concept of the true, and, yes, even with the concept of *arete* [virtue/excellence] which, contained in the well-known expression of *kalokagathia* [goodness], represents the ideal concept of human excellence. On this point, Aristotle, who loves distinguishing one thing from another, gives us a point[5] to ponder when he determines that "good" always has to do with praxis, but "beautiful," in contrast, has to do above all with unchanging things,[6] and therefore with the realm of numbers and geometry. Thus, the three kinds of the beautiful that he names are *taxis* [order], *symmetria* [symmetry], and *horismenon* [the definite]. This corresponds to the line of argumentation in *Metaphysics* M 3 and 4, which lays the groundwork for the critical discussion of the doctrine of Forms and at its end leads into the most authentic domain of Aristotelian thought—the *Physics*.

Aristotle's testimony is so very important here because it brings to light the closeness which exists between the semantic field of *poiesis*, art, and work, on the one hand, and the semantic field of the beautiful and the true, on the other. The beautiful here remains close to the realms of knowing and recognizing. In light of this, it is not surprising that our return to the Greek beginnings in Western thinking, and therewith to the metaphysical role that the concept of beauty played there, is of central importance for hermeneutical philosophy. When I took the experience of art as my starting point in *Truth and Method,* it was in order to show the wide compass of hermeneutics in my topic, and to place it within the universal meaning of *Sprachlichkeit*—linguisticality. And then my return at the very end of the book to the concept of beauty and the breadth of the realm of its significance further serves, I think, to substantiate the universality of hermeneutics.

[A Closer Look at the Concept of the Beautiful]

The concept of the beautiful in Plato brings us into contact not only with the concept of the good but also with the concept of the true, and with the standpoint of questioning in metaphysics, as such. In dealing with the concept of the beautiful, we have to do not only with art as such, but also with the much broader concept of the beautiful as a topic in the Platonic dialogues. Indeed, in these dialogues it is clear that what is meant by the beautiful is not art, as such. One need only think of Plato driving the poets out of the ideal state or his challenging assertion that art stands at a double remove from the truth.[7] In doing this Plato is applying his concept of mimesis: for him, the individual thing is in each case an imitation of the idea. Making a copy in art, according to this concept of mimesis, becomes an imitation of what was itself an imitation. This represents a conscious sharpening of the point by Plato. In contrast, Aristotle sees in "mimesis" not so much the difference between imitations and the thing imitated, the idea; rather, he emphasizes the similarity of both.[8] Therefore what the mimesis really accomplishes, according to Aristotle, is a cognition of something, because cognition, as such, is precisely a recognition. I have discussed this point elsewhere.

When Plato speaks of *aletheia* [truth] and sees truth connected with beauty, he is not thinking of art and he is also not thinking of the poets, who have much to say that is true but as the saying goes, "The poets lie a lot." What Plato has in mind with this connection between truth and beauty is a joy in pure forms and colors, but not in flowers or animals "or copies of them" (*Philebus* 51c). This passage in the *Philebus* teaches quite clearly how little weight Plato actually accords to copying as such. Rather than this, we find in the profound late dialogues of Plato that the concept of the beautiful, the concept of truth, and the concept of the good all step into the foreground. What Plato seeks in these dialogues as "the good life" is not the pure exactness of a mathematical type, but the measured proportionality of a well-mixed drink of life. It is there that the good is to be sought. This is the idea put forward in the *Philebus*.

In connection with this, the famous and much-discussed expression in the *Philebus* (65a) is of special interest: that the good, which

Socrates had been seeking as the right mixture of being, "has taken refuge in the beautiful."[9] When it is emphasized there that the good only permits of being grasped within the threeness [*Dreiheit*] of beauty, symmetry, and truth, this shows how important it is for Plato that the Good be clearly beyond being, and that it contain in itself not only the One but necessarily, the many. This also includes the important point that it is in the "measured" character of appearances that beauty presents itself.

There is a parallel passage in the *Statesman* (283b ff.) where Plato goes into this same topic. In this case, Plato seizes the opportunity to engage in an almost absurd digression. The dialogue partner laments that the way of dialogue is too long and difficult. In reply, the Stranger justifies it through a long debate about the two kinds of measure and the fact that in the end one always comes to the proper measure, to appropriateness. The dialogue partner here is "the young Socrates" and truly not the Socrates of the *Republic* who ridicules the stargazers. But the older Socrates in the *Philebus*, too, is also no longer the one in the *Republic* (which is not to say anything about the time of origin of these dialogues, or indeed of Platonic thought).

In the *Statesman* one finds an elaborately developed presentation dealing with two arts of measure, and there, if I see it rightly, the "proper measure" or the appropriate (*metrion*) is designated as "the exact itself." But in any case, this is not the pure exactness which it is the distinction of mathematics to provide through numbers and measurements. Nor may one see in this expression an allusion to numerological metaphysics in Plato, as Werner Jaeger has maintained. He misses the point completely. Indeed, it is expressly stated in the dialogue that the "exact itself" has to do with doing the appropriate, the fitting, and the needful at the favorable moment.[10]

What this clearly means is the median between opposites. This is not a number mysticism but on the contrary, an anticipation of the doctrine of the mean in Aristotle's *Nicomachean Ethics*. It is through this teaching that Aristotle defines the concept of the ethos and of virtue. Plato emphasizes that both concepts of the measured are indispensable. But if, here in the realm of ethics, he has in mind what he calls "the exact itself," it is clear that we have to do here with what is perfectly suitable because the application of the "pure" knowing found in mathematics does not suffice to indicate the perfectly suitable. So manifestly this is how it is with musical harmony, harmoniousness, with the beautiful. In these cases, in fact, the smallest deviation from the proper is bad. A single bad note in music, as well as in human dealings with each other, already disturbs the harmony and the agreement. In either case one cannot say at all what the appropriate thing would really have been, and yet we know very well that the inappropriate is what has disrupted the harmony.

One would perhaps find such a presentation, which is supposed to establish that the conditioned character of the argument process is inexact, to be not completely in place here. But actually Plato uses this means to give emphasis to his point. He emphasizes here the importance of making correct distinctions, which he calls dialectic, and through dialectic, of turning critically away from those "wise people" who are blind to exactness.[11] These "wise people" make a fundamental mistake if they acknowledge the difference between the pure relationships of number and measuring, but do not recognize the difference that separates this measuring from the "exact itself." In truth, they neglect in this way the true sense of the "pure" and take it to be something which exists in the world. Then they hold something to be a proof of something when, as in the case with the famous squaring of the circle, they are accepting only the sensory appearance as valid. This is like the error into which the architect falls when he insists on taking mathematical exactness as the right measure of exactness. Aristotle criticizes this error in the Platonists.

Our return to ancient times to examine the concept of beauty, to which the closeness of beauty and truth in ancient thinking invited us, admittedly now seems to end in disappointment with regard to the question of art. It looks as if the problem of art and its claim to truth find no support here at all. The discussion of beauty is always about mathematics and the pure relationships to which the mathematical science of numbers and circles was dedicated. In many places Plato gives the appearance of having based his view of sculpture and the pictorial arts as well as poetry on the crudest concept of copying. Against this view, our main interest has been to free ourselves altogether from this concept of art as a copy of something else, and at the same time sought to find a concept of truth which would be valid for both the nonverbal arts and for poetry.

To do this, we need first of all to go more precisely into the formation of certain concepts that were in play within Greek metaphysics. When we do this, we find some very interesting connections that help us defend our standpoint. Now certainly in Aristotle's eyes Plato was a Pythagorean, and indeed one can see Plato as more a meta-mathematician than as a metaphysician. But the inner consistency of the Greek way of thinking moves Plato and Aristotle closer together, and precisely this connection is significant for the question of what makes art art, and of what the absoluteness and contemporaneity of art are based on. In any case, it is not when one sees a picture, statue, or poem as a copy of something that Goethe's exclamation, "So true, so full of being!" becomes understandable. His exclamation does not refer to something special about the muscles in a sculpture, its appearance, its form, or how well it is portrayed; rather, Goethe refers to something that lies beyond our grasp—and precisely its ungraspability is what makes an overwhelming impression on us. Art can be overwhelming for us when it appears to be a copy of something but also when it is a complete departure from all copiedness, as can be the case in abstract painting and sculpture. Clearly, we are dealing here with something quite different from the relationship of original and copy. Works of art possess an elevated rank in being, and this is seen in the fact that in encountering a work of art we have the experience of something emerging—and this one can call truth!

One should not be astonished by the fact that neither in ancient times nor in the Christian Middle Ages was there any discussion of the elevated rank in being that is possessed by works of art. The reason for this is that their "place in life" was already self-evident for the ancient world and its sacred orders. The ecclesiastical as well as secular forms of Christian metaphysics both accepted as fact that the order of the world, which was also the order of creation, included with it a high rank for works of art. This was also true for the literary arts, whose myths and sagas were compellingly brought forth in ever new ways of being presented. Indeed, the discord between poets and the investigators that one called philosophers was based on the fact that they both in their own ways were seeking the truth. The various iconoclasms, too, that swept over eras of the history of the Christian church are an echo of this tension between the true word and the true image.

Only with the advent of humanism, as the Middle Ages came to an end, did the situation change. Here, alongside the creator God of the Old and New Testaments, stepped the creative artist as an *alter deus*—an "other God," a kind of second God. And when the Revolution that belonged to the third stage of modern history, the Enlightenment, came to a head, art achieved its highest rank. For instance, think of Lucile in Büchner's play *Danton's Death* [1835]. Above all, it was the continued influence of Hegel's lectures on aesthetics, including their further development by Heinrich Gustav Hotho (1802–73), that had great influence right up until neo-Kantianism [1870–1920].[12] In this period, aesthetics no longer dealt with the beautiful but with art. Also, Paul Natorp [1854–1924] in the age of the "science" of religion showed religion its place at the limits of reason—a place it had to share with art. As Western culture moved away from the closed, geocentric image of the world and the Copernican turn caused unimaginable infinities to open up, this sparked new directions for scientific investigation. Indeed, the scientific Enlightenment pressed in all directions to explore the unknown. After the early explorers of the globe came the scientists doing research, and from them came the increasing alteration and domination of nature through science and technology. This became the basic cast of mind of the age. Ecclesiastical or secular topics were no longer the means through which a holy world could come to presentation in art. In place of these, it was the experience of order as such, mediated by sculpture and the pictorial arts, poetry, and above all music, that moved to the center of bourgeois cultural life. In the miracle of art the modern era celebrated the last pledge of the holy [*eine heile Welt*].

In other contexts I have shown how in modern times, aesthetics in the form of the philosophy of art took over the place that had formerly been held by cosmology and philosophy of nature in the realm of classical metaphysics. In modern times it is physics that in a certain way has put everything under its jurisdiction. The older areas of teaching lost their validity, but aesthetics or the philosophy of art was given a new, higher rank. The powerful change this represented can be seen if we examine an individual instance in the history of concepts. Astronomy in ancient and medieval times was called *musica caelestis*—"music of the heavens"—in contrast to earthly music with its hearable sounds. What the old doctrine of the Pythagoreans found to be the case with regard to pure relationships of numbers among the stars, and what governed thinking in the Middle Ages as that which was beyond physics, simply lost its validity in modern science. In this way, a problem situation in antiquity basically repeated itself in modernity. In antiquity it consisted in the opposition between the Pythagorean Plato and the physics of Aristotle. In a certain sense this still exists in the present day, if one thinks for example of the way statistics breaks into and disrupts quantum physics. There you find equations but no clear connection to the whole of actually measured results.

[What Is Common to All Art]

Let us now undertake once again to work out with the help of older concepts what is common to all art. Our goal in working with these older concepts will be to grasp conceptually what we today call "art," and what artists create, in such a way that the claim of art to truth becomes clear.

In the *Philebus*, Plato distinguishes in the mixing of the drink of life, which we mentioned before, between pure mathematics and actual practice, which brings us to something quite different from either—and he says this something is indispensable. He names this different thing "accuracy." [13] He expressly says that in the practice of life it is not enough to limit oneself to the divine science of pure numbers, circles, and triangles. For as we know, in the human application of these, a "false" circle and a "false" measure also belong to the human application of mathematics. Only in music and architecture, in which numbers and measure play an especially prominent role, does one find the art of getting it just right. In them this is indispensable. And one must admit that for the good life in general this art is needed "if one is simply to be able to find one's way home." [14]

Here we have the decisive step that Plato takes beyond the Pythagoreans. He supplements the old Pythagorean opposition between the limited and the unlimited through a third type of being. He calls it "coming into being." [15] He used this highly paradoxical formula apparently with full awareness of what he was doing—as he also does in the *Parmenides*[16]—in order to overcome as a false illusion the idea of any actual separation between the two worlds, a world of ideas and a world of appearances.

As if to emphasize his point, Plato varied the expression of this term so that instead of "coming into being" he called it simply "being that has been." [17] In this way he emphasizes still more the unity of becoming and being. This causes us now to think that for Plato the apparent opposition between becoming and being, of becoming other versus being-in-itself, does not have the last word. The purity of mathematics still remains a model for knowing thanks to its exactness and truth. But Plato no longer speaks in the *Philebus* as he does in the *Republic* about how the study of pure mathematics is needed to prepare for the ascent to pure dialectic. Rather, what he now everywhere aims to show is that in the structure of the world as well as in the practice of life we encounter the mixed, and within it we must seek and find the "exact." In the end, only the world of numbers and measure remains connected to the concept of pure knowing. Becoming is no longer simply some kind of nonbeing, that is, something seen as the becoming of something different; now it signifies coming into being [*Werden zum Sein*]. This is the new step, and it finds expression in Plato's *Philebus*. The step from becoming to being leaves to being something of its having come into being. This can already be observed in the manner it is spoken of in the *Philebus*. Being emerges from becoming!

This is a turn in Plato's thinking that it will repay us to ponder. In it we recognize the basic experience we have in encountering a work of art when we say: "That's right! That is the way it is!"—"It is 'right' so." Aristotle needed to go only one step beyond Plato when he made what Plato called "coming into being" [*Werden zum Sein*] into his topic of "the being of becoming" [*das Sein des Werdens*]. In this connection he introduced the concept of *energeia* in order to establish his *Physics*. But let us take note of this term. The word *energeia* is apparently a word newly created by Aristotle. One notices, for instance, Aristotle's seeming embarrassment when he attempts to define *energeia*, because he cannot invoke the use of the word in ordinary language. So he has to define it by analogy to the word *dynamis* in the *Metaphysics*.[18] Plato had already in his *Sophist*[19] carried this term over from its general use in ordinary language to his philosophical discussion. The concept of *energeia* oscillates between actuality, reality and activity [*Aktualität, Wirklichkeit, und Tätigkeit*] and is therefore also helpful in determining the concept of "kinesis" (motion). With the new conceptual expression *energeia*, then, a whole new horizon of problems opens up, a horizon in which new light may be cast on the way of being of the artwork.

This is seen already with regard to a similar, almost synonymous word created by Aristotle, namely *entelecheia* (entelechy). It is an expression that, like *energeia*, attracted some new conceptual determinations to itself on the threshold of modernity. The thing that is common to both words is that they designate something that is not an *ergon* [deed], that is, something that has its existence through an already completed production. The Aristotelian terms that inquire into the being of movement— like *dynamis, energeia,* and *entelecheia*—point to the side of the action in the process of being carried out and not to the *ergon*—the completed action. The process of being carried out, the execution or performance, already has its goal and the fulfilling of its being in itself (*telos echei*). At the same time, it becomes clear that *energeia* does not merely mean the same thing as motion (kinesis) because motion is *ateles* [without goal]. So long as it is ongoing, it is not completed. What is being moved is still under way, has not yet arrived. It is still becoming. In contrast to *energeia*, Aristotle explicitly mentions that becoming and being that has become are not the same. On the other hand, seeing and having seen are the same, as are likewise considering something and having thought about it. Both of these mean a tarrying over what is meant, as when we say, for example, that we are "totally immersed in the matter." I believe that Aristotle described *energeia* with the word for "at the same time" (*hama*) in order to point to the immanent temporality of its duration. In other words, this is not a one-after-another sequence but the at-the-sametimeness that the temporal structure of tarrying [with an artwork] possesses. It is not a doing of this and that, first this and then that; it is a whole that is present in the seeing, and in the considering that one is immersed in—or if we prefer to listen to the deep wisdom of language: *in dem man aufgeht*—"in which one is absorbed." Aristotle adds the example of living. In German too we say that one "is alive." So long as one is alive, one is united with both one's past and one's future.

[The Experience of Art]

Now let's apply this to art. In doing so we will ask not so much what it is that is emerging or showing itself. Rather, we say [with Heidegger] simply: "it" emerges. We say this both in the case of an art image we encounter as well as of language in its powerfulness as poetry. We are having an experience. This "having" does not mean that we are doing something, but rather that we are realizing something as when we understand it correctly. This does not at all mean that we read something into it or put something into it that is not there. Rather, we read to find out what is in it and try to do so in such a way that it comes forth.

An experience of art is like this: it is not a mere copy of something. Rather one is absorbed in it. It is more like a tarrying that waits and preserves in such a way that the work of art is allowed to come forth than it is like something we have done. Again, we can listen to language: we say that what comes forth "addresses us," and so the person who is addressed is as if in conversation with what comes forth. It holds with seeing an artwork as well as with listening to or reading such a work that one tarries with the work of art. To tarry is not to lose time. Being in the mode of tarrying is like an intensive back-and-forth conversation that is not cut off but lasts until it is ended. The whole of it is a conversation in which for a time one is completely "absorbed in conversation," and this means one "is completely there in it."

Reading a poetic work is like this, even though we read it line by line and page by page. It is not like running through a stretch of space until the finish line. Rather, when we read a work we are engaged completely with it. We are there—and at the end the impression grows on us: "That's right!" It is like a growing fascination that hangs on and even hangs on through temporary disruptions because the harmony with the whole grows and demands our agreement. We know this with special clarity in listening to music. Dilthey often used music to illustrate the structural law governing all understanding. It is almost superfluous to say that what is true of the experiencing of an artwork is also true of its creation: it is not merely production. For the creator, the key thing is whether the work succeeds. The perceiver does not know what it is. The famous French explanation, "je ne sais quoi," expresses this well. But the work of art has indeed succeeded and possesses its ungraspable rightness. So when it comes to art, it is meaningless to ask the artist what he or she meant. Likewise it is meaningless to ask the perceiver what it is that the work really says to him or her. Both of these matters go far beyond the subjective awareness of one or the other. It simply goes beyond all thinking and knowing when we say, "That is good." In both cases this means that "it" has come forth. Thus the experience of the artwork is not only an emergence from hiddenness, but at the same time is something really there in its seclusion. It dwells in the work as if in security. The work of art is an assertion, but it is one that does not form an assertive sentence, although it is telling in the highest degree. It is like a myth, like a saga,[20] because in what it says it is equally unfolding things and at the same time holding them back in readiness. The assertion it makes will speak over and over again.

[The Truth of Art, *Vollzug,* and Reading an Artwork]

It has now become clear that our return to the world of Greek concepts has borne fruit for our question. We took as our starting point the special place art holds today and the special ontological rank of the artwork—which is to say we started from a modern viewpoint on art in our questioning. The Greek heritage denied us an answer to our question, to the extent that the Greeks did not distinguish what the artist created—and therewith also the uniqueness of his skill—from what the craftsman produced, which was based on *techne.* At most the Greeks gave the great artists the honorary name of wise ones. Our question, however, is the extent to which we can accord truth to this wisdom. Would modern science, for instance, recognize this truth at all? Could its manner of thinking be broadened enough that the true stands alongside the beautiful and the good, as it did in the ancient world? Certainly in the realm of art one says that something is true or right as it is. This is even a good expression of what one means, but what is named in this way is not something of the kind that we could point to, or about which we could say that it "shines forth" in the way that the beautiful does. Also, when we find everything right in a picture or a poem, this does not mean "correct" in the sense of sentence correctness. For this reason Kant, too, critically distanced himself from the rule aesthetics of eighteenth-century rationalism by referring the aesthetic a priori to the subjectivity of feeling.

As the result of the above considerations, I wish to put forward the following assertion: I take a different approach to the question of what truth, *aletheia,* or unconcealment really means. I invoke the concept of *energeia* here, which has special value because in dealing with it we are no longer moving in the realm of sentence truth. With this new conceptual word Aristotle was able to think a motion that was without path or goal, something like life itself, like being aware, seeing, or thinking. All of these he called "pure *energeia,*" and just this concept leads me to think of art. In Aristotelian metaphysics God is introduced as the Unmoved Mover of the cosmos and is also described as leading a life of pure *energeia,* that is to say, of uninterrupted pure gazing. Apparently the meaning of this sort of being is presentness as such [and to itself]. On the basis of this Aristotelian teaching, one really does not know how to answer the question of what God's contemplative seeing really has as its object—everything or what? What this is for Hegel is being, being as the fulfillment of self-consciousness, and he called it "absolute Spirit." Without doubt he was also thinking of the connection to the Holy Spirit, the third person of the Christian Trinity. But one can also clarify the matter by thinking, for example, of the word *Geistesgegenwart*—the "presence of spirit." In this case we also do not mean something specific that one is aware of and to which one reacts; rather, this simply means that one is awake and aware of everything that is present or that may possibly come to be present. According to the interpretation of it in Greek philosophy, it is the way of living of the gods, who find their complete fulfillment in such looking, which they call *theoria.* Here the original sense of the Greek term *theoria* is important. The word means to participate in a festive act and to be with it. Thus, it is not merely being a spectator. Rather, it means "to be fully there," which is a highest form of activity and reality. Actually, one needs both words to translate the Greek word *energeia,* for the two words are intended in it simultaneously: activity and reality. Whoever participates in a cultic act in this way lets the "divine" emerge, so that it is like a palpable bodily appearance. This applies very well to an artwork. Standing before its appearing we also say: "That right!" [*So ist es!*] What has come forth is something with which we agree, not because it is an exact copy of something but because as an image it has something like a superior reality. It may perhaps also be a copy of something, but it does not need to have anything about it that is like a copy. In thinking of it one thinks of what, for example, the mystery cults protected as a holy secret. Thus the artwork is there and is, as Goethe said, "So wahr, so seiend," "so true, so full of being." In this process it contains the goal of its being (*telos echei*).

This point is quite significant for us. *Aletheia* does not simply mean unconcealment. Certainly we say that "it" comes forth, but the coming forth itself has something peculiar about it. This peculiarity consists in the fact that the work of art presents itself in such a way that it both conceals itself and at the very same time authenticates itself. For what the Greeks called "the shining forth of the beautiful" belongs to a world order that presents itself in its true fulfillment in the starry heavens. So the separation between that which is produced by human craft or machine and that which we call art in the modern sense refers to this "coming forth" in a radical sense. We say that "it" comes forth because something resides within the work, and in a certain sense what comes forth was hidden there. The unconcealment of what comes forth is of something that is hidden in the work itself and not in whatever we may say about it. It remains always the same work, even if in each new encounter it emerges in its own way. We know this well from our experience. The viewer of a painting looks for the right distance from it, a distance from which it truly comes forth. The viewer of a sculpture must go up and down and around it. Viewing an architectural work ultimately requires that one walk around it and gain a range of vantage points from many different distances and perspectives. Who dictates the right distance? Does one have to choose one's own standpoint and firmly hold to it? No, one must seek out the point from which "it" best comes forth! This point is not one's own standpoint. One makes oneself a laughingstock if in front of an artwork one says what one otherwise could say, that one is not standing at one's own standpoint. There is no such distance. If an artwork exercises its fascination, everything that has to do with one's own meaning and one's own opining seems to disappear.

The same thing holds true when one is dealing with a poem. One does well here to recall again Hegel's concept of the Absolute. Indeed, we must ask ourselves if with an artwork one can separate the making function from the product the way one does with a work of craftsmanship, where one just hands the matter over to its useful purpose. No, the artwork is apparently not a "work" in the same sense. When we say about the artwork that to be an artwork "it" must come forth, then I think one would do better to compare it to nature, which lets the flowers come forth, instead of a work of craftsmanship. The work of art is precisely not the product that is finished when the artist's work on it is done. Also, the artwork is not at all an object that one can approach with a measuring tape in one's hand. A real artwork does not allow itself to be grasped by processes of measurement, or through the number of its computer bits. Achievements with information technology, such as one can find in newspapers, illustrations, travelogs, or novels, are no measure of the artistic value of an artwork. What information technology can determine about a picture, for instance, is precisely not the art which gives it its special excellence.

We can also see this point in the limited chance that art history as a discipline [*Wissenschaft*, a science] has of really dealing with an artwork in terms of its function as art. I think, for example, of the iconographic current in the history of art, which as a scientific way of studying artworks has undeniably accomplished a great deal in the twentieth century. But the extent to which art history, treated as a science, possesses the right methical perspective can be seen in the fact that for it the artwork is simply a copy of something. Plato has clearly showed us, and with great irony, what comes from an orientation to the artwork solely as the copy and to its correctness as a copy, when he described a monumental sculpture as "false" because for the sake of the effect on the viewer its upper parts were made bigger than was "correct" (*Sophist* 235e). Certainly the Platonic doctrine of the beautiful immediately testifies against the artwork as a copy, and this view has found followers from Plotinus to Hegel; this latter view describes the work of art as the "sensory appearance of the Idea." Does not Plotinus give us a further hint about this matter when he remarks that a face appears now beautiful and now ugly, even when there has been not the slightest measurable change in it? Plotinus always had in mind the beautiful in art, which is only mentioned in passing by Plato and Aristotle. For us, however, what is essential is that we have to do here with an appearing [*Er-Scheinen*]. As a shining forth [*Scheinen*] this is in keeping with its essence as shifting appearance. And yet there is still the unique shining-forth of the beautiful that is the magic of art, whether it be in our seeing or our hearing, in our experiencing of the sculpture, poetry, or music.

Art has its "being" in the *Vollzug*—the vital, living event of its appearing, or its performance. This conclusion about the artwork agrees with our conceptual reflections on the Greek teaching about beauty and its application. This means, however, that the way of being of the artwork does not reside in its having been created, nor do conceptions like production or reproduction from the side of the receiver hit the mark. Indeed, these concepts are precisely where many such theories go wrong. Certainly the artist, sculptor, painter, or poet does carry out the work that is planned; they draft many designs and make many efforts to carry out their plans. But it is not the artist's construction of a work that another person might wish to have in order to make proper use of it. Both of these ideas—the creation and reproduction of the work—are inappropriate concepts, concepts that cover up the secret selfhood in the creation and in the reception of an artwork. Artistic creating itself is not something that one does [but something that comes through]—and the process of creating will also not be the thing that is reproduced or experienced again. As I have repeatedly said: "It comes forth" or "There is something in the work." But what came forth and how it came forth cannot be put into words. The painter can only say it in his painting, and he can intend to do it successfully there, and the viewer can be caught up in its concentrated power. If one is absorbed in and by the work, then perhaps he or she will find that "it comes forth"—or: "There is really something there in it." But certainly it is not the thing that has been copied that comes forth, such that one knows what it is and recognizes it. This is not the kind of "assertion" that the artwork makes.

Rather, the "it" that comes forth in the exclamation, "It comes forth!" is something that one has never experienced in exactly this way before. Even when one is dealing with a portrait, and the person portrayed knows and finds the picture to be a likeness, it is still as if one had never seen the person before in quite this way. So much *is* the person it. One has, so to speak, been seen into, and the more one looks, the more "it" comes forth. Certainly the portrait is a special case. However, one also says this about an image of a god or about an image of what is holy. The image has its own sovereignty. One says this even about a wonderful still life or a landscape, because in the picture everything is just right. This causes one to leave behind every relation to what is copied. This is its "sovereignty" as a picture.[21]

Or one reads a poem. One reads it again. One goes through it and it goes along with one. It is as if the poem began to speak, as if it began to sing and one sings along with it. In the case of music, whether one makes music oneself and "follows the notes," as we say, or if one only listens along with the music as it is played, it is all *there*—the repetition, variation, inversion, resolution—and it is precisely prescribed in advance. But only if one goes along with it, be it as a musical performer or be it as listener, does it come forward and one receives it. Otherwise it sweeps by and seems empty.

Let us linger a bit longer with the poem. Everything is there to be understood in its plenitude whether one reads it or recites it from memory, and it becomes completely present. When one reads a poem one is filled with a veritable stream of images and sounds, and in the end one perhaps says: "How beautiful!" or perhaps, "Oh, how well it has been worked out, and how right everything is!" One has listened to what is "dictated" by the poem. One can listen to the dictation directly or one can read the poem, but one always gets it even a little bit less correctly in reading than if one had been actually reciting it aloud.

What I have described here is the "sovereignty" of the image in painting and sculpture and the "dictation" by the text in what we call "literature." In both cases, one is dealing with a normative power. As with every norm, one can always come only relatively close to it. But no—that is precisely what we say when we reflect on the matter afterwards. In the *Vollzug*—in the execution, the performance—it is different. In its appearing to you the artwork is "truly there"—the picture, the poem, the song. "It" has come forth. On the basis of this one also understands the original sense of what "critique" means—that one separates the work as an artwork from its being as work that is *not* art (and one should also not assert that one knows the artwork better than the artist).

Today we no longer ask what such an event of appearing [*Vollzug*] "really is," how it begins, ends, how long it lasts; how it remains in one's mind, and in the end how it fades away, and yet somehow remains with us and can surface again. We do not inquire in this way. We have learned this from Aristotle's *energeia*—but we have forgotten how to ask in this way. Certainly one can call this process a "while" [*Weilen*], but this is something that nobody measures and that one does not find to be either boring or merely entertaining.

Certainly an artistic image or a poetic text is constructed sequentially in time, and this "takes time." But again we only say this when we are thinking in terms of what I call "empty time," the kind of time in which things like this are measurable. "Filled time," on the other hand, does not last long nor does it pass away.[22] And yet all kinds of things happen there. The name I have for the way in which this event happens is "reading," whether the encounter is with an art image or a book. In the case of reading, one knows what it means to be able to do this and not be illiterate—which of course is only the first step in the skill that understanding a work of art requires. But at least with reading one does not imagine, as most people think in regard to seeing, that one can already do it. In reality, one must learn how to see artworks and how to hear music. Now the word *Lesen* in German carries within it a helpful multiplicity of harmonic words, such as gathering together [*Zusammenlesen*], picking up [*Auflesen*], picking out [*Auslesen*], or to sort out [*verlesen*]. All of these are associated with "harvest" (*Lese*), that is to say the harvest of grapes, which persist in the harvest. But the word *Lesen* also refers to something that begins with spelling out words, if one learns to write and read, and again we find numerous echo words. One can start to read a book [*anlesen*] or finish up reading it [*auslesen*], one can read further in it [*weiterlesen*], or just check into it [*nachlesen*], or one can read it aloud [*vorlesen*]. All of these also point toward the harvest that is gathered in and from which one takes nourishment.

This harvest is the fullness of sense that is built up into a structure of meaning and similarly with a structure of sound. There are likewise the building blocks of meaning: motives, images, and sounds. But these elements are not letters, words, sentences, periods, or chapters. No, these things belong to grammar and syntax, which belong to the mere skeleton of writtenness and not to its design [*Formgestalt*]. It is the design that comes forth thanks to the means possessed by the language of art in poetry, sculpture, and picture, which in the flow of its play builds up the *Gestalt*. Afterwards the work can be taken apart, and this may enhance the real seeing or hearing of the work so that it gains in differentiation. In general, however, the design of the art image or of the text takes shape without any critical distance from the event. The event of emerging as experienced by the viewer, hearer, or reader, that is, the performance as experienced—the *Vollzug*—is the interpretation.[23]

I have focused on the concept of reading in order to distinguish clearly between the externality of what merely exists—for example, the colors or words or letters—and what the concept of *Vollzug* [reception as an event] has to show us. Here one has only to make clear to oneself how the process of reading takes place. First, note that reading does not wish to be a reproduction of what was originally spoken. This is where Emilio Betti made a great mistake. He distinguished two separate meanings of interpretation, one in the theoretical realm and the other in the realm of the transitory arts, for example in music or the theater arts, where he would like to speak of a "reproduction." But precisely in music it can be shown that interpretation is not just playing the correct musical notes. In exactly the same way, when one reads a linguistic text in a merely reproductive way, one would not call it truly reading; rather, we would just say one is verbalizing it. This shows that the concept of reading must be completely distinguished from what one calls "reproduction," and so the concept of interpretation absolutely must be distinguished from mere reproduction. Whoever truly makes music does not just spell it out by the notes: an interpreter in truth is the fulfiller of the music in such a way that it comes forth. The most perfect mechanical reproduction—and unfortunately this includes tapes and records and every other form of reproduction, even the color reproduction of paintings, for example— really offers only a reproduction without interpretation. In the age of reproducibility we need to remember what interpretation really is.

Of course, polemics as well as justified critiques have been directed against interpretation when it asserts its priority over the artwork and in consequence moves away from the encounter with the artwork. The fact that interpretation arrogates this role to itself in our day is the result of a scientific concept taken directly from the process of objectivizing—from making things into objects. An artwork has its being as a work of art in being brought to fulfillment in experience. That which can be grasped by objectifying the work and by applying scientific methods to it necessarily remains secondary to it and to that extent untrue. The truth that I seek in the artwork's assertion becomes accessible in the encounter. The well-known polemic by Susan Sontag[24] certainly does put its finger on a sore point in relation to most modern scholarly interpretation of poetry and art. The basically scientific methodology used in such interpretation does not allow a work of art to appear in its own light. It tries to "overilluminate" it. Heidegger once said that every interpretation must overelucidate. In the end this is always so, if one is talking about an event of encounter. Only by taking back all individuating objectification can interpretation really serve the encounter itself. In any event, this is the case with an artwork, which has its being in the event of encounter or with the performance. This is also the case in philosophy, if one follows Kant or Plato's *Seventh Letter.*

I was not speaking carelessly and without forethought when I alluded to the flow of the interpretive shaping which accompanies reading, the shaping which is expressed in the right emphasis given to a text in language or in the right phrasing when one makes music. Here it again becomes clear what *Vollzug* in art is. It is certainly not an objectifying process in knowing. Rather, it is the composite multiplicity of elements that enter into it. It is what Aristotle called *energeia.* His creation of this concept arose from a certain pulling back from the Pythagorean mathematizing of the universe and its music. What we call "nature" and what the Greeks called *physis* is above all things what is alive through its being in motion. To run across a mark in a certain stretch of a path or to cross a mark in time certainly makes the motion calculable and construable, but this is not the *energeia* possessed by living things or how the seeing and wakefulness of a person who is thinking takes place. The conclusion I draw from this may at first astonish you, but there is evidence for it: nature and art stand closer to each other than the planned construction of products that come out of the workplace. And our language speaks of "organic unity" in reference to both nature and art. This unity is not something done by anyone. Kant saw this when he grasped the aesthetic and teleological powers of judgment together. Obviously what he had in mind was the fact that in the scientific concept governing modern physics, the concept of purpose was not objectively acceptable either in aesthetics or in the knowledge of nature. Only German idealism ventured to assert this—and in doing so it discovered "art" as art.[25]

What all this amounts to in the end is that art belongs in the neighborhood of *theoria*. We know from the history of thought the inner kinship between art and science, both of which see themselves as being different from all practical and technical activity. So it is something positive, and at the same time it justifies our going back to the basic concepts of theoretical philosophy in ancient times, that one goes back to these when one wants to grasp more deeply the modern meaning of art and its claim to absoluteness. While the work of the craftsman or his industrial successor has a use, the artwork is there for itself, and its way of being is pure *energeia*. Other than this, the Greeks do not make this distinction between works of craft and works of art. Nevertheless, they did distinguish with fundamental sharpness between *techne* and *physis!* What is natural and living is in all the phases of its existence still nature, as seed, as shoot when it comes out of the ground, and in the whole of its maturity, ripeness, and fruit. All of this is the fulfillment [*Vollzug*] of a single process "from nature to nature," as Aristotle says. This same contrast, too, also distinguishes artworks from manufactured products. For the work of art is not constructed for a useful purpose like a manufactured product (even if it is brought to market). When it is in a collection, or in a museum, or is placed somewhere else awaiting our gaze, or when a book waits for us in a library, in order to be experienced in the fulfillment of reading, it is there as a work of art. This kind of reading is not our customary way of doing things in the world; no, it is rather its highest practice, which is what we have already found Greek theory to be. Art as art *is* in *Vollzug,* just as language *is* in conversation.

[On Architecture and Decorative Art: Concluding Remarks]

The topic of "Picture and Poem" [*Bild und Gedicht*], that is, of the pictorial and poetic arts, does not by any means exhaust the compass of what we must keep in mind in connection with the processual or event character [*Vollzugscharakter*] of art. Two important further forms of art need to be discussed. The first of these is architecture.

As I stressed in *Truth and Method*,[26] architecture has a certain weight-carrying and space-creating function, a function which the enactment processes of art as a whole possess. At the same time, architecture is also not merely the construction of a product with a purpose, such as to provide a place in which the play of art can unfold: a theater, an art gallery, or a concert hall, for example, are designed for this purpose. Rather, architecture is true to what it is designed to be in a double respect.

Certainly a work of civic architecture cannot ever be a product of pure art. It serves a purpose and has a place in the midst of the activities of life. At the same time, we often call such buildings as a church, a palace, a city hall, and even occasionally a department store or a railroad station, "architectural monuments." What does this mean? It means that there is something in the building that gives one something to think about. It is certainly not merely there to be looked at but rather also serves its purposes, and yet it is a work of art.

One must emphasize that the rage to reproduce things in an age possessed by technology has created an illusion. The photographic reproduction of buildings, for instance, has the fatal tendency to falsify their effect into that of a picture. This leads us to feel a false sense of familiarity with the building and in consequence a feeling of disappointment when one does not encounter in the building itself the false appearance of a painting but instead for the first time is drawn into its full reality and into the thought it generates. This is similar to the color copies of paintings depicting the image of a painting but not the painting itself, or trying to relate to a work of poetry from just reading the critique of it in the newspaper.

Parallel to this is seeing a building only in terms of its purpose. It emerges as an artwork only when, in the middle of its use, something wonderful shines forth, as with everything that is beautiful. This experience causes us to pause in the midst of our purposeful doing, for example in a room of a church, or in a stairwell, when suddenly we stand there and remain entranced. This does not necessarily mean that one forgets the purposes of one's own activity. For example, in the midst of a cultic purpose being carried out in a room of a church, an aesthetically significant staircase can play an enhancing role in the fulfillment of one's life.

Already we find ourselves dealing here with the second problematic concept I would like to discuss: the concept of the decorative. What we call "decorative" is already thought of in relation to the concept of art, and if we find a painting to be decorative, this is almost a criticism of it. Nothing mysteriously comes forth from it, or perhaps there is nothing in the painting to come forward. What is decorative really should not come forth in the way artworks do, but should have its place as part of the background. When such a background presses forward too much, for example in a very colorfully figured wallpaper, seemingly like the feverish dreams of my childhood, such a decoration loses its true purpose. Nevertheless, we are still dealing with art if we talk of a piece of jewelry that catches one's eye. In this case one may admire the workmanship and good taste of the work, especially if it is not too eye-catching and seems to hold back. A sharp difference between art and handicraft does not always exist, and this is likewise the case with architecture. But this points directly to the tension-filled dialectic of the beautiful, for in decorative art as with all art, the work only has its being as art in its character as something encountered [*Vollzugscharakter*]. With architecture, however, it is different. There we have the artistic thought possessed by the building holding back at first behind the purpose until it takes hold of the viewer's attention in its form. Then the relation to its purpose steps into the background, so that what is distinctive in the building completely fills us. It is then like "music that has fallen silent" (Goethe).

That a presence and an accompanying function are interwoven plays a role not only here but in all encounters with art. All of our seeing, as well as hearing, for instance, is governed by the law of contrast. The field around what we look at, for instance, always plays its part. This applies not only to sculpture and painting but also to poetry. The deadening effect of taste and the increase in attractiveness of the new also play a role. With architectural art it is a bit different. In architecture, the accompanying conditions do not just enter in; the thought regarding its purpose belongs to the very creation of the building. Where a building's relation to its purpose is quite unclear, this fact can be annoying: for example the Porta Nigra in Trier, which has something eerie about it, like a gravesite; or when the Pergamon Altar in Berlin has steps that run right into the wall; or when the choir screen in the Hildesheim church dome just stands against a wall. A building has a pre-given connection with its surroundings with which it has to harmonize. The effect that will be caused by the space is co-intended. Of course, buildings often stand as if forgotten now in an alien environment as stone witnesses to the past, and yet they are an unshakeable phenomenon.

Our discussion of architecture and of the role of the decorative has a special significance today, since it has become characteristic of art in modern times that its "place in life" has become questionable. Architecture confronts the constant task of accomplishing what artworks that are already free in their own function as sculpture, poem, or music are able to do because of the power of their form, namely, to draw people to the work and to have an effect on the quality of their way of living. This influence that a work exercises we call "style." It is a kind of whole that shapes various realms and fits them together. There is style in writing and naturally style in speaking, style in the way humans interact with each other, and in the whole surrounding world in which human life plays itself out. The fact that in the end architecture plays a special role in all this, to shape the style and represent it, is something it owes to its special space-forming task, through which at the same time it offers all the other arts a place-in-life for their own style-creating power and their truth.

Our discussion of architecture and decorative art here is therefore not merely an appendix to the investigation up to now, which has intentionally focused on the concept of art that prevails in modern times. We saw that, in fact, the *philosophical relevance of art* has only recently gotten through to us. And of course this means at the same time that for art its "place in life" has become questionable. Beginning with the cave drawings in primeval times up through the art of earlier eras and right to the end of the eighteenth century, the place of art in the society was self-evident. Of course, architecture and the decorative arts continue to be inseparable from the whole of what gives shape to life. This means that in these art forms the claim of art to absoluteness has to be carried out by an express suspension of any function of serving a purpose. In truth, such a suspension belongs to all appearing of the beautiful. This was understood without further ado throughout the ancient world and posed no problem: the Egyptian and Greek sculptural images of the gods as well as the ancient funeral monuments were tied into the sacred order of life. This was obvious. Even in Periclean Athens, when the great art treasures on the Acropolis had to be hidden away, they remained ready to be brought out for cultic occasions.

This is also true of the Christian era and its beginnings, with a few characteristic changes. Hans Belting quite correctly took up the topic of how the "image" [*Bild*] only gradually faded from cultic observances in the Christian West.[27] Indeed, we have emphasized here that the iconographic standpoint [in art history] is oriented to the artwork as a copy of something. But the iconographic line of research is not simply research into documents, but research into art precisely because the function of copying in art has a special significance with regard to the place in life occupied by art. Ernst H. Gombrich has a quite different methodological orientation when he speaks of the fulfillment of a certain evolving way of thinking in images that can found in the development of painting up to the Renaissance. Nevertheless, this should not lead us to ignore the fact that the representations of Christ as Pantokrator [Ruler of All] that are found in medieval wall paintings or in mosaic art contain a sacred radiance streaming out of them with which the pictures of the Madonna and child in the Renaissance cannot compare. This fact, I think, points in truth to the absoluteness and contemporaneity of all art, two topics which we have inquired into here.

At this point I need not go into the many possible arrangements that people have made of the course of historical development in art. I will conclude only by recalling to you the case of Raphael and the checkered history of his fame. Or the way the status of the baroque was later enhanced. One could draw out lines of development in the history of sculpture and painting, articulating the shifting tastes, their new turns, and the shifting influences from early on up to the present day. In particular, it would be interesting to trace the history of the panel painting, which really opened a new age in painting, from which arose the gallery, the museum, and the general exhibition of collections of art. And however much we may lament the losses in recent centuries that have brought a new homelessness and placelessness to art and to the artist, I still maintain that no political program about art can be taken seriously if it does not recognize the claim of all art to absoluteness. Of course, this does not change the fact that the age of a common European architectural style has come to an end. Still, Mnemosyne remains the mother of the Muses. The presence of the past in the present belongs to the very nature of the human mind. And as Hegel said, "The wounds of the spirit leave no scars."

Translated by Richard E. Palmer

Part 3

Hermeneutics and Practical Philosophy

10

Hermeneutics as Practical Philosophy

In the years and decades after 1960, Gadamer's defense of his philosophical hermeneutics increasingly turned for support to two areas of ancient Greek culture not much emphasized in *Truth and Method:* rhetoric and Aristotle's practical philosophy. Rhetoric was close to hermeneutics in that it was the art of articulating an understanding, while hermeneutics was the art of understanding the articulation, especially when in writing. Each was a reverse version of the other. Each required an underlying ethical understanding to be successful; and each in a way presupposed the other, since rhetoric presupposed understanding and understanding required a persuasive articulation of the meaning of a text. Each discipline was an art more than a science, and Gadamer was at pains to defend hermeneutics against being classified and conceived under the umbrella of science.

Yet a defense of philosophical hermeneutics against the powerful claims of science could not be based on the ancient and modern structural affinity between hermeneutics and rhetoric. And apparently the arguments of *Truth and Method* were not enough. He could not simply explain its arguments over and over again. So in addition to new defenses that appeared as excurses in later editions of his masterwork, Gadamer lectured on and wrote major later essays on Plato. He emphasized especially the dialectical element in Plato as basic to understanding the dialogue of the interpreter with the text. And he explored the foundations of Western art in writings that appear elsewhere in this volume. And finally he turned to Aristotle's "practical philosophy" and tried to spell out this revered concept in classical thinking as a basis for a philosophical hermeneutics. And indeed, not only did practical philosophy offer a basis for Gadamer's further thinking about the encounter with art, but it also provided excellent material for defending his hermeneutics against the encroachments of science and scientific method in modernity.

The first of Gadamer's two key essays in practical philosophy in this volume, "Hermeneutics as Practical Philosophy," can serve as an excellent general introduction to hermeneutics for a wide audience, including those who have not read *Truth and Method.* This essay was first published in 1972 in a volume titled *Rehabilitierung der praktischen Philosophie,* edited by Manfred Riedel (Freiburg: Verlag Rombach). In 1976 he included it in *Vernunft im Zeitalter der Wissenschaft,* a popular Suhrkamp paperback volume of his essays that was eventually translated into eight languages—including one in English as *Reason in the Age of Science* in 1981, a volume which added the later essay "Hermeneutics as a Theoretical and Practical Task" (1978). This comprises chapter 11 of the present volume.

In the essay's opening paragraph, Gadamer points to his purpose as assessing the increased relevance that philosophical hermeneutics has found in the previous decade by reviewing the historical context in which it arose. In other words, he will trace the development of hermeneutics from a specialized field in which interpretation is used as a tool to its present state as "a vast field of philosophic questioning." Instrumental in this transformation is the contribution of Martin Heidegger, who puts forward "a new notion of interpretation and consequently of hermeneutics." This goes beyond the notion of hermeneutics as a methodology and advances a fundamentally new concept of understanding. Heidegger's concept goes beyond mere "self-understanding" and the "legitimacy of objective self-consciousness," and a term like "definitive interpretation" becomes impossible in the light of the interests that guide interpretation.

In the essay's remaining pages, Gadamer explores the link with practical philosophy. He notes "the neighborly affinity of hermeneutics with practical philosophy" and later announces that "the great tradition of practical philosophy lives on in a hermeneutics that has become aware of its philosophic implications." A second essay on practical philosophy will go into the connections between both rhetoric and practical philosophy to hermeneutics. But for now we turn to the present essay as an introduction to and defense of hermeneutics.

* * *

Hermeneutics as Practical Philosophy

In itself hermeneutics is old. But perhaps in the last fifteen years [since *WM*] it has taken on a new relevance. If we wish to assess this relevance and clarify the significance of hermeneutics and its relation to the central problems of philosophy and theology, we need to work out the historical background in the context of which the hermeneutical problem has taken on this fresh relevance. We have to trace the way hermeneutics has expanded from a specialized and occasional field of application to the vast field of philosophic questioning.

By "hermeneutics" is generally understood the theory or art of explication, of interpretation. The usual eighteenth-century German expression for this, *Kunstlehre* (a teaching about a technical skill or know-how), is actually a translation of the Greek *techne*. It links hermeneutics with such *artes* as grammar, rhetoric, and dialectic. But the expression *Kunstlehre* points to a cultural and educational tradition other than that of late antiquity: the remote and no longer vital tradition of Aristotelian philosophy. Within it there was a so-called *philosophia practica* (*sive politica*) [or political philosophy], which lived on right up to the eighteenth century. It formed the systematic framework for all the "arts," since they all stand at the service of the "polis."

To put ourselves right at the middle of the problematic, we have to submit the concepts involved in the nomenclature of the topic to a reflection upon their conceptual history. We will start with the word "philosophy" itself. In the eighteenth century it did not have the exclusive sense we attach to it when we distinguish philosophy from science, even while we still insist that it is a science as well—or even the queen of the sciences. At that time "philosophy" meant nothing other than "science." By the same token, however, science did not consist simply of research grounded on the modern notion of method and the deploying of mathematics and measurement. It connoted both specialized knowledgeableness and any true knowledge, even if it were unattainable by means of the anonymous procedures of empirical scientific labor. Thus, when Aristotle used the expression "practical philosophy," by "philosophy" he meant "science" in a very general sense—indeed as knowledge using demonstration and generating doctrine, but not as the kind of science that was for the Greeks the model of theoretic knowledge, or *episteme*—mathematics. This general, nonmathematical science is called political philosophy in contradistinction to theoretical philosophy as comprised by physics (knowledge of nature), mathematics, and theology (first science, or metaphysics). Since the human being is a political being, political science belonged to the area of practical philosophy as its most noble part, and it was cultivated under the title of classical politics right into the nineteenth century. In the light of this background, the modern opposition between theory and practice seems rather odd, for the classical opposition ultimately was a contrast within knowledge, not an opposition between science and its application.

This implies at the same time that the original notion of practice (praxis) had quite a different structure too. In order to grasp it once again and to understand the meaning of the tradition of practical philosophy, one has to remove this notion [praxis] completely from the context of opposition to science. It is not even the opposition to *theoria* (which is, of course, contained in the Aristotelian division of the sciences) that is really determinative here. This is manifest in the splendid statement of Aristotle to the effect that we name "active" in the supreme measure those who are determined by their performance in the realm of thought alone (*Politics* 1325b21ff.). So *theoria* itself is a practice (πρᾶξις τις).

This strikes modern ears alone as a piece of sophistry because only for us is the significance of practice determined by its application of theory to science—with all the inherited connotations of "practice" that tend to connect such application of theory with every manner of impurity, haphazardness, accommodation, or compromise. In itself this is completely correct. Plato constantly made this contrast more acute for us in his writings on the state. The ineradicable separation that exists between the purely ideal order and the soiled and mixed-up world of the senses (which dominates Plato's doctrine of the Idea) nevertheless is not identical with the relationship between theory and practice in the Greek sense. The conceptual range in which the word and concept of "practice" have their proper place is not primarily defined by its opposition to theory as an often unfortunate application of theory. As Joachim Ritter has shown in his works, practice formulates the mode of behavior of that which is living in the broadest sense. Practice, as the basic character of being alive, stands between activity and situatedness. As such it is not confined to human beings, who alone are active on the basis of free choice (*prohairesis*). Practice means instead the actuation of life (*energeia*) of anything alive, to which there corresponds a life, a way of life, a life that is led in a certain way (*bios*). Animals too have praxis and *bios*, which means a way of life.

Of course, there is a decisive difference between animal and human being. The way of life of human beings is not fixed by nature like other living beings. This difference is expressed by the concept of *prohairesis*, which can only be predicated of human being. *Prohairesis* means "preference" and "prior choice." Knowingly preferring one thing to another and consciously choosing among possible alternatives is the unique and specific characteristic of human being. The Aristotelian concept of practice has yet another specific emphasis, however, in that it is applied to the status of a free citizen in the polis. This is where human practice exists in the eminent sense of the word. It is specified by the *prohairesis* of the *bios*. The free decision takes its bearings by the order of preferences guiding one's life conduct, whether it be of pleasure, or power and honor, or knowledge. Besides these, we encounter in the political makeup of human life together other differences in life conduct such as those between husband and wife, the elderly and the child, and dependents and those who are independent (in former times chiefly the distinction between slave and free). All of this is "practice." So practice is here no longer the sheerly natural component within a mode of behavior, as is the case with animals set in the schemes of innate vital instincts. The Sophistic enlightenment especially insisted that the whole *arete* (performative excellence) of human beings is utterly diverse in each case, even though that *arete* rests upon knowing and choosing and is only realized fully in the free status of the citizen of the polis.

Since "practice" comprises this broad range of significance in Greek, the most important delimitation that it undergoes with Aristotle is not vis-à-vis theoretical science, which itself emerges from the enormous range of life possibilities as a type of the most noble practice. Rather, it is the delimitation over against production based on knowledge, the *poiesis* that provides the economic basis for the life of the polis. In particular, if it is not a matter of the "lower servile" arts but of the kind that a free man can engage in without disqualification, such a knowing and know-how pertain to his practice without being practical knowledge in the practical-political sense. And so practical philosophy is determined by the line drawn between the practical knowledge of the person who chooses freely and the acquired skill of the expert that Aristotle names *techne*. Practical philosophy, then, has to do not with the learnable crafts and skills, however essential this dimension of human ability is for the communal life of humanity. Rather, it has to do with what is each individual's due as a citizen and what constitutes his *arete* or excellence. Hence practical philosophy needs to raise to the level of reflective awareness the distinctively human trait of having *prohairesis,* whether it be in the form of developing those fundamental human orientations for such preferring that have the character of *arete,* or in the form of the prudence in deliberating and taking counsel that guides right action. In any case, practical philosophy has to be accountable with its knowledge for the viewpoint in terms of which one thing is to be preferred to another: the relationship to the good. But the knowledge that gives direction to action is essentially called for by concrete situations in which we are required to choose the thing to be done; and no learned and mastered technique can spare us the task of deliberation and decision. As a result, the practical science directed toward this practical knowledge is neither theoretical science in the style of mathematics nor expert know-how in the sense of a knowledgeable mastery of operational procedures (*poiesis*), but a unique sort of science. It must arise from practice itself and, with all the typical generalizations that it brings to explicit consciousness, be related back to practice. In fact, this constitutes the specific character of Aristotelian ethics and politics.

Its object of study is not only the constantly changing situations and modes of conduct that can be elevated to knowledge only in respect to their regularity and averageness. Conversely, the teachable knowledge of typical structures has the character of real knowledge only by reason of the fact that (as is always the case with technique or know-how) it is repeatedly transposed into the concrete situation. Practical philosophy, then, certainly is "science"; that is, a knowledge of the universal that as such is teachable. But it is a science that needs certain conditions to be fulfilled. It demands of the person learning it the same indissoluble relationship to practice that it does of the one teaching it. To this extent, it does have a certain proximity to the expert knowledge that is proper to technique, but what separates it fundamentally from technical expertise is that it expressly asks the question of the good, too—for example, about the best way of life or about the best constitution of the state. It does not merely master an ability, like technical expertise, whose task is set by an outside authority or by the purpose to be served by what is being produced.

All this holds true for hermeneutics as well! As the theory of interpretation or explication, it is not just a theory. From the most ancient times right down to our day, hermeneutics quite clearly has claimed that its reflection upon the possibilities, rules, and means of interpretation is immediately useful and advantageous for the practice of interpretation—whereas perhaps a fully worked out theory of logic has a more scientifically rarefied ambition than promoting the advance of logical thinking, just as number theory has a loftier aim than advancing calculative finesse. Hence, as a first approximation, we would say that hermeneutics may be understood as a teaching about a technical skill [Kunstlehre] in somewhat the manner of rhetoric. Like rhetoric, hermeneutics can designate a natural capacity of human beings, and then it refers to the human capacity for intelligent interchange with one's fellows. So in a letter to his friend Hitzig, Johann Peter Hebel could say about a theologian that he "possesses and makes use of the most admirable of hermeneutics to understand and humanely interpret human foibles."

Thus the earlier hermeneutics was primarily a practical component in the activity of understanding and interpreting. It was far less frequently a theoretical textbook—which is practically what *techne* meant in antiquity—than a practical manual. Books bearing the title "Hermeneutics" usually had a purely pragmatic and occasional bent and were helpful for the understanding of difficult texts by explaining hard-to-understand passages. However, precisely in fields in which difficult texts have to be understood and interpreted, reflection upon the nature of such activity first evolved, and with this development something like hermeneutics in our contemporary sense was brought forth. This happened especially in the field of theology.

There we can find what is most important and fundamental, for example, in Augustine's *De doctrina Christiana.* Especially when he sought to become more precise about his stance toward the Old Testament, Augustine saw himself forced into a reflection that involved the meaning of "understanding" and compelled him to be clearer about the dogmatic claims of his texts. It was a theological task to discuss why the entire Old Testament cannot be an immediate mirror image or typological prefiguration of the Christian message of salvation. Things as contrary to Christian moral teaching as, say, the polygamy of the patriarchs could no longer be salvaged by allegorical interpretation, and they made necessary a straightforward historical interpretation that drew upon knowledge of the remote and strange morality of the nomads—an essential differentiation of the scope of interpretation. As the Old Testament had been a challenge for Augustine and earlier Christianity, so in the age of the Reformation the holy scriptures in their entirety became the object of a new preoccupation with hermeneutics and the occasion of hermeneutical reflection. The allegorizing method of the dogmatic interpretation of scripture that prevailed in the Roman tradition and so permitted a dogmatic theological tradition to control the meaning of the scripture was supposed to be overcome altogether in favor of the "Word of God." The new slogan of *sola scriptura,* however, proved to be just as difficult a principle of interpretation. As much as it struggled against the dogmatic character of the Catholic tradition of interpretation, even Protestant exegesis was compelled to erect a certain dogmatic canon, and this meant that it had to reflect on the dogmatic results generated by the reading at that time of the holy scriptures in their original tongues. So it is that the new first principle, *sacra scriptura sui ipsius interpres* [sacred scripture interprets itself], became the source of a new theological hermeneutics. But what grew from this was not simply a doctrine concerning a technical skill [*Kunstlehre*]; rather, it comprised a doctrine of the faith [*Glaubenslehre*].

Jurisprudence was another field in which reflection upon the interpretation of texts resulted not only from difficulties within hermeneutical practice, but also from the material significance of these texts. In jurisprudence this reflection was mainly concerned with practical juridical questions that arose from the interpretation of legal texts and from their application in cases of conflict. Mediating the universality of the law with the concrete material of the case before the court is an integral moment of all legal art and science. These difficulties become particularly heightened wherever the legal texts are no longer the authentic expression of our experience of the law, rooted in our actual life experience, and instead represent a historical inheritance taken over from a completely different social and historical situation. A legal order that has become obsolete and antiquated is a constant source of legal difficulties, so meaningful interpretation requires adaptation to the contemporary situation. This general hermeneutical moment of all findings of law becomes even more pronounced in cases in which we speak of reception, particularly in the reception of Roman law in later Europe. However one might wish to evaluate this process of reception and however much a demythologizing of Romantic prejudices may be in order here, the process of making legal administration scientific was introduced with the assimilation of Roman-Italian legal skill north of the Alps. Under the historical conditions peculiar to the modern age, this process led also to the practice of hermeneutics and a theoretical heightening of awareness in the field of law. Thus the exempt status of Caesar (*lege solutus*) under the Justinian code was a matter of dispute for years, and under the changed circumstances of modernity it became an ongoing hermeneutical thorn. The ideal of law implies the idea of equality under the law. If the sovereign himself is not subject to the law but can decide upon its application, the foundation of all hermeneutics is destroyed. Even this example demonstrates that the just interpretation of the law is not simply a doctrine concerning a technical skill (a type of logical subsumption under such and such a paragraph), but a practical concretization of the idea of the law. The art of the jurist is at the same time the administration of the law.

Another significant tension emerged from a very different direction, the resolution of which called for hermeneutics. With the rise of the new humanism, the great Latin and Greek classics, the models of all higher human culture, had to be appropriated anew. The return to classical Latin, as a somewhat exacting and fastidious novelty, particularly in view of its more refined style in comparison with the Latin of the Scholastics, and especially the return to the Greek (and in the case of the Old Testament, to Hebrew) revealed the need for more than all sorts of hermeneutical aids regarding grammar, lexicons, and historical and factual information. This was supplied by the numerous resource manuals called "Hermeneutica." Beyond this chiefly informational aspect, the classics claimed a specific exemplary character that called into question the taken-for-granted self-awareness of modernity. By the same token, the famous *querelle des anciens et des modernes* belongs to the prehistory of modern hermeneutics insofar as it awakened a hermeneutical reflection upon the ideals of humanism. If this *querelle* has now been correctly judged a preparation for the awakening of historical consciousness, then conversely this means that hermeneutics does not just inculcate facility in understanding; it is not a mere teaching concerning a technical skill. Rather, it has to be able to give an account of the exemplary character of that which it understands.

As much as this contradicts the self-understanding of hermeneutics as a *Kunstlehre*—as is manifest in all its different facets—it is more than a mere teaching of a technique, and it belongs in the neighborhood of practical philosophy. And so hermeneutics shares in the reference to self that is essential to practical philosophy. If, for example, ethics is a teaching about the right way to live, it still presupposes its concretization within a living ethos. Even the art of understanding the tradition, whether it deals with sacred books, legal texts, or exemplary masterworks, not only presupposes the recognition of these works but goes further to shape their productive transmission. As long as it remained confined to normative texts, the earlier hermeneutics did not pose a central issue for the conception of the problems of traditional philosophy. To this degree it is still quite a long way from our contemporary interest in hermeneutics. Nevertheless, when the remoteness of the lofty and the remoteness of the recondite needed to be overcome not simply in specialized domains such as religious documents, texts of the law, or the classics in their foreign languages, but when the historical tradition in its entirety up to the present moment moved into the position of having a similar remoteness, the problem of hermeneutics entered intrinsically into the philosophic awareness of its problems. This took place by virtue of the great breach in tradition brought about by the French Revolution and as a result of which European civilization splintered into national cultures.

With the disappearance of its validity as a thing to be taken for granted, the common tradition of the Christian states of Europe, which of course lived on, began to enter explicit consciousness in a completely novel way as a freely chosen model, as the passionate aim of nostalgia, and finally as an object of historical knowledge. This was the hour of a universal hermeneutics through which the universe of the historical world was to be deciphered. The past as such had become alien.

Every renewed encounter with an older tradition was no longer a simple matter of appropriation that unself-consciously added what is proper to itself even as it assimilated what is old; rather, it had to cross the abyss of historical consciousness. The standard slogan became to return to the original sources, and in this fashion our historically mediated image of the past was placed on an entirely new footing. This involved a profoundly hermeneutical task. As soon as one acknowledges that one's own perspective is utterly different from the viewpoints of the

authors and the meanings of the texts of the past, there arises the need
for a unique effort to avoid misunderstanding the meaning of old texts
and yet to comprehend them in their persuasive force. The description
of the inner structure and coherence of a given text and the mere repetition of what the author says is not yet real understanding. One has
to bring the author's speaking back to life again, and for this one has
to become familiar with the realities about which the text speaks. To
be sure, one has to master the grammatical rules, the stylistic devices,
and the art of composition upon which the text is based, if one wishes
to understand what the author wanted to say in the text; but the main
issue in all understanding concerns the meaningful relationship that
exists between the statements of the text and our understanding of the
reality under discussion.

The post-Romantic epoch in its development of hermeneutical
procedures did not actually do justice to this main issue.

What happened was that the self-understanding that grew out of
the tradition of teaching a technical skill [Kunstlehre] first presented itself to the experience of estrangement that emerged with historical consciousness, and so hermeneutics was conceived by the Romantics as a
critical ability in dealing with texts. The mounting logical self-awareness
of the inductive sciences came to the support of this self-understanding
as a powerful aid. Accordingly, they tried to follow the great model of
the natural sciences and considered the ideal in both cases to be the
exclusion of every subjective presupposition. Just as in natural scientific
research the experiment that could be repeated by anyone afforded the
basis of verification, so too in the interpretation of texts one sought to
apply procedures that anyone could check. The age-old procedures of
exegesis, especially the gathering of parallels, underwent a historical-
critical refinement at this time. On this basis, the hermeneutic methodology that the Romantic interest subsumed under its scientific auspices
was constantly compared with the methodology of the natural sciences.
Its objects, the transmitted texts, were to be treated like the data in
a scientific investigation of nature. This sort of self-understanding by
the new critical philology also happened to correspond with Schleiermacher's separation of general hermeneutics from dialectics and, in the
realm of theology, with his separation of the teaching of the technical
skill of hermeneutics from the teaching of the faith [Glaubenslehre]. That
it was thus unable to do justice to the interest in history did not remain
unnoticed by the great historians like Ranke or Droysen, for it did not
match up to the theological pathos so alive in their critical research.
Not without reason, they attached themselves to Fichte, Humboldt, and
Hegel. In spite of this, there was no fundamental recognition of the
older tradition of practical philosophy, even by Dilthey, who managed

to articulate conceptually the heritage of the Romantic school. Insight into the connection between hermeneutics and practical philosophy was completely lacking.

Only when our entire culture for the first time saw itself threatened by radical doubt and critique did hermeneutics become a matter of universal significance. This had a certain persuasive inner logic to it. One need only think of the radicalism in doubting that is to be found especially in Friedrich Nietzsche. His slowly growing influence in every area of our culture possessed a depth that is usually not sufficiently realized. Psychoanalysis, for instance, is scarcely imaginable without Nietzsche's radical calling into doubt of the testimony of human reflective self-consciousness. Nietzsche demanded that we doubt more profoundly and fundamentally than Descartes, who had considered the ultimate unshakable foundation of all certitude to be explicit self-consciousness. The illusions of reflective self-consciousness, that is, the idols of self-knowledge, constituted the novel discovery of Nietzsche, and later modernity dates from his all-pervasive influence. As a result, the notion of interpretation attained a far more profound and general meaning.

Thereafter interpretation leads not only to the explication of the actual intention of a difficult text. Interpretation becomes an expression for getting behind the surface phenomena and data. The so-called critique of ideology called the claim of scientific neutrality into doubt. It questioned not merely the validity of the phenomena of consciousness and of self-consciousness (which was the case with psychoanalysis), but also the purely theoretical validity of scientific objectivity to which the sciences laid claim. The clear claim of Marxism was that the theoretical teachings of the sciences reflected with an intrinsic necessity the interests of the dominant social class, especially that of the entrepreneurs and capitalists. And one of the demands of Marxism, especially when trying to understand the manifestations of economic and social life, was to get behind the self-interpretations of bourgeois culture, which invoke the objectivity of science. In other ways, too, the philosophic career of the concept of interpretation, which has had such success in the last hundred years, has its philosophic grounding in the well-justified mistrust of the traditional framework whose basic terms are not so obvious and presuppositionless as they pretend to be. The pre-understanding implied in them lends in a definite way an antecedent shape to the problems of philosophy. But it not only schematizes philosophic thought; our entire cultural life bears witness to the oldest ontological provenance of our thought from Greek philosophy.

Heidegger's great merit was to have broken through the aura of obviousness with which the Greek thinkers used the concept of being. In particular, he laid bare the way modern thought was shaped by the completely unexplicated concept of consciousness that provides the principle of recent philosophy under the domination of the concept of being. His famous lecture, *What Is Metaphysics?* argued that traditional metaphysics did not ask the question of being itself [*die Frage nach dem Sein*] but on the contrary kept this question concealed, inasmuch as it constructed the edifice of metaphysics from the concept of being as the circumscribed already-out-there-now. The real intention of what was asked by Heidegger's question about being can be understood only in the light of the new concept of interpretation under discussion here. This becomes more evident when one weighs the title of the lecture word-for-word and catches the secret emphasis borne by the word "is."

The intention of the question, "What is metaphysics?" is to ask what metaphysics really is in contrast with what metaphysics wants to be and with what it understands itself to be. What was the significance of the fact that the question of philosophy took the shape of metaphysics? What is the significance of the event in which the Greek thinkers used their heads and freed themselves from the bonds of mythic and religious living and dared to put questions like "Why is it?" and "What is it?" and "Out of what does anything emerge into being?" If one understands the question, "What is metaphysics?" in the sense that one asks what happened with the beginning of metaphysical thinking, then the Heideggerian question first acquires its provocativeness and is disclosed as an instance of the new notion of interpretation.

The new notion of interpretation and consequently of hermeneutics that entered the picture evidently surpassed the limits of any hermeneutic theory, no matter how universally understood. Ultimately it implied a totally new concept of understanding and self-understanding. Interestingly enough, the expression "self-understanding" has today become quite fashionable. It is constantly used even in current political and social discussions, not to mention popular fiction. Words are slogans. They often express what is missing and what should be. A self-understanding that has become unsure of itself was talked about by everyone. But it was the first appearance of a word that marked its succeeding history. The expression "self-understanding" was first used with a certain terminological emphasis by Johann Gottlieb Fichte. Because he felt he was dependent upon Kant, he claimed that his *Wissenschaftslehre* at the same time provided the single reasonable and authentic interpretation of Kantian philosophy. One ought to require coherence of a thinker. Only in the radical consistency of his thought would a philosopher be capable of attaining a genuine self-understanding. In Fichte's eyes, however, there is only one possible way to be completely and without contradiction in agreement with one's own thought, and that is when one derives everything that could claim validity in our thought from the spontaneity of self-consciousness and grounds it therein. If one were to affirm that besides his teaching on self-consciousness and the deduction of the root concepts, the categories, Kant assumed a thing-in-itself, and thus that mind is affected by the sense faculties, then one would have to affirm that he was not a thinker at all but a half-wit, as Fichte so shrilly and coarsely put it. Fichte took for granted that everything that is supposed to hold true must be brought forth by activity. By this he of course means a mental construction. And this has nothing to do with the absurd notion of solipsism that haunted the foothills of nineteenth-century philosophy. Construction, production, and generation are transcendental concepts describing the inner spontaneity of self-consciousness and its self-unfolding. Only in this way may there be a real self-understanding on the part of thought.

Today [1972] this concept of self-understanding has broken down. Was it not a truly hybrid ambition to assert with Fichte and Hegel that the total sum of our knowledge of the world, of our "science," could be achieved in a perfect self-understanding? The famous title of Fichte's foundational philosophic work is indicative of this pretension. *Wissenschaftslehre* has nothing whatsoever to do with what is called the "philosophy of science" today. *Wissenschaftslehre* meant instead the all-encompassing knowledge consisting of the derivation of all the contents of the world from self-consciousness. It is characteristic of the new basic stance of philosophy and of the new insight brought home to us by the experiences of the last hundred years not only that this sense of science is no longer capable of being fulfilled, but also that the meaning of self-understanding has to be understood differently.

Self-understanding can no longer be integrally related to a complete self-transparency in the sense of a full presence of ourselves to ourselves. Self-understanding is always on the way; it is on a path whose completion is a clear impossibility. If there is an entire dimension of the unilluminated unconscious; if all our actions, wishes, drives, decisions, and modes of conduct (and so the totality of our human social existence) are based on the obscure and veiled dimension of our animality; if all our conscious representations can be masks, mere pretexts, under which our vital energy or our social interests pursue their own goals in an unconscious way; if all the insights we have, as obvious and evident as they may be, are threatened by such doubt; then self-understanding cannot designate any patent self-transparency of our human existing. We have to repudiate the illusion of completely illuminating the darkness of our motivations and tendencies. This is not to say, however, that we can simply ignore this new area of our minds that looms in the unconscious. What comes in for methodical investigation here is indeed not only the field of the unconscious that concerns the psychoanalyst as a physician; it is just as much the world of the dominant social prejudices that Marxism claims to elucidate. Psychoanalysis and critique of ideology are forms of enlightenment thinking, and both invoke the emancipatory mandate of the Enlightenment as formulated by Kant in terms of the "exodus from the condition of self-inflicted immaturity."

Nevertheless, when we examine the range of these new insights, it seems to me that we need to cast a critical eye upon just what sort of untested presuppositions of a traditional kind are still at work in them. One has to ask oneself whether the dynamic law of human life can be conceived adequately in terms of progress, of a continual advance from the unknown into the known, and whether the course of human culture is actually a linear progression from mythology to enlightenment. Actually, one should entertain a completely different notion: that of whether the movement of human existence does not issue in a relentless inner tension between illumination and concealment. Might it not be just a prejudice of modern times that the notion of progress that is in fact constitutive for the spirit of scientific research can and should be transferable to the whole of human living and human culture? One has to ask whether progress, as it is at home in the special field of scientific research, is at all consonant with the conditions of human existence in general. Is the notion of an ever-mounting and self-perfecting enlightenment ultimately questionable?

If one wishes to appraise the significance or the task and the limits of what we call hermeneutics today, one must bear in mind this philosophic and humane background—this fundamental doubt about the legitimacy of objective self-consciousness. In a certain way, the very word "hermeneutics" and its cognate word "interpretation" furnish a hint, for these words imply a sharp distinction between the claim of being able to explain a fact definitively 1) by deriving all its conditions; 2) by calculating it from the givenness of all its conditions; and 3) by learning to produce it in an artificial arrangement—the well-known ideal of natural scientific knowledge; and on the other hand, the claim (say, of interpretation) which we always presume to be no more than an approximation: only an attempt, plausible and often fruitful, but clearly never definitive.

The very idea of a definitive interpretation seems to be intrinsically contradictory. Interpretation is always on the way. If, then, the word "interpretation" points to the finitude of human being and the finitude of human knowing, then the experience of interpretation implies something that was not implied by the earlier self-understanding when hermeneutics was coordinated with special fields and applied as a technique for overcoming difficulties in troublesome texts. At that time hermeneutics could be understood as a teaching about a technical skill—but no longer.

Once we presuppose that there is no such thing as a fully transparent text or a completely exhaustive interest in the explaining and construing of texts, then all perspectives relative to the art and theory of interpretation are shifted. Then it becomes more important to trace the interests guiding us with respect to a given subject matter than simply to interpret the evident content of a statement. One of the more fertile insights of modern hermeneutics is that every statement has to be seen as a response to a question, and that the only way to understand a statement is to get hold of the question to which its statement is an answer. This prior question has its own direction of meaning and is by no means to be gotten hold of through a network of background motivations, but rather in reaching out to the broader contexts of meaning encompassed by the question and deposited in the statement.

What has to be held up as a first determination that will do justice to modern hermeneutics in contrast to the traditional kind is this notion that a philosophical hermeneutics is more interested in the questions than the answers—or better, that it interprets statements as answers to questions that its role is to understand. That is not all. Where does our effort to understand begin? Why are we interested in understanding a text or some experience of the world, including our doubts about patent self-interpretations? Do we have a free choice about these things? Is it at all true that we follow our own free decision whenever we try to investigate or interpret certain things? Free decision? A neutral, completely objective concern? At least the theologian would surely have objections here and say, "Oh no! Our understanding of the holy scriptures does not come from our own free choice. It takes an act of grace. And the Bible is not a totality of sentences offered willy-nilly as a sacrifice to human analysis. No, the gospel is directed to me in a personal way. It claims to contain neither an objective statement nor a totality of objective statements but a special address to me." I believe that not only theologians would have doubts about the notion that one ultimately encounters free decisions when interpreting transmitted texts. Rather, there are always both conscious and unconscious interests at play determining us; it will always be the case that we have to ask ourselves why a text stirs our interest. The answer will never be that it communicates some neutral fact to us. On the contrary, we have to get behind such putative facts in order to awaken our interest in them or to make ourselves expressly aware of such interests. We encounter facts in statements. All statements are answers.

But that is not all. The question to which each statement is an answer that is itself motivated in turn, and so in a certain sense every question is itself an answer again. It responds to a challenge. Without an inner tension between our anticipations of meaning and the all-pervasive opinions and without a critical interest in these generally prevailing opinions, there would be no questions at all.

This first step of hermeneutic endeavor, especially the requirement of going back to the motivating questions when understanding statements, is not particularly an artificial procedure. On the contrary, it is our normal practice. If we have to answer a question and we cannot understand the question correctly (but we do know what the other wants to know), then we obviously have to understand better the sense of the question. And so we ask in return why someone would ask us that. Only when I have first understood the motivating meaning of the question can I even begin to look for an answer. It is not artificial in the least to reflect upon the presuppositions implicit in our questions. On the contrary, it is artificial not to reflect upon these presuppositions. It is quite artificial to imagine that statements fall down from heaven and that they can be subjected to analytic labor without even once bringing into consideration why they were stated and in what way they are responses to something. That is the first, basic, and infinitely far-reaching demand called for in any hermeneutical undertaking. Not only in philosophy or theology but in any research project, it is required that one elaborate an awareness of the hermeneutic situation. That has to be our initial aim when we approach what the question is. To state this in words expressing one of our more trivial experiences, we must understand what is behind a question. Making ourselves aware of hidden presuppositions, however, not only and primarily means illuminating our unconscious presuppositions in the sense of psychoanalysis; it means becoming aware of the vague presuppositions and implications involved in a question that comes up.

Elaborating the hermeneutic situation, which is the key to methodical interpretation, has a unique element to it. The first guiding insight is to admit the endlessness of this task. To imagine that one might ever attain full illumination as to one's motives or interests in questions is to imagine something impossible. In spite of this, it remains a legitimate task to clarify what lies at the basis of our interests as far as possible. Only then are we in a position to understand the statements with which we are concerned, precisely insofar as we recognize our own questions in them.

In this connection, we must realize that the unconscious and the implicit do not simply make up the polar opposite of our conscious human existence. The task of understanding is not merely that of clarifying the deepest unconscious grounds motivating our interest, but above all that of understanding and explicating them in the direction and limits indicated by our hermeneutic interest. In the rare cases in which the communicative intersubjectivity of the "community of conversation" is fundamentally disrupted so that one despairs of any intended and common meaning, this can motivate a direction of interest for which the psychoanalyst is competent.

But this example is a limit situation for hermeneutics. One can sharpen any hermeneutic situation to this limit of despairing of meaning and of needing to get behind the manifest meaning. The labor of psychoanalysis would, it appears to me, be based on a false estimation of its universal legitimacy and its unique meaning, if its task were not regarded as a task at the limit and if it were not supposed to set out from the fundamental insight that life always discovers some kind of equilibrium and that also belonging to this equilibrium a balance between our unconscious drives and our conscious human motivations and decisions. To be sure, there is never complete concord between the tendencies of our unconscious and our conscious motivations. But as a rule neither is it always a matter of complete concealment and distortion. It is a sign of sickness when one has so dissimulated oneself to oneself that one can know nothing further without confiding in a doctor. Then in a common labor of analysis, one takes a couple of steps further toward clarifying the background of one's own unconscious—with the goal of regaining what one had lost: the equilibrium between one's own nature and the awareness and language shared by all of us.

In contrast to this, the unconscious in the sense of what is implicit in our direct awareness, is the normal object of our hermeneutic concern. This means, however, that the task of understanding is restricted. It is restricted by the resistance offered by statements or texts and is brought to an end by the regaining of a shared possession of meaning, just as happens in a conversation when we try to shed light upon a difference of opinion or a misunderstanding.

In this most authentic realm of hermeneutic experience, the conditions of which a hermeneutic philosophy tries to give an account, the affinity of hermeneutics with practical philosophy is confirmed. First of all, understanding, like action, always involves a risk and is never just the simple application of a general knowledge of rules to the statements or texts to be understood. Furthermore, where it is successful, understanding means a growth in inner awareness, as a new experience enters into the texture of our own mental experience. Understanding is an adventure and, like any other adventure, is dangerous. Because it is not satisfied with simply wanting to register what is there or said there but goes back to our guiding interests and questions, one has to concede that the hermeneutical experience has a far lower degree of certainty than that attained by the methods of the natural sciences. But when one realizes that understanding is an adventure, one realizes that it affords unique opportunities as well. It is capable of contributing in a special way to the broadening of our human experiences, our self-knowledge, and our horizon, for everything that understanding mediates is mediated through ourselves.

A further point is that the key terms of earlier hermeneutics, such as the *mens auctoris* or the intention of the text, together with all the psychological factors related to the openness of the reader or listener to the text, are not adequate to what is most essential to the process of understanding to the extent that it is a process of communication. For indeed it is a process of growing familiarity between the determinate experience, or the "text," and ourselves. The intrinsically linguistic condition of all our understanding implies that the vague representations of meaning that bear us along get brought word by word to articulation and so become communicable. The communality of all understanding as grounded in its intrinsically linguistic quality seems to me to be an essential point in hermeneutical experience. We are continually shaping a common perspective when we speak a common language and so are active participants in the communality of our experience of the world. Experiences of resistance or opposition bear witness to this, for example, in discussion. Discussion bears fruit when a common language is found. Then the participants part from one another as changed beings. The individual perspectives with which they entered upon the discussion have been transformed, and so they have been transformed themselves. This, then, is a kind of progress—not the progress proper to research in regard to which one cannot fall behind, but rather a progress that always must be renewed in the effort of our living.

The miniature of a successful discussion can illustrate what I have developed in the theory of the fusion of horizons in *Truth and Method,* and it may provide a justification as to why I maintain that the situation of conversation is a fertile model even where a mute text is brought to speech first by the questions of the interpreter.

The hermeneutics that I characterize as philosophic is not introduced as a new procedure of interpretation or explication. Basically, it only describes what always happens wherever an interpretation is convincing and successful. It is not at all a matter of a doctrine about a technical skill that would state how understanding ought to be. We have to acknowledge what is, and so we cannot change the fact that unacknowledged presuppositions are always at work in our understanding. Probably we should not want to change this at all, even if we could. Understanding always harvests a broadened and deepened self-understanding. But that means hermeneutics is philosophy, and as philosophy it is practical philosophy.

The great tradition of practical philosophy lives on in a hermeneutics that becomes aware of its philosophic implications, so we have recourse to this tradition about which we have spoken. In both cases, we have the same mutual implication between theoretical interest and practical action. Aristotle thought this issue through with complete lucidity in his ethics. For one to dedicate one's life to theoretic interests presupposes the virtue of *phronesis* [practical wisdom]. This in no way restricts the primacy of theory or of an interest in the pure desire to know. The idea of theory is and remains the exclusion of every interest in mere utility, whether on the part of the individual, the group, or the society as a whole. On the other hand, the primacy of "practice" is undeniable. Aristotle was insightful enough to acknowledge the reciprocity between theory and practice.

So when I speak about hermeneutics here, it is theory. There are no practical situations of understanding that I am trying to resolve by so speaking. Hermeneutics has to do with a theoretical attitude toward the practice of interpretation, the interpretation of texts, but also in relation to the experiences interpreted in them and in our communicatively unfolded orientations in the world. This theoretic stance only makes us aware reflectively of what is performatively at play in the practical experience of understanding. And so it appears to me that the answer given by Aristotle to the question about the possibility of a moral philosophy holds true as well for our interest in hermeneutics. His answer was that ethics is only a theoretical enterprise, and that anything said by way of a theoretic description of the forms of right living can be at best of little help when it comes to the concrete application to the human experience of life. And yet the universal desire to know does not break off at the point where concrete practical discernment is the decisive issue. The connection between the universal desire to know and concrete practical discernment is a reciprocal one. So it appears to me that heightened theoretic awareness about the experience of understanding and the practice of understanding, like philosophical hermeneutics and one's own self-understanding, are inseparable.

Translated by Frederick G. Lawrence

Hermeneutics as a Theoretical and Practical Task

This 1978 essay, *Hermeneutik als theoretische und praktische Aufgabe,* was originally presented to two different audiences on two successive days: first, the Heidelberg Academy of Sciences (January 18, 1978) and then the International Organization for Legal and Social Philosophy [*Internationale Vereinigung für Rechts- und Sozialphilosophie*] meeting in Münster (January 19, 1978). Later he expanded the essay for publication in a special double issue of the *Revue Internationale de Philosophie* [vol. 33, nos. 127–28 (1979): 239–59], that carried the title [translated from the French]: "The New Rhetoric: Homage to Chaim Perelman." The first two audiences were mostly nonphilosophers, and the reading audience of the journal was more general, those interested in Chaim Perelman, but not necessarily conversant with Gadamer's hermeneutics. Perelman, the famous Brussels and later Penn State University professor of law, had something in common with Gadamer. Both turned to ancient rhetoric, one to support a new rhetoric and the other to support a new hermeneutics. One of Perelman's half-dozen books in French, *Traité de l'argumentation: la nouvelle rhétorique* (1958), originally cowritten with Lucie Olbrechts-Tyteca, was translated into English as *The New Rhetoric* (1969) and was widely read in the United States and elsewhere.

These contexts help to account for several aspects of Gadamer's essay. Its target audience for the original two lectures was made up of those largely unfamiliar with hermeneutics, so Gadamer goes to some length to explain hermeneutics and to defend his own hermeneutics. In the case of the publication of his essay in a French journal, Gadamer consciously finds common ground with Perelman in that Perelman "rediscovers" ancient rhetoric. Gadamer was already familiar with it. Philosophically, Perelman does not share Gadamer's underpinnings in ancient or modern philosophy, turning rather to British empiricism as a professor of law, but the common ground is sufficient. Gadamer finds in Perelman's new rhetoric an ally for his hermeneutics, and he ventures to tie his own philosophy not only to Aristotle's rhetoric but also to his practical philosophy. In doing so, he argues for a form of hermeneutics that has practical effects.

Indeed, the theme of this essay is that his hermeneutics has not only a theoretical dimension but a practical dimension, also, a practical dimension rooted in Aristotle's practical philosophy. Gadamer hastens to make clear that the usual modern conception of theory and its relation to practice is not what he has in mind. Rather, he goes back to Aristotle not only for rhetoric but for practical philosophy and attempts to shape a hermeneutics that is both theoretical in its universal dimensions but also practical in not using the abstract methods of science but a practical philosophy that seeks the Good, in the ancient sense.

This essay, then, is of value not only as defense and elaboration of important dimensions of Gadamer's hermeneutics, but also important in the way it links up with rhetoric. Like rhetoric, Gadamer's hermeneutics thinks in terms of reception, of application. Like rhetoric, his hermeneutics seeks an event of understanding that is transformative, although not as directly pointed to a desired action. But in its link with ancient practical philosophy his hermeneutics achieves a greater depth even than the new rhetoric, but in his friendly approach he finds a new ally for his hermeneutics and perhaps will win some rhetoricians over to support his hermeneutics, which is also rooted in ancient philosophy.

* * *

Hermeneutics as a Theoretical and Practical Task

Not only the word "hermeneutics" is ancient. The reality designated by the word may be properly rendered today with such expressions as "interpretation," "explication," "translation," or even only with "understanding." At any rate, it precedes the idea of a methical science developed by modernity. Even modern linguistic usage itself reflects something of the peculiar two-sidedness and ambivalence of the theoretical and practical perspective under which the reality of hermeneutics appears. In the late eighteenth as well as in the early nineteenth centuries, the singular emergence of the term "hermeneutics" in certain authors shows that at that time the expression, coming probably from theology, penetrated the general language usage; and then it obviously denoted only the practical capacity of understanding, in the sense of the intelligent and empathetic entry into another's standpoint. It comes up as a term of praise among the pastoral types. I discovered the word in the German author Heinrich Seume (who of course had been a student with Morus in Leipzig) and in Johann Peter Hebel. But even Schleiermacher, the founder of the more recent development of hermeneutics into a general methodological doctrine of the *Geisteswissenschaften* [human sciences and humanities], appeals emphatically to the idea that the art of understanding is required not only with respect to texts but also in one's verbal exchanges with one's fellow human beings.

Thus hermeneutics is more than just a method of the sciences or the distinctive feature of a certain group of sciences. Above all it refers to a natural human capacity [for understanding].

The oscillation of an expression like "hermeneutics" between a theoretical and a practical meaning is encountered elsewhere too. For example, we speak of logic or the lack of it in our day-to-day exchanges with our fellow human beings, and by this we are not at all referring to the special philosophical discipline of logic. The same holds true for the word "rhetoric," by which we designate the teachable art of speaking, as well as a natural gift and its exercise. Here it is altogether clear that without any native endowment the learning of what can be learned leads only to quite modest success. If natural giftedness for speaking is lacking, it can scarcely be made up for by methodological doctrine. Now this will surely be the case as well for the art of understanding, for hermeneutics.

This sort of thing has its significance for the theory of science. What kind of science is it that presents itself both as a cultivation of a natural gift and as a theoretically heightened awareness of it? For the history of science this question presents us an unsolved problem. Where does the art of understanding belong? Does hermeneutics stand close to rhetoric? Or should one bring it more into proximity with logic and the methodology of the sciences? Recently I have tried to make some contributions to these questions for the history of science.[1] Like linguistic usage, inquiry into the history of science also indicates that the notion of method, fundamental to modern science, tended to dissolve the notion of science that was open precisely in the direction of being a natural human capacity.

So there arises the more general question as to whether there survives into our own day a sector within the systematic framework of the sciences that is more strongly tied to the earlier concepts of science than to the notion of method that is proper to modern science. It may still be asked whether this is not at least the case for the clearly circumscribable domain of the so-called *Geisteswissenschaften*—and this without prejudice to the question of whether a hermeneutic dimension does not play a role in every instance of the desire to know, even that of the modern sciences of nature.

Now there does exist at least one example of this sort pertinent to the theory of science, which could lend a certain legitimacy to such a reorientation of the methodical heightening of awareness on the part of the *Geisteswissenschaften*. This is the practical philosophy established by Aristotle.[2]

Aristotle claimed a peculiar independence for practical philosophy in relation to Platonic dialectic because he understood the latter as theoretic knowledge. He began a tradition of practical philosophy that exercised its influence right down into the nineteenth century, indeed until it was dissolved in our own century into what is called political science. Despite all the specificity with which Aristotle set the idea of practical philosophy against Plato's unified science of dialectic, the aspect of practical philosophy that is relevant for theory of science has remained quite obscure. Right down to our own day there have been attempts to see in the method of Aristotelian ethics, which was introduced by Aristotle as a form of practical philosophy and in which the virtue of practical reasonableness (*phronesis*) takes up a central place, nothing more than the exercise of practical rationality. (The fact that any human action falls in the category of practical rationality, and hence also of the contribution of Aristotelian thought on the matter says nothing about the method of practical philosophy.)

It is not surprising that there is dispute about this point because general statements by Aristotle about the methodology and systematic aspects of the sciences are relatively scarce, and when they occur they evidently have the methodological specificity of the sciences less in view than the diversity of their objective fields. This is especially the case for the first chapter of book epsilon [book VI] of the *Metaphysics,* and its doublet at K 7. There, of course, physics (and in Aristotle's ultimate intention, first philosophy in general) is distinguished as theoretical science from practical and poetic science. But if one examines how the distinction between theoretical and nontheoretical sciences gets grounded, one discovers that the discussion focuses solely on the differences in the objects of such knowing. Now this surely corresponds with Aristotle's general methodological principle that method must always be directed toward its object and what is relevant to its objects. Thus the matter is clear. In the case of physics its object is distinguished by self-movement. In contrast, the object of the productive sciences, the work to be produced, has its source in the producing agent and his knowledge and ability; likewise, what guides a person engaged in practical and political action is determined by the agent and his or her knowledge. Thus it can appear as if Aristotle were speaking here about technical knowledge (for instance, that of the physician) and about the practical knowledge of one who makes a reasonable decision (*prohairesis*) as though such knowledge itself constituted the practical science that is correlative to the theoretical knowledge of physics. But this is obviously not the case.

The sciences being differentiated here (besides which in the theoretical realm one finds the further distinguishing of physics, mathematics, and theology) are introduced as the sort that strive to know the *archai* and *aitiai*—the principles and determining factors. It is a matter here of inquiry into the *arché* [*Arché-Forschung*]; and this does not mean the knowledge a physician, a craftsman, or a politician has, which is always found in application, but knowledge about what may be said and taught in general about such knowing.

It is characteristic that Aristotle does not reflect upon this distinction at all. Obviously for him it is taken for granted that in these realms knowledge of the universal raises no independent claim whatsoever, but rather constantly entails being transformed in the concrete application to a single case. Yet our consideration of the matter shows that it is necessary to make a sharp distinction between other sciences and the philosophical sciences which thematize the practical or poetic performances of acting or producing (including poetry and the "making" of speech), and also to distinguish the investigation of these performances from the performances themselves. Practical philosophy is not itself the virtue of practical reasonableness.

Of course, one hesitates to apply the modern notion of theory to [Greek] practical philosophy, which by its own self-characterization already wants to be practical. Thus it is a problem of the utmost difficulty to work out the specific conditions of the scientific quality that holds sway in these areas, especially since Aristotle himself characterizes them with only the vague indication that they are less exact. In the case of practical philosophy the matter is particularly complicated, and for this reason it called forth a certain methodological reflection on Aristotle's part. Practical philosophy, then, needs a unique kind of legitimation. Obviously the decisive problem is that this practical science is involved with the all-embracing problem of the good in human life, which is not confined to a determinate area like the other modes of technical knowledge. In spite of this, the expression "practical philosophy" intends precisely to say that it makes no determinate use of arguments of a cosmological, ontological, or metaphysical sort for practical problems. Although we are here restricted to the practical good, to what is of importance for human beings, it is still clear that the method for handling these questions of practical action is fundamentally different from practical reason itself.

Already implicit in the apparent pleonasm [redundancy] of a theoretical philosophy, and most specifically in its self-designation as practical philosophy, something is mirrored in the reflection of philosophers right down to our own day: that philosophy must claim not merely to know but also to have a practical effect. In other words, as the science of the good in human life, ethics promotes that good itself. In the case of the productive sciences, the so-called *technai,* this is obvious even for us today. They are precisely teachable skills or techniques [*Kunstlehren*] for which their practical use alone is the decisive issue. But in the case of political ethics it is completely different, for it is hardly possible to repudiate such a practical intent. Thus this claim has almost always arisen right down to our own day. Ethics does not simply propose to describe valid norms; it also wants to establish their validity or even to introduce more adequate norms.

At least since Rousseau's critique of the rationalist pride of thinkers in the Enlightenment, this has become a real problem. How should the philosophic science of moral affairs legitimate its claim to exist at all if it is true that the undistorted character of natural moral consciousness knows how to recognize the good and duty with unsurpassable exactitude and the most delicate sensitivity? This is not the place to spell out *in extenso* the way Kant grounded the enterprise of moral philosophy in reply to Rousseau's challenge, or even to expound the way Aristotle sets for himself the same question and tries to do it justice by bringing out the special preconditions needed for a student to meaningfully receive theoretical instruction about the "practical good."[3] Practical philosophy functions in our context here only as an example of a tradition in which such knowing does not correspond to the modern notion of method.

Our theme is hermeneutics, and for this theme the relationship of hermeneutics with rhetoric stands in the foreground. Even if we did not know that early modern hermeneutics had been developed as a construction parallel to rhetoric in conjunction with Melanchthon's renewal of Aristotelianism, the problem of rhetoric for a theory of science would be a ready-made point of orientation. Clearly the ability to speak has the same breadth and universality as the ability to understand and interpret. One can talk about everything, and everything one says should be understandable. Here rhetoric and hermeneutics have a very close relationship. The skilled mastery of such abilities in speaking and understanding is demonstrated to the utmost in the case of writing in the writing of speeches and in the understanding of what is written. Hermeneutics may be precisely defined as the art of bringing what is said or written to speak again. What kind of an art hermeneutics is, then, we can learn from rhetoric.

What rhetoric is as a science, or what rhetoric as an art consists of, is a problem that was already considered in the initial phases of reflection on the theory of science. It was the well-known antagonism between philosophy and rhetoric in the Greek educational setup that provoked

Plato to pose the question concerning the cognitive character of rhetoric. Although Plato in his *Gorgias* characterized all of rhetoric as an art of flattery equating it with the art of cooking and set it in opposition to any serious knowledge, in another dialogue, the *Phaedrus,* he dedicated himself to the task of endowing rhetoric with a more profound meaning and endowing it a share of a philosophical justification. Thus it was asked there exactly what facet of rhetoric is a *techne.* The perspectives laid open in the *Phaedrus* were also at the root of Aristotle's *Rhetoric,* which presents more a philosophy of human life as determined by speech than a technical doctrine about the art of speaking.

Such a notion of rhetoric shares with dialectic the universality of its claim, insofar as it is not confined to a determinate realm as usually holds true for the specialized capability required for a *techne.* This is precisely the reason why rhetoric could enter into competition with philosophy and rival it as a universal propaedeutic. The *Phaedrus* wants to show that if a rhetoric posited with such a breadth wishes to overcome the narrowness of merely rule-governed technique, which according to Plato contains only *ta pro tes technes anankaia mathemata* [the knowledge preliminary to it] (*Phaedrus* 269b), it ultimately has to be taken up into philosophy, into the totality of dialectical knowledge. This process of demonstration is of interest to us here because what is said in the *Phaedrus* about elevating rhetoric beyond a mere technique to the status of true knowledge (which Plato, of course, called *techne*) may also apply to hermeneutics as the art of understanding.

It is widely accepted that Plato understood dialectic (that is, philosophy itself) as a *techne,* and he distinguished its uniqueness in contrast to the other *technai* only in the sense that it is the highest form of knowledge, indeed the knowledge of the most sublime thing given for human beings to know, the good (*megiston mathemata*). Mutatis mutandis the same had to hold true for the philosophic rhetoric called for by him as well, and hence ultimately for hermeneutics too. Aristotle was the first to draw that distinction between science, *techne,* and practical rationality (*phronesis*), a distinction which was to have great consequences.

The concept of practical philosophy, in fact, rests upon the Aristotelian critique of Plato's idea of the Good. Only when one looks into the issues more carefully does it become clear (as I have tried to make plausible in a recent investigation)[4] that the question of the good was actually posed as if it were the highest fulfillment of that same idea of knowledge pursued by the *technai* and by the sciences in their own proper fields. But this question is not really fulfilled in a highest learnable science. The supreme objective of inquiry, the good (*to agathon*), comes up constantly in Socratic argumentation but in a negative demonstrative function. For instance, Socrates refutes the claim of the *technai* to be genuine knowledge. His own knowledge is *docta ignorantia*, and it is not called dialectic for nothing; only the individual who knows is capable of standing his ground right down to the final speech and response. Thus—something that is also relevant for rhetoric—this knowledge can only be a *techne* or science if it becomes the dialectic! Only the individual is truly capable as a speaker who has acknowledged as good and right the thing about which he is trying to persuade people and is thereby able to stand up for it. This knowledge of the good and this capability in the art of speaking does not mean a universal knowledge of "the good"; rather, it means a knowledge about that to which one has to persuade people here and now, a knowledge of how one is to go about doing this, and a knowledge of those whom one has to persuade. Only when one sees the concretization required by the knowledge of the good does one understand why the art of writing speeches plays such a role in the broader argumentation. It too can be an art. Plato acknowledges this with his explicitly conciliatory turning to Isocrates; but only in the eventuality that, beyond realizing the weakness of the spoken word, one also recognizes the weakness of anything written and is capable of coming to its aid at any time, just as one would do for all spoken discourse—in the manner that the dialectician stands behind what he says.

This point is of fundamental significance. In addition to all that goes into knowledge (which ultimately includes everything knowable, or "the nature of the whole"), real knowledge also has to recognize the *kairos*. This means knowing when and how one is required to speak. But this cannot be acquired merely by learning rules or by rote. There are no rules governing the reasonable use of rules, as Kant stated so rightly in his *Critique of Judgment*.

In Plato this comes out in the *Phaedrus* (268ff.) by means of an amusing exaggeration: if anyone were to possess only all the physician's information and rules of thumb without knowing where and when to apply them, he would not be a physician. Were a tragedian or musician only to have learned the general rules and techniques of his art and yet produced no work using that knowledge, he would not be a poet or musician (280ff.). In the same way, the orator has to know all about where and when to speak (*hai eukairiai te kai akairiai;* 272a6).

Here one notices in Plato an overinflation of the model of *techne* as a learnable science, in that he stretches supreme knowledge in the direction of the dialectic. For Plato, neither the physician nor the poet nor the musician knows the good. Even the dialectician or the philosopher, who really is one and not just a Sophist, does not possess a special knowledge, but is in his person the embodiment of the dialectic, that is, of philosophy. Parallel to this is the way the true political art emerges in the dialogue of the *Statesman* as a kind of artistry in weaving, an artistry by which one has to weave together opposing factors into a unity (305e). It is in fact embodied in the statesman. Likewise, in the *Philebus* knowledge of the good life comes about as an art of right mixing, which the individual in search of happiness has to bring about *in concreto*. In a beautiful work, Ernst Kapp has shown this well with regard to the *Statesman,* and in my own early works as a beginner criticizing Werner Jaeger's construction of the history of the development [of Greek thought], I had similar points in mind with respect to the *Philebus*.[5]

It is against this background that the elaboration of the distinction of theoretical, practical, and productive philosophy, which appears in its initial stages in Aristotle, has to be considered. So too must its status as theory of science be determined. The dialectical overstretching of rhetoric tried out by Plato in the *Phaedrus* is suggestive of a direction. Rhetoric is indissoluble from dialectic; and persuasion that is really convincing is indissoluble from knowledge of the true. To the same degree, understanding has to be thought about from the vantage point of knowledge. It is a capacity to learn. And Aristotle stresses this as well when he deals with *synesis*.[6] What is at issue for the truly dialectical rhetorician, as well as for the statesman and also in the leading of one's own life, is the good. And this does not present itself as the *ergon*, which is produced by making, but rather as praxis and *eupraxis* (and that means as *energeia*). Accordingly, even though it is supposed to make good citizens, Aristotelian politics does not actually treat education as productive philosophy. Instead Aristotle deals with politics just as he handled the doctrine about constitutional forms—as practical philosophy.[7]

It is certainly correct that the Aristotelian idea of a practical philosophy did not live on in its totality but only in its limitation to politics. This limitation put it closer to the notion of a technique because it proposes to mediate a sort of philosophically grounded specialized knowledge in the service of a law-giving reason. This allowed it to be integrated into the scientific thinking of modernity, at least for a while. On the other hand, Greek moral philosophy determined following ages, and especially modernity, less in its Aristotelian than in its Stoic form of expression. Similarly, Aristotle's *Rhetoric* remained relatively uninfluential within the tradition of ancient rhetoric. It was just too much philosophy for the masters of the art of speech with their guidelines toward a masterly art of speaking. But just because of its philosophic character, which, as Aristotle says, linked it with dialectics and ethics (*peri ta ethe pragmateia; Rhetoric* 1356a26), it found its new hour in the age of humanism and the Reformation.

The use made of Aristotelian rhetoric by the Reformers and especially Melanchthon is quite relevant for us here. Melanchthon transformed rhetoric from the art of making speeches into the art of following discourses with understanding—which means he transformed it into hermeneutics. Here two elements came together: first, the new emphasis upon the characteristic of being written and the new cultivation of reading that set in with the invention of the art of book printing; and second, the Reformation's theological turning against the tradition and toward the principle of scripture. The central role of the holy scriptures for the preaching of the gospel led to its translation into vernaculars, and at the same time the doctrine of the universal priesthood of all believers gave rise to a use of scripture in preaching and reading that was in need of new guidance. Now, wherever laymen took up reading, it was no longer a matter of people directed to an understanding by way of a spoken lecture. No longer did the impressive rhetoric of the jurist, the priest, or a literate elite come to the support of the reader.

We ourselves realize how very hard it is to read a text out loud in a foreign tongue or even a difficult text in one's own language on short notice in such a way that one can make good sense of it. If, in a classroom, one asks a beginner to read a sentence aloud—whether it be in German, Greek, or Chinese—it always ends up Chinese whenever one reads aloud what one does not understand. It is only when one understands what one is reading that one can modulate and introduce a rhythm in such a way that what is meant really comes across.

Thus a heightened difficulty arose, the difficulty involved with reading, that is, of bringing the scriptures to speak. In the modern period this raised the art of understanding in its diverse dimensions to methodical self-awareness.

The characteristic of having been written down is not something that is encountered for the first time during our centuries of a general culture marked by reading—whose end we are perhaps approaching in our day. From its very outset, the hermeneutic task posed by something's having been written down has to do not with the external technique of deciphering written signs so much as with the task of correctly understanding the meanings that are fixed in writing. Whenever writing exercises the function of univocal determination and controllable warrant, both the composition as well as the comprehension of a text that originated in this fashion are tasks requiring the exercise of an art, whether one is dealing with tax lists, contracts (which, to the joy of our investigators of language, are sometimes composed bilingually), or religious or other legal documents. So the exercise of the art of hermeneutics is based on an age-old practice as well.

The peculiarly hermeneutical dimension of such an exercise makes us aware of what went on in such practice. Reflection upon the practice of understanding down through time can hardly be dissociated from the tradition of rhetoric. And so it was one of the most important contributions of hermeneutics, already achieved by Melanchthon, to have developed the doctrine of the *scopi,* the perspectives. Melanchthon noticed that just as orators do at the beginning of their writings, Aristotle too points to the viewpoint under which one has to apprehend his elucidations. It is clearly one thing to have to interpret a law and quite another to have to interpret the holy scriptures or a "classical" work of poetry. For the meaning of such texts is determined not by an understanding that is neutral but by their claim to be accepted.

There were especially two areas in which the problem of interpreting written texts found available a long-standing technical expertise and brought forth a heightened theoretical consciousness: the interpretation of legal texts, which made up the stock-in-trade of jurists, especially since the codification of Roman law under Justinian; and the interpretation of holy scripture in the sense of the ecclesiastical dogmatic tradition of the *doctrina Christiana.* The legal and theological hermeneutics of modern times were able to link up with these older traditions.

Quite apart from any codification of law, the task of making a finding based on it and coming up with a verdict necessarily contains a tension that Aristotle had already thematized clearly: the tension between the universality of the accepted legal framework, whether codified or uncodified, and the individuality of the concrete case. Of course, the concrete passing of judgment in a legal question is no theoretical statement but an instance of "doing things with words"; this is almost too obvious to bear mentioning. In a certain sense the correct interpretation of a law is presupposed in its application. To that extent, one can say that each application of a law moves beyond the mere understanding of its legal sense and fashions a new reality.

This process is similar in the performing arts, where one goes in interpretation beyond the given work, whether it be the musical notes or a dramatic text, to such an extent that new realities are shaped and determined by the performance. In the case of the performing arts, however, it still makes sense to say that each performance is based upon a determinate interpretation of the given work, and it clearly still makes sense to recognize and affirm different degrees of adequacy among the many possible interpretations offered by the performances. But at least in the cases of the literary theater and of music, and in relation to its ideal determinacy, the performance itself is not a mere re-presentation but an interpretation. And so especially in the case of music, we take it completely for granted that we speak of the interpretation of a work by the artist who reproduces it.

In an analogous manner, then, the application of a law to a given legal case seems to me to contain an act of interpretation. This means, however, that every application of legal prescriptions that appears to do justice to the issue at stake both concretizes and further clarifies the meaning of a given law. Max Weber, it seems to me, was completely right when he said, "Prophets alone have been *consciously* 'creative' in their conduct towards the existing law, in the sense of fashioning new law. For the most part, it is by no means specifically modern, but, from an objective point of view, proper to the most 'creative' legal practitioners that they felt themselves *subjectively* to be no more than mouthpieces for already existing—perhaps often even latently—norms, as their interpreters and appliers, but not as their creators."[8] It accords with age-old Aristotelian wisdom that the finding of the law always requires the enlarging consideration of equity and that the perspective of equity does not stand in contradiction with the law, but precisely by relinquishing the letter of the law it brings the legal meaning to complete fulfillment.

On account of the reception of Roman law down through history, this problem of making a legal finding was experienced more sharply at the beginning of the modern period because the traditional forms of legal administration were called into question by the new law put forward by the jurists. Hence the jurist's hermeneutics, as his doctrine of the interpretation of the law, has to be accorded a special significance. In discussions during the early modern age from Budeus to Vico, the defense of *aequitas* took up a lot of space. But one might well also mention the fact that the legal erudition characteristic of the jurists is with good reason called jurisprudence, which means sagacity in judgment. The very word itself recalls the heritage of practical philosophy that considered *prudentia* the highest virtue of practical rationality. It is a sign of the loss of recognition of the special methodological uniqueness of this legal erudition and its practical determinacy that in the late nineteenth century the expression "legal science" came to predominate as a designation of the discipline of law.[9]

The situation in theology is similar. To be sure, since late antiquity there has been a kind of art of interpretation in theology, and there was even a rather differentiated doctrine of the diverse modes of interpreting the holy scriptures. But the various forms of scriptural interpretation from the time of Cassiodorus basically served as guidelines for making the holy scriptures useful to the dogmatic tradition of the church. They were not at all intended to supply by themselves a way of interpreting holy scripture for the sake of mediating correct doctrine.

On the other hand, with the Reformation's return to scripture itself and especially with the spread of Bible reading outside the guildlike tradition of the clerics (which was implicit in the Reformation doctrine of the priesthood of all believers), the hermeneutical problem became pressing in an altogether different way. The decisive point here is not that one was dealing with the holy scriptures in texts in a foreign tongue, whose adequate translation into the vernacular languages and whose exact understanding brought into play an entire armature of linguistic, literary, and historical information. No, the decisive factor was rather that by reason of the radicality of the Reformation's return to the New Testament and in virtue of the demotion of the church's dogmatic tradition, the Christian message itself now confronted readers with a new, uncanny radicality. This went far beyond using philological and historical aids, aids that were actually useful in interpreting any ancient text in a foreign language, not just the Bible.

What Reformation hermeneutics turned up and what Flacius especially emphasized was that the very message of the holy scriptures stood in the way of the natural prior self-understanding that human beings had of themselves. Not obedience to the law and the performing of meritorious works but faith alone—and that means faith in the incredible fact of God's becoming man and in the resurrection—promises justification. To make this convincing in the face of a reliance upon oneself and one's own merits, one's "good works," is what the interpretation of the holy scriptures demands. As a result, since the Reformation the church has set this in the foreground even more decisively than it had been in the older Christian tradition. The entire form of the Protestant Christian worship service becomes confession, empowerment, and call to faith. It rests as much as possible on the correct interpretation of the Christian message. Once the interpretation of scripture in the sermon entered more and more into prominence in the worship service in the Christian churches, the special task of theological hermeneutics came to the fore. Hermeneutics did not serve to advance a scientific understanding of the scriptures so much as the proclamation of it by which the Good News is supposed to reach the simple person in such a way that he or she realizes that he or she is addressed and intended. Consequently, application is not a mere "application" of an understanding but occupies true core of understanding itself. So the interpretive process of application, which was certainly exaggerated to an extreme in pietism, not only represents an essential moment in the hermeneutics of religious texts, but also makes visible the philosophic significance of hermeneutic questions as a whole; so hermeneutics is much more than a methodological instrument.

Hence it was a decisive step in the unfolding of hermeneutics that in the age of Romanticism it was developed into a universally applicable "teachable art" [a *Kunstlehre*] by Schleiermacher and his successors. This was supposed to legitimate the peculiarity of theology as a science possessing equal methodological rights in the garland of the sciences. For Schleiermacher, the understanding approach toward others was a natural endowment of his own genius, and he could surely be called the most congenial friend during an age in which the cultivation of friendship reached a true high point. And he did recognize that one could not restrict the art of understanding to science alone. Instead, understanding as an art plays a major role in the sociable life, and if one simply seeks to understand the words of an intellectually gifted man to which one finds no immediate entry, one makes constant use of this art. One tries to hear what lies between the words used by one's intellectual conversation partner just as one sometimes has to read between the lines of texts.

Nevertheless, precisely in Schleiermacher the pressure brought to bear upon the self-understanding of hermeneutics by the modern notion of science becomes clear. He finds himself distinguishing expressly between a laxer and a more rigorous practice of hermeneutics. The laxer practice begins with the assumption that, when confronted with the utterances of another, correct understanding and agreement is the rule and misunderstanding the exception. On the other hand, the more rigorous practice starts with the assumption that misunderstanding rules and only by way of a skillful exertion can one avoid misunderstanding and reach a correct understanding. It is obvious that with this distinction, the task of interpretation has been uprooted from the context of an intelligent consensus within which the authentic life of understanding gets constantly negotiated. Now it has to overcome a complete alienation. The imposition of an artificial apparatus that is supposed to open up whatever is alien and make it one's own now takes the place of the general communicative ability by which people live together and mediate themselves with the tradition in which they stand.

In accord with the universal thematics of hermeneutics opened up by Schleiermacher and especially with his most distinctive contribution—the introduction of psychological interpretation (which would have to enter in alongside the normally used grammatical interpretation)—is the fact that in the work of his successors, the development of hermeneutics into a methodology became determinative in the nineteenth century. Its object is texts as an anonymous stock which confronts the researcher. Among the followers of Schleiermacher, Wilhelm Dilthey in particular sought to establish hermeneutics as the foundation of the *Geisteswissenschaften* [social sciences and humanities] in order to establish their equal birthright with the natural sciences, by building on Schleiermacher's accentuation of psychological interpretation. Thus Dilthey considered the proper triumph of hermeneutics to be an interpretation of works of art that raises to consciousness the unconscious productions of genius. In relation to artistic works, all the traditional methods of hermeneutics (the grammatical, historical, aesthetic, and psychological) attain a higher realization in the ideal of understanding only insofar as all these means and methods serve the comprehension of the individual structure as such. Here, and also especially in the field of literary criticism, the progressive development of Romantic hermeneutics [in the direction of a science and a skill] redirects a heritage in such a way that right down to its linguistic usage it belies its ancient origin in being criticism, or discerning the singular structure in its validity and its content and of discriminating it from all that does not match up to its standard. Dilthey's effort was, of course, aimed at extending the notion of method proper to modern science to the task of "criticism" and scientifically elucidating poetic expression by means of an interpretative [*verstehenden*] psychology. This detour in the history of literature led to the emergence of the term "literary science" [*Literaturwissenschaft*]. It reflects the fading away of an awareness of tradition, a fading that had taken place during the age of scientific positivism in the nineteenth century. In the areas where German is spoken, the gradually increasing assimilation of the ideal of modern science had even reached the point of changing the name of the field it designates [i.e., *Literaturwissenschaft*].

If we now look back from this overview of the evolution of modern hermeneutics as an evolving doctrine of a teachable art or skill to the Aristotelian tradition of practical philosophy, we are faced with a question: how can the notable tension in Plato and Aristotle between a technical notion of knowledge and a practical, political notion of it which includes the ultimate end of human beings, be made fruitful within the matrix of modern science and the theory of science? As far as hermeneutics is concerned, it is to the point to contrast the separation of theory from practice that is entailed in the modern notion of theoretical science and its practical-technical application, with an idea of knowledge that takes an opposite path, a path leading from practice toward making practice aware of itself theoretically.

In doing so, the problem of hermeneutics can achieve a stronger clarification than is possible from within the immanent problematic of the doctrines of scientific methodology. This seems to me to follow from the twofold relationship of hermeneutics first to rhetoric, which precedes it, on the one hand, and secondly to Aristotle's practical philosophy on the other. It is hard enough, in any case, to determine a place within the theory of science for a discipline like Aristotle's rhetoric. In fact, we have good cause to locate it in the vicinity of poetics, and we would be hard put to dispute the theoretic intention of both writings preserved under Aristotle's name [*Rhetoric* and the *Poetics*]. These writings do not intend to take the place of technical manuals and to serve as aids in a technical sense to the arts of speaking and poetry. Would they, in Aristotle's view, belong at all in series with the art of healing and of gymnastics, which he gladly calls technical sciences in such a context? Did he not himself, even in the place where he really has theoretically elaborated an immense amount of material concerning political knowledge in his *Politics,* enlarge the horizon of problems proper to practical philosophy to such an extent that over and above the manifold of constitutional forms that he studied and analyzed, the question about the best constitution and therewith a practical problematic, the question regarding the good, remained in the forefront? How, then, would the art of understanding that we call hermeneutics have been situated within the horizon of the Aristotelian way of thinking?

In dealing with this question it seems to me instructive to note the way the Greek word for the act of understanding and for being habitually understanding toward others, *synesis,* tends as a rule to be encountered in the neutral context of the phenomenon of learning and in exchangeable proximity to the Greek word for learning (*mathesis*); whereas in the framework of Aristotelian ethics, *synesis* stands for a kind of intellectual virtue. This is no doubt a narrower designation of a word otherwise used by Aristotle as well in a neutral sense, and it corresponds to a similar terminological narrowing of *techne* and *phronesis* in a like context. Still, it says a lot. "Being habitually understanding toward others" [*synesis*] is encountered here in the same sense mentioned at the outset of the usual eighteenth-century use of hermeneutics for knowledge of or understanding of the state of people's souls. "Being habitually understanding toward others" reflects a modification of practical reasonableness, the insightful judgment regarding someone else's practical deliberations.[10] It obviously implies much more than a mere understanding of something said. It also entails a kind of communality in virtue of which the reciprocal taking of counsel, the giving and taking of advice, is meaningful in the first place. Only friends and persons with an attitude of friendliness can give advice. In fact, this points right to the center of the questions connected with the idea of practical philosophy, for moral implications are entailed by this counterpart to moral reasonableness (*phronesis*). What Aristotle analyzes here in his *Ethics* are virtues, normative notions that always stand under the presupposition of their normative validity. The virtue of practical reason is not to be thought of as a neutral capacity for finding the practical means for correct purposes or ends, but it is inseparably bound up with what Aristotle calls ethos. Ethos for him is the *arche*, it is the "that" from which all practical-political enlightenment has to set out.

For analytic purposes, Aristotle distinguishes between ethical and dianoetic virtues and traces them back to their origin in the so-called parts of the rational soul. But just what is meant by "parts" of the soul and the question of whether they ought not rather to be thought of as two different aspects of the same thing, like the concave and the convex, are questions Aristotle himself does not fail to ask (*Nicomachean Ethics* A 13, 1102a28ff). Ultimately, even these basic distinctions in his analysis of what the practical good for human beings is have to be construed in the light of the methodical intent raised by his practical philosophy as a whole. They do not intend to invade the proper place of practically reasonable decisions, which are required of the individual in any given situation. All his sketchy descriptions of the typical are rather to be understood as oriented toward such a concretization. Even the famous analysis of the structure of the mean between the extremes, which is supposed to be predicated of the Aristotelian ethical virtues, is an empty determination that suggests a great deal. It suggests not merely that they receive their relative content from the extremes, whose profiles possess a far greater determinacy in people's moral convictions and reactions than the praiseworthy mean; it is the ethos of the *spoudaios* [the mature person] that is being schematically depicted in this way. The *hos dei* [like God] and *hos ho orthos logos* [the correct principle] are not evasions relative to a more stringent terminological exigency, but pointers to the concretization in which alone *arete* can reach its determinacy. Achieving this concretization is the real concern of one who possesses the virtue of *phronesis*.

In the light of these considerations, the much-discussed introductory description of the task of practical and political philosophy in Aristotle takes on a more precise contour. What Burnet held to be a conscious adaptation on Aristotle's part to the Platonic use of the term *techne*[11] has its true cause in the interference that arises between the "poetic" knowledge of *techne* and the practical philosophy that clarifies the good in sketchy universality and yet is not itself *phronesis*. And here as well stand such terms as praxis, *prohairesis, techne,* and *methodos* in series, forming a continuum of gradual transpositions.[12] But then Aristotle reflects upon the role that the *politike* [citizen-like] is capable of playing in practical life. He compares the intention of such a practically oriented pragmatics with the target being sighted by the archer when he aims at the goal of his hunt. He will more easily hit the mark if he has his target in view.

Of course, this does not mean that the art of archery consists merely in aiming at a target like this. One has to master the art of archery in order to hit the target at all. But to make aiming easier and to make the steadiness of the direction of one's shooting more exact and better, the target serves a real function. If one applies this comparison to practical philosophy, then one has to begin with the fact that the acting human being as the one who is who he is—in accord with his ethos—is guided by his practical reasonableness in making his concrete decisions, and he surely does not depend upon the guidance of a teacher. Even so, practical philosophy can be of assistance in consciously avoiding certain deviations that ethically pragmatic instruction is capable of pointing out inasmuch as it aids in making present for rational consideration the ultimate purposes of one's actions. It is not confined to a particular field. It is not at all applying a capability to an object. It can work out methods—they are more like rules of thumb than methods—and it can be elevated, like an art that one possesses, to the stage of genuine mastery. In spite of these things, it is not really a "know-how" which like some knowing-how-to-make just chooses its task (on its own or upon request); it is posed precisely in the way that the practice of one's living poses it. Thus the practical philosophy of Aristotle is something other than the putatively neutral specialized knowledge of the expert who enters upon the tasks of politics and legislation like a non-participating observer.

Aristotle expresses this clearly in the chapter that forms the transition from the *Ethics* to the *Politics*.[13] Practical philosophy presupposes that we are already shaped by normative conceptions [*Vorstellungen*] in the light of which we have been brought up and that lie at the basis of the order of our entire social life. This does not at all suggest that these normative perspectives remain fixed immutably and would be beyond criticism. Social life consists of a constant process of transformation of what previously has been held valid. But it would surely be an illusion to want to deduce normative notions *in abstracto* and to posit them as valid with a claim of scientific rectitude. The point here is to work out a conception of science that does not allow for the ideal of the non-participating observer, but instead endeavors to bring to our reflective awareness the communality that binds everyone together.

In my own works, I have applied this point to the hermeneutic sciences and have stressed that the being of the interpreter belongs intrinsically to the being of what is to be interpreted. Whoever wants to understand something already brings along something that anticipatorily joins him with what he wants to understand—a sustaining agreement in understanding. Thus the orator always has to link up with something like this if his persuading and convincing about disputed questions is to succeed.[14] So, too, any understanding of another's meaning, or that of a text, is encompassed by a context of mutual agreement, despite all possible miscomprehensions; and so too any understanding strives for mutual agreement in and through all dissent. This includes the practice of any truly vital science as well. It, too, is never a simple application of knowledge and methods to an arbitrary object. Only a person who already stands within a given science has questions posed for him. How much the problems, thought experiments, needs, and hopes proper to an age also mirror the direction of interest of science and research are common knowledge for any historian of science. But especially in the field of the sciences devoted to that understanding whose universal theme is humanity as embedded within traditions does the claim to universality live on, a claim which Plato had long since laid to the charge of rhetoric. Hence that same neighborly relationship of rhetoric to philosophy which had been the provocative outcome of the discussion of rhetoric in the *Phaedrus* also holds good for hermeneutics.

This does not in any way suggest that the methodical rigor of modern science will be either given up or constrained here. The "hermeneutical sciences," or the *Geisteswissenschaften* [humanities], fall under the same standards of critical rationality that characterize the methodical procedures of all sciences, even though their angle of interest and procedures differ essentially from those of the natural sciences. However, they may justly be permitted to invoke the model of a practical philosophy that was also called politics by Aristotle. Politics was named the "most architectonic"[15] of sciences by Aristotle insofar as it embraced within itself all the sciences and arts of the ancient system. Even rhetoric belonged to it. So, also, the claim to universality on the part of hermeneutics rests on being able to integrate all the sciences into it, of perceiving the opportunities for knowledge on the part of every scientific method wherever it may be applicable to given objects, and of deploying it in all its possibilities. But just as politics as practical philosophy is more than a highest technique, this is true for hermeneutics as well. Hermeneutics has to bring everything knowable by the sciences into the context of the mutual agreement in which we ourselves exist. Because it brings the contribution of the sciences into this context of mutual agreement, a context that links us with the tradition that has come down to us in a unity that is efficacious in our lives, it is not just a repertory of methods (as the methodological doctrine for the philological sciences had been, a doctrine that was worked out in the nineteenth century from Schleiermacher and Boeckh down to Dilthey and Emilio Betti) but rather philosophy. Hermeneutics [as philosophy] not only accounts for the procedures applied by science, but also gives an account of the questions that are prior to the application of every science, just as did the rhetoric intended by Plato. These are the questions that are determinative for all human knowing and doing, the greatest of questions, questions that are decisive for all human beings and their choice of the good.

Translated by Frederick G. Lawrence

Greek Philosophy and Modern Thinking

"Greek Philosophy and Modern Thinking" is an important public state-ment by Gadamer of the way that classical Greek philosophy outstrips modern thinking and has much to offer to it. It was originally presented as a radio lecture in May 1977 and was first published in 1978 as Gad-amer's contribution to a seventieth birthday Festschrift celebrating the great legal historian Franz Wieacker, who died in 1994.[1] (His now-classic history of European private law since the Middle Ages was recently translated into English.)[2] Two marks of the thematic importance of this essay to Gadamer are (1) its placement as the opening essay in volume 6 of *Gesammelte Werke,* the second of three volumes of his writings on Greek philosophy in the collection;[3] and (2) its selection by Gadamer and Grondin as one of the sixteen essays to be included in the paper-back collection of his shorter writings intended for the general reader, the *Gadamer Lesebuch.*[4] The greatness of Greek thought is thematic to Gadamer, and this essay offers a brief and accessible statement of this for a radio audience. Because of this it has no notes, although the trans-lator has added one.

Gadamer could have mentioned many, many contributions of Greek philosophy to modern thinking, such as the first breakthroughs of pre-Socratic philosophy and ontology explored by Heidegger, the ge-nius of the Platonic dialogues as a way of exploring a topic, or the sub-tlety of Aristotelian terms and systematic thought, including their value for thinking in aesthetics, but he focused in this essay on four ways in which Greek thinking goes beyond the limitations of modern thought.

The first is the role of objectivity and the will to control in modern scientific thinking. In contrast to this he calls attention to a way of think-ing, the Greek way, that tries to understand the world instead of control it. He traces modern scientific thinking back to the mathematical and objectifying scientific thinking of the seventeenth century as it shook off the chains of Aristotelian thinking. Certainly this represented an escape from an Aristotelian way of thinking that tended to anthropolo-gize the natural world, but Gadamer raises the question of whether the new way of thinking has not gone too far and has covered over a "truth" that is offered by the ancient heritage. This first truth is the limits of objectification and the tendency to abstraction in modern science. The Greeks taught us to be at home in the world without making the objects in nature into things, how to be at home in a realm of social practices and institutions, how to reflect on man's way of being in the world.

This leads to Gadamer's second topic: human freedom, friendship, and the solidarity on which the working of institutions, economic orders, legal orders, or social customs is based. This solidarity, this ethical realm, this realm of human freedom, is something that goes beyond modern scientific thinking, and here Greek thought stands ready to offer truths to a modern thought that with its abstractive and objectifying way of thought has forgotten them. Gadamer dedicates many other essays to these truths. Here he only alludes to them.

The third modern phenomenon that Gadamer focuses upon is "self-consciousness." This is the Cartesian rock of reason on which modern scientific thought rests. It is a presupposition of science that now needs to be questioned. In fact, recent thinking by Marx, Freud, and Nietzsche has called into question the proud modern self-consciousness and its set of illusions. Indeed, the unquestioned primacy of self-consciousness and its methodical doubting now comes itself quite justifiably to be doubted.

Finally, Gadamer takes up arms against the modern scientific concept of language as an instrument of man, as a "means of communication." Language, he argues, is perhaps the most non-objectifiable element in our world. It takes shape not through scientific manipulation but through "the praxis of social life itself, which must always reclaim its practical responsibility for the power that has been placed in the hands of man." Here Gadamer plays on the weakest point in modern scientific thought: its inability from within itself to place limits on its own power. Here the Greek way of thinking about a world in which man can live well and be at home offers something to modern man who finds himself in an alien world of capital, industry, and technology that is spinning out of control. Our modern concept of language, then, is just another symptom of our scientism and of the need to reexplore the Greek way of thinking about man and his relationship to the world.

* * *

Greek Philosophy and Modern Thinking

Greek philosophy and modern thinking—this is a topic with which [modern] philosophy, and especially German philosophy from its beginnings, had concerned itself. Indeed, German philosophy has even been accused of Greco-mania—a preoccupation with Greece. This issue can quite validly be brought up not only in relation to Heidegger or the Marburg school of neo-Kantianism but also in relation to the great movement of German philosophical idealism inspired by Kant that from Fichte to Hegel immediately returned to Greek philosophy to be stimulated by the thinking contained in Platonic and Aristotelian dialectic. Nevertheless, a confrontation with Greek philosophy is an ambiguous challenge for modern thought in a special sense. On the one hand, one should not forget that Greek philosophy does not mean philosophy in the narrow sense in which we now use the term. Philosophy in the larger sense refers to their whole theoretical interest, and this includes their scientific interest, for there is no doubt that the Greeks were the ones who through the creation of science introduced a crucial decision into world history and decided the path of modern civilization. What distinguishes the Occident—that is, Europe and indeed the so-called Western world—from the hieratic cultures of the countries in Asia is precisely the awakening of the will to know that is bound up with Greek philosophy, Greek mathematics, and Greek medicine, with their theoretical curiosity and their intellectual mastery. Thus, the confrontation between modern thinking and Greek thinking represents a kind of self-encounter.

In the effort by Greek thinking to envision the way human beings are at home in the world there emerges an inner parallel between it and the way of becoming at home that generally characterizes the craftsman, expert, or creator of new combinations or forms—the *technitēs* [the person who has mastered a technique]. At the same time this way of inventing one's own place and one's own free space is one that takes shape in the midst of a pregiven natural world of the forms and shapes that constitute the ordered totality of the world. So philosophy in Greece arises when persons start becoming aware in their thinking of the tremendous abandonment that human beings experience in being in the world [in the *there*], the experience of being thrown into the narrow space of freedom, the freedom which the ordered whole of nature grants to the human will and to the human capacity to act. But it is precisely this sense of abandonment as it becomes conscious in their thinking that leads to the posing of tremendous questions, such as: "What was at the beginning? What does it mean that something *is*? What does it mean to say that nothing *is*? Does nothing actually mean something?" The posing of these questions marks the beginning of Greek philosophy, and its basic answers can be summed up in two words: *physis* [nature], that which is there from out of itself in the order of the whole [science], and *logos* [reason], the insight and insightfulness of and into the whole—including also the logos contained in the human skill to create art. Thus in its confrontation with modern science we can see that Greek philosophy stands as almost the very opposite of modern science, and not its forerunner and the blazer of the path of theoretical ability to control [technology]. It is the Greeks who made us aware of the contrast between the world we can come to *understand* and live in and the world insofar as we are able to *control* it.

The latter was actually the great beginning in the seventeenth century with the creation of Galilean mechanics, in which the great researchers and thinkers of that period began a special kind of reflection dedicated to gaining new knowledge and new ways of knowing. In it the world is the object of methodical research by modern experimental science, conceived mathematically and in such a way that science abstracts and isolates the object from the researcher. To reduce this new development to a single formulation, one can say that it gives up the anthropomorphism with which the Greeks had viewed the world. As magnificently simple and persuasive as the physics of the Aristotelian tradition had also been, which told us that fire goes up because it is the nature of fire to do so, for it wants to be above, and it is the nature of a stone to fall downwards because it is only at home where it is below things—this interpretation of nature which is articulated on the basis of humans and their self-understanding was, as we now know and nobody who belongs to the modern world can deny, really an anthropological cover-up of the possibilities for grasping and controlling the world through knowledge.

Even if modern science were not intended to fulfill some kind of interest to come later on, but rather simply intends to offer its own special kind of access to the world via technology, forms, doing, changing, and constructing—even so, there still continues to exist alongside it the great heritage of ancient philosophy, in which we regard our world as something that is understandable and not just manipulable. In contrast to the constructivism of modern science, which holds that only what we can reproduce is known and understood, the Greek concept of science is characterized by the scientific concept of *physis,* that is, in the horizon of what points to itself from itself and exists in itself as a self-regulated order of things. The question that is posed for us by virtue of this confrontation between modern thinking and the Greek heritage is in how far the ancient heritage offers a truth that is covered up by the special conditions of knowledge that we have developed in the modern age.

A word that points to the difference opening up before us here is *Gegenstand,* the German word for "object." At least in the foreign words "object" or "objectivity," it appears to be a self-evident presupposition of the concept of knowledge employing this term, that we are able to know "objects" [*Gegenstände*] as things standing over against us; that is to say, we are able to gain "objective" knowledge of a thing's own being. The question that is raised by the ancient tradition and which is part of the heritage of antiquity is: how far are limits placed on this project of objectification? Is there a certain non-objectifiability that in principle escapes the grasp of modern science with an inner necessity that somehow resides in things themselves? By presenting some test cases to you, I will try to show that in fact the lasting heritage of Greek thought is to make us aware of the limits of objectification.

The leading example of clear limits in our power to objectify, it seems to me, is our experience of the body. What we call our "body" is quite certainly not the *res extensa* of the Cartesian designation of the human *corpus*. The way the body is perceived by us is clearly not in terms of mere mathematical extension. The body is perhaps essentially removed from objectification. How does a human being experience its being in a body? Is this bodily being encountered only in its standing over against us in its possible objectivity when its functioning is disturbed? No, the body announces its presence in any disturbance of the way it is given to us in our own livingness, in an illness, or in displeasure, and so on. The conflict in this case between our natural experience of the body, this mysterious process of unnoticed health and well-being, and the effort that is put forward to bring its unwellness under control through objectification has been experienced by everybody who is in the situation of becoming an object, that is, in the situation of a patient being treated by technological means.[1] This expresses the self-understanding of our modern medical science, which seeks to make controllable with the means of modern science all the disturbances of our rebellious bodilyness.

In reality, the concepts of "objectivity" and of "object" are so alien to the immediate understanding with which a human being seeks to make himself at home in the world, that the Greeks characteristically had no such concepts. They could scarcely even speak of what we call a "thing." The Greek word they used about this whole realm is that word which is now not so foreign to us—*pragma*—a word that means the realm in which one finds oneself involved in the practice of life. This realm of practice does not stand over and against us as something to be overcome, but as something in which one moves around and does things. Being immediately involved in this world constitutes an orientation that now, in the era of modern world mastery structured by science and grounded on technology, has been pushed to the margin.

A second example—and here I take an especially provocative example—is human freedom. Freedom, too, has the structure that I have designated as essentially non-objectifiable. It has of course never been fully forgotten, and the greatest thinker of the thought of freedom that there has been in modern times, I mean Kant, has with full consciousness of the basic orientation of modern science and its theoretical possibilities for knowledge, developed the thought that freedom is not theoretically graspable and provable. Freedom is not a fact of nature but is, as his challenging paradox has formulated it, a fact of reason, something that we have to think because we can no longer understand ourselves at all without thinking of ourselves as free. Freedom is a *factum* of reason.

Nevertheless, there is in the realm of human activity not just this one limit case of all objectivity. I believe the Greeks were right when they placed alongside the *factum* of reason the socially formed thing that they call the ethos. "Ethos" is the name that Aristotle found for it. The possibility of conscious choice and free decision is always carried with us as something we always already are—and we ourselves are not an "object." One of the greatest legacies of Greek thought for our thinking, it seems to me, is that in establishing its ethics on the basis of really lived life, they left us another phenomenon with broad space, which in modern times has scarcely become the subject of philosophical reflection; namely the topic of friendship—of *philia*. This is a word that for us has acquired such a narrow sound, conceptually, that we must first broaden it in order even to know what is meant by it [in Greek thought]. Perhaps it will suffice to recall the famous Pythagorean saying: "Between friends everything is mutual, shared." "Friendship" in philosophical reflection is a term for solidarity. But solidarity is a form of experiencing the world and social reality which one cannot bring about and make possible through objectivistic plans to overcome this solidarity through artificial institutions. On the contrary, solidarity exists before all possible overt acceptance and before the working of institutions, economic orders, legal orders, or social customs. It *carries* them and makes them possible. The jurist is not the last to know this. This, it seems to me, is another truth which Greek thought, once again, is ready to offer to our modern thinking.

And now for a third phenomenon, which is connected with this: I mean the role that *self-consciousness* plays in modern thinking. As is well known, the very pivot of modern thinking since Descartes is that our self-consciousness possesses a methodological primacy. Methodical knowledge is for us a process of self-consciousness in which every step is taken under self-checking. Thus, since Descartes, self-consciousness is the basis on which philosophy, too, gains its ultimate evidentness and the certainty of science its highest legitimation. But the Greeks were right when they saw that self-consciousness is a secondary phenomenon compared to the giving in to the world and being open to the world that we call consciousness, knowledge, or openness to experience. Has not the modern development of science begun to cause some doubts about the assertions of self-consciousness? Against the radical doubt that Descartes employed to establish knowledge, Nietzsche said: "We must doubt more thoroughly!" Freud taught us how much the masking of life tendencies is hidden behind our self-consciousness. The critique of society offered by the "critique of ideology" school in Frankfurt shows us how much that is accepted as self-evident and held as unquestioned certainties in our self-consciousness only mirrors quite other interests and realities. In short: the idea that self-consciousness possesses the unquestioned primacy that modern thinking has accorded to it may now quite justifiably be doubted. Here, too, it seems to me that Greek thinking has a lot to offer in the wonderful self-forgetfulness with which it regarded its own power to think, and in the way the Greeks thought through their own experience of the world with the wide-open eyes of the mind. This is a major contribution that Greek thinking makes toward circumscribing modern illusions of self-knowledge.

With this, let's take one final step and look at the one thing that has come completely into the foreground of contemporary philosophy, a thing that can only with force and violence attempt to hold on to the concept of objectivity and objectifiability: namely, the phenomenon of *language*.

Language, it seems to me, is one of the phenomena most persuasive in showing its non-objectifiability, in that an essential self-forgetfulness resides in the character of speaking as something that is carried out or performed. When the modern description of language tries to picture language as an instrument or means of speaking, this is always already a technology-based distortion in which words and word-combinations are imagined to be held in readiness in a kind of stockpile, and are simply applied to something that one encounters. The superiority of the contrasting Greek view of language is overwhelmingly evident here. The Greeks had no word at all for language. They only had a word for the tongue which brought forth the sounds of language—*glotta*—and they had a word for the thing that is communicated *through* language: logos. Precisely with the word "logos" something is brought into view which is essentially related to the inner self-forgetfulness of speaking, which is evoked through that speaking, and which is raised into presence by speaking. One moves into a world that is created by the availability and communicative sharing that happens in speaking. In our speaking about things, the things *are there* in the speaking and exchange with each other, and through this the world and the experience of the world by human beings is built up—*not* through a process of objectification that, in the face of the communicative mediation of the insights of one person to another, now calls for objectivity and aspires to a knowledge that will be for everyone. In the articulation of the experience of the world through the logos, in speaking with each other, in the communicative sedimentation [in language] of our world experience which encompasses everything that we are able to exchange with each other, there comes forward a form of knowing that presents the missing other half of the truth, a truth that stands alongside the great monologue of the modern sciences and their growing collection of [unexploited] experiential potential.

So our topic of the contrast between modern science and Greek philosophical thinking possesses a continuing relevance today. What is at stake here is the way in which the great results and achievements of the modern science of human experience and how it deals with the world eventually will come into the social consciousness, into the experience of the world of individuals and groups. In the end, the molding of our consciousness really does not take place through the methods of modern science and its method of constant self-checking; rather, it takes place in the praxis of social life itself, which must always reclaim its practical responsibility for the power that has been placed in the hands of man, a responsibility that has to defend the setting of limits, for there are things which human reason must oppose with its own power and with reckless daring. No special proof is required to assert that for people today it is the *world to be understood*—a world in which man is indigenous and a world in which he feels at home—that remains our last court of appeals in the alien world of modern industry and technology wherein it can now only claim a secondary, ancillary function.

Translated by Richard E. Palmer

On the Possibility of a Philosophical Ethics

This essay is significant because it presents Gadamer's criticisms of Kantian and neo-Kantian systems of ethics and argues persuasively for a philosophical ethics based on Aristotle. It was originally presented as a paper at the seventh meeting of the Albertus Magnus Academy in Walberberg University in 1961, and then revised and published in the first volume of *Walberberger Studien* (1963),[1] which was dedicated to publishing distinguished papers presented at the academy. The essay has so far been translated into French, Spanish, Italian, and Japanese. And it has been translated into English twice, first by Michael Kelly, in *Kant and Political Philosophy,* edited by Ronald Beiner and William James Booth (New Haven: Yale University Press, 1993), 361–73, and more recently by the distinguished Gadamer scholar and translator, Joel Weinsheimer in his collection of Gadamer essays, *Hermeneutics, Religion, and Ethics,* translated by Joel Weinsheimer (New Haven: Yale University Press, 1999), 18–36. It is the latter translation which is reprinted here.

Heidegger was once asked by a famous French follower, Jean Beaufret, when he was going to write an ethics. He replied with the luminous and wide-ranging "Letter on Humanism" (1947), one of his first publications after the war. In it he stated in the opening line that "We are still far from pondering the essence of action decisively enough."[2] The parallel is irresistible: a year after the publication of his masterwork, *Truth and Method* (1960), Gadamer was perhaps asked the same question or at least anticipates it here, and replies by reaffirming the enduring value of an ethics based on ethos, as Aristotle's was, in contrast to the duty ethics put forward in Kant's transcendental philosophy.

But there is more to the matter than this accidental parallel, as Jean Grondin's recent monumental biography of Gadamer makes clear.[3] Gadamer's habilitation, written under Heidegger, was a study of Plato's ethics in the *Philebus,* but originally this was to serve as a preface to a study of Aristotelian ethics, which remained a lifelong interest of Gadamer. His dissatisfactions in the early 1920s with the neo-Kantianism of Nicolai Hartmann and to a lesser degree with Max Scheler that were part of his dissertation, come through here with substantial refutations of their projects while omitting to deal with other forms of ethics, such as utilitarianism. In any case, behind this casual paper lies a lifetime of commitment to Aristotle's *Ethics* in the horizon of Heidegger and phenomenology and little else. It is not a comprehensive consideration of various systems of ethics in the nineteenth and twentieth centuries, but is a more narrowly focused effort aimed at the rehabilitation of Aristotle's ethics. And as one reads it, the parallels with Heidegger are also clear, insofar as Heidegger based his ontology on the finite lifeworld of Dasein, while Gadamer suggests an ethics relying on the Aristotelian ethos of finite human institutions and training, without recourse to transcendental subjects or subjectivity. It would seem that Gadamer is going back to Heidegger's source and actually articulating an ethics. This is Gadamer's answer to the question that was presented to Heidegger. It is an answer that grows out of the analysis of historical consciousness in *Truth and Method,* a more moderate answer that goes back to Aristotle's ethos as the basis for an ethics.

As it appears here, Gadamer's essay has been divided into four untitled sections. In the first section of the essay, Gadamer asserts the fact that ethics is not theory in the modern sense of this word, and already in the first paragraph refers to the fact that in both Plato and Aristotle, one does not just seek knowledge of the good for its own sake but in order to be good oneself, to live well. He also alludes to both neo-Kantianism and Scheler's material value ethics. Furthermore, he notes Kierkegaard's critique of "knowing at a distance," and he finds philosophical ethics "sharpened to the utmost extreme" of moral questionableness. He frames this issue in the closing paragraph as a conflict between the law-ethics of Kant and an ethics that attempts to deal with the concrete situation.

In response to this situation, Gadamer in the second section sees two alternative paths: Kant's ethical formalism and Aristotle's way of thinking. In this section, Gadamer takes up Kantian formalism. He first offers a review of Kantian ethics before raising questions about it. The first question about it has to be how testing by reference to law takes place at all, given the propensities of human beings to evil. He gives the example of suicide, where Kant says that the suicide needed to have insight into the moral unacceptability of suicide, but this is precisely what the prospective suicide lacks. Likewise with the conflict between duty and inclination which comes up for discussion, and Gadamer presents his reasons for finding "Kant's way out [of the dilemma] unsatisfactory," since it entails recourse to a metaphysics of morals. Kant's approach is found to be unrealistic and transcendental.

In the third section, Gadamer considers another way out of the dilemma posed by the formalism of Kantian ethics: the material value-ethics of Nicolai Hartmann and Max Scheler. They consider the concrete situation, but in such a way that one reintroduces an infinite subject. Gadamer concludes that a wide gap still yawns between the immediacy of value-consciousness and a philosophy of morals.

In the longest and final section of the essay Gadamer takes up what it would mean to "orient ourselves . . . on Aristotle" in thinking about ethics. He points out that Aristotle's concept of *phronesis* is a way of being moral that is not separable from the whole concretion of what Aristotle called ethics. In looking for what is "advisable," one considers a concrete situation and what is advisable within it. Here Gadamer finds a mediation between logos and ethos, between reason and situation, "between the subjectivity of knowing and the substance of being." The individual has to make a decision about what is good and right, but this "follows from our general ideas about what is good and right." What is right and good is not just useful for achieving a certain goal but also what a right-minded person would do. Thus, moral action "depends so much more on our being than on our explicit consciousness" (as *eidos*). It is not a matter of the abstract application of rules, but a vision of what a good life is like. Ultimately, Gadamer points out, the actions we choose "spread out into the whole of our external social being." Thus, ethics involves politics. It is always related to the life of action, and to the right management of actions.

Here Gadamer asserts the superiority of the Aristotelian way of thinking:

> It is in this way, however, that the sense for the multiply conditioned, which constitutes Aristotle's speculative genius, becomes fruitful for moral philosophy; for here and here alone emerges an answer to the question that has been plaguing us: namely, how a philosophical ethics . . . is possible without requiring a superhuman self-transcendence.

The rest of the essay is dedicated to setting forth the respect in which Aristotle's thinking confronts "what is multiply conditioned." And he goes back to how Kant failed to take into account "the conditionedness of all human being and also, therefore, of our use of reason." For instance, Gadamer argues that the role that education plays in our thinking shows its conditioned character.

Again, the polis reenters the picture because it has "the social and political determinacy of the individual as its positive content." And yet Aristotle also found a "counterpoise" for the conditioned character of all moral knowledge in the fact that "the system of being is powerful enough to set limits to all human confusion." In the end, then, there is an unconditioned element in thinking about the moral, but it is not to be found in Kant's formalism or in the material value-ethics of Scheler, but in the practical reflection and insight generated in the tension between logos and ethos as presented by Aristotle.

* * *

On the Possibility of a Philosophical Ethics

It is by no means evident that a "philosophical" ethics, a moral philosophy, is something different from a "practical" ethics, that is, from constructing a list of values to which the agent appeals, and from the knowledge of how to apply them that guides the agent's appeal to this list of values in practice. In antiquity, by contrast, it was obvious that the philosophical pragmatics which, since Aristotle, has been called "ethics" was itself a "practical" knowledge. Aristotle gave expression to what was basically already implicit in the Socratic and Platonic doctrine about the knowledge of virtue—namely, that we do not just want to know what virtue is, but to know it in order to become good. For Aristotle, too, this is what is special about ethical pragmatics; yet it belongs to the ancient concept of knowledge generally that the transition to praxis is inherent in it: knowledge [*Wissenschaft*] is not an aggregate of anonymous truths, but a human comportment [*hexis tou aletheuein*, habit of telling the truth] (εξις τοῦ αληθεύειν). Even *theoria* does not stand in absolute opposition to praxis, but is itself the highest praxis, one of the highest modes of human being. As Aristotle recognized, this obtains for the highest knowledge, the knowledge of first things, philosophical knowledge, even if there is a tension between epistemic knowledge (επιστήμη, τέχνη) and experiential knowledge, so that the experienced practitioner is often superior to the "learned" expert. This non-dichotomy is wholly the case in the ethical sphere, where there can be no such tension between theory and practice, because there are no experts at applying it.

On the other hand, there is the modern concept of rational "theory," defined from the ground up by reference to its practical application—and this means by an opposition to its practical application. In certain ways, there has always been an opposition between books and life. But it is only with the dawning of modernity, especially in the age of humanism, when the Hellenistic ideal of *sapientia* was revitalized and combined with the critique of Scholasticism, of *doctrina*, that it emerged fully into consciousness. Nicholas of Cusa put his perspicuous doctrines in the mouth of the layman, the *idiota*, who sees more perspicuously than the "orator" and *philosophus* with whom he is speaking. It is with the rise of modern science that the opposition as such becomes fully fixed and at the same time the concept of theory acquires a new profile. Theory now means an explanation of the multiplicity of appearances, enabling them to be mastered. Understood as a tool, it ceases to be a properly human action, and in contrast to such, it claims to be more than a relative truth.

Such a conception of theory, one that has become pretty much patent to us all, leads to a nearly indissoluble aporia when applied to moral phenomena. It seems to be unavoidably tied to an optimistic progressivism, since the course of scientific research aims at producing ever newer, ever more exact theoretical knowledge. Applied to the moral world, however, it becomes an absurd belief in moral progress. Here Rousseau's critique of the Enlightenment has pronounced a veto that cannot be overridden. Kant himself acknowledged as much: "Rousseau set me straight." Kant's *Foundation of the Metaphysics of Morals* allows no doubt that moral philosophy is "the universal knowledge of moral reason"—that is, the consciousness of an obligation to do what a simple heart and level head says is right can never be superseded. Nevertheless, moral philosophical reflections, according to Kant, do not present themselves as mere theory. Rather, so forceful is Kant's moral reproof of the Enlightenment's pride in reasoning that he teaches the necessity of the transition to moral philosophy; thus it has basically remained the case that moral philosophy can never completely disavow its own moral relevance. Max Scheler, founder of the material ethics of value, was taken to task by one of his students because he explained the system of values and its normative power so clearly, yet followed it so little in the conduct of his life. Scheler replied, "Does the signpost go in the direction it points?" This is obviously unsatisfactory. Tellingly, Nicolai Hartmann, who systematically elaborated Scheler's ethical conception, could not avoid ascribing to the philosophy of value a moral significance as well. It has, he suggests, a maieutic function for the consciousness of moral value; that is, it affords an ever richer explication of the moral, in that it reveals forgotten or unrecognized values. This is all that is left of the old expectation that the philosopher is held to: namely, that in the midst of moral perplexity and confusion, he should not merely pursue his passion for theory, but rather ground ethics anew—that is, construct new tables of binding values. Admittedly, it may well be that Heidegger is right when he begins his "Letter on Humanism" with the answer to the question "When will you write an ethics?": "For a long time we have not considered the essence of action decisively enough."

In fact, it does appear that there is an inescapable difficulty in the idea of moral philosophy itself. It was first brought to our awareness in Kierkegaard's critique of Hegel and of the Christian church. Kierkegaard showed that all "knowing at a distance" is insufficient for the fundamental moral and religious situation of humankind. Just as the meaning of the Christian revelation is to be experienced and accepted as "contemporaneous" [*gleichzeitig*], so also ethical choice is no matter of theoretical knowledge, but rather the brightness, sharpness, and pressure of conscience. All knowing at a distance threatens to veil or to weaken the demand that is implicit in the situation of moral choice. In our century, we recall, the critique of neo-Kantian idealism coming from theological and philosophical quarters, under Kierkegaard's influence, brought the fundamental questionability of ethics to our cognizance. Insofar as ethics is understood as knowledge of the universal, it is implicated in the moral questionableness associated with the concept of the universal law. It is to the Epistle to the Romans that one turns first of all. The idea that sin comes from the law is understood not in the sense that the forbidden is tempting and thus encourages sin, but rather in the sense that keeping the law is precisely what leads to the real sin—which is not just the occasional transgression of the law, but that *superbia* that prevents those obeying the law from obeying the commandment to love. It is not the priest and the Levite but the Samaritan who accepts and fulfills the requirement of love deriving from the situation. From the philosophical side, too, it is by beginning with the concept of the situation that the questionableness of the idea of ethics is sharpened to the utmost extreme—for example, by Eberhard Grisebach, the philosophical friend of Gogarten.

In this context, philosophical ethics does indeed seem to be in an insoluble dilemma. The reflexive generality which is necessarily its philosophical métier entangles it in the questionableness of law-based ethics. How can it do justice to the concreteness with which conscience, sensitivity to equity, and loving reconciliation are answerable to the situation?

There are, I believe, only two ways to extricate philosophical ethics from this dilemma. One is that of ethical formalism, stemming from Kant; the other is the way of Aristotle. Neither can do justice to the possibility of philosophical ethics per se, but both can do so for their parts of it.

Kant inquires into the sole kind of obligation which, because of its unconditional universality, will suffice for the concept of ethics. He discerned that the only mode of ethical obligation capable of serving as an ethics is the unconditional duty that obliges the agent against interest and inclination. Kant's categorical imperative is to be understood as the first principle of every moral system precisely because it does nothing but present the form of obligation implicit in Ought—that is, the unconditional quality of the moral law. If there is a moral good will, then it must be adequate to this form. That such unconditional good will does exist, or that the categorical imperative is capable of really determining our will, is not of course demonstrated through this knowledge of the universal "form" of the moral. To this question the metaphysician Kant gives a prepared answer in the *Critique of Pure Reason*. To be sure, every factical determination of the will belonging to the phenomenal realm is subject to the basic principles of experience, and among them an unconditionally good action is certainly never to be met with. But the self-limitation of pure reason has shown that outside the phenomenal order, where there is only the relation of cause and effect, there exists yet another intelligible order, to which we belong not as sensible but as rational beings and within which the standpoint of freedom, the self-legislation of reason, can be rightly understood. That we "ought" is something we know with practical reason's unconditional certainty, which is not contradicted by theoretical understanding. Freedom is theoretically not impossible, and it is practically necessary.

On this basis, Kant derives an answer to the question of why moral-philosophical deliberation is necessary without moral philosophy's thereby transcending the law-creating simplicity of the simple consciousness of duty. Specifically, Kant says, "Innocence is a wonderful thing, and conversely it is really too bad that it cannot be preserved but is easily seduced."[1] The innocence of the simple heart that knows its duty unerringly consists not so much in not being led astray by overpowering inclinations; rather, the heart's innocence manifests itself in the fact that whenever it deviates from the path of justice, which always happens except in a completely "holy will," it nevertheless still unerringly recognizes what is unjust; it absolutely resists not overpowering inclinations, but only the errors caused by reason itself. That is to say, among affective promptings, practical reason unfolds a specific dialectic through which it knows how to attenuate a given duty's power to obligate. It makes use of what I would like to call the "dialectic of the exception." It does not contest the validity of the moral law but, rather, tries to underscore the exceptional nature of the situation in which the agent finds himself— in the sense that whatever the validity of the law, exceptions are nevertheless justified under certain circumstances. Moral-philosophical reflection can come to the aid of moral reason threatened by such temptations. It needs such aid all the more when moral-philosophical reflection in its "universal" form itself abets this temptation. In that Kant's *Foundation* discerns the essence of moral obligation in its being without exception—that is the meaning of the categorical imperative— it establishes the purity of the decisions of moral reason.

The meaning of Kantian formalism, then, consists in certifying the purity of such decisions against all the turbidity coming from the viewpoint of inclination and interest—in the naive consciousness as in the philosophical. To this extent Kant's rigor—where the only cultivated will that possesses moral value is the one that acts purely out of duty and against all inclination—has a clear methodological significance. In Hegel's terms, what emerges here is the form of reason that tests laws. [2]

Here, however, the question arises of how such testing occurs at all, given human reason's dependence on experience and its deep-rooted "inclination to evil." As Gerhard Krüger has pointed out,[3] Kant's moral-philosophical reflections presuppose recognition of the moral law. The formulas which, as types, lie ready at hand to the judgment—for example, that of natural law or that of purpose in itself—are so unreal that in themselves they never have any persuasive power. Recall the person who commits suicide, for example: Kant says that if such a person is still sufficiently in possession of his reason that he can test his decision to commit suicide against the model of such a formula, then he will arrive at the insight that his decision is untenable. That, however, is obviously a mere construction. It is precisely the person haunted by thoughts of suicide who lacks that much reason. Though the ethical impermissibility of suicide could be perceived in this way, the very fact that a person is prepared to think things through (which is the only way someone would come to this insight in the first place) presupposes, even more, a motivation for examining one's conscience. Where does that come from? Kant's formula seems to be of merely methodological relevance to reflection, since it teaches us to exclude all the muddiness of "inclination."

Kant's rigor has still another moral meaning beyond the methodological contrast between duty and inclination. What Kant has in mind are the following: extreme cases—in which, against all inclination, a person takes to heart his true duty—let him, as it were, internalize the power of his moral reason and thus build a firm foundation for his character. He comes to an awareness of the moral laws that guide his life. He is formed by the exceptional situation in which he has to pass the test that he, as it were, sets himself (see, for example, the doctrine of method of the pure practical reason in the *Critique of Practical Reason*).

On the other hand, we need to ask what defines such exceptional situations wherein the contrast between duty and inclination is sharpened to the point of decision. It is not just any situation that can be elevated into an occasion for preserving genuine moral resoluteness and testing one's conscience. Hegel's well-known critique of the immorality of the Ought—because Ought already presupposes a contradiction to Want and thus also presupposes the evil will—comes in here. Isn't he right when he discerns the essence of ethics not in the self-necessity of an imperative ethics, but in the ethos—that is, in the substantiality of the moral order that has its embodiment in the great objectivities of family, society, and state? The truth of moral consciousness lies not merely in the scrupulousness with which it continually tries to become tortuously conscious of impure motives and inclinations. Of course there are occasions of conflict when such moral self-examination takes place. Conscience, however, has no permanent *habitus;* instead, it is something by which we are struck, by which we are awakened.[4] And how? Isn't there such a thing as a "broad" conscience? It can hardly be denied that the wakefulness of conscience depends upon orders of substance in which one always already lives. The autonomous moral reason, therefore, assuredly has the character of intelligible self-determination; but that does not exclude the fact that all human action and decision are conditioned by experience. At the very least, in judging others—and this too belongs to the moral sphere—one cannot ignore their being conditioned. What one can demand of others (morally and not just legally) is not the same as what one can demand of oneself. Indeed, recognizing human conditionedness (in a charitable judgment) is quite compatible with the sublime unconditionality of the moral law. It is indicative of Kant's reflective thematic that he is not interested in the difference between a judgment of conscience about oneself and one's moral judgment of another. For this reason, Kant's way out of our question about the moral meaning of moral philosophy seems to me finally unsatisfactory. We can concede, of course, that no one is spared situations of moral conflict, and to that extent the temptation to consider oneself an exception is a universal human situation. From this does it not follow, however, that the transition to a metaphysics of morals is necessary for everyone? Kant does indeed draw this conclusion. His grounding of the moral is meant to bring the secret metaphysics of every ethics to greater clarity—but also to give it greater moral fixity. But is such a conclusion tolerable? Has not Kant sublated Rousseau in himself again?

So it seems to me that another kind of testing is valuable: a moral-philosophical deliberation that chooses to orient itself not via the exceptional case of conflict, but the regular case of following a moral custom. We might consider the objection to an ethics of the pure Ought and orientation to the reflective form of moral consciousness that has been raised in our century especially by the ethics of material value that Max Scheler and Nicolai Hartmann developed. It has consciously situated itself in opposition to Kant's formalism. In Scheler's work it has immoderately and unjustly misinterpreted the rational character of Kant's formalism of duty; nevertheless, it has also performed the incontestably positive function of making the object of moral-philosophical analysis the substantive content of morality, not just the conflict between Ought and Want. The concept of value that is raised here to systematic significance is meant to break open the narrow focus on the concept of duty—that is, the focus on the mere goals of effort and the norms of the Ought. There are morally valuable things that cannot be made the object of effort and cannot be demanded. There is, for example, no duty to love. Kant's fatal revision of the Christian commandment that we love one another into a duty to perform tasks of practical charity speaks volumes in this respect. Love, even viewed in moral terms, is something nobler than the charitable acts that duty requires. Relying on the phenomenological theory that the laws of essence and of the a priori generally are immediately evident, Scheler grounded an a priori system of value upon the immediacy of the a priori consciousness of value. This not only comprehended the proper goals for which moral will strives; it also delved down into the vital sphere and the sphere of utilitarian values, as well as reaching up into the sphere of the holy. Such an ethics really comprehends the substantive contents of morality, not just the reflective phenomenon of the reason that tests laws.

Even if such an ethics of value expressly includes the concept of ethos and the changing forms it takes, however, it cannot escape the inherent consequence of its methodological claim to intuit a priori systems of value. This is especially clear in the case of Nicolai Hartmann, who conceives of the a priori hierarchy of values not as a self-enclosed system whose highest value is the holy, but rather as an open region of values, a boundless object of human experience and at the same time the subject of unbounded research. The progress of research discovers ever finer structures and relationships of value and thus justifies being itself dominated by value-blindness. Ultimately this must imply, however, that research in ethics as value itself requires and refines ethical consciousness. For that reason, moral philosophy certainly cannot teach with authority—that is, posit new values; but it can develop moral consciousness in such a way that it discovers these values in itself. As Nicolai Hartmann says, moral philosophy therefore has a maieutic function.

Such a theory founders, however, on the necessity (rightly recognized by Scheler) that every morality is a concrete ethical form. If it is made the guiding idea of an ethics of material value, the idea of an infinite refinement of value consciousness must quite unavoidably also imply and ground its own ethos—indeed, one to which other ethical forms can be juxtaposed. One thinks, for example, of what is specially emphasized by Hartmann: the value of abundance violated by "passing by" (Nietzsche). The ethics of value has an immanent and ineluctable limitation: it itself constructs an ethics which contradicts the methodological claim to be aprioristic research in value. This methodological claim can be fulfilled by no human (and that ultimately means by no historically applicable) moral system at all. What the fundamental idea of an a priori value system essentially calls for is an infinite subject. Thus an ethics of material value, while including the substantive content of morality, unlike Kantian formalism, does not find the way out that we are searching for. Moral philosophy and the immediacy of value consciousness remain split asunder.

Let us, then, orient ourselves instead on Aristotle,[5] who has no concept of value, but rather "virtues" and "goods," and who became the founder of philosophical ethics by correcting the "intellectualism" of Socrates and Plato without sacrificing its essential insights. The concept of ethos with which he began makes precisely this explicit: "virtue" does not consist merely in knowledge, for the possibility of knowing depends, to the contrary, on what a person is like, and the being of each one is formed beforehand through his or her education and way of life. Perhaps Aristotle's view is focused more intensely on the conditionedness of our moral being, on the dependence of the individual decision on the practical and social determinants of the time, and less on the unconditionality that pertains to the ethical phenomenon. It was precisely the latter that Kant successfully worked out in its purity, the same purity possessed by its wonderful complement in antiquity: namely, Plato's inquiry into "justice as such," which undergirds his whole projected state. Aristotle succeeded, however, in rendering the nature of moral knowledge so clear that (under the concept of "choice of") it covers just as much the subjectivity that judges in the case of conflict as the substance of law and custom which determines its moral knowledge and its particular choices. His analysis of *phronesis* recognizes that moral knowledge is a way of moral being itself, which therefore cannot be prescinded from the whole concretion of what he calls ethos. Moral knowledge discerns what needs to be done, what a situation requires; and it discerns what is doable on the basis of a conviction that the concrete situation is related to what is considered right and proper in general. It has, therefore, the structure of a conclusion in which one premise is the general knowledge of what is right, as that is adumbrated in conceptualized ethical values.

At the same time, what is happening here is not mere subsumption, merely a successful judgment, for whether such deliberation is undertaken without deviation depends on the being of the person. People who are overwhelmed with emotion get lost in these deliberations—that is, in the process of orienting themselves on the basis of moral conviction. They are, as it were, momentarily benighted.[6] Aristotle explains this by reference to the intoxicated: the unaccountability of someone who is drunk involves no moral unaccountability, for he had it in his power to drink moderately.

The crux of Aristotle's philosophical ethics, then, lies in the mediation between logos and ethos, between the subjectivity of knowing and the substance of being. Moral knowledge does not climax in courage, justice, and so on, but rather in the concrete application that determines in the light of such knowledge what should be done here and now. It has been rightly brought to our attention that Aristotle's last pronouncement concerning what is right consists in the vague phrase "as befits it" [hos dei, as required] (ως δει). It is not the grand conceptualizations of an ethics based on heroic exemplars and its "table of values" that are the real content of Aristotelian ethics; it is, rather, the undeluded and undeceptive concrete moral consciousness [hos ho logos ho orthos legel, according to reason, right reason] (ως ο λόγος ορθὸς λέγει) that finds expression in such unmeaning and all-inclusive concepts as what is "fitting," what is "proper," what is "good and right." It is a mistake for people to take Aristotle's emphasis on this universal formula for concretization and turn it into a pseudo-objectivity, seeing a special "value of the situation" written therein (N. Hartmann). Quite the contrary, this is precisely the meaning of the doctrine of the "mean" that Aristotle develops: that all conceptual definitions of traditional virtues possess at best a schematic or typical correctness, which is produced from the legomena [things spoken]. This means, however, that philosophical ethics finds itself in the same situation as everyone else. That which we consider right, which we affirm or reject, follows from our general ideas about what is good and right. It achieves its real determinacy, nevertheless, only from the concrete reality of the case. This is not a case of applying a universal rule. Just the opposite: it is the real thing we are concerned with, and for this the generic forms of the virtues and the structure of the "mean" that Aristotle points out in them offer only a vague schema. Thus it is *phronesis*—the virtue enabling one to hit upon the mean and achieve the concretization—which shows that something can be done (πρακτὸν αγαθόν), not some faculty special to philosophers. On the contrary, those who deliberate on what is good and right in general see themselves as referring to this practical logos just like everyone else who has to put their ideas of what is good and right into action. Aristotle explicitly refers to the mistake of people who resort to theorizing and, instead of doing what is right, just philosophize about it.[7]

Thus it is certainly not true, as sometimes appears to be the case in Aristotle, that *phronesis* has to do with finding the right means to a pre-given end. This concrete moral deliberation defines the "purpose" for the first time by making it concrete—that is, by defining what "should be done"[*prakton agathon*, the practically good] (as πρακτὸν αγαθόν).

Kant is certainly right to view the ideal of happiness as an ideal more of imagination than of reason, and to that extent it is completely right to say that no determinate content can be specified for the determination of our will that would be universally binding and capable of being defended as a moral law by our reason. Yet we need to ask whether the autonomy of practical reason—defending the unconditional nature of our duty against the persuasions of our inclinations—represents nothing more than a check upon our caprice, and is not determined by the entirety of our moral being, which whole (permeated by the patency of what is right) comports itself practically in each case whenever it chooses what to do. (By *hexis* is meant not a capacity for being this or that, like knowing and understanding are, but instead an ontological category like nature, a "thus and not otherwise.")

What should be done: this is admittedly not just what is right, but also what is useful, purposeful, and in that sense "right." The interpenetration of these two senses of "right" in humankind's practical conduct is clearly what for Aristotle constitutes the humanly good. Obviously those who act in a morally right manner do not comport themselves in the same way as does a craftsman who knows his business [*techne*] (τέχνη). Moral action is not right by reason of the fact that what is thereby brought into existence is right; rather, its rightness lies primarily in ourselves, in the "how" of our conduct, in the manner in which the person who "is right" does it (the σπουδαῖος ανήρ). It is also true, on the other hand, that in our moral conduct, which depends so much more on our being than on our explicit consciousness (ειδώς), we ourselves are drawn forth as well—as we are (and not as we know ourselves). Yet, insofar as the whole of our being depends upon capabilities, possibilities, and circumstances that are not simply given over into our hands, *eupraxia* [good practice] the end of our conduct, and *eudaimonia* [well being] at which we are aiming and for which we are striving, comprehend more than we ourselves are. Our actions are situated within the horizon of the polis, and thus our choice of what is to be done spreads out into the whole of our external social being.

Ethics proves to be a part of politics. For the concretization of our selves—whose circumference is sketched out in the forms of virtue and their being ordered toward the highest and most desirable form of life—reaches far into what is common to us all, which the Greeks named the polis, and to the true form of which everyone is at all times answerable. Only now does it become intelligible that friendship is a central object of Aristotle's pragmatics—not as "love of friends," but as that mean between virtues and goods which is only *met'aretes* [shared values]. Without it—and it is always a precarious possession—a full life is unimaginable.[8]

Thus Aristotle does not emphasize the sublime unconditionality in moral decision-making that Plato and Kant demand. Of course, Aristotle too knows that moral conduct does not simply pursue arbitrarily chosen purposes, but rather chooses something for its own sake, because it is "fine" [*schön*]. But on the whole it is always the task of a being that is limited and conditioned in multifaceted respects to see and master this. Even the noblest ideal of human existence, pure contemplation— toward which the whole structure of Aristotle's ethics, like Plato's,[9] always gravitates—remains tied to governing well the life of action on which that very ideal itself depends.

It is in this way, however, that the sense for the multiply conditioned, which constitutes Aristotle's speculative genius, becomes fruitful for moral philosophy; for here and here alone emerges an answer to the question that has been plaguing us: namely, how a philosophical ethics, a human doctrine of the human, is possible without requiring a superhuman self-transcendence.

The moral-philosophical deliberation that is implicit in the practice of philosophical ethics is not a theory that must be made practically applicable. It is not at all a knowing in general, a knowing at a distance, which would in fact conceal what the concrete situation calls for, like the priest and the Levite's sense of fidelity to the law by contrast to the Good Samaritan's. The universal, the generic, that can be expressed only in a philosophical inquiry dedicated to conceptual universality is in fact not essentially different from what guides the usual, completely untheoretical sense of norms present in every deliberation on moral practice. Most important, it is not different from this untheoretical deliberation, in that it includes the same task of application to given circumstances that obtains for all moral knowledge, for the individual as well as the statesman who acts on behalf of all. It is not just *phronesis*, moral knowledge that guides concrete action, that has a moral being, an *arete* [virtue]; it is a εξις [*hexis*], admittedly it is a *hexis tou aletheuin* [habit of adhering to truth]. The philosophical practice of ethics too has a moral relevance, and that is not a hybrid "academic" claim divorced from "life," but rather a necessary consequence of the fact that it is always situated within circumstances that condition it. It is not something for anyone and everyone, but only for those whose education in society and state has brought their own being to a point of such maturity that they are capable of recognizing general rules of thumb in concrete perplexities and putting them into practice. The audience of Aristotle's lectures on ethics themselves needed to get beyond the temptation only to philosophize and to abstract themselves from the claims of the situation. To keep this danger always before one's eyes: this, I think, is why Aristotle is still not outmoded. Like Kant with his "formalism," Aristotle too distanced himself from all false claims incident to the idea of a philosophical ethics. Whereas Kant destroyed the moral-philosophical rationalizations of the Enlightenment and its blind pride in reason by releasing unconditional practical reason from all the conditionedness of human nature and presenting it in transcendental purity, Aristotle, by contrast, placed the conditionedness of human life at the center and made it concretizing the universal, by applying it to the given situation, as the central task of philosophical ethics and moral conduct alike. We owe Kant our unending thanks for disclosing the consequential impurity of moral reasonings, that "disgusting mishmash" of moral and practical motives which the "practical worldly wisdom" of the Enlightenment validated as a higher form of morality. From this madness Kant helped us recover.

There is another aspect of things, however, which makes it necessary for us to take into account the conditionedness of all human being and also, therefore, of our use of reason. Above all, it is the aspect of education that makes manifest humankind's essential conditionedness. Kant too knows about this, but the limits of his truth become visible in the way he knows about it. Kant shows very impressively how much power the ideas of moral reason, duty, and justice itself are capable of exercising over the mind of a child, and he shows that it is wrong always to employ reward and punishment as educational devices, because that strengthens and confirms the student's egoistic impulses. There is certainly something true about this—and yet the fact that reward and punishment, praise and blame, exemplar and imitation, along with the ground of solidarity, sympathy, and love upon which their effect depends, that all these still form the "ethos" of humankind prior to all appeals to reason and thus make such appeals possible in the first place: this is the heart of Aristotle's ethics, and Kant does not do it justice. The limitations that necessarily underlie our insight into what is morally right do not have to lead to that corrupt mixture of motives that Kant exposed. In particular, ancient *eudaimonia* [well being]—as distinct from the worldly wisdom of the Enlightenment—cannot be accused of heteronomy, of muddying the transcendental purity of the moral. That is proved preeminently by the utopian rigorism of Plato's *Republic* (book 2). Aristotle too does not for a moment overlook the fact that people are concerned with justice for its own sake, and that no considerations of a hedonistic, utilitarian, or eudaimonistic kind can be allowed to prejudice the unconditionality of a genuine moral decision. Indeed, even the conditionedness of our insight—where what is concerned is not decision in the eminent sense of the word, but rather the choice of the better (*prohairesis*)—represents in general no deficiency and no obstacle. It has the social and political determinacy of the individual as its positive content. This determinacy, however, is more than dependence on the changing conditions of social and historical life. Everyone is undoubtedly dependent on the ideas of their time and world, but from this follows neither the legitimacy of moral skepticism nor the exercise of political power in the form of technical manipulation of opinion. The alterations that transpire in morals and modes of thought that, especially for the elderly, portend the utter dissolution of all morals, come to pass upon an enduring basis. Family, society, and state determine the essential constitution of the human being, in that its ethos replenishes itself with varying contents. Of course, no one knows how to predict what might become of humankind and all its forms of communal life—yet this does not mean that everything is possible, that everything is directed by arbitrariness and caprice and can be determined by the powers that be. There are things that are naturally right.[10] Against the conditionedness of all moral knowledge by moral and political being, Aristotle counterbalances the conviction he shares with Plato that the system of being is powerful enough to set limits to all human confusion. Amidst all distortions, one idea remains indestructible: "How strong, though, is the polis by reason of its own nature."[11]

Thus Aristotle's ethics is able to take cognizance of the conditionedness of all human being without having to deny its own conditionedness. A philosophical ethics that is not only aware of its own questionableness in this way, but takes that very questionableness as one of its essential contents, seems to me the only kind that is adequate to the unconditionality of the moral.

Translated by Joel Weinsheimer

Part 4

Gadamer on Plato, Hegel, Heidegger, and Derrida

14

Plato as Portraitist

This is a late essay on Plato by Gadamer dating from 1988. It was prompted by an invitation from the Glyptothek (Museum for Antique Sculptures) in Munich to celebrate the acquisition of a sculptured bust of Plato. His paper was delivered on February 29 in proximity to the sculpted head of Plato, which was a Roman copy of a Greek original attributed to the sculptor Silanion, who lived in the fourth century BC. Gadamer substantially revised and expanded the essay for its inclusion in his collected works (*Gesammelte Werke*, 7: 228–57), and it is this later version which was taken into the *Gadamer Lesebuch*. The translators, Jamey Findling and Snezhina Gabova, have added about a dozen notes in addition to the dozen already in the essay and have also added English translations of Gadamer's citations where possible.

The title of the essay plays on the fact that the sculpted head of Plato was in effect a portrait, and Plato himself as portraitist gave us priceless verbal portraits of Socrates in the dialogues. Gadamer goes into the definition of a portrait before discussing the portraits of Socrates that Plato gives us in the *Phaedo* and *Symposium*. He distinguishes two types of Platonic dialogue. In the first type, the image of Socrates is vague because the purpose is to draw the reader into realizing that he or she is the person whose ignorance is disclosed. The second type shows us the figure of Socrates not only in his critical superiority but as a visionary of the true. The *Phaedo* and *Symposium* fall into this latter category, and Gadamer goes into considerable detail about the figure of Socrates that Plato presents in each of these two dialogues. He discusses "the new world of thinking" that is opened up, a world of *nous*, "a word that evokes a wholly new realm of meaning for Socrates." He notes that Socrates in the *Symposium* opens up another new realm, that of eros. Gadamer suggests that it is always already Socrates who has Diotima's wisdom about love. But Gadamer is not satisfied with these remarks about Plato; he examines the path to the good in the *Republic* and the reference to the "exact itself" in the *Statesman*. And in the *Parmenides* and *Philebus* he is led into several other concepts on which he sheds important light, such as the mixture, individuality, *methexis*, and mimesis. As he does so, this essay becomes a major statement of his Platonic philosophy.

* * *

Plato as Portraitist

My choice of Plato as portraitist for the theme of this essay represents the inspiration of a passing moment. Whenever one is asked to speak about Plato, one is in truth always invited into a wide space, a space which in my view offers many aspects and always holds ready something new and challenging. And that is just how I felt about this new portrait of Plato. However, before I come to Plato himself, I must navigate an enormous stumbling block. What is a portrait? Had I no obligations to the wonderful occasion that brings me here, I should prefer to speak solely about this question: What, in fact, is a portrait? Is something like this head a portrait? If I were to attempt to explain what I think a portrait is, I would probably say: it is the likeness [*Abbildung*], the image [*Bild*] of an individual or a person that would enable us to recognize it, if we know it. But what kind of words do we use here? "Person"? In Greek, this is called *prosopon*—the role, or better, the mask that one wears. This is surely something other than what we mean in our everyday use of the word "person." Were I to be more precise, I might say that what I mean is an individuality, an individual; translating that into Greek, it would be called *atomon*. But this leads us far from what we are really seeking, namely, the words that let us describe what we take a portrait to be.

My initial impulse turned out to be a matter for serious reflection. What does it mean for us to possess a portrait of Plato, the head of a portrait statue, which through fortuitous circumstances and the special efforts of Herr Vierneisel has been preserved until now? Just what do we have here—an image, a portrait, a *ritratto,* something torn from reality instead of something real? We all know that what characterizes a portrait as such poses a unique problem, above all for the Greeks. What can we say, for example, about images [*Bildern*] of the gods, whom no one has ever seen? Archaeologically speaking, this is one of the most important questions regarding the concept of the portrait—how the depicting [*Bildwerdung*] of the gods came about in this art form. What was the importance of Homer for something like vase-painting? Scholarly research deals with questions like these. Upon reflection, I then realized that it is not so very different for ordinary people like ourselves when it comes to our portraits. A portrait is not just a random shot, such as today's cameras take. Nor does it come about simply as a result of sitting for someone, as one says so quaintly. But here again, there is already much to ponder. What can we still call reality when one sits for a portrait? I have recently heard it suggested, to my great surprise, that Plato actually sat for Silanion. That is something I really do not believe. But in any case, what makes such images or busts into portraits is something completely different. In truth, a portrait is much more. With regard to the depicting of the gods, an image emerges, as we know, through recurrent reproductions of cult images, constantly modified and repeated. As a result of this, a god becomes its image. But perhaps with human beings it is not so very different, and it is the case even there that one becomes one's own image only gradually. Only thus, namely through becoming one's image in such a way, can a person have an image, and it is precisely this image which, in the portrait, has become valid for everyone.

Clearly the most distinctive element of a portrait is its intention to be recognized as such. Phenomenology has taught us that it is good to clarify such questions by being attentive to variations in the way language is used. So, for example, we say of a face, or a figure, or a single face in a group picture, that it has the quality of a portrait, that it is portraitlike [*porträthaft*].[1] Here language has already carried out an abstraction for us. And so we ask how one can use the word "portraitlike." In general, what does one mean in saying this? The word seems self-evident, and yet it presents a difficult problem: what a portrait is. This problem has occupied me for over fifty years in the course of my studies in art history. Holding in view the difference between a historical picture and a picture of similar events which is not a historical picture, we could perhaps say of the latter that it is a genre picture. The word "genre" already indicates that it is in a specific sense something universal. But is not the historical picture, as a picture, also something universal, since it is indeed not the events themselves, but rather the events as captured in a picture? And yet it is something unique, which is represented in the picture so meaningfully that it is there for all and, as such, is universal. Hence, I would say that the portraitlike consists in the universal becoming visible in the individual and in the fact that one must, as the one portrayed, completely coincide [*erfüllen*] with one's own image. Hegel once wrote under a portrait of himself, "Our knowledge [*Kenntnis*] should become recognition [*Erkenntnis*]. Whoever knows me will here recognize me." From this statement of the great thinker one can begin to see just how much is required for knowledge to become recognition and for a likeness to be a portrait.

However, after this abstract introduction—perhaps something like an organ prelude—I want to turn to the wonderful occasion which brought me here. What was it like for me to be able to see for the first time this new head of Plato, previously known only from reproductions? I think that in cases such as these, one should not read what others have said. It is important that one see with one's own eyes. I have probably seen too much with my eyes. So I must confess that the appearance of this head surprised me tremendously. One immediately feels the immense power concentrated in it. The steep vertical lines on the forehead are especially pronounced, more so than in numerous replicas we knew already. I must further confess that I found the head surprisingly beautiful. It remains for us to reflect on the importance of this fact, and why it signifies something other than the value of the artwork. However, what stood out to me next about the head, and which until then I had not seen at all—I don't know whether anyone else has already said this—was this: I saw in it most of all the Attic wit, something extremely skeptical and farsighted, distant and satirical, especially in the region of the mouth and in the eyes. What I perceived there was something which to me surely counts as an Attic virtue, one that in general we lack and that, perhaps for this reason, we easily miss. After all, the Platonic dialogues, those descendants of Attic comedy, show ample use of this Attic humor, and Plato's thinking of utopia would be impossible without it. On top of that, we know how Plato loved Epicharmus, and we know from the *Symposium* how he admired Aristophanes. The third thing that struck me was this: how Roman it is! Granted, it is a Roman copy of a Greek sculpture. And I can fully understand the inclination of the archaeologist to take the replica's similarity to the unavailable authentic bronze as being of chief importance. In my view, however, what stands out most is that it is so Roman. It has something of the greatness of those gripping Roman portraits from the time of the republic, which we all know to be a true perfection of the art of portraiture. Here this has been powerfully unified and wedded with that type of portrait which depicts the philosopher. It is a philosopher, and yet it is unmistakably the portrait of a completely singular man. Only through a lucky coincidence, the inscription on a late replica, do we know with any certainty at all that this is really meant to be Plato. But one does believe it. I see a particular benefit in the fact that this head strikes me as so Roman. One encounters here the effective history to which we ourselves belong, if I might call upon this hermeneutical guiding concept.

Plato's influence, his spiritual legacy, passed through this Greek-Roman mediation. One need only think of Plotinus and Augustine. When we come upon this head today, it is as if we are led back through this masterful copy to him, to Plato himself, and indeed through our very own spiritual history. We should in no way imagine that we could see this head in the way that Plato's contemporaries saw it. I will leave open whether much about this head seems Roman to me only because of my great familiarity with the Roman portraits from the time of the republic which are in Boston. Nor do I want to foreclose the possibility that Silanion already experienced something of the transition from the image which is of a type [*Typusbild*] to the individual portrait which was initiated in the fourth century. However, other replicas of the head do not really confirm this. It seems more likely to me that such a splendidly crafted marble copy of a bronze original is a unique creation in itself, and that the creator of a copy of such quality necessarily had to contribute something of his own, something which had emerged for him out of his time and environment—namely, the period of transition from the republican portrait to the imperial portrait. This was perhaps not the case with the original, if indeed the original stems from a similar transition period, only in the reverse direction—from type to individual portrait.

But we should also ask whether we are able to see this development in this way only because we bring our own spiritual history along from the start. The history that has taken shape as the transformation of the Greek to the Roman, of the Roman to the Christian, and thence to the reflected inwardness of modernity—this history, rooted in Plato, is ours. We do not dream this; we see it. And here, through this Roman copy of the Greek original, it is brought to life right before our eyes.

Admittedly, I would never have ventured to speak on this topic in such a way—by profession I am no archaeologist—if there were not also the Greek literary portrait. Here then is the second question I must ask myself, namely, whether this literary portrait does not also contribute something to how we today see this head of Plato. With regard to this question, I feel more qualified to speak. In the end, the great writings of Plato, which have come to us wholly intact, comprise the first genuinely complete corpus of an ancient prose author. It was not edited and pruned through the censorship of Alexandrian teachers, as is the case with the Greek tragedies. Indeed, our *corpus Platonicum* contains a few pieces more than Plato himself wrote. In any case, we may assume that the entire production of Plato is a unique portrait, a portrait of Socrates, and that at the same time it also represents a self-portrait of Plato. But we should be rather cautious with the expression "self-portrait" with regard to these literary portrayals. We will see how little what Plato here gives of himself has the character of a portrait. We are also fully aware of the tension that necessarily exists between a sculpture and a literary portrait. "Leave the Greek his earth and clay into forms compressing, through their child his hands in play thrill on thrill expressing"—these verses from the *West-Eastern Divan* continue: "We, though, grasp our own delight in the Euphrates river, in the liquid element roaming hither, thither"—and the poem ends: "Purely scooped by poet's hand, water is cohering."[2] These verses vividly demonstrate the difference between the plasticity of sculptural forms and the fluid element of poetic language.

We are all familiar with the difficulties involved in illustrating books. Consider a praiseworthy example, such as the artistic high point that was English illustration in the nineteenth century. These illustrations do not limit and confine the imaginative wealth of the literary text, such as that of Thackeray or Dickens, but rather offer a wide playspace, guiding the reader's fantasy with dancelike ease. It is likewise exceptional when a literary portrait, through its imaging power, leads to an actual picture or a portrait statue—something we can find in particular in the literary work of a great author. One can guess, of course, that I speak of the image of Socrates, which has taken shape both in a pictorial type [Typusbild] and at the same time in an actual literary portrait.

We might ask ourselves what language is, what it is capable of, and how it can do what it is capable of. Let us consider as an example the written life history, the biography. One could look at the biographies Plutarch wrote, which unfortunately are no longer as vivid in our cultural consciousness as they were in the eighteenth century. In Plutarch, description and narrative alternate, almost like two different aspects of the same thing. Description corresponds to the typological element in Aristotelian anthropology, which is a Greek cultural legacy and is naturally present in Plutarch. The other aspect is narrative, which contains moments unattainable for any of the visual arts. Flowing time, in which a literary creation lets something arise before us, claims the listener and reader in a curious way. One becomes, if I might say so, a co-creator. In listening as well as in reading, we experience a text in ever new ways, through a stream of images and impressions which a great writer can inspire without imposing them on us. This is one of the wonders that language and writing accomplish. How the visual arts speak to us—that is another wonder.

What standards, then, apply to a portrait? One thinks here of the opposition between ideal and realistic portraits, which is in truth a completely false opposition. There are only ideal portraits. There is only the one idealizing look, through which what is transitory or ephemeral in a face or even the appearance of a whole figure—grasped either in formation or decline—is raised to an enduring form. It is not just a single moment—even a "fertile" one—that is captured in the portrait. Everything is there, what came before and what came after, and a whole life history is "narrated" as the eye of the artist reads it. In a certain way, an ideal portrait follows what Johann Gustav Droysen once said so beautifully: "You must be like that, for that is the way I love you—the secret of all education." For a case of realism taken to the extreme—or, we might say, of failed idealization—a case of realism which, through its very exemplarity, has become unforgettable for me, consider Lovis Corinth's portrait of the poet Eduard von Keyserling, which now hangs in the New Pinakothek in Munich. This endlessly delicate, decadent, suffering poet and author (unfortunately no longer read enough), one of the foremost narrators of the German language since Fontane, stares at us with large, frightened eyes. "Here a breath and we tremble from decay." That is also what his poems in the series "Evening Houses" portray, a magical portrait despite the strangeness of these gaunt necks and almost lifeless, flickering eyes. Here too we would say that one could recognize him if one had known him, and, like me, would never forget him even if one did not know him—indeed, even if one had never read a line of his. Whether a picture is a portrait, or a literary portrayal is portraitlike, depends on the intention of the representation and the "conception" of the represented. In contrast, the model used by a painter does not as such have the effect of a portrait. But what is more, one must guard against inserting into the portrait one's own conception of the portrayed—whom one knows or thinks one knows—which is not there at all, instead of seeing what is really there. And so here as well we should not attempt to read into the bust of Plato our own image of him. Only then does one see lips somewhat resigned and an eye that glances over the world in spirit. That is what I could not see in it. Yet just as every head has many faces, the same is true for the portrait, and to that degree what we think we recognize therein is justified.

It is no different with literary portraits, especially Alcibiades' portrayal of Socrates in the *Symposium,* in which the figure of the implacable Socrates reaches an incomparable plasticity. Alcibiades introduces himself and says he would like to praise Socrates using "images," and then adds: "But please do not laugh."[3] He knows exactly what he is saying. The Greek word for "image," *eikon,* has a double meaning here. It designates not only "image" but also a "similitude" through which one could express what is truly meant. Thus the comparison with Silenus and Marsyas alludes to the actual appearance of Socrates, and everyone quite naturally laughed, because the actual appearance of Socrates did have something markedly ugly about it, something absurd, with his protruding eyes and peculiar snub nose. Aristotle, as I once suggested,[4] alluded to this when he referred to Socrates while arguing against Plato's doctrine of ideas, which he charged with *chorismos,* with the separation of the idea from the appearance. Even in the word *simos,* the snubness can be meant only of a nose—just as, with an idea, something can be meant only if it "appears."

Hence this is an indirect reference to Socrates. He had just such a nose, and Theaetetus was proud to look like him. That is how Plato's literary portrait, here voiced by Alcibiades, characterized the appearance of this extraordinary man and indeed his whole being, and itself created a model for the visual arts. Similarly, there was an entire literary genre, the Socratic dialogue, belonging to the so-called Socratics. There were many who aspired to this genre in Platonic times. But in general we cannot characterize these dialogues as portraits, even if such features might occasionally have appeared in them. Yet a great author like Plato, even if he makes people say abstract things, will still reveal something of their humanity wherever he can. The speech of Alcibiades in the *Symposium* is a shining example of this.

But let us turn first to the image of Socrates that appears in the typical Socratic dialogues of Plato. Plato's intention here is a different one. Socrates and his interlocutors remain curiously vague—with the consequence that we as readers suddenly see ourselves in the role of the person whose ignorance is disclosed. The intention that Plato the artist here pursues is simply to force one to think through questions and answers. Hence these dialogues are rightly called leading dialogues, and the vagueness of the characters is thus not an artistic weakness but rather the fulfillment of a task that these texts pose. These dialogues do not claim to assert Plato's true doctrine, nor are these assertions simply put in the mouth of Socrates. If I were to choose an example from this group of dialogues, which belong to the early time of Plato, I would select the *Euthyphro*. This is a famous dialogue in which the Socratic art of argumentation (which one can admittedly correct with modern logic) is presented in a dramatic situation. Socrates meets a *mantis* (a seer), who boasts about being especially able at his art. He meets Socrates just as the charge of impiety is being brought against him. There follows a long conversation about what impiety or its opposite, piety (*eusebeia*), really is. This provides a wonderful indirect portrait of Socrates[5] as a man who is *eusebes* and who now behaves as if he wants to learn the science of piety from the seer. In truth, he knows better than anyone else that one must already be what one wants to know. The story to which this relates speaks clearly enough. Euthyphro has brought his father up on charges for letting a slave die out of negligence, and regards his act as a heroic moral deed. Socrates tries to show him his mistake. But he fails, since Euthyphro simply has no idea what *eusebeia* is. This is shown by his committing such an error in reverence as to bring his own father up on charges (in a dubious case). The conversation concludes with the refutation, in the eyes of the reader, of the seer's definition of piety as the manner in which one best conducts business with the gods.

In my view, this conversation is a key for all Platonic dialogues insofar as one maintains that Socrates taught virtue to be knowledge, and that finding definitions was his goal. Surely in this sense Socrates can only be a not-knower [*Nichtwissender*]. Whenever a definition is sought in such cases, it can never be found. The *Euthyphro* represents in my view a first phase in Platonic writing, in which the element of portraiture in the dialogues was consciously moderated. Everything is directed at having one pose the question of the good oneself, without relying on finding an answer man—whether a seer or someone else who, due to their profession, knows better. This knowledge is the learned ignorance of Socrates.

The second type of Platonic dialogue differs from the first in an essential way. It shows the figure of Socrates not only in his critical superiority, but at the same time as a visionary of the true. This is the mythical Socrates—surely different than the not-knower, and yet the same. Here the portraitlike element lies not only, as in the first type of dialogue, in the implicitness of his knowing ignorance [*wissenden Nichtwissens*], on which the apparently knowledgeable foundered. Now the superior not-knower, in the full potency of his physical presence and his teaching, with all the vigor of his charismatic personality, goes beyond himself. This is indeed something remarkable: the strength of his arguments receives a new and higher validation in the appearance of the man who here vouches for himself. The portraitist in Plato, who shines through everywhere in his work, is here called upon to employ the full range of his art in order to breathe such life into the figure of his master that it itself becomes an argument. The fact that we no longer have a simple dramatic exchange of question and answer, but rather account, testimony, and narrative, is hence completely justified. Narrated conversations have the strongest portraying effect—which is to be expected, considering the difference between visual art [*Bildwerk*] and the literary portrait. For the latter has the advantage of being able to unite plastic imaging and the description of action. Written in this style are, first and foremost, two of the best-known Platonic dialogues, namely the *Phaedo* and the *Symposium*. Both dialogues are narrated, permitting the figure of Socrates to appear in his full vitality.

The *Phaedo* reports the conversation concerning the immortality of the soul that Socrates led in prison, with his Pythagorean friends, on the last day of his life. It is told by someone who was there. Plato himself, says the narrator, was not there because he was sick. I have always asked myself whether he was really sick, or whether this is another subtle literary fiction, one which raises the person who is absent to a higher presence and, in this way, does not allow the author to disappear behind his work. But perhaps it was true in this case. It was indeed significant for later readers of Plato whether the one sentenced to death by the public court was still faithfully followed by his friends, who wanted to be together with him until the last moment. This would by no means endear a person to the rulers of the day. One hardly needs to recount the story itself, how the conversation begins, how Socrates reported that he had begun to render the Aesopian fables into verse because he had dreamed that Apollo said to him repeatedly, "Socrates, practice music." Since Apollo continued telling him this, even during the last night of his life, Socrates concluded that he must follow this bidding on paths other than those he had taken his whole life long in conversation. And so he tried to render the Aesopian fables into verse. An incredible invention. I lip-read it from this head of Plato; a joke, satire, and deeper meaning as well are hidden here. In any case, Plato underlines Socrates' fidelity to the religious life of the city through the absurd and comical consequence of changing Aesopian fables, with all their instructional clarity and moral usefulness, into verse, and of Socrates being the one to do so. Plato himself could not have won much fame as a poet with such material.

Equally famous is the second example of a narrated conversation: the banquet, the *Symposium,* in which the entrance of Alcibiades finally brings about the above-mentioned portrait of Socrates. The entire recounting of the banquet occurs as a narrated conversation. At the start it is reported that Socrates stayed behind on the way to the banquet. The hosts were becoming anxious as to whether he would come at all. But something had occurred to him, and so he went no further but rather stopped to reflect. This is certainly a very portraitlike touch. However, it is the end of the dialogue which forms a unique portrait of this extraordinary man. This happens specifically with the speech of a drunken Alcibiades, inspired by both hatred and love, which disrupts the whole banquet scene.

The two dialogues which I here place in the foreground have very different subjects. Yet they are so essentially tied up with the life and death of Socrates that each of them can be described as a portrait of Socrates. Let us begin with the first, which describes the last hours of Socrates' life. What is told here represents not only an outstanding high point, as well as end point, in the life of Socrates; it represents at the same time a crucial turn in Plato's own life and in his entire body of written work.[6] One understands immediately how the idea of letting these last conversations be told by someone else creates distance and thereby lets Plato portray Socrates as he was and acted, not just in terms of what he had to say. Thus Plato could obviously go far beyond mere remembrance—

in contrast, for example, to the "Memorabilia" of Xenophon, which belong to the memorial literature of this unique man who, until they finally got rid of him, was just as known in the streets of Athens as he was unwelcome there. But now we face the task of showing the Platonic art of portraiture in its philosophical significance. Plato portrays only because he argues. He does not portray solely in order to achieve a poetic effect, but rather in order to say something—as a thinker—through poetic representation.

The subject of the *Phaedo* is the immortality of the soul, which was a question of real concern for the century of enlightenment in which this scene plays out. The two main participants in this final conversation, Simmias and Cebes, come from the Pythagorean world of science. It is obvious from the start that they are not members of a religious sect. They trust far more in the mathematics, medicine, and biology of the time. They know, for example, that the material of the human body transforms itself completely in a very short time. No organism keeps the same cells its whole life long, as we would say today. Now the Pythagoreans certainly knew nothing of cells. But they did know what is essential—that the stuff of which the living body consists is used, and is renewed, like a garment. Socrates provides extensive explanations in an attempt to show the two participants, against their objections, that the soul cannot die because it is first and foremost what brings life. One can in no way imagine a soul, this airy breath which at once awakens the spirit and grants it presence, other than when it ensouls a person. In this way, the immortality of the soul could be, so to speak, logically proven. Plato, or his Socrates, prepares this proof insofar as he comes to speak of mathematical things. He shows that numbers are obviously something. But what are they really? Numbers have a peculiar being. It is not the kind of being possessed by those things which are counted by them. Nor are numbers like the last breath of the dying, which one sees and hears. So a new tension enters the dialogue. Socrates shows something about numbers, that is, without one's knowing what it is, from where it comes, or to where it goes. One knows, however, that it is such and such. All of us, even we laypersons, are conscious of the simple fact that there are prime numbers, that they occur less and less often the higher one goes on the number line, and that nevertheless no one can say where the sequence of prime numbers really stops. Our mathematicians have developed theories and models in order to solve these riddles of the human spirit. Yet it remains mysterious how something can be produced in the numbers themselves which exerts on us the compulsion of reality. It is not the way we would like it—although it seems so simple, always adding one and one and then another one, endlessly one plus one. Our mathematicians—even our schoolchildren—rub their hands with delight at the simplicity of this task. And yet, in the end, there is still no easy answer when, for example, a child wants to know the largest number there is. It is a strange being that numbers have. This leads finally to the fact that there exists something we cannot lay our hands on, something that even the natural scientist with his methods cannot grasp in its proper being.

Perhaps matters with the soul are just as they are with numbers, or with the normative ideas and ideals by which the community orders its life. The Platonic Socrates loves to give two examples: the same itself is, so to speak, an ideal pair of two sames, and justice itself is the just itself. One perceives a certain kinship between the former and the latter, the same and the distributive justice that gives each side the same. One also senses that both are a complete mystery, and that much more still lies behind them. So the proof is finally to show how the soul cannot take part in death, because life is always with it. Death is always closed off from it, and the soul is *athanatos,* immortal like the immortals. Both seem inseparable, the soul and the gods, both inseparable from immortality. Here we must be aware that the immortals of whom the myths and the poets tell have the character of appearance for mortals. Likewise, the soul appears only in life and as life—while death is shrouded in the darkness of the *ignoramus.* But then the dialogue surprises us with a new question: whether the soul is also indestructible. Certainly this is an old linguistic pair, *athanaton kai anolethron,* "immortal and indestructible." They sound like one and the same. The new argument concerning "indestructible" is hard to understand. Only one goal becomes clear, to make mathematical truths valid for those beings that can think.

In the end, of course, it comes out that Socrates himself knows his arguments are able only to refute rational reasons put forward against immortality, but do not represent any positive proof of it. For us, the real meaning of the dialogue as a portrait of Socrates lies here. Only the practical consequence, the adherence to the world of religious representations in which everyone lives, is supported by this example of the Socratic attitude in view of the unprovable and unknowable. Hence, the portrait of one eager for knowledge and of one unshaken by the fear of death becomes the strongest of all arguments. After the Socratic proof, Simmias confesses that he is not yet completely convinced. He obviously means that the child in us, the part of us that fears, which had been spoken about earlier, has still not been completely placated and that further doubts could yet come. Socrates rightly praises him for this. Throughout one's life, one should never feel certain about such a question. And yet, despite this, one should comport oneself morally and socially as if one had such knowledge, and in such a way that one would be well-received by the gods in Hades. Thus should we all live. Here again Socrates shows himself to be the *eusebes* that we know. He too does not know how things really are. But whatever is the case, one must lead one's life in a way that seems good and just. That much he knows.

The portrait that the *Phaedo* presents is a true masterpiece among literary portraits, for which we owe thanks to Plato. It shows Socrates in the hour of his death. One need only recall his famous last words, when, as his limbs were already growing cold, he said to his friends: "You must still slaughter a cock to Asclepius." There is nothing here of the deeper meaning that Nietzsche, in the spirit of Schopenhauer, found in these words. It is much more like the opening scene with the dream that leads Socrates to write poetry. Once again we see that meticulous compliance with holy conventions ordained through custom and practice—even when Socrates once again remains ignorant.

The second shining example of a Platonic literary portrait is found in the *Symposium*. Again, our task will be to recognize the portrait that emerges here as the completion of an argument. The banquet itself is a celebration of speech. In the end, it has to do with the Greek people. Anyone who has been to Greece knows the endless waves of sound which pound and roar through every nook and cranny of the streets of Athens, evidence of the Greek gift of speech, and of their tremendous love of it. At the banquet described here, a circle of friends has come together, including, among others, the prizewinning tragic poet Agathon, the comic poet Aristophanes, and Socrates himself. It is decided not to have a wild drinking party, but rather an exchange of philosophical speeches. The theme of the speeches is to be Eros, the passion of love. Each of the participants gives praise to all-powerful Eros and his beauty with profound and spiritually moving speeches—even Aristophanes. At the end comes Socrates, and a Socratic dialogue ensues.

Socrates begins by asking what Eros really is. It is a desire—but a desire means longing for something, indeed, something which one lacks. From this Socrates concludes that Eros himself is not really beautiful, as everyone has said, since he is actually the one who desires the beautiful. Eros is therefore not the beautiful boy who is always in the retinue of Aphrodite, but the unshodden one, the one whose desire remains unstilled. He is himself not beautiful, but rather directed longingly towards the beautiful. This is vintage Socrates, an argument of uncanny logical consistency.

A new world of thinking is indeed opened up here. The *Phaedo* contains the first introduction to this new world. This is seen in the famous self-portrayal of Socrates, the story of how he bought Anaxagoras's book in the market. Knowing that it cost so-and-so many minas, the Americans have calculated how long the manuscript, and therefore the book, must have been on the basis of the pay for writers at that time. It was apparently quite a short book. It speaks of nous, which we would call "spirit." This word evoked a wholly new realm of meaning for Socrates, regarding which he anticipated the help of Anaxagoras. Now we are aware that Socrates was not content with Anaxagoras's account of how nous gave the decisive impetus to the formation of the world. He did not want to know how nous puffed and pushed, but why the ultimate order of the world is as it is, and why it is such a good order. That is the nous for which he sought. It is not something good in itself, the finest, the purest, that which pervades everything, as Anaxagoras describes it, but rather something which looks upon the good. Socrates expected in nous not so much something that sets the formation of the world in motion as something that is directed to what is good and beautiful in the order of the world. Nous, the thinking, the spirit, is not one distinct being among all others, but rather that which differentiates all beings.

The same idea is found in connection with love, with Eros, in the *Symposium;* Socrates shows that Eros is the desire for the beautiful and not itself something beautiful. Socrates indeed knew of the vigorous power of passion that overcomes one; however, he saw that Eros is not only a natural power, but also a desire for something. Eros is always *eros tinos* [desire *for* something 199e], and it always pursues the beautiful. But if this demon, as Diotima calls it, loves the beautiful, it must distinguish between the beautiful and the ugly. If so, then it is, in truth, thinking: *eros philosophos* [desire for wisdom]. Whoever is unconsciously enraptured by passion is thereby directed toward something, spellbound by something that has come over one. An observer would perhaps assume that this passion takes from the person all reason and ability to decide. But it is always the beautiful, and never the ugly, which attracts someone. Thus Socrates continues the dialogue with Agathon until the superficiality of his praise of Eros and his ignorance become conscious to him.

At this point, however, Socrates breaks off the dialogue with Agathon. He goes on to relate his conversation with the priestess Diotima, who taught him the ways of love. Again, there is a subtle irony in Socrates' appeal to the priestess Diotima of Mantineia. Plato artfully hints that, whether Diotima is posing questions or answering them, it is in fact Socrates speaking, and that it will still be Socrates speaking when Diotima begins to lead the dialogue herself and gives her speech (*Symposium* 202e). This will be true even when Diotima no longer believes that Socrates will be able to follow (210d)—which she repeats often, exhorting Socrates to strain himself. Even then, it is not actually Diotima who speaks, but rather Socrates, going beyond himself and laying out the entire vision of the way of love. Here we must be attentive to how the distance between Diotima and Socrates increasingly diminishes. It is always only Socrates, beginning with the slight mockery of Diotima, who portrayed Eros to him as a universal principle of life, "like a real sophist" ($208c_1$). "You must know," this really means, "you can believe me about that." She then goes on to refer everything back to the desire for immortality and to recognize Eros, desire itself, in all forms of human life and creation. Although the homoerotic and pedagogical passion of Plato and his readers is not primarily for women, but rather for young, talented boys, the love of the feminine is included in love for procreation and continued life, for having and rearing children ($208e_2$). The higher desire, for the right ideas, the logoi—to awaken these things in other souls and above all to see in them the beautiful, this is the complete wisdom of love that Socrates here learns from Diotima. No doubt because it is irrelevant, the question of whether Socrates only finds his pedagogical Eros after the lesson of the fictional priestess remains open. (This happens in other Platonic dialogues as well; for example, in the *Apology*, the question of the justification of Socratic practice as obedience to the Delphic oracle remains open.) Not without reason does Diotima say that Socrates could be initiated into the rites of love ($209e_5$). We easily understand this about Socrates in the description of the passage from one beautiful youth to another, and in the assertion that what we seek in others are the logoi—which in truth motivate this passage ($210c_1f$). Is it not, in the end, always already Socrates who has this wisdom about love?

One has cause, however, to ask oneself what Diotima leaves in doubt, namely, whether Socrates will really be able to follow her until the end. Does the Platonic Socrates ultimately doubt himself and the ascent to the beautiful, which like a sudden revelation becomes visible in its truth, purity, and unity, or is Socrates driven out beyond himself as it were? It sounds like a step in the direction of onto-theology, a step which Aristotle the physicist will take and thereby become the founder of metaphysics, the ancestor of Christian Scholasticism, and in the end the founder of the modern world of science. The renewed account of the ascent becomes clearer and clearer, becomes too clear—that is, transparent—when the ascent leads from one beautiful body to another and thence to the beautiful soul. One may feel somewhat perplexed, reading about this upward path. Yet it is the well-known problem of the constitution of the universal, of *epagoge* (which of course has nothing to do with *enumeratio simplex* [complete enumeration] and which involves a transition to *noein*). What is reminiscent in this account of the path of love is nothing else than the experience of the dialectician, as described by Aristotle in the *Posterior Analytics* (B 19). Diotima's doubt as to whether Socrates could follow her is itself a deeply grounded irony. It is no longer Socrates who projects this dialectical structure into the pedagogical experience of love. The Socrates of the *Phaedrus,* who otherwise does not spare logical argumentation, is here, as Diotima, more reticent. Indeed, he sees in the sweet madness of loving the elevation and transition to truth, but not in such a run-through of every beautiful body and every beautiful soul. This is, as it were, only an expression for the unsayability of the universal. Or is it still more?

We encounter another hesitation and half-evasion, similar to Diotima's here, when Socrates is asked about the good in the *Republic.* There he has succeeded in making the four Platonic cardinal virtues convincing. But then he is also required to answer the question about the greatest good, the *megiston mathema,* which is defined by him as incomprehensible and unattainable, not teachable like the other *mathemata.* Finally he suggests the simile of the sun, and later the myth of the cave in order to sketch the new educational path for the future rulers of the ideal state. We should take note of the parallels between this path, the path to the good in the *Republic,* and the path to the beautiful in the *Symposium.* When here the Socratic art of argumentation no longer produces only negative results and failed definitions, one indeed realizes that the explanatory power of the logos is exceeded by the beautiful as well as by the good. As much as Plato is inclined to continually change from the beautiful to the good and from the good to the beautiful as if they were the same, the *Philebus* confirms that it is difficult to find a concept for either the beautiful or the good. In the end, the beautiful itself can only be described as the appearance of the good in a threefold way (*sun trisi*), in a triad of determinations. In the *Statesman* it is even called "the exact itself" (*auto to akribes*), which is in everything, but not over everything, as the inner measure.[7] How does Plato address this difficulty in the *Symposium?* I think that, here as elsewhere, the solution has long been clear. One must simply read the dialogues and not just use the material to reconstruct his doctrine—or the Kantian doctrine, or even the unwritten dialectic of Plato himself—which in any case could not be learned. The figure of Socrates, his whole life, enriches these dialogues to a dimension that the conceptual only suggests. Socrates is not simply a role into which Plato slips. In the end, his conversation partners are often we ourselves, we thinking readers. This might well be ignored—in particular by those who, bewitched by the spell of modern, so-called scientific philosophy, saw the Platonic "system" in Plato, the Aristotelian "system" in Aristotle, the Scholastic "system" in Thomas Aquinas, the

Counter-Reformational "system" in Suarez, and lastly thought about the concept of system in German idealism, always seeking only to recognize the proper system of philosophy from the point of view of such false objectivity. In the case of the *Symposium,* we cannot reconstruct any such system, and yet neither can we disregard the dramatic ending, which interprets Diotima's entire account of the way of love in terms of Alcibiades' portrait of Socrates. One is not being prepared here for something that Plato himself knows and could state better.

The dialogue describes the entrance of Alcibiades: how he is startled at the sight of Socrates, how he admires him—and how he finally loses all measure and all inhibition in the almost shameless telling of his intimate experience with Socrates. What he gives here is a unique testimony of what Socrates has learned from Diotima and what he was. The Platonic ideal of the Doric harmony of logos and *ergon* is brought vividly to life in the figure of Socrates. The strategy of seduction that Alcibiades describes does not succeed because Socrates was unseduceable. Alcibiades even accuses him of that. Socrates would always only give the illusion that he was in love. In truth, he wants only to be loved by us. This is the image that Plato draws here.

In the eyes of Alcibiades, it seems as if Socrates has learned all too well from Diotima, and as a result could never love him. Or is it reversed in the end: Is it Alcibiades who did not know how to love, since he always wanted only to be loved? Is it for this reason that such a promising man became the *homme fatal* of Athens? Whatever the case may be, Alcibiades was one of the greatest disappointments Socrates ever had. Plato's readers knew how he eventually became responsible for the destruction of Athens in the Peloponnesian War. They would have been able to recognize in this Socrates the Platonic answer to the breakdown of the Socratic pupil.

The two aspects of Plato's literary portraits which we have examined now present us with the task of drawing philosophical consequences. They are of a radical kind. We had concluded from the structure of the speech of Diotima that the description of the ascent to the beautiful follows the stepwise conceptual scheme of *epagoge.* From that we determined that the ascent to the beautiful consists of nothing else than learning to see the beautiful, which is in everything. Now this admittedly sounds too much like modern nominalism, or like the projection of concepts back into Plato. In reality, however, what emerges before us in this portrait of pedagogical Eros has a higher truth. It is immediately clear even for us that love does not blind, but rather makes one see, in the sense that one strives to see the other and to let him be in his true possibility. Hence there lies in the passion of love, if one does not allow oneself to be enchanted by its "false" madness, an intellectual longing for the other which is the foundation of all true love. In Plato, an intellectual longing means that true Eros is directed toward the "logoi," and the logoi always refer to that which is valid for everyone. What is proper, good, and beautiful—this is the one beautiful, that which is itself meant in all love of the beautiful. And yet the beautiful as such cannot be separated from this or that particular thing. It can never be detached from its appearance. The beautiful must appear; otherwise it is not the beautiful. For it is pure shining [*Scheinen*], and as such it is not dependent on what kind of being it is, whether human or god or any other beautiful thing. As pure shining, appearance [*Erscheinen*], shining forth [*Herausscheinen*], the beautiful is like that "splendor" which is, according to Plotinus, as if poured out over that which appears, because this shine [*Glanz*] has its being in the *diffusio sui*, in its diffusion [*Austeilung*]. Plato has shown this in a wonderful myth in the *Phaedrus,* in which the soul, imprisoned in the body, feels its wings grow again at the sight of the beautiful and uplifts itself anew. In the *Phaedrus* it is said that the beautiful stands out above all others, because it shines forth (*to ekphanestaton*).[8] Thus the beautiful is conceptualized in Platonic terms as something to whose essence it belongs to appear. Of course, we usually hear Plato saying that all appearances participate more or less in the essence, in the *eidos,* and also that beautiful things are never pure beauty, but are always mixed with something else and are to that extent impure. Yet it belongs to the unique essence of the beautiful to appear. One of the foremost questions in the entire tradition of the metaphysics of light is whether the Platonic doctrine of ideas actually holds that the essence is in the appearance—which is what the young Socrates, with his example of the daylight, has in mind in the *Parmenides.*[9] What does this claim mean as a philosophical assertion?

I begin with a remark found in Aristotle that Plato was actually a Pythagorean, that he had simply introduced the word *methexis* in place of the word "mimesis"—just another expression for the same thing.[10] It is difficult to translate these Greek expressions. The word "imitation" cannot rightly stand for what "mimesis" means here. Better would be "re-presentation" [*Darstellung*]. For that is the Pythagorean teaching: "The sun-orb sings, in emulation, 'mid brother-spheres, his ancient round: his path predestined through Creation, he ends with step of thunder sound."[11] Thus Goethe describes the Pythagorean harmony of the spheres in his verses. The paths of the stars follow the numerical proportions according to which they are ordered. On this thesis, then, the stars represent the numbers, and, to this extent, the appearances fulfill the ideality of the numbers. Thus it is a mathematical vision of the cosmos which immediately presents itself in the Pythagorean view of the world: the numbers are what things fundamentally are. The Pythagorean doctrine effects a kind of identification of being and number.

Plato did in fact change the expression, as Aristotle claims. Instead of "mimesis," he says *methexis*. But here translation becomes extremely difficult. *Methexis* actually means "participation" [*Teilhabe*], and if one says it in Latin, it will be yet further misunderstood: *participatio*. For here the idea of the whole and the parts intrudes, which, in the Greek expression, as with German equivalents, such as *Teilnahme* and *Teilhabe*, is really not relevant. Can one really speak of taking a part [*Nehmen eines Teils*] when one takes part [*Anteil nimmt*]?

However, to say that the appearance participates in the idea and is not like the stars, which imitate or represent numbers, indicates more than a mere change of expression. Yet Aristotle dilutes the distinction, as if there were no difference. He even tries to equate Plato's doctrine of ideal numbers with the Pythagoreans in order to emphasize its untenability. In reality, a wholly new ground reveals itself in this change of expression, a ground on which Plato establishes both his proximity with and his departure from the Pythagorean worldview. It is the Socratic-Platonic ground which Plato entered with the flight into the logoi and which he introduced to the world with the name "dialectic." When the stars bring the numbers to representation through their paths, we call this representation "mimesis" and take it to be an approximation of the actual being. In contrast to this, *methexis*·is a wholly formal relationship of participation, based on mutuality. "Mimesis" always points in the direction of that which one approaches, or towards which one is oriented, when one represents something. *Methexis,* however, as the Greek *meta* already signifies, implies that one thing is there together with something else. Participation, *metalambanein,* completes itself [*erfüllt sich*] only in genuine being-together and belonging-together, *metechein.* Now Plato himself certainly used the expression "mimesis" in various ways, but only in order to emphasize the ontological difference between, on the one hand, a copy [*Nachbild*] and likeness [*Abbild*] and, on the other hand, the original [*Urbild*] and model [*Vorbild*] of the idea. It is also worth noting, as I emphasized in my first study of Plato,[12] that the problem of *methexis* will not really provide an answer concerning the relationship of appearance and idea. Not without reason is Plato quite indefinite in his choice of expression for this relationship. That was not his problem, since this relationship was already presupposed in his flight into the logoi. In contrast to this, the presupposition under which one sought to adapt Plato to neo-Kantianism and its theory of knowledge was unexamined. Hence Nicolai Hartmann, following

Natorp, developed the theory of descending *methexis,* which necessitated returning to the question of individuation and concretion. According to this theory, the constitution of the individual was first developed fully in Plotinus and, in this way, what Plato's dialectic of *methexis* strove for was attained. So the binding of the *eidos* to the logos is disregarded, and language is consequently replaced with mathematical calculus. However, that is really a modern (nominalist) turn. Against it, Aristotle retains logos as the starting point. But, for him, both expressions, "mimesis" and *methexis,* are only metaphors. He himself gave a conceptual answer to the question of the difference between the individual thing and its *eidos:* it is the introduction of the concept of *hyle*—of stuff, of material— which, through its being-together with the form, is the concrete, which he called the *synolon.* This is not the place to delve into the Aristotelian step to concept formation and his implicit dependence on the logos- and *eidos*-doctrines of Plato.[13] Our starting point is the separate valence which Plato can claim for the manner of representation of his thinking. This has allowed him to become not only the great portraitist whose capacity for plastic representation we see and admire in the *Phaedo* and in the *Symposium.* Plato has also understood the need to indicate, even in the conceptual language of his dialectic, the limit that is set for the concept and the language of humans with regard to the appearances of reality.

One can therefore see that it is no accident when Plato uses *methexis* [participation] rather than "mimesis" for the relationship to the ideas. The problems posed by *methexis* are pushed to the limit in the first part of that most mystifying of dialogues, the *Parmenides.* There the most important difficulty for the hypothesis of the ideas is that knowledge of the ideas would be accessible only to the gods and knowledge of the world of appearances only to humans—a *chorismos* [separation] of complete absurdity. Actually, this is a premonition of the later Platonic dialectic, which dissolves Parmenides' objections against Socrates and the hypothesis of the ideas. Not until the *Sophist,* in which the formulation and elaboration of the problem found in the *Parmenides* is taken up in a positive way, do we really learn what is at stake for Plato himself in the question of *methexis.* It was a wonderful and bold idea to introduce the young Socrates into conversation with the master of rational consistency. This idea has cost historical research and its quest for historical facts much misguided effort.

Once again, one must be able to read what is said implicitly in a dialogical argumentation. At the beginning of the *Parmenides,* Socrates criticizes the inferior dialectic that Zeno has presented against the hypothesis of the many. There is nothing unusual about this. Socrates would have found it astonishing only if a corresponding dialectic of the ideas themselves were possible, a participation of the ideas in each other and not just the participation of the individual in the idea. What is revealed here, so to speak, is the subversive role that Socrates plays in the dialogue with Parmenides. He anticipates the problem of the participation of the ideas in each other, even while regarding such a thing as altogether incredible. Stenzel correctly observed how, in the dialogue with Parmenides, Socrates is forced step-by-step into the difficulties which accompany a general doctrine of ideas and of participation in the ideas. In the hypothesis of the beautiful and the good, Socrates does not doubt that "it itself" would be different and separate from everything that participates in it. Here it is self-evident that with the good, the beautiful, and the just, we are dealing with an ideal toward which we all strive. On the other hand, Socrates' embarrassment increases (as he expressly admits at *Parmenides* 130d) when the hypothesis of ideas is expanded to absolutely everything that one can say and claim as meant. Of course, I cannot believe that in this one could see an embarrassment of Plato; still less does the first part of the *Parmenides* as a whole catch Plato in a crisis of the doctrine of ideas. To assert this would seem to me a hermeneutic naïveté that misses the sense of the whole.

But it is also incorrect to view Socrates as if he did not understand the problem of participation, even though he does not know how to counter the Parmenidean critique and is, in the end, soundly thrashed by him. In fact, Socrates is treated from the start with great respect by the old Parmenides, even when he is unable to refute the objections that Parmenides directs at the doctrine of ideas. Plato indicates that Socrates finds the use of the concepts of whole and part inadequate, especially in the reified form in which Parmenides employs them for his refutation. This is shown by the profound statement that Plato puts in the mouth of Socrates which seeks to evade the aporias of participation: participation is like the daylight, distributed over everything, yet without light being separated from light and day being separated from day (131b). Likewise, when the day example is replaced with that of a sail spread over many, Socrates yields to this reification only with hesitation and a "perhaps." And he makes yet another significant claim in response to the third-man argument with which Parmenides confronts him, revealing the process of iteration of each third man to be a simple thought game. It is hardly unreasonable to want to reserve ontological status only for the *eidos* itself, nor does it indicate the kind of nominalistic weakening of the *eidos* that Parmenides assumes it does. Certainly the young Socrates is not yet ready for the conceptual clarification of participation. But again, Plato takes every precaution to show that it is not a simple lack of understanding on the part of Socrates. Parmenides praises him for his persistence and encourages him to practice still more in "what the world calls idle talk."[14]

Through such practice in idle talk he will perhaps learn that there must be participation of one idea in the other—and this means there must be the one and the many—if there is to be logos at all. Later the stranger from Elea, to whose conversation Socrates is only a listener in the *Sophist,* will help him with that. It had by then become clear that the absurd *chorismos* [separation], against which Aristotle would direct his critique, already in the *Parmenides* represented the critical point in the hypothesis of the ideas. This means that, in the final analysis, we cannot speak of such separation of the ideas in Plato, as Aristotle supposes. "You have sought too soon to determine a particular *eidos*"—these are the last critical words Parmenides has to say to Socrates. They indicate that the relation of ideas to each other, the participation of ideas in each other, which seemed unthinkable to the young Socrates, will be the genuine basis of the Platonic dialectic. All logos contains such participation of ideas in each other.

That appearances participate in ideas remains the presupposition which lies beneath the hypothesis of the ideas. It shines through clearly in the *Parmenides,* as in all the magnificent visions to which Socrates attains. This is confirmed just as much in the ascent to the good in the *Republic,* through the myth of the cave, as it is in the ascent to the beautiful, which Diotima represents to Socrates as the way of love. In the *Parmenides,* when Socrates uses the daylight analogy to illustrate how a universal (the *eidos*) relates to the particular, this presupposition becomes explicit. That this participation exists is, in the end, the condition for the very possibility of thinking and speaking, of the binding together of ideas and understanding. The "splendor" of the beautiful and the light of day describe *methexis* more truly than the relation of whole and part, in which the Eleatic dialectic entangled Socrates. In the good, as in the beautiful, as in the light, the ubiquity of participation is made known.

The signifying power of the syllable *meta* lends *methexis* the sense of "being-with." We find the same sense of the syllable *meta* in the original text of the Parmenidean poem (fragment 9). There it is said of light and of night that neither has any share of nothing (*meta mēden*). In the concept of mixture, which admittedly makes a reifying interpretation easy, we encounter a problem similar to that found in "participation." But in connection with the philosophy of ideas, something like the concept of mixture is no longer incomprehensible. It is reported of Eudoxos[15] that he used the concept of mixture to interpret the participation of the appearances in the idea and that he taught the inherence of the ideas in appearances. Similarly, the metaphor of mixture, in which the good of human life should be sought, is used in Plato's *Philebus*. However, that does not mean an actual mixture of separate components, of the *hedone* and of knowledge. What is meant is being-with. The number too is with the idea, with being. Thus the path of thinking always goes through differentiations of the one from the other. But that is precisely the way of logos: it expresses the being-with of one *eidos* and another *eidos*. The anamnesis takes place as *dihairesis* [division]. In the Pythagorean metaphor of mimesis, it was still unclear how number could be being itself. In the *Phaedo* this is immediately evident in the Socratic flight into the logoi. Precisely with that, statements become possible which also have validity for the individual, so that the sentence "Theaetetus flies" must be false.

The strongest evidence for this relation between the ideas and the concrete individual, however, is the teaching of the four kinds in the *Philebus*. There the Platonic Socrates relies on the Pythagorean doctrine of opposites and draws the conclusions that lie in the relation of limit and unlimited. The point is that the being-mixed-together of the opposites of limit and unlimited makes a third kind of being unavoidable. So here one encounters, as the third kind, the concept of the *metrion*, the measured and limited. It could seem trivial that there must also exist the limited. But this result in the *Philebus* is followed by another conclusion which leads just as necessarily to a fourth basic kind of being. The third in addition to limit and unlimitedness represents the true wonder of being: coming into being, being which has become. This is not a mere application of thinking, number, and measure to the undefined and unlimited. Measure here belongs rather to being. It lies in the *metrion* [due measure], which the *Statesman* speaks of as the genuine measure that is proper to the being itself. As a concrete existent, this measured being points back to an original being, to the cause, the nous, that governs and steers everything, so that it is appropriate and corresponds with the whole—like the good, the healthy, or the beautiful.

When one grasps the internal logic according to which the four kinds derive from one another in the *Philebus*, one immediately sees that, in this doctrine of the kinds, the old problem of *methexis* reappears. Both additional kinds, the measured (that is, the appropriate) as well as the last ordering cause, represent all that is beyond the reach of thinking, of number, of measuring, and, in the end, of logos: the concrete. The attempt to deduce the concrete from measure and number alone is here immediately derailed. The concrete is undeniably tied together with "nous," and so the fourth kind in the *Philebus* repeats the mythical account of the reality of the real. This is the participation of the idea in the appearances, precisely as the demiurge in the *Timaeus* is responsible for the reality of the universe.[16]

A further illustration of what remains implicit in the Platonic way of thinking is the so-called second principle that, according to Aristotle, was introduced by Plato in his famous lecture on the good together with the *hen,* the one. Here I might refer in particular to my work "Plato's Unwritten Dialectic."[17] The "indeterminate dyad" takes the place of the *apeiron,* to which an entire series of Pythagorean concepts refer. Just as Plato replaced mimesis with *methexis,* so also did he confer a new, purely "logical" sense to the concept of *apeiron* [boundless], clearly in order to release it from the connotations which burdened the older, cosmological concept of *apeiron* since Anaximander. In his physics, Aristotle showed that the indisputable validity of the concept of *apeiron* is based on the unbounded progress of thinking and on the infinitude of the number line. From this point of view, Plato was likely to accept the Pythagorean *tetraktys* [ten dots in four lines to form a triangle] as the guiding schema of the number line. He apparently looked at the first "ten" as an original schema for all order and filled it with variable content, if we can trust Aristotle's account.[18] The closed pyramid of the number ten, however, opens the possibility of counting into the infinite. Number is the many in the one, and to it corresponds the schema of the dyad, to which no determinate content can be assigned. This schema is the principle of all thinking and all differentiation. It transcends the numerically theoretical meaning of *peras* [bounded] and *apeiron* [boundless], which the Pythagoreans had also applied to astronomy and music. It exceeds any possible content, and goes beyond even the concept of *hyle,* which Aristotle referred to it. For the sake of the numbers and in view of mathematics, Aristotle is compelled to purify *hyle* to its genuine conceptual sense, raising *hyle* to *noete hyle,* "intelligible stuff."[19]

This consideration teaches that Plato saw in the *aoristos duas* [undefined twoness] the limit of number and of logoi. In this respect he stands closer to Aristotelian metaphysics than to the Pythagorean identification of being and number. Aristotle himself has recognized the *atomon eidos* [no longer divisible form] as constitutive for defining the what-being [*Was-Sein*], because the *tode ti* can only be shown, not spoken. The different and also, in a certain sense, the superiority of Plato consists in the fact that, insofar as he holds fast to the dialogical character of all speech, this limit of logos is "suddenly" transgressed in dialogue again and again. This is the reason why Plato dedicated no real attention at all to the participation of the individual in the *eidos*—something which Aristotle criticized. What Aristotle had in mind is confirmed when, in the *Phaedo* (100d), Plato offers any number of concepts that one might use for the relation of the individual to the idea, the participation of the individual in the idea. Above all, however, the real force of the Socratic arguments for the immortality of the soul, which are tied to the hypothesis of the ideas, depends entirely on the participation of the ideas in each other, and takes it as self-evident that this will be valid for the individual soul as well. Hence the proof of immortality passes without hesitation over the *eidos* and from there to the god. Both obviously belong to the realm of the ideas.

We seem to be far afield from the topic when we bring the problem of *methexis* [participation], which belongs to the Platonic doctrine of ideas, and the doctrine of ideal numbers into relation with Plato as portraitist. And yet replacing mimesis with participation, *methexis*, and taking part does not seem to me a bad way of describing the essence of the art of portraiture and of the portrait. In our introductory considerations, we had reason to reflect on what is called a realistic portrait, and we could hardly describe our reflections other than with the conceptual tools that we find in the problem of *methexis*. A portrait is not a mere mimesis in the style of that automatic reproduction of modern technology that we call a "photograph" [*Aufnahme*]. A human face "torn out" of nature does not establish how the face in fact looks. The portrait—and even the "picture" [*Aufnahme*] made with photographic materials—is only a portrait if it is a portrait and not a passport photo. What we call *eidos*, therefore, is something valid drawn from the individual appearance. Are we not all, finally, in this sense Platonists?

Let us once again allow the wisdom of language to lead us. When one says "an individual" and "individual," language reminds us of a concealed truth. We tend to speak of an individual and of individuality when we have before us, whether in a picture or in reality, that which eludes words: the concrete, living presence of a person. But when we want to comprehend somebody in their individuality or in a portrait that reproduces this individuality, there is always in this act a certain recognition of ourselves, namely, of the human in the other individuality. Does not the word "individual" already tell us this? A glance at the history of the word is instructive. The word is the Latin translation of "atom." When Plato identifies the last differentiable thing in the differentiation of the "ideas," which can always be further distinguished from each other, he still says *atmeton eidos*—"indivisible *eidos*." He does not use the expression "atom," obviously in order to keep the specification that he called *dihairesis* [separation, differentiation] in mind and to avoid falsely recalling Democritus, who had thus named the last indivisible components of nature. In contrast, Aristotle uses the word frequently, and in the same logical sense it had in Plato's expression—namely, as the limit of specification and not of material division. In any case, the word- and concept-history of "atom" point to an emergence out of the universal and to the limit of the universal. What Aristotle called the *tode ti* is that to which one can point only if one means a "this." We, of course, speak of the individual without consciously realizing that what we mean by this is one limit of the specification implied when we call something "unique." Here linguistic practice supplies an example of the irresistibility with which language and thinking appropriate even what they cannot reach. What they cannot reach is precisely the indivisible, which designates itself as the limit of differentiation. The indivisible always remains in relation to the differentiation. So when we ask what is particular in an individual, we are not conscious even in our own linguistic perception that we treat the individual as "effabile" [utterable].

In metaphysics, one finds oneself entirely in the tradition of the ancients. Today we confront the problem, foreign as such to the ancients, of the *principium individuationis*. It is not coincidental that this principle arises from a later formulation and conceptual development. The claim that Aristotelian matter, *hyle*, is the principle of individuation stems from the measuring, mathematizing attitude of modern science, and thus misses the analogical function of Aristotelian *hyle,* defined through its relation to *morphe,* form, and *eidos.* This language also misses the sense of limit that lies in the concept of individuation. In modern science, we would speak of space and time as principles of individuation, because the measured is thereby rendered unambiguous. In truth, the individual, according to our linguistic practice, represents the limit of all measurability. So what health is does not let itself be described through pure measurements. Likewise, much could be said about the significance of the transformation in meaning which ultimately led to the complete eradication of the concept of the individual from the categorizing thinking of metaphysics, in which the word had its origin. For us, the word means the Christian-mediated mystery of the human heart and the boundaries of the soul—the measure of which, as Heraclitus already knew, one can never take (fragment 45).

So we are led back, by this long excursion through metaphysics and the limits of logos philosophy, which is our ancient heritage, to our opening theme: what is a portrait? Whether we refer to a portrait in poetry or visual art, or simply in the context of what we describe as "portraitlike," we always mean that the represented are persons whose individuality determines what a picture of this type expresses. With regard to such a picture, the assertion that the individual person is "ineffabile" [unutterable] is not valid. At the same time, individuality remains a relative limit concept and does not mean a this-here, but rather the image of a human being that places a person before our eyes. For where the individuality of the person is made visible in the picture, there is a stir in the picture, in this motionless presence, as the ceaseless flow of life overcomes it. The individual is not merely a "here and now," but rather a playing together of many unique features that brings to life what is fixed.

As with the reading of a written or printed text, the process of decoding abruptly converts into understanding. A picture, too, lets the one represented suddenly become living for us. A story places something almost tangible before our eyes—which also happens when one is really convinced by an explanation. In all such cases something is suddenly there. We perceive something common to the good itself, the beautiful itself, and the exact itself, of whose sudden appearance the Platonic dialogue speaks. What it is, that here is "here," is of course unsayable. But at the same time this means that everything that is here in such a way will represent itself differently in everyone, and yet will be the same. So a portrait invites us to recognize it, even when we have seen neither the one represented nor reproductions of him. Hence a myth might be a shocking encounter for us with something we have secretly known. Or a word that is spoken to us, for instance, the word of promise, which goes out to everyone and yet is *pro me* [especially for me].

Let us turn back to the place from which the new bust of Plato brought us to such reflections. I saw it next to that unique bust of Homer, whose blind eye penetrates everything. Beside it now stands—centuries lie between them—the thinker, in whose features are inscribed so much insight, withdrawal, and distance from all that comes to pass. When one then enters the hall in which the monuments of Platonic times stand, one is immediately captured by the spell of several tombstones. We would not speak here of a portrait. It would truly be inappropriate to represent the dead one or his mourning father in a portrait. A tombstone is not a monument of a person, but rather a gesture of remembrance and of departure. The figures that take leave from one another touch each other softly and stand in a silence which creates between the two a space of vibration—even when it is only the young boy and his dog. The one who mourns always reaches out over the space of separation and gently takes hold of the arm of the dead. As I learned in my visit to the Glyptothek, in conversation with Herr and Frau Vierneisel, it is always the survivor who takes the hand of the deceased, as a last embrace. It is the clinging to life that solemnly confesses itself and yet nevertheless accepts the parting without objection. This has the intimacy of a portrait. But it is more a portrait of departure.

These tombstones belong to the same time as Plato himself and his statue, which was certainly made by Silanion after Plato's death and

yet still looks as if done from life. Just as the monuments are not portraits, neither is the image of Socrates that Alcibiades compares with
the statue of Silenus, which opens itself and makes knowable its inner
beauty. In the National Museum of Athens, just as in the pieces here in
Munich, lies an unimaginable spiritual richness. Year after year, we are
presented with new pieces. What has remained spared from the storms
of world history in the Greek landscape has been brought to light in
our day, like gifts from the earth. The Athenians were for the most part
a farming people whose citizens owned and were buried on their own
land. Hence much has been sleeping in the bowels of the earth.

Now the earth teaches us to read Plato. Reading Plato is learning to see. In these dialogues, the Platonic Socrates takes us with him.
The difficult account-giving that he requires, and which constantly fails
and ends in ignorance, reaches beyond itself when in stepwise reflective differentiation it leads to something which we can, with Aristotle,
call a definition (*horismos*). Each dialogue can, or at least should, always continue in another dialogue. Each ending is like a new prospect.
Again and again, the Platonic dialogues display fragments, termina-
tions, transitions—which, as in the case of the *Philebus*, were already
famous in antiquity. The *Parmenides* also ends in an aporia. The ten
books of the *Republic* are certainly an artful composition, and yet they
teem with gaps and tears and breaks, which a misguided philology has
at times marshaled for the purpose of riveting together a historical-
genetic construction.

The pretense of historical-critical reflection which conducts itself
this way falls into error when it deals with Greek dialectic and indeed
with the Greek art of dialogue, and most of all when it has to do with
philosophy. Verifying the authenticity of the *Seventh Letter* was indeed
not necessary to put an end to all claims that giving definitions is the
last word of the philosopher. As the excursus of the *Seventh Letter* confirms, the true experience of thinking is much more the sudden illumination of understanding.[20] Out of the inexhaustible effort to understand, insight is born, suddenly, like that highest inspiration of the good
itself and the beautiful itself, about which we have spoken.[21] When one
possesses Plato's mastery of the poetic art, one finds pleasure in seiz-
ing upon mythical fantasy, opposing the seeming ultimate validity of
everything fixed in writing with stories of playful nonreality and meaning. Likewise, Plato needed the art of portraiture, not in order to make
thinking and account-giving more entertaining, but rather to perpetu-
ally remind thinking of the uncompletability of our human endeavor.
So well did Plato comprehend the limits of all demonstration that he
himself recast the very expression "philosophy" as the epitome of all

detachment from everyday matters and of dedication to theoretical existence, and imposed on it a new inner tension and determination.

It is of course Diotima—in the instruction of Socrates dealt with above—who says: "No god philosophizes and tries to become wise" (for he already is).[22] "To love" wisdom and what is wise here acquires the distinctive sense of not having it and therefore striving for it, being thus between ignorance and knowledge. It is like an unfolding of the knowing ignorance of Socrates, namely what Plato, through Diotima, presents here to Socrates for his education. Of course, the fiction thus continues. Socrates learned it from Diotima, and he fulfills what he has learned in an exemplary way.

With this, the portrait of Socrates that emerges in the Platonic depiction of the banquet becomes in reality a self-portrait of Plato. Not without reason does he prefer the expression *dialektike*—not in the terminological sense of dialectic that has become dominant since Aristotle, but rather in a sense that goes back to the Socratic art of leading dialogues. Arguing through oppositions, which is tied to the Eleatic Zeno, first came to be known by the name *dialektike* through the *Parmenides*. We are inclined to see the difference between the ancient and the modern dialectic since its renewal through Kant, and above all his followers, in the fact that dialectic has just now attained the positive sense of a philosophical method. It was virtually anointed the method of philosophical demonstration by Hegel. That is correct, but only if one presupposes the modern concept of science, the fundamental role of method, and the corresponding ideal of demonstration. A dialectic that knows the limit of logos and holds fast to its embeddedness in the pragmatic unity of life can be called, from this point of view, "negative." In truth, the Socratic ideal of the "Doric harmony of logos and *ergon*"[23] is realized therein, and as long as this holds true, the portrait is a reminder of the responsibility of thinking. For the portrait discloses the universality of the individual—like all genuine knowledge. So I quote once again the profound inscription that Hegel once put under his portrait: "Whoever knows me will recognize me here." I would give it a similar twist. Whoever looks at Plato's head here in the Glyptothek will, insofar as one knows Plato, recognize Plato in it, and then two millennia of our history will remind us of what being human is and what thinking is.

Translated by Jamey Findling and Snezhina Gabova

The Heritage of Hegel

This key essay by Gadamer evokes powerful memories for me of the day in 1965 when I first met Heidegger. He paid a visit to Heidelberg, and I got to talk with him as he arrived to attend a final Gadamer lecture in the course on "From Hegel to Heidegger," to which Heidegger responded at the end. I also attended a private seminar afterwards with Heidegger at Gadamer's home, followed by a two-and-a-half-hour dinner with him at the Golden Hen restaurant along with other Gadamer students, among them Rüdiger Bubner, who is now a distinguished senior professor at Heidelberg. It was July 24, 1965. I know because Heidegger inscribed and dated my copy of *Sein und Zeit* on that day, now a treasured possession. Of course it was a special day for all of Gadamer's students, but most of all for me, since it cemented the whole course of my scholarly life, a life of studying and writing about Heidegger, Husserl, and Gadamer, and also translating several writings by the latter two. At that time I was a professor of comparative European literature with an interest in literary criticism, but I gradually changed to teaching philosophy and humanities (possible in a small college). Now, forty years later to the day, I am submitting this collection of translated essays by Gadamer to my publisher, over half of which I translated myself.

"The Heritage of Hegel" is a key essay of Gadamer because the legacy of Hegel was a bone of contention between a disappointed Heidegger and his ever loyal and respectful student, Hans-Georg Gadamer. For Gadamer, Hegel's philosophy was a creative and positive element in his philosophical hermeneutics. For Heidegger, Hegel was another figure against whose absolute idealism he rebelled and in doing so he could profile the originality of his own philosophy. And this profiling was always vital to a philosopher who struggled for the language (Gadamer called it *Sprachnot,* a lack of words), and the right path to express his rich, radical philosophy.

This essay of Gadamer is also important among his writings because other than Heidegger, Hegel is probably the modern philosopher that Gadamer most admired and built upon. Gadamer seldom criticized him but instead defended and sought to rehabilitate him. When he wanted to profile his own philosophy, he chose Kant. Kant was the foil. I took a seminar from Gadamer on Hegel's *Phenomenology of Spirit* in which we spent the whole semester explicating the first four pages! Another illuminating Gadamer seminar was on Heidegger's "Letter on Humanism," where about half the period each time was spent on a student reading and Gadamer's commenting on the protocol of the previous meeting! From that seminar I have retained a special love for this trailblazing text of Heidegger. Outside of ancient philosophy, Hegel and Heidegger were the two great sources of Gadamer's thinking, with Heidegger being much more important, of course.

Anyway, I offer here a few choice morsels from that fateful day in 1965: 4:00 PM walking with Gadamer and company over to the Alte Aula, I fell in step with Heidegger (accidentally, of course) and said: "You must be very proud of your student Gadamer." I was just wanting to be polite. He paused, meditating on what to reply. Then he asked me: "You know his *wirkungsgeschictliches Bewusstsein*?" I answered: "Yes, of course." Then he said suddenly: "Straight out of Dilthey!" I was stunned. I then asked: "Well, in general what do you think of philosophy today?" He answered: "Going to the dogs!" That was the end of our conversation. We ran out of time. 4:15 PM: Gadamer presented the final lecture of the semester series titled "From Hegel to Heidegger." I remember at the beginning Gadamer and Heidegger entering together down the center aisle of the Alte Aula auditorium to deafening applause (knocking on the desktops). Heidegger was so short compared to Gadamer! (I thought of Mutt and Jeff in the comic strip.) Heidegger listened patiently to the nearly two-hour lecture, in which Gadamer tried to show that elements of Hegel show up in Heidegger's writings: the historical content of Dasein's consciousness, the dialectic of *Lichtung* and *Verbergung* (clearing and concealment), the truth of essence being *Wesen*, and so on. At 5:45: after Gadamer finished the final lecture for the semester a little early, he turned and asked if Heidegger would like to make any remarks. Heidegger came to the podium. He said he disagreed with the whole premise of the lecture because, didn't Gadamer remember that Hegel's phenomenology culminates in absolute knowledge? This makes everything impossible! He went on, waving his arms, for about ten minutes.

At 6:30 PM: a private Heidegger seminar at Gadamer's modest apartment in Handschuhsheim, to which I, as the visiting American scholar, was invited. The number of guests exceeded the number of chairs, so several cushions from the sofas were confiscated for students to sit on. In this seminar, Heidegger did not begin with any preliminary words but a simple question: what does "Ich bin hier" ["I am here"] mean? He rejected each answer, one after another, and the eager German students did not hesitate to try! They took a phenomenological approach, for the most part. Finally, not getting the answer he wanted, he said, "Zu viel Leiblichkeit!" ["Too much bodilyness, too much relating things to the body."]. The discussion went on until ten o'clock, at which time Gadamer said that they did not want to exhaust their guest. Besides, they must be hungry. He asked Heidegger if he would like to go with the group to dinner. Heidegger said yes.

So the whole group descended the hill together on foot to dine at the Golden Hen restaurant—until 1:00 AM! I do not remember much of the conversation, although I was only two seats away from Heidegger's place at the end of the table. Heidegger talked about the unfairness of taking away his teaching rights after the war when he was a harmless philosophy professor. He felt very much misunderstood by the occupying forces. It was at this point that I pulled out my copy of Heidegger's *Sein und Zeit* and asked him if he would sign it, which he did: "Zur Erinnerung" ["To the memory"], followed by his name and the date. A priceless memento. It was an unforgettable nine hours.

"The Heritage of Hegel" is here excellently translated by Frederick G. Lawrence, who generously permitted me to make any minor editorial changes I might wish to make it flow more smoothly. Gadamer originally presented the essay (without the afterword) in April 1978 in Naples under the title "Hegel e l'ermeneutica" ["Hegel and Hermeneutics"]. Then, when he was awarded the Hegel Prize by the city of Stuttgart in 1979, Gadamer presented it again on June 13 of that year, this time in German, under the title "Das Erbe Hegels." It was published the same year as a book by Suhrkamp with the afterword under the title *Das Erbe Hegels*. I have a feeling that the afterword was written to make it of a more suitable length for a book. It is really two essays because the afterword is over half as long as the original essay and extends its scope.

Despite its title, this essay is really a continuation of Gadamer's dialogue with Heidegger over Hegel, a dialogue which grew out of the 1965 lecture course, and was continued in an exchange of letters, one of which is quoted *in extenso* in the notes. It could have been called "In Defense of Hegel." Heidegger died in 1976, but Gadamer continued the dialogue with Heidegger over Hegel without his partner.

One of the first things one notices in reading this essay is its explanatory and even reminiscent character. It does not focus on any specific text of Hegel but on why Hegel and his followers, like Dilthey, Croce, and Collingwood, were important to his own hermeneutical philosophy. And he is also not afraid to discuss his debt to Aristotle and to Heidegger and how these fit with Hegel. Even in 1978 he is still explaining his hermeneutics and where it came from, as we see by the original title, "Hegel and Hermeneutics." Nearly two decades after *Truth and*

Method (1960) and all the discussion it provoked, as he was nearing the age of eighty and at the height of his career, Gadamer reminisces to a captivated audience and continues to explain why Hegel was important to him. He replies to Heidegger's accusations regarding absolute spirit by noting that the finitude of spirit is in its manifestations, and he says that Heidegger exaggerated Hegel's absolute idealism in order to profile his own philosophy. Gadamer does not have to do this. He wants to see other sides of Hegel. He notes Hegel's influence on Dilthey in this essay. He finds a personalized and dialogical Hegel, coming from Plato. He notes Hegel's view of art as the self-disclosure of spirit. Toward the end of the first essay, Gadamer explains his attraction to Aristotle's practical philosophy, and surprisingly finds in the debunking of the illusions of self-consciousness by Marx, Nietzsche, and Freud support for the universality of hermeneutics. He drifts into an explanation of the central role of language in his hermeneutics, language as the medium of access to the world. And taking up another point of difference with Heidegger, he again defends the role of metaphysics in philosophy and history. He concludes with a defense of Hegel's doctrine of absolute spirit, but in the end, the essay is as much an explanation and defense of his philosophical hermeneutics as it is about Hegel.

In the afterword, written subsequent to the lecture for the publication of the book by Suhrkamp, with the same title,[1] Gadamer continues his dialogue with Heidegger over Hegel two years after Heidegger's death. He begins by noting the renewal of interest in Hegel by Croce in Italy, McTaggart and Bradley in England, and Bolland in Holland. He mentions the address of Windelband to the Heidelberg Academy of Sciences in 1910. Hegel was a professor at Heidelberg from 1816 to 1818 before being invited to Berlin, and there is a seminar room in the philosophy seminar dedicated to Hegel. Gadamer notes how the interest in Hegel was continued in Germany by Emil Lask, Richard Kroner, Julius Ebbinghaus, Georg von Lukacs, and Ernst Bloch, among others. And he notes the decisive stimulus brought by Nietzsche, Dilthey, Bergson, and the philosophy of life to broadening the reception-horizon of Hegel.

Gadamer notes that "for Heidegger and his students it had to be a constant preoccupation to determine the proximity to and distance from Hegel." Gadamer asserts that Heidegger's seminar on *Hegel's Concept of Experience*[2] followed the explication so closely that "the resistance of his own thinking was almost unnoticeable." Gadamer notes that his hermeneutics was based on finitude and the historical character of Dasein as he found it in Heidegger, and he attempted to continue Heidegger's turn away from transcendental philosophy, but when Heidegger turned to poetry Gadamer "returned to the open dialectic of Plato."

Again in this essay, Gadamer is explaining himself and his own philosophy, and he does not hesitate to go back to Plato and Aristotle to do so. He also refers to the debate centered around the theologian Wolfhart Pannenberg on hermeneutics and universal history, which explored the relevance of Hegel's concept of history to theology, and against Heidegger's deconstruction of metaphysics he defends his own return to Plato, Platonism, and Hegel. But in the final parts of his essay he returns to his personal dialogue with Heidegger and refers to his correspondence with Heidegger about Hegel and to Heidegger's change of the term "overcoming metaphysics" to "*recovering* from metaphysics," as if it were a disease. In the latter case, one still feels the aftereffects of metaphysics. And Gadamer says that whether one overcomes, recovers from, or steps back from metaphysics, one still has to presuppose it!

. While Hegel is a main focus in this essay, it remains a valuable general defense and discussion by Gadamer of his philosophical hermeneutics in the context of the heritage of Hegelian philosophy. It thus has value that goes beyond a discussion of the heritage of Hegelian thinking. Like the preceding essay, it is a readable discussion and defense of his philosophical hermeneutics.

* * *

The Heritage of Hegel

No one should take upon himself the task of measuring all that has come down to us in the great heritage of Hegelian thought. It should be enough for each person to be the heritage oneself and to give an account of what one has received from this inheritance. But least of all can someone undertake to evaluate this heritage whose contribution to philosophic thought lies decades in the past; and to do so for the younger generations who have entered upon this heritage on their own and who confirm the limits of his competence precisely by the fact that they value his merits. Moreover, no one should imagine himself able to reap the harvest of an entire epoch or indeed even merely to assess it. Even Hegel himself did not do this—Hegel whom overzealous epigones want to burden with the notion that the idea he thought through and named "absolute knowledge" comprised the actual end of history. Hegel knew better when he—ultimately to be sure in regard to himself as well—cited the following: "See, the feet of those who are going to take you away are already standing in front of the door." [1]

So instead of delivering a pretentious contribution to scholarly research or a comprehensive report on the state of research in the field, please allow me simply to narrate how in my opinion the heritage of Hegel has been transposed in my own attempts at thinking.

The philosophic turn which I, in connection with impulses from the thought of Heidegger, have tried to give to Romantic hermeneutics and its progressive development by way of the historical school through Ranke, Droysen, Dilthey, and his disciples is inseparable from the all-encompassing synthesis of Hegel.[2] Here for the first time the notion of the logos that the Greeks had worked out for the apprehension of the world in its totality was extended to the historical world without assuming the suprarational data of a salvation history. To come to know reason in history was Hegel's bold claim, and in the end it drew upon itself just as much resistance as his attempt—long since antiquated and doomed to fail from the outset—to bend the modern investigation of nature, in spite of its essentially provisional character and its way of constantly overtaking itself, under the concept of a science that would be a totality of truth (*doctrina*), that is, which affirmed an absolute, rational truth. In the end, the dialectic of absolute knowledge—in the domain of the historical spirit—had just as little chance of escaping the resistance of historical research. It could hardly avoid following a path very similar to that traveled by the idealist philosophy of nature through the victorious course of the scientific investigation of nature. The open dialectic of the Platonist Schleiermacher must have appeared far more promising as the foundation for a methodology of the historical sciences than Hegel's construction of world history. And so Dilthey, Schleiermacher's biographer, and the methodology of the historical school of which Dilthey was the philosophical interpreter, undertook an epistemological grounding of the *Geisteswissenschaften* under the motto of hermeneutics. But it was within philosophy itself that Hegel's conceptual achievement, the speculative method of dialectics, met with the sharpest resistance.[3] For it is of such a sort that before it one's understanding literally stands silent, full of astonishment and protest. This sort of response came about in the neo-Kantianism that was having an ever greater influence. Its slogan, "Back to Kant," referred not least to the speculative hubris of absolute idealism; from a Kantian basis and in dependence upon Lotze, it proposed in its turn the critical grounding of the *Geisteswissenschaften* [human sciences and humanities] upon the concept of value.[4]

Be that as it may, Hegel's legacy and especially the notion of the objective spirit ultimately gained renewed power over Dilthey and even over neo-Kantianism and the phenomenology that was emerging in our century. Here a way was indicated of overcoming the one-sidedness of modern subjectivism and especially that of the "psychological" interpretation, which Schleiermacher's genial gift for empathy not only added to the traditional methods of the theory of interpretation but singled out for special distinction. The theory of objective spirit became the most effective heritage of Dilthey's school (Spranger, Litt, Freyer, E. Rothacker) and of neo-Kantianism just as it was going into dissolution (E. Lask, E. Cassirer, N. Hartmann).[5] And so I had to decide—between the alternatives of the "psychological reconstruction of past thought" and the "integration of past thought into one's own thought"—against Schleiermacher and in favor of Hegel.[6] To be sure, Hegel's *Philosophy of World History* remained caught in the insoluble contradiction of an open progress of history and a conclusive apprehension of its meaning, and it could not be repeated if one were intent on taking historicity seriously.

In this way I became an advocate of the "bad infinite" for which the end keeps on delaying its arrival—something that for Hegel is not merely an untruth but a truth as well. In particular, the philosophical energy with which Martin Heidegger had set up the paradox of a hermeneutics of facticity as a counterpoise to the transcendental phenomenology of Husserl and his program of a new science of consciousness inspired me.[7]

That precisely the unilluminable obscurity of our facticity—which Heidegger called "thrownness" [*Geworfenheit*]—sustains and does not merely set limits to the projective character of human Dasein, had to bestow a new weight on the historicity of human Dasein and on the significance of history for our Dasein. Our understanding of history is not only a matter of acquiring knowledge and familiarity or of the development of the historical sense; it is also a matter of the shaping of our destiny. For understanding is not so much an act of consciousness as a challenge that one comes up against and in which the historical richness of the spirit builds up; understanding is also and above all a happening and makes history. It was heresy to assert these things over against Husserl's program of philosophy as a rigorous science, with its grounding in the apodictic certitude of self-consciousness. In truth, however, the thinking out of the historicity of Dasein was just as little capable of being written off by Husserl as historicism and relativism as Dilthey's "Construction of the Historical World in the *Geisteswissenschaften*." One could learn this from Heidegger. Heidegger's turn toward the hermeneutics of facticity was a turn away from the idealism that stresses consciousness in the neo-Kantian mold from which Husserl too was cast; however, it was not a form of relativism *but a philosophic counter-project*. It included an ontological critique of the notions of objectivity and subjectivity, which had remote origins in the beginnings of Greek thought, so it was redolent precisely of Hegel's critique of extrinsic reflection when Heidegger distinguished the ontological dimension of questioning from every ontic question. Especially when Heidegger, in the development of his thinking, toned down the existential pathos of his great pioneering work and came to acknowledge his own transcendental self-understanding as inadequate, it came ever more starkly to light that Hegel's doctrine of the objective spirit had not exhausted its real relevance. When one reflects today upon the thoughtworthy discussion that Ernst Cassirer (who had further developed neo-Kantian idealism in the direction he took in his *Philosophy of Symbolic Forms*) held in 1930 with the young Martin Heidegger in Davos, one realizes clearly how Hegel's heritage lived on in *both* thinkers and how the younger of the two should have felt himself compelled to a lifelong dialogue with Hegel.

It may be shown that Hegel's "reflection in itself" represents a figure of thought in which an Aristotelian legacy predominated and was renewed and which at the same time was not utterly remote from Heidegger's thought, which had been nourished upon the critique of Greek ontology. Being [*das Sein*] as "being true" [*Wahrsein*], the self-presentation of coming-to-presence [*Wesens*], which one calls "thinking"; this was the central motif that inspirited Heidegger's early interpretations of Aristotle (which have not yet been published).[8] The emphasis placed by the young Heidegger upon the way that disclosure (*aletheia*) does not have its primordial place in propositions [*Sätze*] but in being [*Sein*] was a prelude to the later Heidegger's turn away from transcendental self-interpretation; and it prepared that thinking upon being [*Sein*], which as the lighting process [*Lichtung*] of being was the being [*Sein*] of the lighting process, is the "there" [*Da*] that opens upon its own and antecedes every possible self-manifestation by any entity.[9] In any case, the well-honed metaphors such as *Differenz, Lichtung,* and *Ereignis* in which Heidegger later attempted to speak about being [*Sein*] which is not the being of any entity [*Seiendem*], came far closer to the speculative dialectic of Hegelian concepts than did the academic neo-Hegelianism that had been worked out within the framework of neo-Kantianism, especially in the Heidelberg of the day.

Then, too, one should not fail to note that the motives which compelled Heidegger to undertake his so-called *Kehre* (turn) harmonized with a new sensitivity to the style of the epoch, a sensibility which, exhausted from the subtle sensuality of impressionistic enchantment, called for a new, constructive objectivity. Already in 1907 Richard Hamann, who was one of the teachers during my youthful years after 1918, had concluded his laying to rest of impressionism in life and art with the demand, "More Hegel!" It is known that Hegel found a lasting home in other lands, for instance in Italy, and that the constructive spirit of modern art in our century had hurried far ahead of the German development. Van Gogh and Cézanne and a generation later Juan Gris and Picasso, for example, became symbolic representatives of a new outburst, which subsequently enveloped the German scene. It was similar in literature, where Mallarmé's *poesie pure* represented the poetic correlate of Hegel's absolute knowledge, and German literature later moved in the same direction with the discovery of the late Hölderlin, George's formally stringent art of versifying, and Rilke's thing-poems [*Dinggedichte*]. These were developments that helped bring to the language of poetry as well as the language of thought a new objective power of symbolization. It is no accident that the earliest documentation of the *Kehre* in Heidegger's thought reached verbal articulation in his Hölderlin lecture in Rome in 1936, and in this way the old Romantic assertion of the neighborhood of poetry and philosophy got a new life. These things made a great impression upon me from very early on.

It is true that Heidegger by that time no longer trusted the notion of hermeneutics to keep his thinking free from the consequences of a transcendental theory of consciousness, just as he tried mightily to overcome the language of metaphysics by means of a special half-poetic language.[10] At that point the task of speaking up for the happening that resides in understanding seemed to fall to me, and also the task of overcoming modern subjectivism by an analysis of a hermeneutic experience that becomes reflectively aware of itself. So already in 1934 I had begun with a critical analysis of aesthetic consciousness, concerning which I sought to prove[11] that it did not do justice to the truth claim of art; and, accompanied by a constant interaction with the Greek classics, especially with Plato, I sought to overcome the historical self-estrangement with which historical positivism had deflated ideas into mere opinions and philosophy into doxography.[12] I was helped by the theory of contemporaneity [*Gleichzeitigkeit*] that Kierkegaard, for religious and critical theological reasons, had advanced against "understanding at a distance." This had in 1924 attained a persuasive effectiveness through the Diederich edition of the "religious discourses" (*Works of Love*). Already, however, one of my earliest experiences in thinking—by way of a detour through Kierkegaard, together with a paradoxical enthusiasm for William the Assessor in *Either/Or*—had actually led me to Hegel, without my completely having realized it.

To be sure, then, what shaped my thinking in this way was a personalized and dialogical Hegel behind whom there always stood the daily, thoughtful interaction with the Platonic dialogues. Over and above this, from very early on I had sought to maintain a critical distance toward the academic aridities of *Kathederphilosophie* that I had encountered in a series of experiences with my own teachers. Life experience and the study of Plato had led me quite early to the insight that the truth of a single proposition cannot be measured by its merely factual relationship of correctness and congruency; nor does it depend merely upon the context in which it stands. Ultimately, it depends upon the genuineness of its enrootedness and bond with the person of the speaker in whom it wins its truth potential; for the meaning of a statement is not exhausted in what is stated. It can be disclosed only if one traces the history of its motivation and looks ahead to its implications. From that point on this became one of my guiding hermeneutical insights. Here the heritage of Dilthey merged with the phenomenological clarification brought about by Husserl. Why is it that Socrates, even though he often brings about the downfall of the most reasonable, even the most Socratic, responses of his interlocutors by means of very questionable logic, remains free from any suspicion of being merely one of these negative Sophists who play a game with their dialectical superiority? [13] All honor is due to "logic," but the smiling superiority with which in modern research the Platonic arguments are examined as to their logical validity—and at best are even improved upon in a well-meaning way—always appeared to me to be an almost comic *metabasis eis allo genos* [transition into another kind of thing]. It confuses the scientific procedures of proof with the persuasive power of dialogue and logic with the rhetoric of thought whose old name was "dialectic." But it was many long years before the central position of dialogue and the linguistic character of our experience of the world as a whole made its way into my thinking and theory of hermeneutics.

For that to occur, help was needed from many sides. One sort came to me at the time of World War II by way of the autobiography of Collingwood, the disciple of B. Croce and the last representative of English Hegelianism.[14] There I found that exactly what I was well accustomed to in my philological and interpretive practice, had been made perceptible in masterly fashion in relation to the research experience of the great discoverer of the boundary walls in Roman Britain and had been raised up to the status of a principle as "the logic of question and answer." Just as Collingwood had illuminated the course of the Roman *limes* [boundaries] not by the accident of a lucky archeological discovery but by virtue of the prior posing and answering of the question how such a protective device reasonably would have had to be set up, so too the interaction with the philosophic tradition becomes meaningful only when reason is recognized in it. This means that reason directs its own questions to it. The fact that one only really "understands" a statement when one understands it as an answer to a question is compellingly evident, I think. That I nonetheless could not completely follow the theory of historical knowledge and the theory of reenactment constructed by Collingwood was due to his misleading confusion of practice and action (which often bedevils contemporary thought about these matters), through which the essence and experience of history is voluntaristically distorted. A theory of planning or of action can never do justice to the experience of history, where our plans tend to shatter and our actions and omissions tend to lead to unexpected consequences.

But the short-circuited applications I found in Collingwood did not basically deter me; I had come to know the stronger Hegelian position that lay behind his views, although to be sure in an undogmatic, free fashion. Hegel had illuminatingly demonstrated in his famous doctrine about the cunning of reason [*List der Vernunft*] that the consciousness of the individual—prescinding from the exceptional case of "world-historical individuals"—is no match for reason in history. But must not this knowledge of the finitude and limitedness of the individual who stands as an agent in history affect anyone who thinks? What must this mean for the claim of philosophic thought to truth? The fact that the form of the proposition is not suitable for expressing speculative truths was something Hegel had both known and told us; but Collingwood turned this insight against himself and the methodological compulsion to which he was subject. What I found convincing about Collingwood's logic of question and answer was not its methodological usefulness, which is ultimately trivial, but its validity (which transcends all methodical usage) according to which question and answer are utterly entangled with one another. For what is a question? Surely it is something that one has to understand and that one does understand only when one understands the question itself in terms of something, that is, as an answer; and in doing this one limits the dogmatic claim of any proposition. The logic of question and answer proved to be a dialectic of question and answer in which question and answer are constantly exchanged and then are dissolved in the movement of understanding.

Thus there emerged all at once, behind and beyond all the methodology of the *Geisteswissenschaften* and beyond all epistemology, the unity of dialogue and dialectic that in a surprising manner related Hegel and Plato to one another, and this set the hermeneutic experience free. This experience was no longer confined to the "being-toward-a-text," that is, to a procedure for interrogating and construing pre-given texts by the methodically informed interpreter. Suddenly the mystery of the question, the motivating interest that precedes all knowledge and interpretation, took center stage. A question arises; it imposes itself; it is indemonstrable. It is not hard to realize that there is no method for learning how to ask questions, and one recalls that the old piece of rhetorical doctrine, the *de inventione,* contains at least an indirect indication of the significance of the question for all knowledge. The structure of dialogue proves to be a key to the role that language [*Sprachlichkeit*, linguisticality] plays for all understanding and coming to know.

At the same time, however, another, even greater teacher was brought to my attention. I mean Aristotle, who had first been opened up to me by the young Heidegger when I was quite young. In relation to the Aristotelian theory of *phronesis*, of practical rationality, I had begun to learn how to clarify conceptually the pathos of *Existenzphilosophie* that was typical of the reception accorded Kierkegaard at the time. What Kierkegaard had taught us and what we then called "existential" [*existenziell*] decades before "existentialism" was brought to formulation in France, found in Aristotle its prototype in the unity of ethos and logos that he had thematized as practical philosophy, and especially as the virtue of practical rationality. To be sure, the two-thousand-year tradition of practical philosophy that goes back to Aristotle ultimately fell prey to the pressure of the modern notion of science. The turn away from "politics" as a discipline of "practical philosophy," which was still cultivated by historians until late in the nineteenth century, and to what was called *Politologie* (in German parlance) or "political science," is a telling expression of this. But there remains in the earlier form of politics a moment that offers an exact correspondence to the hermeneutic experience, and especially to what is operative in the sciences. Whoever possesses the virtue of practical rationality is aware of the normative viewpoints he follows and knows how to make them effective in the concrete decisions that are demanded by the practical situation.

In the practical situation one becomes aware of the normative viewpoints that reside in the practical situation in which one stands, not in the sense of their being theoretic knowledge but because of their binding validity. Of course, practical philosophy can in its turn make this awareness an object of its theory, as when Aristotle describes in outline the "ethical virtues." But the theoretician can still only see these viewpoints adequately from the standpoint of their fulfilled concretization, insofar as one experiences oneself as bound by their validity. This is why Aristotle restricted the possibilities of theoretical insight in the practical field. Now it seems to me that the same thing holds true for hermeneutics and hence for the *Geisteswissenschaften*, and ultimately for all understanding in general.[15] The practice of understanding, in ordinary life as in science, is in a similar way the expression of the affinity of the one who understands with the one whom one understands and with that which one understands. The theoretical giving-an-account of the possibilities of understanding is not an objectifying reflection that makes understanding something capable of being mastered by means of science and methodology. It shows forth instead that the universal as something of which one is aware is itself subject to the indissoluble problematic of its rational application. But thereby the problem of hermeneutics proves to be a fundamental problem of philosophy in general. Like practical philosophy, philosophical hermeneutics stands beyond the alternatives of transcendental reflection and empirical-pragmatic knowledge. In the end, it was the great theme of the concretization of the universal that I learned to consider as the basic experience of hermeneutics, and so I entered once again the neighborhood of the great teacher of concrete universality, Hegel.

It was not just theology and jurisprudence that were and are at all times familiar with the hermeneutical task of concretizing the universal, and indeed have been so from time immemorial. The idea that the universality of the rule is in need of application, but for the application of rules no rule exists, one could have learned from Kant's *Critique of Judgment* and from its successors, especially from Hegel, or even from one's own insight.

We stand full of wonder before Hegel's grand synthesis of Christianity and philosophy, of nature and spirit, of Greek metaphysics and transcendental philosophy, which he projected in the guise of absolute knowledge. But this is not completely relevant for us today. The century and a half that separates us from Hegel may not be forgotten. I myself would not want to see in Hegel the destruction of what Habermas called "the certain foundation of transcendental consciousness, in terms of which the a priori drawing of boundaries between transcendental and empirical determinations, between validity and genesis, appeared to be certain." But certainly the overwhelming power of Hegel's synthesis did work in this direction; and we have experienced this effect throughout an entire century, which one names the historical century. During this time, however, Marx, Nietzsche, and Freud exposed limits to the self-certitude of thought thinking itself.

So for me it was not a matter of becoming a disciple of Hegel, but rather of interiorizing the challenge that he represents for thinking. Under this challenge, the basic experience of hermeneutics began to reveal its true universality to me inasmuch as our use of language, or better, inasmuch as the use that language finds in us whenever we think, pervades our whole experience of the world. Language is constantly achieving the concretization of the universal.[16] And so hermeneutics traded its historic service function, a function which it also had possessed as the methodology of the *Geisteswissenschaften*, for a position wherein it became a form of philosophy that was all-determining. The tendencies of our century that I shared in when thinking of language as the true concretization of the universal converge everywhere with the Platonic-Aristotelian heritage of Greek dialectic, which was always my special interest in scholarly research. But these interests still also preserved something of the grand synthesis of reason and history that was risked by Hegel, even though I was not conscious of this at the time. In the linguistic character of our access to the world, we find ourselves implanted in a process of tradition that marks us as historical in essence. Language is not an instrumental setup, a tool that we apply, but the element in which we live and which we can never so objectify that it ceases to surround us.

This element that surrounds us nevertheless is nothing like an enclosure from which we could ever strive to escape. Nor is the element of language merely an empty medium in which one thing or another may be encountered. No, language is the quintessence of everything that can encounter us at all. Language surrounds us as what has been spoken, as the universes of discourse (*ta legomena*). To dwell in language means to be moved in our speaking about something and in our speaking to someone. Even when we are speaking a foreign language, it is not the language that is surrounding us so much as what is spoken in it. But since it surrounds us as what is spoken and not as the threatening field of otherness in relation to which there can only be self-affirmation, conquest, or submission, language gives shape to the space of our freedom. Even though the idealism of freedom developed by Hegel and his generation appears abstract, even though today the freedom of everyone, which Hegel designated as the goal of world history, appears utopian in the face of the mounting lack of the freedom of all, and even though the contradiction between what is real and what would be rational is ultimately indissoluble—all this testifies to our freedom. Neither natural necessities nor causal compulsions determine our thinking and our intending; whether we will and act, fear or hope or despair, we are moved in the space of freedom. This space is not the free space of an abstract joy in construction, but a space filled with reality by prior familiarity.

For this Hegel had the beautiful expression, "making oneself at home." In no way does being at home include becoming a partisan for what has already been passed down. Just as much, it grounds the freedom for criticism and for projecting new goals in social life and action. Precisely therein does it make sense to see oneself an heir of Hegel—not by thinking his anticipation of the absolute as a knowledge that we entrust to philosophy; still less by expecting philosophy to serve the demands of the day and to legitimate any authority that pretends to know what the moment requires. It suffices to acknowledge with Hegel the dialectic of the universal and concrete as the summation of the whole of metaphysics until now, and along with this to realize that this has to be summed up ever anew. Indeed, one talks about the end of metaphysics and about the scientific age in which we stand, and perhaps even about the lack of history proper to the technological age we are now entering. In the end, Hegel could turn out to be right. We would then, of course, be in the position of saying about humanity as a whole what Hegel had said about "a cultured people": that without metaphysics it would be "like a temple without the holy of holies." [17]

Finding oneself having been set outside the grooves of mere naturalness is an experience that distinguishes us as thinking beings. Everywhere and ever again we come up against limits, yet these are limits beyond which our thinking is irresistibly driven. By means of science, by means of the "big bang," the enigma of the beginning comes to life for every man today, an enigma to which the theology of creation once offered its answer—or was it a question?—the enigma of the universe, which took its earliest conceptual form in the logos of the cosmos and which gets ever more deeply revealed in the expanding universe of nature and of history; it is the enigma of human freedom which we experience, as well as of human reason, which we have in order to keep on doubting on the basis of our experience and yet to which as thinking beings we necessarily have to lay claim again; and finally there is the thinking out of our finitude, the thinking through of our end as thinking beings, an idea on which thinking itself can hardly lay hold. All of this does not let go of us. The ancient Greek maxim, "Know thyself!" holds good for us as well, for it meant, "Know that you are no god, but a human being." Self-knowledge really is not the perfect self-transparency of knowledge, but the insight that we have to accept the limits posed by our finite natures. But just as the great Greek thinkers still could not follow the admonition to humility, which especially their poets tended to raise, but rather surrendered themselves to the drive toward questioning for the sake of "becoming immortal as far as possible," [18] so, too, Hegel's heritage will not let go of us.

But this does not mean that metaphysics as a science, this unique form (Gestalt) of our Western civilization that found in Hegel its triumphal completion and its end, would be possible for us. Nevertheless, without this heritage of metaphysics, it would not be possible for us even to comprehend what science is that it determines our age most profoundly, what place it assumes, and what function it serves within our own self-understanding. In full awareness of our finitude, we remain exposed to questions that go beyond us. They befall us—if not the individual in his quietest moments, then all of us, from the vantage point of that in the light of which we all know ourselves. And in this way we all confirm

Hegel's doctrine of the absolute spirit. With Hegel we know about the manifoldness of the encounter with ourselves that reaches beyond every historical conditionedness. We encounter ourselves in art, in spite of all social utilitarianism. We encounter ourselves in the challenge of religion that still lives on in the age of science. No less do we encounter ourselves also in thinking. In thinking we find the questions that we call philosophical and that move us ever further in our interaction with our philosophic tradition. From them in truth no thinking being can ever completely hold himself at a remove. I do not need to demonstrate this further in Swabian country. These questions still hold us in suspense.

Afterword

My Hegel speech, with which I thanked the city of Stuttgart for the distinction I received, tries to present the tension-filled proximity that the development of a philosophical hermeneutics manifests in relation to the magnificent project of thought in Hegel. Even if one would like to treat the final form of speculative idealism in Hegel as the conclusive systematic foundation of philosophy, after a century and a half one cannot propose going back and barricading oneself in the house of this thought. At the start of our century Benedetto Croce had already sensed the need to discriminate what is living from what is dead in Hegel's philosophy, and so to draw a sum from the advancing tradition of Italian Hegelianism. Something similar took place in England (by McTaggart and Bradley) and in Holland (by Bolland). At just about the same time in Germany there set in a new approach to the philosophy of Hegel, that left behind the neo-Kantianism which then dominated the academic scene and was beginning to near its end. Windelband lent his voice to this new movement in his address to the Heidelberg Academy of Sciences in 1910, and the movement was carried along by the circle of his disciples, by Emil Lask and Richard Kroner, by Julius Ebbinghaus, Georg von Lukacs, and Ernst Bloch, as well as many others. But only when the whole mass of the Romantic heritage of the *Geisteswissenschaften* poured into neo-Kantianism's transcendental philosophic continuation, an event which once again repeated the journey from Kant to Hegel, was the consciousness of the epoch as a whole embraced anew by Hegel's philosophic thought.

This actually meant that Hegel was liberated from the thin-blooded academic effort to restore him [*Repristination*] and put him back in the context of his most characteristic motifs. The epochal awareness of the early twentieth century came increasingly under the influence of Friedrich Nietzsche and the philosophy of life, a philosophy which found in Henri Bergson its leading European spokesman. What was new in this was that one now questioned behind the statements of self-consciousness, and then in the name of historical consciousness, of critique of ideology, and of depth psychology, one questioned the truth-claims of philosophy that rested on the notion of transcendental subjectivity and on the general unshakableness of self-consciousness. In this situation, the new familiarity with Hegel's early political-theological sketches, which had been edited by Hermann Nohl at the urging of Wilhelm Dilthey, found a strong resonance and opened up new perspectives. It was the new concretization that the idealist principle of self-consciousness had gained in Hegel that now became visible in his regard.

From the notion of life, which came from Schelling as the potency of the organism, and upon which was grounded the higher potency of self-consciousness, after it had been burst open by the "lightning flash from the absolute," but especially from the Johannine notion of love, which the young Hegel had thematized in its religious and social facets—the total horizon now broadened out in which the thinking of Hegel appeared.

Herbert Marcuse's dissertation, written under Heidegger, is symptomatic of this.[19] It centers on the inner interweaving of life, consciousness, and spirit or mind. And so what Heidegger had in view in his questioning behind the "fantastically idealized subject" of transcendental philosophy could lead to a certain proximity with Hegel. A neo-Kantian and logician basing his thought on "the fact of science" in the style of Cohen, or a phenomenologist of transcendental subjectivity in the style of Husserl, was for me, at any rate, no Hegel. And so, from early on,[20] Heidegger too experienced the attraction from Hegel's side—and precisely for that reason pursued the critical delimitation of his thought over against that of Hegel. Going beyond "subjective idealism," Hegel clearly was close enough to Heidegger to challenge him all the more.[21]

For Heidegger and for his students it had to be a constant preoccupation to determine his proximity to and distance from Hegel. If I should come before the public with my report on the heritage of Hegel and on what I have developed as hermeneutical philosophy, I would at the same time take up the question of how I can believe hermeneutics avoids the consequences drawn by Hegel when he traced out in a comprehensive analysis the necessary course of the spirit through the forms of consciousness in which it has appeared. In an essay in his *Holzwege*, Heidegger entered so deeply into the path of the argument of the *Phenomenology of Spirit* that the resistance of his own thinking in doing so was almost unnoticeable. I have made some contributions to the question regarding the ambivalence of Heidegger's stance toward Hegel;[22] and I have tried to emphasize the lasting heritage of Hegel and especially to purify the dialectic of self-consciousness from short-circuited applications of it by Marx, by Kojève, and by Sartre.[23] But the challenge from Heidegger remains as he took up the critical motifs of Schelling, Kierkegaard, and Nietzsche and from the standpoint of the basic hermeneutic constitution of Dasein drew into his critical destruction of metaphysics the idea of [disqualifying] absolute knowledge, as well as the mutual reflection of Christian religion and absolute spirit hazarded by Hegel's universal synthesis.

The hermeneutics I developed was based upon finitude and the historical character of Dasein, and it tried also to carry forward Heidegger's turn away from his own transcendental account of himself, but I did not follow him in the direction of an inspiration from the poetic mythos of Hölderlin; rather, I returned to the open dialectic of Plato and relied upon the "dampening down of subjectivity," as Julius Stenzel called it, that from early on had attracted me toward Greek thought. It was consistent with this that just as the problem of language came more and more into the foreground in our century as a whole, it did so also in philosophical hermeneutics; indeed, the occurrence of language in understanding and in agreement became my underpinning of finitude in hermeneutics. This corresponded with the intention of Heidegger's thought because he also knew himself to be *unterwegs zur Sprache* [on the way to language]. To be sure, I had good reasons for placing the *dialogical* character of language in the foreground. Not only was the centering in the subjectivity of self-consciousness overcome by this, but above all I strove in this way to support Heidegger in his almost tragic struggle against a fall back into the language of metaphysics.

In my contribution to the Löwith Festschrift, I had already tried by means of a consideration in the opposite direction to overcome Heidegger's view that we cannot escape the language of metaphysics because the grammar of our languages binds our thought to it.[24] I argued that figures of speech, parables, and the many other indirect modes of speech that have been developed in the Near and Far East exhibit a narrative structure and yet still mediate insights of philosophic metaphysics. The language of these texts has nothing to do with the predicative structure of the judgment and is independent of any determinate grammar. Even in translation such discourses and proverbs maintain a profound intelligibility.

On the other hand, Heidegger's attempts at a half-poetic form of discourse are sometimes more expressive of a linguistic need than of its overcoming. So I have pointed in the direction of the interchange involved in dialogue and toward the dialogical structure of language in which an entirely undogmatic dialectic is constantly enacted; and I have shown the way the language of a community is shaped in it beyond the explicit awareness of the individual speaker and how a step-by-step unveiling of being comes about in this way. This, however, is repeated in the conversation of the soul with itself, which since Plato is the way we think of thinking. Certainly it is clear that a disclosure of being occurs in an utterly different, immediate manner in a fully achieved poem; and so we call a poem in which this disclosure is missing "empty." Certainly the dialogical structure of thinking can never attain such immediacy, but it can move toward it in the dimension of the hermeneutical experience. Even in Hegel's speculative displacement of the proposition, the effort of his conceptualization is seeking to overcome the deformation of thought that is embedded in the very form of the judgment and of the proposition, a deformation that pushes one to go beyond a substantialistic metaphysics, and toward expressing speculative truths.

In this context, the dialogical structure of all understanding and all agreement that I have elaborated has proven to be of such wide-ranging importance that our relationship to tradition and especially to the thought history of Western metaphysics is modified by it. Even what appears in Heidegger's perspective to be a growing forgetfulness of being still makes a case for his partnership in the conversation of thought with itself.[25] The extreme consequences of thought heightened with anguished enthusiasm by Nietzsche and with eschatological pathos by Heidegger are counterbalanced [in my hermeneutics] by the continuity of a linguistically interpreted order of life that is constantly being built up and renewed in family, society, and state.

To emphasize this point, as I did in *Truth and Method,* may sound to many like blind optimism in an age of faith in science and technological destruction of all that has previously flourished. In fact, behind this optimism one can also find a profound skepticism regarding the role of "intellectuals" and especially of philosophy in humanity's household of life. Not that I would deny the ubiquity of philosophy. I am even convinced of the fact that there is no one who does not "think" sometime and somewhere. This means there is no one who does not form general views about life and death, about freedom and human living together, and about the good and happiness. These views usually rest upon unacknowledged biases and short-circuited generalizations, and perhaps one can say that in the attempts at thought and the conceptual clarifications of the "philosopher" people may find their own criticism and to that extent a certain legitimation—at least for one who thinks further.

But that is the most that can be expected of it, I think. The great equilibrium of what is living, an equilibrium which sustains and permeates
the individual in his privacy as well as in his social constitution and in
his view of life, also encompasses those who think. Nietzsche may have
formulated this truth a bit too provocatively when he spoke of the "little
reason" of human beings.[26] More serene was the Greek thought which
held that the raising of knowledge to clarity and the happiness of *theoria*
were the supreme form of human life, and which recognized this as the
ideal of the best life. Still, it also knew that such theory is embedded
in the practice of conditioned and lived life and is borne along by it.[27]

So there was a material reason why, in thinking through the hermeneutic phenomenon, I was led more and more toward the model of
Aristotle's practical philosophy. In his Kant book of 1929—certainly a
transitional phase in his thought—Heidegger developed the idea of a
finite metaphysics in appealing to the role of the transcendental imagination, but without wanting to draw the resolute consequences of Fichte
and the other "absolute idealists."[28] Once again this point became interesting to me. No doubt the same underlying problem here had been
given its profile in the comprehensive synthesis of Hegelian thought.
What Hegel called absolute knowledge is inseparable from the entire
path of spirit through all its ways of being conditioned and all its manifestations. As a thinker, Hegel was well aware of his own conditionedness
and limitedness, and hence he left room for improving his "philosophic
science"; and of course the goal of world history, the freedom of all, is in
truth something I hold in suspense even today, perhaps for understandable reasons, in the remoteness of a "bad infinity." The same ultimately
holds true of the unity of history and of his system of philosophy that
sustains Hegel's theoretic and historical work as a presupposition. Hermeneutical philosophy's point is to recall the truth within these things.

This is the sense in which one of my earlier formulations has to
be understood: "Dialectic has to be retrieved in hermeneutics."[29] This
statement may not be reversed, at least not if in Hegel one understands
by dialectic the unfolded form of philosophic demonstration and not
simply the speculative element, which of course bestows upon all the
ultimate basic propositions of philosophy from the days of Heraclitus
onward their tension-filled character. In contrast, Plato's art of dialogue
and the "dialectic" of tireless self-correction of all abstract one-sidedness
that the Socratic dialogue reflects, can provide certain hints as to how
a philosophic figure of thought may be constructed that reunites the
metaphysical question concerning the infinite and absolute with the ineradicable finitude of the questioner. Plato himself designated the network of relationships among the logoi as "dialectic"; and this pertains

to that of being itself, which exposes itself to thought. By this Hegel simultaneously meant that being itself may never be apprehended in the unrestricted presence of some *unus intuitus* (unitary intuition) or of an infinite monad in the sense of Leibniz; but, as with all human clarity and lucidity, it is clouded over by opaqueness, passing away, and forgetfulness. Diotima knew this when she compared the knowing proper to humans with the life of a species that has its ongoing being only in the relentless process of the reproduction of its individual instances.[30] My hermeneutics tries to establish this point inasmuch as it characterizes the context of tradition within which we exist as an ongoing reacquisition that proceeds into infinity. It endeavors to make its own the way that every vital and productive conversation with someone else knows how to mediate the other's horizon with one's own.

So even the debate opened up by Wolfhart Pannenberg about hermeneutics and universal history, in which he sought to bring to my attention the consistency of Hegel's philosophy of history, seems to me ultimately not to have a real point of conflict.[31] There is indeed no disputing that the Christian and non-Christian histories of salvation— and even histories of un-salvation [*Unheilsgeschichten*] such as the Nietzschean one of a mounting European nihilism—are a legitimate need in a human reason that is explicitly conscious of its historical character. To this extent universal history is indisputably an aspect of the experience of our being in history. Like all other history, however, universal history too must always be rewritten insofar as it does not possess its absolute datum as does *Heilsgeschichte;* and each projection of writing a universal history has a validity that does not last much longer than the appearance of a flash momentarily cutting across the darkness of the future as well as of the past as it gets lost in the twilight. This finitude is a point of hermeneutical philosophy that I have dared to defend against Hegel.

I would surely be the last to deny the primordial communality that unites all the attempts by humanity at thinking, including that of our Western tradition. So against Heidegger I have sought to reaffirm the beginning [*Anfang*] in Plato and Platonism and also in Hegel (and not only in Schelling), which Heidegger's destruction of metaphysics was calling into question. I also would not dispute that, say, in Dilthey's thought, and still more in Graf Yorck motifs of *Lebensphilosophie,* impulses are operative that lead beyond the historical positivism to which Dilthey's epistemological foundation of the *Geisteswissenschaften* surrendered all too much.[32] Dilthey's move from psychology to hermeneutics actually carries him well beyond the methodology of the *Geisteswissenschaften* .and so brings him, with a certain inner consistency, into proximity with Hegel. Everything that his school and those influenced by him understood under the notion of objective spirit bears witness to this Hegelian heritage.

On the other hand, one has to see that each initiation in thought on the part of one who thinks, even when, in the end, all are inquiring about the same thing, has to be profiled against the one who happens to be his philosophic partner in conversation, if it is to be capable of articulation at all. When Heidegger made the introductory statement to Hegel's "logic of essence," namely, "The truth of being is the essence" [*Die Wahrheit des Seins ist das Wesen*], the theme of that thought-provoking seminar on the occasion of the Freiburg jubilee of the year 1964, the profile that guided him was fully clear to me. I believed (and still believe), however, that Heidegger could have written this sentence himself—in his sense and in his language, of course. Then he would probably mean, "The unconcealment of being [truth] occurs as the 'coming-to-presence'" [*Die Offenbarkeit des Seins geschiet als das an-Wesen*]. I tried to set this down in a letter to him, but Heidegger, in his answer to me, pushed his self-profiling so far that he totally distorted Hegel's statement and rendered it as follows: *Certitudo objectivitatis reflectitur qua relucentia* ("The certitude of objectivity is reflected as a shining back"), and he explained it to me this way: "The intent of the seminar was to show forth how for Hegel it comes to the quite alienating determination of reflection as 'essence' [*Wesen*]. To *see* this it was necessary from the outset to think truth as certitude and 'Being' as objectivity, within the transcendentality of absolute knowledge."[33]

Perhaps a similar example would be that in both Aristotle's notion of being as *ti en einai* [essence] and in Hegel's notion of *Wesen*, the "has been" [*gewesen ist*], the temporal horizon of being resounds, precisely as Heidegger had shown. In like manner Heidegger saw in Aristotle, just as he had in Hegel, a representative of the vulgar notion of time as measured time, which in fact constituted the object of their thematic analyses of the problem of time. But with this, it was also obvious that both thought time in another sense as well. This struck me as a problem, so I dedicated to Heidegger on the occasion of his eightieth birthday a piece on empty and fulfilled time which referred to other time experiences within the history of metaphysics (in Platonism and in Schelling and Hegel).[34] He replied to me that the actual counter-notion for fulfilled time was not empty time but measured time. That is how strongly he was held fast to his will to have a profile of his own.

In a similar way, Heidegger insisted on understanding Hegel's reflection in itself—which was certainly differentiated expressly enough from "extrinsic reflection"—as testimony for the orientation toward self-consciousness that dominated Hegel, and thus he underemphasized the step Hegel took to objective spirit.

Nevertheless, it remains true about his own project of posing the question of being anew and of overcoming the secular answer given by metaphysics as well as by the language of metaphysics, that the new element he puts forward belongs inextricably with the old. "To overcome" presupposes the status of metaphysics in Heidegger's own thought as not something that lies behind him but as a partner against which he can be profiled.[35] Metaphysics remains just as much a presupposition one needs for the overcoming of metaphysics and for Heidegger's "step back" [*Schritt zurück*]—as the total "forgetfulness of being" [*Seinsvergessenheit*] is a presupposition of the technological thought of our time.

I surely do not need to add that in *Truth and Method* I have also proceeded in an equally (and certainly one-sidedly) profiling way: with Schleiermacher, whose hermeneutics I separated all too much from his dialectics; with Dilthey, whom I measured against the consequences drawn by Heidegger and Nietzsche; and finally with Hegel, to be sure, to whom for this reason I have devoted further studies, and whose challenge I try to pose to myself, in positive as well as in negative aspects, wherever I can.

Translated by Frederick G. Lawrence

Heidegger and the Language of Metaphysics

This essay was originally titled "Remarks on the Theme 'Hegel and Heidegger'" and was contributed to a seventieth birthday celebration volume for Karl Löwith, a noted Jewish professor of philosophy whom Gadamer had brought back to Heidelberg from New York in 1952.[1] When Gadamer added the essay to the collection of his own writings that he brought out in 1972, he changed the title to "Heidegger and the Language of Metaphysics."[2] In 1983, when he included the essay in a collection of his writings on Heidegger, he shortened the title to "The Language of Metaphysics,"[3] a title he retained when it was included in a group of essays on Heidegger in his collected works.[4] But since we are translating the *Gadamer Lesebuch* (1997), we will retain the title given it in our source.

The context of this essay, which was written in 1967, is Gadamer's ongoing dialogue with Heidegger over Hegel which, as we have already noted in our introduction to the previous essay, "The Heritage of Hegel," was going on in 1965, when Gadamer offered a course titled "From Hegel to Heidegger" and Heidegger visited its closing lecture in Heidelberg and even responded to it briefly. This discussion is continued in Gadamer's ongoing dialogue with the "post-metaphysical" Derrida, in which Gadamer in 1986 asserts flatly: "There is no language of metaphysics."[5] As Heidegger's follower, Gadamer also claims to have carried forward the Heideggerian project of renewing philosophy but without having to reject Hegel or Plato, properly read, while Derrida follows Heidegger's effort to "deconstruct" them. So we may say that this essay not only stands in the Hegel-Heidegger controversy but for us also the later controversy with Derrida over the "metaphysics of presence" in Plato.

A point of interest in this piece, although it was written ten years earlier than "The Heritage of Hegel," is that Gadamer goes a step further here, now that Heidegger is dead, and specifies some other areas where Heidegger's philosophy is incomplete. These are especially of interest coming from a loyal follower of Heidegger who has closely read the master. First, there is the problem of the we and the thou, the "we" of intersubjectivity and the "thou" of dialogue. Next, there is the concept of the self and the nature of man among "living beings" which comes up in Heidegger's "Letter on Humanism," and then the fact that being comes to presence in a clearing that "points to a primordial interconnection of being and man . . . man is the guardian of being." Gadamer agrees with Heidegger on the priority of language, language speaking us instead of us speaking it, but he wants to raise the question of the "self" in Heidegger. Also, there is the question of Heidegger's conception of nonhuman living things, vegetation, animals, and so on. So there are many rewarding topics discussed in the essay.

Gadamer's final topic is language itself. Here he agrees with Heidegger in trying to attain a post-technological view of the world as something other than mere tools for human use. But what makes one at home in the world, according to Gadamer, is dialogue with other people, which has complex hermeneutical dimensions. Gadamer says that "the continual coming to language of our being in the world" is not just a matter of the language of metaphysics, but of many other factors. East and West bring this about differently, but they remain in language. Gadamer has a famous saying, "Being that can be understood is language." Here he remains a faithful follower of Heidegger, and he also follows Heidegger's effort to go beyond a philosophy of reflection and subjectivity and toward the finitude of being, but he thinks that dialogue and a more comprehensive idea of language in terms of being offer more than does a project of rejecting or purifying metaphysics and the "language of metaphysics." For Gadamer there is no "language" of metaphysics, but only language itself as the rich medium in which our being in the world discloses itself.

* * *

Heidegger and the Language of Metaphysics

The tremendous power emanating from Heidegger's creative energies in the early 1920s seemed to sweep along the generation of students returning from World War I or just beginning their studies, so that a complete break with traditional academic philosophy seemed to take place with Heidegger's appearance—even before it was expressed in his own writings. It was like a breakthrough into the unknown that posed something radically new as compared with all the mere movements and countermovements of the whole Christian Occident. A generation in Germany was shattered by the collapse of an epoch and wanted to begin completely anew; it did not want to retain anything that had formerly been held valid. Even in the intensification of the German language that took place in his concepts, Heidegger's thought seemed to defy any comparison with what philosophy had previously meant. And this was in spite of the unceasing and intensive interpretive effort that especially distinguished Heidegger's academic instruction—his immersion in Aristotle and Plato, Augustine and Thomas Aquinas, Leibniz and Kant, and Hegel and Husserl.

Altogether unexpected things came to the surface and were discussed in connection with these names. Each of these great figures from our classical philosophical tradition was completely transformed and seemed to proclaim a direct, compelling truth that was perfectly fused with the thought of its resolute interpreter. The distance separating our historical consciousness from the tradition seemed to be nonexistent. The calm and confident aloofness with which the neo-Kantian "history of philosophical problems" was accustomed to deal with the tradition, and the whole of contemporary rhetoric that came from the academic rostrum, now suddenly seemed to be mere child's play.

In actual fact, the break with tradition that took place in Heidegger's thought represented just as much an incomparable renewal of the tradition. Only gradually did the younger students come to see how much appropriation of the tradition was present in his criticism, as well as how profound the criticism was in this appropriation. Two great classical figures of philosophical thought, however, have long occupied an ambiguous position in Heidegger's thought, standing out as much by their affinity with Heidegger as by their radical distance from him. These two thinkers are Plato and Hegel. From the very beginning, Plato was viewed in a critical light in Heidegger's work, in that Heidegger took over and transformed the Aristotelian criticism of the Idea of the Good and stressed especially the Aristotelian concept of analogy. Yet it was Plato who provided Heidegger the motto for *Being and Time*. Only after World War II, with his decisive incorporation of Plato into the history of Being, was the ambiguity in regard to Plato removed. But Heidegger's thought has revolved around Hegel until the end (1976) in ever new attempts at delineation of their difference. In contrast to the phenomenological craftsmanship that was all too quickly forgotten by the scholarship of the time, Hegel's dialectic of pure thought asserted itself with renewed power. Hence Hegel not only continually provoked Heidegger to self-defense, but he was also the one with whom Heidegger was associated in the eyes of all those who sought to defend themselves against the claim of Heidegger's thought. Would this final form of Western metaphysics be outstripped by the radicalism with which Heidegger stirred the oldest questions of philosophy to new life? Or would the circle of the

philosophy of reflection, which dashed all hope of freedom and libera-
tion, force Heidegger's thought too back into its orbit?

The development of Heidegger's late philosophy has scarcely encountered a critique anywhere that does not go back in the last analysis to Hegel's position. This observation is true in the negative sense
of aligning Heidegger with Hegel's abortive speculative revolution,
as Gerhard Krüger[1] and countless others after him have argued. It is
also valid in the positive Hegelianizing sense that Heidegger is not sufficiently aware of his own proximity to Hegel, and for this reason he
does not really do justice to the radical position of Hegel's speculative
logic. The latter criticism has occurred basically in two problem areas.
One is Heidegger's assimilation of history into his own philosophical
approach, a point that he seems to share with Hegel. The second is the
hidden and unnoticed dialectic that attaches to all essentially Heideggerian assertions.

If Hegel tried to penetrate the history of philosophy philosophically from the standpoint of absolute knowledge, that is, to raise it to a
science, Heidegger's description of the history of being (in particular,
the history of the forgetfulness of being into which European history
entered in the century following Hegel) involved a similarly comprehensive claim. Indeed, there is in Heidegger nothing of that necessity of
historical progress that is both the glory and the bane of Hegelian philosophy. For Heidegger, rather, Hegel's history that is remembered and
taken up into the absolute present in absolute knowing is precisely an
advance sign of the radical forgetfulness of being that has marked the
history of Europe in the century after Hegel. But for Heidegger, it was
fate not history (remembered and penetrable by understanding), that
caused the conception of being to arise in Greek metaphysics and that
in modern science and technology carries the forgetfulness of being to
the extreme. Nevertheless, no matter how much it may belong to the
temporal constitution of man to be exposed to the unpredictability of
fate, this does not rule out the claim continually raised and legitimated
in the course of Western history to think what is. And so Heidegger too
appears to claim a genuinely historical self-consciousness for himself,
indeed, even an eschatological self-consciousness.

My second critical motif proceeds from the indeterminateness
and undeterminableness of what Heidegger calls "being." This criticism
tries by Hegelian means to explain the alleged tautology of being—that
it is itself—a disguised second immediacy that emerges from the total
mediation of the immediate. Furthermore, are there not real dialectical
antitheses at work whenever Heidegger explicates himself? For instance,
the dialectical tension between thrownness and projection, authenticity

and inauthenticity, nothing as the veil of being, and finally, and most importantly, the inner tension and ambiguity [*Gegenwendigkeit*] of truth and error, revealment and concealment, which constitute the event of being as the event of truth. Did not Hegel's mediation of being and nothing in the truth of becoming—that is, in the truth of the concrete— already mark out the conceptual framework within which alone the Heideggerian doctrine of the inner tension within truth can exist? Hegel, by his dialectical speculative sharpening of the antitheses in understanding, overcame a thinking dominated by [an analysis of] the understanding. Would it be possible to get beyond this achievement, so as to overcome the logic and language of metaphysics as a whole?

Access to our problem undoubtedly lies in the problem of nothingness and its suppression by metaphysics, a theme Heidegger formulated in his inaugural address in Freiburg. From this perspective, the nothingness we find in Parmenides and in Plato, and also Aristotle's definition of the divine as *energeia* without *dynamis,* really constitutes a total vitiation of nothingness. Even God, as the infinite knowledge that possesses being from itself, is understood basically from the vantage point of the privative experience of man's being (in the experience of sleep, death, and forgetting) to be the unlimited presence of everything present. But another motif seems to be at work in the history of metaphysical thinking alongside this vitiation of nothingness that extends even into Hegel and Husserl. Aristotelian metaphysics culminated in the question, "What is the being of beings?" The question that Leibniz and Schelling asked and that Heidegger even called the basic question of metaphysics, "Why is there anything at all, and not rather nothing?" expressly continues the confrontation with the problem of nothingness. The analyses of the concept of *dynamis* in Plato, Plotinus, the tradition of negative theology, Nicholas of Cusa, and Leibniz, all the way to Schelling—from whom Schopenhauer, Nietzsche, and the metaphysics of the will take their departure—all serve to show that the understanding of being in terms of presence [*Präsenz*] is constantly threatened by nothingness. In our own century, this situation is also found in Max Scheler's dualism of impulse and spirit and in Ernst Bloch's philosophy of the not yet, as well as in such hermeneutical phenomena as the question, doubt, wonder, and so on. To this extent, Heidegger's approach has an intrinsic preparation in the subject matter of metaphysics itself.

In order to clarify the immanent necessity of the development within his own thought that led Heidegger to "the turn" and to try to show that it has nothing to do with a dialectical reversal, we must proceed from the fact that the transcendental-phenomenological conception of *Being and Time* is already essentially different from Husserl's conception of it. Husserl's constitutional analysis of the consciousness of time shows particularly well that the self-constitution of the primal presence (which Husserl could indeed designate as a kind of primal potentiality) is based entirely on the concept of constitutive accomplishment and is thus dependent on the being of valid objectivity. The self-constitution of the transcendental ego, a problem that can be traced back to the fifth chapter of the *Logical Investigations,* stands wholly within the traditional understanding of Being, despite—indeed, precisely because of—the absolute historicity that forms the transcendental ground of all objectivities. Now we must admit that Heidegger's transcendental point of departure starting from the being that has its being as an issue for itself and the doctrine of the existentials in *Being and Time* both carry with them a transcendental appearance; as though Heidegger's thoughts were, as Oskar Becker puts it, simply the elaboration of further horizons of transcendental phenomenology that had not previously been secured and that had to do with the historicity of Dasein.[2] In reality, however, Heidegger's undertaking means something quite different. Jaspers's formulation of the "boundary situation" certainly provided Heidegger with a starting point for explicating the finitude of existence in its basic significance. But this approach only served as the preparation of the question of being in a radically altered sense, and was not the explication of a regional ontology in Husserl's sense. The concept of "fundamental ontology"—following the model of "fundamental theology"—also creates a difficulty. The mutual interconnection of authenticity and inauthenticity, of the revealment and concealment of Dasein, which appeared in *Being and Time* more in the sense of a rejection of an ethicistic, affect-oriented thinking, turned out increasingly to be the real nucleus of the "question of being." According to Heidegger's formulation in *On the Essence of Truth,* ek-sistence and in-sistence are indeed still conceived from the point of view of human Dasein. But when he says that the truth of being is the *un*truth, that is, the concealment of being in "error," then the decisive change in the concept of "essence" which is a consequence of the destruction of the Greek tradition of metaphysics can no longer be ignored. For Heidegger wants to leave behind both the traditional concept of essence and that of the ground of essence.

What the interconnection of concealment and revealment means and what it has to do with the new concept of "essence" can be exhibited phenomenologically in Heidegger's own experience of thought in a number of ways: (1) In the being of the implement that does not have its essence in its objective obstinacy, but in its being ready-to-hand, which allows us to concentrate on what is beyond the implement itself. (2) In the being of the work of art, which holds its truth within itself in such fashion that this truth is not available in any other way but in the work. For the beholder or receiver, "essence" corresponds here to one's tarrying with the work. (3) In the thing, as the one and only reality that stands in itself, which cannot be compelled to serve our purposes, and which contrasts in its irreplaceability with the concept of the object of consumption, as found in industrial production. (4) And finally in the word. The "essence" of the word does not lie in being totally expressed, but rather in what is left unsaid, as we see especially in speechlessness and remaining silent. The common structure of essence that is evident in all four of these experiences of thinking is a "being-there" that encompasses being absent as well as being present. During his early years at Freiburg Heidegger once said, "One cannot lose God as one loses one's pocketknife." But in fact one cannot simply lose one's pocketknife in such a fashion that it is no longer present. When one has lost a long-familiar implement such as a pocketknife, it demonstrates its existence by the fact that one continually misses it. Hölderlin's "Fehl der Götter" ["disappearance or loss of the gods"] or T. S. Eliot's silence of the Chinese vase are not a nonexistence, but "being" in the most poetic sense because they are silent. The breach that is created by what is missing is not a place remaining empty within what is present-to-hand; rather, it belongs to the being-there of that to which it is missing, and is "present" in it. Hence "essence" is concretized, and we can demonstrate how what is present is at the same time a concealment of presence.

Problems that necessarily eluded transcendental questioning and appeared as mere peripheral phenomena become comprehensible when we start from such experiences. In the first place, this holds for "nature." Becker's postulation of a paraontology is justified here insofar as nature is no longer only "a limiting case of the being of a possible inner-worldly being." But Becker himself never recognized that his counter-concept of "paraexistence," which is concerned with such essential phenomena as mathematical and dream existence, is a dialectical construction. Becker himself synthesized it with its opposite and thus marked out a third position, without noticing how this position corresponds to the Heideggerian doctrine of the "turn."

A second large complex of problems is placed in a new light in the context of Heidegger's later thought, namely the thou and the we. We are familiar with this problem complex from Husserl's ongoing discussion of the problem of intersubjectivity; in *Being and Time* it is interpreted in terms of the world of concern. What constitutes the mode of being of essence is now considered from the point of view of the dialogue, that is, in terms of our capacity to listen to each other *in concreto,* for instance, when we perceive what governs a conversation or when we notice its absence in a tortured conversation. But above all, in Heidegger the inscrutable problem of life and corporeality presents itself in a new way. The concept of the living being [*Lebe-Wesen*], which Heidegger emphasized in his "Letter on Humanism,"[3] raises new questions, especially the question of its correspondence to the nature of man [*Menschen-Wesen*] and the nature of language [*Sprach-Wesen*]. But behind this line of questioning stands the question of the being of the self, which was easy enough to define in terms of German idealism's concept of reflection. But it becomes puzzling the moment we no longer proceed from the self or self-consciousness, or from human Dasein, in *Being and Time,* but rather from essence. The fact that being comes to a presence in a "clearing," and that in this fashion thinking man is the guardian of being, points to a primordial interconnection of being and man. The tool, the work of art, thing, the word—in all of these, the relation to man stands forth clearly in essence itself. But in what sense? Scarcely in the sense that the Being of the human self thereby acquires its definition. The example of language has already shown us that. As Heidegger says, language speaks us, insofar as we do not really preside over it and control it, although of course no one disputes the fact that it is we who speak it. Heidegger's assertion here is not without meaning.

If we want to raise the question of the "self" in Heidegger, we will first have to consider and reject Neoplatonic modes of thought. For a cosmic drama consisting in the emanation out of the One and the return into it, with the self designated as the pivot of the return, lies beyond what is possible here. Or one could consider what Heidegger understands by "insistence" as the way to a solution. What Heidegger called the "insistence" of Dasein and what he called errancy are certainly to be conceived from the point of view of the forgetfulness of being. But is this forgetfulness the sole mode of coming to presence? Will this render intelligible the place-holding character of human Dasein? Can the concept of coming to presence and of the "there" be maintained in exclusive relation to human Dasein, if we take the growth of plants and the living being into consideration? In *On the Essence of Truth,* Heidegger still conceived of "insistence" from the point of view of the being that first "raised its head" [i.e., man]. But does not insistence have to be taken in a broader sense? And hence "ek-sistence" too? Certainly the confinement of the living being in its environment, discussed in the "Letter on Humanism," means that it is not open for being as is man, who is aware of his possibility of being. But have we not learned from Heidegger that the real being of the living being is not its own individual being-there, but rather the species? And is the species not "there" for the living being, even if not in the same way that being is present for man in the insistence of the forgetfulness of being? Does it not comprise a part of the being of the species that its members "know" themselves, as the profound expression of the Lutheran Bible puts it? Indeed, *as* knowing, are they not concealed from themselves and yet in such fashion that knowing passes over into them? Is it not also characteristic of "insistence" that the animal intends only itself [*conservatio sui*] and yet precisely in this way provides for the reproduction of its kind?

Similarly, we could ask about the growth of vegetation: Is it only a coming to presence for man? Does not every form of life as such have a tendency to secure itself in its being, indeed to persist in it? Is it not precisely its finitude that it wants to tarry in this manner? And does it not hold for man as well that the Dasein in him, as Heidegger called it, is not to be thought of at all as a kind of highest self-possession that allows him to step outside the circuit of life like a god? Isn't one's entire doctrine of man distorted rather than put in order by modern subjectivism, in that we consider the essence of man to be society (as ζῷον πολιτικόν)? Is it not just this belief that declares the inner tension and ambiguity that is being itself? And does this not mean that it is senseless to pit "nature" against "being"?

The continuing difficulty [for Heidegger] is that of avoiding the language of metaphysics, which conceives of all these matters in terms of the "power of reflection." But what do we mean when we speak of the "language of metaphysics"? It is obvious that the experience of "essence" is not that of a manipulating kind of thinking. If we keep this distinction in mind, we can see that the concept of "recollection" has something natural about it. It is true that recollection itself is something and that in it history has its reality, not that history is simply remembered through it. But what takes place in "recollection"? Is it really tenable to expect something like a reversal in it—like the abruptness of fate? Whatever the case may be, the important thing in the phenomenon of recollection, it seems to me, is that something is secured and preserved in its "there," so that it can never not be, as long as recollection remains alive. Yet recollection is not something that clutches tenaciously at what is vanishing; the nonexistence of what disappears is not at all concealed or obstinately disputed by it. Rather, something like consent takes place in it (of which Rilke's *Duino Elegies* tell us something). There is nothing of what we have called "insistence" in it.

Conversely, we may call "fascination" what arises through the constructive capacity and technological power of "insistence," that is, of human forgetfulness of Being. There is essentially no limit to this kind of experience of being, which, since Nietzsche, we call nihilism. But if this fascination proceeds from such a constantly intensifying obstinacy, does it not find its own ultimate end in itself, precisely by virtue of the fact that the constantly new becomes something that is left behind, and that this happens *without* a special event intervening or a reversal taking place? Does not the natural weight of things remain perceptible and make itself felt the more monotonously the noise of the constantly new may sound forth? To be sure, Hegel's idea of knowledge, conceived as absolute self-transparency, has something fantastic about it if it is supposed to restore complete at-homeness in being. But could not a restoration of at-homeness come about in the sense that the process of making-oneself-at-home in the world has never ceased to take place, and has never ceased to be the better reality, a reality that is not deafened by the madness of technology? Does this restoration not occur when the illusory character of the technocracy, the paralyzing sameness of everything man can make, becomes perceptible, and man is released again into the really astonishing character of his own finite being? This freedom is certainly not gained in the sense of an absolute transparency, or a being-at-home that is no longer endangered. But just as the thinking of what cannot be preconceived [*das Denken des Unvordenklichen*] preserves what is its own, for example, the homeland, what cannot be preconceived regarding our finitude is reunited with itself in the constant process of the coming to language of our Dasein. In the up-and-down movement in coming into being and passing away it—is "there."

Is this the old metaphysics? Or is it the language of metaphysics alone that achieves this continual coming-to-language of our being-in-the-world? Certainly it is the language of metaphysics, but further behind it is the language of the Indo-European peoples, which makes such thinking capable of formulation. But can a language—or a family of languages—ever properly be called the language of metaphysical thinking, just because metaphysics was thought, or what would be more, anticipated in it? Is not language always the language of the homeland and the process of becoming at home in the world? And does this fact not mean that language knows no restrictions and never breaks down, because it holds infinite possibilities of utterance in readiness? It seems to me that the hermeneutical dimension enters here and demonstrates its inner infinity in the speaking that takes place in dialogue. To be sure, the technical language of philosophy is preformed by the grammatical structure of the Greek language, and its usages in Greco-Latin times established ontological implications whose prejudiced character Heidegger uncovered. But we must ask: Are the universality of objectifying reason and the eidetic structure of linguistic meanings really bound to these particular historically developed interpretations of *subjectum* and *species* and *actus* that the West has produced? Or do they hold true for all languages? It cannot be denied that there are certain structural aspects of the Greek language and a grammatical self-consciousness, particularly in Latin, that fix in a definite direction of interpretation the hierarchy of genus and species, the relation of substance and accident, the structure of predication and the verb as an action word. But is there no rising above such a pre-schematizing of thought? For instance, if one contrasts the Western predicative judgment with the Eastern figurative expression, which acquires its expressive power from the reciprocal reflection of what is meant and what is said, are these two not in truth only different modes of utterance within one and the same universal, namely, within the essence of language and reason? Is it not true that concept and judgment remain embedded within the life of meaning of the language we speak and in which we know how to say what it is we mean?[4] And conversely, cannot the connotative aspect of certain Oriental reflective expressions always be drawn into the hermeneutical movement that creates common understanding, just as the expression of the work of art can? Language always arises within such a movement. Can anyone really contend that there has ever been language in any other sense than in the fulfilling of such a movement? Even Hegel's doctrine of the speculative proposition seems to me to have its place here, and always takes up into itself its own sharpening into the dialectic of contradiction. For in speaking, there always remains the possibility of canceling out the objectifying tendency of language, just as Hegel cancels the logic of understanding, Heidegger cancels the language of metaphysics, the Orientals the diversity of realms of being, and the poet everything given. But to cancel [aufheben] means to take up and use.

Translated by David E. Linge

Hermeneutics and the Ontological Difference

It is well known that Gadamer was Heidegger's assistant in Marburg from 1923 to 1928. He even briefly moved to Freiburg in 1923 to study with Heidegger before Heidegger was invited to Marburg. These crucial years were formative for Heidegger's masterwork, *Being and Time* (1927), and Gadamer later became a defender, promoter, and authoritative interpreter of Heidegger's thought, although there were many other very notable interpreters of Heidegger both before and after World War II, like Eugen Fink, Otto Pöggeler, and Friedrich-Wilhelm von Hermann, in addition to innumerable students from abroad who appreciated the radical power of Heidegger's thought. During Heidegger's years in Marburg, Gadamer struggled not to surrender to the powerful spell of Heidegger's teaching and personality by gaining an additional accreditation in 1927 in classical Greek philology. This gave him solid ground to stand on in resisting some of Heidegger's interpretations of Greek philosophers. For the most part Gadamer distanced himself from Heidegger during the Nazi period (1933–45), but he initiated friendly contact with him after the war, and they remained friends for the rest of Heidegger's life. For details on these years, see the excellent biography of Gadamer by Jean Grondin [*GBio*].

No documentation on any original public presentation of this essay is available. It was simply included in the set of seven late papers on Heidegger at the beginning of volume 10 (1995) of Gadamer's collected works with the note, "Entstanden [arose] 1989." Yet it is a valuable memoir of the years 1922–24 and the atmosphere at that time. In addition, it addresses the difficult interpretive topic of the "ontological difference" in Heidegger during this period, and Heidegger's new conception of ontology as the "hermeneutics of facticity." If its title were made longer and more specific, it would read, "Heidegger's View of Hermeneutics and of the Ontological Difference in the Period 1922–1924."

Yet the essay contains even more than this. Gadamer recalls an illuminating conversation with Heidegger about the ontological difference. There is a clear tie of this term to Aristotle and of Aristotle to the fundamental ontology of *Being and Time*. It contains remarks on Kierkegaard and on Heidegger's plan of a critique of traditional theology, and a remark by Gadamer himself on the inadequacy of the Greek *parousia* (appearance and presence with) for the mysteries of Christian theology. There is a clarification of why Heidegger used the term *Hermeneutik* for his interpretive explication of Dasein's being in the world. And we are treated to a series of other themes and areas of dispute with Heidegger: *aletheia* (truth), *Destruktion* (deconstruction), *energeia* (the self-movement of seeing and thinking in Aristotle), the *Unvordenkliche* (that which cannot be anticipated in thought), and the language of metaphysics. By the time one ends this lapidary essay, one has encountered a clear statement in 1989 of the major themes in Gadamer's discipleship and differences with Heidegger. In other words, this essay goes far beyond the topics of hermeneutics and the ontological difference in Heidegger during the early 1920s. The differences center around several things: deconstruction and the downhill history of metaphysics in the West, the centering of hermeneutics in historical consciousness (touched on lightly here), Heidegger's project of "overcoming metaphysics," and finally the nature of language. These are themes Gadamer has discussed at greater length elsewhere, but here they form a colorful bouquet in a general survey of early Heidegger and Gadamer's relationship to him.

Gadamer concludes with his own contrasting view of language as conversation, an indirect criticism of Heidegger's view of language. He agrees with Heidegger that language is not a tool of man but the medium in which we all live and move and have our being. But he goes a step further to see in the interaction of dialogue the very life of language itself. Living language, says Gadamer, is conversation; it is the conveying of an interpreted meaning to another as well as receiving the meaning conveyed by the other. It is the fabric and living medium of our life together.

* * *

Hermeneutics and the Ontological Difference

When I think back to the first lectures of Heidegger that I myself heard back in 1923 in Freiburg and then in 1924 in Marburg, the term "ontological difference" was at that time like a magic word. It was always uttered with the full emphasis that a concentrated thinker gave it, but without going into individual details about the relationships and meaning of what he was really trying to grasp in words. Even without this, one felt that we were zeroing in on something completely decisive. This was the way that the young Heidegger used this term. It almost became like a customary way of speaking, to which we were often treated when we sought in one of his seminars to put forward our own small contributions and efforts at thinking and Heidegger would say. "Yes, yes—but that is ontic, not ontological."

I want in what follows to try to understand what this difference between "ontic" and "ontological" really meant. For over and over again Heidegger used the expression "ontological difference" like a pregnant symbolic term. One never spoke of a "theological" difference. No, the first minting of this new Heideggerian term was too strong for that and too exclusive. But if one looks at the matter more closely, one still has a right to ask about what *das Sein* [Being] means and at the same time what is meant by the divine and God. On the theological side, Rudolf Otto suggested a famous formulation, "the wholly Other" [*das ganz Andere*]. This expression obviously contains a relation to "difference." The different, the other, in Greek is *to heteron,* and the *heteron* is always a *heteron tou heterou,* an "other of the other." In Otto's expression, theology exists in the absolute difference [from God] which Christ knew as the difference between the Creator and his creation. In this case, one really does not understand the "other" in the logical sense of the word *heteron.*

At this point I would like to bring in a phrase that has stuck with me from those earliest times with Heidegger. When you learn a phrase you only half understand, it always sticks with you. One should not underestimate how much one initially picks up—certainly it is more than one is conscious of oneself, and more than one really recognizes when one begins to understand something. Another term like this, which I ponder even now, and which all those who know their Heidegger will immediately recognize, is the phrase, *das Seiende im Ganze* [beings as a whole]. I claim no special advantage over other Heidegger experts in understanding this phrase, but I was among the few then who when they heard this phrase for the first time experienced it as both luminous in meaning and significant. This was an expression that the young Heidegger used in almost the same way as the "ontological difference." It was a very vague formulation. As I would explain it today, by using such terms Heidegger avoided sharpening the meaning of his terms too much, for at that time he did not want to differentiate unequivocally between *Sein* and *Seiendes,* the way that he later took true pleasure in doing, such that in the end *Sein* was seen as not only quite different from *das Seiende* [concrete beings] and their mode of being [*Seiendheit*] but was even written with a *y,* as *das Seyn.* In the terminology of the later Heidegger, all these other expressions articulated the being of what at that time he called "beings as a whole" [*das Seiende im Ganzen*].

The best way to make the meaning of this expression clear is to think back to the very beginnings of Greek thought. This expression named what Heidegger had in mind when, with a certain sharpening of his terminology, he did not say *Sein* but *das Seiende im Ganzen* [beings as a whole]. Today I see in this phrase the best formulation of the intention that Parmenides captured in verse in his famous didactic poem ["On Nature"]. There the topic is Being [*Sein*], and the term for this in Greek is *to on* [*das Seiende*, the being of beings]. What is striking about this word is that it is in the singular. This was the special distinction of Parmenidean thinking: that something arose that banished both nonbeing [*Nicht-Sein*] and the many, and he did this while faced with the powerful emergence of the cosmological, astronomical, geographical knowledge of the world—knowledge of the heavens, knowledge of the stars, and knowledge of the earth—that was taking place in the city of Miletus. Miletus was one of the great centers in the period of colonization when the Greeks opened up for themselves the whole Mediterranean area. Heidegger's term *das Seiende im Ganzen* [beings in general, beings as a whole] described in a striking way exactly what Parmenides' poem was presenting. It was not inquiring there into what the many [specific] beings were, whether water or air or whatever, and how all this was held together in some kind of equilibrium. He was no longer dealing with the processes of rising and decay that mutually limited each other like the changing of day and night, the interaction of water and land, and all that a seafaring nation like Greece could immediately visualize. This neuter word, this singular *das Seiende,* is a first step toward a concept [*zum Begriff*].[1] Heidegger at that time consciously *held back* from his later formulation *das Sein*—perhaps in order that *das Sein* would not be misunderstood as the being of beings, as what-being [*Was-Sein*] in the metaphysical sense. Parmenides has in fact described *das Sein* as this "being as a whole," as everywhere proportionally filling up everything like a single huge Ball. Nowhere do you find nothing.

When Heidegger later on speaks of the "ontological difference," he has in mind something which remains unexpressed in this first formulation. He means by it the difference between being and all the things that are. What this is supposed to mean is rather obscure. Basically no human being knows what the concept *das Sein* means, and yet we all have a first pre-understanding, when we hear the word, and we understand that here the being that belongs to all beings has now been raised to the level of a concept. And so now it is different from all beings. That is what the "ontological difference" means, first and above all. The young Heidegger was always conscious of the fact that it was truly puzzling that we do indeed experience and name many beings, but we also name and think the being of beings [*das Sein des Seienden*].

To illustrate the puzzle of this distinction, let me tell a true story. It took place in Marburg. My friend Gerhard Krüger and I were accompanying Heidegger to his home after a lecture. He lived in the Swan Alley, so I can date it more exactly: it had to have been in the spring of 1924. At that time we were already vigorously discussing the ontological difference, so we asked Heidegger how one really makes this ontological distinction. Presumably we wanted to start out from the concept of reflection by a subject which formed the starting point of German idealism. Heidegger looked at us condescendingly and said, "But no, this differentiation was certainly not something made *by me.*" This was in 1924, long before the "turn." Those who know the later Heidegger know that the difference [*das Unterschied*] he spoke of then was not something that we have made, but rather we are placed into this difference [*Unterschied*], in other words, into this *Differenz* [difference]. *Sein* [Being] shows itself "in" existing things, and this already raises the question of what it means that "there are" beings [*Seiendes*]. By way of introduction, I would also note how Heidegger formulated it in his later work on Nietzsche: our thinking finds itself situated from its very inception on the path to the distinguishing of beings from being. As is well known, French Heideggerianism or Nietzscheanism has endorsed this sense of difference, following Heidegger and inspired by him, and intentionally spelled the word *différence* wrongly as *différance*. Obviously this alteration is intended to make one aware of the double meaning which resides in *différer,* namely, deferring till later or distinguishing between things. Difference, then, is not something that a person makes; rather, it is something that is done to you, or that yawns before you like a chasm. It is something that kicks things apart [*tritt auseinander*]. An arising takes place.

In the later Heidegger this means "the opening up of being," or what he called *das Ereignis* [sometimes translated as the "event of appropriation," *er-eignen*], which the later Heidegger in numerous intellectual efforts tried to conceptualize or somehow intuit [*zur Anschauung zu bringen*]. Under these circumstances, what seemed the obvious thing to do was to return to the first steps of Greek thought. For Heidegger, this was an old topic, the beginnings of Western philosophy, but now it became central. Today, such a project of returning to antiquity probably sounds old-fashioned, but one must remember what these years were like, in which the greatest book success was Spengler's *The Decline of the West.* All of this one heard at the same time as the young Heidegger's lectures on the beginning of Western philosophy. One was hearing something about an end of the West here that belonged to a beginning—and in fact, one may ask: what beginning is a beginning at all that is not the beginning of an end? We can indeed think a beginning only from the standpoint of an end. This key idea of an "ontological difference" extends from the earliest Heidegger to the very last formulations of his thinking. Indeed, even in his last writings, one occasionally finds in him that unanticipated [*unvorgreifliche*] turn of phrase, *das Seiende im Ganzen.*

The other key concept that I would also like to address here in an introductory way is the expression "hermeneutics." This is not a term customarily found in the realm of philosophy. In preceding centuries the lawyer or judge knew what it was, but at that time they did not take it as very important. Likewise with the theologians. Even for Schleiermacher, the grandfather of modern philosophical hermeneutics, hermeneutics is still a help-discipline and in any case is categorized under dialectic. In Dilthey, his successor, hermeneutics is classified under psychology. It was only with the change that Heidegger gave it in his receiving of Husserlian phenomenology—which at the same time meant his reception of Dilthey's writings through phenomenology—that "hermeneutics" took on a fundamentally philosophical meaning. The first course that I attended in the year 1923 had the title "Ontology: The Hermeneutics of Facticity."[2] The whole reach of our topic here is present in the title of this lecture course. Like many academic titles, this too has an academic prehistory. I happen to know that Heidegger at that time had to give up the title he had planned to use because an older colleague had already announced something similar. Presumably Heidegger actually helped himself by narrowing the meaning of "ontology" with the term "hermeneutics." In any case, the title that resulted from this was quite suspense-provoking. What did "ontology" mean in this case—and what was "hermeneutics"? In his introductory lectures, Heidegger could often be rather pedantic. But later, I noticed that as an experienced teacher, which he had become in the meantime, he was constantly deferring the presentation of his enormously rich ideas and the thickness of his thinking because he was worried that in themselves his ideas would not reach to the end of the semester. Of course, a beginning teacher in philosophy would do it in this way—especially when he had something he wanted to say. It was no different with Heidegger—only, he had a lot to say! So in the last weeks of the semester he would let loose a veritable thunderstorm on his students, in which what he had in mind flashed forth like bolts of lightning, things he could not yet bring into language.

But what is a "hermeneutics of facticity"? Certainly one can reach back for help here to the older concept of hermeneutics. According to it, hermeneutics is the doctrine of understanding and the art of explaining what one has understood. Heidegger too had presented this to his students in a somewhat drawn-out way in the introductory lecture of 1923, which is now published.[3] Then, however, after this preparation, he summarized the present problem situation of philosophy. This chapter certainly does not have the clarity we find in most of the later Heidegger. But one can see here how the young Heidegger regarded the situation of philosophy. There were two factors in this situation, he said. One of them was historicism. This was above all represented by the great figure of Dilthey, his school, and its successors. Because of his form of "historical consciousness" all of us now required a new methodical self-awareness [to replace it]. And the way that German idealism spoke of the absolute simply would not suffice anymore.

Rather, we now have constantly to pose to each other the question of how, in light of the rise of historical consciousness, one can make any claim to truth at all in a work of philosophical thinking. The philosophical thinking of my youth [in the 1920s] stood under the challenge of this historicism. In it one found oneself confronted by the problem of relativism. There are people even today who [mistakenly] regard me as a relativist. Heidegger has shown, however, that one could only do this from the fictitious standpoint of an absolute observer, a standpoint in which one is content to determine with objectivity and bring to knowledge that which had been thought in the various periods of the history of thought in the West. Against this, Heidegger put forward another extreme possibility. It sounded very tactful in the Heidegger of that time, but who knows if it might not still have been intended as challenging, even though it sounded polite. I would say that in this case the defendant on trial was the whole system of philosophy. Formally one hears [it directed to] Rickert. Heidegger describes here a thinking that is so order-oriented that ultimately it seeks to place the temporal under the eternal. This is a beautiful and interesting formulation. In it, according to Heidegger, there was a philosophy that stood against relativism and that encompasses the absolute in systematic form and arranges all the problems of the history of philosophy in a grand context. Now the counter-thesis of Heidegger was that in both of these forms [relativism and absolute idealism], what is essential in philosophy is missed and covered up. What one had to do instead was to find the roots of philosophical questioning in [the being of] the concrete, factual human Dasein [*faktischen menschlichen Dasein*]. This is what "facticity" means: the concrete, factual existence of the human [*das Dasein des Menschen*]. In accordance with the subject matter, however, it means still more than this. I have given some thought to the formation of the word that "facticity" comes from. *Factum* is indeed really quite enough. But it happens that in neo-Kantianism the ultimate foundation of apriorism was the *factum* of science. In this case, this word would certainly not be right!

From the standpoint of the history of the word, one might initially deal with the word "facticity" with regard to the theological problem that was posed by Hegel's synthesis of faith and knowledge. The Christian church with its Easter faith has to maintain the *factum* of the Resurrection. "Facticity" as a word emphasizes the factuality of the *factum*. So facticity becomes a formulation that is challenging for our will to understand, something like when in *Being and Time* Heidegger speaks of the "thrownness" of Dasein. For Heidegger, thrownness belongs to human existence in a world that man comes into without being asked, and one is called away from this world also without being asked. In all of life's "thrownness" one also lives toward one's future, a future toward which one is projected.

In this situation hermeneutics [as a hermeneutics of facticity] is focused on something that is *not understandable* [life]. Indeed, this is somehow always the case for hermeneutics. Challenged by something not understood or not understandable, hermeneutics is brought onto the path of questioning and is required to understand. In this process one never has some advance lordship over all meaningfulness. Instead, one is answering an always self-renewing challenge to take something not understood, something surprisingly other, strange, dark—and perhaps deep—that we need to understand. Nevertheless, this tends to render harmless the paradox that lies in the hermeneutics of facticity. For it is not this or that thing that is not understood by it, but simply the not understandable; the fact of being-there and still more, the understandability of not being, are somehow projected toward sense. This is where we come across insights by the young Heidegger that mark him as a contemporary of those who feel the effects of Nietzsche and of life philosophy. His insight is that [human] life does not just awaken and rise like a seed of corn and be open to all beings, the way the seed arises and grows to flower and bears fruit. But this is the way that Aristotle's metaphysics thought of nous and Hegel thought of absolute knowledge. In contrast to this, Heidegger says that life is actually creating disguises and cover-ups constantly, and restores itself [*um sich aufrichtet*]. There is a saying of Heidegger on which many unfortunate Heidegger translators have suffered shipwreck—and many weak interpreters also: *Das Leben is diesig.* One must understand something about sailing and know the sea in order to understand this saying. It has nothing to do with the German word *dies hier,* "this here." *Diesig* means "foggy"! If one continues reading Heidegger's words, they clearly show that the interpreters have not understood them correctly. Carrying it further, the word means, with regard to life, that "It clouds over [*Es nebelt sich*, deceives us] again and again." Certainly waking life is bright and open for everything—but then suddenly everything is covered over and hidden. Thus, we come again and again to the limit of all openness, a limit which always retreats once again.

As a philosopher, Schelling designated such limits with the expression *das Unvordenkliche* [that which could not be thought of in advance]. This is a very beautiful German word. Its magic rests on the fact that we can perceive in it a real trace of this advance movement in our mind which always wants to think ahead and beyond; but over and over, again and again, it comes upon something that could never have been anticipated or planned for by using our imagination or by thinking ahead. That is *das Unvordenkliche*. Everyone knows something of this. The theologian would have still more to say about it than I would. I would remind you, for instance, of the *Unvordenklichkeit* [unanticipatability] of home. And one can never communicate to someone what home [*Heimat*] is for you. A possession? Something lost? Seeing something once again? Memory and return to what one recollected? All of these are unanticipatabilities that come together in human life. They may demand great effort from our understanding. One would like to uncover what is still shrouded in darkness, and yet one finds that it continually escapes us and yet, for all that, it is always still there. This is exactly what the hermeneutic of facticity knows about. Such a hermeneutic obviously does not follow a curiosity addicted to order, an addiction found in the system of philosophy taught from the podiums of our universities. No, it deals in its way with another kind of understanding—with what *life itself* offers us to be understood. The hermeneutics of facticity stands before the puzzle that Dasein, thrown into the *Da* [there], explicates itself to itself, and constantly projects itself on its own possibilities, on what it encounters. Heidegger made this "as" of the interpretation of its future possibilities the hermeneutical "as." [To interpret is to see something *as* something.] Actually, we are dealing with a translation here from the Greek—and suddenly with a leap we are once again back at our beginnings. In Aristotle's grounding of metaphysics we know this "as" in the phrase *das Seiende als Seiendes* (Greek: *on he on*). This phrase does not mean *das Seiende* here, however, but *das Sein;* it refers to whatever it is and that it is, regardless of all—now this, now that—that may happen to it. Later on, being [*das Sein*], that is, that which remains what it is independent and separate from all predications by us and accidents, was formulated into the Neoplatonic conceptual word, "the Absolute." Very early, Heidegger sought help in Aristotle for understanding what being [*Sein*] authentically is. In one of his early lecture notes we find this note to himself: "From the hermeneutics of facticity back to A." This A refers to Aristotle, naturally. When one takes as one's starting point hermeneutical facticity—that is, Dasein's self-explication—then one sees that Dasein always projects itself on its future and therewith is aware of its finitude. Heidegger, in his famous phrase in *Being and Time,* "Vorlaufen zum Tode" [existentially running forward toward death, always having death in mind as one's ownmost possibility], designated this as the authenticity of Dasein. This being in the there, then, is Dasein existing between two darknesses: the future and what one has from the past. This is what the hermeneutic of facticity teaches us. It is directed against the radically opposite concept of Hegel's absolute spirit and its self-transparency.

What *Sein* really means remains obscure, despite all the poems about the experience of one who was brought up in the thinking of the West and its religious horizon.[4] What does "it is there" mean? This is the secret of the *Da* [there], not a secret of *what* is there, or *that* it is there. It does not mean the existence [Dasein] belonging to human beings, as in the term "struggle for existence," but rather it means that the "there" arises in the human being, and yet despite all one's openness it remains at the same time hidden, concealed.

Heidegger took up both of these aspects in his well-known discussions of the concept of *aletheia* [truth] as both unconcealment and concealment. It is especially the tendency to concealment in Dasein that poses a hermeneutical task. One must uncover and explicate whatever the will to understand runs up against. This is what we meant by Heidegger's term *Destruktion* in the 1920s. His usage of the word at that time did not have the destructive sense that some of the English and French translators have given it, namely destruction and nihilism. Rather, it is a dismantling process [*Abbau*] for purposes of explication.[5] It goes against concealment [*Verdeckung*] and undertakes an opening to view [*Freilegung*] of what had been concealed. Concealment, however, happens in all of Dasein's self-explication. Every Dasein understands itself on the basis of its environment and daily life, and articulates itself in the linguistic form in which it lives and moves. To this extent, then, there is always and everywhere concealment—and always also the deconstructive explication of concealments.

Let's move now to a narrower and more technical sense of the word *Destruktion,* a sense that to a large extent Heidegger's philosophical beginnings determined. He showed us how "deconstruction" must be practiced on the concepts in which contemporary philosophical thought was operating. This too was deconstruction, and this too happened for the same purpose of a laying something open to view. What is "consciousness" anyway? This question takes us back from Hegel and Kant to Leibniz and Descartes to late Scholasticism, to Christian Neoplatonism, then to heathen Platonism and ultimately to Aristotle, Plato, and Parmenides. When Heidegger spoke of deconstruction [*Destruktion*] in this connection he had Aristotle in mind, and above all Aristotle as Thomistically interpreted, the tradition in which he was brought up. But now, at the beginning of the twentieth century, the genius of his thinking had worked itself free of this interpretation; so now he returned afresh to Aristotle studies. There he discovered that in Aristotle too the original self-explicatedness [*Selbstausgelegtheit*] of human being-there [*des menschlichen Daseins*], of the being of a human being, was to be found, although it was not immediately to be seen in his *Physics* or *Metaphysics,* both of which of course have a central significance for the history of metaphysics. What Heidegger apparently had in mind when he wrote that note, "Back to A," which we cited earlier, was that he wanted to learn from the self-explication of Dasein [of existence, of the human being] that he found in Aristotle, and from A's wonderful discipline in thinking. So he began with the *Rhetoric*! He found the second book of this work especially important with regard to his explication of the significance of *Befindlichkeiten* [attunements; see *Being and Time,* section 29] for Dasein. We find an important passage at the close of sixth book of the *Nicomachean Ethics,* where Aristotle takes up the doctrine of *phronesis* [practical wisdom, the wisdom of daily life], a doctrine on which I myself later capitalized so much. In this early program Heidegger perceived the illumination that Dasein throws on daily life, and he sought on this basis to develop a quite new way into metaphysics, and thereby to move metaphysics from its scholastic distance from life back into the midst of it.

This is the way that Heidegger himself viewed the matter at that time, and thus it came about that he tried to see the *on he on,* (the *Seiende as Seiendes*), that is, the "being-question," through Aristotelian eyes, and this meant in a counterposition to Plato, whose view perhaps rested on a questionable construction. But going from the matter itself, it is certainly correct that whatever *Sein* [being] is, a movedness must pertain to it that belongs to *Sein.* Indeed, nobody can doubt that in the world around us we see moved beings in their movedness. Thus, in 1922–23 Heidegger, already engaged in the first project he tried on Aristotle, tried to think highest being as movement, and therewith to aim at a concept of God whose essence is motion and who causes all beings to be present. On the basis of this, one can understand that under the sign of Aristotle the pantheistic heresy always played a role in the Christian church. This is less the case in the Aristotelian description of God as the first Unmoved Mover than in the idea that God's divinity is always in the motion of constant perception of all that is (which is to say, all that is present to God). This is no surprise. Therefore Heidegger was especially interested in Siger von Brabant, and when he came to Marburg, he first purchased Mandonet's *The Belgian Philosophers* and the *Summa* of Thomas Aquinas.

Now we must take a further step in order to see how, in the long history of thought, its Greek beginnings have been transformed and indeed minted into a basic schema of ontology and Aristotle's *Physics* came to be called metaphysics. What we mean by "nature" here [in the traditional ontology] is not that something is in motion, but that something is so and not other, that it is itself only in the condition of motion (on the basis of the *arche* of kinesis). But to do this we·must completely separate ourselves from the concept of motion in our [modern] physics. This view leaves entirely aside what is presently in motion, and in this way we derive the basic laws of mechanics from the relationship of place, time, and rate of motion, which belong to motion as such. Thus, Galilean physics abstracts completely from the thing that is actually in motion at the time. I am reminded of my learning from my instruction in physics that a feather in near-vacuum falls almost exactly as fast as a slab of lead. But against this [scientific] approach, I would say that movement or motion refers not only to this event of falling as such, but above all to the being of the *vis motrix* [moving force] of the living being. Heidegger used this idea for several very profound analyses, which we see in his article of 1939 on the second book of the *Physics*.[6] Basically one is already dealing in it with the context of *Being and Time*.[7] So Aristotle's *Physics* was in a certain sense his most important book. For there, in the basic character of pure movedness, the *Da* of *Sein* becomes visible—and exactly through this it is also concealed! In the puzzling miracle of mental wakefulness lies the fact that seeing something and thinking something are a kind of motion, but not the kind that leads from something to its end. Rather, when someone is looking at something, this is when he or she truly sees it, and when one is directing one's thinking at something, this is when one is truly pondering it. So motion is also a holding oneself in being, and through this motion of human wakefulness [*Wachseins*] there blows the whole breath of the life-process [*Lebendigkeit*, liveliness], a process that ever and again allows a new perception of something to open up. These are basic elements of the *Da* [there], elements that allow us to see the categories and concepts which Aristotle first worked out in his *Physics*.

Among these is the concept of *energeia,* the concept of being-at-work or being a workpiece at work. Now in Greek thinking the finished thing is the telos, and in fact the highest distinction and level of living nature is to have motion *in itself* (it is already completely living and already has its telos in itself). For the artistically gifted Greeks with their skills, however, a thing was only truly there that was completely finished, was completely there like things that always are what they are, or are constantly as finished products. Thus the Aristotelian physics leads to onto-theology. When Heidegger was planning his projects on the metaphysics of Aristotle, he was obviously driven by the idea that *Sein*—whether living or not—is motion in Aristotle's sense of it, is in motion; that is, it is motion as the *energeia* of the *dynamei on* [power of being]. Aristotle, by studying the thinking of his predecessors, had worked out the conceptual means for being able to say what being means, in spite of the constant being-other that resides in motion!

As Heidegger was working out these matters, he did so in a farewell effort at a critique of theology. As it happens, in the 1980s I discovered these early writings among my own papers. I hastened to publish them. In writing my introduction to this group of early papers of Heidegger, I chose for them the title "Theological Writings of Heidegger's Youth."[8] This title playfully alludes to Hegel's theological *Jugendschriften* [*Writings in His Youth*], about which scholars quite justifiably have maintained that, indeed, they really contain very little theology and are far more like a political tract. Heideggers "theological" *Jugendschrift*, too, appears to concern itself not with theology but with Aristotle.

And yet it was basically a theological critique which Heidegger, as a troubled Christian, intended. It was this interest that caused him to find Aristotle to be so strong, and it was this interest that caused him to try to understand the basic drives of the human Dasein, in the same ways as Aristotle long ago had understood being human in his *Rhetoric* and in his practical philosophy. Heidegger wanted to put Aristotelian metaphysics to the test in order to see whether its questions about being actually sufficed for what he himself was seeking. What he found there is obviously not what we as persons with a Christian education seek answers for, when confronted with the mystery of the Incarnation of Christ. This mystery is something that absolutely cannot be equated with what the parousia was for the Greeks, where their gods appeared to humans. How is one to cope with understanding the mystery of the Trinity, for instance, which Augustine himself ventured to approach only with very careful analogies? No, these are completely different mysterious things, for which we as thinking beings have not matured to the point of being able to understand. And certainly they are not graspable with the categories of Aristotelian physics and metaphysics, and still less with the categories of modern science. In light of this, the debate between Luther and the other Reformers over the Holy Sacrament is a powerful symbolic expression of the conceptual difficulty of coming to terms with the holy message of the Christian church through thinking. Heidegger's return to Aristotelian metaphysics is to be understood as a return that is intended to be a critique of theology. This is nearly as challenging to understand as the handwritten motto that stood at the beginning of his program. There it said that in the taking up of Aristotle, Christian theology had simply *borrowed a conceptuality*—and indeed a conceptuality that is not suited to express what one deals with in the Christian faith.

We need to remember that we all no longer live back in the time of the Greek beginnings. The reencounter with Aristotle, and indeed with the whole of Greek thinking that has dominated Western history, does not in any way alter the fact that we have been irrevocably stamped by our own complex Western heritage. Certainly it now comes to our attention that in this tradition of thought are contained concealments of the original Greek beginnings. But every cover-up also has its life-function. We all know that. Indeed, what would life be without forgetting? And yet we find ourselves now faced with the task of clearing up these concealments in our thought and of going back to original experiences in order to raise these up to the level of concepts. For this task, Greek thought remains a model. The original experiences represented in Greek thinking—appropriated and yet not thought through by them—have helped to shape the scientific culture of our present day. It required Hegel's highly developed art of thinking to bring about a certain mediation between our modern Enlightenment and the Christian message. And this is exactly why for Heidegger Hegel was a constant challenge to his thinking. Heidegger saw in Hegel the last Greek thinker. But how can a mere dialectical mediation by Hegel help us in our debate with the modern Enlightenment? Heidegger had this question constantly in mind in the last years of his life, and certainly also in his tour of the Greek Aegean Sea where he experienced an island emerging from the morning fog. He wrote to me from there: "We still do not think the Greeks in a way that is Greek enough." ["Wir denken die Griechen noch immer nicht griechisch genug."] And: "What is *Sein* for the Greeks?—Being is 'appearing'!"

What was Heidegger trying to say with this comment? Was it that we are always forgetting our distance from the Greeks? Or was it that to the extent we hold on to the Greeks, we will be able to advance on our own way? Or is he calling to mind Hölderlin's experience of the divine in nature and in history? Any of these may be what Heidegger meant.

Certainly in these early years, Heidegger never imagined that even to the end of his life he would lack the conceptuality he needed for his life task. He himself expressed this point later on when he spoke of the overcoming of metaphysics or of the "language of metaphysics" and spoke about the time of transition in which we found ourselves. For him, the language of metaphysics [of presence metaphysics] was something which we fall back into over and over again—even he. Heidegger recognized this fact again and again in his writings, and he made us feel this all the more through his own audacious use of language. He knew that language was like an element that carried us within it, and yet he himself often had to use violence and turn language against itself!

For instance: What in fact, is the "language of metaphysics"? What does "language" mean here? I myself have not been able to accept many of Heidegger's linguistic violences with language and I have not been able to follow many of his powerful interpretations, but at the same time I have tried to develop further the hermeneutic impulse I received from him. I have not, however, tried to go back [as he did] and trace the steps that thought has taken in the West and then treat this as a wrong path; rather, I have dedicated my own hermeneutical efforts to entering into a conversation with Plato and Plotinus, Augustine or Thomas Aquinas, or whoever, in order to at least partially gain ground in my attempt to find the right language for what I myself was seeking. Certainly we all stand in the ontological difference and we will never be able to overcome it, or want to overcome through thought the theological difference between the divine and the creaturely. Hegel wisely abandoned such a Gnostic effort, rather than completely succumbing to it. In any case, it was not Hegel's path that Heidegger followed. Rather, he took his orientation from Hölderlin's powerfully poetic assertive power. Although he could not claim for himself the power to create the poetic word, he did not allow conceptually dialectical language to become a temptation to him either.

I have tried to follow in the path which Heidegger showed us. What I understood in the old texts, I always held to be present today, certainly not in their words but in our words, even when I only succeeded in getting a little closer to their meaning. But in the present case we are dealing with something quite different from this. Heidegger's deepest insights show a bond with his contemporary, the Norwegian poet Knut Hamsun, and also I think above all about his constant confrontation with Nietzsche. What we have to do with here, I think, is not just the fact that repression is always at work in our consciousness. Certainly the thing we are conscious of is held up in the bright light of consciousness, and at the same time the other is thereby repressed. No, what is repressed is not simply no longer there. The topic of dreams in psychoanalysis is well known and indeed only constitutes a weak testimony to the power of the structure of drives by virtue of which we constantly have to live. For instance, our thinking and our prejudices are constantly threatened with succumbing to *désir*. There is no concealing from ourselves how hard this is, and this shows how indispensable it is that we recognize that we live in conversation. We seek conversation not only in order to understand the other person better. Rather, we need it because our own concepts threaten to become rigid; and also because when we say something we want the other person to understand what we are thinking. My own efforts at thinking are led by yet another evident fact: the problem is not that we do not understand the other person, but that we don't understand ourselves! For precisely when we seek to understand the other person, we have the hermeneutical experience that we must break down resistance in ourselves if we wish to hear the other as other. This is really a basic determinant of all human existence, and also still governs the success of our "self-understanding." What was called "self-love" [*Selbstliebe*] in the eighteenth century we today call "narcissism."

In whatever way we may bring modern views into connection with older insights, one thing is clear: that language itself is a form of life, and like life, it is hazy [*diesig*]; over and over it will surround us with a haze. Again and again we move for a while in a self-lighting haze, a haze that again envelops us as we seek the right word. Life is easier when everything goes according to one's own wishes, but the dialectic of recognition requires that there can be no easy laurels. We learn this from the resistance we feel in ourselves when we let the other person be right. To make ourselves aware of this, the best help may be for us to get as fully as possible into the matter itself, overcome our own biases, and in the end to see ourselves as put in question—and where does this happen best if not in standing before the other person, a person who exists in himself or herself? So I would like to close with a short saying of Kierkegaard that makes this point especially clear and may even suggest the deeper meaning in my insistence on conversation, for conversation is the medium in which alone language is alive. The saying of Kierkegaard is the title of a talk he once wrote. It is: "Über das Erbauliche in dem Gedanken, gegen Gott allzeit Unrecht zu haben."—"On what is edifying in the thought that against God one is always wrong."

Translated by Richard E. Palmer

Hermeneutics Tracking the Trace [On Derrida]

This late essay by Gadamer (1994) is an important final part of the dialogue with Derrida sadly broken off by their deaths: first, that of Gadamer on March 13, 2002, and then that of Derrida on October 9, 2004. The dialogue was largely unspoken on Derrida's side, while Gadamer repeatedly renewed it over the years in published articles. This essay, translated into English for the first time, is Gadamer's closing statement in that dialogue.

The debate between Gadamer and Derrida entered the public sphere in 1981 at a Sorbonne conference in Paris on "Text and Interpretation." Gadamer and Derrida were among a half-dozen distinguished speakers. Derrida's first hesitant steps toward a dialogue were initially published in French,[1] and later documented in more elaborate form as a book in German in 1984 containing the papers from the conference.[2] Five years later the documents of the encounter and several later articles by Gadamer plus twelve commentaries were collected and translated in the book *Dialogue and Deconstruction: The Gadamer-Derrida Encounter.*[3] Of course, there were several other personal encounters over the years in France, Germany, and Italy. A major public continuation of the dialogue came in 1988 in an event sponsored by the French Department at Heidelberg, where Gadamer and Derrida, two famous followers of Heidegger, spoke on the subject of Heidegger's politics. This was in response to a rather sensational book by Victor Farias, first published in French translation, *Heidegger et le nazisme.*[4] The Heidelberg encounter was not documented, and a note sent to me from a friend in Heidelberg at the time claimed that nothing of philosophical interest had transpired there, so our book on the Gadamer-Derrida debate should continue on schedule.

Gadamer's original effort at dialogue with Derrida at the Sorbonne conference, a lecture he titled "Text and Interpretation" (later he lengthened it for publication in 1984), was based on his recognition of the debt they both had to Heidegger.[5] This approach did not work, as is generally acknowledged on all sides, perhaps because of Gadamer's special advantage of having a close lifelong association with the person and philosophy of Heidegger. What ultimately did lay a bridge to Derrida were Gadamer's interpretations of the poetry of Paul Celan.[6] Here Derrida could claim some common ground with Gadamer and some expertise in Judaism and Celan.

Derrida's 2003 lecture in homage to Gadamer arose out of his acceptance of an official invitation by Heidelberg University to speak at a university-wide celebration of Gadamer's life on February 11, 2003, about a year after Gadamer's death. In it Derrida expressed genuine affection and respect for Gadamer. In his lecture Derrida focused on a poem of Celan, a topic that had been interpreted by Gadamer in his 1973 book on Celan's "Atemkristall" cycle of poems, *Who Am I and Who Are You?* (*Wer bin ich, wer bist du?*).[7] Derrida later delivered his homage to Gadamer lectures twice in Paris in the same year.[8] He then immediately published them as a small book, *The Uninterrupted Dialogue between Two Infinities, the Poem.*[9] In it he took his lead from the analysis of a single poem of Celan and in the course of the lecture invoked several important themes in the thought of Gadamer.

Gadamer published his Celan essays and books as a kind of penance in the years after the untimely suicide death of Paul Celan.[10] And it seems that perhaps Derrida too repented of the harshness of his followers' attacks on Gadamer (as a "closet essentialist," for instance, in John Caputo's *Radical Hermeneutics*), so he gave public lectures in Heidelberg and Paris in which he published his affectionate tribute to Gadamer. A year after the publication of this tribute [*Beliers: le dialogue ininterrompu*], in October 2004, he himself succumbed to pancreatic cancer. Thus, the late tribute to Gadamer set an important matter straight, and was among his last significant publications.

The present essay by Gadamer, "Hermeneutics Tracking the Trace" ["Hermeneutik auf der Spur"], was written in 1994 and published for the first time in the final volume of his collected works in 1995.[11] This essay is Gadamer's effort at age ninety-four to sum up his areas of agreement and disagreement with Derrida. The rather lengthy text was not originally given as a lecture, unlike many of his writings, and his choice to write it especially for inclusion in the final volume of his collected works indicates its importance to him. Although it was not included in the original *Gadamer Lesebuch,* I have added it because of the wide interest in Gadamer's relationship to Derrida and Derrida's death in the meantime.

In his essay, Gadamer is at pains to emphasize the common ground between hermeneutics and deconstruction. His opening sentence asserts that deconstruction lies within the purview of hermeneutics. The thrust of the essay as a whole is a certain regret that Derrida did not

choose to place deconstruction in relationship to philosophical hermeneutics, but rather to approach it as a continuation of Heidegger's project of a recovering from metaphysics and in relationship to French literary criticism, to place it in the context of intertextuality. In this context
he takes up Derrida's terms and explores them in the light of the project
of overcoming Western metaphysics. The first term is "logos" as Derrida uses it in "logocentrism" in an argument against the metaphysics
of presence. Here Gadamer goes back to the richness of the term in ancient Greek philosophy, in Heraclitus, Socrates, the Stoics, and the Gospel of John. In Greek philosophy the understanding of the logos is not
tied to phonocentrism (centeredness in sound), but Derrida views metaphysics in this way on account of his argument with structuralism about
the priority of voice over writing. So Gadamer calls for a reemphasis
on the multiple dimensions of the meaning of "logos" in Greek. Likewise, he argues that Derrida's understanding of metaphysics is really
more Kantian than Greek, and that getting back to Greek metaphysics
in its complexity would be a better course than simply writing it off as
something to be overcome. Gadamer claims to be following Heidegger in
seeking a "recovery" (*Verwindung*) from metaphysics as if from an illness
rather than an overcoming it as an opponent in battle. He concludes the
first of the essay's three parts by saying that broad areas of agreement
exist between his philosophical hermeneutics and deconstruction, but
"the usage of the word 'metaphysics' needs to be more circumscribed."
Derrida's conception of metaphysics is not based on Greek metaphysics, says Gadamer, and is also infected with the problems arising from
his confrontation with French structuralism and the modern theory
of signs.

In the second section Gadamer turns to Derrida's concept of writing. He begins by agreeing with Derrida that writing is not a copy of vocal sounds, as structuralists describe it when they argue for the primacy
of the oral element in language. In contrast, however, Gadamer asserts
that writing presupposes the oral element when one reads, because one
voices what one reads. In fact, Gadamer notes in *Truth and Method* that
up to Augustine's time all reading was reading aloud. There was no
silent reading in ancient Greece! He agrees with Derrida in preferring
the term "trace" to that of "sign." He disagrees with Levinas' conception
of the trace in terms of the face of the other, and begins to probe the
process of understanding the trace. This takes Gadamer in the direction of a hermeneutical approach to traces and therefore into what he
describes as a conversation with a text, the question and answer of interpretation, and the being-with that is involved in the process of reading
a text. Here he finds intertextuality actually less helpful to interpreting
the trace than hermeneutics because the former multiplies meanings

and takes one down false paths, whereas hermeneutics seeks the direction of meaning appropriate to the text.

In the third and final section, Gadamer examines Derrida's interpretation of the Greek term *chora*. Here he finds that Derrida's project of overcoming logocentrism and metaphysics to the exclusion of a careful examination of the context of its use in Plato's *Timaeus* leads him into a shallow definition of the term and into attributing to it a misinterpretation of Greek metaphysics in Plato and Aristotle. Here Gadamer lures the discussion into the area of his lifelong specialization, namely Plato. He places the *chora* [primal space] in the context of Plato's effort to define a "third thing" in terms of the underlying mathematical character of reality. He agrees with Derrida, Heidegger, and Vernant that the idea of moving from mythos to logos is shallow and does not apply here. But he says that the trace does not lead us to the beyond of the One or to the Divine. What it leads to is necessity—based on mathematics. He says that intertextuality leads one in many directions; on the other hand, interpretation is a game in which one has to go along with the meaning in which one participates. Gadamer complains that the richness of going along with a meaning and participating in it are not found in deconstruction, however much it may open up new horizons.

He concludes with a discussion of interpretation as *Zwischenrede*—interruption—and of eminent text, another favorite term. Interpreting a text is always an interruption of a process, and an eminent text is text in its highest possible form. His final paragraph poses the following as the essential question of hermeneutics: *What must the reader know? Or what should the reader want to know?* Obviously the most important thing for the reader to know is the context, for it is the context that gives the direction of meaning, and the reader needs to know and be aware of it. Whether Gadamer's appeal to hermeneutics as a better alternative to intertextuality and whether his criticism of Derrida's interpretation of logos and metaphysics are able to invalidate the deconstructive project of Heidegger and then Derrida is open to question. But Gadamer's contention that we will approach this task better if we go more deeply into precisely what Greek metaphysics is and how it was already misinterpreted by Aristotle is less dubious. And since metaphysics is philosophy, as Gadamer says, we will never escape it, kill it, or go beyond it. The most we can hope for is to "recover" from [understand more deeply] the forms of it which have guided Western culture for millennia. That there have been longstanding misinterpretations of Plato and Aristotle, and that we need to confront these, are contentions on which I think Gadamer, Heidegger, and Derrida are all in agreement.

* * *

Hermeneutics Tracking the Trace [On Derrida]

As a topic, deconstruction clearly falls within the realm of hermeneutics. But in categorizing hermeneutics, at least, one cannot imagine any particular method that would show it to belong to a group of scholarly disciplines that stand in contrast to the natural sciences.[1] Rather, hermeneutics offers a description of the whole realm in which humans reach an understanding with each other. In my own writings about hermeneutics, the discussion is never only about the sciences [*Wissenschaften*]. Derrida, too, can also say about deconstruction that he would like it to overcome the narrowing effect of methods. On this point we are in agreement. In spite of this, however, it seems that up to now we have not succeeded in reaching an understanding with each other. Of course, reaching an understanding does not necessarily mean agreeing with each other. On the contrary, where people are in general agreement, the reaching of an understanding is not necessary. Rather, reaching an understanding is always sought and sometimes achieved in reference to something quite specific about which full agreement does not exist. In our encounters in Paris and Heidelberg,[2] it seems that Derrida and I never managed to establish a common ground. Looking at the responses to our discussion historically clearly shows this on both sides. Those on the hermeneutics side complain that Derrida seeks to escape dialogue, whether as a conscious strategy or more or less unconsciously. On the other side, the deconstructionists do not find that my contribution to the discussion in the Paris conversation of 1981, and then in more detail when I revised it for publication,[3] contributes at all to a genuine conversation with Derrida. Instead, hermeneutic philosophy, according to Derrida, has simply behaved in a defensive way and remained completely in the realm of metaphysical thinking. Thus, it basically did not address the concerns of deconstruction.

Such a peaceful separation of the two sides really will not do in philosophy—as if it were somehow possible for different directions of thought in philosophy to operate side by side without ever touching. For each side refers to an experience we can all have. One should be able to resolve differing opinions about this experience and reach some kind of understanding through questions and answers that examine the matter—in other words, through a critical conversation. Thus, the hermeneutics side would certainly not dispute the fact that it too experiences "dissémination," and it will not dispute that such things as agreements, wordplay, and overtones are present in every talk with which one has to do. It would only insist that in each case a new task for thinking is posed, a task that invites us to reach a new agreement in understanding.

Back in the 1960s, when I had finished up my own project in philosophical hermeneutics and offered it to the public, I paused to take a look at the world around me. At that time, two important things struck me, in addition to the works of the later Wittgenstein. One of these was that I met the poet Paul Celan, in whose late works I began to immerse myself. The other was the fact that Derrida's essay "Ousia et Grammè,"[4] published in the *Festschrift for* [Jean] *Beaufret,* came into my hands, followed later by the several important books that Derrida published in 1967, which I immediately began to study. In "Ousia et Grammè" it was fully clear that Derrida, starting from his reading of Husserl, accepted Heidegger's critique of how the concept of being had been obscured by metaphysics [in Western philosophy], and how in him this critique became an effective force. At any rate, in reference to the onto-theology of Aristotle, it certainly is true that for Aristotle the meaning of "being" could be read off the highest existent being. Of course, I had some difficulty in understanding how Derrida took up this Heideggerian critique of the Greek concept of being and carried it further, and how in addition certain motifs of the later Heidegger led Derrida—partly in a positive way, partly in a critical modification—from Heidegger's concept of *Destruktion* to his own concept of *Dekonstruktion.* In particular, what interested me was the fact that Derrida applied his thinking in this area not just to metaphysical constructions in philosophy but also to works of literature—particularly since something I myself also constantly had in mind was the common basis in life that is shared by philosophy and poetry. Even with regard to Heidegger himself and his interpretations of literature and art, often I could only with great difficulty still recognize a text of literature or work of art in terms of what that work was saying to me, although I always found his approach to such "texts" very significant. Actually, both thinkers, Derrida and Heidegger, were interpreting themselves [and their thought] and not that which they intended to interpret. On no account should one disregard these interpretations! Heidegger takes the assertion made by an artwork so seriously that he ventures to use [interpretive] violence in order to accommodate it to his own thinking. But at least Heidegger does not remain stuck in the outer courtyard of aesthetic neutrality. The same thing applies to the way Heidegger lays claim to Nietzsche, and also the way Derrida invokes Nietzsche![5] What Heidegger in *Being and Time* had developed through his distinctions among *Vorhandenheit* (being merely present and on hand), *Zuhandenheit* (being immediately available to hand), and *Dasein* (being-there) was really a critique of the self-understanding of metaphysics. This eventually was sharpened into his slogan, "the overcoming of metaphysics." In doing this, Heidegger found himself in a debate with

Nietzsche, whom he understood to be a kind of last, radical consequence of metaphysics. In contrast to this, in his later writings Heidegger tried to lay the foundation for a new understanding of Being.

Now Derrida, too, turned to Nietzsche for inspiration, but in Nietzsche's *Gay Science* he saw a solitary path into the Open, so he turned his whole energies toward not deserting the huge task of deconstruction. In this connection, both Heidegger and Derrida are well aware that philosophy can never totally and completely cut itself loose from its historical heritage in Western metaphysics. This is why Heidegger introduced the weaker formulation, "*recovering from* metaphysics" [*Verwindung der Metaphysik*], and precisely with this Derrida established the tirelessness of his deconstructive effort. These, then, are clearly some commonalities that initially offer themselves to us.

In light of this, I myself have pondered again and again the relationship between [Heidegger's] *Destruktion* and [Derrida's] deconstruction from the vantage point of my own hermeneutical efforts.[6] Basically I can only try to convey here several questions that show what I see as the common ground on which—perhaps!—all three of us stand.

First question: what actually does the concept of *présence* contain within it such that Derrida with his concept of metaphysics would like to go behind it? Basically, Derrida seems to regard the definition of being as "presence" as the very matrix of the history of metaphysics. He writes, "One could show that all names for grounding or establishing, for principle, or for 'center,' are always only pointing to the *invariant* element of a presence (for example, as *eidos, arche, telos, energeia, ousia*—and essence, *Existenz*, substance, subject, *aletheia*, transcendentality, consciousness, God, man, etc.)." Seemingly, all of this Derrida has united in the term *logocentrism*. But the question is, what does "presence" in the true sense have to do with "logos"? Is he only thinking here of truth in the form of an assertion [*Satzwahrheit*]? If so, one very easily recognizes in it the form of truth that for Heidegger was the target of his *Destruktion*. What Derrida has in mind with the term "logocentrism," however, is actually what Heidegger had in mind with his critique of Husserl. What corroborates my point here is how near this comes to the task of the young Heidegger, in particular, which was to release philosophy from its entrapment in the neo-Kantian logic of judgments. When Heidegger began his studies of Kierkegaard and Aristotle and had in mind the *Metaphysics* of Aristotle, what this really entailed at that time was that *Sein* revealed itself in its beingness [*Seinsheit*] as highest being; as the Divine. This is how I too understood the *Metaphysics* in those days. It fits with this that Heidegger, as he still did in the supplement to his Nietzsche volumes, saw Plato as the preparation for Aristotle's posing of the question of being as being. It is my view today that this is certainly not a very compelling view with regard to Plato himself, when one remembers how, immediately after this, Plato sought to go *beyond being* in his dialectical ascent to the Good itself, the Beautiful itself, or the One itself. This applies more to Aristotle insofar as he erected the doctrine of the Mover God on the foundations of his physics—even though Heidegger himself, as his later interpretation of Aristotle's *Physics* B 1 shows, was always tracking down the *Ereignis* [happening, coming into manifestation, be-ing] of the *Da* [there].

However that may be, the *Metaphysics* of Aristotle was later on taken up into the doctrines of the church (in a Christian transformation of it) as *theologia rationalis* [rational theology], whereas Plato [and his view of Being] was in the Christian Middle Ages seen as close to crossing the boundary into heresy.

Of course, it is obvious that the movement of Greek thinking as a whole is not expressed in the Aristotelian teaching of the Prime Mover [in the *Metaphysics*]. On the contrary, it is significant that Heidegger's own new appropriation of Aristotle does not take its start from the *Metaphysics* but from the *Rhetoric*, and the *Ethics* as well. In particular, the doctrine of practical knowledge [in the *Ethics*] came to have a foundation-laying significance for Heidegger's own path, and with respect to this point I myself have to a large extent taken the same path. Certainly Heidegger would have done better had he adopted Plato's very explicit critique of the logocentrism of metaphysics, which is found in the excursus to Plato's *Seventh Letter*. There one finds Plato's well-known critical remarks that were prompted by a lecture on his writings that had previously been presented to the court of the tyrant Dionysus of Syracuse. In response to this, Plato composed what was obviously an exactly worked out statement on how the communication of thoughts to other persons is possible at all and how thinking can be taught.[7] It was also in this statement that the logical definition was explicitly worked out. But this option was shown to be just as insufficient as had been naming the issue or mere intuition. Even what is mediated by these means [naming, intuition] and what is at work in all thinking and never adequately expressed in assertions, is nevertheless shaped in the soul into knowledge and correct opinion, and finally into the partial gaining of "nous" [mind]. All of these are only mediations of the *Sache selbst*, the matter about which one is concerned, and they remain adapted and subordinate to the living reality of conversation. The decisive point is this: it is not via written means alone, but in general only in *conversation* that the glimmer of an understanding can pass from one partner to another.

In view of the living character of conversation, it is no accident that Plato named the path of his own thinking a "dialectic." And in the *Republic,* when outlining his educational plan for developing future rulers, it was dialectic that was expressly required as the step needed for the ruler to go beyond mathematics. Dialectic is richly exemplified in the thought-play of the Platonic dialogues. These dialogues are not intended to be merely a critical overcoming of counterarguments, nor are they merely demonstrations of the art of argumentation. Rather, a dialogue leads the partner in the conversation to an admission of not knowing, and throws him back on his own thinking. To this extent, dialectic merely has a preparatory function, like the art of creating bewilderment that one finds, for example, in Plato's *Parmenides.* I think it would certainly be hard to subsume this process we have been describing in Plato under the commonly accepted concept of "metaphysical thinking." On the other hand, when one sees Aristotle in his *Physics* turn toward first principles [*archai*] in such a way that the leap beyond the logos is accomplished, namely a leap to the nous, then indeed one could call this new dimension a step toward metaphysics. To the degree that, in this metaphysics, the highest *arche* as First Mover is called "the Divine" and is grasped as pure entelechy [complete actuality compared to potentiality], this step achieves a new accessibility. From the standpoint of folk religion, one could certainly understand this First Mover as the Divine, as a being that is beyond physical nature. But what can metaphysics really mean in Plato? In the *Republic* (509b9) the "step beyond" which Plato has in mind and which finds its expression in transcendence expressly means that it is a step over being to that which is "beyond being" [*Jenseits des Seins*]. Thus, perhaps Derrida should view what he calls "metaphysical thinking" more from the vantage point of this Platonic transcendence than by starting from Aristotelian conceptual determinations which have come to be fixed into writing as "substance" or "essence."

|

If one returns to Derrida after this conceptual-historical clarification I have offered of what metaphysics really is and how it was wrested away from Greek dialectic by logic, one can, I believe, come nearer to seeing what Derrida himself had in mind with the artificial coinage *différance.* First, he takes as his starting point the concept of signs and how in every sign a transgression [*Überschritt*] is accomplished. No sign points to itself alone but always beyond itself, he says. At this point one will have to ask how Derrida thinks he is going to avoid logocentrism if he is going to take this as his starting point. Given the role that structuralism plays in contemporary French philosophy and given the fact that the sign is a concept that actually harks back to American roots, and, furthermore, given what Derrida has in mind by phonocentrism [centeredness in sound], one could very well expect that Derrida would simply leave to the concept of being in metaphysics its determinative role in philosophy. So I am asking myself at this point if we do not here come up against a limit to what we have in common, a limit I would like to call "phenomenology," because phenomenology is directed critically against all constructions. Heidegger had already been stimulated by this project in Husserl, and he has passed this thought on to us exactly in order to direct our thinking against what Derrida has called "logocentrism." So one has only to understand the true direction and goal of Derrida's thinking, which is embodied in his critique of Husserl, when he recognizes not only the dominance of presence-metaphysics in the logos, but also in the voice that "announces." In the end, one can agree with Derrida that the voice here is a *voix pensée,* a thought contained in the voicing [*eine gedachte Stimme*], in the same way that *écriture* [writing] is also only thought embodied in writing [*nur gedachte Schrift ist*].

The conclusion I draw from all this is: writing and voice are both of them truly inseparable from *reading.* What would writing be without reading, what would reading be without writing, and also without the—perhaps soundless—intonation and articulation of the writing? One should not let oneself be misled by the way Husserl in his struggle against psychologism worked out what he called the ideal unity of meaning. One ought in this case to listen to the word "meaning" with French ears. In French, the words that translate *Bedeutung* [significance] are usually *vouloir dire* (to want to say). Exactly this turn of phrase pulls the ground from under [what Husserl called] the "identity of meaning" [*Identität der Bedeutung*]. For in fact, the words *vouloir dire* carry with them the idea that we can never fully say what we had wanted to say. There are strong previous patterns that we all have—in our speaking as well as in our thinking—that are already formed in us beforehand. With the first word we speak we are involved in the whole game and play of language. In this regard, Heidegger pointed to something we all experience when he said, *Die Sprache spricht.* [Language speaks.] In the French expression of it [*vouloir dire*] this is even more clear. It expresses merely approaching and simply coming close to the meaning [*Sinn,* the sense]—and indeed, what does *Sinn* mean if not that it points in a direction and in that way determines meaning? Heidegger's critique of metaphysics as well as Derrida's program of deconstruction must themselves affirm the difference and the *différance* that resides in this *vouloir-dire*. Nobody can simply think his or her way outside and beyond the kind of thinking in which he or she was formed. Even as more and more we come into contact with the languages of other cultures and other cultural worlds, this contact is above all a net gain for ourselves. We are more at home with our heritage and our mother language, which thinks with us [*die mit uns denkt*].

When Heidegger began his teaching as the successor to Husserl in Freiburg [1928], his inaugural lecture posed a question, which like every genuine question leaves something open. It was: "What is metaphysics?" This lecture was most certainly not supposed to be new testimony in favor of metaphysics. Rather, one should understand the question as follows: what is metaphysics really [*eigentlich*] in contrast to what metaphysics thinks it is? When the questioning poses the question of being [*die Frage nach dem Sein fragt*] to itself, it places before itself the totality of existent things [*das Ganze des Seienden*] and perhaps in doing so obscures the thinking of being—precisely the being that is sought through its questioning! For this reason one must perhaps say—and this is also to be considered in reference to other cultures—that there can never be "philosophy" without metaphysics. And yet philosophy is perhaps only philosophy when it leaves metaphysical thinking and sentence logic behind it! On this path we are always moving between Plato's *anamnesis* [recollection] and Hegel's logic. In the singularity of "concept" and "category," philosophy runs through the whole of the process of recollection that is both determining things in advance and constantly returning back to itself. Heidegger speaks of himself as merely preparing the being-question, because he experiences over and over in language and thinking the dominance of an understanding of being as *Anwesenheit* [presentness] and *Präsenz*. This holds true even in Nietzsche and comes powerfully to light in Heidegger's lifelong struggle with Nietzsche.

Also, the fundamental ontology of Heidegger, as one can call *Being and Time*, should not be taken as his final word. Very soon thereafter he left this, his own transcendental self-interpretation, behind and a whole series of paths and forest paths followed. Precisely Heidegger's own intellectual development shows us the extent to which his efforts in thinking are weighed down more and more by an ever-increasing lack of words [*Sprachnot*]. Obviously this is not to say that Heidegger would have recognized the path of deconstruction as his ultimate goal. Is there really no other way to overcome Aristotelian substance metaphysics or its final fulfillment in Hegel's absolute knowledge than to renounce all conceptual thinking or the *logos* as such?

Of course, one may ask: what is the logos? One should certainly not underestimate the fact that the Socratic-Platonic flight into the logoi [words, theories] already represented a turning away for which metaphysics as the logic of conceptual definition and of demonstration had prepared the way. But is the logos not something quite different from this? For instance, what does "logos" mean in Heraclitus? What does it mean in the case of Socrates' not knowing? And what does it mean in Plato's dialectic? What does the *logos spermatikos* [the seminal Word] of the Stoics mean? And what about the logos found in the Gospel of John? Here the "logos" takes on completely different dimensions, and these prepare one much better for the New Testament thinking of the Incarnation than does the renewal of Aristotelian thinking by medieval metaphysics—not to mention its modern post-Kantian death-struggle. So Heidegger (and whoever follows him) could orient himself critically toward the tradition of metaphysics, in order to destroy the traditional understanding of being in logic and metaphysics. At this point I ask myself: is it not generally the case that thinking always has to ask whether the words and concepts in which it operates, in all the multiplicity of their spreading themselves out and always joining together, create ever new contexts of meaning? To this question I think Derrida—if perhaps also with some hesitation—would say that this is once again the logocentrism of our reigning metaphysical tradition. But now we must ask: does not he himself understand Heidegger's ontological difference as a break, as an opening, as *différance*?

What I mean by this is that for Derrida, too, the uncovering of breaks [*Brüche*] involves a certain thinking further. Indeed, his deconstruction can never be accepted simply as a method of interpreting texts. Derrida himself was the first who saw in this view of deconstruction a complete misunderstanding. But precisely the violence of the breaks ultimately points to an inner framework. Certainly not a framework of truth statements, and certainly not something like a system of philosophy. Rather, violent interaction with texts is only justified in cases where it opens up new horizons—and this is certainly what happens for the thinker.

It is hard to think along with and then think further in an alien language world—this is true not only in the German language world in general but also in the Heideggerian language world. Nevertheless, I find the influence of Husserl in Derrida, above all in his early writings, and I also notice the same tendency to objectivize that one finds in structuralism. In this case, a certain philosophical subsoil can be seen. What one finds offered in structuralism is a logic of the mythical world. But no Greek had ever intended or even imagined such a logic.

Nevertheless, it shines through in the most alien heritage of Lévi-Strauss and Foucault, or even Saussure's theory of language. And all this feels like a step back toward a new [version of the] Enlightenment. Doubtless, Derrida wanted to continue on the path opened up by Husserl, and in doing so he radicalized him. But then when he followed the later Heidegger and his debate with Nietzsche, Derrida perceived certain consequences for his own path. Nevertheless, in Derrida as well as in Heidegger, as they take their paths, we scarcely ever find any opposition to metaphysics that amounts to anything [*ganz einlösbare Entgegensetzung*]. One cannot speak in a way completely different from the way one thinks. This also applies to me when I recognize in the difficult Derridean formulation of concepts like *dissémination* and *différance* something similar to my "effective historical consciousness" or "fusion of horizons." Heidegger certainly took special offense at my use of the word "consciousness" [in this term]. To be quite honest, I must admit that the term *wirkungsgeschichtliches Bewusstsein* [historically influenced consciousness] is only an emergency expression (I lacked the proper words) that tries to emphasize the [historical] temporality of being. What I mean is far clearer when I talk about *Sprachlichkeit* [linguisticality], a term in which the Christian tradition of the *verbum interius* [inner word] shines through. But there, too, one is dealing with a kind of quasi-transcendental "condition of possibility" that is actually more a condition of impossibility, you might say, which is what the Incarnation represents for human understanding. In my writings today [1994], I am trying in a phenomenological style to carry forward Heidegger's effort to "recover" from metaphysics, and at the same time to preserve the dialectic of question and answer. What this means is that I take conversation as my starting point. For me, this is where the *différance* is realized: through conversation, in question and answer, the alterity of the true [*die Alterität des Wahren*] is brought to recognition. In the dialogue of question and answer a constant transgression [*Überschritt*, overstepping] takes place. It may well be that in the question as well as in the answer, the unsaid accompanies the spoken and can be deconstructively disclosed. But it does not first speak through the fact that it is disclosed. Indeed, if it is disclosed, perhaps it will not speak any more. In conversation it is no longer a break [*kein Bruch*] if it only happens that ever new viewpoints announce themselves, ever new questions and answers are posed that ever and again displace/postpone/defer everything. [Rather, in a real conversation] one is in spite of everything led closer [to what one seeks]. One begins to understand, even when one does not know where the conversation is leading.

Certainly, where philosophy is concerned, there are good reasons to say with regard to the conceptual language of metaphysics that one falls back into it over and over again. One should never imagine that philosophical concepts lie ready for us like grain in some kind of storage bin simply waiting to be drawn out. No, thinking in concepts is not fundamentally different from thinking as it happens in the ordinary use of language. Indeed, nobody can simply introduce a usage into language. Rather, the language usage introduces itself; it takes shape in the life-process of language, until finally it has won for itself a firm standing. Conceptual thinking always has unsharp edges, as Wittgenstein has said. So one ought to trace the life that meanings have in language—and that means going back from the speaking itself to how the concept arose out of its *Sitz im Leben* [place in life]. This is what happens, for example, in Heidegger's *Destruktion,* this laying open/disclosure. Derrida's deconstruction is not so very far from this. There the construction emerges expressly in naming. It too deals with the gap [*Bruch*], with constructive compulsions which language uses to dangle thinking from its leading strings. The common goal is always to break conventions of speaking and thinking and to provoke new horizons. Thus, the slogan of phenomenology was "To the things themselves!" This can happen in a very dramatic way. An individual word, for example, may leap into a quite different meaning. Through this, what is customary collapses—and precisely in this way new connections become visible. In the end, it is like this with every fortunate inspiration: it comes to a person in the process of thinking and in such a way that the whole direction of thinking is changed. Just for this reason it seems to me that in such thinking, a new goal is always sketched, however vaguely.

In any case, I think one would not be referring adequately to Heidegger's laying open of the Greek understanding of being, if one thought it dealt only with the issue of clearing away the Latin equivalents of Greek philosophy, which as concepts were then taken into common use, like *essentia,* "subject," or "substance," for example. For Heidegger accomplishing this was only a necessary first step. In this connection the really important point is that in Greek the meaning of the philosophical concepts was very close to their regular use in the language, so that all the very telling and very striking concepts of their philosophy were enriched through their resonance with normal usage. A concept that has become rigid in one's mother tongue can also be enriched in this way, for instance when Heidegger finds being to be property and presence [*Sein als Anwesen*] in Greek thought and in so doing uncovers neglected meanings of "being" as a verb (or even when he writes *Seyn* for *Sein*). The turn back to language rests on the fact that in the actual usage of a word in Greek, one finds a wordless experience lurking in it that is allowed to become part of the thinking of the word. Certainly thinking can also get tangled up by this in dead ends [*Aporien*], as Kant shows in his transcendental dialectic. But it can also be that, as happens in the Greek understanding of the world, *the wordless experience of the world presses itself into the concept.* Then one may find in Greek thinking, with the suddenness of an earthquake or a bolt of lightning, that truth suddenly arises like a counter-world. When a new word pushes one toward a new thinking in this way, this is like an event of emergence [*Ereignis*], and in fact language often does this effortlessly, if it can find the words. When a real breakthrough is demanded [*zugemutet*] from thinking, everything that goes against it collapses, as when, for example, Heidegger reversed the meaning of the title, "What is called thinking" [*Was heisst denken*] to mean "What calls us to/ or demands that we think?" [*Was gebietet uns zu denken?*] In such a reversal something goes down and something new arises.

So areas of agreement do definitely exist between deconstruction and hermeneutics as philosophy, a point which ought to take us further. First of all, both of us had a common starting point, namely the critique that Heidegger opened up of the way that a long-forgotten Greek ontology has lived on. As the later Heidegger has shown in "The Era of the World Picture," this critique also includes a philosophical critique of modern science, which has been based on the concepts of method and objectivity. The parallel in sound of Heidegger's watchword, *Destruktion,* and of Derrida's slogan-word of "deconstruction" is impossible to miss. But obviously the concept of metaphysics with which Derrida works needs to be, as I have tried to show, more carefully circumscribed or defined. Basically, in Derrida's definition, for instance, "metaphysics" is not Greek at all! For him metaphysics is what is associated with that word since Kant's *Critique of Pure Reason.* For Derrida in his deconstructionist essays on dialectic [*deconstruktiven Ansätzen von Dialektik*], metaphysics is only naming what in neo-Kantianism was called "dogmatic metaphysics." Also, one can observe in Derrida's language how his theory of signs intrudes into the language of metaphysics; for instance, when he distinguishes the sensible world of signs from the intelligible world of signs. But the decisive point here is that for Kant the critique of the metaphysics of "pure concepts" undergoes a certain restriction from the side of practical reason. The *Critique of Pure Reason,* for instance, does not propose to demonstrate freedom, or to base metaphysics on physics. Rather, for Kant one has to establish reason as a rational factum. For Kant, metaphysics is possible only as a moralistic metaphysics—only "on the borderline of pure reason," as Natorp loved to say.

Today we find ourselves far away from the original experience of the Greeks, an experience that since Parmenides, Plato, and Aristotle has left its stamp on the conceptual language of philosophy in antiquity and later influenced the conceptual beginnings of Christianity when it took up Greek thought. And finally, with the nominalism of the modern age, Greek thought has prescribed the concept of science.

The works of Derrida pose special difficulties to understanding because he also applies the dismantling of all constructions to himself. From this it follows that if Derrida does undertake the project of bringing his theoretical works into line with each other, so to speak, this threatens to seem like a falling back into metaphysical thinking. And indeed he cannot avoid being himself, as one who represents now one and now the other side. Thus, one is not only justified but positively required to persuade the author about his own identity before he can become a partner at all in a conversation. Of course, the identity that a partner in a conversation has is not a fixed identity and is not even expressible as such. It is simply that which one takes with oneself into a conversation. In the end, I think, we will all have to concede [*bestehen* in the text should be corrected to *gestehen*] that the logos is not a monologue and that all thinking is a dialogue with oneself and with another person.

Derrida's critique of Husserl as he published it under the title of *Voice and Phenomenon* seemed to me to contain a special difficulty. It sounded astonishing. Long before *Being and Time,* we as young students of Heidegger had tried to develop a critique of Husserl. At that time we felt far closer in spirit to Wilhelm von Humboldt [1768–1835] and his beginnings of a philosophy of language than we did to the Husserlian theory of meaning as set forth in the *Logical Investigations* (1900). Of course, at that time we were not able to come up with anything from our sense of surprise and alienation that was right. Looking back even today, difficulties still stand in the way as I look back at Derrida's Husserl critique and try to understand it. For instance, the role of the voice in Derrida's critique of Husserl still appears quite odd to me. Husserl was certainly far more a mathematician [than a philosopher of language]; he carried over into his theory of meaning the way that mathematics normally deals with its objects. Thus, for him the meaning of being is the meaning of ideal being [or the being of ideas] seen like the objects in mathematics. This prompted us in those days to invoke Humboldt's philosophy of language against that of Husserl. Now all of a sudden we recognize in Derrida Heidegger's critique of Husserl. Heidegger took that masterpiece of Husserlian phenomenological analysis, the treatise on time consciousness, as the starting point for his critique. Starting out from the concepts of Dasein, facticity, and futurity, Heidegger used the force of his ontological analysis to take away any basis for a concept of consciousness. [Now the question I ask is:] On the basis of this analysis, how is one to find one's way to Derrida's concepts of sign and trace?

Stronger than our idealistic and phenomenological tradition, which Derrida shares, the French style of literary-critical work seems to have an essential role in the works of Derrida. One cannot understand Derrida just on the basis of Husserl and Heidegger. One must also take into account his debate with sign theory and with structuralism. This, too, is a critical debate, but as I have indicated earlier, the thing he criticized in them continues on as an unacknowledged presupposition in himself. For instance, Derrida sounds as if he were a distant observer of the infinite network of all signs and of all references to other things. This is really an example of his use of the language of metaphysics put forward on the philosophical basis of nominalism. One can clarify this by referring to modern science. For example, think of the huge field of tasks that molecular chemistry confronts when, in its research it seeks links which, in light of their immeasurable multiplicity, it must confirm through experiments. But are we ever in a comparable position to that of the researchers into the universal world of signs about which Derrida speaks? No, we stand already in the middle of it! But without the possibility of surveying the whole, we must go after one or the other trace. In doing this, for a long time we do not know if the path we are taking will lead to the goal we seek or whether we have been directed down a false path. Where should we hope to find an answer? One can only ponder what direction the traces along the way could be pointing, or we can look at where the written traces, oracular aphorisms, plays of fantasy, or poetic inspirations might lead us. Paul Celan said that poetic language is "vielstellig" [having many places] and leaves many paths open. At the same time, however, he demanded from the readers of his poems a "right" understanding. For this he advised, "Just read it over and over again!" When the aphorisms of oracles are ambiguous, the gods are toying with man. When poets write their hermetically intricate verses, they place their trust in the inviolability of the intricate web of sound and meaning that expresses itself through the performance for which the poem is a prescription.

II

Given his starting situation, it is quite understandable why Derrida wants to accord a pre-eminent place to writing and to writtenness. The breath of solitude blows through everything written. Also, I have long

accepted the fact that the relation between language and writing is not
to be understood in terms of two givens: a primary and a secondary. Certainly it stands to reason that writing is not a copy of the vocal sounds.
Quite the other way around, writing presupposes that one lends a voice
to what is read. Because of this, the capability of language to be written
is precisely not a secondary phenomenon; in this respect it is also significant, and at the same time natural, to note that there is no really pho-
netic script. In the end, the deeper commonality already resides in the
concept of logos—of course, I do not mean the logic of sentences. The
primordial meaning of "logos," as Heidegger has already underlined,
is *das Lesen,* the gathering together of the *Lese* [harvest]. So, following
Heidegger, I have linked my own hermeneutical efforts to the concept
of *Lesen* [reading].[8] But I have missed in Derrida the recognition that
writing, when it is read, is just as vocalized as language that is actually
spoken.

So I think a good deal here points to the phenomenon of
Sprachlichkeit [linguisticality]. The way the voice is articulated as a speaking voice—perhaps even when one reads without making any sound—
suggests that writtenness [*Schriftlichkeit*], even that of the alphabet, is an
articulation with a high level of complexity. The voice that the writer or
reader "hears" as he or she writes or reads clearly attains a far higher
level of articulation than could any possible writtenness. For instance,
there are many other signs, gestures, winks, and clues [*Spuren,* traces]
[that accompany the voice in the articulation of meaning]. One can
even go so far as to say that everything which presents itself [*sich zeigt,*
points to itself] is a symbol [*Zeichen,* sign]—Goethe even made this concept of the symbolic universal.[9] Each thing that shows itself necessarily distinguishes itself from other existing things that show themselves.
Each thing separates itself from the other thing, even as it at the same
time relates itself back to it. This is certainly correct. But this kind of
complex all-sidedness is reserved for God in the metaphysical concept
of the Deity. As for us mortals, on the other hand, we have only what
Celan calls many-sidedness [*Vielstelligkeit*] and multiple meanings. In
fact, it was quite correct when Derrida ultimately decided to substitute
the concept of the trace [*Spur*] for that of the sign. Paul Celan once put
it this way:

> The multiplicity of meanings derives from the circumstance that we
> observe only a very few facets of each thing, facets that show the thing
> from several angles, in several "refractions" and "component parts"
> [*Zerlegungen*] that are not at all merely "appearances." I endeavor
> linguistically to reproduce clippings at least from the many sides of a

> spectral-analysis of things, but at the same time to show them in *several* aspects and penetrations by other things, such as with the neighboring thing, the next following, or the opposite. Because I am unfortunately not in a position to show *all sides* of things.[10]

One well understands here the ironic expression of regret by Celan in this quotation, and one also grasps why Derrida preferred the concept of the "trace." It frees him from all mathematical combinatorics, and on the other hand also of the restrictions contained in the intentional concept of the sign. Traces [or clues] as such are not intended or willed but just left behind. At the same time, this increases their ontological value [*Seinswert*]. One is not just standing before some random object one cannot overlook. Rather, when one finds a trace, one sees oneself pointed in a certain direction—and when this happens one also feels bound to pick it up, just as one does with written documents that have been left behind.

How is a trace, then, more than a sign? The answer seems simple to me. Every trace points one in a certain direction, and indeed is waiting there for someone who is already under way and seeking his way. I am, of course, not sure whether I have captured the usage of the concept of "trace" in Derrida's sense here. One can also imagine some completely different sides of the concept of the trace. Levinas, for instance, has emphasized in the concept of the trace that the trace is something that is passing away, something disappearing into emptiness, and at the same time represents a silent testimony left behind. Thus the marks of pain and suffering inscribed on a face as traces are left behind by a lived life. Such traces do not want to call back to our minds some specific something. No, it is in this face that one encounters the other, and this is for us always the completely other, so our understanding has to remain silent. This is what the trace of the other means in Levinas. This example shows how *vielstellig* [diverse, multiple] a word is and how much its meaning is carried to us by its context. Here we are not at all dealing with crass opposites in word meaning. In both cases a trace is something left behind. And yet the encounter with a face points in a completely different direction than the context of speaking and writing that Derrida has in mind. In Derrida it sometimes sounds as if the trace (French: *trace*) is something like a powerful inscription, an engram, that is written on one's mind, and then sinks down into one's memory and remains there. Often the trace is shoved off into the realm of mere sign usage. Then the only thing that is seen is that signs beckon to be understood.

Someone who finds a trace/clue certainly also knows that something has existed before and is now left behind. But one does not just take note of this. One begins to search and to ask oneself where it leads. Only for a person who is on his way and in search of a right path, does the trace stand in the context of seeking and detecting [*des Spurens*], only then does picking up that trace mark his beginning.[11] With it one finds a first direction, something is disclosed. But where this trace will lead is still open. One allows it to lead. One tries hard not to lose track of the trace and to keep moving in the right direction. For when one loses track of the trace, one loses the way. Then one does not know how to go farther. One now has to search anew for the trace and resume the quest. In the end, if the trace takes the place of a sign, it forms a field of actions that are all its own. One could say that the trace takes shape at the same time. When it is encountered more often, it becomes one's path. Of course, where this path will lead can still remain completely uncertain. For when one chooses a path and finally chooses it, that path can still be the wrong one. Then one does not get where one really wanted to be. It is then that one is "advised" [*geraten*] of the right path.

It is clear that the role played by the trace in Derrida is that of *écriture*—that is, writing. The individual signs that make up the writing are determined by conventions. If the writing is readable, then as a text it will truly come to stand—and this means it will become something like a meaning-conferring event. As such, the written signs have as little meaning as the individual syllables. The sense of the text first emerges when its meaning dawns on the reader, and this happens only if one reads the writing as a whole with understanding. It is then that the reader will be able to find the right intonation, which must be done if he or she wants to read further with understanding.

We all know how the evidentness of a rightly understood meaning is built up. It goes through a number of stages: the deciphering of individual letters, the right articulation of the word, and in the end it is like a coming together of a whole in which the multiplicity of signs is put together and grasped. Then one gets immersed in the reading. One rightly calls this "concentration." One is directed to a centerpoint from which the whole becomes a structure of meaningful parts. One then says that one feels "captivated" by the reading. One cannot tear oneself away from it, at any rate so long as everything is making sense. One refuses to leave it because one is really engaged with it [*dabei*], ready to go along with it in understanding [*in Verstehen mitzugehen*].

One recognizes in this account the general description of what happens in the pursuit of any trace. The reader too is under way. There may be many things that occur to the reader in the reading; indeed, one may focus on this or that, but in the end the reader follows the path which the text prescribes to him or her. It is like a conversation with another person. One encounters a text the way one encounters another person; one seeks to get closer to it. One tries to do this in one way or another. In the process one gets new ideas, even inspirations. That's just how it often happens to a person in a conversation: the conversation comes to life precisely from the unforeseen ideas that may give the conversation a whole new direction. A conversation is not a discourse that is well programmed in advance. And yet one does seek to give the conversation a direction. For instance, one poses a question. Perhaps one understands in the answer given what the other person has understood or meant. Only to the extent that one has understood the other person can one answer at all. Otherwise, each one just talks past the other. A genuine conversation takes place only where it constantly leads into the open of other possible ways to continue it. The other person's answer can be a surprising one. This puts a new openness before us, an openness in which what is question-worthy presents itself. Possible answers are numerous. The conversation goes forward and one has the feeling of being on the right path, the feeling that one is getting somewhere. This is really the way it also is when one is looking for a trace. One can have to go back in order to search further for it. When one has again found the trace, one takes it up again. And for someone who has lost his or her way, there is not just the one single clue that one can follow up on. Traces can contradict each other, traces can peter out and end up pointing into a distance for which one has no guide. We can recognize this as happening in a conversation with meaningless answers, or in a text where one reads on without making any progress in understanding. One loses what was leading one forward and so gives up the search.

Here the puzzling nature of a question shows itself to us. Questions press themselves on us. Clearly one must pose them because they impose themselves on us, for otherwise the continuation of the process of coming to an understanding finds itself locked hand and foot in the stocks. Actually, the secret of the question contains the miracle of thinking. One knows, of course, that thinking is making distinctions. What this means precisely is to have the one thing and also the other thing in view. This is what happens in questioning. The question requires a decision among possibilities. But even the way one poses the question already includes a decision made in light of the fullness of all the different possibilities. It is therefore not at all easy to pose questions. This is an old, originally Platonic, point: that if the one being questioned no longer knows how to answer, he would like to be the one asking the questions. But then he finds that to pose questions is even harder! The one answering a question is at least led in a certain direction by the question being asked. On the other hand, the person who is supposed to do the questioning must find the trace [the direction-giving clue] and then must stick with the trace [*auf der Spur bleiben*]. In questioning, one cannot just follow the path of another. This is the reason that to ask questions is harder than to answer them. [*Deshalb ist Fragen schwerer als Antworten.*]

It is clear that the kind of question we have in mind here is not one which just asks for information. It needs to be an "open" question, but in such a way that its very posing makes it a fruitful question. An old saying runs as follows: "In science, the standpoint of the question decides [the matter]." [*In der Wissenschaft entscheidet die Fragestellung.*] Throughout the questioning one can by no means know that the path is right just because it leads to an answer. Indeed, the opposite can be the case. The person who is on the right path of questioning will not be the one for whom the answers are easy. On the contrary, the person for whom the answer is difficult to find is the one who learns to see new questions. And even if these turn out to be bypaths and erroneous paths, this is the path research must follow. Paths for research in science, in fact, copy the paths of questioning itself.

In a real conversation, on the other hand, the conditions are different because in living conversation the right understanding is immediately confirmed and misunderstandings are corrected. In a conversation one does not have to weigh every word on a scale of gold and carefully choose one's words so as to exclude all possible alternative meanings or misunderstandings. Still, if one is trying to tell someone something, the words must be the right words, that is, words that will reach out to the other person. Indeed, in a conversation one is certainly always already following the trace [*auf der Spur*]; but one never finds oneself to be off at a distance, the kind of distance in which the incalculably large world of signs lies spread out before one. No, in a conversation one sees oneself as being led. From this one begins to understand how hard writing is, because in writing one seeks to reach an unknown person, the reader. Also, what is written has something frighteningly irrevocable about it. That which is written [in scripture] is made up of pre-given signs. They are, as it were, inscribed—and because of this, it is as if they were prescribed.

They form texts. This means that by itself neither the trace nor the sign points to the sense of the meaning [*Bedeutungssinn*] of the individual word. Words with completely different meanings can represent the same scriptural image. The meaning of the word in each case is only determined by the context. We call them texts only when they are read and read over and over again. A text has the unity of a fabric and presents itself in its texture *as a totality*—and not just in written signs, and not even in the merely grammatical unities that form sentences. All these do not yet make a text a text; it is a text only when it makes a "written statement," as we wisely call it. But basically one understands when one understands completely and has understood the whole [*das Ganze*]. Someone who only half understands can possibly have completely misunderstood—and then one does not know whether one agrees with him or exactly how one should answer him. Therefore, one must question this person once again until one has understood. But of course, this still does not necessarily mean that in the end one will be in agreement with the other person.

In music, the use of written notation has parallels to the use of writing for language. Sometimes linguistic texts are set to music, and in the case of absolute music one can also say that one has not "understood" a composition. Either with regard to the linguistic text or in the case of music, this does not mean that one has failed to apperceive the sequence of words or the sequence of tones; rather, what it means is that a complexly differentiated thing has not presented itself as a unified whole in one's understanding. Scriptural statements, which certainly constitute a text with their letters, syllables, words, and sentences, taken together indicate how to understand the text as a whole. Likewise the musical notation puts forward such a totality, a totality that one does not just read, but also follows as an indication of how the performance is to go. This is why it is always a difficult and dubious enterprise to sight-read a piece of music. A person who wants to understand music needs to be familiar with the whole or at least be "going along with it" [*mitgehen*] as it is performed. If one has "gone with" it, then one also knows when the music has come to its end. For there is a "prior grasp" [*Vorgriff*], an expectation that one has of the work of art, of how the work constitutes a whole in an eminent sense. In poetry I have for this reason called poetic texts "eminent texts." [12]

Texts that are not works of art leave open the question of whether the text is ever really over with or whether it only breaks off, like a conversation, or a life. And perhaps there are still other forms of eminent texts that offer a real conclusion, like the judgment that takes place as one stands before a judge, or like a message that makes a promise, or like the Amen in church. And there is certainly also an art of writing and of speaking that merely puts down an end point. Punctuation, after all, was only a late invention in the history of writing. In any case one thing is quite clear: every such text stands in a context. Even the referential meaning of a sign relies on what it points to. And however much a text may constitute a unity of meaning in itself, it is always dependent on a context, such that this context will often be needed in order to determine a single clear meaning out of several possibilities. This is an age-old hermeneutical principle, which applies to all understanding of texts. One notices this when the surrounding field that forms the context is newly rearranged and suddenly the text receives a new meaning. One should always be conscious of the fact that the unity of a word is determined from the unity of the sentence in which it appears, and the unity of the sentence is itself again determined out of larger textual contexts. This also happens to a person in reading. Whoever has to spell out the words cannot really read and also cannot understand what he or she is reading. In the same way, if one lifts an individual part of a text out of context, it falls silent. It lacks the larger sense given to it by the power of the whole [*überlegene Sinnkraft*].

This is the drawback with all understanding of quotations, and especially the tricky crossing back and forth of borders which the theory of intertextuality involves. Every sentence is not only a unity in itself; rather, it belongs within a unity of sense that gives the text its inner tension and its own particular tone. We all know how music is made in the speaking of the tone, and we therefore also know what a difficult and heavy responsibility it is to read aloud the minutes for a meeting if one has no clearly definable persons sitting opposite, for whom one is trying to find the right tone. Tone and emphasis arise from an ungraspable movement, a movement back and forth between each other in a being with each other. One thinks, for example, of how ungraspable irony is to an outsider and yet how much irony, if understood by the other person, binds two people together. And, on the other hand, one thinks of how a lack of understanding of an irony works to separate people. This particular case serves to remind us of how profoundly the unity of meaning in a text or a conversation rests upon the being-together of people with each other [*im Miteinander*].

Here [with *Miteinander*] we find a completely new field of problems opening up before us, a field that encompasses far wider dimensions than what has been called "logocentrism." Certainly not all random connections [*Anknüpfungen*] and modifications, and not all playful allusions and reminiscences, can be made explicit without disturbing the being-with-each-other that is generated by agreement in understanding. Even though I recognize what Derrida calls *dissémination*, this concept certainly cannot claim to offer the last word. No, it only names a presupposition on the basis of which a new understanding of meaning can make its demand. I readily recognize the power exerted by conventions—or to speak in Heideggerian terms, the "omnipotence of shallow talk"—but neither the demands of logic nor the persuasiveness of deep-seated prejudices can constitute a legitimation of these. On the other hand, it is not allowable that the ideas one follows just be random inspirations. It can be in the case of very refined connections [*Fügungen,* coincidences] in rhetorical as well as poetic usages, that many of these connections of meaning only represent byplay. But then there can also be connections that determine the whole game involved. For these reasons I think it would be wrong to argue that simple intertextuality constitutes the basis of all textual understanding. Actually intertextuality only corresponds to the style of a certain period. It does not always have a claim for thematic discussion. Rather, one must remember that allusions necessarily remain vague in most cases, and recognizing a possible allusion will hardly be a major contribution to the interpretation. Instead, the assertion of art generally resides precisely in its nonemphasis [*Nichtabhebung*] on itself, in the discretion of its allusion—and in its harmony with what else is being said. "Ars latet arte sua." "Art [loves to] hide[s] its art" [Ovid].

When one is dealing with language and art forms in language, one should not fail to grasp the concept of language very broadly. Music [as a language] presents itself from itself, but it is also universally the case that art—and particularly when one takes into account its time period—is stamped with a clear unity even in the most varied arts. One thinks, for instance, of the dominant role that iconography plays in the scholarly study of art today. Certainly it represents an important historical dimension, but the transition is missing that is involved in what I have called the "transformation into structure" [*Verwandlung ins Gebilde*]. This entails that in such [iconographic] studies, the realm of art as such has not yet been reached. Or consider contemporary architecture, in which the citing of other styles plays a major role today. Here for the most part a vague quality of something being well known [*Bekanntheitsqualität*] can be noticed, and precisely this vagueness plays its role in the "statement" that the building is making. If one allows such a quotation to become the central and only object or causes it to be so, one can fail to notice the building itself. This is particularly the case in the historicizing styles of the nineteenth century. There we find neo-Gothic churches, Romantic rail stations, and neoclassical department stores! We recognize in this the answer given by artistic creativity in the century of the Industrial Revolution. In the end, this led in art and literature to a chaotic mixture of many historicizing tendencies. Of course, one must remember that in the experience of art there is always constantly in play the vague memory of styles from past epochs, and one spoils the play of the work of art in the encounter if one tries to mix in observations about precise derivations. One sees what emerges as tastes and styles change like the play of waves on the shore, if one looks at the reevaluation [in the nineteenth and twentieth centuries] of the baroque period and even the art of the period of *Jugendstil* or of Art Nouveau, a reevaluation of which immediately made rediscoveries possible.

This well may be analogous with intertextuality, which corresponds very well to the style of its day in its use of literary citation. Indeed, and completely parallel to this, which is perhaps of historical interest, one finds that in the encounter with the text the unity of the statement is still there! It is not to be denied that an artist is not able to escape completely from contemporary currents in taste, and for this reason one finds alongside artistic works of high value others that are only fashionable imitations. But the basic thesis of intertextuality cannot gainsay the decisively important formative tasks [*Gestaltungsaufgaben*] that the artist faces. What is in real danger of happening is well known in the plastic arts. To make an allusion discreet and unobtrusive, which is practically a formative rule of art, will certainly not be easy against the representational predilections of contemporary viewers who do not have art [but rather realistic copying] in mind at all. Given this problem, it is hardly to be expected that in portrait art, for instance, the person being portrayed will ever be satisfied with the result. But even the gradual change of taste during epochs or during the long course of history under the dictatorial power of an orientation to representation and iconographical copying did not protect even the greatest masterpieces of pictorial or sculptural art from banishment to the storage warehouse or worse, from brutal redoing. One thinks of Rembrandt's so-called "The Night Watch," where the distortion of the side of his face by the newly won light of day is painfully clear, or the miraculous rescue of "The Conspiracy of Claudius (or Julius) Civilis" from an Amsterdam cellar, from whence it was then spirited away to Stockholm.

The closeness of the trace and writing to the reading that articulates writing—especially given the multiplicity of relationships that make up the world of signs and the world of language that is articulated in writing—gives rise to an endless multiplicity of possible connections and relationships. And of course these connections and relationships may open up new avenues of thought. But the question is: How do we know whether a particular path is viable? Is the path that seems right really so? Digressions, similar paths, and changing vantage points can lead one astray. And along with the reading of a written text there can arise tones that make something plausible that is not intended in the text itself. How can one distinguish whether this intonation really belongs to a certain line of thought or not? Some reading may push everything beneath the surface that is in a written thought, or it may bring to light something which one later finds in the process of reading the text was not meant at all. In view of the multiplicity of relationships between words and relationships among things being discussed, are there really no criteria for us to use? Perhaps the logical sequence in a text leads us into error? What is the right path?

III

In this third and final section, it may be helpful to examine some concrete writings we find in this newly established phenomenon we call deconstruction, in order to see what can be called positive in these writings and what will only lead one into errors. In doing so I would like to look at Derrida's very interesting discussion of the Greek term *chora*, which he recently published in an essay that is highly worth reading.[13] In this essay, Derrida does not have in mind simply the word but rather the concept of *chora* [space that originates?] as it is known to the Platonist who appears in Plato's *Timaeus*. You will recall that in this dialogue Socrates narrates the myth of the demiurge, a being who constructed the cosmos—not only the heavenly spheres but also our earthly world consisting of four elements—in accordance with number and measure. It is in this connection we encounter something without which the whole event of creating the order of the world and the interaction of its four elements could not find a place. This is that-which-gives-space [*das Raumgebende*], which here is called *chora*. Now we can of course ask what the *chora* really means. The general usage of the word suggests some completely different contexts, in one of which the term *chora* designates a sovereign administrative realm. But in the context of our story of the construction of the worlds, the word already puts forward a conceptual framework, a framework that presents an original image and copy, a framework in which the story had operated in the beginning and which encompassed everything. But now that-which-grants-space [*das Raumgebende*] enters the scene here like something new, something that until now has not existed at all. Now *what is this third thing?* Here one can point to the perspective which this Third Thing opens up, that is, the language of metaphysics, which offers us this story. That-which-grants-space is neither an intellectual thing [*ein Geistiges*] nor a material thing [*ein Materielles*]. Rather, it is a third thing, so to speak. It is a third sort of thing [*eine dritte Gattung*], something that is neither the one nor the other!

What do we find out here about this *chora?* The extended presentation in the *Timaeus* leaves one seemingly clueless, if we try to say exactly what this third sort of being really is. In the text (from 50a forward) gold is brought up as an analogy, and the fact is discussed that there can be many kinds of golden things but only one gold element, and also discussed is the basic substance that one uses to carry perfume because it in itself has no odor. But both of these examples cause one to think more in terms of the concept of matter, of the *hyle* of Aristotle, of an ultimate matter that has no formal determination at all, rather than the space that creates a place for something [*den Platz machenden Raum*]. Certainly the *chora* that takes in everything, as it says in 50d, is itself expressly called "formless," like the formless dough out of which the baker or potter would make something. Or again, this *chora* is said to be like the mother or the wet nurse who first carries and nourishes the self-forming, living thing—but this is a completely different realm of ideas.

Nevertheless, the introduction of this *chora* in the *Timaeus,* in the form of a surprising interruption of the prevailing story accepted up to then—of the world being created by the demiurge with the help of nous—is presented as a good copy of some original image of the world! This success means that all at once one has to set aside the idea of a logos that simply comes to be out of necessity. Instead, the origin of the world is a *mixture* of nous and *ananke,* of reason and necessity. Reason persuades necessity to concede that something good will come from it in the end. This is the puzzling introduction of that third genus, a genus between being and becoming, idea and appearance, original image and copy. Obviously all the mythical overtones and allusions and changing forms are going to leave us at a loss, so that what is meant by *chora* will be like a completely new beginning. Yes, it was announced, but in such a general form that it is difficult to make this completely independent genus [*Gattung*] intelligible at all. For in it are both: being and becoming, the unalterable in being and on the other hand the formless, a formlessness that, because of its changeability, escapes any easy grasp. This latter is bluntly introduced as "the cause of the form of what wavers" [*Gestaltursache des Schwankenden*].

We will follow here a basic hermeneutical principle, which advises us to inquire into the larger context.[14] Now what does this context teach us in this text? After announcing a completely new beginning, the text nevertheless makes it quite clear that we will still be dealing with the four elements already discussed—these being for Plato given in advance—and with what happens with them ($48b_5$ *pathe*). If one looks more closely into the matter, one perceives that all these varied descriptions of how the *Aufnehmende,* the "receiver" [or "receptacle"], is supposed to be the third genus, finally lead us to the point that the nature of the third sort of thing is to be expressly introduced with the designation of *chora* (52a–f).

And in the summing up at the end, the *chora* is positioned in the middle between being and becoming and is presented as that which mediates (52d). And in order to explain this, the four elements, which according to the prevailing Greek conception in Platonic times (since Empedocles) are the constituent parts of all that is, are now constituted with the help of mathematics and its necessity. Its complexly shaped image in the realm of appearance will form for all beings the unchanging building blocks of reality. Of course, this is not exactly persuasive in terms of their visual appearance! Fire, for Greek thinking, is everywhere present where warmth is, thus not only in the blazing of flames but also in the warmth of life; and water is for them not only this great infinity of the oceans, seas, and rivers, but likewise ice with its stony hardness. Air is not merely the azure blue sky but is likewise the wind and the clouds, the mist and the storm. Unchangeable? When the narrator had introduced them he himself had emphasized how little these elements in their appearance corresponded to the ordering thought. None of them was completely and unalterably this or that. Fire, for instance, is not always pure fire but at most fiery, and likewise with water, air, and earth, which make up in ever-changing ways of appearing these constituent parts of all being. One needs at the same time to show them to be the enduring elements [*das Beständige*] out of which everything is that has its being. To explain this point, mathematics and especially the geometry of the triangle were mobilized. The triangle was the great pattern for knowing, knowledge, and proof, that was under construction in the form of Euclidean geometry. As building elements, triangles were to give the elements their consistency, and for this task the recognized mathematical truth of stereometry was sufficient to show that there can only be five regular bodies. These were simply called the Platonic bodies.

How these five bodies were to be assigned to the four elements has certainly not been without some joking about it. There stands the pyramid representing steep flames. There stands the cube, which stood for the firm earth. The polygon with the most corners, the icosahedron, stands for water that is dispersed into steam and mist. This is all very pretty if also somewhat tiresome. But there is a difficulty with it. There are only four elements but five mathematical bodies. So a special task is assigned to the dodecahedron [a body with twelve plane surfaces] in order to sidestep this embarrassment. It is to serve as the scaffolding for the globe of the world! Even Plato's contemporary readers certainly did not accept the idea that Plato really meant all this literally. In every word of the *Timaeus* one can detect Plato's joyful play with the stories he is telling. If Aristotle nevertheless takes the whole thing literally and then criticizes it, he does so because he is fighting, in reference to this and in many other playful passages in other dialogues, to carry through his own agenda, which is to defend the preeminence of nature and the merely secondary character of mathematics. I think that overall one has to picture the *Timaeus* as a game of Plato [*ein Spiel Platos*].

On the other hand, the necessity that is in play now in the new approach is not just a game. And Plato is fully in earnest when he finds that the traditional depictions of nature and the world based on the dualism of original and copy and on being and becoming are not sufficient! Whatever one may say about Aristotle's misinterpretation of Platonism as putting forward a two-world doctrine, it must be admitted that Plato had long ago anticipated something different in his thinking. We see this in the *Parmenides,* in the *Sophist,* and in the *Philebus.* And now in the *Timaeus* Plato brings it explicitly to language as what he calls the "second beginning" (48b) in his tale of the demiurge creating the world. Derrida has obviously recognized this. For this reason he was immediately attracted to this third genus, because the distinction between being and becoming is here expressly declared to be insufficient. The *chora* of the *Timaeus* actually causes one to think of the modern natural sciences that are based on mathematics, sciences whose development was delayed a thousand years because Aristotle's teleological philosophy of nature, accepted for a millennium, stood in the way.

Let's now examine the textual basis for Derrida's effort to inquire deconstructively behind what he calls "metaphysics." Obviously he identifies metaphysics with the doctrine of two worlds, and this serves as the foundation for his very interesting and imaginative essay on *chora.* But what do the texts themselves tell us? Well, Derrida cites Plato's *Republic.* He represents the *chora* here as that which is "beyond" [*Jenseits*] Being. But in fact, the term *chora* does not occur in the *Republic*! But since in the *chora* in the *Timaeus* there seems to be a beyond, a beyond that is neither sensible nor mental, Derrida believes he recognizes in the *Timaeus* the same beyond that in the *Republic* is introduced as that which is beyond being. In doing so Derrida links this [view of metaphysics] with the late Platonism of the early Christian period. Now it is certainly true that Dionysus the Areopagite speaks in his depiction of the one and divine of the *chora* as the distinctive place of the one. Derrida thinks he can call all three as witnesses to his same anti-metaphysical meaning, and in this way he can pick up on a threefold trace. For in all three directions of meaning something ungraspable is shown: the good as the beyond of being, the beyond that grants space or place, and the beyond of the divine one. In his view, these three form a many-leveled ensemble.

I have my doubts about this. Certainly I very much admire the fireworks in the dazzling allusions that Derrida arranges as he listens in on the preliminary scenes of the *Timaeus*. And I do not at all deny the fact that Plato is here mustering everything he can to be sure that we do not forget that the world structure [*Weltbau*] parallels the structure of the state and the structure of the soul. They do belong together. Plato certainly proves himself a perfect deconstructionist here in this great dialogical drama. Indeed, I share the view of Heidegger, Derrida, and Vernant (whom I listened to with agreement some years ago) that the conventional explanatory formula, "From mythos to logos," is wrong and does violence to both sides in this case. And yet it seems to me that the context in which the *chora* is introduced in the *Timaeus* is quite different from the other two and indeed offers a trace [*Spur*] that leads to something quite different from the beyond of the one or the place of the divine. What it leads to is a necessity—and there can be little doubt what necessity is being referred to here: it is the necessity in mathematics. Certainly the structure of Euclidean geometry is something astonishing and wonderful, and wonderful likewise is the fact that the mathematicians of Plato's time had recognized and proved that only five regular geometrical bodies can be inscribed within a sphere. What kind of puzzling rationality of a third dimension is this, Plato asks, that allows the space-giving [the *chora*] from within itself only these five complete bodies that all fit perfectly into the complete sphere of being? What limits are shown here, and at the same time what concession is shown by necessity, if it grants only to these five regular geometrical bodies something of the perfection of the sphere? Even the demiurge can change nothing about this, because so much necessity is involved in it.

I am dealing with the topic of the *chora* here with the purpose of raising a fundamental question—the question of whether references can just be added and followed up even when they go in various directions, or whether one must decide *in what context* one may follow up on references. Traces have their prior determination; they are not random. While I believe I understand the beyond in the idea of the good, I really do not think in this context of the four this-worldly elements of ordinary bodies. And when one has in mind the beyondness of the one as it appears in Dionysus the Areopagite and in his Christian successors, one tends to think of the beyond of being that is found in Plato's *Republic*. But doing so only allows us to see it within the Neoplatonic interpretation of Aristotelian metaphysics, from which we learned to think of the divine as beyond beings, and as the God granting space to every existing being. For this we are indebted to Aristotle's *Physics*, which introduced God as the prime mover. On the other hand, when we place *chora* in the context of the idea of symmetry and the mathematical ordering in the five "beautiful" bodies as they come closer and closer to the spherical form of the universe and its construction out of triangles, then it serves to give us an intuition of mathematical necessity, which then causes us to understand why the four elements, in spite of their changing ways of appearing, are to be understood as being [*Sein*]. But this is not particularly persuasive, as the narrator concedes. These are sovereign games that Plato plays here with mathematics, as he also happily does elsewhere [*wie auch sonst gerne*]. Mathematics itself, however, is not for this reason itself just a game.

The close of the seventh book of the *Republic* makes it quite clear that one should read the Platonic dialogues as games. There the possibility of creating an ideal state is presented with playful lightness, such as when Plato offers the clever solution to the problem of how one can make the transition to the next state: one must simply drive out of the ideal city-state all its inhabitants that are ten or older. Then the paradise made up of well-trained children will really be able to come into being. In such playful games, one can still refer to serious problems in Athens, and in truth Plato's utopias mirrored the fall of the great culture of Athens and with it the age of the flowering of Greek democracy.[15] Nevertheless, the mathematical construction presented in the *Timaeus* has exercised a powerful fascination on the study of physics in modern times, above all in the twentieth century. Plato's play in the *Timaeus* with the way the world was constructed [his *Weltspiel*] has in fact had a continuing influence over the centuries, via Kepler and the Romantic philosophy of nature offered by Schelling—right up to the present time. As quantum physics teaches us today, it remains a relevant problem in relation to how far mathematical relationships can enable us to get closer to reality. Indeed, this is a very broad field.

The dialogical poetry of Plato works energetically to avoid rigid determinations; instead, it wants to lead our thinking further. Thus, the mirror image of Attic democracy that is held up before us is also full of powerful critical assertions. The way Plato leads thinking preserves something of the secret of language and of the way humans reach understandings in their everyday use of language. We have already cited Plato's only authentic words about this matter, which he uttered for us in the *Seventh Letter*. He said that dialectic must always become dialogue again, and thinking must be preserved in the way we are "with each other" in conversation. This is the Plato I know. It is certainly true that we can find in Plato many traces of pride in logic and in the mathematics of his time, but I am certainly not able to see any "logocentrism" in this at all. Rather, I would label the metaphysics that shaped medieval thinking under the influence of Aristotle and that flowered under the conditions of the reading culture in modernity, "monologocentrism."

With regard to getting at what Aristotle himself thought, however, one should always remember that the works we have of Aristotle were merely dictated notes that served him as the basis for lectures and conversations.

It would require a separate presentation on the basis of a host of industrious scholarly commentators on Aristotle, to show how little the philosophical thinking of Aristotle really corresponded to ideals of the logic of demonstration, so it was required that the commentaries do this for teaching purposes. One finds the best information on how Aristotle's investigation into the principles (*archai*) really proceeded in the appendix to the second *Analytic* (B 19). This chapter of Aristotle should be considered just as important as the excursus from Plato's *Seventh Letter*, for it demonstrates how concepts are formed and how language and the common knowledge that resides in language work together to bring their accomplishments to completion. Aristotle was not incorrect to criticize the demonstrative power of the Platonic dialectic in Plato's use of the concept of *dihairesis* (division).[16] And he was certainly right that the distinctions which are worked out in a live conversation, and equally so in Platonic dialogical poetry, do not at all possess the character of a demonstration through logical necessity. But did Plato ever assume this? What he had in mind were conversations—and everybody admits that among human beings agreement in understanding is only seldom achievable through a rigorous logical demonstration. In the sciences, of course, we are fully aware of the superiority of carrying out logically secured demonstration. But we also know about the realms of freedom that exist in human action—and in addition to this there is the exercise of creative fantasy that goes on in research, and likewise the fantasy that is involved in the language of poetry. One must grant to all of these their right to be. One simply cannot make everything into an object of knowledge. Think of the many important human experiences other than those in science; for instance, having one's breath taken away as a member of the audience in a theater, or being lost in thought before the whole comedy or tragedy of living, or when one witnesses exciting events, or when one is spellbound listening to a suspenseful story. What holds true especially for the poetic language of the lyric poem is certainly not only valid for it: a lyric poem does not strive to be an object of science for us but rather, like all experience of art, it requires our going with [*Mitgehen*] it and participating [*Teilnehmen*] in it. For these reasons, it seems to me that one does not find the task of deconstruction posed in them, although it certainly can open up new horizons.

Interpretation is always a ticklish matter [*heikle Sache*]. The reason for this lies in the fact that by its very nature (and quite literally), it is *Zwischenrede*—"speech between." By its nature it interrupts the process of *Mitgehen*—of going-along-with something, of listening. We all know this experience, for example, when we listen to poetic texts. Such an interruption is not for this reason something superfluous. Wherever we stumble across something we don't understand, the help of interpretation is needed. But interpretation fulfills its true purpose only when it enables us to restart the process of understanding the poem which had temporarily been obstructed by unintelligibility. This is a very broad field of problems which we actually have to confront when we have to do with art. So where, then, are there sharp boundaries?

We must keep in mind that the field of language extends far beyond the poetic text. It also includes thinking meditation—and therewith the use of concepts on which the prose of thought rests. It is in speaking that all this comes to completion. Ultimately, this general point also holds to a certain extent for every interpretation in itself. It may be speaking that takes place between people [*Zwischenrede*]—but interpretation truly is what it should be only when it interrupts in order to enable a thinking conversation to continue. One can take as a model of this the way the book Delta of the *Metaphysics* of Aristotle offers itself as a mere aid or tool. It should serve as a model for interpretation in general. This holds true not only in relation to poetry; it applies to all reading. It is no accident that I have discussed what I call the "eminent text" in relation to the texts that Derrida uses in order to lift the claim of deconstruction.[17] Indeed, in a broad sense I would consider what I am saying to be true of the experience of all art. It encompasses much more than I first thought. Texts and works of art are such that one does not simply take note of them in passing. Indeed, one would like to be able to recite a lyric poem from memory, if possible, so that one can enter more easily into conversation with it. And works of art are in general such that the conversation one has with them is never exhausted but invites us to revisit and reencounter them again and again. Philosophical texts are certainly not eminent texts in the same sense. Even when they do not attain the level of Platonic dialogues, philosophical texts are still a "between speaking" [*Zwischenrede*] in the endless conversation of thinking. Certainly one turns to them again and again for advice, for we all live within a process of having experiences. We clearly do not read philosophical texts like a poem. Rather, we study a philosophical text as written by one who also does not know the answer, but the author of the text has for a long time asked himself about the question and considered what he is saying—and thus he is not so easily influenced by what is presently important or by an involuntary accommodation to his own time. So reading a philosophical text is like a conversation with another person. "It is not my word, whatever I also may say."

But back to language and writing! The whole circle of these problems is, I think, connected to the truly boundless question with which I have long occupied myself: *What must the reader know?* To this question one cannot expect any definite answer. Perhaps one should pose the question differently: "What should the reader want to know?" [*Was darf der Leser wissen wollen?*][18] Perhaps Socrates had something like this in mind when, at the conclusion of his conversation with Phaedrus, he offered a prayer to Pan and the other gods. His prayer there included the wish for riches, but riches reinterpreted into the Socratic sense of that word when he says, "I would like to count him rich who is rich in wisdom and who possesses no more material wealth than a person of moderation can carry with him and manage."[19]

Translated by Richard E. Palmer

Part 5

Concluding Dialogue
with Jean Grondin

A Look Back over the Collected Works and Their Effective History

This dialogue is a fine conclusion for our translation of the Gadamer Lesebuch.[1] Still, although it was conducted when Gadamer was ninety-six, it is not his last word on every topic! Always active, Gadamer published several books after the last of the ten volumes of his collected works came out in 1995, including what amounts to an additional short one-volume addendum to the collected works, Hermeneutische Entwürfe: Vorträge und Aufsätze (2000) [HE],[2] as well as two books documenting a series of lectures on early Greek philosophy he delivered in Naples in 1988, that have recently been translated into English.[3] But one of the liveliest of the very late published works was a book of conversations that took place in 1999–2000 with his longtime student from Rome, Riccardo Dottori. Here Gadamer took the measure of the twentieth century, and Dottori quickly had the conversations published in German in 2000.[4] The New York publisher Continuum promptly brought out a handsome translation of this book in 2004 under the title A Century of Philosophy.[5] This work certainly offers great pleasures for every Gadamerian. It is not an autobiographical reflection but a comment on the century. For autobiography, there also exists the rich and lengthy autobiographical reflection that Gadamer offered in The Philosophy of Hans-Georg Gadamer (1997), half of which he and Grondin chose to have included in the Gadamer Lesebuch as its first essay.[6] But if there was a last word from Gadamer, it would have to be this ten-chapter valedictory with Dottori on philosophy in the twentieth century.

But how does the interview with Jean Grondin in our volume differ from these? It is not another writing but a dialogue on past writings and their reception. It is not an autobiographical sketch, such as that presented in The Philosophy of Hans-Georg Gadamer, nor a wide-ranging commentary on the twentieth century, such as is captured in the Dottori interviews, but a "look back," an assessment of accomplishments, a reply to critics, a clarification of misunderstandings. For this reason it has its own special place as a late word by Gadamer on his writings, some of which are included in this volume. The text is based on two conversations which were held on May 3 and 24, 1996. They have the relaxed tone of looking back with a friend after Gadamer has completed the editing of his collected works.

Jean Grondin is qualified not only by nearly two decades of warm friendship with Gadamer, but also by half a dozen books on Gadamer and hermeneutics that he had published even by the time of the interview. Later on he completed a monumental biography of Gadamer, which has been translated into English and published by the Yale University Press,[7] and he has written several books on Gadamer in several languages, two of which are his *Introduction to Philosophical Hermeneutics*[8] and *The Philosophy of Gadamer.*[9] It could be said that no one is more qualified by long acquaintance, publications, and ongoing work on Gadamer to conduct this interview with him.

What are a few highlights of this conversation? Grondin opens by asking what the main goal was that guided his whole career as a philosopher. Gadamer's answer is interesting because it separates him sharply from his teacher, Heidegger. His goal was to restore respect to the arts and humanities in an age when the scientific perspective has delegitimized them. About this topic Heidegger cared nothing. Then Grondin took up three basic misinterpretations of *Truth and Method:* that it is a form of aestheticism, that it is a form of relativism, and that it is preoccupied with language (linguisticism). Gadamer rebuts all three terms vigorously, and this is probably the most valuable and interesting part of the conversation. The conversation lingers on the topic of language, and Gadamer brings up Augustine's view of the Trinity and his philosophy of the inner word, a favorite topic of Grondin. In this connection Gadamer again stresses that there are forms of language that are not focused on control and domination. It is these forms he has dedicated his life to defending.

In the final part of the conversation, Gadamer's tone becomes prophetic as he warns of the consequences of the global spread of scientific culture and the retreat of other forms of knowledge. Here he invokes his teacher Heidegger's warnings against a preoccupation with technology in his 1938 essay, "The Age of the World Picture."[10]

At the end, the interview turns to the future in terms of Gadamer's own future projects. He anticipates work on the rehabilitation of ethics and rhetoric, on both of which, he notes, the later Heidegger did not focus. There are other topics in the conversation, such as the religious element in Heidegger's early education in contrast to his own, but our introduction here should at least have given a taste of this remarkable dialogue.

* * *

A Look Back over the Collected Works
and Their Effective History

JEAN GRONDIN: Professor Gadamer, you are now [at age ninety-six] in a position to look back on a long path of thought. Your teacher, Martin Heidegger, once said that every thinker pursues one thought in his life, follows one star. Of course, I know that you hesitate out of modesty to use this term in reference to yourself and would deny being a thinker comparable to Heidegger. But still, as you now look back to the very beginnings of your career, what may have been your basic thought, your guiding question? Or do you perhaps regard this question as meaningless?

HANS-GEORG GADAMER: Oh no, the question is surely quite reasonable, since at the end of a long life, one does indeed become aware of structures in one's life that do not seem to have been planned at all. In my case, I came out of a natural scientific milieu but from the beginning I was drawn to art, although art did not play any special role in my parents' home or in my relationships in school at the time. Nevertheless, I found that I was very receptive to great poetry from very early in my life. I remember reading Shakespeare early; I was a very enthusiastic theatergoer, too; and even in my school years I loved lyric poetry. Even that early I was enchanted by the poetry of Stefan George. In the last year of the war [1918] I was as a student drawn to aesthetics, art history, history, and German studies. But at that time I had no inclination at all to pursue classical studies. You see, instruction in Greek and classical studies in the pre-university schools found itself in a difficult [staffing] situation and classics had only very old instructors, so although I learned Greek and Latin very well, I was not drawn to classics the way I was to Shakespeare and to the classical and modern theater. For this reason, when I entered Breslau University in 1918, I unfortunately bypassed the classical philologists—Wilhelm Kroll was there at that time. Also, at the university, German Studies [*Germanistik*] was a disappointment to me when I found that this area involved only the study of the German language and not of what the language communicated. So it came about that I felt more and more frustrated as I tried to formulate my own questions, and for this purpose I found that I could gain the most from working in philosophy. It came about in this way. What I was trying to do above all was to uncover a place for what seemed important and true [in art and the humanities] in the face of the overwhelming power of the historical standpoint. So I would answer your question by saying that from the very beginning the study of philosophy was for me supposed to be more than merely a reflection on the sciences. It was also hopefully going to open up a space for the experience of art and its neighborhood to the standpoint of philosophical questioning. And that has basically remained my task, even if it has taken some long detours.

GRONDIN: Without any doubt, your philosophy has been put under the heading of "hermeneutics." Even Heidegger once said in a letter, "Hermeneutical philosophy? Oh, that is Gadamer's thing!"[1] To what extent is it your thing, in contrast to Heidegger, and how can one explain to a lay person—and that is always what we are in philosophy—what hermeneutics is?

GADAMER: Surely Heidegger's comment on me is quite ambiguous—is it a critique or a recognition?—as is everything that he tended to say in such cases. There is a critique in it in the fact that in my philosophical work I defended hermeneutics as my thing, while the later Heidegger gave up the use of this word, which had originally been a term familiar to him in his theological studies. As to what hermeneutics is: well, back at that time it was of course merely an ancillary science, above all for theologians and jurists. But in Heidegger it was a development of phenomenology into a hermeneutical phenomenology that I found convincing. As this new concept of hermeneutics finally came to be filled with its own content for me, I became fully aware at the same time that I always had the later Heidegger in mind, without of course using his vocabulary of the "turn." What gradually became very clear to me on this path was that the questions of philosophy that Heidegger raised and developed in his critique of the metaphysical tradition will only become truly persuasive if one is able to reach the other person to whom one is speaking. This would explain why, for example, in view of the resistance of the publisher at that time to having the concept of hermeneutics in the title [of *Truth and Method*], I obediently accepted it. For me hermeneutics was not a matter of a theory of science or even a theory of the human sciences. On the contrary, I wanted to show that in the "human sciences" not only science and method played a role, but there was above all the mysterious presence that the artwork has— and that the ever-recurring questions of metaphysics and religion also possess.

GRONDIN: You have referred very charitably to your publisher having doubts about your proposed title, *Elements of a Philosophical Hermeneutics*. Because of this you came up with the present title, *Truth and Method*. But now in your collected works the term "Truth and Method" not only covers the first volume, *Truth and Method* itself, but also the accompanying second volume of hermeneutics essays in which you bring forward prior steps, expansions, and further developments. What did you intend by actually extending the title "Truth and Method" so that it covered both of these volumes?

GADAMER: Speaking from my perspective as a phenomenologist, my goal was above all to get at the *Sache selbst* [thing itself] and to get back to the lifeworld, and not to take the goal of neo-Kantianism, which was the bare facts that are sought by science. Indeed, what drew me to Heidegger above all was how closely he moved toward grasping things. This was also the reason that later on I preferred to deal with Greek philosophy, because the Latin terms had colored the whole language of philosophical concepts and forced prior decisions on the use of language in philosophy as it was pursued among all the languages of modern cultures. With the Greeks, in contrast to this, one could get back to the everyday experience of the world. This led me to assert the encompassing role of language [in culture]. Of course, I was also acutely conscious of the fact—and here I come to the answer to your question—that the third part of *Truth and Method* was only a sketch and I had not said everything I really had in mind. This prompted the wonderful [Odo] Marquardian joke about the third part, that instead of being-toward-death, in the hermeneutics I offered instead a "being-toward-the-text"! In truth, I did want to show that in texts experiences open up that belong much closer to art, religion, and philosophy than they do to science.

GRONDIN: Your hermeneutics, and I am referring above all to *Truth and Method,* has provoked many critical reactions and we cannot go into each of them without taking up its own "effective history," as you call it. I think it would be pointless here to go back into specific objections, so I would like to limit myself to a few concrete topics. I would like to focus on three headings. Each deals with one of the three main parts or topic realms of *Truth and Method,* namely art, history, and language. Three not very adequately formulated counter-headings that refer to critiques of your main theses are: aestheticism, relativism, and linguisticism. Under the heading of aestheticism lurks the suspicion that in the end you have put forward an aesthetic conception of truth. Granted you criticize the "aesthetic consciousness" because it looks away from the truth claim of art, but in fact the moment of truth that you have in mind in *Truth and Method* is formulated with the help of the concept of the beautiful and of the Platonic metaphysics of light. This gives rise to the thought that you have in mind truth in a purely aesthetic sense.

GADAMER: First of all, one must keep in mind that I borrowed the idea of the beautiful at the end of *Truth and Method* from the Greek concept of the *kalon* [the fine, the beautiful], and that includes the inseparability of the good and the beautiful. That is one thing that I would say right away [against the charge of aestheticism].

And I would say that hermeneutics is anything but an aestheticizing approach, because my whole argument begins precisely with art and not with aesthetics. There I would rather speak of the transcendence that goes beyond everything one encounters in the experience of life. Take for instance, ingratitude, the lack of thankfulness. This is something *King Lear* teaches us. This is also what Aristotle meant when he found poetry to be more philosophical than history. The writing of history deals with things as they have really happened; poetry in contrast shows how they always happen.

In *Truth and Method* I attacked the distorted idea in the first part of Kant's *Critique of Judgment* that one could characterize art with the concept of "disinterested pleasure." As our century developed it seemed to desire [from art] in the end to have nothing more than disinterested pleasure. In contrast to this, I have tried to show something that of course is not generally perceived, namely, that Kant had sought to make the transition to what art is by starting with the aesthetic question. For this reason, he thought first of all of natural beauty, and with the help of the feeling of the sublime he sought to make the transition from the wider aesthetic dimension to art. It is a mistake and a misuse of the *Critique of Judgment,* if one thinks that Kant here allows us to speak in support of objectless art. What one fails to recognize here is that modern and postmodern works can be art too [in the higher sense] and not mere decoration. To support modern and postmodern art in this way [from Kant] was in my opinion a misunderstanding. Thus, in my 1983 essay "Text and Interpretation," which I included in the second volume of my collected works [and also in the present volume], I have shown the general direction of my later writings.

The goal of my critical writings on aesthetics, then, was to free aesthetics from all mere historicism. Art history under the sign of historicism had more or less just become iconography.

GRONDIN: So how does art transcend historicism?

GADAMER: It seems persuasive to me that a work of art stands firm against every transforming of it into some other form of statement. Thus, as a philosopher, I am defending a kind of experience for which a mere playing around with ideas cannot be substituted. Defining "transcendence" in this sense means that every mere heightening of precision in discussion is out of place. A work of art is good or bad, strong or weak. But one experiences through it a certain presentness or presence [*Gegenwärtigkeit*]. This I call transcendence.

GRONDIN: Under the heading of relativism, one thinks especially of your rehabilitation of prejudgments [or prejudices] as conditions for the possibility of understanding. By doing this you raise historicity to a hermeneutical principle. Is this not some form of historical relativism?

GADAMER: There was no word "relativism" so long as there was no doubt in absolute truth, which was to be embodied in metaphysics. Neo-Kantianism had especially struggled to uphold an apriorism free of history while making the silent reservation of the relativity of experience. This was what one had to understand by the a priori. In the philosophy of art in the nineteenth century, above all in the magnificent projects of Fichte's and Hegel's idealism, one had to do with absolute knowledge. But for a finite nature there can be no knowledge of the absolute. Most of what we call science today is really a collection of sciences of experience—with the exception of mathematics and logic—and sciences of experience cannot be absolute knowledge. Greek philosophy seems to me to offer the right answer to the objection of relativism, when it only called mathematics science and all our world of experience was settled in the boundless realm of linguisticality and rhetoric. In this realm not everything is provable. What must be accepted as true here aims at what is believable.

In reality it has already been shown by Plato, in the *Phaedo* and the *Philebus,* and the same is done by Aristotle in detail in the *Ethics,* that for ethics the concept of mathematical truth was not valid. In mathematics and its necessities everything depends on the invention of proofs. But one cannot demand the exactness of mathematics in the being of and the dealings of humans. That does not mean that in ethics we don't have to do with truth, but rather in ethics there can be no proof that has the compelling power of mathematics. In rhetoric basically there are not syllogisms, but rather enthymemes [arguments from probability]. In rhetoric we are dealing with believability, and this holds for all ideas of what is true in the classic concept of rhetoric. This even holds for physics, insofar as one is dealing with the sublunar world; for there, too, the accidental happens. In truth, on account of this Aristotle compels us to accept a quite narrow concept of *episteme* as science, which he only finds acceptable in mathematics. Only in mathematics are there real proofs, and only there can there be no exceptions.

One would really honor the realm of the *Geisteswissenschaften* [human sciences] much more adequately, I think, if we brought them back under the older concept of rhetoric, where one deals with believable statements and not scientifically compelling proofs. This also applies for historical research, as well as for the sciences of law and theology, and as a matter of fact it also applies to the experience of art. In it there may be ever so much knowledge and science, but nothing that has to do with an artwork as a statement.[2]

GRONDIN: As your starting point [in *Truth and Method*] you emphasize the pre-structure of understanding and at the same time you talk about getting to the "thing itself," the phenomenological slogan in both Husserl and in Heidegger. How can you bring both of these together: the *Vorgängigkeit* [the event character] of the structure of prejudgment [as you present it] and the disclosure of the thing itself [*die Sache selbst*]? Doesn't the one exclude the other?

GADAMER: Here one only has to be clear about what *die Sache* [the matter] truly means. The matter is always the thing in dispute [*die Streit-sache*]. We erring human beings should never forget this, because all our efforts to overcome our prejudices rest on it. Of course, Husserl also used "the thing itself" to name the intentional object, and I remember how Heidegger was asked in a proseminar in Freiburg what the intentional object really was. Sharp anticipation [was aroused by the question], and the answer that he himself gave was that the intentional object was *das Sein* [being]—apparently in contrast to what is [*das Seiende*]. When Hei-degger speaks of the thing itself and of the thing that shows itself as phenomenon, what he means is the deconstruction of what is covering the thing over, and here the whole temporal and historical substructur-ing is implicitly implied. The uncovering of prejudices to which this is supposed to lead when being shows itself is a consequence of the analysis of *Zeitlichkeit* [time-ing] in *Being and Time*. The prejudices on the basis of which one makes judgments are not conscious. To this extent, the matter [*die Sache*] is always the issue in dispute [*die Streitsache*]. The thing against which one struggles if one is intending *die Sache* is wishful think-ing, and here one needs to defend the being of the other. This goal is especially of service when I and thou dispute with each other in a con-versation. For the conversation depends on the other person participat-ing in the dispute also realizing that he too has unconscious prejudices. This belongs to the nature of a fruitful conversation. When we do not listen with such clear good will that the other recognizes in you his view of what he means, then we are merely sophists. In any case that is what the term means when I speak of sophists. The sophist does not want to understand what you are saying but rather maintains that he is right. What we call "sophistic" is the illusory character of such refutations.

GRONDIN: In the third major part of *Truth and Method* you deal with what you call the universal dimension of linguisticality [*Sprachlich-keit*], and in the course of this you uncover an ontological dimension of hermeneutics. Here being, understanding, and language appear to be completely interwoven with each other. Many have interpreted this as a kind of "panlinguisticism." Above all, they are led in this direction by your famous formula, which is indeed the most often-cited quotation from your work, namely: "Being that can be understood is language." What do you mean by this formula?

GADAMER: Above all it means: being that can be experienced and understood, and it means that Being speaks. Only via language can being be understood. This formula that you cite is certainly a little ambiguous in its meaning, but an important aspect of speculative assertions is that they can come to speech from various sides. One often has this experience in practice, too; depending on how the person asking asks, or what he means, or who he is, one answers a little differently. It seems to me that this is not something we need to criticize, but rather it corresponds exactly to what Aristotle in the *Rhetoric* calls the enthymeme.[3] In it is expressed the paying attention to the other person that characterizes true rhetoric. Using an enthymeme does not assure that one reaches a compelling conclusion, but it is not for this reason without meaning nor without persuasive power and claim to truth. All discourse is such that the thing meant can be shown from various sides and thus allows of being repeated in various ways. This is the kind of conclusiveness which expresses itself in a powerfully persuasive way without being a compelling proof.

Let me give you an example. One day Heidegger says to us, "Die Sprache spricht" [Language speaks]. I must confess that for a long time I resisted the forced paradox in this formulation of Heidegger. It certainly did not please me very much, and I learned that even the most loyal followers of Heidegger were furious that he had come out with it. It is certainly clear that the person who is now speaking to you is the one who speaks. But in the meantime I think I have grasped what Heidegger meant when he said that language speaks. Of course there is a person who speaks, but not without being restricted by language, for it is not always the right word that comes to one. Hermeneutics helps us to realize that there is always much that remains unsaid when one says something. There is a lot in the same direction of meaning that almost completely escapes our attention because of the abstraction contained in the concepts of modern science. Thus I have designated as a central point of hermeneutical procedures that one is never supposed to have the last word.

GRONDIN: If I understand you correctly, you are emphasizing with this assertion the limits of language, but one gets the impression from *Truth and Method* that the universe of language is boundless.

GADAMER: No, no! I have never thought and never ever said that everything is language. Being that can be understood, insofar as it can be understood, is language. This contains a limitation. What cannot be understood can pose an endless task of at least finding a word that comes a little closer to the matter at issue [*die Sache*].

GRONDIN: Why [in *Truth and Method*] do you invoke Saint Augustine's doctrine of the inner word in this connection?

GADAMER: Precisely because it took Augustine no less than fifteen books to get closer to the secret of the Trinity without falling into the false way out of Gnostic presumption. This has become a very important point for me, a point which I would emphatically say I must defend. In truth, I am not at all talking about a Tower of Babel; that is to say, a multiplicity of languages and a confusion of languages is not the problem, one that according to the Old Testament, the tower illustrated and after which man is turned away to his own destiny. In reality, the multiplicity of languages does not represent an insurmountable barrier to the hermeneutical task. Every language is teachable. Thus a person is always capable of overcoming all boundaries [represented by language], when that person seeks to reach an understanding with the other person. Indeed, in the experience of a limit that resides in the word as such one really finds an infinite task.

I later followed up on this issue in some essays on the limits of language.[4] So my present effort to be understood is apparently justified. If I hear a foreign language that I only know a little of, I still believe that I am on the way to a basis for conversation. Even now in the midst of the present welter of languages in which we find ourselves, I have the same meaningful experience over and over. It consists in the fact that human beings who try to express themselves in a foreign language, however badly things go, will still find a great good will on the side of the local speaker. It sounds paradoxical, but it is true: one more easily makes oneself understood in the stuttering of a foreign language than when one tries to be understood by each speaking his or her own mother tongue.

I have regularly had an experience of this. It happens quite often, that one person makes the other person the following offer: "Oh, we will make it simple—you speak German and I will talk to you in English, French, Spanish, or whatever." But it does not work. If two people want to talk to each other, after a while one or the other language is chosen. What in my opinion comes out in this experience which we have all had is how concrete a reality conversation and linguisticality represent. They are not just abstractions from the general concept of language. If one goes back in ancient history and finds the natural root of language in the words *graphein* and *gramma,* this is also definitely misleading. Words are nothing written. Nor are words buried deep in the brain. Rather, what is there, so to speak, is the capacity to establish new combinations and in this way to make speaking possible. This is what I call linguisticality, and this expression refers to that "inner conversation" which the Stoics called the *logos endiathetos* [the Word latent in the Godhead from all eternity]. Now Augustine very impressively developed the point that this inner conversation can explain a mystery of the Christian religion. Indeed, I have learned a great deal from Augustine's *De trinitate*. These books contain a fine excess of metaphors that try to make understandable a great mystery of the Christian faith, the Trinity. Augustine took his bearings from the concept of the logos and the processes in God. In the end he is always inspired by Neoplatonism, and thereby achieves the overcoming of gnosis. If that is so, then one actually finds a limit to human understanding here, and this is what requires faith.

GRONDIN: If the Trinity refers to a process in God, does this mean for you that there is in it a boundary against Gnosticism, knowability, instrumentalism, and nominalism?

GADAMER: Yes. It is the Augustinian doctrine with all possible emphasis, that the *trinitas* exactly means the boundary. In this case, we can only come closer to it through human analogies.

This is certainly not a proof of God. It is only a way of understanding the revelation. Augustine's attempt in his books is to say that the greatest mystery of the Christian proclamation and revelation can nevertheless be made somewhat understandable through analogies. To this extent he believed that by using this approach he went beyond the Gnostic attacks.

GRONDIN: Very illuminating! But against this, would not everybody eventually grant you that in understanding the Trinity, even if this is not to be, one can at least get closer? Humans can handle the more trivial realities, of course. It is obvious that one can only approach an understanding of the Trinity because it is the Trinity of God, because it exceeds our understanding, but at least the other regions of human knowledge can certainly be brought under human control.

GADAMER: Brought under control? In knowing, it is not always a matter of ruling and dominating. There is such a thing as being familiar. Augustine presented fifteen analogies to the mystery of the Trinity— precisely to show that not everything is governable by humans. There are things that are close and intimate, like the things that are familiar to us and for which we have language. But how that comes about remains mysterious to us. This was enough for the theologian Augustine to say: Don't act as if this is something totally new to us, this mystery.—No, there are many things that we basically do not understand with which we are still familiar.

We all know about such mysterious things. One thinks for example of memory, of forgetting and remembering. There is a deep truth in Plato's doctrine of amnesia [forgetting]. For instance, one can search for a word that one absolutely cannot think of, but when one thinks again, it is simply there. How many times does one vainly search for the same word over and over again? Thus, the linguistic expression stands in a remarkable closeness to the concept.

Now one can ask whether this association of the word with the concept is not perhaps also meaningfully related to another much discussed problem: the way that Aristotle presents practical philosophy and the knowing involved with practical insight, with *phronesis*, under the general conceptual perspective that Aristotle in A 1 and Z 1 [*Metaphysics*] calls *skopos* [reach, scope, *epi skopos* = oversight, supervision], and the fact that Aristotle uses *skopos* as a concept containing both, although one term [*Wissen*] is in itself not practical but really theoretical, while the other term [*phronesis*] refers to praxis itself. On this observation hinges the much discussed question of how philosophy and practical philosophy are connected to practical knowledge in *phronesis*. Indeed, there is a whole debate over just this one question. One side says that *phronesis* is a kind of ethics, because Aristotle maintains that philosophy itself is also of service to virtue and should be helpful to it. There seems to be no exact boundary between word and concept in this realm. But the nominalistic way of thinking in modernity, which regards all words as merely tools, no longer recognizes that life relationships are actually shaped and take shape in words. Question and answer do not always have to be in words. A look can be a question and another look can express an answer and an understanding.

GRONDIN: Is there then such a thing as nonlinguistic understanding?

GADAMER: Doubtless there is.

GRONDIN: And would you still call this language [*Sprachlichkeit*, linguisticality]?

GADAMER: Why yes! Language in words is only a special concretion of linguisticality. And the same thing also applies to gestures, for example. A dog for whom you show the direction to go by pointing with your hand does not run in that direction but leaps up at your hand. Also, there is a language for the mute, and even for the deaf-mute. For Wilhelm von Humboldt this is also a truth, and for me this is especially persuasive, because his true charisma consisted not only in the fact that he was a magnificent linguist. He always took as important the things that were accessible in various individual languages. One thinks of his introduction to the language of the Kawi.[5] This holds for the whole problem area that makes the *Phaedrus* so difficult and to me so unforgettable. It is shown there how philosophical dialectic stands linked with genuine rhetoric. This raises many questions that I am only slowly posing to myself.

One of these is the problem of how it came about that medieval Scholasticism was finally so completely dominated by Aristotle. When one reads Augustine, for instance, one breathes Platonic air. Also, in reading Plotinus one is carried along by a soulful Greek that recalls the greatest secrets of the Platonic spirit. Would perhaps the later transition to Aristotle in Christian theology have been possible without Arab theology? That is the question. It is certainly no accident that in the passage of Aristotle through Arabic culture one finds many traces of that culture echoing in our language. For instance, we call the Arabic numerals we use by their Arabic names. There is nothing left of the famous Roman numerals, in which one always recognizes something of the multiples of one. In the Arabic numbers we have symbols that have been set free, that don't copy anything. The idea of algebra is of Arabic origin. With Arabic we have a completely strange language before us, one that indeed does not know of a copula or anything developed in Greek and Roman logic and grammar. Language is never free of metaphors. But not every language is as logical as Latin. If one tries to transform everything until it fits into generic concepts and their specifications, there are always little pieces that still fall outside them. [In Latin] things get weaker, paler. The whole fate of Western civilization is foreshadowed here in this nominalistic turn, and perhaps already in the dispute over the reality or nonreality of universals [*Universalismusstreit*], to such a degree that one no longer merely strives to carry on a conversation but also wants to maintain something as compellingly provable. To see this point more clearly, one should remember the inseparability of rhetoric and dialectic which is maintained in the *Phaedrus*. Plato's work is particularly striking in expressly taking rhetoric as a topic and its use for demagogical, populist purposes, which one calls sophism. Socrates is often presented as in dialogue with the Sophists. This is a brilliant invention by Plato.

GRONDIN: Socrates in conversation with the Sophists—that is something Plato *invented?*

GADAMER: Certainly, and with what great poetic power! One knows, of course, that the great Sophists were almost all foreigners who came to Athens. So this view of them was held in general about intellectual youth, and other people who were attracted by these teachers, and one day their wrath against these new fashions fell on the only person they could get their hands on, namely Socrates. The whole of the writings of Plato wonderfully present this general confusion of Socrates with the Sophists. In order to carry through his critique of the demoralizing consequences of the movement for Sophist enlightenment, Plato in his way stylized Socrates[6] and through this made Socrates' famous knowing of not-knowing immortal, although it was something that Xenophon in his recollections of Socrates apparently never noticed. Later, in the *Phaedrus*, Plato even seeks something like a reconciliation between rhetoric and dialectic, and Aristotle continued this reconciliation by teaching both logic and rhetoric in Plato's academy.

Whether practical philosophy, which Aristotle developed, somehow presupposed *phronesis* or is indeed itself such a moral insight is something one must really be able to clarify. But the fact that Aristotle, too, did not place logic in the highest place seems to me very significant. I am more and more persuaded that Aristotle, like Plato, through his kind of thinking undertook conceptual experiments, and that his writings are not, or are not in every case, intended for some kind of publication. So one should transpose his writings into dialogues, also, if one wants to understand them.

Regrettably, we no longer possess the dialogues that were written by Aristotle himself, which were praised around the world. From Cicero we can go so far in reconstructing them that we know they did not just deal with matters for teaching and they left a lot undecided. One listens to a debate in them in which a third person mediates, but in the end much remains open. Of course, Plato aimed for an even stronger effect in this direction. When he presents Socrates in conversation, one always has the feeling that the person addressed is ultimately oneself. The monotone on the part of the other, who mostly only says "yes" or "perhaps," results in one very soon forgetting altogether that these are dialogues!

GRONDIN: The central place of the expression *Sprachlichkeit* [linguisticality] in your philosophy really seems rather mysterious if it does not necessarily involve a concrete language in words. Could you explain this?

GADAMER: I already talked about this somewhat when I referred to the language of gesture. Apparently this is the thing we humans have in common, that even household animals who cannot speak, often scarcely need to receive a signal from us. Why is this? What is it that is held in common? Obviously a dog lacks the capacity to understand the symbolic, namely, that by referring to something one does not mean one is able to make known something that one does mean, whatever it may be, and to do so in such a way that it is understood, like the *tessara hospitalis* that even after generations will identify a traveler as an old friend of the family.

GRONDIN: So language [*Sprachlichkeit*, linguisticality] would refer to the quite general capacity to mean something by something and to communicate it?

GADAMER: Yes, to understand something as a sign of something else, and not to understand the outstretched finger the way the dog will who snaps at it in trying to take hold of it, but rather to understand that it means something.

GRONDIN: But what about the relationship between logic and rhetoric? Nowadays logic stands for a rigorous, scientific, well-grounded knowledge, while rhetoric is regarded as a kind of sophism.

GADAMER: Certainly rhetoric today is almost an invective! I regard this as a weakness of our civilization. In Vico [1668–1744], the full sense of rhetoric is still there. You know the Latin writing, *De ratione studiorum*, I assume.[7] It has always attracted me very much, much more than its application, which he carried out himself in *The New Science*. In it one stumbles across many philosophical oddities. Still, even there the basic point is very enlightening. You certainly remember that the Latin expression for science in Vico is *critica*. What this word really means, however, is not "communication with something" but distinguishing something from something else. Thus, the whole modern concept of objectivity begins to take shape in this time period. Originally objectivity meant what shows itself to the subject, that which stands over against it [*den Gegenstand*]. Vico was already aware of the Cartesian turn. So one could say that linguisticality is also found in the capacity to make symbols. And with the poet Stefan George I would perhaps also say the capacity to dream.

GRONDIN: In connection with this I would like to ask: how do you generally react to the common complaint that hermeneutical thinking is hostile to science, logic, and objectivity? This complaint is quite widespread.

GADAMER: Certainly.

GRONDIN: Is this a misunderstanding?

GADAMER: As my answer to this, I would cite the excursus from [Plato's] *Statesman*, in which the two forms of measuring are placed next to each other and it is expressly said there: to man, who is, as such, a political being, both forms belong. Science, which is power and which claims to be able to control things, is only one form of knowledge. There is another form of knowing, however, and it is this that I would like to defend: [it is the capacity] to come up with the right word at the right moment, this kind of exactness itself. This was the ancient, honorable concept of rhetoric.

Thus, this is a misunderstanding that actually misleads us. I mean, it is completely self-evident when I say: everyplace where the procedure of measuring and logic gives rise to blindness, the true blindness does not reside in this knowledge itself but in the fact that one regards it as the whole of knowledge. It is this viewpoint that I would like to defend against. In art [*Kunstwissenschaft*] and particularly in the human sciences [*Geisteswissenschaften*] I have encountered the same thing. Yet what attracted me to these areas was precisely not what was achieved through method. Rather, it is once again this symbolic presentness. One recognizes *oneself* in history, for example. But in the methodical science of historical research they regard this as completely wrong. They want you to be "objective"!

These are, of course, very deep matters, things that now, at the end of my working life, are accompanied by the question: What will the consequences be of the present global extension of our scientific culture? Will there now perhaps be a return to certain forms of ritual? I would like to mention in this connection my two late essays on art in word and image and on the phenomenology of ritual and language.[8] What I wanted to do in these two essays is something I will always defend. Ritualizing is for us something infinitely strange and exotic that is found in China or Japan. I will always remember how much self-control a Japanese has to exercise in order not to laugh when he sees a European bouquet of flowers. For we do not see how symbolic a bouquet of flowers is. Oh, these Europeans, who put just any colors whatever together! In truth, flower arrangement is a great art, and a great educational achievement of Japanese culture. It is a supremely artistic matter, in which ritual is accomplished and finds expression.

GRONDIN: But isn't it the case that in our society the technological ability to do things has become the new ritual, so that there can be no turning back?

GADAMER: No, not at all! Ritual is anything but the automated regulation of things. Ritual is something one carries out which expresses reverence. Ritual is also not something useful. Rather, it brings a tremendous elaborateness [*Umständlichkeit*] into life, and it has probably reduced many explosive dangers in the emotional life of the person who practices it. In it you do not think of any use. In principle, I had this in mind when I cited that place in the *Statesman*. Nobody talks about the fact that science is no longer science. This is something one really does have to admit.

The genuine insight that Heidegger had with regard to the technological era and what he called *das Gestell* [framing] consists in the fact that the result was that all this technology no longer held any kind of fascination for him. That is the decisive point.

GRONDIN: Your relationship to Heidegger is of course a very complex one. According to one's perspective one can see you as a follower or as. . . .

GADAMER: Or as one who stayed behind, who can be seen as lagging behind Heidegger. Both are certainly justified.

GRONDIN: It all depends. One can regard your hermeneutics as a further development of Heidegger or as an alternative to him. In what way are you his follower, and in what respect might you be offering a counter-concept? In general, how do you see your relationship to Heidegger?

GADAMER: That is a very central question. First of all, one cannot think of my becoming who I am without Heidegger. And the question can only be asked after Heidegger; now that he is, so to speak, no longer there, how is he still basically with me? About this I would say: his radicalism always bore the stamp of his religious background. For his whole life, his radicalism was driven by an endless search for God. I also search in my own way, but with the difference that I did not have any important childhood influences in this direction. But for the young boy Heidegger in Messkirch growing up as a church sexton's son, it was of course completely different.

[From early on] I was an admirer of Heidegger, and I would still say today that my first book, *Plato's Dialectical Ethics,* was all too much molded by the general position Heidegger defended: that Plato is only a preparation for Aristotle. Today I would say Heidegger was not fair to Plato, so he did not see what even Hegel saw. If I pick up any volume of Hegel's history of philosophy, as bad as this whole edition is, and turn at random to any particular place and have not noticed whether it is his commentary on Plato or his commentary on Aristotle, I cannot tell which it is! Is it about Plato or Aristotle that he is speaking? His commentary on Plato and that on Aristotle change places almost at random. Hegel has seen something! Of course, this was from the standpoint of his presuppositions. What I am indebted to Heidegger for is that I was forced to study classical philology [in the 1920s] and thereby learned to maintain a somewhat better-disciplined following of his tendency to show from language what the true lineage of concepts is. To the basic question that you pose of what my relationship is to him, I would answer: I greatly admired his imaginative thinking and his power of thinking. Whatever one may criticize in Heidegger, one must consider this: a person who can think as powerfully as he did was also able in a flash to sidestep self-criticism! He followed his vision. That he succeeded so well in doing this also explains his political mistake. Already from the beginning he had a bad conscience about it. First I received the news from Freiburg about his trafficking with Nazi circles. I did not take it seriously. I never believed that he would ever venture into politics. That he had no talent for it was all too evident. And so I was actually not surprised that it went wrong. It is quite clear to me he was led into his political mistake by the fact of his having foreseen the domination of the industrial revolution over humanity. This he had seen. This was more clearly seen by the farm boy from Messkirch than by us, who from early on had adjusted to the civilization and had even been educated for it. This was also what Heidegger, in my view, was right about in his discussion of technology, as I said before. He was right when he said it is not the technology that is dangerous, but the fascination that comes from it. This is what humankind has to overcome. One must come to see that this is something that reflects a powerful backwardness in our European culture. One sees this especially in the Latin European countries. I see very clearly the role of the Catholic Church in this. One can view this very critically, especially if one is educated in another confession! But this is what I would say today about Catholicism: alongside the other great religions of the world it nevertheless manifests a form of awe, while Puritanism ultimately represents, as Heidegger writes, a "forgetfulness of being."

GRONDIN: In 1985 you undertook personally to supervise a ten-volume authorized edition of your collected works. The final volume appeared in 1995. This is an unusual piece of good fortune, that an author lives to see his own authorized edition of collected works through to the end. The final approval of each writing for this edition has always been your own. What were your guidelines in putting this collected edition together?

GADAMER: This is actually a paradox. Because my very first thought was that I really do not want people to make a classic figure out of me, a person of whom everything I ever wrote is gathered up. So the edition of my writings does not offer my complete works—my publisher Siebeck very rightly agreed with me on this—but rather my "collected" works. I collected some for the edition and left others out. That was the first step in this whole project. Now I had to reckon with the fact that I could scarcely hope to live to complete this task. The first volumes I chose were those on Greek philosophy. Through working on these three volumes, I found out how many different publishers had brought out my studies in Greek philosophy in foreign countries, most of which I knew but not all. So I received many questions to read, and based on my answers the edition was ultimately printed. I asked the publisher, the father of the present publisher Siebeck, if he could perhaps bring out a collection of these Greek studies. He readily agreed to this, although he himself preferred to do all of them. So we agreed on this: okay, I will choose them myself, and will do my best to include in addition to my Greek studies the most important of the works I have done in the course of the last fifteen years. Of course, in doing it this way the chronological and thematic order is basically mixed up.

But with this little balancing, and after the successful completion of the edition, I can now take my leave of it saying to myself, "At least there will never be a posthumously arranged complete edition. This will substitute for it." By doing this people will be done with it, and there will never be one of those great monuments of a posthumous complete edition of my works. I must confess I see in this a gain that has in part accrued to me.

GRONDIN: Now that this edition is completed, what works would you still most like to tackle?

GADAMER: I would still like to do some basic investigations of the line that goes back and forth marking the separation between word and concept.[9] One of these essays would deal with the topic of what ethics is, and what it means that one can talk about something practical in theoretical terms. Also, could we perhaps bring back to life the ancient meaning of rhetoric? As far as I know, the later Heidegger no longer dealt with either topic. Instead he pursued Nietzsche to the farthest extreme. There he was no longer able to come out with anything without borrowing from poetry, and he found no real language for his thoughts. That he saw far I do not dispute. I defend him above all by referring to his work from 1938, "The Age of the World Picture." Is this essay something from yesterday or is it not rather from tomorrow? Or even the day after tomorrow?

Translated by Richard E. Palmer

Abbreviations

(Works listed are by Gadamer unless another author is given.)

BW   Heidegger, Martin. *Basic Writings: From Being and Time (1927) to The Task of Thinking (1964)*. Edited by David Farrell Krell. Revised and expanded edition. San Francisco: HarperSanFrancisco, 1993.

DD   *Dialogue and Dialectic: Eight Hermeneutical Studies on Plato*. Translated by P. Christopher Smith. New Haven: Yale University Press, 1980.

EH   *The Enigma of Health: The Art of Healing in a Scientific Age*. Translated by Jason Geiger and Nicholas Walker. Cambridge: Polity / Stanford: Stanford University Press, 1996.

GA   Heidegger, Martin. *Gesamtausgabe*. Frankfurt: Klostermann.

G-B   Makita, Etsuro. *Gadamer-Bibliographie (1922–1994)*. Frankfurt: Peter Lang, 1995.

GBio   Grondin, Jean. *Hans-Georg Gadamer: A Biography*. Translated by Joel Weinsheimer. New Haven: Yale University Press, 2003. Published first in German as *Hans-Georg Gadamer: Eine Biographie* (Tübingen: Mohr Siebeck, 1999).

GDE   *Dialogue and Deconstruction: The Gadamer-Derrida Encounter*. Edited by Diane P. Michelfelder and Richard E. Palmer. Albany: State University of New York Press, 1989.

GL   *Gadamer Lesebuch*. Edited by Jean Grondin. UTB [Unitaschenbücher] 1972 Tübingen: Mohr Siebeck, 1997.

GOC   *Gadamer on Celan: "Who Am I and Who Are You?" and Other Essays*. Translated and edited by Richard Heinemann and Bruce Krajewski. Albany: State University of New York Press, 1997. A translation of *WBI*.

GW   *Gesammelte Werke*. 10 vols. Tübingen: Mohr Siebeck, 1985–95.

GW 1   *Wahrheit und Methode: Grundzüge einer philosophischen Hermeneutik.* 1986.

GW 2   *Hermeneutik II: Wahrheit und Methode.* Ergänzungen und Register. [Additional materials and index.] 1986, revised 1993. Contains twenty-five articles on hermeneutics, the supplements to each of the five editions of *WM,* the "*Selbstdarstellung*" [Self-Presentation] of 1977, plus an index to *GW* 1.

GW 3   *Neuere Philosophie I: Hegel, Husserl, Heidegger.* 1987.

GW 4   *Neuere Philosophie II: Probleme, Gestalten.* 1987.

GW 5   *Griechische Philosophie I.* 1985.

GW 6   *Griechische Philosophie II.* 1985.

GW 7   *Griechische Philosophie III: Plato im Dialog.* 1991.

GW 8   *Ästhetik und Poetik I: Kunst als Aussage.* 1993.

GW 9   *Ästhetik und Poetik II: Hermeneutik im Vollzug.* 1993.

GW 10   *Hermeneutik im Rückblick.* 1995.

HE   *Hermeneutische Entwürfe: Vorträge und Aufsätze.* Tübingen: Mohr Siebeck, 2000. A supplement to the *GW,* containing new and previously omitted essays.

HD   *Hegels Dialektik: Funf hermeneutische Studien.* Tübingen: Mohr, 1971; second edition, 1980.

HDE   *Hegel's Dialectic: Five Hermeneutical Studies.* Translated by P. Christopher Smith. New Haven: Yale University Press, 1976.

HI   Multiple authors. *Hermeneutik und Ideologiekritik.* Frankfurt: Suhrkamp, 1971. Paperback collection of essays by various authors.

"HtJ"   "Heideggers 'theologische' Jugendschrift." *Dilthey-Jahrbuch für Philosophie und Geschichte der Geisteswissenschaften* 6 (1989): 228–34. Gadamer's introduction to his rediscovered Heidegger texts in the same volume.

HW   *Heidegger's Ways.* Translated by John W. Stanley. Albany: State University of New York Press, 1994. A translation of *Heidegger's Wege* (Tübingen: Mohr Siebeck, 1983).

IG   *Die Idee des Guten zwischen Plato und Aristoteles.* Sitzungsberichte [minutes] der Heidelberger Akademie der Wissenschaften [Transactions of the Heidelberg Academy of Sciences]. Heidelberg: C. Winter Universitätsverlag, 1978. See *IGE.*

IGE   *The Idea of the Good in Platonic-Aristotelian Philosophy.* Translated by P. Christopher Smith. New Haven: Yale University Press, 1986.

KS 1   *Kleine Schriften I: Philosophie, Hermeneutik.* Tübingen: Mohr, 1967.

KS 2   *Kleine Schriften II: Interpretationen.* Tübingen: Mohr, 1967.

KS 3   *Kleine Schriften III: Idee und Sprache: Platon, Husserl, Heidegger.* Tübingen: Mohr, 1972.

KS 4   *Kleine Schriften IV: Variationen.* Tübingen: Mohr, 1977.

M   Aristoteles. *Metaphysik XII.* Greek-German. Translation and commentary by Hans-Georg Gadamer. Frankfurt: Klostermann, 1948. Subsequent editions in 1970, 1976, and 1984.

"NSH"   "Natural Science and Hermeneutics: The Concept of Nature in Ancient Philosophy." Translated by Kathleen Wright in *Proceedings of the Boston Area Colloquium in Ancient Philosophy,* vol. 1, ed. J. J. Cleary (Lanham, 1986), 39–52.

PA   *Philosophical Apprenticeships.* Translated by Robert R. Solomon. Cambridge, Mass.: MIT Press, 1985. A translation of *PL.*

PD   *Plato und die Dichter.* Frankfurt: Klostermann, 1934.

PdE   *Platos dialektische Ethik: Phänomenologische Interpretationen zum Philelos.* Leipzig: Meiner, 1931. Updated in a second enlarged edition as *Platos dialektische Ethik und andere Studien zu platonischen Philosophie.* Hamburg: Meiner, 1968. *PdE* 1968 is also in *GW* 5: 3–163.

PDE   *Plato's Dialectical Ethics.* Translated by Robert M. Wallace. New Haven: Yale University Press, 1991. A translation of *PdE* 1968.

PH   *Philosophical Hermeneutics.* Edited and translated by David E. Linge. Berkeley: University of California Press, 1976.

PHGG   *The Philosophy of Hans-Georg Gadamer.* Edited by Lewis Edwin Hahn. LaSalle: Open Court, 1997.

PL   *Philosophische Lehrejahre.* Frankfurt: Klostermann, 1977.

QCT   Heidegger, Martin. *The Question Concerning Technology and Other Essays.* Translated by William Lovitt. New York: Harper and Row, 1977.

RAS   *Reason in the Age of Science.* Translated by Frederick G. Lawrence. Cambridge, Mass.: MIT Press, 1981.

RB   *The Relevance of the Beautiful and Other Essays.* Translated by Nicholas Walker, edited by Robert Bernasconi. Cambridge: Cambridge University Press, 1986. "Relevance of the Beautiful," 3–53.

"RHI"   "Rhetorik, Hermeneutik und Ideologiekritik." In *KS* 1: 113–30. Also appeared later in *HI* 283–317.

"RHIE"   Translation of "*Rhetorik, Hermeneutik und Ideologiekritik*" under the title "On the Scope and Function of Hermeneutical Reflection," translated by Richard Palmer and G. B. Hess in *PH* 18–43; reprinted in Joself Bleicher's *Contemporary Philosophy: Hermeneutics as Method, Philosophy, and Critique* (London: Routledge & Kegan Paul, 1980),

128–40; in *Hermeneutic Tradition: From Ast to Ricoeur*, edited by Gayle L. Ormiston and Alan D. Schrift (Albany: SUNY Press, 1990); and under the title "Rhetoric, Hermeneutics and Ideology-Critique," in *Rhetoric and Hermeneutics in Our Time: A Reader*, edited by Walter Jost and Michael Hyde (New Haven: Yale University Press, 1997), 313–34.

"TAI" "Text and Interpretation." In *GDE* 21–51.

TI *Text und Interpretation: Eine deutsch-franzosische Debatte mit Beiträgen von Jacques Derrida, Philippe Forget, Manfred Frank, Hans-Georg Gadamer, Jean Greisch und François Laruelle*. Edited by Philippe Forget. Stuttgart: Fink, 1984.

TM *Truth and Method*. Second revised edition. Translation revised by Joel Weinsheimer and Donald G. Marshall. New York: Crossroad, 1989. A translation of *WM*.

VB *Über die Verborgenheit der Gesundheit: Aufsätze und Vorträge*. Frankfurt: Suhrkamp, 1993.

VGDH *Volk und Geschichte im Denken Herders*. Frankfurt: Klostermann, 1942. In *GW* 4: 318–35.

VZW Vernunft im Zeitalter der Wissenschaft. Frankfurt: Suhrkamp, 1976.

WBI Wer bin Ich und wer bist Du?: Eine Kommentar zu Paul Celans Gedichtfolge "Atemkristall." Frankfurt: Suhrkamp, 1973. Translated in *GOC*.

WM Wahrheit und Methode. Tübingen: Mohr, 1960. Also *GW* 1. Translated as *TM*.

Notes

The notes for the chapter introductions are by Richard E. Palmer. The notes for Gadamer's texts are by Gadamer himself. The translator has sometimes supplemented Gadamer's notes or has added entirely new notes to explain or document references that may be unfamiliar to the English-speaking reader; where authorship is unclear, translator additions have been enclosed in brackets.

Chapter 1

Introduction

1. *Philosophie in Selbstdarstellungen,* vol. 3, ed. Ludwig J. Pongratz. (Hamburg: Meiner, 1977), 60–101. Gadamer's contribution to the volume did not carry a title, since all three essays were self-presentations.
2. *PL* and *PA*.
3. *GBio.*
4. Hans-Georg Gadamer, "Reflections on My Philosophical Journey," in *PHGG*, 3–63 (part 1: 3–18, part 3: 26–40).

Autobiographical Reflections

[The text of this essay is from Hans-Georg Gadamer, "Selbstdarstellung, born February 2, 1900, written 1975," in *GW*2: 479–508. For the English translation, see parts 1 and 3 of "Reflections on My Philosophical Journey" in *PHGG*, 3–18, 26–40 (all four parts take up 3–63).]
1. [For a review of the earlier years of Gadamer's life, I refer English-speaking readers to the first chapter of his *PL*. *PL* has been translated into English as *Philosophical Apprenticeships (PA)*.]
2. Paul Ernst, *Der Zusammenbruch des deutschen Idealismus,* 2 vols. (Munich: Beck, 1920–22).
3. Oswald Spengler, *Der Untergang des Abendlandes: Umriss einer Morphologie der Weltgeschichte,* 2 vols. (1918, 1922).
4. [See Wilhelm Dilthey, *Selected Works,* ed. Rudolf A. Makkreel and

Frithjof Rodi (Princeton, N.J.: Princeton University Press), vol. 5 (1985) and vol. 1 (1989).]

5. [Ernst Troeltsch, *The Social Teaching of the Christian Churches,* 2 vols., trans. Olive Wyon (Chicago: University of Chicago Press, 1981).]

6. [The Marburg school was a school of neo-Kantian philosophy represented by the Marburg philosophers Hermann Cohen (1842–1918) and Paul Natorp (1854–1924), as well as Nicolai Hartmann (1882–1950) and Ernst Cassirer (1874–1945).]

7. Hans-Georg Gadamer, "Zur Systemidee in der Philosophie," in *Festschrift für Paul Natorp zum 70. Geburtstage* (Berlin: De Gruyter, 1924), 55–75.

8. Hans-Georg Gadamer, "*Metaphysik der Erkenntnis:* Zu dem gleichnamigen Buch von Nicolai Hartmann," *Logos: Internationale Zeitschrift für Philosophie der Kultur* 12 (1923–24): 340–59.

9. Hans-Georg Gadamer, "Der aristotelische *Protreptikos* und die entwicklungsgeschichtliche Betrachtung der aristotelischen Ethik," *Hermes: Zeitschrift für klassische Philologie* 63 (1928): 138–64. Also in *GW* 5: 164–86.

10. See Julius Stenzel, *Studien zur Entwicklung der platonischen Dialektik von Sokrates zu Aristoteles* (Leipzig, Berlin: Teubner, 1912; 2nd ed. 1931); and *Zahl und Gestalt bei Platon* (Leipzig, Berlin: Teubner, 1924).

11. In this regard, see also my essay "Praktisches Wissen" in *GW* 5: 230–48. Walter Brocker later demonstrated this in his *Aristoteles* (Frankfurt: Klostermann, 1935).

12. In this regard, see also my essay "Praktisches Wissen" in *GW* 5: 230–48.

13. Hans-Georg Gadamer, "Gibt es die Materie?" in *GW* 6: 201–17. [There is also a deleted sentence here (see *GW* 2: 487): "My uncompleted (early) commentary on Aristotle's *Physics* will perhaps still one day be published."]

14. Hans-Georg Gadamer, "Antike Atomtheorie," *Zeitschrift für die gesamte Naturwissenschaft* 1 (1935–36): 81–95. Also in *GW* 5: 263–79.

15. *PdE.* Also in *GW* 5: 3–163. English: *PDE.*

16. See my article, "Idea and Reality in Plato's *Timaeus,*" in proceedings of the Heidelberger Akademie der Wissenschaften, 2. Abhandlung (1974), and *GW* 6, 242–70.

17. ["Ihr Verhältnis zur historischen Kritik ist schon dann ein positives, wenn diese in der Meinung, keine Förderung durch sie zu finden—das was sie sagt, fur selbstverständlich befindet." Hans-Georg Gadamer, introduction to *Platos dialektische Ethik,* 13 (p. 10 in 2nd ed., and p. 13 in *PDE*). The review appeared in *Archiv für Geschichte der Philosophie* 41 (1932): 246.]

18. [*PD;* and Hans-Georg Gadamer, "Platos Staat der Erziehung," in *Das neue Bild der Antike,* vol. 1, ed. Helmut Berve (Leipzig: Koehler und Amelang, 1942), 317–33. Both works were reprinted in *PdE* (1968), 179–204 and 205–20; and in *GW* 5: 187–211 and 249–62. English translations in *DD,* 39–72 and 73–92, as well as subsequently in *PDE.*]

19. I have taken up this point recently in "Platos Denken in Utopien," *Gymnasium* 90 (1983): 434–55, and in *GW* 7: 270–89. [Untranslated.]

20. [For a more detailed discussion of these years and of this promotion,

see the chapter titled "Dozentenjahre" in *PL*, 44–59 and 57–58, cited in note 2, and the corresponding pages in the English translation, *PA*, 69–81.]

21. [Robert Musil was a major twentieth-century German author, best known for his three-volume novel, *The Man Without Qualities.*]

22. *VGDH*. Also in *GW* 4: 318–35.

23. Karlheinz Volkmann-Schluck, *Plotin als Interpret der Ontologie Platos* (Frankfurt: Klostermann, 1941).

24. Hans-Georg Gadamer, *Kleine Schriften II: Interpretationen* (*KS* 2).

25. *M*.

26. Wilhelm Dilthey, *Grundriss der Geschichte der Philosophie* (Frankfurt: Klostermann, 1949).

27. *WM*.

28. I have in mind especially the work of the "Poetik und Hermeneutik Arbeitsgruppe," a selection of whose writings from various volumes and years of their meetings has been translated into English in *New Perspectives in German Literary Criticism*, ed. Richard E. Amacher and Victor Lange (Princeton, N.J.: Princeton University Press, 1979).

29. [In German the same word, *Spiel*, is used to mean both "play" and "game." Our translation will sometimes use one term, sometimes the other, depending on the context, and sometimes also "playing the game," in order to suggest the overtones of motion.]

30. [As the German word shows, *sein* is part of "consciousness" in German; thus Gadamer is suggesting that even when he uses the word "consciousness" the emphasis should be on the *sein* that contains historically conditioned structures and not on an empty, flickering awareness. Gadamer has used this slogan elsewhere, generally in explanation of "historically affected consciousness." For instance, in "RHI" he says, "Denn wirkungsgeschichtliches Bewusstsein ist auf eine unaufhebbare Weise mehr Sein als Bewusstsein" (*GW* 2: 247); "For historically affected consciousness is in an inescapable way more being than consciousness." The English translation of this essay is titled "On the Scope and Function of Hermeneutical Reflection" and was published in *PH*, 18–43.] In Hegel, *Sein* [being] refers to the thing in its immediacy, and *Wesen* [essence] is the "truth" of that immediate thing. The *Begriff* [concept] unites these two without losing either side. Thus a "concept" here has a rootedness in being that is not associated with it in merely nominalist uses of this term.

31. [Heidegger's "Die Zeit des Weltbildes" was presented as a lecture in 1938 and published in his *Holzwege* (Frankfurt: Klostermann, 1950), 69–104. In English it is "The Age of the World Picture" in *QCT*, 115–54.]

32. ["I conceive (experiments) through the mind." In other words, it is the mind which first grasps, integrates, and projects. Galileo here is discussing his famous experiment regarding the indefinitely continued motion of bodies projected on a plane in space. He first constructed the experiment in his mind. See *Le opere di Galileo Galilei*, 1st complete edition (1842–56), ed. Eugenio Albèri, vol. 13, *Dialoghi delle nuove scienze* (Florence: Società Editice Fiorentina, 1855),

"Giornata Quarta" ("Fourth Day"), 221–22 (first two pages of chapter). I am indebted to Donatella diCesare for this reference.] See my lecture given in 1983 at both Lund, Sweden, and in Boston. In German, the article carried the title "Naturwissenschaft und Hermeneutik" and appeared in *Philosophie und Kultur,* ed. Arno Werner (Lund: University of Lund Press, 1986), 3: 39–70. It is also in *GW* 7: 418–42. [English translation: *NSH.*]

33. [This is clearly a reply to Habermas.]

34. My contribution to that volume may be found translated into English in *PH* under the title "On the Scope and Function of Hermeneutical Reflection," 18–43; this is a translation of the essay titled "Rhetoric, Hermeneutik und Ideologiekritik" in *HI.* See also Josef Bleicher's *Contemporary Hermeneutics* (London: Routledge and Kegan Paul, 1980).

35. See Giambattista Vico, "The Academies and the Relation between Philosophy and Eloquence," trans. Donald Phillip Verene, in Vico, *On the Study Methods of Our Time,* trans. Elio Gianturco (Ithaca, N.Y.: Cornell University Press, 1990).

36. [See Chaim Perelman and L. Olbrechts-Tyteca, *The New Rhetoric* (Notre Dame, Ind.: University of Notre Dame Press, 1969).]

37. Paul Friedländer, *Platon,* 2 vols. (Berlin: De Gruyter, 1928–30 [1st ed.]; 1954–60 [2nd rev. ed.]). In English: *Plato,* 3 vols., trans. Hans Meyerhoff (New York: Pantheon Books, 1958–69).

38. See *GW* 6 and *GW* 7, esp. *IG,* in *GW* 7, 128–227. [English: *IGE.*]

39. [For a trenchant critique of the use of the term *Geist* in Heidegger, see Derrida's *De l'esprit: Heidegger et la question* (Paris: Galilee, 1987); English translation as *Of Spirit: Heidegger and the Question,* trans. Geoffrey Bennington and Rachel Bowlby (Chicago: University of Chicago Press, 1989).]

40. [See Michael Polanyi, *Personal Knowledge: Towards a Post-Critical Philosophy* (London: Routledge and Kegan Paul, 1958).]

41. [In the summer semester of 1965, Gadamer offered a lecture course titled "Von Hegel bis Heidegger" that raised these questions. Heidegger attended its final lecture and offered some remarks afterward. Basically, in those remarks Heidegger continued to emphasize the fact that Hegel's thought culminates in a form of absolute knowledge.]

42. See my discussion of the "eminent text" in "Text und Interpretation," in *TI,* 24–55, esp. 44–45. [Also in *GW* 2: 330–60, esp. 350–52.] [English translation in *GDE,* 21–51, esp. 41–42, and this essay is included in the present volume.]

43. *WBI.*

Chapter 2

Introduction

1. "Hermenraetic" [*sic*], in *Grosses Universal Lexicon aller Wissenschaften und Künste, welche bishero [sic] durch menschlichen Verstand und Witz erfunden und verbes-*

sert worden (Halle and Leipzig: Johann Heinrich Zedlers, 1735), vol. 12 (H.–He), columns 1730–33. No author given.

2. E. F. Vogel, "Hermeneutik," in *Allgemeine Encyklopädie der Wissenschaften und Künste,* ed. J. S. Ersch and J. O. Gruber (Leipzig: Verlag von Johann Friedrich Glebitsch, 1829), second section (H–N), ed. G. Hassel and A. G. Hoffmann, 5th part (Heinrich–Hequaesi), 300–322.

3. Heinrich Dobschütz, "Hermeneutik, biblishe," in *Realencyklopädie für protestantische Theologie und Kirche,* 3rd ed. (Leipzig: J. C. Hinrich'sche Buchhandlung, 1899), 719–35.

4. Gerhard Ebeling, "Hermeneutik," in *Die Religion in Geschichte und Gegenwart,* 3rd edition done in collaboration with Hans von Campenhausen, Erich Dinkler, Gerhard Gloege, and Knud E. Løgstrup, edited by Kurt Galling, vol. 3 (H–Kon), columns 242–62.

5. I had at one time intended to translate all five of these encyclopedia articles into English, and add introductions, but other more urgent projects intervened. All of these articles may be found in the Sterling Library at Yale University.

6. Edmund Husserl's "Phenomenology" article in the 1927 *Encyclopaedia Britannica* met a tragic fate at the hands of the English translator. It was not only hastily translated; it was cut by a third. Thus, the publication of the full original German text of the article in the *Husserliana,* vol. 9 (Amsterdam: Nijhoff, 1962), was an important event. At the suggestion of Herbert Spiegelberg, I translated the article for the *Journal of the British Society for Phenomenology* in 1970, and he wrote a foreword for it. This translation has recently appeared in the *Collected Works* of Husserl in English, vol. 6: *Psychological and Transcendental Phenomenology and the Confrontation with Heidegger (1927–1931),* ed. and trans. Thomas Sheehan and Richard E. Palmer (Dordrecht: Kluwer, 1997), 159–79.

7. See Hans-Georg Gadamer, "Hermeneutik," in *Contemporary Philosophy,* vol. 3, ed. Raymond Klibansky (Florence: La nuova Italia, 1969), 360–72.

8. This information is from Gadamer's bibliographer, Etsuro Makita, in *G-B,* A74/01, giving the data for Gadamer's 1974 encyclopedia article, "Hermeneutik," in *Historisches Wörterbuch der Philosophie,* ed. Joachim Ritter (Basel: Schwabe, 1974), columns 1061–73. This text is basically the same, except for the ending, as the Italian article of 1977 and *GW* 2: 92–117.

9. Hans-Georg Gadamer, "Ermeneutica," in *Enciclopedia del Novecento* (Rome: Istituto dell'Enciclopedia Italian, 1977), 2: 731–40.

10. The added material can be found as pp. 115–16 of the *GW* 2 article.

11. For a more extensive list of texts important in the historical development of hermeneutics, see the hypothetical table of contents for a six-volume Hermeneutics Compendium never realized, given at www.mac.edu/faculty/richardpalmer/compendium.html.

12. See Martin Heidegger, "The Origin of the Work of Art," in *BW,* 139–212.

13. See *GDE.*

14. According to Etsuro Makita, *Truth and Method* has been translated into Japanese, Chinese, Russian, Hungarian, Turkish, Serbo-Croatian, Polish,

Spanish, French, Italian, and other languages. See *G-B*, B60/01. In addition, my own 1969 book introducing philosophical hermeneutics has so far been translated into Chinese, Turkish, Farsi, and Spanish. Interest in Gadamer's philosophical hermeneutics is clearly continuing to spread throughout the world.

15. *G-B*, B60/01.

Classical and Philosophical Hermeneutics

1. [Recent research by Benveniste on the etymology of the Greek word *hermeneus* has cast doubt on whether this word is related to the god Hermes, as seemed obvious in its ancient use and etymology. —Grondin's note.] [When Heidegger was asked about the word "hermeneutics" in relation to his thought in his dialogue with a Japanese, he obliquely refers to this questionability, saying that "the noun *hermeneus* is referable to the name of the god Hermes by a playful thinking that is more compelling than the rigor of science." Martin Heidegger, *On the Way to Language*, trans. Peter D. Hertz (New York: Harper and Row, 1971), 29; and Martin Heidegger, *Unterwegs zur Sprache* (Pfüllingen: Neske, 1959), 121. Gadamer appears to be following the playful thinking of Heidegger in this respect. —Translator's note.]

2. Plato, *Statesman* 260d.

3. See Plato, *Epinomis* 975c.

4. See Photius, *Bibliotheca* 7; Plato, *Ion* 534e; Plato, *Laws* 907d.

5. See Karl Holl, *Untersuchungen zu Luthers Hermeneutik: Luthers Bedeutung für den Forschritt der Auslegungskunst* (1920); [see Karl Holl, *Luther*, vol. 1 of his *Gesammelte Aufsätze zur Kirchengeschichte*, 3 vols. (Tübingen: Mohr, 1928–32)] and its continuation by Gerhard Ebeling first in his *Evangelische Evangelienauslegung: Eine Untersuchung zu Luthers Hermeneutik* (Munich: Christian Kaiser, 1942, repr., Darmstadt: Wissenschaftliche Buchgesellschaft, 1962), then in "Die Anfänge von Luthers Hermeneutik," *Zeitschrift für Theologie und Kirche* 48 (1951), and "Hermeneutische Theologie?" in his *Wort und Glaube*, vol. 2 (Tübingen: Mohr, 1969), 99–120.

6. See the presentation of this by Lutz Geldsetzer in his introduction to the reprint of Georg Friedrich Meier, *Versuch einer allgemeinen Auslegungskunst* (Düsseldorf: Stern-Verlag Janssen, 1965, reprinting the 1757 edition), esp. xff.

7. Christian Wolff, *Philosophia Rationalis sive Logica* (2nd ed., 1732), 3rd part, section 3, chapters 6 and 7.

8. Johann Martin Chladenius, *Einleitung zur richtigen Auslegung vernünftiger Reden und Schriften* (1742; repr., Düsseldorf: Stern-Verlag Janssen, 1969).

9. Quintilian, *Institutio oratoria*.

10. [Parts of the *Clavis* have recently been published with a translation into German facing the Latin: Matthias Flacius Illyricus, *De Ratione Cognoscendi Sacras Litteras: Über den Erkenntnisgrund der Heiligen Schrift*, ed. and trans. Lutz Geldsetzer (Düsseldorf: Stern-Verlag Janssen, 1968).]

11. Richard Simon, *Histoire critique du texte du Nouveau Testament* (1689; repr., Frankfurt: Minerva, 1968); and *De l'inspiration des livres sacrés* (1687).

12. [Gadamer added the following note in *GW*:] See my critical discussion of Strauss's interpretation of Spinoza in "Hermeneutics and Historicism," contained in *GW* 2: 414ff. [English: *TM*, 532ff.]

13. J. J. Rambach, *Institutiones Hermeneuticae Sacrae* (Jena: I. W. Hartung, 1723, 1764).

14. See Immanuel Kant, *Kritik der Urteilskraft*, 2nd ed. (1799), vii. [English: *Kant's Critique of Aesthetic Judgment*, trans. James Creed Meredith (Oxford: Clarendon, 1911).]

15. [Johann August Ernesti, *Institutio Interpretis Novi Testamenti* (1761); and J. S. Semler, *Abhandlung von freier Untersuchung des Canon* (1771–75). See Ernesti, *Elements of Interpretation*, translated from the Latin of J. A. Ernesti and accompanied by notes, with an appendix containing extracts from Morus, Beck, and Keil (Andover: M. Newman, 1827.)]

16. See Gianni Vattimo, *Schleiermacher filosofo dell' interpretazione* (Milan: Mursia, 1968). [Several editions of Schleiermacher's *Dialektik* are available today (2007) in German, and one translation into English.]

17. Heymann Steinthal, *Einleitung in die Psychologie und Sprachwissenschaft* (Berlin: Dümmler, 1871; 2nd ed., 1881).

18. See Erich Rothacker, *Einleitung in die Geisteswissenschaften*, reproduction of the 2nd edition of 1930 (Darmstadt: Wissenschaftliche Buchgesellschaft, 1972). [Although this book has not been translated, many other titles by this author are available in English.]

19. [For a discussion of Boeckh and Steinthal, see Maurizio Ferraris, *History of Hermeneutics*, trans. Luca Somigli (Atlantic Highlands, N.J.: Humanities, 1996), 92–94. The original Italian volume was published by Bompiani in Milan, 1988.]

20. Wilhelm Dilthey, *Gesammelte Schriften*, vols. 4, 8; and published in the meantime, see vols. 18, 19. The more recent volumes of the *Gesammelte Schriften* were edited by Frithjof Rodi (Leipzig: Teubner, 1914–58, and continued by Göttingen: Vandenhoeck and Ruprecht, 1961–). An English translation of certain writings is: Wilhelm Dilthey, *Hermeneutics and the Study of History: Selected Writings*, edited with an introduction by Rudolf Makkreel, vol. 4 of Dilthey, *Selected Works* (Princeton, N.J.: Princeton University Press, 1996).

21. Emilio Betti, *Zur Grundlegung einer allgemeinen Auslegungslehre* (Tübingen: Mohr, 1954); Emilio Betti, *Teoria generale della interpretazione*, 2 vols. (Milan: Dott. A. Giuffré, 1955). A slightly shortened one-volume translation by Betti of the *Teoria* into German as *Allgemeine Auslegungslehre als Methodik der Geisteswissenschaften* was published in Tübingen by Mohr in 1967.

22. J. G. Fichte, *Werke*, 11 vols., ed. Immanuel Hermann Fichte (Berlin: De Gruyter, 1845–48; repr., 1971), 1: 434.

23. See Dieter Henrich, *Die Einheit der Wissenschaftslehre Max Webers* (Tübingen: Mohr, 1952).

24. Günther Bornkamm, "Die Theologie Rudolf Bultmanns in der neueren Diskussion," *Theologische Rundschau* 29, nos. 1–2 (1963): 33–141.

25. On the questionableness of such a supposedly "neutral" use of existential philosophy, see Karl Löwith, "Gründzüge der Entwicklung der Phänomenologie

zur Philosophie und ihr Verhältnis zur protestantischen Theologie," *Theologische Rundschau* (1930): 26ff. and 333ff.

26. See Georg Misch, *Phänomenologie und Lebensphilosophie: Eine Auseinandersetzung der Diltheyschen Richtung mit Heidegger und Husserl*, 3rd ed. (Stuttgart: Teubner, 1967), unchanged from the 2nd ed. of 1931 except for an added afterword.

27. *KGW* [Critical edition of the *Collected Works*], vol. 7, pp. 3 and 40 (line 25). See also lines 10 and 20 on p. 40.

28. Karl Löwith, *Das Individuum in der Rolle des Mitmenschen* (Munich: Drei Masken, 1928).

29. See Dilthey, *Gesammelte Schriften*, vol. 8.

30. R. G. Collingwood, *Denken: Eine Autobiographie* (1955). English translation: *An Autobiography* (New York: Penguin, 1944).

31. Günther Stachel, *Die neue Hermeneutik: Ein Überblick* (Munich: Kösel, 1967); Eugen Biser, *Theologische Sprachtheorie und Hermeneutik* (Munich: Kösel, 1970); Emerich Coreth, *Grundfragen der Hermeneutik: Ein philosophischer Beitrag* (Basel: Herder, 1969).

32. Hans Robert Jauss, *Literaturgeschichte als Provokation* (Frankfurt: Suhrkamp, 1970; translated in *New Literary History*, ca. 1970); and *Ästhetische Erfahrung und literarische Hermeneutik* (Frankfurt: Suhrkamp, 1977); translated as *Aesthetic Experience and Literary Hermeneutics* by Michael Shaw (Minneapolis: University of Minnesota Press, c. 1982). Wolfgang Iser, *Die Appellstruktur der Texte* (Constance: Universitätsverlag, 1970); and *Der implizite Leser* (Munich, 1972); in English as *The Implied Reader: Patterns of Communication in Prose Fiction from Bunyan to Beckett* (Baltimore: Johns Hopkins University Press, 1974). E. D. Hirsch, Jr., *Validity in Interpretation* (New Haven: Yale University Press, 1967); and Thomas Seebohm, *Zur Kritik der hermeneutischen Vernunft* (Bonn: Bouvier, 1972).

33. C. Fr. Walch, foreword to *Hermeneutica Juris*, by C. H. Eckard (Lipsiae: Libraria Weidmanniana, 1779, 1802).

34. See, among others, P. Koschaker, *Europa und das römische Recht*, 3rd ed. (1958).

35. A. F. J. Thibaut, *Theorie der logische Auslegung der römischen Rechts* (1799; 2nd ed., 1806; repr., 1967).

36. Karl Engisch, *Die Idee der Konkretisierung in Recht und Rechtswissenschaft unserer Zeit*, treatise for the Heidelberg Academy of Sciences, 2nd enlarged edition (Heidelberg: C. Winter, 1968).

37. See E. Rothacker, *Die dogmatische Denkform in den Geisteswissenschaften und das Problem des Historismus* (Mainz, 1954).

38. See E. Spranger, *Über die Voraussetzungslosigkeit der Wissenschaften*, treatise of the Berlin Academy of Sciences (1929), which documented the development of this slogan word [i.e., *Voraussetzungslosigkeit*] from the mood of cultural struggle after 1870 without raising the slightest suspicion of its unlimited acceptance at the time.

39. Hans Sedlmayr, *Kunst und Wahrheit* (1959).

40. K-O. Apel, "Wittgenstein und das Problem des Verstehens," *Zeitschrift*

für Theologie und Kirche 63 (1966). [Now in *Transformations of Philosophy* (Frankfurt, 1973), 1: 335–77.]

41. See the important contributions to be found in *Hermeneutik und Dialektik*, 2 vols., ed. Rüdiger Bubner, Konrad Cramer, and Reiner Wiehl (Tübingen: Mohr, 1970). [Selections by Habermas and Apel are in vol. 1.] Also see my reply published as an appendix to the third edition of *TM* (1972), and now available in *GW* 2: 449–78.

42. See pp. 96–97 above [See the reference to Quintilian above in note 9.]

43. Klaus Dockhorn, review of *WM* in the *Göttingsche Gelehrte Anzeigen*, 218 (1966). [See also Dockhorn's *Macht und Wirkung der Rhetorik* (Bad Homburg: Gehlen, 1968).]

44. See *Philosophy, Rhetoric, and Argumentation*, ed. Maurice Natanson and H. W. Johnstone, Jr. (University Park: Pennsylvania State University Press, 1965).

45. Aristotle, *Posterior Analytics* B 19.

46. Karl R. Popper, *The Logic of Scientific Discovery* (New York: Basic Books, 1958). German: *Logik der Forschung* (Vienna: J. Springer, 1935), with many later editions.

47. Michael Polanyi, *Personal Knowledge* (Chicago: University of Chicago Press, 1958)

48. See my article "Die Begriffsgeschichte und die Sprache der Philosophie" in *GW* 4: 78–94; [translated by Jeff Mischerling and Jakob Amstutz as "The History of Concepts and the Language of Philosophy," *International Studies in Philosophy* 18, no. 3 (1986): 1–16].

49. Thomas Kuhn, *The Structure of Scientific Revolutions* (Chicago: University of Chicago Press, 1963).

50. Charles Taylor, "Interpretation and the Sciences of Man," *Review of Metaphysics* 25 (1971): 3–15; translated into German in 1975.

51. See J. Habermas, *Zur Logik der Sozialwissenschaften,* volume supplement of the *Philosophische Rundschau* (1967); Habermas's article in *HI* (1971); and Hans Albert, *Konstruktion und Kritik* (1972). Habermas's later work also discusses hermeneutics; see his *Theory of Communicative Action,* 2 vols. (Frankfurt, 1981), vol. 1.

52. Paul Ricoeur, *Freud and Philosophy: An Essay on Interpretation* (New Haven: Yale University Press, 1970); *Conflict of Interpretations: Essays in Hermeneutics* (Evanston, Ill.: Northwestern University Press, 1974); *Herméneutique et critique des ideologies dans demythisation et idéologie,* ed. E. Castelli (1973); *The Rule of Metaphor: Multidisciplinary Studies of the Creation of Meaning in Language* (Toronto: University of Toronto Press, 1977); *Hermeneutics and the Social Sciences,* ed. John B. Thompson (Cambridge: Cambridge University Press, 1981); *Time and Narrative,* 3 vols. (1984–88); *Oneself as Another* (Chicago: University of Chicago Press, 1992); and Jacques Lacan, *Écrits: A Selection,* trans. Alan Sheridan (New York: Norton, 1977).

53. See my reply to Habermas in the essay "Rhetorik, Hermeneutik und Ideologiekritik" ["RHI"], and in English ["RHIE"], translated at first under a quite different title.

54. See Jacques Derrida, *Writing and Difference,* trans. Alan Bass (Chicago: University of Chicago Press, 1978).

55. See Joachim Ritter, *Metaphysik und Politik* (1959); and Manfred Riedel, *Zur Rehabilitierung der praktischen Philosophie* (1972).

56. Hans-Georg Gadamer, "Theorie, Technik, Praxis," in *Neue Anthropologie,* vol. 1: *Einführung* (1972). [Also in *GW* 4: 243–66.]

Chapter 3

Introduction

1. Hans-Georg Gadamer, "Die Universalität des hermeneutischen Problems," *Philosophisches Jahrbuch* 73 (1965–66), second half-volume, 215–25. The next year Gadamer included this essay in his *KS* 1: 101–12, and he finally included it in *GW* 2: 219–31. It was also chosen for the lead essay in his first collection of essays in English, *PH,* 3–17.

2. Gadamer as chairman of the department aggressively recruited Habermas to come to Heidelberg. Habermas taught at Heidelberg from 1961 to 1964 as his first professorship after habilitating at Marburg and before going on to Frankfurt. Gadamer told me with pride of his efforts to bring the already brilliant and productive young Habermas to Heidelberg, and he also mentioned his friendship with another very famous member of the Frankfurt school of thinkers, Theodor Adorno. Gadamer's philosophy was a major influence on Habermas, and they remained friends throughout the rest of Gadamer's life.

3. The page numbers cited here are to the essay as it appeared on pp. 3–17 of *PH.*

4. Johannes Lohmann, *Philosophie und Sprachwissenschaft* (Berlin: Duncker und Humblot [*sic*], 1975).

The Universality of the Hermeneutical Problem

1. See my 1958 article on this topic in *GW* 8: 9–17, now translated into English by E. Kelly: "On the Problematical Character of Aesthetic Consciousness," *Graduate Faculty Philosophy Journal* 9, no. 1 (Winter 1982): 31–40.

2. See Otto Vossler, "Rankes historisches Problem," his introduction to the book, L. Ranke, *Französische Geschichte;* this essay is also contained in Vossler's *Geist und Geschichte: Gesammelte Aufsätze* (Munich: Piper, 1964), 184–214.

3. It is certainly a misunderstanding to interpret my discussion of "The Example of the Classical" in *TM* as a declaration of a Platonizing classical idea of style and not as the working out of a historical category. See, for example, Hans Robert Jauss, *Aesthetic Experience and Literary Hermeneutics,* trans. Michael Shaw (Minneapolis: University of Minnesota Press, 1982; German original, 1979).

4. See *GW* 1: 281; *TM,* 277ff. See also *GW* 2: 57–65; in English, "On the

Circle of Understanding," in *Hermeneutics versus Science? Three German Views* (Notre Dame, Ind.: Notre Dame University Press, 1988), 68–78.

5. On the concept of the "new," see *GW* 4: 154–60; and in English see my address, "The Old and the New: Opening of the Salzburg Festival 1981." Both the German and English texts are in the *Offizielles Programm der Salzberger Festspiele,* 19–23/24–28.

6. Plato, *Protagoras* 314a.

7. The problem of the responsibility of science that has arisen since I wrote this article and that has been much discussed is in my view a moral problem.

8. See Johannes Lohmann, *Philosophie und Sprachwissenschaft* (Berlin: Duncker und Humblot, 1975). Published as no. 15 in the series "Erfahrung und Denken," dedicated to forwarding the relationship between philosophy and science.

9. Aristotle, *Posterior Analytics* B 19, 100a3ff.

Chapter 4

Introduction

1. Hans-Georg Gadamer, "Sprache und Verstehen," *Zeitwende* 41, no. 6 (November 1970): 364–77. In German, *Zeitwende* means "axis of time," that is, the birth of Christ.

2. Hans Hörmann, Hans-Georg Gadamer, and Hans Eggers, *Sprechenlernen und verstehen: Gesellschaft und Sprache im Umbruch* (Stuttgart: Radius, 1971), 19–34.

3. *KS* 4: 94–108.

4. *GW* 2: 184–98.

5. See my translation of Gadamer's essay, "Rhetorik, Hermeneutik, and Ideologiekritik," in *PH,* 18–43, under the title "On the Scope and Function of Hermeneutical Reflection" [see "RHIE"].

6. Among a dozen of Habermas's translated later writings, see especially his two-volume *Theorie der kommunikatives Handelns* (Frankfurt: Suhrkamp, 2000; earlier edition in the mid-1980s); and recently, the collection of essays under the title of *The Inclusion of the Other* (Cambridge, Mass.: MIT Press, 1998). In my essay "Habermas vs. Gadamer: Some Remarks" in the valuable collection *Perspectives on Habermas* (Chicago and LaSalle: Open Court, 2000), 487–500, I have argued that the two thinkers complement each other and we do not have to choose either thinker to the exclusion of the other.

Language and Understanding

1. The term *Existenz* refers in Heidegger to future existential possibilities. For this reason, "existence" is not quite the right translation. I do not know whether Gadamer is citing this phrase from a particular source.

2. Hans Lipps, *Untersuchungen zu einer hermeneutischen Logik* (Frankfurt: Klostermann, 1938), now in his *Werke,* vol. 2 (Frankfurt: Klostermann, 1977).

3. See J. L. Austin, *How to Do Things with Words* (Cambridge: Harvard University Press, 1955).

Chapter 5

Introduction

1. Hans-Georg Gadamer, *Die Moderne und die Grenze der Vergegenständlichung* (Munich: Bernd Klüser, 1996), 12.

From Word to Concept: The Task of Hermeneutics as Philosophy

1. Oswald Spengler, *Der Untergang des Abendlandes: Unrisse eine Morphologie der Weltgeschichte,* vol. 1: *Gestalt und Wirklichkeit* (Vienna: Wilhelm Braumüller, 1918); vol. 2: *Welthistorische Perspektiven* (Munich: Oscar Beck, 1922). There are innumerable editions by Beck, and the work has been translated into English and six other languages. The English translation is *The Decline of the West,* vol. 1: *Form and Actuality;* vol. 2: *Perspectives of World History* (New York: Alfred Knopf, 1926 and 1928, then in one volume in 1932).

Chapter 6

Introduction

1. The page numbers cited in this introduction are to *PH.*

Aesthetics and Hermeneutics

1. It is in this sense that I criticized Kierkegaard's concept of the aesthetic (as he does himself). See *GW* 1: 101–2/*TM,* 95–96.

2. *GW* 1: 478/*TM,* 474.

Chapter 7

Introduction

1. Hans-Georg Gadamer, "Von der Wahrheit des Wortes," in *GW* 8: 37–57.

2. Hans-Georg Gadamer, "Von der Wahrheit des Wortes," in *Jahresgabe der Martin-Heidegger-Gesellschaft* (privately printed, 1988), 7–22.

3. Hans-Georg Gadamer, "Dichten und Denken im Spiegel von Hölderlins 'Andenken,'" in *GW* 9: 42–55. English translation: "Thinking and Poetizing in Heidegger and in Hölderlin's 'Andenken,'" trans. Richard Palmer, in *Heidegger toward the Turn: Essays on the Work of the 1930s*, ed. James Risser (Albany: State University of New York Press, 1999), 145–62.

On the Truth of the Word

1. [Gadamer may be referring here to Wittgenstein and Habermas.]

2. [Since a sentence "combines" subject and predicate.]

3. [The translation of *Ant-worten* as "answering words," which Gadamer hyphenates, calls our attention to the hermeneutic element involved in every instance of answering. An answer (*Antwort*) is always a response to a question, here represented as the word (*Wort*) that initiates the questioning.]

4. [Ernst Cassirer, *The Philosophy of Symbolic Forms*, 3 vols., trans. Ralph Mannheim (New Haven: Yale University Press, 1953, 1955, 1957).]

5. [Here it should be clarified that in German, *das Wort* has a far wider range of meanings than does "word" in English. For instance, *das bekannte Wort Schillers* means "the well-known quotation from Schiller," and *Dr. Meyer hat das Wort* means "It is Dr. Meyer's turn to speak." At the same time, there are some usages in English that do carry this sense of a whole sentence rather than one word, or of speaking in words, which we will try to work into the translation when possible.]

6. The significance that the religious tradition possesses for stimulating poetic style has entered general awareness since Northrop Frye's *Anatomy of Criticism* (Princeton, N.J.: Princeton University Press, 1957). See also Paul Ricoeur's remarks on the critical limitations of structural "geometry." [Source not given.]

7. One thinks here of the συναγωγη τεχνων [*synagoge technon*] of Aristotle.

8. On the concept of mimesis, see nos. 8 and 9 in *GW* 8: "Dichtung und Mimesis" and "Das Spiel der Kunst." [Both are translated by Nicholas Walker in *RB*, as "Poetry and Mimesis" (116–22) and "The Play of Art" (123–30).]

9. In this regard, see "Die Wahrheit des Kunstwerks" in *GW* 3: 249–61. [This essay, which served as Gadamer's afternote to his paperback edition of Heidegger's *Ursprung des Kunstwerkes* (Stuttgart: Reclam, 1960), 102–25, has been translated under the title "Heidegger's Later Philosophy" in *PH*, 213–28, and as "The Truth of the Work of Art" in *HW*, 95–110. In relation to the material that follows, see also "Philosophie und Poesie" in *GW* 8: 232–39, translated by Nicholas Walker in *RB* as "Philosophy and Poetry," 131–39.]

10. One finds this gone into more extensively in the following two essays, "Stimme und Sprache" (*GW* 8: 258–70; "Voice and Language") and "Hören—Sehen—Lesen" (*GW* 8: 271–78; "Listening—Seeing—Reading"). [Neither is yet translated into English.]

11. [See Thrasybulos Georgiades, *Nennen und Erklingen: Die Zeit als Logos* (Göttingen: Vandenhoeck und Ruprecht, 1985).]

12. [German expressionist painter, 1867–1956.]

13. See Lothar Spahinger, *Ars Latet Arte sua,* a book on Ovid in German published in 1996 by Tuebner Verlag.

14. [See Beda Allemann, "Die Metapher und das metaphorische Wesen der Sprache," *Weltgespräch* 4 (1968): 23–29, which Gadamer is likely to have read.]

15. [On the interpretation of this Stefan George poem as a whole, see Hans-Georg Gadamer, "Ich und du die selbe seele (*sic*)," in *GW* 9: 245–48. Untranslated.]

16. See *GW* 1: 139–49; "The Ontological Valence of the Picture," in *TM,* 134–44.

17. See Max Warburg, "Zwei Fragen zum 'Kratylos,'" *Neue Philologische Untersuchungen* 5 (1929).

18. In reference to this and also what follows, see my "Philosophy und Poesie" in *GW* 8: 237–39; in English as "Philosophy and Poetry" in *RB,* 131–39.

19. [In the text Gadamer quotes this in English: "The silence of the Chinese vase," apparently from a poem in English, possibly Wallace Stevens(?).]

20. [German: *In seiner letzten Verborgenheit ist es das Bergende.*]

Chapter 8

Introduction

1. Jacques Derrida, "Interpreting Signatures (Nietzsche/Heidegger)." For a translation of the texts of this debate and discussion of it by twelve leading scholars, see *GDE.*

2. Derrida's "Interpréter les signatures (Nietzsche/Heidegger)" first appeared in French in his *Psyché: Inventiones de l'autre* (Paris: Galilée, 1987).

3. Hans-Georg Gadamer, "Le défi hermeneutique," *Revue internationale de philosophie,* 38th year, vol. 151 (1984).

4. *TI,* 24–55.

5. Hans-Georg Gadamer, "Text and Interpretation," trans. Dennis Schmidt, in *Hermeneutics and Modern Philosophy,* ed. Brice R. Wachterhauser (Albany: State University of New York Press, 1986), 377–96.

6. After the discussion of antitexts, this portion of the essay begins with the sentence: "But not in the case of literature!" This refers to the idea that an ordinary text disappears in the act of understanding it, but not the literary text, which retains a vivid presence.

Text and Interpretation

1. [As previously stated in the introduction to this chapter, the first translation of Gadamer's essay "Text and Interpretation" was by Dennis F. Schmidt in *Hermeneutics and Modern Philosophy,* ed. Brice R. Wachterhauser (Albany: State University of New York Press, 1986), 377–96. It was incomplete, however, be-

cause Gadamer decided to add about fourteen pages of text to his original lecture when it was published in *TI*, 41–55 (the full essay is pp. 24–55).]

2. [There is no equivalent in English for *für etwas Verständnis haben*. We have rendered it "to have an appreciation for something," but *Verständnis* also suggests to sympathize, to comprehend, to have insight into something. It involves such considerations as those Gadamer immediately raises here—of language, community, and the happening of understanding in conversation.]

3. See the collection of my studies on the later Heidegger in *HW* and *GW* 3: 175–332.

4. See "Correspondence concerning *Wahrheit und Methode:* Leo Strauss and Hans-Georg Gadamer," *Independent Journal of Philosophy* 2 (1978): 5–12.

5. [See *WM*, 450/*TM*, 432.]

6. Already in 1959 I sought to show this in "On the Circle of Understanding," an essay dedicated to Heidegger which is contained in *GW* 2: 57–65.

7. See Moritz Schlick, "Über das Fundament der Erkenntnis," in his *Gesammelte Aufsätze 1926–1936* (Vienna: Gerold, 1938), 290–95, 300–309.

8. In this regard, one should refer to more recent developments in the theory of science. For these in relation to my own work, see J. C. Weinsheimer, *Gadamer's Hermeneutics—A Reading of Truth and Method* (New Haven: Yale University Press, 1985).

9. See Erich Rothacker, *Das "Buch der Natur": Materialien und Grundsätzliches zur Metapherngeschichte,* edited by W. Perpeet from Rothacker's posthumous papers (Bonn: Bouvier, 1979).

10. [See *WM*, 370/*TM*, 353ff. and esp. *WM*, 373/*TM*, 356, where Gadamer concludes, "The concept of the original reader is crammed full of unreflected idealizing (*Idealisierung*)."]

11. [From the beginning of the next paragraph to the end, the present translation follows *TI* except that a few additional footnotes from *GW* 2 have been indicated. This portion of the essay appeared as pp. 37–51 in the English translation in *GDE*, 21–51.]

12. See an essay of mine which has appeared more recently, "The Hermeneutics of Suspicion," in *Hermeneutics: Questions and Prospects*, ed. Gary Shapiro and Alan Sica (Amherst: University of Massachusetts Press, 1984), 54–65.

13. In this regard, see various essays on literary theory which I have collected together in *GW* 8.

14. [This sentence was added in *GW* 2: 354–55, with the following footnote: "See Max Warburg, "Zwei Fragen zum 'Kratylos,'" *Neue philologische Untersuchungen* 5 (1929).]

15. [This poem is represented in a footnote on the same page as the reference in *TI*, *GW* 2, and *GL*. We have inserted it into the text here rather than put it in a footnote to keep it close to the reference. In the footnote under the poem, Gadamer notes:] "Philippe Forget, the editor of *TI*, cites Uwe Japp, *Hermeneutik* (Munich, 1977), 80ff. [for a more detailed analysis]. In that analysis three levels are distinguished (borrowing from Rastier). In this case what they call 'saturated analysis' is carried to absurd extremes: *salut* is no longer understood as 'greeting' but as 'rescue' (*récif*!!) and the white care [*blanc souci*]

as 'paper.' This is something not encountered at all in the text, not even in the self-related *vierge vers*. This is indeed method without truth!"

16. [J. W. von Goethe, "Shakespeare und kein Ende," *Artemis Gedenkausgabe der Werke, Briefe, und Gespräche,* ed. Ernst Beutler (Memorial edition of Goethe's works, letters, and conversations in 24 volumes) (Zurich: Artemis Verlag, 1948–54), 14: 757.]

17. [A *Gebilde* is something shaped into a certain form or structure. See the discussion in *WM* of *Verwandlung ins Gebilde*, "transformation into structure."]

18. [The interchange between Emil Staiger and Martin Heidegger to which Gadamer alludes here is documented in Emil Staiger, *Die Kunst der Interpretation* (Munich: Deutscher Taschenbuch, 1971), reprinted from the original 1955 edition (Zürich and Freiburg: Atlantis), 28–42.]

Chapter 9

Introduction

1. A lengthy and as yet untranslated essay is paired with this one at the end of *GW* 8, "Zur Phänomenologie von Ritual und Sprache," 400–440. It is another indication of Gadamer's late turn to anthropological sources in ancient Greece. And there are many other important shorter essays offered in the same volume in English in *The Relevance of the Beautiful and Other Essays* (1986).

2. See *TM* on this topic. On the absoluteness of art, I would refer the reader not only to Hegel but to the contemporary philosopher of art, Christoph Menke, and his book *The Sovereignty of Art: Aesthetic Negativity in Adorno and Derrida,* trans. Neil Solomon (Cambridge, Mass., and London: MIT Press, 1998).

3. The Chinese translation of this essay (based on my English translation of it) has been done by Sun Li Jun, but I do not have the documentation of it. Also, my 2003 article on this essay published in English and Chinese, "Eleven Assertions about 'das Bild' in Gadamer's 'Wort und Bild: So Wahr, So Seiend!'" can be found in the Taiwanese journal *Universitas: A Monthly Journal of Philosophy and Culture* 346 (2003): 3–20 (English), 21–36 (Chinese).

The Artwork in Word and Image: "So True, So Full of Being!"

1. [The subtitle of *WM, Elements of a Philosophical Hermeneutics,* is not given in the English translations.]

2. [*Das Bild* normally means a "picture" or "illustration," as for example in the popular German illustrated magazine *Das Bild.* But it can also mean "image," and Gadamer uses the term here to refer both to painting and sculpture and even architecture, so I have decided on "image" rather than "picture" to translate *Bild* in the title of this essay.]

3. [This essay can be found in *GW* 2: 330–60 and is translated in *GDE.* The essay is included in the present volume.]

4. [Gadamer indicated to me that his preference was for "simultaneity" over "contemporaneousness" to translate *Gleichzeitigkeit* because it suggested the element of presence, of being present for us in our time, whereas "contemporaneous" could suggest a similar event in two countries. I have used both depending on the case.]

5. Aristotle, *Metaphysics* M 3, 1078a31–32.

6. εν τοις ακινητοις.

7. In this regard, see also my essay "Plato und die Dichter" in *GW* 5: 187–211. ["Plato and the Poets" in *DD*, 39–72.]

8. In this regard, see *GW* 1: 118ff. and the relevant works of volume 8: "Art and Imitation" (no. 4), "Poetry and Mimesis" (no. 8), and "The Play of Art" (no. 9).

9. In this regard, see my *Plato's Dialectical Ethics* (*GW* 5: 149ff.), as well as "The Idea of the Good between Plato and Aristotle" (*GW* 7: 185ff.). [See *The Idea of the Good in Platonic-Aristotelian Philosophy*, trans. P. Christopher Smith (New Haven and London: Yale University Press, 1986).]

10. (Plato, *Statesman* 284e ff.): "το μετριον και το πρεπον και τον καιρον και το δεον." [Fowler in the Loeb classics edition translates this into English as "the moderate, the fitting, the opportune, the needful."]

11. Plato, *Statesman* 285a: οι κομψοι.

12. These dates are according to the 1964 *Encyclopedia of Philosophy*.

13. In German, *Treffsicherheit*. Gadamer references *Philebus* 55e7 and the Greek word στοαχαοτική.

14. Plato, *Philebus* 62b8.

15. Plato, *Philebus* 26d8: γένεσις εις ουσίαν.

16. Plato, *Parmenides* 155e ff.

17. Plato, *Philebus* 27b8: γεγενημενη ουσία.

18. Aristotle, *Metaphysics* IX, 6.

19. Plato, *Charmides* 168d ff.; Plato, *Sophist* 247e ff.

20. On the rise of the concept of "mythos" in the times prior to the Romantic period, see "Der Mythos im Zeitalter der Wissenschaft," in *GW* 8: 180–88. [Not translated.]

21. [See Christoph Menke, *The Sovereignty of Art: Aesthetic Negativity in Adorno and Derrida*, trans. Neil Solomon (Cambridge, Mass., and London: MIT Press, 1998), for a very subtle treatment of this sovereignty phenomenon as aesthetic negativity.]

22. On distinguishing between empty and filled time, see my essay "Über leere und erfüllte Zeit" in *GW* 4: 137–53. English translation, "Concerning Empty and Ful-filled Time," by R. Phillip O'Hara in *Southern Journal of Philosophy* 8, no. 4 (Winter 1970): 341–54.

23. In this regard, see "Hören—Sehen—Lesen" in *GW* 8: 271–78; and "Über das Lesen von Bauten und Bildern" in *GW* 8: 331–38. [Neither essay is translated into English yet. By the way, the word *Vollzug* means the carrying out, the execution of something, its fulfillment, and in art the event in which the perception of an image or poem as a tarrying in time takes place. See the next paragraph.]

24. [See Sontag's 1963 essay "Against Interpretation" in *Against Interpretation and Other Essays* (New York: Farrar, Strauss and Giroux, 1966), 4–14.]

25. See the very solid study by Jürgen-Eckardt Pleines, *Ästhetik und Vernunftkritik* (Hildesheim, Zurich, New York: Georg Olms, 1989); and his article "Einheit und Mannigfaltigkeit in ästhetischen Urteil," *Zeitschrift für Ästhetik und allgemeine Kunstwissenschaft* 33 (1988): 151–75.

26. [*GW* 1: 161–65/*TM*, 156–59.]

27. [See Hans Belting, *Bild und sein Publikum in Mittelalter* (Berlin: Mann, 1981). English: *The Image and Its Public in the Middle Ages: Form and Function of Early Paintings of the Passion*, trans. Mark Bartusis and Raymond Meyer (New Rochelle, N.Y.: Caratzas, ca. 1990).]

Chapter 11

Hermeneutics as a Theoretical and Practical Task

1. See my "Rhetorik und Hermeneutik" and "Logik oder Rhetorik?" in *KS* 4: 148–63, 164–72, and also in *GW* 2: 276–91 and 292–300. [Neither essay is presently available in English.]

2. When I was speaking on the theme of this essay in Munster in January 1978, I used the opportunity to pay tribute to the memory of my colleague, Joachim Ritter, whose works contain so much that has advanced the issues under discussion. [See the preceding essay, "Hermeneutics as Practical Philosophy."]

3. In this regard, see my essay "On the Possibility of a Philosophical Ethics" in *GW* 4: 175–88. [English translation in the present volume.]

4. In *IG* and *IGE*.

5. Ernst Kapp, "Theorie und Praxis," *Mnemosyne* 6 (1938): 179–94; Hans-Georg Gadamer, "Der aristotelische Protreptikos und die entwicklungsgeschichtliche Betrachtung der Aristotelischen Ethik," *Hermes: Zeitschrift für klassische Philologie* 63 (1928): 138–64 and *GW* 5: 164–86 [not translated into English]; and in *PdE* and *GW* 5: 3–163. English: *PDE*.

6. Aristotle, *Nicomachean Ethics* 211.

7. Aristotle, *Politics* H 1, 1337a14ff.

8. [Regrettably, Gadamer does not refer to a specific writing by this well-known Heidelberg sociologist.]

9. The origin of the German translation of *jurisprudentia* as "legal science" (instead of the earlier "legal erudition") may reach as far back as the beginnings of the historical school, to which Savigny and his *Zeitschrift für die historische Wissenschaft* belong. There the analogy with historical science and the critique of a dogmatic notion of natural right both play a part. Otherwise, the possibility always lay ready for accentuating the *scientific* element more strongly than *prudentia* and for relegating the consideration of equity entirely to the realm of practice. (See, for example, the critique by François de Connan [1508–51] of this tendency toward *juris scientia* in his Commentaria 1 11 [presumably *Commentariorum juris civilis libri x*, 2 vols. (Naples: Franciscum Antonium Perazzo,

1724)].) See also Paul Koschacker, *Europa und das Römische Recht* (3rd ed., Munich: Beck, 1958), 337.

10. Claus von Bormann, *Der praktische Ursprung der Kritik* [subtitle: *Die Metamorphosen der Kritik in Theorie, Praxis und wissenschaftlicher Technik von der antiken praktischen Philosophie bis zur neuzeitlichen Wissenschaft der Praxis* (Stuttgart: Metzler, 1974)]. On page 70 of his otherwise highly useful work, the author stands the foundations on their head, when he wants to ground understanding of others on "critical self-understanding."

11. Burnet comments on this in his edition of the *Nichomachean Ethics*, discussing A 1.

12. Aristotle, *Nichomachean Ethics* A 1, 1094a1ff.

13. See Aristotle, *Nichomachean Ethics* K 10, 1179b24–25 and 1180a14–15.

14. Here Chaim Perelman and his school, drawing on the experience of jurists, have revived age-old insights into the structure and significance of argumentation as a rhetorical procedure.

15. Aristotle, *Nichomachean Ethics* A 1, 1094a27.

Chapter 12

Introduction

1. Hans-Georg Gadamer, "Die griechische Philosophy und das moderne Denken," in *Festschrift für Franz Wieacker zum 70. Geburtstag* (Göttingen: Vandenhoeck und Ruprecht, 1978), 361–65.

2. Franz Wieacker, *A History of Private Law in Europe: With Particular Reference to Germany,* trans. Tony Weir (Oxford: Oxford University Press, 1996).

3. *GW* 6: 3–8.

4. *GL,* 200–205.

Greek Philosophy and Modern Thinking

1. [In elaboration of this, see Gadamer's later book, *The Enigma of Health: The Art of Healing in a Scientific Age (EH)*.]

Chapter 13

Introduction

1. Hans-Georg Gadamer, "Über die Möglichkeit einer philosophischen Ethik," in *Sein und Ethos: Untersuchungen zur Grundlegung der Ethik,* ed. Paulus M. Engelhardt (Mainz: Matthias-Grünewald, 1963), 11–24.

2. Martin Heidegger, "Letter on Humanism," in *BW,* 217.

3. *GBio,* 134–36.

On the Possibility of a Philosophical Ethics

1. Immanuel Kant, *Grundlegung zur Metaphysik der Sitten* (Berlin, 1902), 4: 404–5.

2. G. W. F. Hegel, *Phänomenologie des Geistes,* ed. J. Hoffmeister (Leipzig and Hamburg, 1905), 301ff.

3. Gerhard Krüger, *Philosophie und Moral in der Kantischen Kritik* (Tübingen, 1931, 2nd enlarged ed., 1967).

4. As the editor of the *Walberberger Studien* remarks, Thomas Aquinas emphasizes that "conscience" refers to an act, and only in an extended sense to a *habitus* underlying it (*Summa theologica* 1: 79, 13; vol. 6).

5. Underlying my discussion here is my essay "Praktisches Wissen" of 1930, which has been published for the first time in *GW* 5: 230–48.

6. Aristotle, *Nicomachean Ethics* book 6, chapter 5, 1140b17: ευθὺς ου φαίνεται ἡ αρχή [*euthus ou phainetai he arche*].

7. Aristotle, *Nicomachean Ethics* book 2, chapter 4, 1105b12ff. επί τὸν λόγον καταφεύγοντες [*epi ton logon katapheugontes*].

8. See my essay "Freundschaft und Selbsterkenntnis" in the *Festschrift für U. Höllscher: Würzburger Abhandlungen zur Altertumswissenschaft,* Neue Folge 1, Beiheft 1 (1985): 25–33. (Also in *GW* 7: 396–406.)

9. See my review of Gauthier-Jolif's commentary on the *Nicomachean Ethics* in *Philosophische Rundschau* 10 (1962): 293ff. (Also in *GW* 6: 302–6.)

10. More on this in *Truth and Method* [*TM*], 318ff. (Also in *GW* 1: 324ff., 2:401ff.)

11. Plato, *Republic* 302a.

Chapter 14

Plato as Portraitist

[*Translators' introductory note:* This essay represents an important contribution by Gadamer, inasmuch as it brings together two fields which have long occupied Gadamer's thinking. The study of Greek philosophy, and especially of Plato, has been an abiding interest of Gadamer's for over seventy years. His first book, *Plato's Dialectical Ethics,* was published in 1931, and succeeding decades have witnessed a steady stream of essays on numerous aspects of Greek philosophy (to which three of the ten volumes in Gadamer's collected works are devoted). However, Gadamer has also maintained a long-standing interest in art and art history, evidence for which is readily apparent in the first part of *Truth and Method,* which presents the experience of the work of art as the paradigm for hermeneutic experience in general. The section on "The Ontological Valence of the Picture," which also contains a discussion of the portrait, is of particular relevance to this essay. In addition, volumes 8 and 9 of the collected works, which comprise a two-volume subset entitled "Aesthetics and Poetics," gather together many of Gadamer's most significant essays in this field. The translators would like to gratefully acknowledge the assistance of Dennis Schmidt and Walter Brogan in the preparation of this translation.]

1. [In addition to the sense of having the quality of a portrait, the German word *porträthaft* connotes both similarity or likeness to a portrait (compare *kindhaft*, childlike) as well as a certain capacity or appropriateness for being portrayed (compare *glaubhaft*, believable). Thus, as Gadamer suggests, one might speak of a range of things as *porträthaft:* an image that is, or is like, a portrait, as well as an actual face or figure that would readily lend itself to being portrayed.]

2. [English translation from J. W. von Goethe, *West-Eastern Divan,* trans. J. Whaley (Oswald Wolff, 1974), 19. Goethe's German text reads: "Mag der Grieche seinen Ton zu Gestalten drücken—an der eignen Hände—Sohn steigern sein Entzücken; Aber uns ist wonnereich, in den Euphrat greifen und im flüss'gen Element hin und wider schweifen. . . . Schöpft des Dichters reine Hand, Wasser wird sich ballen."]

3. Plato, *Symposium* 215a.

4. Hans-Georg Gadamer, "Amicus Plato magis amica veritas," in *GW* 6: 71–89. [English: *DD*, 194–218.]

5. See also Hans-Georg Gadamer, "Sokrates' Frömmigkeit—des Nichtwissens," in *GW* 7: 88–117, esp. 108ff. [An earlier version of this essay has been translated by Richard Velkley as "Religion and Religiosity in Socrates" in *Boston Area Colloquium in Ancient Philosophy,* vol. 1 (1985), 53–75.]

6. On this point, see also my work on the proofs of immortality in Plato's *Phaedo* in *GW* 6: 187–200. [See "The Proofs of Immortality in Plato's *Phaedo,*" trans. P. Christopher Smith, in *DD*, 21–38.]

7. Plato, *Statesman* 284d.

8. Plato, *Phaedrus* 250d.

9. Plato, *Parmenides* 131b.

10. Aristotle, *Metaphysics* 987b12.

11. [J. W. von Goethe, "Prologue in Heaven," in *Faust I,* trans. Bayard Taylor (Houghton Mifflin, 1870). The German text reads: "Die Sonne tönt nach alter Weise, in Brudersphären—Wettgesang, und ihre vorgeschriebne Reise vollendet sie mit Donnergang."]

12. Hans-Georg Gadamer, "Platos dialektische Ethik," in *GW* 5: 3–163. [Also in *PdE* and *PDE*.]

13. On this point, see my "Amicus Plato magis amica veritas" in *GW* 6: 71–89. [English translation: "Amicus Plato magis amica veritas," in *DD*, 194–218.] See also "Die Idee des Guten zwischen Plato und Aristoteles" in *GW* 7: 128–227. Also in *IG* and *IGE*.

14. Plato, *Parmenides* 135d.

15. Alexander on Aristotle's *Metaphysics* 97, 17–18 (Hayduck). [Alexander of Aphrodisias, *On Aristotle's Metaphysics* 1, trans. William E. Dooley (Ithaca: Cornell University Press, 1989).]

16. On this point, compare my "Idee und Wirklichkeit in Platos *Timaios*" in *GW* 6: 242–70. ["Idea and Reality in Plato's *Timaeus,*" in *DD*, 156–93.]

17. In *GW* 6: 129–53. [Translated by P. Christopher Smith in *DD*, 124–55.]

18. For example, Aristotle, *Physics* G 6, 206b32; Aristotle, *Metaphysics* M 8, 1073a20; *M* 8, 1084a12.

19. See my essay "Gibt es die Materie?" in *GW* 6: 201–7.

20. Plato, *Seventh Letter* 344b.

21. On this point, compare my treatment "Dialektik und Sophistik im siebenten platonischen Brief," in *GW* 6: 90–115. ["Dialectic and Sophism in Plato's *Seventh* Letter," trans. P. Christopher Smith, in *DD*, 93–123.]

22. Plato, *Symposium* 204a.

23. On this principle, see my study of logos and *ergon* in Plato's *Lysis* in *GW* 6: 171–86. ["*Logos* and *Ergon* in Plato's *Lysis*," in *DD*, 1–20.]

Chapter 15

Introduction

1. Hans-Georg Gadamer, *Das Erbe Hegels: Zwei Reden aus Anlass der Verleihung des Hegel-Preises 1979 der Stadt Stuttgart an Hans-Georg Gadamer* (Frankfurt: Suhrkamp, 1979). Also in *GW* 4: 463–74, afterword 4: 474–83.

2. Martin Heidegger, *Hegel's Concept of Experience* (New York: Harper and Row, 1970).

The Heritage of Hegel

1. Acts 5: 9. Compare Hegel, *Werke,* 13: 29. The quotation comes up only in Michelet's edition, not in the manuscripts in Hegel's own hand; and it is related in a critical fashion to a "perspective of the various philosophies" that Hegel finds unsatisfactory but precisely *sub specie aeternitatis.*

2. It was the merit of Erich Rothacker's *Einleitung in die Geisteswissenschaften* (1930) to have demonstrated the historical debt of the historical school to Hegel.

3. The most influential critique of Hegel's dialectic was that of Adolf Trendelenberg, who in turn obviously affected Hermann Cohen. The most visible manifesto of the "back to Kant" movement was the book by Otto Liebmann in 1865, *Kant und die Epigonen* (repr. Erlangen: Harald Fischer, 1991).

4. See my 1971 essay "Das ontologische Problem des Wertes" in *KS* 4:205–17. [Also in *GW* 4: 189–202.]

5. See Wilhelm Dilthey, *Die Jugendgeschichte Hegels* (1904, [see *Gesammelte Sohriften* 4]); and Wilhelm Dilthey, *Gesammelte Schriften,* vols. 7–8.

6. See my presentation in *TM,* 164–69.

7. On the notion of facticity, compare Martin Heidegger, *Being and Time,* trans. J. Macquarrie and E. Robinson (New York: Harper and Row, 1961), 82–83, 225–26, passim.

8. The particular emphasis Heidegger put upon this point is documented now in his Marburg lecture series, *Logik: Die Frage nach der Wahrheit* (1925–26;

GA 21), in which Aristotle's *Metaphysics,* book 9, chapter 10, is treated in detail in nos. 13b and 14. [Also, Gadamer discovered the lecture on Aristotle from 1922–23 among his papers and published it in the *Dilthey-Jahrbuch;* see "HtJ."]

9. As is well known, Heidegger's new "turn" first entered the public sphere after World War II in virtue of his *Brief über den Humanismus* (1947); but it was already substantially implied in some of his lectures, especially those on *Der Ursprung des Kunstwerks.* [Both the "Letter on Humanism" and "The Origin of the Work of Art" are available in English translation in *BW.* In the latter, the "Origin" essay is complete.]

10. On Heidegger's later avoidance of the concept of hermeneutics, see Martin Heidegger, *Unterwegs zur Sprache* (Pfüllingen: Neske, 1959), 98, 120ff. [English translation: *On the Way to Language,* trans. Peter D. Hertz (New York: Harper and Row, 1971), 12, 28ff.]

11. My first publication in this area was a contribution in the *Festschrift for Richard Hamann* (1939): ["Zu Kants Begtundung der Ästhetik und dem Sinn der Kunst"].

12. This was clear even before *Truth and Method,* in my 1958 lectures in Louvain (Chaire Cardinal Mercier, 1957), which have been published under the title *La connaissance historique* (1963). [Now in English translation: "The Problem of Historical Consciousness," *Graduate Faculty Philosophy Journal* 5 (1975): 8–52.]

13. See my Plato book of 1931, *Platos dialektische Ethik* [*PdE* and *GW* 5:3–163], and especially my essay, "*Logos* und *Ergon* in Platos *Lysis,*" in *KS* 3: 50–63 [*GW* 6: 171–86]; [now also in English translation: "*Logos* and *Ergon* in Plato's *Lysis,*" in *DD,* 1–20].

14. Collingwood's *Autobiography* has been translated into German at my instigation by J. Finkeldei and published with an introduction by me under the title *Denken* ([Stuttgart: Koehler,] 1955).

15. See my recent piece, "Hermeneutics as a Theoretical and Practical Task" [in the present volume] as well as my contribution to the congress in Thessaloniki in 1978 on Aristotle's practical philosophy ["Die Idee der praktischen Philosophie," in *GW* 10: 238–46].

16. On this rests the universality of hermeneutics, which furnishes one of the objects of discussion in the Suhrkamp volume *HI.*

17. G. W. F. Hegel, "Vorrede," in *Wissenschaft der Logik.*

18. See Aristotle, *Nicomachean Ethics* K 7, 177b3ff.

19. Herbert Marcuse, *Hegels Ontologie and die Grundzüge einer Theorie der Geschichtlichkeit,* (Frankfurt, 1932). [*Hegel's Ontology and the Theory of Historicity,* trans. Seyla Benhabib (Cambridge, Mass.: MIT Press, repr., 1989).]

20. See the concluding sentence in Heidegger's habilitation, *Die Kategorien- und Bedeutungslehre des Duns Scotus* (1916). There he speaks of "the great task of a foundational confrontation with the system of a historical Weltanschauung that is the most forcible in fullness as well as in depth, experiential richness, and concept-formation, which sublated in itself all prior fundamental philosophic problem motifs, namely, with Hegel."

21. From a letter of Heidegger of December 2, 1971: "I myself do not know clearly enough how my 'position' vis-à-vis Hegel is to be determined—it would

not be enough to put it down as a 'counterposition'; the determination of 'position' is connected with the question concerning the mystery of the 'beginning' [*Anfangs*]; it is far more difficult because—simpler than the explanation Hegel gives for it before the start of the 'movement' in his *Logik*—I have repeatedly opposed talk about the 'breakdown' of the Hegelian system. What has broken down, and that means to have sunk away, is what came after Hegel—Nietzsche included."

22. See my *Hegels Dialektik: Funf hermeneutische Studien* [1971; *HD*]. The letters of Heidegger cited in the afterword are in reference to this publication. [English: *HDE*.]

23. Hans-Georg Gadamer, "Hegels Dialektik des Selbstbewusstseins," in *Materialien zu Hegels Phaenomenologie des Geistes* (Frankfurt: Suhrkamp 1973), 217–42 [*GW* 3: 47–64]. English: "Hegel's Dialectic of Self-Consciousness," in *HDE*, 54–74.

24. [Now published as Hans-Georg Gadamer, "Heidegger und die Sprache der Metaphysik," in *KS* 3: 212–20; also in *GW* 3: 229–37. English: "Heidegger and the Language of Metaphysics," in *PH*, 229–40. Also included in the present volume.]

25. In the letter mentioned in note 21, Heidegger himself made the following remark about my Freiburg lecture on "Hegel and Heidegger" [of 1972; see *HD*, 100–116]: "But I think you bring the dialectic of consciousness and of 'being' too closely together with the Platonic dialectic—in view of the 'conversation' perhaps justifiably." This admission was precisely my concern and what I explicated somewhat further in my memorial speech, "Sein Geist Gott," in *GW* 3: 320–32.

26. [Nietzsche says in *Thus Spake Zarathustra:* "The body is one great reason, a variety with one sense, a war and a peace, a herd and a herder. A tool of your body is also your little reason, my brother, which you call "spirit"—a little tool and toy of your great reason." See "Of the Despisers of the Body" in *Thus Spake Zarathustra*. One's reason is really a tool of the larger wisdom of the body.]

27. The widespread prejudice that Aristotle placed the ideal of the theoretic life first on account of his dependence upon Platonism while in fact, however, the practical-political ideal of life was the consequent outcome of the argument of the *Ethics* I opposed in my lecture in Thessaloniki ["Die Idee der praktischen Philosophie," in *GW* 10: 238–46], where I said: "We are not placed before the choice whether we will be gods or human beings."

28. See my "Kant und die philosophische Hermeneutik" in *KS* 4: 196–204. [Also in *GW* 3: 213–22. English: "Kant and the Hermeneutical Turn," in *HW*, 49–59.]

29. From a letter of Heidegger of February 29, 1972:

"Insofar as I have looked over your studies on Plato and Hegel and thought them through, they clarify and at the same time ground the suggestion with which you close your Freiburg lecture: 'Dialectic has to be retrieved in hermeneutics.' Thereby is productively opened up for the first time a way towards getting over [*Verwindung*] dialectic. The closer specification of hermeneutics nevertheless at the same time forces us to the question whether and in which way the peculiarly universal claim of information-technique can be recovered in hermeneutics as a deficient (in the utmost measure) mode of 'mutual understanding' in hermeneutics. The assumption of both tasks has for its execution not only to suffer through and acknowledge the linguistic poverty of thought, but to ponder it in a way that precedes all reflection and is on the way toward an initial 'de-termination' [Be-Stimmung] of phenomenology."

Heidegger is surely correct when he regards information technique as an extreme case that poses for hermeneutics its utmost task. But even here I ask what the linguistic poverty of speech really means. In his letter Heidegger continues:

"Why does thinking necessarily remain in the language-poverty of word discovery? Presumably because the utterance of thinking has to utter being (even more so, its difference from entities), while any given historical language still addresses and expresses the entity in a way that is oblivious of itself. The word is fashioned for the uttering of entities. But it is again only capable of so speaking because it speaks out of the lighting-up process of being, and speaking even names this. Indeed, how enigmatic are the names of *this* naming. How does it stand with the hermeneutics of *such names?*"

I would like to suggest here that Heidegger, because he so looks to names and naming, gets close to using a "puzzling" metaphor here. But does not a metaphor become enigmatic and puzzling precisely by reason of the fact that it becomes dissociated as a name from the flow of the discourse? Perhaps the poverty of language [in Heidegger] itself arises from the ideal of naming and ultimately gets overcome by itself, as it were, in the dialogical movement of thought?

30. See Plato, *Symposium* 207a ff.

31. Wolfhart Pannenberg, "Hermeneutik und Universalgeschichte," *Zeitschrift für Theologie und Kirche* 60 (1963): 90–121.

32. Collingwood especially has stressed and criticized this in his *Idea of History*. On the other hand, recent investigators try to stress the positivistic side in Dilthey with a positive intent. See the well-balanced presentation by Manfred Riedel, *Verstehen oder Erklaren?* (1978), esp. 42ff.

33. The precise context of the passages cited from Heidegger's letter of December 2, 1971, is as follows:

"In order to go into the question as to whether on p. 94 you have 'noticed something correct,' I refer you to both of the enclosed photos that Schadewalt sent me last September. [Marginal comment by Heidegger: the thrice-underlined *en* in *to ti en einai* (the already *has been* of mediation).]

"The intention of the seminar was to demonstrate how for H. [Hegel] it comes to the quite alienating determination of reflection as 'essence' [Wesen]. To see this it is necessary beforehand to think about the truth as certitude and 'being' as objectivity in the transcendentality of absolute knowledge.

"The sentence, 'The truth of Being is Essence' [Die Wahrheit des Seins ist das Wesen] in Latin would have to go: Certitudo objectivitatis reflectitur qua relucentia. But even stated in this way, the Latin language does not speak philosophically in Hegel's sense as you convincingly demonstrate.

"If Oskar Becker were still alive—by the way, an outstanding picture from Schadewalt—he could testify that already in 1922 I spoke of the *Reluzenz* in Dasein. The word is meant to say something other than reflection as an act of consciousness—namely, the shining back of the coming-to-presence [*des Anwesens*] upon and within Dasein. This belongs to the Descartes critique I attempted in the first Marburg lecture.

"Accordingly, the working note of page 67 is to be thought about in a different way. 'The undomesticated element' [*Das Unheimische*] does not consist in the fact that reflection 'can settle down nowhere,' but in the fact that the *aletheia* itself and as such is *not* experienced and grounded, that it does not come to *Wesen* [verbally construed as 'presencing'] as the *Ereignis* ['event of appropriation']. See my lecture on Identity.

"This experiencing of *aletheia* is the step back to the 'most ancient of what is ancient' (see *Aus der Erfahrung des Denkens,* 19), the turning to the 'other beginning,' that is, the one and the same single beginning of Western European thought, but this beginning of thought in another manner. While for decades I already thought and tried to cherish this tradition, I fell into the completely inadequate talk about the *Sprung* [leap] in a lecture, 'Der Satz der Identität,' that was contemporaneous with the jubilee seminar under discussion; if you were to see my copy, you could verify the corrections I made immediately after I had the printed text in front of me. This briefly in response to your rhetorical questions, p. 90, section 2, below."

34. Hans-Georg Gadamer, "Über leere und erfüllte Zeit," in *KS* 3: 221–36, and in *GW* 4: 137–53. [English: "Concerning Empty and Ful-filled Time," translated by R. Phillip O'Hara in *Southern Journal of Philosophy* 8, no. 4 (Winter 1970): 341–54. Reprinted in *Martin Heidegger in Europe and America,* ed. Edward G. Ballard and Charles Scott (The Hague: Nijhoff, 1973), 77–89.]

35. Heidegger himself had thoroughly recognized this connection and later set himself against the misuse of his slogan about the "overcoming [*Ueberwindung*] of metaphysics." He suggested as a new expression "getting over" or "recovering from [*Verwindung*] metaphysics"; and in my essay on "Hegel and Heidegger" I have explained this new turn of speech: what one gets over does not simply lie behind one as simply overcome or eliminated, but keeps on making a difference for one. [*GW* 3: 87–101; translated by P. Christopher Smith in *HD,* 100–116.]

Chapter 16

Introduction

1. Hans-Georg Gadamer, "Anmerkungen zu dem Thema 'Hegel und Heidegger,'" in *Natur und Geschichte: Karl Löwith zum 70. Geburtstag,* ed. Hermann Braun and Manfred Riedel (Stuttgart: Kohlhammer, 1967), 123–31.

2. Hans-Georg Gadamer, "Heidegger und die Sprache der Metaphysik," in *KS* 3: 212–20. Translated by David Linge in *PH,* 229–40.

3. *HW,* 61–69. English translation from *PH,* 229–40, reused in *HW,* 69–79.

4. *GW* 3: 229–37.

5. Hans-Georg Gadamer, "Hermeneutics and Logocentrism," in *GDE*, 121.

Heidegger and the Language of Metaphysics

1. See Gerhard Krüger, "Martin Heidegger und der Humanismus," *Theologische Rundschau* 18 (1950): 148–78.

2. See Oskar Becker, "Von der Hinfälligkeit des Schönen und der Abenteuerlichkeit des Künstlers," originally published in the *Festschrift für Husserl* (1929), 27–52; repr., Berlin: Alexander, 1994.

3. Martin Heidegger, *Brief über den Humanismus* (Frankfurt: Klostermann, 1947), 15–16. [For the English, see "Letter on Humanism," in *BW*, 217–65, esp. 226–27.]

4. [Footnote added later:] Certainly Derrida would not agree with this rhetorical question. Rather, he would see in it a lack of radicality that refers back to "metaphysics"—and this includes Heidegger. In his eyes Nietzsche is the one who truly can be credited with overcoming metaphysical thought, and consequently he subordinates language to *écriture*—[see his *L'écriture et la différence* (Paris: Seuil, 1967); *Writing and Difference,* trans. Alan Bass (Chicago: University of Chicago Press, 1978)]. Regarding the contrast between hermeneutics and this post-structuralist following of Nietzsche, see two of my newer works in *GW* 2: "Text und Interpretation" (1983), 330–60; and "Destruktion und Dekonstruktion" (1985), 361–72. [A retranslation of "Text und Interpretation" is contained in the present volume, and an English translation of "Destruktion und Dekonstruktion" can be found in *GDE*, 102–13. In addition, Gadamer's last essay on Derrida, "Hermeneutics Tracking the Trace" (1994), has been translated for the present volume.]

Chapter 17

Hermeneutics and the Ontological Difference

1. In this regard, see also my "Parmenides oder das Diesseits des Seins" (1988) in *GW* 7: 3–31. [Untranslated.]

2. [Martin Heidegger, *Ontology: The Hermeneutics of Facticity,* trans. John Van Buren. (Indiana University Press, 1999).]

3. Martin Heidegger, *Ontologie (Hermeneutik der Faktizität),* ed. Käte Bröcker-Oltmanns (Frankfurt: Klostermann, 1988), 9ff. Also in *GA* 63.

4. [See Martin Heidegger, *Aus der Erfahrung des Denkens,* 2nd ed. (Pfullingen: Neske, 1965); written 1947. Gadamer did not take these poems seriously as poetry. He told the translator that they were written as part of Heidegger's therapy treatments for depression after the war.]

5. For greater detail, see my "Destruktion und Dekonstruktion" in *GW* 2: 361–72 [translated with other essays on this topic in *GDE*, 102–13]; and see also

my explanation of the term "deconstruction" in "Heidegger und die Sprache," in *GW* 10: 17. [Untranslated.]

6. Martin Heidegger, "Vom Wesen und Begriff der Φ ύ σ ι ς. Aristoteles, *Physik* B, 1." Available both in his *Wegmarken* (Frankfurt, 1967) and in *GA* 9 (1976).

7. [*Zeit und Sein*, a lecture given in 1962. See the translation, Martin Heidegger, *On Time and Being*, by Joan Stambaugh (New York: Harper and Row, 1972).]

8. Hans-Georg Gadamer, "Heideggers 'theologische Jugendschrift" ["HtJ"]. [Gadamer accidentally found these early writings of Heidegger among his papers as he was working on his own collected writings and published them in the *Dilthey-Jahrbuch* with an explanatory introduction.]

Chapter 18

Introduction

1. "Bonnes volontés de puissance (une réponse à Hans-Georg Gadamer)," *Revue internationale de philosophie*, 38th year, no. 151 (1984): 341–43.

2. See *TI*.

3. *GDE*.

4. Victor Farias, *Heidegger and Nazism* (Philadelphia: Temple University Press, 1989), a translation of *Heidegger et le Nazisme* (Paris: Livre de Poche, 1987).

5. Hans-Georg Gadamer, "Text and Interpretation," trans. Dennis Schmidt and Richard Palmer in *GDE*, 21–51.

6. See *GOC* for many of Gadamer's essays on Celan. For Derrida and Celan, see Jacques Derrida, *Sovereignties in Question: The Poetics of Paul Celan*, ed. Thomas Dutiot and Outi Pasanen {New York: Fordham University Press, 2005). This volume contains Derrida's tribute to Gadamer: "Rams: Uninterrupted Dialogue—Between Two Infinities, the Poem," pp. 135–64.

7. See *GOC*.

8. See Anthony Smith, "Memory and Friendship: Jacques Derrida Week," in *The Weblog*, an Internet source. See also the lengthy commemorative article by Robert Maggiori, "Derrida, la pensée de la difference," in *Liberation-fr* (October 11, 2004), available on the Internet.

9. Jacques Derrida, *Beliers: Le dialogue ininterrompu: Entre deux infinis, le poeme* (Paris: Galilée, 2003). In German translation, see *Hans-Georg Gadamer, Jacques Derrida: Der ununterbrochene Dialog*, ed. Ralf Konersmann (Frankfurt: Suhrkamp, 2004). A considerably shortened English translation by Thomas Dutoit and Philippe Romanski appeared as Jacques Derrida, "Uninterrupted Dialogue: Between Two Infinities, The Poem," *Research in Phenomenology* 34 (January 2004): 3–19; available online.

10. Gadamer once told me that he and his wife made a trip to Paris in order to present to Celan a full-page newspaper statement of solidarity with Celan signed by a hundred German scholars in the face of a vicious accusation of

plagiarism by the widow of a dear friend. Celan, however, actually regretted this effort because he did not want to carry the matter any further in public. It seems that the plagiarism was actually done by the widow's late husband and friend of his, a fact he wanted kept quiet. So the whole project of the German effort to support Celan in this matter backfired on Gadamer, and Gadamer felt terrible about this. In the years after Celan's death he sought other means of supporting his work through writing on the poetry of Celan. This important episode is not mentioned in Jean Grondin's definitive biography of Gadamer, now available in English translation by Joel Weinsheimer. See *GBio*. Perhaps it was too early to do so. Grondin sent me a clarifying e-mail, so he was aware of the situation.

11. *GW* 10: 148–74.

Hermeneutics Tracking the Trace [On Derrida]

1. [As Wilhelm Dilthey did.]
2. [In 1981, 1988, and 1993. The first encounter took place in Paris on April 25, 1981. It was at a conference on "Text and Interpretation" at the Goethe Institute. The second encounter took place in Heidelberg under the auspices of the French Department in 1988, for which no documentation is available to this author, and I was advised at the time that nothing important happened there. On November 19, 1993, Gadamer presented a talk in Paris that is documented by Dieter Thomä's "Elefantentanz: Gespräch über das Gespräch," in the *Frankfurter Allgemeine Zeitung*, December 8, 1993. See also Jean Grondin, "La définition derridienne de la déconstruction," *Archives de philosophie* 62, no. 1 (1999), documenting a later convergence of hermeneutics with deconstruction. Derrida's respectful tribute to Gadamer shortly after Gadamer's death on March 13, 2002, may be found in the *Frankfurter Allgemeine Zeitung* on March 28, 2002: "Wie recht er hatte! Mein Ciceronne Hans-Georg Gadamer" ("How right he was! My Ciceronian Hans-Georg Gadamer"). And later came his official tribute to Gadamer in Heidelberg and in the book *Beliers* in 2003. The regrettable death of Derrida himself from pancreatic cancer on October 11, 2004, followed the death of Gadamer by only two and a half years and has been lamented worldwide.]
3. [See Hans-Georg Gadamer, "Text und Interpretation," in *GW* 2: 330–60; and "Text and Interpretation" in *GDE*, 21–51. Gadamer extended his essay by a dozen pages for the later publication in *TI*. Gadamer added a second reply to Derrida in 1982, "Und dennoch: Macht des guten Willens," which appeared in *TI*, 59–61.]
4. [This essay was later included in Jacques Derrida, *Marges de la philosophie* (Paris: Minuit, 1972), and became widely available in German and English.]
5. [In particular, see Derrida's essay in the conference with Gadamer in 1981, "Interpreting Signatures: Nietzsche/Heidegger," in *GDE*, 58–71.]
6. [Among other sources, see Hans-Georg Gadamer, "Destruktion und Dekonstruktion," in *GW* 2; and two preceding essays in volume 10: "Frühromantik,

Hermeneutik, Dekonstruktivismus" (1987) and "Dekonstruktion und Hermeneutik: (1988). These three essays are available in English in the volume dedicated to the Paris encounter with Derrida, *GDE,* under the respective titles "Destruktion and Deconstruction," 102–13, "Hermeneutics and Logocentrism," 114–25, and "Letter to Dallmayr," 93–101.]

7. I have discussed this point in greater detail in *Dialektik und Sophistik im siebenten platonischen Brief* (1964), in *GW* 6: 90–115; [in English as "Dialectic and Sophism in Plato's *Seventh Letter,*" in *DD,* 93–123].

8. Some relevant works in this regard can be found in *GW* 8: "Stimme und Sprache" (no. 22), "Hören—Sehen—Lesen" (no. 23), "Lesen ist wie Übersetzen" (no. 24), and others.

9. [Gadamer is alluding to the final stanza of *Faust,* part 1, where the opening lines go, "Everything finite / Is only a likeness (a symbol) . . . "]

10. See Hugo Huppert, "Spirituell: Ein Gespräch mit Paul Celan" in *Paul Celan,* ed. Werner Hamacher and W. Menninghaus (Frankfurt, 1988), 321.

11. [*Seinen Anfang,* a word with Heideggerian overtones.]

12. [As poetry, it is a text in the highest possible, most eminent, sense of that word.]

13. [See Jacques Derrida, *Chora* (Vienna: Passagen, 1990), now out of print but available in *Uber die Namen,* etc., by the same press.]

14. For a more detailed discussion, see my essay "Idee und Wirklichkeit in Platos *Timaios*" in *GW* 6: 242–70; in English as "Idea and Reality in Plato's *Timaeus,*" in *DD,* 156–93.

15. See my "Platos Denken in Utopien" in *GW* 7: 270–89. [Not yet translated.]

16. [The term *dihairesis* refers to the idea that a concept in a conversation can be broken down into its individual parts in order to move to a higher level of unity that includes a knowledge of the identity of the separated parts.]

17. See in this regard "Der 'eminente' Text und seine Wahrheit" in *GW* 8: 286–95. [Originally published in English as "The Eminent Text and Its Truth," trans. Geoffrey Waite, *Bulletin of the Midwest Modern Language Association* 13, no. 1 (Spring 1980): 3–10 (discussion 11–23). Gadamer enlarged the text somewhat for inclusion in his collected works. It is also included in *The Horizon of Literature,* ed. Paul Hernadi (Lincoln: University of Nebraska Press, 1982), 337–47, discussion 347–68.]

18. In the context of Celan interpretation, see my essay "Was muss der Leser wissen?" in *GW* 9: 443ff.

19. 279c. Quoted from *Plato's Phaedrus,* trans. R. Hackforth (Cambridge: Cambridge University Press, 1972), 166.

Chapter 19

Introduction

1. Hans-Georg Gadamer, "Dialogischer Rückblick auf das Gesammelte Werk und dessen Wirkungsgeschichte" (1996), in *GL,* 280–95.

2. Tübingen: Mohr-Siebeck, 2000, 244 pp.

3. Hans-Georg Gadamer, *The Beginning of Philosophy*, trans. Rod Coltman (New York: Continuum, 2000); and Hans-Georg Gadamer, *The Beginning of Knowledge*, trans. Rod Coltman (New York: Continuum, 2001).

4. Hans-Georg Gadamer, *Die Lektion des Jahrhunderts: Ein philosophischer Dialog mit Riccardo Dottori*, translated into German by Tobias Günther, Britta Hentschel, and Daniela Worf (Münster: LIT, 2000).

5. Hans-Georg Gadamer, *A Century of Philosophy: A Conversation with Riccardo Dottori*, trans. Rod Coltman and Sigrid Koepke (New York: Continuum, 2004).

6. *PHGG*, 3–64, and *GL*, 1–30.

7. *GBio*.

8. Jean Grondin, *Introduction to Philosophical Hermeneutics*, trans. Joel Weinsheimer (New Haven: Yale University Press, 1997).

9. *The Philosophy of Gadamer* (Montreal: McGill-Queens University Press, 2004).

10. Marin Heidegger, "Die Zeit des Weltbildes," in *Holzwege* (Frankfurt: Kostermann, 1950), 69–104. English: "The Age of the World Picture," in *QCT*, 115–54.

A Look Back over the Collected Works and Their Effective History

This conversation with Jean Grondin took place on May 3 and 24, 1996. The transcribed text was reviewed several times by Gadamer and amplified at some points.

1. [A letter from Martin Heidegger to Otto Pöggeler dated January 5, 1973, cited from Pöggeler, *Heidegger und die hermeneutische Philosophie* (Freiburg: Karl Alber, 1983), 395. This book is not translated, but another work by Pöggeler, *Heidegger's Path of Thought*, has been translated.]

2. [For Gadamer, an artwork makes a "statement." In his collected works, he groups volumes 8 and 9 under the heading *Ästhetik und Poetik*, and gives to volume 8 on the theory of art the title *Kunst als Aussage* (*Art as Statement*), while volume 9 interpreting specific works is *Hermeneutik im Vollzug* (*Hermeneutics in Performance*).]

3. [In Aristotle, this is an argument based on probability.]

4. For example, see my "Grenzen der Sprache" (1985) in *GW* 8: 350–61.

5. [Kawi is a language from the islands of Java, Bali, and Lombok. It is now extinct as a spoken language, but is still used in Bali and Lombok as a literary language and is the main language used for the Lombok cultural practice of reading and writing literature on the leaves of the lontar palm. —Grondin's note, from Internet *Wikipedia*.] [The book Gadamer is referring to is Wilhelm von Humboldt, *Über die Kawi-sprache auf der Insel Java*, nebst einer Einleitung über die Verschiedenheit des menschlichen Sprachbaues und ihrren Einfluss auf die geistige Entwickelung des Menschengeschlechts, 3 vols. (Berlin: Royal Academy of Sciences, 1836–39). —Translator's note.]

6. See my essay "Plato as Portraitist" in this volume.

7. [Presumably Gadamer is referring to Vico's book, republished in 1974 with a German facing translation, *De Nostri Temporis Studiorum Ratione: Vom Wesen und Weg der geistigen Bildung,* Latin and German edition.]

8. See "The Artwork in Word and Image" in this volume [1993; German title, "Wort und Bild: 'So Wahr, so seiend!'"] as well as my [untranslated] essay "Zur Phänomenologie von Ritual und Sprache" (1992), in *GW* 8: 373–99 and 400–440, respectively.

9. See my essay, "From Word to Concept: The Task of Hermeneutics as Philosophy" (1995) [in the present volume].

Index of Persons

Index of Subject Matter

a priori, 283, 415
absolute idealism, 52, 322, 325, 327
absolute knowledge, 112, 135, 197, 323,
    326–27, 330, 334, 339, 341, 343, 348,
    363, 382, 415
absolute spirit, 32–33, 124, 197, 213, 325,
    337, 339, 365
accuracy, 209
Aesopian fables, 302
aesthetic consciousness, 8, 74, 78–79, 81,
    83, 124, 330, 413
aesthetics, vii, 27, 43, 59, 61, 64, 123–26,
    128, 130, 138, 142–43, 189, 192,
    207–8, 213, 219, 266, 411, 414
"Age of the World Picture, The" (Hei-
    degger), 24, 386, 410, 427
aletheia, 132, 134–35, 204, 213–14, 329,
    357, 365, 378
allegorical hermeneutics, 42, 46, 65, 233
allegory, 46
amnesia, 419
anamnesis, 315, 382
ancient rhetoric, 254
anticipation of meaning, 123–24, 129,
    170, 242
antitexts, 156, 176
apeiron, 316
application, 38, 42, 48–49, 61–62, 174,
    247, 256–58, 285, 287, 334
apriorism, 167, 284, 363, 415
Arabic numerals, 421
architecture, 142–43, 155, 193, 195–96,
    209, 220–23, 396
areté, 203, 231, 262, 287
argumentation, 9, 25, 56, 69, 203, 246,
    252–53, 300, 308, 312, 380
Aristotelian thought, 28, 135–36, 166,
    203–4, 205, 206, 210–11, 213, 230–31,

249–50, 254–55, 256, 260–63, 268–
    69, 274–76, 284–89, 298, 308, 312,
    316, 317–18, 329, 333, 366, 368–69,
    379–80, 382–83, 402
art, 4–8, 13, 15, 21, 23–27, 29–31, 35, 37,
    42–46, 51, 53, 57, 61, 65, 69, 72, 74,
    77–81, 112–13, 115–17, 120, 123–32,
    142–43, 147–48, 150–52, 154–55,
    159–60, 163, 182, 186–88, 190,
    191–204, 206–15, 217–24, 227, 229,
    233–36, 241, 248, 251–55, 257, 259–
    61, 263, 269, 294–96, 300–301, 303,
    308, 317–18, 320–21, 325, 329–30, 337,
    352, 361, 369, 377–80, 394, 396–97,
    404–5, 411–15, 423–24
art history, 61, 115–16, 215, 411
art of dialogue, 341
artwork, 8, 58, 79, 115, 123, 131, 143,
    148, 154, 192–95, 199–200, 202,
    210–21, 223, 296, 377, 423, 426
authentic word, 136
authenticity, 55, 135–37, 173, 181, 195,
    320, 348, 350, 365
authority, 75–78, 82, 99, 142, 232, 283,
    335
autonomy, 37, 95, 144–46, 184, 191, 286

bad infinity, 34, 328, 341
beautiful, the, 87, 126, 142, 191–93,
    203–5, 207, 212, 214–15, 223, 305–10,
    313–15, 319–20, 335, 413
beauty, 78, 91, 124, 126, 203–6, 215, 305,
    310, 320, 414
being, x, 12, 14, 23, 31–32, 35, 55, 57, 74,
    130, 136–37, 159, 160–62, 168, 190,
    192, 195, 209, 211, 261, 270, 329, 343,
    346–47, 350–52, 356, 358–60, 363,
    365–67, 377–79, 382, 387, 401, 416–17

Hans-Georg Gadamer (1900–2002) was a leader in the development of hermeneutics during the twentieth century. The most influential of his works is *Truth and Method.*

Richard E. Palmer is President Joseph R. Harker Professor Emeritus of Philosophy and Religion and Hermeneutics Scholar in Residence at MacMurray College in Jacksonville, Illinois. His most recent publication is *Gadamer in Conversation: Reflections and Commentary.*